Robert B. Ridinger, MA, MLS
Editor

Speaking for Our Lives
Historic Speeches and Rhetoric for Gay and Lesbian Rights (1892-2000)

Pre-publication
REVIEWS,
COMMENTARIES,
EVALUATIONS . . .

"The vast majority of examples included in Robert B. Ridinger's compilation, *Speaking for Our Lives,* date from the early 1960s through 2000. While the earlier coverage is sparse, this dearth acknowledges the challenges Ridinger encountered collecting speeches about gay and lesbian issues, many of which were never published. Much work and analysis remains in this field, but *Speaking for Our Lives* is an admirable beginning. It documents the diversity of concerns and issues, even the controversies, within the queer community: lesbian feminists, butch/femme identities, leather sexuality, AIDS, racism, and feminism.

Ridinger's collection opens the door to the closet that stores all the testimony, manifestos, public affirmations, speeches, and letters comprising gay and lesbian rhetoric in the past century. Amid the voices of activists such as Barbara Gittings and Eric Rofes are the supportive words of diverse political figures such as Harold Washington and Nancy Pelosi. This book not only preserves an important aspect of American gay and lesbian history for future scholars, but also introduces the heart and soul of a significant social movement to the wider audience it deserves. Academic libraries should be sure to take the initiative to introduce this work to their users."

Faye A. Chadwell, MLS
Head of Collection Development and Acquisitions,
University of Oregon Libraries

More pre-publication
REVIEWS, COMMENTARIES, EVALUATIONS . . .

"Robert B. Ridinger has compiled a book that will be the primary source of original rhetoric on GLBT issues for many years to come. He has done the legwork for researchers in putting together this collection. The speeches Mr. Ridinger has collected are enormously important in the history of the GLBT movement for equality. They range from early homophile organization addresses to more recent mainstream political pronouncements. The diversity of individuals represented in the book, from Mel Boozer and Joseph Beam to Barbara Gittings and Bella Abzug, shows the depth and breadth of this balanced collection. Every library will want this title in their reference collection."

Stephen E. Stratton
Associate University Librarian
for Technical Services and Collections,
California State University,
Channel Islands;
Co-Chair, American Library Association,
GLBT Roundtable;
Author, *Encyclopedia of HIV and AIDS*

"Ridinger has uncovered an eclectic array of important primary source material that might otherwise, as so much of gay and lesbian history, have been lost. Arranged chronologically from 1892 to 2000 these approximately 200 speeches, letters, poems, manifestos, testimonies, organizational statements, proclamations, and other ephemeral addresses individually provide a glimpse into the long history of the struggle for gay and lesbian civil rights. Assembled, they demonstrate the richness and diversity of the many pioneers who have dared to speak out against bigotry and ignorance. Their power and righteousness shouts from these exciting, if little-known, documents. This collection is a boon to researchers, ensuring that these voices will endure into the next millennium and reiterating the importance of the courage to tell the truth."

Jim Van Buskirk, MLS
Program Manager,
James C. Hormel Gay & Lesbian Center,
San Francisco Public Library

More pre-publication
REVIEWS, COMMENTARIES, EVALUATIONS . . .

"To his already impressive list of reference works on anthropology and the GLBT movement, Ridinger adds what may be the most indispensable volume to date. *Speaking for Our Lives* includes not only the essential position papers and speeches from the last half-century, but also a surprising and illuminating assortment of secondary statements that add considerable depth to what is known about the history and evolution of the GLBT movement. From Ingersoll's obsequies over Whitman's grave to reflections on the Leather Movement and silver commemorations of Gay Pride, the collection reminds modern readers of how tentative any claim to novelty is that excludes the prescience of the pioneers: gay marriage, adoption, civil rights, ordination, and the dangers of both assimilation and separatism. These issues have been with us for longer than current activists seem to realize.

Ridinger's introductions are unobtrusive but thorough, and provide a great deal of historical context besides, and his selections represent an astute and delightful tour through the major political and social terrain staked out by gay activists at various historical turning points. This is a collection full of startling incidental information dropped in the course of delivering a rallying cry to the troops, and it warrants careful reading and referral by all of those who consider themselves knowledgeable about GLBT history, politics, or culture. This book is one of the most unusual and certainly one of the most essential documentary collections in the GLBT canon."

James V. Carmichael Jr., PhD
Professor, The University of North Carolina at Greensboro

"This is a fascinating collection of primary source materials chronicling the history of the GLBT rights movements in the United States. This will become a major sourcebook for anyone teaching GLBT civil rights, history, or literature courses. Hardly an entry goes by that the reader doesn't learn a new fact, hear a new quote, or reflect on his or her own place in this history. I was pleasantly surprised several times while reading the entries to suddenly think, 'Oh, I remember that' or in more frequent cases 'I didn't know that.' The documents range from speeches given to thousands of people to manifestoes read by only a few. Some of the authors are well known, some are not. Emotions run the gamut from the somberness of the 1892 eulogy for Walt Whitman to the pent-up anger no longer under the surface from a flyer titled 'I Hate Straights' distributed widely in June 1990. The early documents pave the way for what's to come. Documents from the eighties illustrate well the gaining force of the Gay Rights Movement right into the nineties. To quote Barbara Gittings in entry number 168, 'With so many bigotries and barriers still to erase, we need all hands and all hearts to help. Keep up the good work.'"

Roland C. Hansen, MLS
Head of Access Services, Columbia College Chicago Library

NOTES FOR PROFESSIONAL LIBRARIANS AND LIBRARY USERS

This is an original book title published by Harrington Park Press®, an imprint of The Haworth Press, Inc. Unless otherwise noted in specific chapters with attribution, materials in this book have not been previously published elsewhere in any format or language.

CONSERVATION AND PRESERVATION NOTES

All books published by The Haworth Press, Inc. and its imprints are printed on certified pH neutral, acid free book grade paper. This paper meets the minimum requirements of American National Standard for Information Sciences-Permanence of Paper for Printed Material, ANSI Z39.48-1984.

Speaking for Our Lives

Historic Speeches and Rhetoric for Gay and Lesbian Rights (1892-2000)

THE HAWORTH PRESS
Titles of Related Interest

Bisexual Politics: Theories, Queries, and Visions by Naomi S. Tucker

Gay/Lesbian/Bisexual/Transgender Public Policy Issues: A Citizen's and Administrator's Guide to the New Cultural Struggle edited by Wallace Swan

Love and Anger: Essays on AIDS, Activism, and Politics by Peter F. Cohen

Rough News—Daring Views: 1950s' Pioneer Gay Press Journalism by Jim Kepner

Trailblazers: Profiles of America's Gay and Lesbian Elected Officials by Kenneth E. Yeager

Before Stonewall: Activists for Gay and Lesbian Rights in Historical Context edited by Vern L. Bullough

Reclaiming the Sacred: The Bible in Gay and Lesbian Culture, Second Edition edited by Raymond-Jean Frontain

Scandal: Infamous Gay Controversies of the Twentieth Century by Marc E. Vargo

Lost Gay Novels: A Reference Guide to Fifty Works from the First Half of the Twentieth Century by Anthony Slide

Anything but Straight: Unmasking the Scandals and Lies Behind the Ex-Gay Myth by Wayne R. Besen

Dangerous Families: Queer Writing on Surviving by Mattilda, a.k.a. Matt Bernstein Sycamore

Speaking for Our Lives
Historic Speeches and Rhetoric for Gay and Lesbian Rights (1892-2000)

Robert B. Ridinger, MA, MLS
Editor

Harrington Park Press®
An Imprint of The Haworth Press, Inc.
New York • London • Oxford

Published by

Harrington Park Press®, an imprint of The Haworth Press, Inc., 10 Alice Street, Binghamton, NY 13904-1580.

EDITOR'S NOTES
Punctuation, spelling, and style have been corrected or altered in some instances in order to improve consistency and clarity while maintaining the authors' original intent.

The editor has attempted to the best of his ability to obtain from copyright holders permission to reprint these individual texts and speeches. If you have any information regarding copyrights that the editor has not credited, please send this information to Robert Ridinger via e-mail at rridinger@niu.edu or to ISE Founders Library, Northern Illinois University, DeKalb, Illinois 60115-2868.

Cover design by Lora Wiggins.

Library of Congress Cataloging-in-Publication Data

Ridinger, Robert B., 1951-
Speaking for our lives : historic speeches and rhetoric for gay and lesbian rights (1892-2000)/ Robert B. Ridinger, editor.
p. cm.
Includes bibliographical references and index.
ISBN 1-56023-174-2 (cloth : alk. paper)—ISBN 1-56023-175-0 (pbk. : alk. paper)
1. Gay and lesbian studies—United States. 2. Transsexualism—United States. 3. Bisexuality—United States. I. Title.
HQ75.16.U6R53 2004

2003006746

This book is dedicated to the works and memory
of the leather poet, composer, singer, and Golden Bear
John Eric Larsen
(July 25, 1965-April 2, 2001)

ABOUT THE EDITOR

Robert B. Ridinger, MA, MLS, a veteran of the United States Peace Corps, holds the rank of Full Professor in the Northern Illinois University Libraries. He earned his MLS from the University of Pittsburgh and an MA in anthropology from Case Western Reserve University. For many years he has been working to recover and preserve the history of the gay and lesbian community of the United States. He is the author of numerous books, including several annotated bibliographies, and a contributor to *The Bear Book* (Haworth, 1997) and *The Bear Book II* (Haworth, 1998). He is a member of the board of directors of the Leather Archives and Museum in Chicago.

CONTENTS

SECTION III: THE 1960S

SECTION V: THE 1980S

Acknowledgments

For a book of this type, one ought properly to thank all the people whose work is contained in it. In this case, regrettably, many of them are no longer alive to be thanked in person. Some of the people I met or collided with along the long and challenging path that led to this book deserve special thanks.

A large bear hug to Eric Rofes, for sharing his own speeches and pointing me to others he considered of note; Barbara Grier of Naiad Press, for encouragement, participation, and being willing to tell me "where all the old lesbians were"; Barbara Gittings, for keeping an *incredibly* full record of her public addresses and being willing to share them; Jack Nichols, for surprising me on the Internet and restoring his 1967 Bucknell University speech to the public record; Dr. Franklin Kameny, for encouragement and for coining the phrase "Gay Is Good"; Alvin Fritz of the University of Washington Libraries for helping to decode blurry microfilm of the *Seattle Gay News;* Sally Gearhart for writing *Wanderground: Stories of the Hill Women* and for being Sally Gearhart; Del Martin for encouragement; Ginny Vida for being there; Ben Heath for the Mattachine permissions; master Alex Keppeler for sharing the life and legacy of our Golden Bear; Joseph Bean for telling me about the lost copy of his inaugural speech at the Leather Archives; Douglas Sanders for the letter from Thailand; and Hannele Lehtikuusi for her ILGA (International Lesbian and Gay Association) address from Helsinki.

I would also like to thank the staff of the IDS office at the University Libraries, Northern Illinois University, for helping me to track down a few elusive bits of text, and to give special thanks to Vicki Smith for being willing to cope with the files of this unusual project.

And, always and forever, to my life partner, John Schultz, for putting up with me in the middle of yet *another* book.

Robert Ridinger,
De Kalb, Illinois, October 6, 2003

Introduction

The first word of gay and lesbian rhetoric, wherever and whenever verbalized, was spoken to deny the darkness and the silence on the subject of same-sex love and the cultures built around it, to assert the presence of such individuals in the particular social era, and to signify a refusal to accept a wide range of categories and assumptions as to the essential natures, characteristics, and qualities of gay and lesbian people. Yet within the body of scholarship produced by Western society until the late twentieth century, the subject has served more as a source of information for historians and writers engaged in retrieving the past of the movement than as a distinct field of analysis. This is due in part to the fact that many of the speeches given at demonstrations in the early days of the gay liberation movement were sometimes given extemporaneously or from notes and outlines, there being no prepared text preserved beyond notable quotations cited in local alternative newspaper coverage of the events. Another factor complicating the study of this aspect of gay and lesbian history was the low priority frequently given to these speeches by the gay and lesbian press; although, given the space limitations of publications forced to try to be many things at once, this is understandable, if regrettable.

When did the tradition of speaking in public about gay and lesbian issues begin? What role did this type of rhetoric play in contributing to and defining more general goals of the gay and lesbian movement? What issues frequently were not addressed using this strategic technique? How did it change over time, and what were the forces driving this change, if it occurred? Such questions presuppose the existence of a collected body of lesbian and gay rhetoric spanning several decades that can be analyzed. *Speaking for Our Lives* is intended to serve as both a beginning compilation of this elusive genre of gay and lesbian historical sources and as a wake-up call to those same historians and activists to consider the preservation of this most public aspect of their verbal contributions to the struggle for gay and lesbian civil rights.

The beginnings of public rhetoric by openly gay and lesbian individuals acknowledging and addressing the existence and civil rights of homosexuals may be said to lie with the placement of Karl Heinrich Ulrichs on the program of the Society of German Jurists meeting in Munich on August 29,

1867. His intention was to deliver a paper reviewing a proposal that same-sex relationships not be criminalized by the German states. In his account of the day's events, Ulrichs states that the clearly divided audience was already somewhat familiar with the nature of his proposed speech and considered it highly controversial, if not actually obscene. He attempted to begin presenting his text, only to be interrupted by outcries and uproar from the floor. Upon the restoration of quiet, he was informed by the president of the society that he would be allowed to proceed only if he spoke in Latin.

By the end of the nineteenth century, public speeches touching on the issues raised by Ulrichs (who died in exile from his home state of Hanover at L'Aquila in Italy on July 14, 1895) were being made on a more regular basis in the newly united Germany by the second significant gay male orator of the developing movement for same-sex rights, Dr. Magnus Hirschfeld of Berlin. With several associates he founded the Scientific Humanitarian Committee in 1897 and, as its representative, made many public appearances in cities throughout Germany. His lectures were given to both public audiences and societies of the various professions. Much of the printed legacy of this period of homosexual-supportive rhetoric was destroyed in the raid on the Institute for Sexual Science in Berlin by Nazi Brown Shirts and Hitler Youth on May 6, 1933, during which the entire library of books and manuscripts (some said to have been written by Ulrichs) was carried off to the Opernplatz and later burned as part of the Nazi effort to purify the libraries of all "un-German" materials.

Although the works of Ulrichs and Hirschfeld and their colleagues in the women's movement, such as Dr. Anna Rueling, provided a foundation for the later emergence of national gay and lesbian organizing in Europe, which culminated in the formation of the International Lesbian and Gay Association on August 8, 1978, in Coventry, England, their principal counterpart in the United States at that time was the poet Walt Whitman. The absence of such a rhetorical tradition in America (and the ignorance of the prior accomplishments of the German movement until its rediscovery during the 1970s with the beginning of contemporary gay and lesbian historical writing) placed both the homophile and gay liberation movements at something of a disadvantage, depriving them of role models while forcing them to develop their own means of expression, including reclaiming the word *gay*.

To a certain extent, the homophile movement's rhetoric was limited to and developed most fully in the articles published in the pages of *The Ladder*, the *Mattachine Review*, and *ONE Magazine*, some of which were transcriptions of papers presented at their meetings by invited members of the clergy and the medical and psychiatric professions. Included among these are a few addresses by the leaders of the Mattachine Society. Given the homophile emphasis on education rather than confrontation, it is perhaps not surprising that such speeches as have been recorded reflect a low-key gradualist approach to liberation.

With the riot at New York City's Stonewall Inn in June 1969 that birthed the second gay liberation movement came an explosion of demonstrations of all types in all venues, each characterized by public verbal affirmations of the worth of lesbians and gay men as human beings deserving of civil rights and respect. Some fumbled with existing language to communicate ideas central to the expansion of consciousness called for as part of the philosophy of gay liberation, and others, rejecting the culturally limited and limiting definitions of available words, coined new terms and phrases to militantly call for the replacement of the old sexual order by a new, more utopian world in which openly gay and lesbian people could express their realities freely in a language then being forged. Many of the speeches in the subsequent twelve years, until the appearance of AIDS in 1981, were marked by a continuation of this thread as a foundation for the claiming of rights in many different contexts. The pain and anger generated by AIDS in the lesbian and gay community added to the emotional content and coloring of many of the speeches given in the last two decades of the twentieth century. A more interesting shift over the three decades after Stonewall is the transformation of the basic terms *gay* and *lesbian* into the more generic *GLBT,* which was simultaneously accepted by the mainstream society and repudiated by sections of the communities it attempted to cover.

Speaking for Our Lives has two purposes: to begin the retrieval of this genre of primary source material of the gay and lesbian movement and to restore to a broader audience the hidden voices of men and women who ranged in political and cultural affiliation from lesbian feminists to leathermen, but for whom activism meant placing their thoughts and emotions on public records in person as testimony to the existence of issues and values important to them. The anthology's coverage begins with the eulogy delivered by Robert Ingersoll at the funeral of Walt Whitman in Camden, New Jersey, in 1892 and includes speeches, letters, poetry, manifestos, testimony at public hearings, proclamations by city officials, and remarks at venues ranging from gay and lesbian pride parades to the floor of U.S. Congress and the marches on Washington. Entries have been arranged in chronological order to permit the casual reader and scholar alike to trace the evolution of language and ideas within this genre.

The idea for this book originated when I was in the middle of completing *The Gay and Lesbian Movement: References and Resources.* In the process of assembling that bibliography, I had happened across one or two speeches given by American activists which had been reprinted in sources as varied as the *Seattle Gay News, Windy City Times,* and *The Advocate.* Prior to that time, I was not aware that this type of primary source material had been preserved in any way outside of possible drafts surviving in the personal papers of individuals, which some of the gay and lesbian archives held. I put the idea on the back burner for two years until another book project on the archaeology of India had been completed. The Haworth Press expressed interest in the idea at the American Library Association convention in New Orleans in 2000, and the search began.

Where do you look to find a class of literature that may or may not have been written down, performed by people who may or may not have given permission for it to be published in any form, and so preserved for others outside the groups who attended the rallies and conventions and dinners where it was originally given? I started by selecting the full texts of those items located during my earlier book project, then moving chronologically forward through back runs of the major gay and lesbian newspapers of record for the major cities of the United States. In the process, it quickly became clear that the original idea of limiting the work to speeches would have to be abandoned, as there was so much useful material available in forms such as open letters, manifestos, organizational statements of purpose, and even sermons that had been publicly read or were intended to be placed in the public domain for everyone to see. This enabled me to significantly expand the time frame of the book to include items from the European homosexual rights movement and the eulogy delivered at Walt Whitman's funeral in 1892. I was pleasantly surprised to find that some texts were available via Internet sites specializing in gay and lesbian historical materials, and even more so to learn that the more recent additions included the full organizational affiliation of the person who provided them, along with e-mail contact information. The true challenge lay in determining how many of the speakers were still alive and where they might be, and tracking them down to obtain permission to use their words. I was able to learn that some had died and others had simply vanished from the knowledge of any activist with whom I spoke. The most rewarding connections in building this book were the phone conversations with people whose careers and work I had known only from the printed page, many of whom were astounded that I had found a copy of a speech they recalled giving but which they themselves had long since lost or mislaid. Their delight that these materials still existed and would be put back into the public record, as well as their positive and solid support for this book was gratifying. The resulting collection indicates both the range of possible sources for this type of documentation and the amount of research and conservation still to be done in this area, a challenge to future librarians, archivists, and historians.

SECTION I: PRE-1950

March 30, 1892

Address at the Funeral of Walt Whitman

Robert G. Ingersoll

This speech was given by Ingersoll, a prominent orator and friend of Whitman, at the funeral services held in Harleigh Cemetery in Camden, New Jersey. Whitman's funeral was attended by several thousand people.

Again, we, in the mystery of Life, are brought face to face with the mystery of Death. A great man, a great American, the most eminent citizen of this Republic, lies dead before us, and we have met to pay tribute to his greatness and his worth.

I know he needs no words of mine. His fame is secure. He laid the foundations of it deep in the human heart and brain. He was, above all I have known, the poet of humanity, of sympathy. He was so great that he rose above the greatest that he met without arrogance, and so great that he stooped to the lowest without conscious condescension. He never claimed to be lower or greater than any of the sons of men.

He came into our generation a free, untrammeled spirit, with sympathy for all. His arm was beneath the form of the sick. He sympathized with the imprisoned and despised, and even on the brow of crime he was great enough to place the kiss of human sympathy.

One of the greatest lines in our literature is his, and the line is great enough to do honor to the greatest genius that has ever lived. He said, speaking of an outcast, "Not until the sun excludes you will I exclude you."

His charity was as wide as the sky, and wherever there was human suffering, human misfortune, the sympathy of Walt bent above it as the firmament bends above the earth.

He was built on a broad and splendid plan—ample, without appearing to have limitations—passing easily for a brother of mountains and seas and constellations; caring nothing for the little maps and charts with which timid pilots hug the shore, but giving himself freely with the recklessness of genius to winds and waves and tides; caring for nothing so long as the stars were above him. He walked among men, among writers, among verbal varnishers and veneerers, among literary milliners and tailors, with the unconscious majesty of an antique god.

He was the poet of that divine democracy which gives equal rights to all the sons and daughters of men. He uttered the great American voice; uttered a song worthy of the great Republic. No man has ever said more for the rights of humanity, more in favor of real democracy, of real justice. He neither scorned nor cringed; was neither tyrant nor slave. He asked only to stand the equal of his fellows beneath the great flag of nature, the blue and the stars.

He was the poet of life. It was a joy simply to breathe. He loved the clouds; he enjoyed the breath of morning, the twilight, the winds, the winding streams. He loved to look at the sea when the waves burst into the whitecaps of joy. He loved the fields, the hills; he was acquainted with the trees, with birds, with all the beautiful objects of the earth. He not only saw these objects, but understood their meaning, and he used them that he might exhibit his heart to his fellow men.

He was the poet of Love. He was not ashamed of that divine passion that has built every home; that divine passion that has painted every picture and given us every real work of art; that divine passion that has made the world worth living in and has given some value to human life.

He was the poet of the natural, and taught men not to be ashamed of that which is natural. He was not only the poet of democracy, not only the poet of the great Republic, but he was the poet of the human race. He was not confined to the limits of this country, but his sympathy went out over the seas to all the nations of the earth.

He stretched out his hands and felt himself the equal of all kings and of all princes, and the brother of all men, no matter how high, no matter how low.

He has uttered more supreme words than any writer of our century, possibly of almost any other. He was, above all things, a man, and above genius, above all the snow-capped peaks of intelligence, above all art, rises the true man.

He was the poet of Death. He accepted all life and all death, and he justified all. He had the courage to meet all, and was great enough and splendid enough to harmonize all and to accept all there is as divine melody.

You know better than I what his life has been, but let me say one thing: Knowing as he did, what others can know and what can not, he accepted and absorbed all theories, all creeds, all religions, and believed in none. His philosophy was a sky that embraced all clouds and accounted for all clouds. He had a philosophy and a religion of his own, broader, as he believed—and as I believe—than others. He accepted all, he understood all, and he was above all.

He was absolutely true to himself. He had frankness and courage, and he was as candid as light. He was willing that all the sons of man should be absolutely acquainted with his heart and brain. He had nothing to conceal. Frank, candid, pure, serene, noble, and yet for years he was maligned and slandered simply because he had the candor of nature. He will be understood yet, and that for which he was condemned his frankness, his candor—will add to the glory and greatness of his fame.

He wrote a liturgy for mankind; he wrote a great and splendid psalm of life, and gave to us the gospel of humanity—the greatest gospel that can be preached.

He was not afraid to live; not afraid to die. For many years he and Death lived near neighbors. He was always willing and ready to meet and greet this king called Death, and for many months he sat in the deepening twilight waiting for the night, waiting for the light.

He never lost his hope. When the mists filled the valleys, he looked upon the mountain tops, and when the mountains in darkness disappeared, fixed his gaze upon the stars.

In his brain were the blessed memories of the day and in his heart were mingled the dawn and dusk of life.

He was not afraid; he was cheerful every moment. The laughing nymphs of day did not desert him. They remained that they might clasp the hands and greet with smiles the veiled and silent sisters of the night. And when they did come, Walt Whitman stretched his hand to them. On one side were the nymphs of day, and on the other the silent sisters of the night, and so, hand in hand, between smiles and tears, he reached his journey's end.

From the frontier of life, from the western wave-kissed shore, he sent us messages of content and hope, and these messages seem now like strains of music blown by the "Mystic Trumpeter" from Death's pale realm.

Today we give back to Mother Nature, to her clasp and kiss, one of the bravest, sweetest souls that ever lived in human clay.

Charitable as the air and generous as Nature, he was negligent of all except to do and say what he believed he should do and say.

And today I thank him, not only for you but for myself, and for all the brave words he has uttered. I thank him for all the great and splendid words he has said in favor of liberty, in favor of man and woman, in favor of motherhood, in favor of fathers, and I thank him for the brave words he has said of death.

He has lived, he has died, and death is less terrible than it was before. Thousands and millions will walk down in to the "dark valley of the shadow" holding Walt Whitman by the hand. Long after we are dead the brave words he has spoken will sound like trumpets to the dying.

And so I lay this little wreath upon this great man's tomb. I loved him living, and I love him still.

October 8, 1904

What Interest Does the Women's Movement Have in Solving the Homosexual Problem?

Anna Rueling

This address was given by physician and women's rights activist Dr. Anna Rueling at the Prinz Albrecht Hotel in Berlin to the Scientific Humanitarian Committee, the organization working for the civil rights of what were then known as "Urnings" (homosexuals as members of a third sex), which had been founded in Berlin by Dr. Magnus Hirschfeld in 1897. This address is one of the earliest to acknowledge the existence of female homosexuals and to center attention specifically on their condition, foreshadowing the rise of the lesbian feminist movement in the United States some sixty-eight years later. The comment on "penal code paragraphs" refers to Paragraph 175, which criminalized homosexual behavior. Paragraph 175 was repealed after World War II. The original German text may be found in volume seven of the *Jahrbuch für Sexuelle Zwischenstufen* for 1905 on pages 131-151. This translation was done by Michael Lombardi-Nash.

Ladies and Gentlemen,

The Women's Movement is an historico-cultural necessity.

Homosexuality is an historico-cultural necessity, and is an obvious and natural bridge between man and woman. Today this is an undisputed scientific fact about which ignorance and impatience cannot dispute. Many have asked how I came to this conclusion and have uttered the truth about historico-cultural and natural-historical concepts in the same breath, two things which on the surface seem to be opposite.

The interest to research the reason for this extended viewpoint is that one in general, when the matter concerns homosexuals, thinks only of male Urnings and overlooks how many female homosexuals there are. They are of course less discussed because they—I was just about to say "unfortunately"—have had no unjust cause to fight against such as penal code paragraphs which arise out of having false moral views.

No cruel justice menaces women nor does the penitentiary if they follow their natural instincts. But the mental pressure under which Urninds are is just as great, indeed even greater than the yoke which their male fellow-sufferers must bear. To the world which judges by outward appearances they are even more obvious than the female Urning. Only too often they are overwhelmed by people's moralized misunderstandings.

In our total social life, however, Uranian women are at least just as important as their male counterparts because they influence our lives in many ways, even if they are not discussed. If one would just observe, one would soon come to the conclusion that homosexuality and the Women's Movement do not stand opposed to each other, but rather they aid each other reciprocally to gain rights and recognition, and to eliminate the injustice which condemns them on this earth.

The Homosexual Movement fights for the rights of all homosexuals, for men as for women. The Scientific Humanitarian Committee has distinguished itself by taking interest in this fight to the advantage of all other movements which should have, and has also participated in the interest of Urninds with such lively dedication.

The Women's Movement strives to have its long-despised rights recognized. It fights, namely, for as much independence as possible and for a just and equal standing of women with men, married or unmarried. These latter strivings are especially important because firstly, of the condition of our present economical state, and secondly, because a great number of women will remain unmarried due to a statistical nominal surplus of women in the population of our fatherland. These women are forced, when a sufficient means of earning money is not at their disposal away from the home—which is only the case of approximately 10%—to take up the fight for life and win their bread by any means available.

The homosexual women's position and participation in the Women's Movement in its all-important problem is of the greatest and the most decisive importance and deserves the most basic and extensive analysis.

One must differentiate between the homosexual woman's personality as well as her sexual instinct. Most important, of course, is her personality in general. In the second place is the tendency of her sexual drive, which, without the exact knowledge of her tendency, no unbiased evaluation could be rendered, because of the incapability to make full and just considerations of the same, because the physical sex drive is almost always just an overflow, naturally following psychical characteristics; i.e., in persons with dominant masculine characteristics it is directed toward women and vice versa, always without taking into account the outer bodily structure.

Homosexual women have many characteristics, inclinations and abilities which we usually consider as valid for men. They take a much less interest in the emotional life than the average woman. While for the expressly heterosexual woman, feeling is almost always—even here exceptions prove the rule—dominant and decisive, while mostly a sharp clarity and reason predominate in the Urnind. She is, as in the average, normal man, more objective, more energetic and goal oriented than the feminine woman; she thinks and feels like a man; she does not imitate men; she is conditioned as he; this is the all-decisive point which haters and calumniators of so-called "men-women" always ignore, because they do not even take the time to do basic research on the homosexual. It is easy to judge what one does not understand, and it is just as easy, as it would only seem to be difficult to correct a pre-established and false opinion, to correct them by reasoning. I would like to note that there is an absolute and a separate psychic homosexuality, that, therefore, masculine characteristics do not necessarily and unconditionally result in the sexual drive being forced towards one's own sex; because each Urnind naturally possesses numerous feminine characteristics to a certain degree, which may be expressed in one of the numerous intermediate stages in the transitional stages between the sexes, even by being sexually attracted to a man.

Of course, the drive in these cases is in most cases directed to a very effeminate man, as a natural completion of the woman who has a strong masculine soul.

I recall, for example, George Sand and Daniel Stern, who both loved men, those of the side of the feminine, Friedrich Chopin and Franz Liszt. Klara Schumann, the great artist, also, was married to a man who had strong feminine characteristics—Robert Schumann. It seems, moreover, as if in the women I have characterized as psychic homosexuals, the sex drive was never especially strongly developed; even George Sand and Daniel loved their artists much more with their souls than with their senses; therefore, I am include to speak of psychic homogenic women somewhat as "sexless" natures.

Since a woman who has a masculine nature and masculine traits would never satisfactorily fulfill a full-fledged man, without further ado, it is clear that the Urnind is not suitable for marriage. Even Uranian women know this is true or feel this way. Unconsciously and naturally they voluntarily refuse to walk up the aisle to the justice of the peace.

But how often had they to deal with parents, cousins, aunts, and other dear friends and relatives who, day in and day out, tried to talk them into the necessity of marriage and make life a misery with their wise advice. Often, as young girls, they had to blindly fall into marriage, and thanks to our stunted education, without having a clear view and understanding of sexuality and sexual life.

As long as it remains the opinion of so-called society that late spinsterhood, namely, unmarried women, experience unpleasantness, indeed, that it is something demeaning, then it will occur only too often that the Urnind will allow herself to be driven to marry by exterior conditions, where she will find no happiness and be incapable of creating happiness. Such a marriage is far more immoral than the love which ties two persons when a powerful nature attracts them forcefully together.

The Women's Movement wants to reform marriage. It wishes to change many rights so that the inconsolable conditions of the present cease, so that discontent and injustice, arbitrary and slavish subjugation disappear out of the home of the family, so that a healthier and powerful race blossoms.

While striving for these reforms, the Women's Movement should not forget the amount of guilt it bears in the false, unfriendly evaluation of homosexual women. I say expressly, "how much guilt." Obviously far from it that I would want to burden the Women's Movement with full responsibility for this false evaluation. But for the sake of this portion of the guilt it is a simple and inescapable duty of the Women's Movement to explain to as many persons as possible by speaking and by writing how very destructive it is for homosexuals to enter into marriage.

First of all, naturally, for both partners' sake, the man is simply duped, because aside from its ideal meaning, entering into marriage is a two-sided contract in which both partners undertake duties and assume rights. A homosexual woman, however, can only fulfill her duties to the man with disinclination, in the best case, with indifference. A forced sexual communion is, without a doubt, a misery, and no conventional man could see anything to strive for or find happiness with a Uranian woman whom he wanted to marry.

It happens very often, that such a man will avoid sexual intercourse with her out of friendly sympathy and searches for sexual satisfaction of his drives in the arms of a mistress or with a prostitute. True morality and the health of our people concern the Women's Movement, which must do everything in its power to prevent homosexual marriages. And the Women's Movement can do much in the work of explaining to all circles that the marriage of Urninds creates a three-fold injustice: to the state, society and an unborn race. Because experience teaches that the successors of Uranian persons are only seldom healthy.

The unfortunate, unloved creatures are received unwanted and make up a great percentage of the number of weak-minded, idiotic, epileptic, chest-diseased degenerates of all sorts. Even unhealthy sexual drives such as sadism and masochism are often inherited by Uranian persons who have children against their nature. State and society should show an urgent interest to prevent Uranians from marrying, because later they must bear not such a small portion of the care for such unhealthy and weak beings, from whom they may hardly expect a profit. A substantially more practical point for heterosexual women, it seems to me, is that if Urninds could remain unmarried without ruining [their] social reputation, they would find it much easier, as is their nature, to find the great satisfaction they do in the circle of the wife, housekeeper, and mother.

Still lacking, unfortunately, is an exact statistical survey of the number of homosexual women, but, taking into consideration my immense experience and thorough studies in this field, the result yielded by the statistical survey by Dr. Hirschfeld on the extensiveness of male homosexuality may also be applied to women.

According to this survey, there are as many Urninds as there are unmarried women. This should not be misunderstood. For example, I mean that there may be as many as two million unmarried women. Among the two million unmarried women there is a greater percentage of Urninds, let's say 50%, thus one million; among the homosexuals, however, there are again as many, approximately 50% who, because of external circumstances, are married, therefore, you may calculate that 50% of normal unmarried women have lost the opportunity to marry. The consequences are easy to deduce according to these figures. When Urninds are free of having to marry, the possibility of marriages for the heterosexual women would increase enormously.

But I do not mean to say that I present here a universal means to prevent late spinsterhood, because increasing animosity from men toward marriage has its roots more in social relationships. But this is not the place to speak about that. If, however, the Women's Movement forcefully takes the side of the homosexual in the marriage question, then it takes a step forward toward reaching beautiful and lofty goals, the original idea of marriage, and the love ties between men and women would then be allowed to attain their rightful place. It is an ethical requirement in order to daily smash the face of public contempt, which causes numerous marriages of circumstance, so that persons may enter into marriage because they love one another.

I noticed that many homosexual women marry because they become aware of their nature too late and thus become unhappy in their innocence and make themselves unhappy. Here, too, the Women's Movement may take a stand by speaking about the question of their education as youths—which they often do—also by demonstrating how important it is for those parents who notice the homosexual bent in older children and youths, to make a long, loving and exact observation—and honest and understanding observers can recognize it in many ways—to explain in an understandable way the essence of homosexuality and their own natural inclinations.

Doing this prevents early misery enormously, instead, as often happens, of trying by all kinds of means to force homosexual children to take the heterosexual path. One need not fear that effeminate heterosexual children may be considered homosexual and thus be made into homosexuals, because, in the first place, such a diagnosis would naturally have to come from an experienced medical doctor, and secondly, as experience has taught, neither education nor any such a thing can change the heterosexual drive into a homosexual one and vice versa.

Of course, a heterosexual person can be seduced into homosexual behavior, but this occurs out of curiosity, search for pleasure or as a surrogate for the absence of normal intercourse—the latter occurs in the case of the navy—but the innate drive is not changed because of this, because under normal circumstances this does not occur.

At this time I would like to repeat what Dr. Hirschfeld has often explained, that homosexuality is not class specific, that it occurs among the upper class no less than among the lower or vice versa. No father and no mother, neither of them, ladies and gentlemen, can know without a doubt if there is an Uranian child among their offspring.

In middle-class circles they believe, oddly enough, that among them homosexuality has no place, and from these circles the most annoying enemies recruit each other against the movement to free Uranian people. I would like to give as an example, that my father, when by chance he came to speak about homosexuality, explained with conviction, "nothing of the sort can happen in my family." The facts prove the opposite. I need add nothing to that statement.

To return to the question of marriage, I would like to make note that a homosexual woman never becomes what one refers to with the expression "old spinster." The situation is worth investigating because it easily makes the Urninds especially recognizable at a later age.

Just take a look at an unmarried woman between the ages of 30 and 50 years. You will notice none of the joked-about characteristics of the average unmarried, heterosexual woman. This observation is instructive. It proves that a reasonable and moderate gratification of the sexual drive keeps a woman happy, fresh, and active, while absolute abstinence easily develops those characteristics which we feel unpleasant in old spinsters, for example, unfriendliness, hysteria, etc.

In order to create the possibility for homosexuals and all women in general to be able to live according to their own nature, it is necessary to actively join the strivings of the movement, which wishes to open immense possibilities of education and new occupations.

Now I am touching a sore spot in the evaluation of the sexes. I believe that all people, in all good will, would agree, if we research again here what intention nature, which is never wrong, had when it created man, woman and the transitional stages between the two. And one would have to agree that it is wrong to place one sex higher than the other, as it were, to speak of a first class—the man—a second class—the woman—and a third class sex—the Uranians.

The sexes are not to be evaluated differently, because they are distinct. The facts which show clearly and naturally that men, women and Urnings are not qualified for all occupations cannot be altered by the Women's Movement—and it does not wish to. A feminine woman is already organically by nature determined above all to become a wife and mother. And she has the right to be proud of her natural destination, because an occupation more highly esteemed than motherhood does not exist.

The woman, wife and mother or who is one of both, should not forget the rest of the world—she should take part all the more in all events of public life—that she may be capable is the goal of the Women's Movement, and that is, indeed, one of its finest goals.

To the normal, I mean, to the totally masculine man, other functions are given by nature and are shown other ways, than to a woman. He is—it cannot be denied—predestined for the most part to undertake a rougher battle than the woman, and so, occupations are open to him which obviously remain closed to women, for example, the military, all occupations which demand heavy labor, etc. Obviously there is also a bridge upon which some occupations rest, ones which both men and women are able to equally fill according to each person's abilities.

The logic of enemies to the Women's Movement falls apart because it equates all women under the label "woman" without considering that nature never created two persons alike, that the opinion whether an occupation be for a man or a woman is solely a matter of inner, masculine or feminine character.

From this we may differentiate between a feminine individuality in which feminine characteristics dominate, a masculine one dominated by masculine characteristics, and finally a masculine-feminine or feminine-masculine individuality in which there is an equal mixture of both.

Because nature created different kinds of sexes does not mean to say that there is only one sphere of activity for women—the home—and for the man another—the world—rather, nature's intention was and is without a doubt that each person has the opportunity to reach the goal which one is able to fulfill by one's own means and merits.

The interrelationships of masculine and feminine characteristics in people is so endless that common sense tells us that each child—whether it is male or female is all the same—must reach independence. The adult will have to decide for itself whether its natural drives lead to home, world, marriage or unmarried life. There must be a freedom of the play of the energies, then one can make the best and surest decision between becoming one of the women who can and wants to take up an artistic or academic occupation outside the home, or one of those women who does not feel enough energy to do this. And again it is the responsibility of the parents, who should feel this as their holiest duty, to be just toward each child's individuality and to avoid a make-believe system of education to fit all circumstances.

Schools are another story which, naturally, cannot do without certain methods, but it must be agreed upon, when it concerns girls and boys, to get rid of the old madness that the brains of girls have a weaker aptitude than boys' brains. One need not fear that competition in all the occupations will get out of hand because of the possibilities of co-education—especially, as the enemies' side believes, in academic occupations. It is for these scientific occupations which homosexual women are best suited, because they have the ability of a greater objectivity, energy, and endurance which is often lacking in very feminine women.

These facts do not exclude the very capable heterosexual women doctors, jurists, etc., but in spite of this, I feel that, with her own interest in mind, the heterosexual woman will always find happiness in the most favorable way or find it more meaningful to marry and make herself a partner to a man who feels the same way about her, who not only loves her sexually but also esteems her as his equal mentally and who recognizes that his rights are, of course, just as valid as hers.

Men, women and homosexuals, thus would have equal opportunity in a goal-oriented education, and a broader range of opportunities in education would open to male and female youths. Men would become the breadwinners of a thinking and understanding partner, women would slowly reach a worthy and just and respected position, and the Urninds would be able to devote themselves freely to the occupation of their choice.

Just as a man oftentimes prefers to take up an occupation which is typical of a woman's occupation—for example, women's designing, nursing, the occupation of the cook, the servant—there are also occupations which Uranian woman are especially attracted to. As a matter of fact, a great number of homosexual woman show up in the fields of medicine, law, and business and even in the creative arts. There are men who, like Weininger, believe that all great historical literary, scientific or otherwise known, important or famous women have been homosexuals.

According to my past statements, I do not have to especially accentuate that this highly one-sided view is unproved, because not only history, but also our own eyes daily show us the weakness in this theory. On the other hand, I would not deny that many important women have been homosexual, just to mention Sappho, Christine of Sweden, Sonja Kowlewska, Rosa Bonheur. However, it would seem strange if one wanted to classify Elizabeth of England and Catherine the Great of Russia as Uranian persons; the latter was perhaps bisexual—her many male and female "friendships" seem to imply this—a pure homosexual, however, she was not.

In opposition to the anti-feminists who claim that the female sex is inferior and who acknowledge only those women who exhibit strong masculine characteristics, I accept both as equals, but I am convinced that a homosexual woman is especially best suited to play a leading role in the enormous movement for the rights of women which is worldwide. And, in fact, from the very beginning of the Women's Movement to the present day it has been more often than not homogenic women who took over the leadership in numerous battles, who only means of their energy does the average woman, indifferent to her nature and easily subjugating herself, be brought to the awareness of her worth as a person and of her inalienable rights.

I cannot and will not name anyone, because as long as homosexuality remains something criminal and is considered to be against nature, as in many circles, as something unhealthy, some women may be offended whom I would like to indicate as being homosexual. We must always be proper and dutiful and not be indiscreet, and the noble feelings of the Uranian love of a female Women's-Rights-Fighter, as heterosexual sentimentality, do not belong before a public forum. One who has only just superficially followed the development of the Women's Movement, one who is acquainted with a few or many leading women, one who has a spark of understanding for homosexuals would soon pick out those female Women's-Rights-Fighters and would recognize that not the worst is among them.

If we weight all the contributions which homosexual women make to the Women's Movement, one would be astounded that its large and influential organizations have not lifted a finger to obtain justice in the state and in society for the not so small number of its Uranian members, and that they have done absolutely nothing to this very day to protect so many of its most well-known and most worthy female predecessors in this battle from ridicule and scorn when they explain to the greater public about the true essence of Uranism.

One should never have found it so difficult to point out how the characteristics of the homosexual tendency express themselves more involuntarily and without the slightest personal, intentional assistance of appearance, speech, behavior, gesture, clothing, etc. And the Urninds concerned are most unjustly given up to the ridicule of unknowing persons. Also, notice that many homosexual women naturally do not always appear masculine, which would be in harmony with her nature. There are also numerous Urninds who appear completely feminine, who go through all the motions to hide their homosexuality, a comedy which makes them uncomfortable and under which they suffer.

I am well acquainted with the reason why this doubly exceptional hesitation exists, because the Women's Movement has handled even general sexual matters with an odd frankness and matter-of-factness. It is the fear that the movement would suffer because of the broach of the homosexual question by becoming active by flashing the human rights of homosexuals in the blind eyes of the ignorant masses. I cannot deny that having this fear so early in the movement is justified, and it should be avoided in order not to lose friends again, and there should be a fully unconditional apology made for the total ignorance of the homosexual problem in earlier times.

Today, however, when the movement is moving incessantly forward, when no bureaucratic wisdom, no bourgeois ignorance can be victorious over it any longer, today I must point out that a total rejection of the doubtless very important question is unjust, is an injustice which is brought upon the Women's Movement by itself in many cases.

The so-called "moderate" tendency will not help homosexuals one bit for the simple reason that deeds of this kind have no tendency at all. Victory will come as a sign of radicalism, and we expect that the radicals will change the direction and for once make it honestly and openly recognized; indeed, there is a great number of Urninds among us, and we owe them a word of thanks for their efforts and their work and for many a fine success.

I do not mean to say that all questions of the Women's Movement will be handled from the homosexual viewpoint, just as I do not ascribe all this success to the Urninds or even a greater portion of it—that would be just as insane as it is wrong to take no notice at all of the homosexual problem. The Women's Movement doubtless has greater and more important concerns than the freedom of homosexuals—but only by taking care of the lesser matters can these greater efforts be accomplished.

Therefore, the Women's Movement should not ascribe to the homosexual problem such a great importance; it does not need to go out into the streets to preach against the injustice of Uranians—it should not do this, because it would surely hurt our cause—I do not underestimate this at all; it needs only to act by giving due consideration to the homosexual question when it discusses sexual, ethical, economic, and general human relationships between the sexes. This it surely can do; and by doing this it will slowly carry out its educational goal without much ado.

Now I am coming to a point which in recent years has especially come into the sphere of our work in the Women's Movement—I am going to speak of prostitution. One may wish to speak of this from an ethical standpoint. No matter, one will have to deal with it now as in the past and as in the future. Personally, I consider prostitution to be a pitiful but necessary evil, which we will be able to put a halt to in more favorable times—a goal which is worth the effort in the long run.

The importance of the battle of the Women's Movement against the increase of prostitution and against genocidal venereal disease, it seems to me, is that approximately 20% of prostitutes are evidently homosexual. At first you may find it unusual that homosexuality and enduring sexual intercourse with men appear as the most paradoxical thing that could ever exist. To my question how it is possible that an Urnind becomes a prostitute, a "woman of the street" once answered that she views her sad task as a business—her sexual drive does not come under consideration at all. She satisfies this with her lover.

These women have conducted some foul business in the streets. When the Women's Movement has succeeded in opening all suitable occupations for women, carrying through an equal respect of the abilities and inclinations of each person, then there will no longer be any homosexual young women among prostitutes, and a great number of the heterosexual women will be able to nourish themselves better and with more humanity than by the bad social conditions of prostitution today. They would be able to immediately take up an occupation, because women would be taught understanding and independence in their youth.

A young woman who is hardened early for the struggle to make a living will end up on the streets less often than a young woman who lives without a knowledge of the most basic and natural facts of life. In a certain sense the battle of the homogenic woman for her social recognition is also a battle against prostitution, and again I stress, that in this struggle it is only a matter of restraining it and never of suppressing it fully.

One must not forget that when a more correct judgment of Uranism is reached in general, a great number of homosexual men who now, out of fear of being discovered go to a prostitute, which is very much against their nature, may abstain from them. This would naturally decrease the amount of venereal disease, although it would not cause a great decrease. But I believe it would be a worthwhile cause, because each individual case of syphilis or some other venereal disease which would be prevented means a contribution to the health of the people and thus one to the next generation, which is in the long run a gain for the fatherland.

The Women's Movement is fighting for the rights of free individuals and of self-determination. Therefore, it must recognize the despised spell which society casts on Uranians even today, which oppresses their rights and their duty to take a stand and fight the battle on the side of the Uranians as they do unwed mothers, women workers and many others who need it, and to fight for their rights and for their freedom in their battle against old-fashioned false opinions of morality, but when it is really immoral to render a morality which is the worst immorality when women have inalienable rights torn from them and when they now must struggle in bloody battle to recover them; when Uranians have inalienable human rights to their kind of love torn from them, a love which is just as pure and noble as heterosexual love when they are good people who so love. There are as many good people among homosexuals as among so-called "normal" people.

Most of all, I would like to avoid the appearance of estimating homosexuals too highly. I can assure you, ladies and gentlemen, I will not do that—I am well aware of the problems of homosexuality, but I also recognize its good side. Therefore, I would like to say that Uranians are no better or no worse than heterosexuals—they should not be treated differently, but only in a different way.

To conclude my statements I would like to emphasize again that homosexual women have done their part in the greater Women's Movement, that they are mostly responsible for activating the movement. They have suffered because of their masculine inclinations and natural characteristics, and because of the many, many injustices and hardships caused by laws, society, and the old morality which concerns women. Without the power and cooperation of the Urninds, the Women's Movement would not be so successful today, which it certainly is—which could easily be proven.

The Women's Movement and the movement for homosexual rights have thus far traveled on a dark road which has posted many obstacles in their way. Now it will become brighter and brighter around us and in the hearts of the people. This is not to say that the work of securing the rights of women and of Uranians has come to an end; we are still in the middle of two opposing sides, and many a bloody battle will have to be fought. There will be many victims of the injustice of laws which will deal the death-blow before both movements have reached their goal—to gain the freedom of each person.

Our ultimate goal will be reached when both movements recognize that they have many common interests for which to fight when it becomes necessary. And when, at times, as they will, hard times come to either side—that will not be the time for hesitation to stand up in defense against injustice and to march on to the victory which will surely be ours.

Revelation and truth are like the rising sun in the East—no power can force it out of its orbit. Slowly but surely it rises to its glittering zenith! Perhaps not today or tomorrow, but in the not too distant future the Women's Movement and Uranians will raise their banners in victory!

Per aspera ad astra! (Reach for the stars!)

1928

Appeal . . . on Behalf of an Oppressed Human Variety

Kurt Hiller

The full title of this speech is "Appeal to the Second International Congress for Sexual Reform on Behalf of an Oppressed Human Variety," and it was delivered at the meeting of the congress in Copenhagen, Denmark. The text had been prepared by Kurt Hiller of Germany's Scientific Humanitarian Committee, who was unable to attend the Danish meeting due to financial considerations. It was therefore delivered by Dr. Magnus Hirschfeld, founder of the committee and then serving as president of the Sexual Reform Congress. The comment about rebutting Monsieur Barbusse refers to Henri Barbusse (1873-1935), a Marxist writer and novelist.

Honorable President, distinguished members of the Congress!

I thank you for giving me the opportunity to express my thoughts to you—indirectly; I should have presented them myself in your midst, had my economic situation not prevented me from making the trip to Copenhagen.

I wish to use the international forum you have set up to cry out to the world: From time immemorial there has existed among all peoples an unusual, but otherwise perfectly worthy, harmless, guiltless variety of human being, and this variety—as if we were still living in the darkest Middle Ages—is senselessly and horribly persecuted by many peoples, following the lead of their legislators, governments and courts. Let the intellectual world, the researchers, and policy makers of all nations stand up against this barbarism and demand in the name of humanity: Halt!

The variety of which I speak is that minority of human beings whose love impulses are directed, not toward a member of the other sex, but rather toward a member of their own; these are so-called homosexuals, Urnings, or inverts.

They are outlawed, it is said, because their feelings and acts are "contrary to nature." However, their feelings and acts are rooted in their constitution, components of their character, something dictated to them by nature. And since the history of all primitive and all civilized peoples demonstrates that such a minority has existed in all ages, then this fact means that we are obligated to recognize this nature as being indeed perfectly natural—shocking, perhaps, but nothing that deserves to be either denied or defamed. A phenomenon of nature that is incomprehensible or discomfiting to the majority does not cease on that account to be a phenomenon of nature.

Same-sex love is not a mockery of nature, but rather nature at play; and anyone who maintains the contrary—that love, as everyone knows, is intended to serve the propagation of the species, that homosexual or heterosexual potency is squandered on goals other than procreation—fails to consider the superabundance with which Nature in all her largesse wastes semen, millions and billions of times over. As Nietzsche expressed it in *Daybreak,* "Procreation is a frequently occurring accidental result of one way of satisfying the sexual drive—it is neither its goal nor necessary consequence." The theory which would make procreation the "goal" of sexuality is exposed as hasty, simplistic and false by the phenomenon of same-sex love alone. Nature's laws, unlike the laws formulated by the human mind, cannot be violated. The assertion that a specific phenomenon of nature could somehow be "contrary to nature" amounts to pure absurdity. Nevertheless, this absurd claim has persisted for many centuries in literature and in legislation, and even quite celebrated sex educators have come out with this nonsense.

Just recently, an internationally renowned spokesman of the European left, Henri Barbusse, exhibited his knowledge and brainpower most unfavorably when he answered, in response to a circular inquiry (in the Paris magazine *Les Marges* of March 15, 1926): "I believe that this diversion of a natural instinct is, like many other perversions, a sign of the profound social and moral decadence of a certain sector of present-day society. In all eras, decadence has manifested itself in over-refinements and anomalies of the senses, feelings and emotions."

One must reply to Monsieur Barbusse that this alleged "over-refinement" of which he speaks, uncritically parroting a popular misconception, has always manifested itself just as much at times when a race was on the ascent as when it was in decline that, for example, love between man and youth was no more excluded from the heroic and golden ages of Ancient Greece than it was from the most illustrious period of Islamic culture, or from the age of Michelangelo; and that a Marxist is making a fool of himself when he tries to connect the homosexuality of the present with the class struggle, by pointing to it as a symptom of the "moral decadence" of "a certain sector" of society, namely, the bourgeois sector: as though same-sex love did not occur among proletarians of all kinds—among workers, peasants, employees, little people in all occupations—just as much as among the possessing classes.

The experience of sexologists and psychotherapists proves the contrary. Nature does not stop at any social class when creating her marvelous varieties of human beings. It is true that the proletariat as a rule has less time and means than the propertied classes to devote to the pursuit of sexual pleasure, even to the sublime forms of sublimated eroticism; and this is one reason which, among many others, leads—or ought to lead—the fighter for human happiness toward socialism. But this is just as true for the broad mass of proletarians considered heterosexual as for the minority considered homosexual.

The public hears much less about the homosexuality of the modest little people than it does about that of the luxury circles of the big bourgeoisie, but it would be extremely superficial to infer on this basis that homosexuality is some kind of monopoly of the bourgeoisie. One must realize, rather, that the outlawing of same-sex eros strikes the homosexual proletarian even harder than the homosexual capitalist, because the capitalist has the resources at his disposal to evade it more easily.

At any rate, the homosexually inclined worker owes little gratitude to Monsieur Barbusse when he attacks the alleged "complacency" with which some authors place their "delicate talents" at the service of the homosexual question, "while our old world convulses in terrible economic and social crises," venomously asserting that their doing so "does no honor to this decadent intellectual phalanx" and that it "can only reinforce the contempt which the young and healthy popular force feels for the advocates of this unhealthy and artificial doctrine."

The "terrible economic and social crises" in which the world is "convulsing" apparently prevent Monsieur Barbusse from relinquishing a prejudice which he shares with the most backward people of all nations. The Emperor Napoleon and his Chancellor Cambaceres were more revolutionary four generations ago when they freed homosexual acts from the penal code, than this revolutionary of today. Barbusse sings the same moralizing tune on this matter, of which he understands nothing, as the most reactionary ministers in the German government when their "theme" is to draft bills on matters of which they likewise understand nothing. "Contempt," "healthy popular force," "unhealthy doctrine"—we have long heard phrases like these from the conservative and clerical jurists of the Wilhelmine era.

At this moment, when Soviet Russia has abolished the penalties on homosexual acts (per se); when fascism is on the rise, appearing in Italy for the first time in generations; when reaction and progress are locked in furious combat over the homosexual question in Germany and several other countries, along comes Comrade Barbusse, member of the Third International. Unburdened by any relevant knowledge, he delivers a bigoted, agitational tirade against a species of human being that is already sufficiently agitated against, and he unscrupulously stabs in the back those who are waging a good fight on behalf of freedom, even if by its nature the cause is unpopular. I regret that I find it necessary to speak the truth so bluntly to a master whose poetry and political philosophy I once admired; but the higher someone stands, who disseminates false and reactionary theories, the more sharply he must be rebutted, for his theories are all the more dangerous.

It is not true that homosexuality is a sign of "decadence" or something pathological. Men of glowing physical health, of undeniable mental soundness, and of great intellectual powers have been bearers of this inclination—just as often as have been the weak, the unstable, and the inferior. There are inferior, average, and superior homosexuals—exactly as there are inferior, average, and superior heterosexuals. To belong, not to the rule, not to the "norm," but rather to the exception, to the minority, to the variety, is neither a symptom of degeneration nor of pathology. Likewise, having red hair is neither decadent nor sick.

If it is true that there are higher percentages of the mentally weak, the eccentric, the unbalanced, the hypersensitive, and the hypertense among homosexuals than among those oriented in the usual way, the blame should not be placed upon the predisposition, but rather upon the circumstances in which these people find themselves. One who lives constantly under the onus of attitudes and laws that stamp his inclination as inferior must be of an unusually robust nature to retain his full worth in every respect. If the terrible weight of contempt and persecution that bears down on homosexuals were to be lifted from them, the neurotic traits within would to the same degree vanish, and then the intrinsic creative worth of their nature, especially the pedagogical ability of which Plato wrote, would come into play. It is necessary to incorporate homosexuals in the general culture of society, to assign homosexuality a place in society where it can act productively, for it has its own fertility. Hellas, and above all Sparta, understood this and knew how to draw the practical conclusions from this knowledge.

But before homosexuality can be assigned this positive and even sublime role in the state, which corresponds to its particular character and at the same time is of service to the state, we must first carry out a negative, liberating, and humanitarian action directed against the worst injustice: that the public outlawry, under which this variety suffers, must be abolished in all countries. To be sure, it is not just the penal code that is involved, but it is the penal code that must be dealt with first.

Homosexual acts committed by fully competent and mutually consenting adults are still punished in England (one may recall the tragedy of Oscar

Wilde); and in the United States, along with Argentina and Chile; in Germany and Austria; in several Scandinavian, East European, and Balkan countries; and also in the German Canton of Switzerland—only homosexual women are for the most part privileged. In these countries, the threat of a long prison sentence is real. The German draft penal code of 1925 provides for a maximum of ten years in the penitentiary!

It is not society in these countries which profits thereby, but rather the tribe of blackmailers, and thousands of socially valuable lives are ruined. Despite Monsieur Barbusse, France, and along with France the great majority of Latin countries, no longer have the penalty; likewise, the Islamic countries, China, and Japan do not have it; and the Soviet Union, as I have already mentioned, has abolished it.

It is clear that socially harmful conduct in the sphere of same-sex love should remain punishable to the same degree as socially harmful conduct in the sphere of opposite-sex love; that therefore the free sexual self-determination of adults and the inexperience of sexually immature youth should be protected by law; and that the misuse of economic or official dependence for lascivious purposes should be forbidden, as well as indecent behavior in public places—with complete parity between heterosexual and homosexual acts. If anyone claims that the homosexual liberation movement would like to see *carte blanche* given to unrestrained and antisocial debauchery, or that such liberation would place the interests of the abnormal above the interests of society—then he is lying. The interests of society come first; but I question whether the interests of society demand that human beings be thrown in prison, disgraced, and ruined socially for acts that harm no one, merely because their erotic taste differs from that of the majority. I question whether the interest of society is served when a minority of its members are forced through severe penalties into lifelong sexual abstinence or chronic self-gratification (the situation imposed upon convicts serving life sentences)—a minority which, we know, causes not the slightest harm by following its own nature. That child molesters or homosexual lust-murderers should be protected is not the thrust of my argument.

Prudishness, along with false and monstrous notions about the forms that same-sex lovemaking takes, prevents a general public discussion of the problem—especially in countries where it is most needed. And even more than prudishness; the apathy of those not personally involved, both in the masses and among the intelligentsia. One must have a great sense of justice and noblesse to take on the cause of a persecuted minority to which one does not personally belong. But fortunately there are still a certain number of people distinguished by such fairness. These people comprehend that an age in which concern for national minorities is so extraordinarily keen and active must find the courage to protect a minority which, to be sure, is not an ethnic one, but which can be found in all states, and is especially deserving of protection, since there is no state in the world where they are the majority and with which they, like the national minorities, could identify. International minority rights, which are slowly taking shape, should defend not only the national, the racial, and the religious minorities, but also the psycho-biological, the sexual minorities, so long as they are harmless; and if the Second International Congress for Sexual Reforms chooses to speak out in favor of these ideas, it would be a courageous act of ethical rationality.

SECTION II: THE 1950s

September 1952

Address to the International Committee for Sexual Equality

Donald Webster Cory

This address was given to the International Committee for Sexual Equality meeting at the University of Frankfurt, Frankfurt am Main, Germany. Cory was the author of the groundbreaking book *The Homosexual in America,* which had been published in 1951. The group in Los Angeles mentioned in his coverage of activism on behalf of homosexuals is the Mattachine Society. Donald Webster Cory was the pseudonym used by the gay activist writer Edward Sagarin (1913-1986), who would later reject this advocacy and publish antigay articles in sociology under his own name.

The United States of America today occupies a position unique in Western culture. As a result of the decline of the British Empire, the rise in influence of the Soviet Union in Eastern Europe and in Asia, and the resultant division of the world into two great and perhaps mutually antagonistic forces, the United States, with its vast reservoirs of raw materials, its industrial efficiency and wealth, has emerged in international affairs in a position of influence and affluence such as has been centered in no single nation since the decline of the Holy Roman Empire. In every field of human endeavor, the peoples of the free world are watching America, hopeful that out of this land will come new vistas of progress, yet skeptical of the meaning of American democracy and culture in terms of human values. Thus, despite the very slow and halting steps forward that emerge from this land, such progress is watched with greater interest outside the borders of the forty-eight states than are similar developments in other countries. The changes now taking place in American attitudes towards sex, as in other fields, therefore have significance far greater than would be apparent if such changes were to be found in another land, be it France or India or England or the Dominican Republic. Yet the new outlook, simultaneously revolutionary and evolutionary as it paradoxically must be, is formulated in an atmosphere so devoid of the free interchange of thought (the very essence of that highly publicized American democracy) that outside of a professional few, people are for the most part unaware of what is occurring.

More than any other power, the United States was founded on traditions of puritanism. The concept of sex as a necessary evil, an ugly pursuit enjoyed by man because of the devil incarnate in the flesh, was taught by the early cultural leaders of this country. The varying and diverse elements that made up the American melting pot vied with one another to appear before the masses as pure and good, one group not to be outdone by another in the antisexual repudiation of physical desire. Thus the struggle of the Protestant puritans to maintain a rigid and self-avowedly virtuous ban on all things sexual was strengthened by the several minorities that found conformance the road to acceptance and possibly integration into American life: the immigrants so anxious to abandon their European culture which was to them a stigma; the Jews, who found in their Talmudic codes a reinforcement of sexual repudiation; the Negroes, freed from slavery and desirous of appearing "good" and "moral" and "pure" in the sense that these words were being used and misused; and the Catholics, who succeeded in wresting the leadership from the puritan Protestants in the antisexual culture.

It was in this milieu that sex became the unmentionable subject in nineteenth century America. Birth control information dared not be disseminated through the mails; and the education of young people in things sexual consisted in the main of long sermons by ignorant hypocrites who warned that masturbation would lead to insanity.

A revolutionary change has taken place in America during the decades since the First World War. American thinking has begun to catch up with the American practice. The activities which were indulged in so frequently by men and women, never admitted, always frowned upon, seldom discussed or written about, now became topics of open conversation. No longer did people suffer great shock when they learned the elementary facts of life.

Thus, the changing social scene made it possible for leadership to arise that would provide the scientific data, in psychological and sociological areas, to substantiate the amorphous ideas beginning to formulate in the minds of the people, and at the same time such leadership could capture the imagination of large segments of the population. For America has been a land where the masses move slowly, seldom more than passingly alert to an issue, and always seeking to designate the responsibility in the hands of a hero, a movement, a leader. As Gunnar Myrdal reported:

> *The idea of leadership pervades American thought and collective action. The demand for "intelligent" leadership is raised in all political camps, social and professional groups, and, indeed, in every collective activity centered around any interest or purpose . . . If an ordinary*

> *American faces a situation which he recognizes as a "problem" without having any specific views as to how to "solve" it, he tends to resort to two general recommendations; one, traditionally, is "education," the other is "leadership." The demand for leadership . . . is a result less of a conscious ideological principle than of a pragmatic approach to those activities which require the cooperation of many individuals.*

Until a few years ago, this need for leadership, so acutely felt by all those striving to break through the morass of misinformation, hypocrisy, and censorship, was left unanswered. Then the report of Kinsey and his associates was published. This book, bombshell that it was in the complacent scene of puritanical hypocrisy, denounced as it was from all sides, could never have found the light of a printed page in America some two or three decades earlier. Professor Kinsey, still looked on with some skepticism by die-hards who are more intent on retaining preconceived ideologies than on verifying their scientific validity, nevertheless became an acknowledged leader overnight in an area of American thinking. Yet, to understand the full significance of the American scene, let it be emphasized that this scientist would have been stoned and lynched had his findings been proclaimed in the nineteenth century. Thus, the Kinsey report is in the first instance a manifestation, a proof, of the change that was taking place in this country, although more than that, it facilitated and expedited this changing process. It is therefore one—perhaps the most dramatic, certainly the best known—of many dynamic occurrences, which are made possible by the very events that they, in turn, make more possible.

It is against this background that the status of the homosexual in America must be studied. It is today generally recognized that the homosexuals constitute a sociological minority, a factor most important in America, a land in which the minority problem, particularly as concerning the rights and the integration of ethnic groups, has admittedly become the most important domestic situation facing this country. The mutual antagonisms between the various ethnic groups have produced several phenomena that must be noted.

The intellectual and cultural leadership of this country has almost unanimously endorsed the ultimate aims and the immediate struggles of the ethnic minorities. As a result, novelists, journalists, statesmen, church and lay leaders today proclaim the principles of brotherhood, espouse a philosophy based on the recognition of the rights of man, state that all men are brothers and that minorities must be given equal rights in all walks of life. Although many of these leaders would be the first to denounce the homosexual, to deny that they favor rights for this maligned group, their propaganda, to the extent that it has any impact on American thinking, is one which coincides with the aspirations of all minorities, not excluding the sexual.

However, a great gap exists between American leadership and the American people on the ethnic minority problems. The great mass of American people, not only in the South, but even in the North, certainly do not practice equality with Negroes, and continue to a large extent to practice anti-Semitism in their social and economic affairs. This cultural gap results from the lesser influence of tradition, superstition and outworn ideology on the thinking of the more intelligent, the more educated, and the more enlightened. It is a gap that will in due time be closed by the process of education and enlightenment that is in the hands of the leadership, but most important of all, it is a gap which, I maintain, I can already find in existence so far as the homosexual minority is concerned.

The segmentation of the population into mutually antagonistic ethnic groups causes certain divisive influences within the homosexual minority. First, some homosexuals (although the proportion is smaller than among heterosexuals) reflect the antagonistic attitudes toward some ethnic groups, and hence a unified minority is difficult to fuse. Secondly, some members of the Jewish-homosexual and the Negro-homosexual double minorities fear to conduct a struggle on behalf of their sex group because it might, they reason, vitiate their struggle on behalf of their ethnic group. The latter is usually considered by these people to be their first loyalty, their original and their lasting group identification. They are furthermore unconvinced of the propriety of the struggle for sexual rights on the same level and with the same righteous vigor as the struggle for ethnic rights.

Nevertheless, most homosexuals do participate in a greater amount of inter-ethnic mingling than do heterosexuals, and this, too, is a double-edged sword. On the one hand, it aids the unity within the homosexual group, but it creates an antagonistic attitude toward homosexuals on the part of many individuals who, still under reactionary influences as far as minorities are concerned, look upon the Negro-white alliances as further proof, not of liberalism and emancipation, but of degeneration.

The current status of the American homosexual is characterized by the following main phenomena: (1) increasing awareness of the existence of the group, and of the widespread adherence to its practices, on the part of the large masses of people; (2) increasing expressions of support and sympathy for the group by leadership in psychological, sociological and other areas of American thought; (3) tendency to accept the existence of the group as an unfortunate necessity, a problem that cannot be erased, but a continued unwillingness to accept the individual members who become adherents of it or identified with it; (4) tolerance toward certain group activities so long as they remain anonymous and hide behind a façade of respectability, no matter how thin the veil; (5) a tendency within the group to feel that (a) this status is not unbearable, (b) a better one is not deserved, and (c) the struggle for change may bring down the wrath from law-makers and other authorities.

These are characteristics that differ considerably from the situation that prevailed some thirty or forty years back. At that time, the manifestations of homosexuality were carefully hidden, the word unspoken and unknown save in medical circles, the members of the group concealing their activities in the most complete and utter fear. The problem could not be mentioned in newspapers or magazines, and many educated people lived for decades without any awareness of it. Historians of the American scene have even been deluded into believing that the complete cloak of silence existed because there was no homosexuality at the time, and they denounce those who interpret in this manner the writings of Herman Melville, Walt Whitman, and Henry James as being inconsistent with the prevailing puritanical codes of nineteenth century America.

This change that has taken place is not so much one of greater acceptance of the homosexual on the part of American society, but rather an acknowledgment of the existence of the minority and of the problem involved therein. Once "homosexual" was the most unmentionable, the most unprintable, of any word, except for the so-called obscenities, in the English language. Today it is mentioned and printed everywhere, but, to use the expression of Menninger, it is today the "most electric" word in our language. From silence to discussion, even without enlightenment, is progress, for enlightenment becomes inevitable through discussion, and impossible without it.

Within the most advanced cultural circles, it is today rare to find outright condemnation of homosexual activities. Whether one looks to Kinsey, who reaches an audience far wider than any other leader in sex thinking in the history of America (and possibly in world history, save for Freud), or whether one looks to psychiatrists, church leaders, and others, it is today not at all uncommon to find the homosexual defended by men of the highest intellectual integrity.

For example, on the question of arrests, Kinsey recently spoke before the National Probation and Parole Association, and stated that there are cities in the United States where more than half of the alleged sex offenses are initiated by police intent on obtaining blackmail. Furthermore, he said, "there are cities in which there is no greater blackmail racket than that operated by police against homosexuals." This statement received wide publicity in the newspapers, and it is a statement that is of utmost importance because it is characteristic of a new thinking and a new approach: namely, the homosexual is no longer a pariah without his intellectual defender.

Permit me to cite a few other examples. Dr. Robert W. Laidlaw, speaking before the Section on Marriage and Family Counseling of the National

Council on Family Relations, stated: *"It happens that I act as psychiatric consultant in a theological seminary, where one finds a very high type of individual—particularly in the music school—who is beset by homosexual conflicts . . . A few months ago, in a seminar with the faculty of this seminary, we had quite a discussion in regard to whether homosexuality, per se, should disqualify a man from the ministry. I steadfastly upheld the platform that it should not."*

Those who are unable to find a change in American attitudes should ask themselves whether a psychiatrist could have taken this position twenty or thirty years earlier, and whether he could have defended it at a public gathering without eliciting a single word of disagreement.

Finally, in psychiatric and psychological circles, it is becoming increasingly apparent that, despite the emphasis of these professionals on the disturbances of homosexuals, many of the difficulties can be overcome by a correction of the attitude of society. In his brilliant book, *The Folklore of Sex,* Dr. Albert Ellis writes:

> *The banning of certain sexual outlets—e.g., homosexuality—which would be, under normal circumstances, merely peculiar and idiosyncratic modes of behavior serves to make the users of these outlets neurotic—and to make neurotics use these outlets. In this sense, sex "perversion" does not render society sick, but society makes sick people out of "perverts"—and induces individuals to use "perversions" as neurotic symptoms.*

This concept, that the ills of society may be the cause of the difficulties of the homosexual, rather than the effect, was expressed by the eminent physician Dr. Harry Benjamin, in the *American Journal of Psychotherapy,* as follows: *"If adjustment is necessary, it should be made primarily with regard to the position the homosexual occupies in present day society and society should more often be the patient to be treated than the invert."*

But if society is sick, what is to be done about it? And if the homosexual's disturbance is, at least partially, the result of the hostility of society, how can he be helped?

First, not all homosexuals think that something should be done, although most are somewhat dissatisfied with the current situation. There are some people in the group who, recognizing the status quo as being less hostile, more possible to live with, than none might have expected, fear the consequences of a struggle, and fear public reaction to a fast-moving change. They believe that any effort to broaden the rights of these people would bring forth the wrath of the police and reaction in public attitudes, and they contend that the current situation is as liberal as the present American culture might permit. These same people, therefore, go a step further and justify some of the hostility toward the group, claiming that the homosexuals themselves, because of promiscuity, instability, exhibitionism, violence, and other alleged factors, are unworthy of better treatment and responsible for their own status. That the attitude briefly summarized here has its psychological foundations in the guilt of the individuals, and is a defensive justification of hostility which they require for self-condemnation, are too apparent to require elucidation. Whatever the causes, the inaction of these people, so far as social protest is concerned, is difficult to alter.

The struggle for social betterment is furthermore impeded by the secondary interest taken therein by the heterosexuals who have spoken out for improvement in status (as Kinsey, Ellis, Benjamin, and others) and by the fear surrounding the homosexuals who might be expected to have the motivation and incentive to give leadership to a more militant movement.

It is unrealistic to expect to find, within the group of sociologists, psychologists, and others, those people who are themselves heterosexual and yet are anxious to devote themselves to a cause with the perseverance, the fervor, the willingness to withstand calumny, that are required if any success is to be attained. These people, in the first instance, have certain reservations, not of a moral but of a psychological nature, and in the second place they are involved only intellectually, not emotionally.

So that the leadership would have to fall on those most vitally concerned, but a complete anonymity surrounds the individual members of this enormous group. Particularly those most capable of offering leadership, the college professors and university officials, the many authors, philosophers, journalists; the popular heroes in the sports and entertainment worlds, the prize fighters and baseball players and movie actors; the sociologists already engaged in a struggle for ethnic minority rights—these people have a vested interest in retaining their anonymity. What chance would a politician have, not only for election, but even for appointment to a position for which he was eminently qualified, if he should openly proclaim himself as part of a great movement to struggle for the rights of the homosexuals?

Without leadership, where can a movement originate and how can it gather strength? How can public attitudes be changed if those most capable of facilitating such a change have an interest in remaining silent on the one hand, or, on the other, can devote themselves to this situation only as a secondary pursuit?

It would seem, on the face of it, that we have here an insolvable contradiction. There can be no change without guidance from the more advanced, and no individuals offering such guidance dare to come forth unless a change is first effected to make it possible to function without martyrdom to oneself and one's immediate associates. As a matter of fact, the situation is even more complex, because any homosexuals who might conceivably acknowledge their drives in order to head a struggle would find themselves cut off from larger numbers of their own followers, who could not afford association with one who had dropped the mask of concealment.

And, after all, what could such a leadership do, if it should arise, and if it were possible to conduct such a struggle? It would have little access to the popular newspapers and journals, to the lecture platforms, to the air waves so influential in the shaping of American thought. It could not formulate an ethic and an outlook that would reflect the developed thinking of many intelligent men and women, because there is no medium for the argument and exchange of opinion so necessary in the evolution of a group ideology. Yet, without such a development, a leadership can only reflect its own narrow outlook, which may be far removed from that of the people who are ostensibly the followers. Thus, on such fundamental issues as to whether the movement for recognition should be one of militant protest or quiet accommodation; whether it should be one of struggle to effect changes in the laws or to educate the group to abide by certain laws; whether it should be one of teaching the public to accept the concept of variety in sexual expression or of teaching the group to accept the concept of monogamous fidelity to a single loser [*sic*]; whether the orientation should be to look inward toward an inner group minority and an almost segregated life or toward integration as human beings with those of all temperaments—on all of these questions the leadership could not develop an outlook that would reflect the viewpoint of those millions of Americans who are partisans of this minority.

Under these circumstances, a few people who believe militantly in the necessity of struggle have become demoralized. The situation, they state, is hopeless. Hostility prevents the emergence of the forces that are necessary to educate the public and the gay group, but without such forces hostility will continue its indefinite reign. Such pessimistic nihilism is not infrequently encountered.

Nevertheless, with the diminished hostility in the most advanced circles of American public opinion, with open espousal of the rights of homosexuals by many leaders who have access to America's eyes and ears, with the increasing attention given to the problem by many of the most prominent and talented writers, a new dynamic process is set in motion that will counteract the vicious circle of do-nothingism that has hitherto strangled the possibilities for effective homosexual action.

The gap that exists between important American thinkers, on the one hand, and large numbers of men and women, on the other, is a sociological phenomenon that cannot remain stagnant. The writers, philosophers, lecturers, jurists, even though they may reach but a few people with their message, impress their thought on teachers, preachers, journalists, and others, whose new outlook, once it has been formulated, is made known to many others. This is a long, drawn-out, and often a discouraging process, with the difficulties multiplied many times by prejudices and fears, but eventually the masses do catch up to their teachers, and then the lawmakers, politicians, rabble-rousers, begin to reflect this new attitude of the people, no longer finding it profitable to exploit a waning prejudice.

Thus, as the American cultural leaders speak up, on lecture platforms, in books and magazines, and through the channels of newspapers and occasionally even on the radio—speak up in defense of the victimized deviant, larger numbers of people, both inside and outside the group, are influenced in their attitudes. The diminished hostility resultant therefrom makes it possible for heterosexuals to believe in and express their friendly attitude, and likewise reduced are the guilt and fear within the homosexual group. As the fright at the specter of self-expression is lessened, the homosexual finds it possible to give a certain limited leadership to the protest, and this very small, frequently anonymous struggle can continue to spread a word of enlightenment, both to other homosexuals, and to heterosexuals, thus setting in motion a new cycle. As the shame is diminished with the increasing acceptance, both by one's self and one's associates, the righteousness of the cause of protest is impressed upon the minds of many homosexuals, and in fact the guilt of being homosexual is replaced by the guilt of not defending one's cause.

This is a new situation, and in recent years, it has already begun to manifest itself and to produce some small results. The law in some states has been relaxed, and in others many people have called for a change. Lecture groups of gay people have been initiated in several cities; private clubs and veterans organizations have been formed; a social-work group, having the open cooperation of numerous ministers, psychiatrists, and other professional men, has been incorporated and is now functioning to help those who run afoul of the law or who have other difficulties; a correspondence society is in existence; and in Los Angeles, where police terror is particularly outrageous, a group is functioning openly to raise funds and to conduct a public campaign against entrapment and police brutality.

The next steps are not easy to predict. The publishing program, both of fiction and non-fiction, can be better controlled, so that there is a wider influence of the group upon the thinking of those who become spokesmen. A magazine, perhaps quite unlike those published in Europe, may be able to be established in the United States, concentrating on literary and other cultural aspects of the group problem, or perhaps not devoted exclusively to this one group. Efforts must be made to enlist friends among the medical, psychological, legal and other professions to conduct a campaign more vigorous than heretofore in defense of the group and of its individual members.

Church leaders can be particularly effective in making representations against newspapers and magazines in protest against their one-sided hostility. An educational program to convince the homosexuals themselves of the propriety of their activities is urgently needed.

These are but meager beginnings. Each of these is amorphous, all of them disconnected, many functioning at cross-purposes to the others. But let us not fail to see the enormous importance of the beginnings. For these are the beginnings of the groups, the movements, the activities, and the struggles that will make possible the next step forward, that will spread the friendly word of truth both within and without the group, and this in turn will make it both necessary and possible for more such movements, and stronger ones, to arise, and for the influence to spread far and wide. With the greater influence, it will become less difficult for such activities to take place, and with the increased activity, the influence spreads to new circles with new messages. This is a new cycle and a dynamic one, whose aim and goal of sex equality are not beyond human reach.

January/February 1955

An Open Letter to Senator Dirksen

Anonymous

This letter, printed in the January/February issue of the *Mattachine Review,* was written by an official of the California Republican Party. It is intended as a response to what the accompanying note refers to as "critical remarks about sex variants" made by Senator Everett M. Dirksen during the 1954 campaign on September 22 at the Biltmore Hotel in Hollywood before a gathering of Republican women. The note accompanying the letter states that "because the writer admitted having homosexual tendencies, no name can be revealed."

TO: Senator Everett M. Dirksen
Senate of the United States
Washington, D. C.

Dear Senator Dirksen,

Because I have admired you and applauded your career as a great Republican from a State which has meant much to me, I trouble to write you this letter. I write, not only for myself however, but as a self-appointed spokesman for a large group of misunderstood and maligned people. A group to which you referred in your speech before the Republican women on September 22.

We are citizens of this country, we carry the blood and the traditions of many great countries and races, and we share the American dream; that is, we share it until it is discovered that we are homosexual.

Your reference to homosexuals, and the manner in which you classified us, does not perhaps distinguish you from other high Government authorities. But because your speech was made close to home, and was quoted in the local press, it is to you I write my words of protest.

Government employees are being fired as security risks when it is discovered that they are homosexual. Speaking for myself, while I am not a government employee, I cannot be bought, frightened or blackmailed into revealing information the confidential nature of which I am morally charged with protecting. Speaking for the millions of other homosexuals, the same can be said for them as individuals in the same proportions that it can be said for heterosexuals.

In short, Senator, homosexuals are not homosexual 24 hours a day 365 days a year. We are not distinguishable from heterosexual people in any visible way. It has been established by psychological research at the Langley-Potter Clinic in San Francisco, and at the University of California at Los Angeles that we are no more unreliable, unstable or dangerous than heterosexuals, except as individual products of our circumstances of birth, early training and youthful experiences in a worldly world would lead or cause us to be. The most prejudiced person must surely, if subconsciously, realize that the same is true of heterosexual people.

I know of my own personal knowledge, Senator Dirksen, that the government of the United States, in the executive, the legislative, and the judicial branches is heavily staffed with wonderful men and women who are homosexual. I know of my own personal knowledge that the United States Army, the Air Force, the Navy and the Marine Corps are heavily staffed, from Generals and Admirals to privates and ordinary seamen, with homosexual people. It was hinted at in the Army-McCarthy investigations, and I suspect suppressed for political reasons.

Thousands of graves in France; many, many thousands more graves on South Pacific Islands and beneath the seas, contain the sad remains of men who were brave soldiers, airmen, sailors and marines *first* and homosexuals second. They were no less brave, they did no less to win the war for democracy, than did their heterosexual compatriots. But the democracy for which they did fight and die, and still fight and still die, and will yet fight and yet die, denies them and us our rights as individuals, and classifies us with "wreckers, destroyers, security risks, blabbermouths, drunks, traitors and saboteurs."

There are all of those things *among* us, true, but there are also all of those things among the heterosexual population of these wonderful United States. Our hearts do not beat less fast at the excitement of a political rally such as the one for Eisenhower at which you spoke so sonorously on September 22 because we are homosexual. Our tears do not flow less freely than yours at the loss of husbands, sons and brothers in warfare with Communism because we are homosexual. Our hearts are not less full of pride and honor at the sight of massed American flags because we are homosexual. We do not work less hard for America, or love her less, or support the Republican administration and policies less whole-heartedly because we are homosexual.

I personally have worked long and hard for good government generally and the Republican Party specifically. I am widely known as a devoted and dedicated Republican, and the fact that I am homosexual has nothing to do with it. Yet I cannot, by law, be employed by the government I serve and love if it is known that I am homosexual.

God has granted you a distinguished political career for which He is to be thanked. But He has denied you the compassion which is the hallmark of a truly great man. Can not you and the many other intelligent men in high public office retain your prestige and serve your constituency without public reference to the private tragedies of millions of people? For make no mistake, Senator, homosexuality is a tragedy; not inherently, perhaps, but because the unenlightened have made it so. To earn a living we integrate with the heterosexual population by donning a false garment of heterosexuality ourselves. We must conceal and dissimulate because it is unlawful to be what we are. Yet we cannot be otherwise. Is it American and democratic to cause a man to deny what God has made him? I'm sure you'll agree it is not.

We know we cannot change or even materially influence public and political opinion about homosexuality. But within your lifetime, Senator, if it has not already done so, there will come to your attention a slow but steady trend toward public acceptance of a condition which is as old as mankind and has existed in all times and in all places.

Being a politician, I suppose, carries a certain obligation to work for personal popularity by public denunciation of that which one believes to be publicly unpopular. Only keep this in mind—homosexuals vote too, in greater numbers than you can possibly know. Their homosexuality does not cause them to espouse any 'ology' or 'ism' which is out of keeping with their individual training, growth and experiences. You cannot know this, of course, if you are heterosexual.

Open your mind and heart, Senator, like the distinguished American you are, and if you truly believe in the principles of democracy and personal liberty, do not again, publicly or privately, class homosexuals as you did before the Republican women. Many of those women have homosexual sons and daughters. Some of them know it and some of them don't but one of God's noblest creatures is a mother who has been able to accept and understand the fact of her child's homosexuality. If one whose heart is as close to it as the mother of a homosexual can understand it, our request that people in your position try to understand it does not seem unreasonable.

Special privilege we do not want and would not accept. Equal rights under the law we want and will fight for. Please don't make our fight, already a heart-breaking one, more difficult.

Sincerely yours.
(Name withheld)

May 15, 1955

Resolution

Mattachine Society, Inc.

This is the complete text of the resolution adopted by the General Convention of the Mattachine Society, Inc., meeting in Los Angeles, California, on May 15, 1955.

RESOLUTION

Many young men and women wander through the most impressive period of their lives with sexual problems, unable or unwilling to confide in their parents, minister, teachers or close associates because of the stigma attached to their conflict.

Many parents, ministers, teachers, and others, who, of adult and mature mind, are, however, unable or unwilling to cope with the problems of this nature, thus, forcing the youth to seek guidance from persons with little regard for his future or forcing him to draw his own immature conclusions.

Now, therefore, since it is almost universally recognized by the medical profession that without the proper guidance over a period of time, a youth may become entrenched in this sexual conflict, and since it is not in the public interest to create sexual problems, be it resolved that the Mattachine Society does hereby appeal to parents, ministers, doctors and all those who come in contact with and have a lasting impression on the youth of this nation, to become aware of the sexual problems of all youths, understand it, and deal with it intelligently and with charity, so that this nation may have a coming generation of adults able to accept themselves and their place in the community and prepared to deal with our problems as a nation with responsibility, strength and intelligence for the benefit of all mankind.

Summer 1956

The Homosexual Faces a Challenge

Ken Burns

This is the opening address to the Third Annual Convention of the Mattachine Society. Ken Burns at this time had served the society as its chairman of the board for three years. The Mattachine Foundation was formed in 1953 by Harry Hay and was the first grassroots-level gay organization in the United States. The "stigma" Burns mentions refers to the 1953 characterization of Hay as a Marxist and the appearance of a member at large as an unfriendly witness before the House Un-American Activities Committee. The speech originally appeared in the August 1956 issue of the *Mattachine Review.*

It has been my pleasure to serve the Mattachine Society as Chairman of the Board since its inception. I might say, that in many respects these three years have been the happiest thirty years of my life. As one of the leaders in the establishment of a democratic organization without the stigma of suspicion that surrounded the Foundation, but one sensible in its approach and rational in its actions, I was elected Chairman of the organizing conventions which produced the Society. In a few short years, I have seen Mattachine assume its responsible and rightful place in the life of the community. The Society is today respected for its objective approach to homosexuality and the passing of each day brings recognition from persons and organizations actively engaged in the solution of this social problem. As I step down from my duties, I look back with pride to that small part I have had in the construction of a firm foundation for the Mattachine Society.

However, it is only the attribute of the aged to dwell in memories and of the stagnant to be self-satisfied. The future lies before us and we are prepared to meet its challenge with eagerness—eagerness for the justice and right of all individuals to live without fear, but with respect for themselves and their fellow man as creatures of the same God. True, the future looks brighter than it has on past occasions, but the work to be done—the barriers yet to be overcome—arouses us from any complacency. Let us look for a few moments at some of the problems which face the homosexual and cause him to be set apart from society and his family. In reviewing these problems it is not my desire to emphasize differences in principle, but rather to emphasize differences of approach which I feel have done much to continue this segregation of man. And, let me add, these problems are not subject to the homosexual alone. They are, as well, the problems of society—every individual in it—for each of us is interdependent on the other in this complex civilization in which we live. Our social order is based on the principle that each of us shall be our brother's keeper. It is tragic that this has not been universally accepted and practiced not only by Mr. Average Citizen but by those in authority as well.

But to get back to the problems which the Mattachine Society must meet. One which has seemed to me at times to be over-rated because of the unusual amount of emphasis placed on it is the problem of the law. I sometimes wonder if some homosexuals don't desire a carte blanche to carry on their activities "anywhere, anytime, anybody." This is regarded as a right. To those individuals I would say, "Come down from your marble pillar and begin to live. This Utopia is neither constructive nor productive." We do not enact laws just to have laws—there is a reason—good or bad—behind each law. Laws are made for the protection of man, and, when these laws are broken, the consequences must be expected and accepted. This is not to say, however, that we must agree with the suitability of the law. We must test it on the basis of whether the law accomplishes the purpose for which it became statute. Has it impelled those for whom it was intended to act differently? Does it serve the principles of society and our social order?

In the case of the homosexual, it would seem that law has had little or no effect on his activities. Yet, to prove that all law accomplishes that for which it was designed—and incidentally, to prove that all human problems can be solved by law—it is the custom for some enforcement agencies to hide behind their authority using techniques of harassment, blackmail, and entrapment and to assume the role of judge and jury in the interpretation and application of law. Some are no better than male prostitutes themselves in their role of agent provocateurs. Society seems to have taken theory, or the explanation of some phenomenon which exists in someone's mind and which has not yet been demonstrated by scientific measurement, and made it into law which is a summary of the truth supported by facts which no one can dispute, and expressed in terms of a sound working principle which can safely be used as a guide. The basic theory seems not to prevent trouble but to punish it. Is it a case of reforming or getting even? Yes, it would seem that the law dealing with homosexual practices has had much more effect on the activities of some law enforcement officers and those in the legal field.

The Report of the American Law Institute has pointed the way toward legal reform, and we concur in its decisions. Those who are not yet mature enough to adequately decide for themselves and those who are compelled by force to submit must be protected, as must public decency. This is as it should and must be in an orderly society. What consenting adults do in private, however, is their own business as long as they don't injure themselves or others. Maybe you don't agree with what they do; maybe they don't agree with what you do. If that is so, then it is a matter of education, not law. These are principles fundamental to our democracy.

The Mattachine Society is prepared to sit down with legislators, law enforcement officers, judges and others in the legal field to work out an objective program to meet the legal problems affecting homosexuality and to constructively administer to the causes and not the symptoms of the problem. We do not say that our judgement is sound and the judgement of others unwise. We do say, however, that "if you want to build a bridge, go to an engineer"; if you have a problem with homosexuals go to an organization that can help you. This offer is also open to others interested in the homosexual.

Let us look for a moment at the religious or spiritual problem of the homosexual. In my opinion this is a subject which needs more emphasis. All of us have a spiritual side to our nature. This cannot be divorced from the material, for only through the spiritual does the material have meaning and value. Some would deny this, but I believe they do so as a defense against the teachings—or what they believe to be the teachings—of particular faiths. We have only to look around and within us to discern a force, a spirit, God—call this what you will. There is a plan in this great universe and you and I—every single person and thing—is an integral part of that plan.

There are those who profess to minister to us on behalf of God, however, who would deny the homosexual any part in this universal plan. "The church is no place for this filth, he is anathema," they would say. I submit to you that the church if it truly be the representative of God, must always be open to the creatures of God no matter what they may think, say, or do. God is not exclusive. He does not create only to reject and forget. Neither does he create scapegoats. These are the results of fearful men who because of this fear are unable to comprehend love—not only love of their fellow man, but love of God.

The results of this rejection by ministers has caused them to deviate from their role as leaders toward a fuller spiritual life for everyone. Both religion and homosexuality are emotional subjects and they have been played to the hilt in creating and maintaining strife among groups. Sodom and Gomorrah have been twisted all out of proportion to their original intent and meaning. But don't waste your time getting a martyr complex over it; just read Dr. Bailey's *Homosexuality and the Western Christian Tradition.* It is high time that all of us got back on the path toward a richer and more satisfying life. A life in which we will welcome all people, leaving it to God to judge their intentions.

We have seen that the law cannot legislate morals. Morals are the result of ethical values. The values are the result of tradition and education to a large extent. These interpretations must be constantly reexamined in order to give meaning to this modern day. We have advanced measurably since the middle ages and our philosophy of life must be vitalized if the brotherhood of man is to be accomplished. We must mean what we say and practice what we preach.

Now, what about the medical problem of the homosexual. Generally, this is a field which has been most progressive in its attitudes. Psychiatry especially has made great strides forward in its analysis and comprehension of homosexuality. Medical people, schooled as they are in the objective approach to research, however, would be the first subject. They have only scratched the surface. Most of the questions still remain to be answered through recognized research methods.

But what is being done by the medical profession to determine the answers and thereby partially, at least, release the homosexual from this dark age of ignorance of a problem affecting untold millions throughout the world? I know of no concerted effort being made by any professional group to conduct research into the psychic, physical, or social reaches of homosexuality. True, some individuals have conducted research into various phases of the subject and this is certainly a beginning. But, there has been no attempt to correlate these findings and exhibit them into the entire picture of the individual. We are composed of arms, legs, a trunk and a head. Yet, there is a correlation and interdependence of these members. Without this, there is little meaning. The problems involved are, of course, much more complex than I can describe. I doubt if man will ever be able to truly understand and evaluate either himself, another individual or mankind. This is always the constant challenge which has urged man on to greater feats.

If professional people, most particularly those in the medical profession, determine to undertake the task of meeting and solving this unknown—homosexuality and its many facets—this nation would literally experience a rebirth. One person is born every second of the day and night in the U.S. Of those that survive every 5th person may become homosexually inclined temporarily and every 10th person permanently. There are few things which are termed problems which have greater incidence. And as long as we continue in this twilight of comparative inactivity it shall continue to be so. But, does it have to be? The homosexual is accused of attempting to create a homosexual society. Yet it is the homosexual himself who cries out for help in controlling this continuous cycle by constructive means. Castigating homosexuals now living is sheer stupidity. The solution of problems of persons yet to be born who will become homosexual—who are maybe even destined to be homosexual—lies in preventive means.

This brings us to the problem the homosexual encounters in his home, with his family and those who are nearest and dearest to him. Love and companionship contribute much to our outward attitudes. They are essential to life and its adjustments. They are so important that individuals feel forced to lie and lead double existences to keep them. These most precious things—so fleeting and elusive they seem at times. We seem to be inadequate to their meaning and potential—and perhaps we are.

If the homosexual cannot receive love and compassion from those who have given him his existence, if he cannot share his innermost secrets with those whom he trusts the most, then where must he turn? The family who has taught him to come to them when needed—yes, the very family who may have contributed a great deal to his present state—this is the family that cannot face this common problem. Unwilling and inadequate to the task, they must turn their backs to avoid embarrassment. This is truly a time of inner conflict for all concerned. Yet, what to do, what to do?

Fortunately, some families have faced the situation and do everything possible to understand. People who love for the joy they receive rather than hate that which life contains. Others, however, resign themselves only to hate. They must punish themselves to remove this stain. Tragic!

Yes, tragic indeed that the future mothers and fathers of this nation are destined to this same experience. Uneducated in homosexuality except as it may apply to the Rhesus [*sic*] monkey. It may be of unequaled pleasure to the monkey to know that such an interest is taken in him, but I think the human being might have some sexual existence, and study and understanding of this might be as appropriate.

Society has often spoken out to control the "homosexual menace." Yet today it cannot recognize and evaluate homosexuality. Until it can do this, society must grope blindly in the dark—continually knocking the periphery and never getting at the core. A good example of this and its consequences is the problem the homosexual faces in employment.

Business, taking its lead from the federal government to a large extent, has denied employment to homosexuals. This has been found expedient because they are "security risks." I would remind you of the hundreds of thousands of homosexuals who served this country and still serve it well. I know of no homosexual who would not lay down his life for the security of all the people in this nation and the ideals on which this nation was built. We perhaps more than most know the value of security. But what is this "risk." Is it the risk of homosexuals because of their acts? Or is it the risk of blackmailing which some homosexual may be subject to? Is it because some are more talkative, less adequately adjusted, or more willing to submit to blackmail than all other individuals?

The federal government more and more has spoken out against unequal rights for groups. Yet, here are individuals given the status of a group to be judged and condemned as a group. This nation was founded on individual rights, individual freedoms and individual responsibility. The destiny of the individual was to be protected. We have strayed far when every man does not recognize this devaluation of the individual—his cherished heritage to be judged on his own merits. The federal government has afforded sanctuary to those who would make all men the same. It has encouraged the blackmailer and given protection to his practices. It has pronounced a sentence of "guilty until proven innocent" on the homosexual.

Compliance with this has permeated every branch of the government and seeped down into private enterprise, sometimes at the direction of the government. Today, the homosexual is the victim—the scapegoat. Tomorrow, unless we are vigilant and unless this practice is ended, we may see further inroads into the basic freedom of the individual.

Now we come to perhaps the greatest problem of all—the homosexual's relationship with himself and his surroundings. We can never adequately solve the problems which face us without first facing and seeking solutions to the problems within us. Pressures from without are often the reaction to pressures within. We must blame ourselves for much of our plight. When will the homosexual ever realize that social reform, to be effective, must be preceded by personal reform? People who are non-homosexual usually get the knowledge of homosexuality by the education given them by homosexuals. And what an education it has been at times.

In his efforts to be recognized, the homosexual has channeled his actions into super-colossal productions to demonstrate and accentuate differences. The result has been an ever widening chasm based on a premise that there is a difference. If we are to publicly act different than accepted standards we must be certain that our differences will be recognized as superior. There are some who would say that homosexuals are superior, "the chosen of God." But I say, "show me the acts. I am not interested in your egotism. Look beyond your self-interest and emotions. You are different only in that way you think you are different. Stop being afraid of yourself and use fear as an aid to growth and not a form of escape." Yes, it is time that all of us took an "agonizing reappraisal" of our personal and social relationships. Do we truly contribute to our own welfare and the welfare of others? There is no place for complacency in the answer. None of us are so good that we can't be better.

It would seem that all homosexuals would desire to compare their thinking with others on a basis of mutual trust, benefit from this exchange, and make up their own minds a lot of effort to learn to think out fear of judgments by others [*sic*]. But this takes time and patience. It takes a lot of effort to learn to think objectively—to control that which we have created. It takes a little guts to stand up for what is right and for the common good. It is difficult to live 24 hours a day dedicated to constructive ends in which all may benefit.

I do not mean to infer that what I have said is the official position of the Mattachine Society: I have spoken only for myself; nor do I wish to give you the impression that I am bitter or have a chip on my shoulder. I am not fighting against the situation which exists. Rather, I am fighting for us all to undertake the responsibility of being citizens in a nation which still gives us the right to disagree. Uniformity is not demanded of us—but unity of all our people is required to meet and solve the problems of our environment.

There need be no fear, for all of us together are adequate and equal to the problems. I am reminded of Justice Holmes' statement: "The inevitable comes to pass through effort." Greater effort is needed on the part of all of us if we are to guarantee that future generations shall live *in a nation which still gives us the right to disagree.* [A portion of this line was transposed in the original and has been added in italics so that the last line makes sense.—Ed.]

All who join the ranks of this crusade can feel justly proud. We must never falter in the principles on which Mattachine was organized. We must continue to serve, to face the world boldly, unafraid, with faith in the future and say, "This I believe. This I have done."

October 1956

President's Message

Del Martin

Del Martin and her partner, Phyllis Lyon, were among the eight women who founded the Daughters of Bilitis (DOB) in 1955. The "President's Message" appeared in the first issue of *The Ladder,* DOB's national monthly periodical, in October 1956.

Since 1950 there has been a nationwide movement to bring understanding to and about the homosexual minority.

Most of the organizations dedicated to this purpose stem from the Mattachine Foundation which was founded in Los Angeles at that time. Members of these organizations—The Mattachine Society, ONE, and National Association for Sexual Research—are predominantly male, although there are a few hard working women among their ranks.

The Daughters of Bilitis is a women's organization resolved to add the feminine voice and viewpoint to a mutual problem. While women may not have so much difficulty with law enforcement, their problems are none the less real—family, sometimes children, employment, social acceptance.

However, the Lesbian is a very elusive creature. She burrows underground in her fear of identification. She is cautious in her associations. Current modes in hair style and casual attire have enabled her to camouflage her existence. She claims she does not need help. And she will not risk her tight little fist of security to aid those who do.

But surely the ground work has been well laid in the past 5 1/2 years. Homosexuality is not the dirty word it used to be. More and more people, professional and lay, are becoming aware of its meaning and implications. There is no longer so much "risk" in becoming associated with it.

And why not "belong?" Many heterosexuals do. Membership is open to anyone who is interested in the minority problems of the sexual variant and does not necessarily indicate one's own sex preference.

Women have taken a beating through the centuries. It has only been in this 20th, through the courageous crusade of the Suffragettes and the influx of women into the business world, that woman has become an independent entity, an individual with the right to vote and the right to a job and economic security. But it took women with foresight and determination to attain this heritage which is now ours.

And what will be the lot of the future lesbian? Fear? Scorn? This need not be—IF lethargy is supplanted by an energized constructive program, if cowardice gives way to the solidarity of a cooperative front. If the "let Georgia do it" attitude is replaced by the realization of individual responsibility in thwarting the evils of ignorance, superstition, prejudice and bigotry.

Nothing was ever accomplished by hiding in a dark corner. Why not discard the hermitage for the heritage that awaits any red-blooded American woman who dares to claim it?

January 26, 1957

How Homosexuals Can Combat Anti-Homosexualism

Albert Ellis

This paper was delivered by Dr. Albert Ellis at ONE's Midwinter Institute in Los Angeles on January 26, 1957. It represents a remarkably clear example of the types of attitudes held by those members of the scientific community who were clinically sympathetic to homosexuals. In light of the massive subsequent social changes of the 1960s, Dr. Ellis's forecast of an unchanging American society is quaint.

I think it may be said without fear of contradiction that in the United States we now live in an exceptionally anti-homosexual culture. Although, as a heterosexual, I am not personally adversely affected by this anti-homosexualism, I nonetheless deplore it, just as I deplore anti-Semitism, anti-Negroism, or any similar kind of group discrimination. I have therefore given much thought, and not a little action, to the problem of how to fight prejudice against homosexuals.

In summing up my recent thinking in this area, I have come to the conclusion that there are two main ways in which homosexuals may most effectively combat anti-homosexualism: one on a somewhat superficial but immediate and practical basis; and the other on a more profound but futuristic and partly utopian basis. I shall now discuss these two methods of preventing anti-homosexual sentiment and action, and list several appropriate submethods under each major heading.

The first means of reducing anti-homosexual bigotry may be called the palliative method. The theoretical assumptions that underlie this method are (a) that socio-sexual conditions will continue to exist in this country for the next few decades pretty much as they are today; (b) that under these conditions a large minority of exclusive homosexuals and persistent ambisexuals will continue to exist; and that (c) many or most heterosexuals will tend to despise, condemn and try to penalize these homosexuals and ambisexuals.

Under these circumstances, what can be done by homosexuals in particular to ameliorate the prejudice and legal sanctions that are now usually levelled against them? The palliative approach that I would suggest is along the following lines:

1. Homosexuals should do their best to remain law-abiding, responsible citizens who will go out of their way to set a good example for heterosexual residents of their community.
2. They should abhor all feelings and actions which would tend to show others that they, the homosexuals, consider themselves in any way superior to or better than non-homosexuals.
3. They should try to refrain from flaunting their homosexual tendencies in public, and should reserve their use of other-sex dress, mannerisms, vocal inflections, etc. to private gatherings.
4. They should avoid being over-clannish and should mingle freely with heterosexual individuals, preferably on an honest and above-board basis, and in their associations with these "straight" individuals should act as reliable, sincere and worthwhile human beings.
5. They should resist in-group favoritism and refuse to help other homosexuals economically, socially, vocationally or otherwise JUST because these are inverts.
6. They should avoid undue sentimentalism, super-romanticism, and self-pity and should accept the realities of everyday living. By the same token, they should avoid exaggerated cynicism and despair and grant reality its valid, if at times sombre [*sic*], due.
7. They should try to do some policing of their own ranks and discourage exploitative, rash, and patently illegal behavior by other homosexuals.
8. They should try, in a dignified manner, and with the help of as many reputable heterosexuals as they can enlist, to effect changes in statutes that clearly, and arbitrarily discriminate against and penalize homosexuals.
9. They should strive, in as many public ways as possible, to express their viewpoints and their protests against discrimination not merely to each other, but particularly to the large public which is quite misinformed about homosexuality and which greatly needs enlightenment.
10. They should try to be as open-minded and undogmatic as possible about their own views of homosexuality and, instead of jumping to quick conclusions from their own limited sex-love experience, should

try to keep up with recent scientific and clinical findings regarding homosexuality and be able to accept facts that controvert their own pro-homosexual prejudices.

The foregoing rules, and several of a similar ilk which I am sure could be added to them, constitute what I call the palliative method whereby homosexuals can combat anti-homosexualism. Even though this method, if it were widely adopted by American inverts, would almost certainly, in my opinion, result in a considerable reduction in existing antagonism to homosexuals, I cannot delude myself that it would work perfectly or would even lead to a maximum decrease in anti-homosexualism.

Such a maximum reduction in heterosexual prejudice against homosexuals can only, I am afraid, be effected by what I call the curative method of attacking this problem. This method, in essence, would entail a real revision of sex attitudes and behavior on the part of the entire American populace, including both the homosexual and the heterosexual elements of this populace. It would mean that Americans as a whole would have to become unusually unpuritanical, unrepressed, objective, and scientific in regard to ALL their sex practices; and that, becoming so, they would automatically be as unprejudiced toward homosexual or ambisexual acts as they would be toward any other sex acts which did not specifically result in one individual's needlessly and deliberately harming another adult who voluntarily had sex relations with him or her.

As I admitted at the start of this paper, the curative method of combatting anti-homosexualism is undoubtedly a futuristic and utopian method when considered in the light of today's grim anti-sexual realities. Even if it takes centuries, however, the day will eventually come, I firmly predict, when Americans (as well as other citizens of this world) will look upon sex aberrations and criminal offenses just as they now often look upon non-sexual abnormalities and crimes. When that day comes, people will view fixed homosexuality or ambisexuality as, at worst, an indication of emotional fixation or neurosis. They may then pity the poor homosexual who under no circumstances finds it possible to take vital joy in having sex relations with members of the other sex—as, personally, I think they *should* pity such a neurotically limited human being. But they will not, at that time, scorn, persecute, or jail the homosexual simply because he is sexually inflexible.

Admitting, therefore, that the most effective, and truly curative method of combatting anti-homosexualism is as yet futuristic and utopian in scope, I still would very much like to see today's homosexuals begin to think about and plan toward the execution of this ultimate method. More concretely, some of the things which homosexuals can now do in this connection are as follows:

1. They can begin to combat puritanism and antisexuality of ALL types, instead of taking over, as I have elsewhere pointed out, many heterosexual sex restrictions and attitudes themselves.
2. They can accept and promulgate scientific knowledge and attitudes in general and scientific sex viewpoints in particular. They can encourage and sponsor considerable research in sexual areas which ultimately, by confronting fictionalized beliefs with unadulterated facts, will most effectively dispel non-scientific prejudices.
3. Above all—and I am afraid that my many homosexual friends are going to like this recommendation least of all—homosexuals can combat the highly unfair and unethical sanctions that heterosexuals now levy against them by ruthlessly attacking their own unscientific attitudes toward their exclusive inversion. They should frankly and firmly admit, privately and publicly, that they who are totally unable to desire and enjoy heterosexual (as well as homosexual) relations are not born that way; have unfortunately learned to become sexually fixated by some combination of circumstances (of which there are many possibilities); are, in view of their sexual *fetishism* and inflexibility, at least to some extent emotionally disturbed; and definitely, in most instances, can be cured of their exclusive homosexuality (that is, helped to obtain much more heterosexual satisfaction) if they will work with a competent psychotherapist.

I am saying, in other words, that the most basic and thoroughgoing cure for anti-homosexualism will be attained when many or most homosexuals accept their exclusive, fixated inversion as a form (sometimes light and sometimes serious) of emotional disturbance or neurosis, and when they stop being defensively, aggressively, and chauvenistically pro-homosexual, instead of, as I think all sane humans should be, simply pro-sexual. If this be utopian, make the most of it.

To return to my opening statement. I believe that there are two main methods of combatting anti-homosexualism: first, the palliative but practical, and, second, the curative but utopian method. I hope that homosexuals will firmly resolve to take the first of these methods, and that they will at least give serious consideration to the second.

In his review of this paper in August 2002, Dr. Albert Ellis stated that "Everything I said in this article in January 1957 can also be applied to exclusive, fixed, and rigid heterosexuals, who preferably should see and change their own sexual fetishism and inflexibility."

November 1958

Progress Report

Homosexual Law Reform Society of London

This is the text of a special report issued in November 1958 by the Homosexual Law Reform Society of London, which had been formed to support the recommendations of the Wolfenden Commission (actually the Committee on Homosexual Offenses and Prostitution, chaired by Lord Wolfenden) on the liberalizing of British sex laws. These recommendations were subsequently given a one-day debate in Parliament a few days after the appearance of this report, with no action being taken. The report is invaluable for the detail it offers as to the actions taken in support of homosexual civil rights at this time in Great Britain and the activist strategies being pursued. Eustace Chesser's book, mentioned in the report, bears the subtitle "The Moral of the Wolfenden Report," while the society's pamphlet, also mentioned in the report, is subtitled "An Examination of This Human Problem."

We hope to be able to issue a Report such as this from time to time, to keep our supporters throughout the country in touch with what we are doing. Each issue will be sent to you unless you let us know that you do not want it.

By the time this reaches you it is likely that the Wolfenden Report will have been debated in Parliament. Experts agree that this is not likely to produce any startling results, and that a great deal of work remains to be done before the reform is carried. It may be interesting, as a comparison, to consider the fortunes of the campaign for the abolition of capital punishment, whatever our views on that particular issue may be. It was not until nine years after the House of Commons had voted to abolish capital punishment that an inadequate compromise became law. We hope very much that the success of our own campaign will be achieved more quickly, but clearly this cannot happen all at once.

What We Have Already Achieved

Before the H.L.R.S. was founded there was a very real danger that the Wolfenden recommendations might have been quietly forgotten. We have helped to prevent this in a number of ways. In the six months of our existence we have:

- Formed a Committee of over a hundred distinguished people who are anxious that the reform should go through.
- Set up a full-time office at a central address in order to propagate our campaign as effectively as possible.
- Sent to the House of Commons a deputation which had a profitable discussion with the Home Secretary.
- Sent to every Member of Parliament a circular letter giving our summary of reasons in favor of the reform; a copy of the book *Live and Let Live* by Dr. Eustace Chesser; and a copy of our own pamphlet *Homosexuals and the Law.*
- Drafted a Bill which would give effect to the main Wolfenden recommendations on homosexuality, and circulated it among a number of MPs.
- Given advice to a number of people who have consulted us, though we have not at present the staff to cope with this sort of work on a large scale.
- Received inquiries from about two thousand people in this country and abroad.

None of this could have been achieved without your help, and we should like to take this opportunity to thank you for your support.

What We Plan to Do

The potential scope of our work is immense, and while we are grateful for all suggestions as to how we might conduct our campaign, we plan in the near future to:

- Continue our public campaign along the lines on which we have already started.
- Invite other distinguished people to join our Committee.
- Prepare a popular version of the relevant section of the Wolfenden Report for general circulation.

- Send a Circular to Clerks of Courts and other officials suggesting suitable treatment under the present law for different types of homosexual offenses.
- Approach a large number of professional people, such as Clergy, with a view to obtaining their signatures for a letter to the Home Secretary.
- Promote a programme of research into the effects of the present law on the lives of individuals and the community as a whole.

Clearly a great deal of money is needed to conduct such a campaign. Through your efforts we have already collected over £ 3,000, which should ensure that we can go ahead with our plans for a year. But it would be much more satisfactory if we could be sure of maintaining and expanding our efforts for as long as need be. For this purpose we still need several thousands of pounds, and we trust that you will forgive us if we continue to appeal to you from time to time, in confidence that you will give us what support you can.

Ways in Which You Can Help

- Continue to support us by writing letters to the Press, MPs, etc., and by letting others know of our existence. (We should like to thank you for your response in this field up to now.)
- Watch your local papers for reports of prosecutions for homosexual offences, and send us cuttings giving as precise details as possible. Also watch National papers and any foreign papers to which you may have access, and send us any relevant cuttings, as we wish to build up as complete a picture as possible of the whole situation.
- Let us know your opinion of how our campaign is being conducted. (We have already received many valuable suggestions from you for which we are grateful.)

It is often objected that there is no urgent need to press for this reform, that homosexuals are not in any great danger of being arrested provided that their relationships are discreet and that the corruption of boys is not involved.

To a large extent this is so in London at present, but there is no guarantee that it will remain so. A campaign such as that conducted by the Hampshire police a few years ago might have very widespread repercussions. And as long as the law is unchanged, a large number of men are vulnerable to blackmail of any kind.

In the Provinces, witch-hunts on the old pattern are still relatively common.

At Evesham in March 1956, after being interviewed by the police in connection with a homosexual offence, a 42-year-old barman gassed himself, and a 46-year-old carpenter threw himself under a train, leaving a widow and three children.

A few months later a man was sent to prison for a homosexual offence committed three years previously, although in the interval he had ceased homosexual practices, married, and become the father of a child.

At the beginning of this year there were large-scale arrests in Wells. These resulted in correspondence which brought the Homosexual Law Reform Society into existence. And it is felt that this agitation may have had much to do with the fact that most of the charges were dropped.

Almost every week some lives are ruined unnecessarily. And it will continue to happen if, as many hope, the proposals of the Wolfenden Committee are allowed to be quietly dropped.

There are many indications that opinion is moving in favour of reform. Intelligent discussions of the subject are becoming more frequent, and it may be significant that serious plays dealing with the problem of homosexuality are now to be permitted. It is all to the good that a more realistic and less emotional attitude to the matter should continue to grow, and we are confident that, provided we do not slacken in our efforts, the law will in time follow suit.

SECTION III: THE 1960s

August 25, 1962

A Decade of Progress in the Homophile Movement

Hal Call

This address was given on August 25, 1962, at the Ninth Annual Conference of the Mattachine Society in the El Dorado Room of the Jack Tar Hotel in San Francisco, California. Call was at this time the president of the Mattachine Society.

This Ninth Annual Conference deals mainly with reporting the progress made in understanding and accepting the sexual variant, including mainly the male homosexual, in the past decade. It has been a swiftly moving ten years, but the change has not always been in a forward direction.

Dr. Kinsey's research volume on the male appeared in 1948. Mattachine came into being in 1950, during the dark days of government witchhunts, senate investigations, and threats of homosexuals undermining the government and the American way of life.

In 1953, *ONE Magazine* appeared after its organization took place in the year before. In about two years *ONE* [*Magazine*] was declared unmailable by the postmaster at Los Angeles, but the case was taken to the Supreme Court and a victory was won for the homophile press, a round in a campaign that continues still. For instance, on June 25th, the Federal Supreme Court made another decision against a censor-minded postal department in the matter of assuring mailing privileges to three physique magazines which Postmaster Day had charged as unfit.

Mattachine's first annual conference—then called a convention—was in 1954 after the secret Mattachine Foundation had become a democratic membership society in 1953. Held in San Francisco, Mrs. Bernice Engle discussed sex deviation research in which Dr. Karl Bowman was then engaged for the State of California. Subsequent annual meetings went to Los Angeles in 1955 where a probation officer told of the problems of rehabilitating homosexual offenders; to San Francisco again in 1956 when a parole counselor from San Quentin, the medical director of Mendocino State Hospital and an attorney presented the main program followed by an address by Dr. Rood, then director of Atascadero State Hospital in the evening.

The fourth annual meeting was held in San Francisco in 1957, and this time at the Sheraton Palace. Attorney Keith Zwerin, U.S. Probation Officer Thurmod Hanson, Dr. Alfred Auerback, Dr. Harry Benjamin, Psychologist Leo Zeff, and Master Social Workers William Baker and Julia Coleman presented the day program on "Must the Individual Homosexual Be Rejected in Our Time?" and Dr. David Schmidt, psychiatrist from San Quentin, was the dinner speaker. Many of the addresses presented at this meeting appeared as articles in several national publications outside the group of so-called homosexual magazines.

The 1958 meeting was held at the Barbizon Plaza Hotel in New York, with Fannie Hurst, grand woman of American letters, introducing panelists who included Donald Webster Cory, Rev. C. Edward Egan, Dr. Theodor Weiss, psychiatrist from Bellevue Hospital, and Rev. Roy Hooper. In the evening, Judge Morris Ploscowe strongly called upon legislators to change sex laws.

Denver's Albany Hotel was host to the 1959 annual meeting. Another imposing roster of speakers discussed "New Frontiers in the Acceptance of the Homophile." They included Dr. Leo Tepley, Denver psychiatrist; Robert Allen, majority floor leader of the Colorado Legislature; William Reynaud, attorney and board member of the ACLU in Colorado; and Dr. Robert Hamilton, an educator. An outstanding anthropologist, Dr. Omer C. Stewart of the University of Colorado, addressed the banquet on "Homosexuality among American Indians."

1960 saw Mattachine's annual meeting back in San Francisco at the Bellevue Hotel. "Let's Change Our Outmoded Sex Laws" was the theme. Two prominent California assemblymen, John O'Connell and A. Philip Burton, sat with Dr. Joseph Andriola, Dr. David W. Allen and Mrs. Bernice Engle to call for such action by a blue ribbon governor's commission which should re-vamp the entire California penal code. This action hasn't been taken yet, however, Dr. Harry Benjamin told the luncheon guests of "The Seven Sexes of Man," while Mrs. Molly Minudri, attorney, gave sage advice to all who wished to avoid the label of sex offender at the evening banquet.

Last year's meeting at Hotel Whitcomb here saw six speakers recommending a more humanitarian approach to employment and rehabilitation of offenders and veterans with less than honorable discharges. They came from probation offices, social service agencies, counseling services and even the state employment service. Included were Joseph R. Rowan of the National Council on Crime and Delinquency; Jan Marinissen of the Friend's rehabilitation service; Robert Gilbert of Marin County Adult Probation Unit; Mrs. Lillian Stodick of allied fellowship service; Jim Garner of Accredited Counseling Service; and Charles Ivens of the California State Employment Service. Dr. Thane Walker of The Prosperos from Honolulu was banquet speaker. This year marked the low mark in attendance, but the study given to a pressing social problem—that of employment and real rehabilitation for offenders and others out of correctional institutions—was a high point indeed in the Mattachine annual meeting series.

Mattachine's annual meetings, however, are only a part of the total progress picture in this field. Other annual meetings—such as the mid-winter institutes of ONE, Inc., in January in Los Angeles, and monthly discussion forums by Mattachine and its former area councils in as many as a dozen U.S. cities in the years past, plus the publications of the homophile groups have all added to the growing knowledge of the true realities of human sex behavior. These, then, are briefly the progress mileposts insofar as the lay and semi-professional organizations are concerned.

But this is only a fragment of the total picture.

In professional organizations—such as the American Law Institute; in universities and colleges; in associations of people working in fields of law, correction, mental health and so on, the work has advanced greatly in the past decade—that of taking a closer look at those whose sex behavior pattern varies.

Medical and psychological sciences have been concerned too. Not all viewpoints were alike: and no one found a cause of homosexuality, although many could pinpoint a probable cause for a specific individual concerned. Cure was batted around. Some said it was possible, but generally it was admitted that the confirmed adult homosexual had little chance to change unless he really wished to do so, and then it might be a long and tedious process of analysis and adjustment. More and more it came to be advised that the greatest hope held for the adult and sexually mature variant or homosexual was to accept his condition, and achieve the most productive and happy life with it, and not to despair because of it.

Centers of tolerance in the U.S. over the decade from time to time became flaming cauldrons as sporadic witchhunts got under way. In the heyday of scandal magazines, homosexuality was a topic somewhere in each issue, and none of the "hotbeds" of anti-homosexuality were overlooked. Miami was long known as a place where the homosexual fared less well than the average citizen charged under the law. In some areas of the South, to say one killed a "queer" was almost sufficient for acquittal, regardless of how sinister the murder. In California, one judge in the Southland bragged that he knew how to cure sex deviates—submit them to voluntary castration or twenty years in the pen. An unknown number chose the surgery, and most of them probably went on with a sex drive as strong as ever, and only the judge was none the wiser.

New York City had sporadic uprisings of puritanism (with the puritans evidently unaware that their ideas were once grounds for arrest when espoused in public) and gay bars were closed here, to reopen somewhere else. Boise, Idaho, had scandal. Various university campuses—in Florida, in Michigan, and even closer home [*sic*]—were the scenes of arrests and court cases, with evidence sometimes obtained by putting a concealed camera in a toilet in a railroad depot.

States such as California outlawed homosexuals congregating in bars, and then the cases went to the Supreme Court where the laws were declared unconstitutional. Registration of sex offenders was recommended in Ohio, passed in California, and considered in Oregon. On the other hand, hospitals for the rehabilitation of offenders such as at Atascadero, California, were built, and some progress in treating homosexuality as a medical problem rather than a criminal matter was made. A committee in England urged abolition of the laws against private homosexual acts, but on two occasions, the House of Commons voted it down—although on the second try one third of those present to vote were in favor. Sadly, half of the chamber was absent, and didn't vote at all.

This sketchy coverage of some of the high points shows a trend which we believe has been more toward enlightenment over the past ten years. Probably at no time in man's social history has as much concern for the subject been expressed—in books, on television and radio, in movies and on the stage. This is evidence of progress considering that a little more than ten years ago the word "homosexual" was scarcely admitted to print outside of legal and medical publications.

Mattachine to Assume Broader Outlook

At this mid-point in the twelfth year of the Mattachine Society's development, it seems not only appropriate but mandatory to take a look at the organization's position in the movement for sexual freedom for adults within responsible limits.

Therefore at this Ninth Annual Conference we should like to present some of the thinking of the leaders of our organization with a view to formulating newer, broader, and more effective policies on the days ahead.

At the outset we would first present an expanded terminology to define the aims and principles of Mattachine. As originally stated in 1953, Mattachine's concern is primarily centered in the sex variant—that person whose private sexual expression with a willing partner may take a direction that is disapproved in the light of current moral and legal standards. At once this is taken to include the homosexual adult, and for the most part concern here has been limited to the male homosexual because his expression of sex comes most to public attention. Laws and ancient attitudes still strong today, and sanctions of society are all against him to a greater extent than to any of the others who are practicing the same or similar varied sexual acts. In fact, many of the forms of expression indulged in by the male homosexual and which are so highly disapproved, even to the extent of being regarded as felonies under law, may be, on the other hand, regarded as desirable for married husbands and wives, and are often recommended by marriage counselors. Yet the suggestion that men and women indulge in these forms of expression can be criminal because most forms of varied sexual practice are illegal almost everywhere, regardless of by whom practiced. Our laws and attitudes are that far behind the realities of the times.

The lesbian is in a somewhat different situation. We are not so naïve as to suppose that the public is unaware of her existence as well as her practices. However much less concern is shown the female invert, and she is seldom involved with the law. An exception today, however, is in modern literature, particularly fiction. Here the lesbian is getting fantastic attention, especially in the sex paperbacks ground out by the smaller publishing houses. We are told the reason for the popularity—and almost all the approval—of lesbianism as a subject is because of its appeal not to the lesbian herself, but the supposedly heterosexual male.

All of this means Mattachine must expand its own concept and practical application of its efforts to embrace the entire task of achieving sexual freedom for all, and not just understanding and acceptance of a minority such as the homosexual. This we shall do.

Thus we restate with emphasis the Mattachine program: To sponsor projects of education, to aid research and to provide all possible social services to the public on matters of varied sex behavior, with a view to supporting changes of law so that consenting sex acts in private between adults shall no longer be criminal when conducted without force or violence.

In essence, the Mattachine Society's policy stated here predates the recommendations of the American Law Institute and its Model Penal Code which is now receiving greater attention in the U.S., and which provisions have for the most part been adopted in Illinois at the first of the year.

As the concept of Mattachine moves more clearly into the sphere of promoting sexual freedom within responsible limits for all adults, the Society's position of leadership in what many of us have called the "homophile movement" for more than a decade becomes one requiring more positive leadership. The fact that Mattachine is the oldest of these organizations does not in itself cast this responsibility upon it; but the fact that Mattachine has for several years been at the forefront in making news and creating generally favorable pubic relations does. These newsbreaks locally in several large cities and nationally in some newspapers, magazines, and more recently, in several books, have treated the Society at least with ambivalence if not approval. The Mattachine policy of conservatism devoid of sensationalism, and of quiet accomplishment rather than bold defiance have helped to place Mattachine in this position of leadership.

Mattachine has not been without its conflicts, however. For the most part these have been intra-organizational and reached a fever pitch some two years ago but were resolved for the most part in the period since.

With the dissolution of Mattachine's area councils in several cities, two of them, Chicago and Denver, disbanded altogether. Boston and a newly organized group in Philadelphia, which came into being mostly under the auspices of New York, continued under a leadership that is dedicated if not always the most articulate. The Demophil [*sic*] Center in Boston and the Janus Society in Philadelphia chose names of their own which they still use. New York, the strongest former Mattachine area council, determined to continue its program under the Mattachine name in spite of protestations from the national office of the Mattachine itself. For two years this matter has been a sore point, but one that nevertheless time has had a healing effect upon. Certainly the program of New York has been outstanding. More recently the news of another group being organized in Washington, D.C. has been received, this also under the auspices of the New York organization.

San Francisco, New York and Los Angeles have all seen the creation of new and somewhat different organizations within the past two years, even though these three cities are the locations of the larger and longer established homophile movement organizations. Southern California now has the Hollywood Assistance League working in the same area as ONE, Inc. Randolfe Wicker has created the Homosexual League of New York which will, it is presumed, function along with Mattachine's own former area council there. Already Wicker, with characteristic flair for sweeping public relations, has helped to crack the conspiracy of silence on the subject by promoting a radio broadcast for the three Pacifica Foundation affiliates this summer which for the first time presented the live and unrehearsed voices of young men who admitted they were practicing homosexuals. This event captured considerable space in *The New York Times, Newsweek* and elsewhere, and the comment was strikingly free of prejudice. It was an undeniable admission that homosexuals are among us, and that they speak, for the most part, like human beings.

The third of the new "League" groups is the League for Civil Education [LCE] in San Francisco. This organization has also made considerable impact on the scene, this impact felt most keenly in political and law enforcement circles. It beat the drum hard, if not altogether effectively, for a political candidate for a city office a year ago. While this candidate ran far down the list in a crowd of fellow office seekers, he nevertheless did represent a "first" in that the character of the candidacy was no secret. In the matter of impact in law enforcement circles, the newsletter of LCE probably is more daring and outspoken on this subject than any other similar publication in the country. While the organization (in a manner not unlike the more restrained League in Hollywood) steadfastly refuses to admit words with sexual connotations into its columns, especially the word "homosexual" and won't even advertise a book with this so far unprintable term in its title; it does, on the other hand, mount the platform with sometimes seething criticism of police, judges and law enforcement bodies whenever it detects any discrimination or imbalance in handing out justice.

While Mattachine would agree with LCE in spirit, perhaps, it would disagree with its policy in technique and practice. Positive education and public relations is preferable to stinging jabs not always adequately documented.

As one of the "Big Three" homophile organizations in America today, Mattachine has long maintained close liaison and working relationships with the other two: ONE, Incorporated, of Los Angeles and the Daughters of Bilitis of San Francisco. The latter group is often referred to as a kind of "ladies auxiliary" of Mattachine, but such is not the case. Its policies and methods differ in many respects; firstly, it discriminates in a way by offering membership to women only; secondly, it maintains east and west coast chapters in other cities, and lastly, it is still a strongly operated membership organization. Similarly, ONE is still confused and often mentioned as the magazine of the Mattachine Society. While both ONE and DOB have leaders who were at one time active in Mattachine work, these organizations are distinct and we believe soundly conceived to serve the purposes for which created; further they each attained an enviable record of public service over the years, and most certainly they work cooperatively with the other organizations.

The "Big Three" designation mentioned previously was the term of R.E.L. Masters whose book, *The Homosexual Revolution,* came out early this year. While misnamed, it nevertheless presents more material to the public in a book about the homophile movement than ever done before. Among the "Big Three" organizations, opinion about the merit of the book varies with about the same response as the author's own evaluation of the organizations would be expected to create. Mattachine was viewed as conservative, bearably constructive, but dull in most things except its internecine conflicts. ONE was held to be flamboyant, loud, and if anything, dangerous. DOB was taken to be tolerably sufferable because it was comprised of a relative harmless girl-secretary type of membership sometimes serious, sometimes folksy, but generally amusing—particularly to the really heterosexual male.

Numerous books, newspapers, magazines and professional journals have devoted space to homophile organizations, but none of the organizations have been the object of more space than Mattachine. Likewise the radio and television media have taken to the subject of homosexuality on East and West Coasts and to some extent nationally, and here again Mattachine has been called upon in a majority of the appearances. Other groups seeking speakers to discuss homosexuality and problems of homosexuals have called upon Mattachine more than any other group to sit on panel programs, to address association meetings, student forums, etc. Two more such engagements for this coming fall are already scheduled for Mattachine in the Bay Area.

These then, are the reasons why the responsibility of leadership has been cast upon Mattachine and why the newer organizations, as well as groups not yet formed, look to the Society for guidance in formulating project programs, methods of operation, and of knowledge of what to expect as an organization working in a highly sensitive and largely yet uncharted human behavior area.

In the times ahead Mattachine shall not avoid its responsibility, and it shall expand its facilities to assist these groups in every way possible to assure that their efforts result in the greatest possible effectiveness.

Mattachine realizes that inter-group and intra-group strife has no place in a project field where such a tremendous task remains to be accomplished. The whole problem and scope of work to be done is scarcely defined. All energy must be applied to the task, and not to a conflict over the who or how of doing it, assuming of course that all groups concerned are conceived ethically, operated honestly, and dedicated faithfully to public service.

Many areas of disagreement will continue. But there must be a single purpose among all the homophile organizations. We in Mattachine believe this purpose can still be best described as stated in the Society's "Aims and Principles," first published almost ten years ago.

AIMS AND PRINCIPLES OF THE MATTACHINE SOCIETY

TO SPONSOR PROJECTS OF EDUCATION

- Education of the general public so as to give them a better understanding concerning sex variation, so that all persons may be accepted as individuals for their own worth and not blindly condemned for their emotional make-up; to correct general misconceptions, bigotries, and prejudices resulting from lack of accurate information regarding sex variants.

- Education of variants themselves so that they may better understand not only the causes and conditions of variation, but formulate an adjustment and pattern behavior that is acceptable to society in general and compatible with recognized institutions of a moral and civilized society with respect for the sanctity of home, church and state.

TO AID THE VARIANT THROUGH INTEGRATION

- Since variants desire to be accepted by society, it behooves them to assume community responsibility. They should, as individuals, actively affiliate with community endeavors, such as civic and welfare organizations, religious activities, and citizenship responsibilities, instead of attempting to withdraw into an invert society of their own. For only as they make positive contributions to the general welfare can they expect acceptance and full assimilation into the communities in which they live.
- The long-term aid is not only to support well-adjusted variants with full integration into society, but to give special aid to maladjusted homosexuals for their own welfare as well as that of the community.

TO CONDUCT A PROGRAM OF SOCIAL ACTION

- To secure the active cooperation and support of existing institutions such as psychology departments of universities, state and city welfare groups, mental hygiene departments, and law-enforcement agencies in pursuing the programs of education and integration.
- To contact legislators regarding both existing discriminatory statutes and proposed revisions and additions to the criminal code in keeping with the findings of leading psychiatrists and scientific research organizations, so that laws may be promulgated with respect to a realistic attitude toward the behavior of human beings.
- To eliminate widespread discrimination in the fields of employment, in the professions and in society, as well as to attain personal social acceptance among the respectable members of any community.
- To dispel the idea that the sex variant is unique, "queer" or unusual, but is instead a human being with the same capacities of feeling, thinking and accomplishment as any other human being.

GENERAL AIMS

- To accomplish this program in a law-abiding manner. The Society is not seeking to overthrow or destroy any of society's existing institutions, laws or mores, but to aid the assimilation of variants as constructive and responsible citizens. Standard and accepted democratic processes are to be relied upon as the technique for accomplishing this program.

- The Society opposes indecent public behavior, and particularly excoriates those who would contribute to the delinquency of minors and those who attempt to use force or violence upon any other persons whatsosever.
- Although the Mattachine Society is a non-sectarian organization and is not affiliated with any political organization, it is, however, unalterably opposed to Communists and Communist activity and will not tolerate the use of its name or organization by or for any Communist group or front.

March 1963

Towards a Sexually Sane Society

Antony Grey

This address was delivered as one of the "Winter Talks" sponsored by the Albany Trust of London, which operated the Homosexual Law Reform Society. Grey was at this time the secretary of the society and the trust. He had been connected with the society since its founding in 1958 and had served as treasurer since 1960. "Antony Grey" was the pseudonym of activist A. E. G. Wright. The "Quaker report" refers to *A Quaker View of Sex,* published in London by the Friends Home Service Committee in 1964. The full name of the Dutch organization C.O.C. is the Cultuur en Ontspannings Centrum (Center for Recreation and Culture).

Mr. Chairman, ladies and gentlemen, the title which I chose for this talk is a deliberately vague title—but I hope it is not going to be a deliberately vague talk. I did, in fact, have a fairly precise idea in my mind of what I meant by this title, "Towards A Sexually Sane Society," because I believe that the society we are living in today, at any rate in this country, is not a particularly sane one in this respect. It might even be described as a sexually insane society, or at least one that is mad about sex in various ways. This, I think, is an unfortunate state of affairs which we should try to put right.

I believe it was Bernard Shaw who said that there has been more nonsense talked about sex than about any other subject; and if one reads the newspapers or listens to debates in Parliament, one certainly gets the strong feeling that this is true. I once talked to a rather eminent member of the House of Lords who had previously sat in the Commons for many years, and he said to me: "You know, when those fellows get up and talk about sex they completely take leave of their senses. From the way they carry on, you would think that every girl was a shrinking young virgin and every young man was a brute who wanted to rape the first woman he came across, and it is terribly difficult to get them to be in the least balanced or sensible about anything of this kind."

Sex, of course, is just one aspect of life. It is a very important aspect—indeed, a fundamental appetite, like sleeping or eating or thinking—and one cannot ignore it. By trying to ignore it or suppress it, one merely succeeds in making it into an overwhelmingly important thing which gets out of all proportion in life, and lots of people nowadays make far too much fuss about it, usually in quite the wrong ways. Three main categories of these spring to mind. First of all, there are the puritans—the people who think the whole thing is dirty and ought to be suppressed. These are the people who provide the censors and the punishers, and unfortunately they still dominate our law-making and law-giving. Secondly, there are the people who set out to exploit sex in a commercial way; not just the people who live on prostitution and make big profits out of that, but the sexual titillators, among whom I would include not merely the pornographers, but also the sensational Press, who do it under the guise of preaching good behavior and saying "How shocking all this is," while all the time they are really creating more relish for it. And then there are the unfortunate people who as a result of all this titillation and repression become utterly obsessed by sex, so that it gets out of all proportion in their lives and their whole thought and life-drive is dominated by the unsuccessful search for satisfactory sex.

I think that all these English attitudes are particularly unbalanced and immature; in fact, we are quite rightly regarded as the laughing stock of the Continentals in this respect (although I sometimes wonder whether they are all that much better than we are). You may have read Mr. Malcolm Muggeridge in this week's *New Statesman,* commenting on the Quaker report. He said: "Sex, to the French, remains pleasurable or humorous. They cannot grasp it as a duty. The wrongs of homosexuals condemned to seek their pleasures in public lavatories, which so harrowed the Quakers, leave them cold." So those who seek a healthier and more matter-of-fact approach are themselves sensationalised in this sort of way. The Quaker report has been commented upon in the Press in ways which are simply a grotesque garbling of what they did in fact say—I am sure Mr. Wedmore will agree with that.

> [At this point, the representative of the Quakers agreed with Grey's statement emphatically.]

The more one tries to do social work to help people who have sexual problems, the more one realises that workers in all the fields of family difficulties and sex matters come up against a mountain not merely of prejudice, but of wilful ignorance. People don't want to know about sex; they not merely don't know about it, they actively don't want to know. This is especially true of homosexuality, because homosexuality is a subject about which one either knows a good deal or else one knows nothing at all; and those who don't want to know will not be told. I have been told of an eighteen-year-old boy who was troubled with homosexual feelings, and who, having hesitated for months, finally screwed up his courage to the sticking-point, came down to breakfast one day, and said to his parents: "Mummy and Daddy, I've got something very important to tell you: I'm homosexual." His mother, who was pouring out the coffee, did not even bother to look up. She said, in reproving tones, "Don't be silly, dear, that's not a funny joke at all." In other words, "This couldn't possibly happen to *my* child—it's always those nasty people down the road." I have also had the extraordinary experience of discussing this subject with one of the Members of Parliament who had expressed himself most violently against the Wolfenden Report in a House of Commons debate, and who, after a certain amount of quite friendly and reasonable conversation with me, suddenly looked very puzzled and asked: "Is it true that these homosexuals actually find the idea of going to bed with a woman distasteful?"

This is the basic problem which we at the Albany Trust are up against. Almost in spite of ourselves, we are becoming a social service agency for quite a lot of our time, and in the process we are learning quite a lot about all sorts of people. The ignorance which exists about this problem of homosexuality is quite appalling. I have heard of a couple of cases only this week of parents who have been so shocked and upset by finding that their children had homosexual tendencies that they either turned them out of the house or assaulted them. And the children, the people who come to us for advice, will often say: "Well, I have lived with my parents for ten, fifteen, or twenty years, and I don't know what to do, and life is very difficult." Usually I ask them whether their parents have any idea about their homosexuality, and they reply: "Oh, no—I couldn't possibly tell them. I would not know how to start." This is a very difficult problem, which everybody has got to solve for themselves, but which far too few people are making any attempt to solve at all.

These attitudes are of course largely due to the law, which is why we want to change the law but it is not the only factor. I believe that quite apart from any question of the law, there is a genuine fear among the population at large of the unknown, and a dislike of the different. However silly it may be, there are many people who feel that homosexuals are a threat to their security—to their emotional security, if not to their physical security—and that is why it is not sufficient for us to speak of "persecution," and to present homosexuals as a minority which has a legitimate grievance, in order to get the law changed. This is, of course, true; but we have got to take a more positive approach, and somehow to make society surer than it is at present that the homosexuals in its midst are not a danger to it.

How are we to move towards a more sexually sane society? First of all, I think that everyone who wishes to do so could usefully begin by making an honest self-criticism of their own lives and characters, seeing if they could be more objective about them and moving towards a better outlook in themselves. And those who are homosexual must be sufficiently honest with themselves to think seriously about some of the most common criticisms of homosexuals which are made by the public at large, in the Press, in Parliament and so forth, even if they feel that these criticisms are largely unfounded and born of ignorance. I would ask everyone, nevertheless, to try and think what they can do about these things, both as individuals and as members of a community; and in discussing them, I would like people also to speculate how far the situation with respect to these matters will or ought to be different a few years after the law has been changed?

The first of these very common criticisms is that far too many homosexuals are indiscriminately promiscuous, and that they positively enjoy indulging in furtive and sordid sexual activities, often in public places—not merely because they are forced to do this, but because they prefer it that way and get a kick out of it. Possibly there are far worse things than promiscuity; and much of the public misbehaviour which goes on may not bother anybody else. But, to say the least, it does not help to improve the public's idea of homosexuals one little bit; and I think we should lose no opportunity of stressing that the present state of the law against private relationships tends to increase the amount of promiscuous and public misbehaviour, rather than to curb it.

Then there is the common belief that homosexuals are a danger to youth, because they would all like to seduce teenagers if they got the chance. This also may be a wild exaggeration, but I cannot help being conscious that behaviour of this sort does go on. Of course, it is unrealistic to expect that teenagers who are homosexual will happily refrain from all sexual activity until they reach their twenty-first birthday: and it may be that implementation of the Wolfenden Report will create a difficult situation for youngsters if the law is altered to make twenty-one the consenting age. As you know, the Homosexual Law Reform Society stands for the Wolfenden Report, and for this particular recommendation; but I think there is no harm in discussing its possible consequences. Perhaps, with the spreading frankness that there is these days about heterosexual teenagers' sexual activities, there may also come about a greater degree of frankness and understanding about homosexual teenage behaviour as well. But it would surely be a good thing for anyone who does have contact with teenagers in this category to think very hard about the desirability, in their own best interests, of discouraging them from a path which we all know is fraught with personal difficulties and dangers, and also with some inevitable unhappiness.

In *Towards A Quaker View of Sex,* the authors deny the notion that all homosexual relationships are necessarily sinful just because they are homosexual. This is rather a remarkable view for a Christian body to put forward, and some of the Press commentaries on the Quaker report have said, quite rightly, that it is not remarkable for what it says, but it *is* remarkable because of the people who are saying it as this is the first time that a Christian group has come out so clearly and explicitly in favour of revising entirely our ideas about what is and what is not sinful. To the Quakers, what matters is the quality and depth of any human relationship—the extent of sincere care and feeling for the other person. It is this which determines whether or not any relationship, whether heterosexual or homosexual, is good or evil. "Members of this group," they say

> "have been depressed quite as much by the utter abandon of many homosexuals, especially those who live in homosexual circles as such, as by the absurdity of the condemnation rained down upon the well-behaved. One must disapprove of the promiscuity and selfish-ness, the utter lack of any real affection, which is the stamp of so many adult relationships, heterosexual as well as homosexual. We see nothing in them often but thinly disguised lust, unredeemed by that real concern which has always been the essential Christian requirement in a human relationship. But it is also obvious that the really promiscuous and degraded homosexual has not been helped by the total rejection he has had to face. Society has not said 'if you do that, that is all right, but as to the other, we cannot approve of that.' It has said 'whatever you do must be wrong; indeed you *are* wrong.' We must consider whether it is not the relationship that matters, rather than the acts that it may involve. Then homosexuals will be helped to face the moral implications of thin selfish relationships, and society will accept homosexuals as human beings."

This brings me to my third critical talking point. It has been said that homosexuals can usually have some lovers and plenty of acquaintances, but they have very few friends. Is this true, and if so need it be true? Is there anything, in other words, in the essential nature of a homosexual which makes him inevitably bound to be more self-centred and less capable of friendship than a heterosexual is, because he is unreliable, or even downright dishonest, in his treatment of other people? I do not think so, and I know a lot of homosexuals who are the opposite of all these things. But there are also a great many who are like this, and what can we do to persuade them that it is unnecessary, and a mistake, both for themselves and for everyone else?

In Holland, there exists an organization called the C.O.C., which you have read about recently in *The Observer.* It has worked in sixteen years with considerable success to foster a degree of *esprit de corps* among both men and women homosexuals in a way which unfortunately is still impossible here until the law is changed, but which points a way ahead. This is much more than just a social club, although there is quite a good clubhouse. They aim at helping people to resolve their personal problems in the most fruitful and constructive way they can: and wherever possible, to establish permanent relationships based on affection in place of casual, promiscuous ones. And not only do they encourage people to face up to their own position and accept themselves honestly; they also help them to establish franker and more sincere and honest relationships with their families, with their employers, even, and with the community around them. Their whole aim is not to separate homosexuals off from society and bring them together in a little cliquish group, but to integrate them with the community. In other words, they do not encourage them to live the whole of their social lives with the homosexual group; they rather try to provide an atmosphere of background relaxation which will enable their members not only to be friendly amongst themselves, but to be more sociable with other people and to mix in heterosexual society. This, I think, is a good thing—this aim at personal integration into the community, rather than at separating the homosexual's life as a homosexual from the rest of his life. If the Dutch can do it, why is it so impossible in this country? Even if it cannot yet be done in an organised way, because of the law, why is it impossible for people to attempt it individually, by bringing more of this sort of spirit into their own lives and into the lives of others?

I ask this because I do feel that the sort of attitudes and behaviour that one finds among numbers of English homosexuals are not particularly healthy, or particularly helpful to other people. At the Albany Trust we do come up against some hard cases, and one cannot help seeing what a large part human selfishness plays in creating a lot of needless unhappiness. The callousness with which so many people treat others, when they ought to be only too aware from their own experience of life how vulnerable other people can be, is quite lamentable. Over the past month, for instance, I have seen about twenty people whose basic trouble was the same in every case: they were all lonely. And several of them had reached the pitch of depression needed to drive them into our office to talk about it because somebody else had let them down.

I should like to think that most of the Albany Trust's active supporters are not in the habit of letting people down, and that they would even make a point of seeking out—instead of running away from—the difficult person who presents a bit of a problem, and trying to repair some of the damage. I do think that a lot of the personal problems which homosexual people have in their lives and the dangerously nervous states which many of them get into, are caused by the legal and social attitudes of our society, because these cause a "splitting off" of the sexual part of a homosexual's nature, and of his sex life, from all the rest of it—his working life and his family life—so that everything becomes unnecessarily difficult and confused for him. In these circumstances, it is scarcely surprising that some homosexuals develop rather fragmented personalities, and become incapable of sustaining a really deep mature relationship with anyone.

Now, you may fairly ask me, "What are you doing about it at the Albany Trust?" So for the rest of my talk, I want to give you a brief outline of what we are doing, and what we hope to do in the future if we have the resources. I am not going to say a great deal about law reform tonight, because we have had two talks on this and it has been fairly exhaustively discussed, but the Homosexual Law Reform Society is continuing as much active publicity as it can afford. Executive Committee members are giving various talks, there are quite a lot of articles being written, and altogether we are campaigning as hard as we can. Recently I have taken part in two university debates, which I won respectively by 147 votes to 1, and by 63 votes to 3. We are going ahead with selective local advertising in various large towns, in the hope that this will stimulate support in these particular areas. When the time seems suitable—which probably will not be until after the next General Election—we shall of course promote a Bill or have the subject raised again in the House of Commons.

I believe that our main achievement in the five years that we have existed is to make it possible to discuss this subject openly at political meetings, university union debates, rotary clubs, religious groups and sometimes even Mothers' Unions. Until about five years ago, homosexuality was totally unmentionable, and it is a very good thing that it is now an accepted topic for the average discussion group's winter programme, so that over this winter we have been getting a request for about two talks a month.

The Albany Trust is pursuing three main aims—those of education, research and social help. In the field of education, we publish, besides *Man and Society,* various pamphlets and literature aimed at parents, teachers, magistrates, doctors and other people who have influence or authority, and who should know about this problem, with the aim of making them more acquainted with the facts (as distinct from the myths) about homosexuality. We have just co-operated with the National Council for Civil Liberties in producing a booklet called *Arrest,* which is a guide to the citizen's rights if he is taken into custody by the police.

As regards research, we have two projects in blueprint, and are only waiting for the necessary funds in order to get them started. Fund raising is a long and difficult business, and one has to be patient, however unwillingly. The first of these research projects is for a study of court cases during a specified period in the London area, and also in a provincial centre. The second proposed research would attempt to find out what public opinion about homosexuality is, as distinct from what we are told it is. We are always being told, by Home Secretaries and Members of Parliament and other knowledgeable persons, that there is a terrific weight of opposition to this reform. Yet whenever we go around speaking, we always win debates by huge majorities; we always find everybody we talk to agrees with us once we have put the case for reform to them, and they are often quite indignant that the law has not been changed long ago. Perhaps we would find, through some research, that most people who have not had it drawn to their attention, have no strong views on the subject at all, but are probably mildly hostile on the strength of reading or hearing occasional things such as court reports. A lot of these people probably know very little about homosexuals, and it would be very useful to find out if this is so, and what their impressions are.

In the sphere of social help we have, as I said earlier, a continuous stream of people coming to us at our office, whom we try to help as best we can by putting them in touch with suitable doctors, clergymen, lawyers and other advisers. If we had sufficient time and money to advertise the fact that we help people in this way, we would get more than we could cope with. The fact that all the people who come to us just arrive, without our doing any advertising to bring them in, does make us feel that there is a great need for very much more positive social help than exists at present for people who are puzzled and worried about their sexual lives. Some of the people who come to us are in quite dire straits, and we had men admitted as in-patients to psychiatric hospitals within twenty-four or forty-eight hours; but most of them are just people who feel much better for a friendly chat, and go away after it with a rather more balanced outlook on life. Our counsellors in this work give a great deal of time and trouble to it—far more than we could do ourselves. We are especially grateful to people like the Camberwell Samaritans, who have been a great help to several people with quite serious problems just recently, and also to such bodies as the Voluntary Hostels Conference, who had a very interesting symposium on homosexuality a few months ago, attended by a great many probation officers, hostel workers and others who wield a great deal of influence in the social work field.

We find that people who have been in prison and come to us asking for help in finding jobs are a big problem, because unfortunately there is more prejudice against ex-prisoners who have been in prison for a homosexual offence than there is against somebody who has merely stolen a few thousand pounds from the petty cash, for instance. This is a fault in social attitudes which is going to take a long time to put right, but we do what we can for ex-prisoners, even if it is not very much—I know of some professionally qualified men who have been six or nine months without succeeding in getting even the most menial job after they have come out of prison.

Growing out of these small beginnings, there is a very healthy realisation among social workers of all kinds that homosexuals are human beings with problems—not people who automatically deserve punishment; that in this respect the law is an ass, and that the social and human problems of homosexual people have got to be coped with rather regardless of what the law theoretically demands. All this growing awareness of the problems that homosexuals are up against is a hopeful sign, and it has made us feel that the time may be riper now than it was two years ago (when we first suggested it) to get funds and backing for the idea of a psychosexual out-patients' clinic, where not only homosexuals but anybody with sexual difficulties and problems can go for help and guidance which is skilled, sympathetic and inexpensive. The Albany Trust convened some meetings about this at Church House two years ago. They came to nothing, unfortunately, but we are now trying to revive the idea and get wider support for it.

From what I have been saying, you will see that there is a great deal to be done and not nearly enough people, money or time to do it with. I have been helping the Albany Trust and Homosexual Law Reform Society in one capacity or another ever since they started, and I am more than ever convinced as a result of doing so that law reform is an essential step towards a sexually sane society. I have also come to realize that law reform by itself is not enough; it will be merely preliminary to the real job which the Albany Trust must continue doing after the law is changed, of helping everybody in this country who has a sexual problem, whether it is a heterosexual one or a homosexual one, to find the way towards a happier, a healthier and a fuller life. After all, our lives here on earth are very short, and we should not be having to waste a minute of them on unnecessary or artificially created problems.

1964

Open Letter to the Florida Legislature's "Johns Committee"

Hal Call

This is the text of the open letter written by Hal Call, president of the Mattachine Society, following the evaluation and bibliographic review of a report (issued earlier in 1964) titled "Homosexuality and Citizenship in Florida," the product of a Florida legislative committee initially named for former Florida Governor Charley E. Johns. Due to its inclusion of what were purported to be photographs of homosexual acts in public places, the report was promptly declared to be obscene by the prosecuting attorney of Miami. Leaked copies of the report created such a furor of criticism that the committee chairman and working staff resigned and the appropriation was rescinded. A lengthy discussion of this incident may be found in James T. Sears's account of southern gay and lesbian history, *Lonely Hunters: An Oral History of Lesbian and Gay Southern Life, 1948-1968* (1997). Edmund Bergler was the author of the 1962 book *Homosexuality: Disease or Way of Life?,* and Alan Guttmacher was a sex researcher and advocate of birth control.

As president of the Mattachine Society, Inc., I would like to join with other responsible Americans in expressing my shock and concern at the report on homosexuality recently issued by the Florida Legislative Investigation Committee. No wonder that I was unable to obtain a copy of the report from the office of the staff director or that the committee seems now—despite its original intent to do precisely the opposite—to be doing everything in its power to prevent further circulation and discussion of its notorious masterpiece. Rarely do legislative bodies come up with material that is so irresponsible, inaccurate, inflammatory or obviously biased.

The committee did not perform its appointed task of presenting evidence on the "extent" that homosexuals have "infiltrated" agencies supported by public funds, the effect of this infiltration, of the policies of various state agencies (except for the State Department of Education) in dealing with this infiltration. Instead, it came up with a report which is naïve and recommendations which are unjustified. The committee affirms the necessity of understanding homosexuality, but its own efforts have only contributed to a further confusion and misunderstanding of the subject. The committee's criticism of others for "a serious lack of responsible research" are words which can best describe its own efforts. Recent articles on homosexuality to be found in *Harper's, Greater Philadelphia Magazine, Maclean's* and *LIFE* reveal how feeble and irresponsible in comparison was the committee's undertaking. And those magazines did not spend five years and heaven only knows how many tax payers' dollars in doing their studies either. The colossal abdication of responsibility by the committee is most blatantly revealed in its statement that it would not study or weigh the conflicting theories, contentions, or claims regarding homosexuality, but would rather let each individual "choose" that view which best "jibes" with his own. This is the height of legislative irresponsibility. But then, to compound that irresponsibility, the committee emotionally suggests the Biblical term "abomination" has stood well the test of time. I submit that such an approach would not be tolerated on any other important issue reflects an inadequate knowledge of the religious position, and makes more difficult an effective treatment of the problem. Any responsible treatment of the subject of homosexuality must involve a scientific rather than an overly moral or religious approach if it is to have any meaning.

I was quite disappointed in the incompleteness, misinterpretation, and emotional slanting of the material in the article as a whole. If only the "homosexual" organizations had but a small portion of the power and influence attributed to them, we would be able to do a better job in educating the public, in reaching large numbers of homosexuals so as to help them live more satisfactory lives, and in creating a better atmosphere between all elements in society. I fear the truth is we get more support from scientists, social scientists, ministers, lawyers, and judges than from homosexuals and that these groups have often helped the homosexual and society to understand each other better than homosexuals themselves.

The example the committee cited to show who homosexuals are and what they do were deliberately chosen for emotional and propagandistic purposes. Any serious consideration of the great bulk of homosexuals is excluded except for a grudging and low-key statement that some are "constructive and contributing members of their communities."

The committee's report unfairly and incorrectly implies that homosexuals spend all their free time frequenting special hangouts where repeated and/or unending sexual acts are committed, devote the major portion of their energies to "bringing out" the young, spreading venereal disease like wildfire, etc. Actually, most homosexuals are just as responsible and moral as anyone else. Most of them live quiet lives and are circumspect in their activities. It is doubtful that homosexuals have any greater interest in youth than others in our youth-centered culture; it has not been proved that one or more homosexual acts converts a normal male into a homosexual though the opposite has been proved time and again; it is pure fantasy to say that a homosexual gets "more stimulation" from pictures in physique magazines than a heterosexual male gets from the fold-out of *Playboy*; and it is not quite the proper chronological designation to describe high school boys as "extremely young." Nor is it justifiable to use quotations which are incomplete and taken out of context as was done when "just as the reverse is true in some cases" was omitted after the words "The urge for a younger companion is almost basic to the gay life."

Especially distressing was the committee's failure to quote the "authorities" (except for Kinsey, Bergler, and Guttmacher) by name. The use of "faceless" and nameless men in a supposedly serious study raises doubts about the data and the sources as well as the purpose for which they are used. This uncertainty is further reinforced when extreme statements are not balanced by moderate ones. People today are becoming more and more knowledgeable on many subjects. It behooves legislators and public officials to recognize this crucial fact. Ignorance and prejudice, as recent activities in this country show, are not so easily fostered as they once were.

It is a bit surprising to a thinking person to observe what strong, condemnatory, and self-righteous views are expressed when homosexuals do wrong, but what total lack of concern when homosexuals become victims of blackmail, assault, battery, and the like. Somehow or other, Christian morality and a sense of decency seem to be lacking here—causing some suspicion as to the sincerity of those who so loudly profess their principles. The report again manifests irresponsibility in its charges that homosexuality is a factor in other forms of sexual deviations, in major crime occurrences, and in security matters. Each of these allegations is serious enough to warrant careful documentation and discussion. Yet, as before, the committee runs away from important and difficult matters which do not lend themselves to gross oversimplification or to popular and emotional treatment and limits itself to those lesser and isolated bits of information which do.

Noteworthy, after pages of hellfire and brimstone, is the climax of the report. Out of 40,000 teachers in Florida we learn that so far 54 have lost their teaching certificates (with 83 cases pending) for "morals" charges. For some odd reason, the report deliberately chooses to omit any figures on the number of those teachers who were dropped for the commission of homosexual acts. On wonders how many were guilty of adultery, fornication, drunkenness, forgery, lewd and lascivious acts with women, etc. We know that two of these teachers, as the newspaper clipping reveals, were specifically charged with misconduct against six high school girls. What about the rest of them?

The committee's recommendations are open to considerable doubt as to actual intent. Under the guise of protecting young people—most states already have plenty of laws to do this—the committee proposes to deny certain basic rights, to harass homosexuals because they are different, and to deny them the possibility of employment at other than menial jobs. The use of psychiatric examinations and outpatient treatment for persons convicted of homosexual acts with minors seem reasonable enough recommendations. The implication of the proposal to keep a first arrest confidential until the individual has pleaded guilty or has been convicted and the automatic elevation of a second homosexual offense to a felony causes consternation. There is, for example, no indication what the specific nature of the offense might be. It would seem that any homosexual act, even one engaged in by consenting adults in private, would fall within the language of the committee's recommendations. If the committee had really wanted to show its sincere and enlightened concern, it would have come out firmly for the recommendations of the Wolfenden Committee, the American Law Institute, and a number of church groups. But this the committee most assuredly did not do. The proposal to create a central records repository for all homosexuals arrested and convicted in Florida and to make these records available to public employing agencies smacks of the police state, of self-incrimination, and of denial of an individual of a right to earn a living in accordance with his interests and abilities. The result of such a policy would be a further stigmatization of an individual whose homosexual offense may not have involved acts committed against a minor, by force, or in public. I am confident the good people of Florida will not permit the committee's rash measures to be enacted into law or to create a new group of "second class" citizens.

The Appendices are as irresponsible and out of focus as the body of the report and the tasteless photographs. Only about one-third of the material in the section on Florida laws has anything whatsoever to do with homosexuality. One can only conclude the remaining two-thirds was included in order to associate homosexuality with everything else that is considered abnormal or arouses emotional responses. The glossary of terms is so written up and arranged (inconveniently in nonalphabetical order) as to shock and provide very little that is constructively pertinent or informative. Its approximately 120 terms include 14 which appear twice and 47 which are either neutral or have no special association with homosexuality—e.g., complex, creep, cute, fetish, flagellation, libido, nymphomania, pyromania, sadism, etc. Worst of all, because it cannot be seen through as readily as the other appendices, the bibliography is anything but "complete and responsible" a list as can be compiled on the subject. It is limited for some reason to an incomplete coverage of material published between 1933 and 1959. Perhaps the list was thrown together at the request of the committee back in 1959 and has never been altered since. Its 338 items include 43 books (only 5 specifically on homosexuality), 20 reports (only 6 specifically on homosexuality) and 275 articles (only 45 primarily on homosexuality). Thus 56 items, or less than one-sixth of the total, are wholly pertinent to the subject of the report. The rest of the bibliography is stuffed with material dealing only in part with homosexuality and with material on such subjects as adultery, prostitution, incest, rape, alcoholism, obscenity, pornography, and psychopathology. Omitted from the list are the pioneer studies of Freud, Havelock Ellis, Wilhelm Stekel, Edward Carpenter and Krafft-Ebing. Specifically missing are 34 books published no later than 1963 dealing wholly with homosexuality, and hundreds of articles on the subject. Any college freshman could have found most of this data by consulting card catalogues and standard guides. For example, a quick check would reveal the following items; *Psychological Abstracts*—491; *Reader's Guide to Periodical Literature*—43; *Education Index*—20; *International Index to Periodicals*—41; *Subject Index to Periodicals*—29; and *Index to Periodicals*—29; and *Index to Legal Periodicals*—32. These 656 references, some of which are duplicated, all deal directly with the subject of homosexuality rather than with a variety of other subjects. Diligence and persistence would probably produce several hundred more articles, books, and pamphlets on the subject. (For the committee's convenience, a short list of some of the many omitted references is appended to this letter.) But even more serious than the magnitude of its omissions is the obvious failure of the committee members, as revealed in the report, to read or comprehend most, if any, of the works included on their modest list.

If the committee is to pursue the subject of homosexuality further, I should like to suggest that it carefully consider (1) factors contributing to homosexuality (e.g., the possibility of a biological "predisposition," the role of the family—especially the parents, and the implications of the "emancipation" of women), (2) what can or cannot be done about these contributing factors, (3) those facets of homosexuality which can or cannot be considered constructive or acceptable, (4) psychotherapy as a practical as well as theoretical form of treatment, (5) revision of the law to remove homosexual acts between consenting adults in private from the roster of illegal and punishable acts, and (6) ways in which society can best accommodate homosexuals and homosexuals can best adjust to society without undue discrimination or recrimination by either party. Further, if the committee and other public officials would consult and cooperate with responsible homosexuals, as well as with recognized specialists and persons of good will, I am sure, in view of our experience over the past fifteen years, that greater understanding and significant gains can be quickly achieved. We recommend this approach to you for your most serious consideration.

July 22, 1964

Civil Liberties: A Progress Report

Franklin Kameny

This speech was delivered in the summer of 1964 by Dr. Franklin Kameny, at that time president of the Mattachine Society of Washington, DC, as the 100th monthly public lecture sponsored by the Mattachine Society of New York at Freedom House in New York City. The bill referred to in the text (HR-5990) was later passed by the House of Representatives, but Congress adjourned without Senate action being taken on the measure. The statement opposing federal employment discrimination issued by the Capitol Area chapter of the ACLU is the next chapter in this book. ECHO was the East Coast Homophile Organizations, and the San Francisco meeting referred to by the Methodist clergyman was the beginning of the Council on Religion and the Homosexual.

Good evening, ladies and gentlemen. It is a pleasure and a privilege to appear before you this evening, as your 100th monthly speaker.

My talk tonight will fall into two major parts. Because I have done and am doing my best to lead my organization—the Mattachine Society of Washington—in directions somewhat different from those traditional to homophile organizations in this country, the first part of my talk will be a presentation of the homophile movement as a civil liberties and social rights action movement, and of the philosophy and rationale behind what I have been trying to do.

I usually try to tailor my talks to my audience and so my talk this evening is directed to some extent to an audience which as I believe you are, is a mixture of both "in-group" and "out-group." And part of it will be directed to those active in the homophile movement.

My approach is one of strong and definite positions, unequivocally held—I feel that the nurture and presentation of controversy are not as virtuous as many in the movement would have them be, nor is the cultivation of an outward neutrality on questions upon which we should be taking a firm, clear, no-nonsense stand.

Let me make it clear at the outset that, like any organization based upon strongly-held beliefs, and composed in its active part of people of strong personality, there exists a considerable range of viewpoint within the Mattachine Society of Washington on many matters directly relevant to the homophile movement. For this reason, the views I express this evening are my own, and are not necessarily those held in any formal sense by the Mattachine Society of Washington.

It seems to me that there are three primary directions in which a homophile organization can go—social service, information and education, and civil liberties—social action. These are complementary, of course, neither mutually exclusive nor competitive, and usually become matters of a difference of emphasis from one organization to another—the placing of the emphasis resulting from a mixture of the setting in which the organization finds itself and the interests and personalities of those leading the particular group.

As I understand it, the Daughters of Bilitis, for example, devotes itself primarily to social service; the Mattachine Society of New York, in the well-established Mattachine tradition, emphasizes the information and education role. The Mattachine Society of Washington, from the outset (because of my own interests, and because in Washington, it seems the clear and obvious direction to take) has placed its emphasis in the area of civil liberties and social action. It is an exponent of that emphasis that I speak this evening.

My reasons for placing emphasis where I do are the following. In regard to social services: No *lasting* good can be accomplished by administration of social service *alone*. Let me give an example by analogy. One can supply virtually unlimited amounts of money, food, clothing, and shelter to the poor, but unless one gets to the roots of poverty—the economic system which produces unemployment, the social system which produces lack of education, and the one which over-produces people, etc.—one will accomplish little of lasting value. Similarly, we can refer homosexuals to lawyers, we can find jobs for those who have lost jobs, or have been denied them because of homosexuality, and we can assist them in other ways, but unless and until we get at and eliminate the discrimination and prejudice which underlie—and, in fact, which *are*—the homosexuals' problems, we will accomplish nothing of lasting value, either, and our job will go on literally without end.

Obviously we cannot easily turn away people now in need with the argument that we are working in order that those in the future will not need; so there is clearly a place in the homophile movement for the social services—and the Mattachine Society of Washington does its share—but only, I feel, to supplement work of a more fundamental nature, dealing with changes of attitude, prejudice and policy.

We come next to the area of information and education. While this is important, I feel that any movement which relies solely upon an intellectually-directed program of information and education, no matter how extensive, to change well-entrenched, emotionally-based attitudes, is doomed to disappointment. The Negro tried for 90 years to achieve his purposes by a program of information and education. His achievements in those 90 years, while by no means nil, were nothing compared to those of the past 10 years, when he tried a vigorous civil liberties, social action approach and gained his goals thereby.

The prejudiced mind, and that is what we are fighting, is not penetrated by information and is not educable. This has been shown in a number of studies of the mental processes associated with prejudice, and has been confirmed by a recent study which showed that tolerance is only slightly promoted by more information; that communication of facts is generally ineffectual against predispositions: that prejudiced opinions, attitudes, and beliefs, usually change only when people are forced to change.

The prejudice against homosexuality is primarily one of an emotional commitment, not an intellectual one; and appeals based upon fact and reason will, for the most part, not be effective.

Where a program of information and education *will* be useful and very important is in presenting our position to that minority of the majority who are potentially our allies anyway, but who have not thought about the matter before—such as the clergy, as just one of a number of examples—who are looked to as leaders by the masses of people.

Even there, however, a vigorous and outgoing program is necessary. Let me illustrate this point with an anecdote. Late in 1962, when the Mattachine Society of Washington was about a year old and had begun to establish itself in the homophile movement by more than its mere existence, I wrote letters to all of the other homophile organizations in the country introducing our group and describing some of the endeavors in which we were then engaged. I mentioned our dealings with the Washington chapter of the ACLU. One of the organizations wrote back, saying that they too had contacted their local ACLU affiliate, and that ACLU representatives had spoken to their membership on several occasions. I replied by saying that representatives of the ACLU had never addressed our membership, but representatives of the Mattachine Society of Washington had addressed the ACLU's membership. I think the difference is illustrative of my point and is important. It has served us exceedingly well.

Information and education, yes—but *not* to inform and educate us. The homophile movement does not, I feel, exist in any major degree for the edification of its own members. In its information and education role, it exists primarily to inform and to educate the public. We should appear before the public in the role of authorities on questions of homosexuality—as indeed we are. I am truly pleased to see growing, particularly on the East Coast, a strong trend toward the bringing of the talks, the lectures, the discussions, outside our own group, and before other groups—before the heterosexual public.

This brings us to the area of civil liberties and social action. Here, we get into an area in which we are engaging in what is fundamentally down-to-earth, grass-roots, occasionally tooth-and-nail politics. We are dealing with emotions of people, and the policies of officialdom, and our methods must be in accord with this.

Let me digress briefly. Official policies—laws, regulations, etc., on the one hand and popular opinion and prejudice on the other hand, interact strongly and circularly. This is obvious. It is therefore obvious, too, that if we work almost infinitely long to change public attitudes and are successful in doing so, or wait for them to evolve, then after another long wait, we might see laws and official policies change. The reverse process is much faster, and much more efficient and is especially suited to a group located, as mine is, in Washington.

The current issue of *Scientific American* magazine has an article which bears directly upon this matter. In a study of changes of attitudes on integration in various parts of the country it is pointed out "that official action has *preceded* public sentiment, and public sentiment has then attempted to accommodate itself to the new situation." This lesson should not be lost upon us.

Prejudiced official attitudes and policies reinforce private discrimination. The private employer, for example, may or may not hire homosexuals, if the government *does* hire them; he will *not* hire them if the government does *not*. That is over-simplified, of course, but in terms of large-scale policies and practices, it is true.

For these reasons, lightly touched upon here, I feel that the primary direction of endeavor and the one likely to be most fruitful should be the changing of the attitudes and policies of those who are, or to whom the community looks, as constituted authority. Wherever discrimination is officially sponsored, it is amenable to attack within the framework of administrative and judicial procedure. This has been the backbone (but let it be emphasized, not the totality) of our approach in Washington; and I would very much like to see such an approach extended elsewhere, including New York.

I would suggest that here in New York you have at least one beautiful example of the kind of situation which needs this sort of approach, and which is much more fundamental than would appear upon first thought. I refer to the continued closing of gay bars. This seems to me to be an obvious infringement upon the right of the homosexual citizen to freely associate, to assemble, and to make use of public accommodations of his own choice on a basis of equality with other citizens. I have suggested that (strategy, tactics, and timing permitting) this is a matter which a group such as Mattachine Society of New York might well take up. I am told that it is difficult to get a bar owner who will cooperate. *This is not a matter for the bar owners. This is a matter for homosexuals*. The lawsuits which brought an end to school segregation were not initiated by schools which wished to integrate; they were brought by Negro school children who wished to attend. The parallel is valid.

One homosexual or several homosexuals in a group, *as homosexuals,* and as potential or actual patrons of otherwise legal establishments which, by stated public policy, they may not patronize, should bring the necessary suit against the proper officials. I feel that it is very much the role of the homophile organizations to encourage, to support, and to create such test cases.

I will extract an item from the second part of my talk to illustrate our position in Washington. We have an all-night restaurant, patronized by numbers of homosexuals. One night the police came in and requested a show of identification of all those who they thought were homosexuals. One of our members, well-coached in his rights, refused to show identification (citizens do not have to do so). He was arrested and I had to bail him out in the wee hours of one Sunday morning. Not only did the case go to court, with the support, elicited by us, of the ACLU, but more important, a formal complaint was made to the Police Department by the ACLU about certain aspects of the case. The Mattachine Society of Washington, on its own, also made a complaint—not only to the Police Department, but to the President of the Board of Commissioners, our closest equivalent to a mayor. In our complaint we pointed out that homosexuals, whether singly or in groups, are entitled to the same use of public accommodations of their choice as are all other citizens, and that the Mattachine Society of Washington was prepared to take all measures legally within its power to ensure that those rights were not infringed upon. A similar letter was sent to Senator Morse, who takes an interest in police practices in the District of Columbia. We have received replies indicating that the matter is being pursued. We intend to follow it up.

It is in matters of this sort that a civil rights philosophy is, I think, effective.

Returning, however, to matters of rationale of approach—I feel that in going before the public, it is absolutely necessary to be prepared to take definite, unequivocal positions upon supposedly controversial matters. We should have a clear, explicit, consistent viewpoint and we should not be timid in presenting it.

In presenting our view to a generally prejudiced public, we are not presenting data to a scientific body. If one presents to a scientific audience nine points in favor of a particular viewpoint, and a tenth point which is doubtful, the scientific audience will grant that the viewpoint has a 90% chance of being correct. Present the same nine points to a person of prejudiced mind, and the first nine points will slide off, as water off a duck's back, and in seeking to retain his prejudices he will seize upon the uncertainty in the tenth, and will say "See, even they agree with me, so I must be right." And become more confirmed in his beliefs than before. Thus it behooves us to take and to present clear, explicit, firm positions.

There are those in the movement who seem to feel that whenever controversy exists, we should be impelled to impartially present both or all sides of the question. I disagree. Having examined the issue, and decided which side is, in our view, correct and consistent with the aims of the homophile movement, we should then present that side alone, presenting the other only to refute it, and as not having equal merit with the view we espouse. We should certainly not sponsor the presentation of opposing views. The Democrats don't present the views of the Republicans as having equal merit with theirs. Our opponents will do a fully adequate job of presenting their views, and will not return us the favor of presenting ours; we gain nothing in virtue by presenting theirs, and only provide the enemy—and let us not think of them as less than an enemy—with ammunition to be used against us.

We are not dealing with scientists; let us not employ the scientific method where it is not applicable. To do so is naïve and unrealistic to an almost suicidal degree.

As our dealings with some of the government officials in Washington have indicated, we are dealing with an opposition which manifests itself—not always, but not infrequently—as a ruthless, unscrupulous foe who will give no quarter and to whom any standards of fair play are meaningless. Let us respond realistically. We are not playing a gentlemanly game of tiddlywinks or croquet or chess. An impractical, theoretical intellectualism is utterly unrealistic and can be completely self-destructive in this context.

Now, a few particular points. My starting point is one now well accepted among the homophile organizations, although still novel elsewhere—that the homosexuals make up a minority group comparable to other, what might be called sociological minorities, such as the Negroes, the Jews, etc. I think that this should be explicitly justified, however, since direct challenges to the concept are frequently posed.

I feel that a little consideration will show that aside from the obvious statistical basis, a minority group in the sense in which we speak, must possess four characteristics.

First, the members must possess, in common, some single characteristic or closely related group of characteristics, but otherwise be heterogenous.

Second, on account of this characteristic, but *not* in reasonable, rational or logical consequence of it, the majority about them must look down upon the members of the group, and must discriminate adversely against them.

There is a third facet of minority-majority group relations which is a little more subtle, but which I think is always present in regard to a group which is a sociological minority. The consequences of the faults and the sins of the individual members of the minority are visited upon all members of the minority. Let a white, heterosexual, Anglo-Saxon Protestant commit a crime, and he alone is blamed. Let a Jew, a Negro, or a homosexual commit a crime, and epithets and blame are depicted against all members of his minority. Let a few members of the majority be personally objectionable or ridiculous to large numbers of people, and the reactions to their offensiveness will be directed against them individually. Let a few members of a minority group be offensive or ridiculous to large numbers of people, and a stereotype will be created which will be applied indiscriminately to all those known to be members of the minority group. This is true of the Negro and Jewish minorities; I hardly need to point out that it is also true of the homosexual minority.

A fourth criterion for the establishment of a sociological minority group is a feeling on the part of members of the minority of cohesiveness, of belonging, and of identity among themselves. This does not have to imply a feeling of belonging to an organization or movement—much as the members of the homophile movement might like all homosexuals to feel—but a feeling of kinship to others whom they know to be members of this minority group. This feeling is clearly present among homosexuals, and strongly so.

With this as a starting point, I look upon the homophile organizations as playing for the homosexual minority the same role as is played by the NAACP or CORE [Congress of Racial Equality] for the Negro minority.

We cannot ask for our rights as a minority group, and I will elaborate briefly upon just what it is we are asking for; we cannot ask for our rights from a position of inferiority or from a position, shall I say, as less than whole human beings. I feel that the entire homophile movement, in terms of any accomplishments beyond merely ministering to the needy, is going to stand or fall upon the question of whether or not homosexuality is a sickness, and upon our taking a firm stand on it. I feel that *The New York Times* article of last December 17, and the recent *New York Academy of Medicine Report* have made this abundantly clear. The Question arises every time there is serious discussion of homosexuality, and I feel that an unequivocal position must be taken.

I do not intend this evening to go into a lengthy or detailed discussion of this question. Suffice it to say for the moment that a reading of the so-called authorities on this matter shows an appalling incidence of loose reasoning, of poor research, of supposedly generally applicable conclusions being derived from an examination of non-representative samplings, of conclusions being incorporated into initial assumptions, and vice versa, with the consequent circular reasoning. A case in point is the recent, much relied upon study by Bieber. Not only were the homosexuals in his study all patients of his, and therefore, *a priori,* disturbed, but he makes the statement: "All psychoanalytic theories assume that adult homosexuality is pathological." Obviously if one assumes that homosexuality is pathological, then one will discover that homosexuality is a sickness, and that homosexuals are disturbed, just as, if one assumes that two plus two equal five, one is likely to discover that three plus one are equal to five. In both instances, the assumption requires proof before it can be seriously entertained.

There seems to be no valid evidence to show that homosexuality, *per se,* is a sickness. In view of the absence of such valid evidence, the simple fact that the suggestion of sickness has been made is no reason for enteratining it seriously, or for abandoning the view that homosexuality is not a sickness, but merely a liking or preference similar to and fully on a par with heterosexuality. Accordingly, I take the position unequivocally that, until and unless valid, positive evidence shows otherwise, homosexuality, *per se*, is neither a sickness, a defect, a disturbance, a neurosis, a psychosis, nor a malfunction of any sort.

I will go further, and say that I feel so strongly that the rationale for the homophile movement rests, and rests heavily upon this position, that should evidence arise to show conclusively that this position is in error, I shall give serious thought to leaving the movement. I do not anticipate that I shall ever need to do so.

Another question which has a way of intruding itself upon any general discussion of homosexuality—much less so, of late, than it formerly did, although it still is the basis for the Federal Government's approach to the question—is that of morality and immorality. It is a point upon which I have rarely heard a straight, direct statement of position from persons in the homophile movement—even when expressing publicly their own views.

Matters of morality, of course, are ones clearly of personal opinion and individual religious belief so that, except for an affirmation of the right of all individuals to adopt their own viewpoints upon those matters, without penalty therefore, and without the official imposition of orthodox views, the homophile movement would be in error in proscribing a position.

However for myself, I take the stand that not only is homosexuality, whether by mere inclination or by overt act, not immoral, but that homosexual acts engaged in by consenting adults are moral, in a positive and real sense, and are right, good and desirable, both for the individual participants and for the society in which they live.

There is another point which comes up frequently in discussions of homosexuality: the matter of the origins of homosexuality and the possibility of re-orientation to heterosexuality. While, as a person dealing in all aspects of homosexuality, I find that these questions are ones of some passing interest; from the viewpoint of civil liberties and social rights, these questions interest me *not at all.*

I do not see the NAACP and CORE worrying about which chromosome and gene produces a black skin or about the possibility of bleaching the Negro. I do not see any great interest on the part of the B'nai B'rith Anti-Defamation League in the possibility of solving problems of anti-semitism by converting Jews to Christianity.

In all of these minority groups, we are interested in obtaining rights for our respective minorities, *as* Negroes, *as* Jews, and *as* homosexuals. Why we are Negroes, Jews or homosexuals, is totally irrelevant, and whether we can be changed to whites, Christians, or heterosexuals is equally irrelevant.

Further, as implied a moment ago, I look upon the assumption that it is somehow desirable that we be converted to heterosexuality (with the implied assumption that homosexuality is an inferior status) as being presumptuously arrogant and an assault upon our right to be ourselves on a par with those around us, as would be similar attempts for example, to convert Jews to Christianity—something which, for just that reason, has become unfashionable in this country.

There is one final point of basic approach, before I become somewhat more specific—and this is a somewhat subtle one, one which is difficult to express clearly. In reading through many statements put out by the homophile movement, there is easily perceptible a defensive tone—a lightly-veiled feeling that homosexuality really is inferior to heterosexuality but that, since we have to live with it, it must be made the best of. While I do not, of course, take the ridiculous viewpoint discussed in the recent *New York Academy of Medicine Report* that homosexuality and homosexuals are superior to heterosexuality and heterosexuals, I am unwilling to grant even the slightest degree of inferiority: I look upon homosexuality as something in no way shameful or intrinsically undesirable.

Now, from the civil liberties and social rights viewpoint, just what do we want? I feel that we want, basically, what all other minority groups want and what every American citizen has the right to request and to expect—in fact, to demand: To be judged and to be treated, each upon his own merits as an individual and only on those criteria truly relevant to a particular situation, not upon irrelevant criteria, as homosexuality always is, having to do only with the harmless conduct of our private lives. We wish, AS HOMOSEXUALS, to be rid of the contempt directed against us by our fellow citizens—contempt which exists without reason, which serves only to render contemptible those manifesting it, and which is reinforced and perpetuated by present official attitude and policy—and it is the latter which, in great measure, is the target of a civil rights endeavor.

In short, as homosexuals we want (to quote from a portion of the statement of purpose of the Mattachine Society of Washington) "the right, as human beings, to develop our full potential and dignity, and the right, as citizens, to be allowed to make our maximum contribution to the society in which we live." These rights are ours in fact, though we are currently denied them in practice.

I feel that with due regard for strategy and tactics, we must take a bold, strong, uncompromising initiative in working for these rights; that the established framework of authority, constituted and otherwise, must be challenged directly by every lawful means at hand.

There will, of course, be reactions to any such attempts—both *The New York Times* article and the *New York Academy of Medicine Report,* to mention but two of several possibilities, are examples of the heterosexual backlash which is a parallel to the white backlash in the Negro rights movement—and we can expect them with somewhat increasing intensity. Such backlash, too, must be faced squarely and responded to fully. Most important, that such backlash may occur must not be allowed to act as a deterrent to further action.

It would be possible to discourse on these matters at greater length, but time is getting on, and my topic of major concern is the Washington homophile scene, so I'll proceed to the second part of my talk.

The Mattachine Society of Washington has a short history; the organization was founded only two and a half years ago—so it is reasonable to first review all of the organization's significant activities to date, and then proceed to proposed projects and those already underway.

Our first major project (in August two years ago) was the sending of a letter to every member of Congress, to the President and his Cabinet, to other members of the Executive Branch, and to members of the Judicial Branch of the Federal Government, as well as to officials of the Government of the District of Columbia. This letter informed the recipients of our existence and goals. It was accompanied by a copy of our statement of purpose and by a news release asking for changes in Federal policy toward homosexuals, in the areas of Federal Civil Service employment, the issuance of security clearances, and policies of the Armed Forces.

As might be expected, the results were few but not nil. We received favorable replies from Congressman Ryan of the 20th District of Manhattan's West Side, and Congressman Nix of the 4th District in Central Philadelphia. We visited the offices and spoke to Nix in person.

We also received from Mr. John W. Macy, Jr., the Chairman of the U.S. Civil Service Commission and a man whom I consider to be the Federal equivalent, for our minority, of Alabama's Governor Wallace or Mississippi's ex-Governor Barnett, an explicit statement of policy which has served us well.

This mailing also led to an explanatory conference at the Pentagon with the Defense Department's top security officials in regard to policies on security clearances for homosexuals.

In the following year, we approached the Selective Service officials, which resulted in a conference with General Hershey, head of the Selective Service, in regard to the question of confidentiality of replies to draft questionnaires. The information involved is not open, under any circumstances, to private citizens but *is* open to other Federal and state officials. We objected to this.

This project has moved slowly over to the Department of the Army. The Office of the Secretary of the Army has indicated to us that they are neither willing to alter their policy, to restrict disclosure of information only to those in the Department of the Army who require it for administration of the draft regulations, nor are they willing to engage in discussion of the matter with us.

This being the case, and acting individually and on my own in my capacity as an independent, private citizen, I wish to state publicly, that I encourage anyone, homosexual or heterosexual, who is subject to the draft, and who feels strongly about the confidentiality of the information he supplies, or about the Army's savage policies toward homosexuals, to refuse, outright and firmly, on principle, to give any response at all to the question asked at the physical examination, as to whether or not one has or has had homosexual tendencies. This refusal should be based upon two grounds:

- That this is information which is of no proper concern to the Government of the United States under any circumstances whatever, and which the Government does not have the need to know, and;
- That this information is open to improper persons (i.e., the FBI, Civil Service Commission investigators, state officials, etc.).

If anyone wishes to make a test case out of this, I will be pleased to offer every possible assistance. We can make a forum out of the court room and get our grievances on these matters before the public.

Another area of our Society's activity was the celebrated matter of the Congressional Bill HR-5990. In order to raise funds and in compliance with the laws of the District of Columbia, the Mattachine Society of Washington, in 1962, obtained a license under the so-called Charitable Solicitations Act, allowing us to solicit for funds.

This came to the attention of Rep. John Dowdy (Democrat of East Texas) who is one of the banes of the existence of the Government of the District of Columbia. As chairman of a subcommittee of the House of Representatives' Committee on the District of Columbia, he introduced a bill, HR-5990, requiring that every organization registering be found affirmatively to contribute to the health, the welfare, and the morals of the District of Columbia, in the expectation that we could not qualify. The second portion of the bill, later deleted, explicitly revoked the certificate of registration held by the Mattachine Society of Washington.

We alerted the District of Columbia Government and the local ACLU and requested hearings on the bill. The hearings were held. The District of Columbia government testified for three-quarters of an hour against the bill: I testified for four and a half hours; our vice-president testified for one-half hour; and an ACLU representative testified for an hour. The D.C. Republican Committee sent in a letter opposing the bill, as did others, and an editorial opposing the bill appeared in *The Washington Post.*

Rep. Dowdy expected to make something of a circus of the hearings at our expense. Instead, we received much favorable publicity, became well-established in the eyes of the Government of the District of Columbia as a reputable group, and, in general, reaped such a favorable harvest from the hearings that we seriously considered citing Dowdy as the Federal official who did the most in 1963 for the homophile movement.

In the autumn of last year under pressure from Dowdy, the Government of the District of Columbia called a hearing to revoke our license. At my suggestion, our attorney pointed out to the District of Columbia's attorney that this hearing was not going to be a bed of roses for the District, because we intended to ask each member of the hearing board whether he was sufficiently unprejudiced against homosexuals to render an unbiased decision. If he were not, then the hearing, and any revocation stemming from it, would be invalid. If he were, he could count on pressure from the Dowdys to deprive him of his job.

At the District Government's request, a conference was held a few days later among the lawyers, in order to find a way out of the situation without a hearing. It was found that, according to one provision of the Charitable Solicitation Act, we didn't need a license anyway, so we turned it in with the clear proviso, stated in a letter, that our fund-raising activities would continue without restriction.

The newspapers picked up the story in somewhat distorted form. We wrote a letter which was printed, again stating that our fund-raising activities were not restricted in any way and closing with the sentence: "Solicitations for funds continue actively."

Further Congressional hearings were held in January, then in March in a report which very nicely quoted some of our purposes, the House District of Columbia Committee favorably reported the bill out to the floor. We immediately alerted the ACLU who sent telegrams to 40 congressmen; we also sent telegrams. Two weeks later a minority report opposing the bill was issued by 9 of the 24 committee members, including Rep. Multer of Brooklyn.

The minority report started out by saying: "In our judgment, HR-5990 is an ill-considered, unnecessary, unwise, and unconstitutional measure. It is a danger to the people of the District of Columbia and should be rejected."

The publication of this report was a necessary pre-requisite under House procedures for full-scale debate of the bill on the House floor. At that time, an editorial appeared in *The Washington Post* titled "Piety By Fiat" and referred to an "oddly inept little bill by that Master of Morality, Rep. Dowdy." It closed by suggesting that Rep. Dowdy's bill be consigned to oblivion.

District of Columbia bills can come up on so-called District Mondays (the 2nd and 4th Mondays of each month). I have called the Capitol each Monday: the bill has not come up. The Chairman of the local ACLU has stated publicly that he considers it dead.

In March of 1963, we presented to the U.S. Civil Rights Commission a 9-page statement entitled "Discrimination Against the Employment of Homosexuals" and we testified at hearings held at that time by the Commission.

At our instigation, the Washington ACLU's Committee on Discrimination has devoted a considerable portion of its time to the problems of homosexuals. Most recently, the Washington ACLU has adopted, as an item of its policy, a statement strongly opposing the U.S. Civil Service Commission's policies against the employment of homosexuals.

We have done our best to encourage the bringing of court test cases against the Government in the areas mentioned before: U.S. civil service employment, security clearances, and military discharges, in an effort to bring about changes in Federal policies on these matters. If anyone here this evening has a potential case against the Federal Government in those areas, I would be most interested in hearing about it and I encourage its being brought to court. We have several cases now in progress.

In May of 1963, for the first time within the memory of anyone, a gay bar in Washington was raided. I spent much of the month of June last year collecting affidavits from those arrested. A formal complaint was filed by the Mattachine Society of Washington against the Police Department. A conference was held involving high police officials and Mattachine Society of

Washington officials. As a consequence, I don't think that any more gay bars in Washington will be raided.

In December of last year, within a very short time, two cases of attempted blackmail were brought to our attention. We took both cases to the head of the so-called Morals Division of the Metropolitan Police Department. They were handled tactfully and with a minimum of embarrassment. One of the cases resulted in a mid-afternoon arrest of the blackmailer in a downtown resturant complete with all the trappings of a TV melodrama, including marked money, envelopes filled with newspaper clippings instead of bills, pre-arranged signals to the police and so forth. The blackmailer is now in prison.

Following these cases *The Washington Post* printed a letter from our Society commending, on behalf of the Washington homosexual community, the head of the Morals Division and his chief subordinate for their handling of these cases. I am quite sure that they never expected a commendation from that source.

In other areas of activity, we have, as has the Mattachine Society of New York, set up a professional referral service—doctors, lawyers, psychiatrists, clergymen—for homosexuals in need.

At our initiative, a series of conferences on venereal disease has been held with District Public Health Service officials. Our VD pamphlet, printed by the District of Columbia, is soon to come out. A major portion of the work in distributing it will be the responsibility of the Mattachine Society of Washington. A TV broadcast on the subject is planned soon with Mattachine Society of Washington participation.

Mattachine Society of Washington representatives have appeared on two hour-long radio programs in Washington, one in Philadelphia, and a two-hour TV broadcast in Chicago.

That, in hasty summary, brings up-to-date the accounting of the Society's past activities. We have a number of projects under way and some which have been proposed.

We are considering approaching all of the various District of Columbia licensing boards to inquire about their policies in the licensing for various occupations and professions of persons known to be homosexual. We are also considering approaching the bar and medical associations in the same fashion.

In a similar vein, we are considering approaching the local universities to inquire as to their policies toward homosexual students and staff—I might point out, by way of digression, that in this country an individual known to be a homosexual would find it more difficult to get an education, at any level, in the schools of his choice (or, in fact, in any school at all)—than would a Negro in the South or a Native in the Union of South Africa.

Our approach to the problem of employment of homosexuals who have lost jobs on account of homosexuality is somewhat different from that taken by the Mattachine Society of New York. You have here, in a certain sense, placed yourself—non-remuneratively, of course—in the employment agency business. We choose not to do so. Therefore we are about to send a letter to every employment agency in the greater Washington area, pointing out to them that a problem exists, that there are competent people looking for work, that they—the agencies—have their fingers on the employers in a fashion and to an extent to which we never could have, and asking for their cooperation—with no remuneration to come to us, of course—in finding jobs for these people, if we send them to the agencies. We hope for at least some favorable responses.

In an attempt to broaden the scope of the project, and to tie it in more closely with a civil rights viewpoint, we are also writing similarly to the largest employers in the District of Columbia area, in order to call attention to the existence of the problem.

A proposed project has to do with the publication of two leaflets. One will deal with the rights of and the procedures to be followed by persons arrested. It will stress the point—as true in New York City as in the District of Columbia and as little realized here as there—that persons arrested *do not* have to tell the police where they work or anything else for that matter.

The second leaflet will deal with methods for the handling of Federal investigations and interrogations—FBI, Civil Service, military investigators, etc.—dealing with homosexuality. In view of the obviously harmful effects to the whole country of present Federal policies on homosexuality in their needlessly depriving the nation of the service of competent citizens, it is the patriotic duty of every citizen to do his best in the interests of his country, to resist, to flout, to thwart, to render totally ineffective such investigations and interrogations of homosexuals. Questions on homosexuality, homosexuals, etc., are never the proper concern of the Government and should not be answered. One is never required to answer such questions under any conditions—you don't even have to give FBI investigators and others the time of day—and you shouldn't. The leaflet will advise on these matters.

We have formed a Research Committee now engaged in a number of projects related to the gathering of published information for the Society's own internal use. In addition, it has two major projects just starting and a third proposed. The proposed project comes to us from the local ACLU, and has to do with Federal employees who have been fired. One of the other two projects is a questionnaire to be sent to all the psychiatrists in the area, asking for information on their views on, and approaches to, matters having to do with homosexuals and homosexuality.

The third—and by far the most important of these projects—has to do with blackmail.

One of the most successful brainwashing jobs in human history has been that done by our Federal Government on the American public—including all too many in the homosexual community—in convincing them, to the point that it has become part of American folklore, that (1) all homosexuals are poor security risks because of susceptibility to blackmail; and (2) that exclusion is the only remedy. We don't believe either of these.

We are thus preparing a survey of the homosexual community on various aspects of the question of blackmail, its prevalence, and the susceptibility of individual homosexuals to it. As far as I know, no one has ever done this before and the homophile organizations obviously can do it better than anyone else. It should provide definite, publishable data to help dispel some of the myths upon which the Government bases some of its policies.

We come now to the last of our current areas of major endeavor, religion. Last December, I gave a talk, followed by discussion, to part of the congregation of Temple Sinai, one of the reformed Jewish congregations in Washington. The talk was well received.

In January, just before one of the radio broadcasts which I mentioned earlier, one of our members telephoned every Unitarian minister in the greater Washington area to tell them of the broadcast; shortly thereafter he sent them a letter, including a copy of Cory's *The Homosexual in America.* This resulted in a sermon by one of the ministers. The sermon was titled "Civil Liberties and the Homosexual" and couldn't have been more satisfactory if I had written it myself. The sermon was followed by two discussion groups—both well attended—at which I was asked to preside.

Subsequently, with the member just mentioned as chairman, I formed a new committee—our Committee on Approaches to the Clergy—which has informally approached perhaps two dozen clergymen of several faiths and denominations, with a considerable and gratifying degree of favorable response. The Committee's bases of approach are two—of equal emphasis. First, we feel that the homosexual finds himself rejected by almost every religious body to the loss and detriment both of the religious bodies and of the homosexuals. We seek to remedy this by working for closer integration of the homosexuals with the religious life of their community.

Second, we wish to enlist the aid of the clergy in our battle for civil rights.

Our committee has drawn up a formal statement of purpose, which, in its present proposed form, pleases me greatly. This very nicely covers all three directions of endeavor discussed above. We plan to send this statement of purpose, our Society's statement of purpose, and a covering letter to the entire clergy of the greater Washington area asking for their assistance and inquiring about their interest in participating in a conference with us.

Most recently, at his initiative, I had lunch with a high official of the Methodists' national headquarters in Washington (we have had very favorable responses from the Methodists). He had just come from a retreat in the San Francisco area, attended by members of the clergy and the homophile movement. He indicated to my pleasure that he felt that we in Washington had done far more in the direction of making contact with the local clergy than had all of the West Coast groups. He was completely with us and wished to assist. He is now rounding up a group of sympathetic ministers of a variety of faiths to meet with us in the very near future. He will try to appear on the program of our forthcoming ECHO conference.

In that connection, I might mention in passing, that the Methodists will have their 5-day national conference in Washington at the same time as the 1964 ECHO conference. Informal plans are now afoot to explore the possibility of some sort of coordination.

I feel that these activities with religious leaders are of the utmost importance because the commitment of most people to their religion and to the leaders thereof is an emotional one. They will follow the lead taken by a minister where they will not follow the intellectual lead set by other leaders and persons in positions of constituted authority. If we can get any substantial portion of the clergy to support us—and a surprising number do—and to support us openly and actively, we can go a very long way, very quickly, toward remedying some of the situations in our regard which are so badly in need of remedy.

That completes a quick accounting of our activities, past, present, and proposed, in all three areas—civil liberties and social rights—information and education—and social service. I hope that the pressures of a somewhat hasty preparation have not made this presentation too unclear, too perfunctory, or too uninteresting.

August 7, 1964

Resolution of the National Capital Area Civil Liberties Union on Federal Employment of Homosexuals

It is widely recognized that the homosexual in the United States is the target for prejudice, discrimination and abuse in many areas of life. It is of particular concern to the NCACLU that an important source of such discrimination is the Federal Government.

It is the present official policy of the United States Civil Service Commission that homosexuals are not suitable for Federal employment. Under present policies a record of homosexual activity, past or present, is sufficient to deny a citizen Federal employment of any sort. Such a record leads to disqualification as a candidate for a position or for retention of a position already held. Disqualification occurs without regard for the individual employee's capability and talent, often results in a permanent denial of livelihood inconsistent with training and background, and this constitutes a waste of manpower which is not in the national interest.

These employment practices are discriminatory, for they involve the prejudging of an individual with no regard to his job qualifications solely upon the basis of attributes which bear no necessary relation to job qualifications. These practices are inconsistent with basic Federal employment policies which seek to ensure that the selection and retention of employees is not determined by irrelevant factors, but rather by the ability of the individual to perform his work. The exclusion policy operates to bar those who have homosexual preferences, those who have had only an isolated homosexual experience at some remote time in the past, as well as those who may have occasional or continuing homosexual relationships in the present, but always without any reference to actual fitness for Federal employment.

In addition, serious problems arise in connection with efforts to enforce the policy of exclusion based upon sexual behavior which takes place in private between consenting adults, or even upon sexual preferences not accompanied by action. Such efforts almost necessarily lead to the use of demoralizing, degrading and oppressive inquiries and methods, including entrapment, designed to ferret out the offending attitude, practice, or past history.

Three principal arguments are commonly offered in support of the present policy. First, it is argued that homosexuals should not be admitted to Federal employment because the presence of a homosexual in a governmental office would be detrimental to the morale and efficient operation of the office. The Civil Service Commission has offered no evidence to support such a conclusion, and in any event it appears to constitute insufficient justification for discriminatory policies.

Disruptive and improper behavior on the job is easily and rapidly ascertained by supervisory personnel and is clearly grounds for dismissal in private and in Federal employment. There is no valid justification for policies which discriminate against capable people on the supposition that they might present personnel problems when there is no clear indication to this effect in the individual case and there are adequate means of eliminating those who are responsible for disruptive behavior when it actually occurs.

Secondly, it is argued that homosexuality constitutes "immoral conduct" and is therefore grounds for disqualification from Federal employment. This is the argument principally relied on by the Civil Service Commission. In affixing the label "immoral" upon homosexuality or other conduct which takes place in private between consenting adults, the Civil Service Commission raises grave questions. The complex issues involved in judging the propriety or morality of private consensual sexual behavior of adults are matters of personal opinion and individual ethical and often religious belief. The Federal government should not seek to enforce conformity in such areas, or incorporate its moral judgments on such matters into its formal policies.

Government policy towards homosexuals is a part of the general problem of government policy respecting private actions and morality. Without determining whether the Government *ever* has a legitimate interest in such matters, it can be said that *some* matters of morality and private conduct should be reserved solely to the judgment of the individual and should not be the subject of government policy or inquiry. One such matter is the area of individual sexual thoughts, preferences and practices as between consenting adults. Sexual acts, whether homosexual or heterosexual, if committed in public, might justify dismissal or disqualification from Government employment, because of their effect on persons other than the participants. Certainly a substantial and specific showing of harm to the public must be shown to warrant any Government inquiry into or policy regarding so personal a matter as private sexual behavior.

The NCACLU therefore believes that the use of the criterion of "immoral conduct" as a basis for disqualification of homosexuals from Federal employment is invalid and contrary to fundamental principles of individual freedom and the right to privacy.

Thirdly, it is argued that homosexuals should not be employed by the Federal government because of their greater susceptibility to coercion through blackmail by reason of which they would constitute a serious security risk for the country. This argument fails on three counts. First, although many positions in the Federal service do not involve the need for access to security information, homosexuals are presently barred from all Federal employment. Second, the vulnerability of individuals to coercion and blackmail varies greatly from one to another regardless of sexual preferences. History is replete with instances where heterosexual behavior has led to serious difficulties, yet heterosexuals are not barred from government employment. A discriminatory practice which categorizes an entire group of people as potentially disloyal to their country is unjust and does not take into consideration the individual variations which certainly exist. Third, to the extent that an individual homosexual is vulnerable to blackmail, a principal basis for pressure is the fear of the loss of job which would result from exposure. That fear stems directly from the Government's policies against employment of homosexuals. Thus the Federal government by its policies against homosexuals is creating one of the important bases for susceptibility to blackmail, a problem which would substantially be less if homosexuality were not a bar to Federal employment.

CONCLUSION

The NCACLU calls upon the United States Civil Service Commission to reconsider its policies under which homosexuals are considered to be unsuitable for employment or retention in the Federal service, simply by virtue of past or present homosexual preferences, tendencies or private practices. This is consistent with the view that it is not the concern of the Government, in employment or otherwise, to scrutinize sexual activities which take place in private between consenting adults. If equal employment opportunity is to be denied to a particular group on the basis of sexual preference and activities, a clear relationship must be established between such activities and job performance. The burden of proof rests with those who would impose the discriminatory policies and such proof lacking, each case must be judged on its individual merits.

It is not the contention of the NCACLU that homosexuals are invariably good Federal employees, but only that homosexual behavior *per se* is irrelevant to Federal employment and that current policies of the Civil Service Commission do not provide equal opportunity for all people. On the contrary, those policies discriminate against homosexuals for reasons which have not been shown to have basis in fact.

We suggest that the Federal government end its policy of rejection of all homosexuals on that ground alone. Exclusion of any individual from government employment should be based only upon considerations which are relevant to that individual's qualifications for the job in question.

November 16, 1964

On Getting and Using Power

A. Cecil Williams

Reverend A. Cecil Williams, director of church and community services at the Glide Urban Center of the Glide Memorial Foundation of San Francisco, gave this address at a meeting of the Society for Individual Rights (SIR) in late 1964.

I have been asked to address this group about the problems of confronting the power structure in our society. As a Negro, and a minister, I have been in a position to understand some of these problems. It is this whole arena that the Negro has to consider in his struggle to get his civil rights. It is this sort of thing which the church has lately begun to recognize for what it is; a concrete reality which is, as a pat of society, something it can no longer afford to ignore. And it is, I feel sure, what homophile organizations will find to be the real key to any meaningful success in their struggle for the civil rights of the homosexual.

We of the civil rights movement have discovered that if the revolution is to be sustained there are basic things we need to know and understand. If our thrust in society is to be meaningful and effective, we must ask some definite questions about ourselves and what we are doing.

The first question to be asked is: "Who are we?" Homosexuals must face what they are and who they are; they must develop self understanding, self identification and a greater capacity for self realization. I mean by this what I call "gut" understanding, in a sense the deepest part of existence which gives the individual his orientation and his community a center of mutual concern and interest. What does it mean to be a homosexual? What are the needs and special problems that homosexuals have in common? How does the homosexual fit into his society? How can the homosexual best realize his self potential as a human being under present conditions?

Most of all, this "gut" understanding implies self acceptance, the realization that human beings can be homosexual and still have pride, a sense of worth and a belief in individual dignity, despite what society has to say.

From awareness of self and the self in others, common bonds and interest can be created.

The second question we must ask ourselves is: "What are we really about?" What are the big issues, the important considerations with which we as individuals and as an organization have to deal? Most of us are naïve about the forces that are hurled at us; and because of this, we never have the power to influence the people or the groups which basically decide what society in general is going to do. We all must talk about what we want to accomplish and what strategy we must use to be successful. Homophile organizations must find ways to deal with the people who can effect change, basically: the power groups which really make the decisions in our society. And I think we must recognize that there are many ways of dealing with the various power structures which we must influence. The civil rights movement has demonstrated that there are a variety of different approaches to solving the main problem; and that each in its own way does some good.

The third question to be asked is: "Do we really see things as they are?" All people, in the church or in the civil rights movement, homosexual or not, must begin to recognize certain realities in our society. Long ago the church decided the world was evil and dirty, so it turned its face from reality and looked to heaven. And then it awoke one day to discover that the world had gone on by; and not only that, but the world had also reached the point where, like it or not, it was painfully affecting the church. We must not let the world go by nor turn our faces from it. We must deal with it as it is, when it is savagely beautiful and joyful; and when it is painful, evil and dirty. We must understand that the world today revolves around a sense of power, the capacity to do things or get them done.

So, we must access the power structure, find out who makes the big decisions, what influences those decisions, how these decisions affect us; and how we can affect those who make them. Our society rejects many more people than it affirms. The Negro, the homosexual, the Mexican, the farm worker, the poor and deprived in general, the drunks; you name it—the list of people society doesn't like is almost endless. However, it is impossible to do anything about this reality unless we first find out what people really think about problems and why they think that way. Public opinion, the reality of what society really thinks about an issue is terribly important; and it must be understood if it is to be influenced.

The fourth question we must ask is; "What are the written laws, the rules which govern us?" Before we can successfully defend them, we must know what our legal and civil rights are. I remember some years ago when I was living in Kansas City and actively involved in civil rights work. I was driving through a residential neighborhood when a policeman pulled my car over. When he came up to the car and asked who I was, I told him Rev.

A. Cecil Williams. I was well known in those parts; and right away the officer said "Oh, Rev. Williams, your rights are . . ." And he started to reel them right off. Without asking him, I was fully informed of legal and civil rights; whereas other Negroes in the same circumstances could have been arrested, abused, roughed up and denied every legal right other Americans are supposed to have.

It is good to let the lawyers help, and good to ask their advice; but there can be no substitute for each man knowing what his rights are. Lawyers are certainly equipped to handle their part; but it is up to the individual to know what he should or should not have to do on his part. Not only must the average citizen know what his rights are, and the basic laws under which he lives; but he must be sure to demand that these rights are respected by everyone. If we don't do this, our civil rights will be taken away from us, one by one.

The fifth question we must ask ourselves is "How are we going to do what we have to do?" There are many different ways, and I want to discuss a few fundamental ones with you.

We must talk about strategy, about the best ways to get the job done. To do this, we must decide who the decision makers are, what public opinion is, what our rights are, then we must be ready to confront the right people with the actual issues in the most effective way. We must involve the decision makers in what we are doing. We must get them to recognize our voice, and certainly we must not ignore what they are doing. They get by because we let them get by.

The most practical way to confront these leaders is to force them to recognize that you exist and must be reckoned with. Therefore, you must organize yourselves, and then involve other groups in what you are doing even if their immediate concerns seem far away from yours. Whenever you get people over twenty-one together, you have power because you have votes. The more support you get from other people and groups, the more influence you will be able to exert either through votes or by other means.

Perhaps the best way to do this is to present a specific, immediate and feasible plan of action. This program should be based on self awareness, group interest and a recognition of power for what it is, and how to use it. This means the political realm of action must be your first choice; to know the realities of society and its political power groups. An action group can learn to use power without being afraid of it, and it can also learn to face naked power in others when it has to. Never believe that you can't beat city hall. You can.

Since there is no doubt that power is in the political realm, the problem is to get votes, or to influence enough of them so that the politicians learn to respect you. An action group must find out what means are available to do this; then determine what resources there are. And then decide what means will be specific, immediate, feasible and effective. Then do it.

We have had enough dialogue about these issues. The Negro has heard about his rights for over one hundred fifty years; but today, he has precious few more than his ancestors did as slaves. So he has decided to stop listening to the talk of others, and of his own; and has decided to get out and do something about it. One of the very first things was controversy.

I think that we must not be afraid of controversy or tension. We in the civil rights movement have learned how to rock the boat, how to disturb complacent middle class people, how to root out complacency. It is good to have strong disagreement because from it comes movement and reaction. Controversy is the need; it stimulates communication and the exchange of ideas. Rejection once in a while is a good thing too. It forces one to find one's self, to reexamine the issues from a personal viewpoint; and then to rejoin the community's action. Tension leads to resolution, to movement; at least, it lets people know that a living, fulfilling movement is on its way.

It is equally important to get this controversy, this tension, into print. S.I.R. and the other organizations now have publications of one sort or another. They should be used to stir up dialogue, to stimulate thinking and the exchange of ideas. As more people read these publications, and sense the involvement of the organizations in action, they too will join in.

I also think we should remind ourselves of our self interest in these issues. We should remember that in this world and working with the power structures we must make deals. You support me, and I'll support you. We must be able to keep our end of the bargain, but we must also have enough power to see that they keep theirs, too.

You know, the Anti-Poverty Program is a perfect example. Here in San Francisco we will get about two or two and one half million dollars for an anti-poverty program. But do you know that it is possible that the middle class people will reap the greater benefit—the people who really don't need the money, and for whom the program was not intended. It happens all the time. So we must be careful not to be fooled by deals of one sort or another which promise one thing, but actually do another.

The time is now. Decisions and action must be made now. Those who have the courage to be counted must be relied upon, and the others will have to be recognized for what they are—of no help. We have all heard the talk of tomorrow, and tomorrow, and tomorrow. Yet we are all required to live today. We have all heard the talk of begin, and begin, and begin; yet we find that nothing has been begun. The beginning must be now, or there may not be very much of tomorrow to worry about.

I sometimes end my talks with a statement I use when I run into people who discriminate against me:

"If you consider me irresponsible, I'll make myself responsible. But if you discriminate against me because of my color, I can only refer you to God who brought us all into being."

December 1964

SIR's Statement of Policy

Society for Individual Rights

The Society for Individual Rights was one of the earliest homosexual rights organizations to be founded in San Francisco. This text was printed on the first page of the group's newsletter, *Vector,* in December 1964.

SIR is an organization formed from within the Community working for the Community. By trying to give the individual a sense of dignity before himself and within his Society, it answers the question of how we can maintain our self-respect. SIR is dedicated to belief in the worth of the homosexual and adheres to the principle that the individual has the right to his own sexual orientation so long as the practice of the belief does not interfere with the rights of others.

We must not forget that there are certain rights connected with being a man which are, despite peculiarities of color, of creed or of sexual orientation, guaranteed to all men. These inalienable rights must be constantly defended against the erosion of public power and ruin by personal apathy. There should be an end to dismissals from our jobs; an end to police harassment, and the interference of the state with the sanctity of the individual within his home. To assure that these reprisals cease, we believe in the necessity of a political mantel [*sic*] guaranteeing to the homosexual the rights so easily granted to others.

We find ourselves scorned by the very society which may in fact be largely responsible for our creation, our rights as persons as citizens before the law imperiled, our individuality suppressed by a hostile social order, and our spirit forced to accept a guilt unwarranted by the circumstances of our existence. Believing as we do that there is no strength but through organization, SIR is determined that through its actions and through cooperation from within the Community, these conditions will be changed. In those areas where we need to change, let us change ourselves.

Other organizations have done good and necessary work, but there are still many areas which desperately call for attention. There is the need for political action, the need to provide adequate and responsible legal counsel, the need to establish cooperation with the churches, the need to educate all men in their rights as citizens, and the need to provide our people with an honorable social fabric. These are but a few of many worthwhile projects which will occupy the efforts of SIR in the months to come.

But also, we must learn from the experiences of other organizations, their successes and failures, adding to their efforts SIR's specific dedication to the democratic process. Rejecting inwardness, the strife of personality and politics, and languishing under a forever unchanging dictatorial control, we intend to give service where service is due. Through action we shall demonstrate a serious comprehensive program of financial stability and resourcefulness, a provision for active and responsible participation of individuals in our efforts, a willingness to get necessary jobs done, and in particular to provide an attractive, meaningful and healthy social fabric for the well-being of our Members.

While we are still dedicated to a spirit of free competition, eventually we hope to achieve the coordination of all organizations working on behalf of the homosexual. Recognizing that we live with an urgency of need, in a time when change is constant and often dramatic, we respond to the call to action, certain that a feeling of Community has been established. Working toward that goal, and an accord to that belief by all people, SIR is pledged to act.

July 1965

What's in It for Me?

Roland Keith

At the first open meeting of Mattachine Midwest, held at the Midland Hotel in Chicago in July 1965, Roland Keith, at that time secretary of the organization, gave this address. The "widely publicized Scott case" mentioned is *Scott v. Macy* (1965).

"*What's in it for me,* if I participate in the homophile movement?" This is a fair question and deserves an equally fair answer. Actually, there are quite a number of things in it for you.

Imagine, if you will, the day when social acceptance becomes a reality for the homosexual; when he will be able to look his fellow men in the eye with the full realization that homosexuality is considered of no more significance than lefthandedness. That's one thing in it for you.

Significant strides have been made toward legal acceptance of the homosexual in Illinois, but there is much yet to be accomplished before the homosexual completely sheds his second class citizenship. For example, his right to assemble without police interference has yet to be reaffirmed. It will come, though, and this is another of the things that are in it for you.

Most employers, and especially the federal government, consider homosexuality adequate grounds to deny an individual employment. Recently, a first break-through was made in this area by the widely publicized Scott case. But, again, there is much ground to cover before the homosexual will be judged on his ability to do a job. This day will come and it is one more of the things that is in it for you.

"But," you may say, "by the time that this discrimination ends I'll be too old to benefit from it." This may be true, but there are more subtle but equally important rewards to be gained from participating in the homophile movement.

Some of these rewards are an increase in self-respect, self-knowledge, and self-confidence. When homosexuals stand up in a positive manner for their rights, when they take their destiny into their own hands to make a world for themselves and their fellows that is free of fear, confusion, and discrimination, they are casting aside their own fears and confronting the forces of intolerance and prejudice with a healthy vigor. They cannot help but benefit from their assertion of human freedom and dignity. That's what's in it for you.

The psychological effects of being a member of a minority group subject to intensive discrimination has been explored by psychologists as distinguished as Harvard's Gordon Allport. In his book *The Nature of Prejudice* he discusses the ego defenses, hypersensitivity, and withdrawal which can develop. We've all seen these characteristics in our acquaintances. It takes a strong individual to withstand these pressures. Participation in the homophile movement can help the homosexual by making him constantly aware of his humanity and his oneness with mankind.

There is also the intellectual stimulation and development provided by working in the homophile movement. Likewise, we can't overlook the personal satisfaction involved in doing a job which we all know must be carried out, but which has never been done before.

These are just some of the things that are in it for you.

"Well then," you might ask, "how do I go about this?" Simple: affiliate with *MATTACHINE MIDWEST* and become an active member of those committees which are working in areas of special interest to you. It's as easy as that. In a few minutes you will hear about these committee activities. As you listen, think about this question, *"What's in it for me?,"* and I believe that you'll conclude that there's plenty in it for you.

July 1965

Introductory Address

Robert Sloane

This text was delivered as the introductory address to the first open meeting of Mattachine Midwest, held at the Midland Hotel in Chicago, Illinois, in July 1965. Robert Sloane was at that time the president of Mattachine Midwest. The "Scott case" mentioned is *Scott v. Macy* (1965).

A lack of rights is often taken for granted. People are used to being put upon by government authority. It sometimes takes centuries of dreamers, philosophers, and finally revolutionaries to shake people out of their lethargy, to open their eyes to the fact that they don't have to accept the oppression that has been taken for granted by the oppressed and the oppressors through the ages.

In 1776 our forefathers not only posted notice of their independence from colonial bondage, but proclaimed man's inalienable right to life, liberty and the pursuit of happiness. They pledged their lives, their fortunes and their sacred honor to support these newly formulated principles. More and more people rallied around their ideas, giving support that would have been unimaginable a generation or so before. Of course, there were those who said, "What's the use? You can't win," or that old chestnut, "you can't change human nature," as though there were no hope of civilizing people. But as you know, the rebels led by Washington did win their independence.

In the nineteenth century there were those who believed that the institution of slavery would always be with us. After all, it had existed since biblical days, and "you can't change human nature." Yet when the time was ripe, out went slavery. The abolitionists had many well-wishers who agreed that they were right, but never lifted a hand because they were defeatists, without faith.

Until a couple of generations ago the standards of our society kept women from the so-called universal suffrage. Women were kept in an inferior position in the home and on the job, and deprived of the right to vote. But in spite of public lethargy women finally won their rights. The fight still goes on for implementing these rights through equal pay, broader job and professional opportunities and wider political participation.

Each generation has the responsibility to guard those rights already achieved and to advance the cause of freedom for all people. As Lincoln said at Gettysburg, "It is for us the living rather to be dedicated here to the unfinished work which they who fought here have thus far so nobly advanced . . . that this nation, under God, shall have a new birth of freedom."

Who could have imagined, a generation ago, the 1964 Supreme Court ruling barring segregated schooling, the 1964 Civil Rights Act, the law soon to be enacted on voting rights? The NAACP took cases to the Supreme Court. The Civil Rights Movement got a quarter of a million people to march on Washington, organized the Mississippi Summer project and the marches on Selma, Montgomery and Bogalusa. Under the banner of nonviolence, tremendous progress is being made in spite of those who take the old way for granted.

In our time, homosexuals have been the victims of abuses winked at by the law authorities. They have been arrested without due process of law, victimized by odious police methods such as entrapment, manhandled by the police and deprived of legal redress when physically assaulted by gangs. They have been treated as second-class citizens by civil service. This attitude has made some of them vulnerable to blackmail.

De Tocqueville noted that Americans are great joiners, that every cause has its devotees ready to organize. This is true for the homophile. During the past fifteen years homophile organizations have sprung up all over the country. Each has developed its own program of activity, quite similar in proclaiming the right to be different and still claim the full protection of the law and protection in one's career. These groups have organized to rededicate themselves to the right of all people including homosexuals, the inalienable right to life, liberty and the pursuit of happiness. They do not ask for special privileges; they demand equal rights.

There are still pessimists who say, "You can't change human nature." Yet the State of Illinois did pass the Model Penal Code, making private relationships between consenting adults legal. The Mattachine Society of Washington, with the cooperation of the National Capital Civil Liberties Union, defeated the U.S. Civil Service Commission in appealing the Scott case. Great progress is being made in New York, Philadelphia, and other East Coast cities and in San Francisco, Los Angeles and other West Coast areas. In San Francisco, when the Society for Individual Rights holds a public meeting more than 250 people turn out.

The existing organizations have hoped for a long time that Chicago would catch up, and set up its own organization. With their encouragement this has finally been accomplished. All of us here today are participants in that historical development.

On May 11, less than three months ago, an Ad Hoc Committee of 17 persons gathered to structure a Chicago-based homophile organization. After a series of meetings we broke up into committees to further the launching of a soundly structured group. At our meeting of June 22nd, we adopted a constitution and bylaws, voted ourselves a name, Mattachine Midwest, and elected officers and a board of directors to serve in the interim period until the first elections in November 1965. We have a hard-working board of directors, each with committee responsibilities, and envisage a hard-working membership, with each individual participating in some form of committee activity.

Our work will help many people who will never support or understand our purpose for existence. Nevertheless, those of us who are here tonight have the responsibility to give of ourselves—our money, our time, our minds, our enthusiasm—to strengthen and advance Mattachine Midwest. It is our vehicle in this generation for advancing the rights of the homosexual.

As we discuss the various activities and committees, think what you can do to strengthen this effort. We have an appointment with destiny in our generation, just as the patriots of 1776 had in theirs. Our success will make available to our country all the potential that lies dormant in inhibited and suppressed individuals, perhaps more than fifteen million of them. Let us use all the instruments we have at hand to continue the good fight, to win full equality of treatment for the homosexual.

Just as the civil rights movement draws support from decent white people, so does the fight for the rights of homosexuals draw to it support from decent heterosexual people. Let us continue to broaden the base of our membership and our support. Let us invite and encourage membership and help from all, regardless of sex or sexual orientation. We may not become a mass movement, but we can hope for tremendous achievements in our time—with *your* help.

February 19-20, 1966

Homophile Organizations Adopt Statement

National Planning Conference of Homophile Organizations

The text of this statement originally appeared in the March 1966 issue of *Vector,* the publication of the Society for Individual Rights, in San Francisco. The planning conference itself took place in Kansas City, Missouri, in February 1966.

Laws against homosexual conduct between consenting adults in private should be removed from the criminal codes. Homosexual American citizens should have precise equality with all other citizens before the law and are entitled to social and economic equality of opportunity. Each homosexual should be judged as an individual on his qualifications for Federal and all other employment. The disqualification of homosexuals, as a group or class, from receipt of security clearances is unjustified and contrary to fundamental American principles.

Homosexual American citizens have the same duty and the same right to serve in the armed forces as do all other citizens; homosexuality should not be a bar to military service. Even under existing military standards, a person dismissed for homosexuality should be given a fully honorable discharge.

For too long homosexuals have been deprived of these rights on the basis of cultural prejudice, myth, folklore and superstition. Professional opinion is in complete disagreement as to the cause and nature of homosexuality. Those objective research projects undertaken thus far have indicated that findings of homosexual undesirability are based upon opinion, value judgments or emotional reaction rather than on scientific evidence or fact.

A substantial number of American people are subjected to a second class citizenship, to the Gestapo-like "purges" of governmental agencies and to local police harassment. It is time that the American public re-examine its attitudes and its laws concerning the homosexual.

Organizations signatory to this statement were Citizen's News (San Francisco); Council on Religion and the Homosexual, Inc. (San Francisco); Daughters of Bilitis, Inc. (San Francisco, New York City, Chicago); Janus Society of America (Philadelphia); Mattachine Society of Florida, Inc. (Miami); Mattachine Midwest (Chicago); Mattachine Society of Philadelphia; Mattachine Society Inc., of New York (New York); Mattachine Society, Inc. (San Francisco); Mattachine Society of Washington, DC; ONE, Inc. (Los Angeles); ONE, in Kansas City, Missouri; Tangents (Los Angeles); Tavern Guild of San Francisco, Inc.; and the Society for Individual Rights (San Francisco).

August 20, 1966

A Challenge to San Francisco

William Beardemphl

This statement originally appeared in the October 1966 issue of *The Ladder,* the nationally distributed magazine produced by the Daughters of Bilitis. Beardemphl was at this time the president of the Society for Individual Rights.

On this day, August 20, 1966, the homosexual community begins to reexamine itself. For ten days we shall seek answers to the dilemma of our socially ostracized existence.

We live in a nation that purports to be the citadel, the vanguard, of individual rights for all persons on this earth. Specifically, we dwell in a city that beacons a liberality of approach that lights the way for others in our nation to follow.

Since the beginning of time the homosexual has served his community well. Who can support the claim that homosexuals have expressed less genius or have performed less service than anyone else? Some have said that mankind owes unpayable debts to his homosexual brethren. Even while the homosexual has served his community well, his community has not served him. He has been victimized and degraded.

There is unequal enforcement of our laws. Homosexuals are selected as the objects of extra surveillance, special intimidations, entrapment and enticement procedures that are not employed against any other group. When a homosexual is placed in legal jeopardy, such guilts have been instilled in him that he is fearful of seeking redress. When those few who still have courage try to seek justice, lawyers' fees double, cases are rejected by many competent attorneys, District Attorneys' offices do not cooperate in protection of their rights. But if a just decision is reached in court, the social stigma of any arrest connected with a homosexual offense brings quick, undeserved punishments. Employment discrimination is practiced against known homosexuals: the right to hold a professional license or to obtain almost any business license is denied. The Constitutional right of assembly in this city has been historically abridged for homosexuals. Federal, State and local governments have always discriminated against us. Professional services, and in many cases public services, have been denied to known homosexuals. Even the Christian Church has been no better.

This is the record of your leadership.

You, the "respectable" members of society, have created these distortions in the lives of individuals; and then you disparage the results of what you have done. You turn with evil indifference on those you have maimed and sadistically hurt—and hurt again—and take advantage of helpless fellow human beings because they happen to be homosexuals?

What are you going to do now?

We will not accept compromise or tolerate injustice any longer. The way ahead for us has been plainly determined by the history of our country. We hear the drums of equality from the American Revolution. We hear the cannons of unity from our great Civil War. We hear the bombs of universal peace from World War I. We see the awesome mushrooming cloud of freedom, of complete individual freedom from World War II. Our banners shall read the same as for all men—Equality, Unity, Peace, Freedom.

In our day-to-day existence, we still hear the catcalls of "fruit," "fairy," "queer," "faggot." All the reactions of subjective inequality are still practiced by our neighbors and continue to dwell in man's civilized heart.

We demand our rights. First, we shall use the framework of established order, But if existing circumstances do not answer our demands, we shall create new approaches. Our approach to social action shall be to act out our rights as legally as possible, and letting society adjust to us.

If the police do not protect homosexuals as they have not protected us in the past, then I can see in the near future a separate police force paid for and operated by the homophile community. Unless restrictive laws are changed, unless the courts uphold the rights of homosexuals, we shall have no alternative but to go to the Supreme Court and overturn these laws that state all men are treated equally in our courts except for homosexuals. If politicians do not openly address themselves to homosexuals, it will be because they do not need our 90,000 votes in San Francisco. We shall put in office public servants who will talk to homosexuals.

We ask no special favor. We want only ordinary rights like every other citizen of these United States—jobs, homes, friends, social lives, safety and security.

Here is our challenge to San Francisco: FACE REALITY—FACE HOMOSEXUALITY.

November 1966

What Concrete Steps Can Be Taken to Further the Homophile Movement?

Shirley Willer

At the time of this address, Willer was the president of the Daughters of Bilitis. The "recent DOB Convention" refers to the Fourth National Conference of the Daughters of Bilitis held in San Francisco on August 20, 1966.

To an extent it is difficult for me to discuss what the homophile movement should be doing. I have some very clear ideas about what the Lesbian should be doing but the problems of the male homosexual and the female homosexual differ considerably.

Most perceptive authorities have stated that the basic problems in relations between the sexes arise from the completely artificial dichotomies of role and appearance ascribed to each sex by society. From the median beds where we lie, few persons, homosexual or heterosexual, arise whole and healthy individuals.

The social conformist is wracked by anxieties in his ambivalent clinging to the social artifacts which require his denunciation of his nature. The social non-conformist is driven to propound his personal revelation as being above reproach and beyond question. In such a society Lesbian interest is more closely linked with the women's civil rights movement than the homosexual civil liberties movement.

The particular problems of the male homosexual include police harassment, unequal law enforcement, legal proscription of sexual practices and for a relatively few the problem of disproportionate penalties for acts of questionable taste such as evolve from solicitations, wash-room sex acts and transexual attire.

In contrast, few women are subject to police harassment and the instances of arrest of lesbians for solicitation, wash-room sex or transexual attire are so infrequent as to constitute little threat to the Lesbian community beyond the circle of the immediately involved. The rare occurrences serve to remind the Lesbian that such things are possible, but also that they rarely happen.

The problems of importance to the Lesbian are job security, career advancement and family relationships.

The important difference between the male and female homosexual is that the Lesbian is discriminated against not only because she is a Lesbian, but because she is a woman. Although the Lesbian occupies a "privileged" place among homosexuals, she occupies an under-privileged place in the world.

It is difficult for a woman to be accepted as a leader in any community or civic organization and the woman who does succeed in breaking down the barriers in recognition is usually greeted with a mixture of astonishment and sympathetic amusement. There are few women who desire to emulate Carrie Nation, chained to a fire hydrant and swinging a battle-axe—but the few women who achieve community, professional or civic leadership are compared to that image, sometimes rightfully so, since despite legal recognition of feminine equality, the road to public recognition for each woman leads across the battlefield.

Lesbians have agreed (with reservations) to join in common cause with the male homosexual—her role in society has been of mediator between the male homosexual and society. The recent DOB Convention was such a gesture. The reason we were able to get the public officials there was because we are women, because we offered no threat. However, they did not bargain for what they got. They did not expect to be challenged on the issues of male homosexuality. In these ways we show our willingness to assist the male homosexual in seeking to alleviate the problems our society has inflicted on him.

There has been little evidence, however, that the male homosexual has any intention of making common cause with us. We suspect that should the male homosexual achieve his particular objectives in regard to his homosexuality he might possibly become a more adamant foe of women's rights than the heterosexual male has ever been. (I would guess that a preponderance of male homosexuals would believe their ultimate goal achieved if the laws relating to sodomy were removed and a male homosexual were appointed chief of police.)

This background may help you understand why, although the Lesbian joins the male homosexual in areas of immediate and common concern, she is at the same time, preparing for a longer struggle, waged on a broader base with the widest possible participation of the rank and file Lesbian. It shows why, to the Lesbian leader, diffusion and consensus are as important as leadership and direction. Demonstrations which define the homosexual as a unique minority defeat the very cause for which the homosexual strives—

TO BE CONSIDERED AN INTEGRAL PART OF SOCIETY. The homosexual must show that he is, in fact, NOT a unique "social problem." That concept is too widely held to require endorsement from homophile organizations. Demonstrations that emphasize the uniqueness of the homosexual may provide an outlet for some homosexuals' hostilities, but having acted out his revolt, he loses a part of the drive that might have been available for more constructive approaches to problem solving.

The basic objectives of the homophile organizations must continue to be open to avenues of in-depth communication. Its energies must not be channelized—its attempts must be repetitive—its approaches must be as diverse as imagination will allow. To put this more specifically, THE MORE WAYS WE CAN GET MORE PEOPLE INVOLVED IN THE GREATEST VARIETY OF APPROACHES TO THE WIDEST POSSIBLE CONFIGURATION OF THE PROBLEMS RELATED TO HOMOSEXUALITY, THE MORE LIKELY WE ARE TO ACHIEVE SOME MEASURE OF SUCCESS.

I can name a few dozen of the concrete steps your organizations should be taking. I do not doubt that you have tried them. Then, I say continue these and add more and more and more.

The argument that concentration is more productive than diversity is false when applied to homophile organizations. You cannot "retool" the talents of your membership to meet a current market. The only thing you may do is warehouse talent which could be of use to the common cause. Because this is a fact, one also hears the notion that instead of re-tooling the members, we should retool the organizations and perhaps, eventually, each person will find the organization of his level and interest.

Accordingly, proceeding from our statement [of] wish to offer a few constructive steps—steps we do not like to call concrete, but in full knowledge of the shifts of time and structure, we believe to be firm and treadworthy.

- To affirm as a goal of such a conference: to be as concerned about women's civil rights as male homosexuals' civil liberties.
- To suggest that homosexual men attempt to appreciate the value of women as PEOPLE in the movement, respect abilities as individuals, not seek them out as simple "show-pieces."
- That those philosophical factors of homosexuality which engage both sexes be basic to our concepts of reform.
- That the number of one sex not be a determinate factor in decisions of policy, but that a consideration of all arguments be heard and the CONSENSUS be the goal of the conference. Insofar as we do find trust and value in the male-oriented homophile organizations, we will find common ground upon which to work.

April 21-23, 1967

Homophile Movement Policy Statement

Western Regional Planning
Conference of Homophile Organizations

This statement was written and adopted by the conference meeting in Los Angeles, California, in the spring of 1967.

Since the homosexual Community is composed of all types of persons, we feel that the movement ought not be constricted by any limiting concept of public image. The homosexual has no reputation to protect.

It is true that the image that an organization projects inside the homosexual community may affect the support it gets from that community. But we would support the right of individuals to do what they want and should educate the homosexual to accept himself as a homosexual and to accept all other persons.

We assert the right of individuals to be what they are and do what they wish so long as it does not infringe on the rights of others.

One purpose of homophile groups is to explain the various alternatives open to the individual and the possible consequences of such alternatives, and to help individuals achieve full personhood.

We do not feel that drag, sado-masochism, and other aspects of sexual behavior can be summarily dismissed as necessarily invalid expressions of human love. As human beings and as homosexuals, we have a special interest in understanding all sexuality.

May 1967

Why I Joined the Homophile Movement

Jack Nichols

This is the text of the address given by activist Jack Nichols in the spring of 1967 at a joint appearance with Barbara Gittings at Bucknell University in Pennsylvania, under the invitation of a student group. The event is mentioned on page 183 of Kay Tobin (now Lahusen) and Randy Wicker's *Gay Crusaders* (1972). The noting of marchers at Independence Hall on July 4 refers to the Annual Reminder, held every year between 1965 and 1969 by homophile organizations to remind the American people that homosexuals did not enjoy the full benefits of liberty and were still being treated as second-class citizens.

Why did I join the movement to equalize the status of the homosexual? Because I found out that there were rewards. When I stand up in a positive fashion for my own rights I feel self-respect, self-knowledge, and self-confidence. I see that it's helpful when homosexuals stand up for their own rights and take their destiny into their own hands, trying to make a world for themselves that's free of fear, confusion and discrimination.

There is something to be said for casting aside one's fears and confronting the forces of darkness and despair with a healthy vigor. People who work in our movement can't help but benefit from putting their focus on human freedom and dignity.

The effects of discrimination which have reigned over homosexual people are subtly pernicious. In centuries past homosexuals were burned at the stake. The dry sticks thrown at their feet were called "faggots." That's the origin of that pejorative word.

It may be argued that homosexuals can avoid such pitfalls without belonging to the Homophile Movement. True. But it is also true that homosexuals must be made of the strongest stuff if they are not to fall prey to insidious confusions that trickle into their minds from an ocean of misunderstandings.

The Homophile Movement to which I belong gives to the homosexual a constant awareness of his humanity, of his oneness with the rest of mankind.

It makes him realize that homosexuality should mean no more than left-handedness and that he is a full member of the human race.

These are just a few of the rewards the Homophile Movement grants to those in its ranks. There is also the satisfaction of doing a job never done before. And there is the joy of collaborating with my fellows on projects bringing comfort and hope, aid and solace to millions who have never heard of this movement or who are unable to align themselves although they may hope every day for its success.

Without this movement, what do we find? Look first at the masses of young homosexuals; often bewildered, uninformed, searching for guidance, wondering about their inner feelings, and fighting what Edward Carpenter called "a solitary and really serious inner struggle." A veil of complete silence has been drawn over the subject of homosexuality and this often leads to the most painful misunderstandings.

Look at the agonized face of a parent as he or she learns for the first time the "dreadful" secret of an offspring. Here is an area in which many homosexuals are painfully sensitive. To see the faces of those we love contorted in disbelief, dismay, revulsion, or rejection and anger, is an experience all too common among those who have, in one way or another, revealed life's facts to parents.

The Homophile Movement works toward breaking down not only the prejudices effecting young homosexuals and their parents, but also those which affect homosexuals throughout their lives. When the homosexual community itself stops believing the nonsense that society has been proclaiming, the Movement will have begun to accomplish its goals.

Dr. Wardell B. Pomeroy, co-author of the Kinsey Report, states that when homosexuals "are called nuts and neurotics and goofers by therapists, immoral by the clergy, criminals by lawyers and judges, and perverts and child molesters by the public" they need a very "special kind of faith in themselves" and "faith in their fellow man." The Homophile Movement exists to give that faith to its members and to those who share, without being members, its aspirations for a brighter future.

The Homophile Movement has distinct roots in the American dream. It is, in great measure, a social protest movement, but these words alone do not describe it adequately. It is another chapter in the Book of Freedom, asking as it does for the rights of the individual, for the sanctity of privacy in an area—sexual behavior—which is certainly the most personal of concerns.

In a sense, the Homophile Movement is thus protecting not only homosexuals but all people resenting the intrusion of government, employers, and others who pry into their private lives seeking excuses for condemnation and discrimination.

There was a time not long ago when private employers felt free to discriminate against citizens, to hire and fire them on the basis of their political beliefs, religion, or race. Today such employers are thought to be misguided, if not immoral, but we live in a nation where an individual's private sexual behavior behind the closed doors of his own home, is still considered relevant to employment.

In the Great Society this nation is building, the Homophile Movement is lending new meaning to the primacy of the individual, protesting the ever-watchful eye of Big Brother while it demands freedom of assembly, freedom of the press, and of the right of a person to be the sovereign of his thoughts and feelings.

Homosexuals are mistreated by officialdom not only because of what they have done—their actions—but for their inclinations. No policy could be further from the principles on which this country is founded. To dismiss a man, to hound him through the remainder of his life for his thoughts and feelings are the tactics of totalitarianism. A person joining the Homophile Movement is waging war on the growing tendency of officialdom to judge men and women by their private sexual inclinations. This person will help protect fundamental freedoms.

Adlai Stevenson used to say that "the American Revolution is never complete. America is a continuing revolution." The many men and women who annually march in front of Independence Hall on July 4 to remind America of the plight of the homosexual contribute peacefully and lawfully to the meaning of the Revolution from which American principles developed.

Two heterosexuals stood watching the protest. "It's terrible, just terrible," said one to the other. His friend turned to him and said, "At last I am convinced that freedom in this country is meaningful. This demonstration makes me realize that America is really going somewhere."

The Homophile Movement belongs to the revolution with which Thomas Jefferson allied himself when he swore "eternal hostility against every form of tyranny over the mind of man." There is no tyranny more morbid than that dictating to love and affection and no slave more pitiful than he who succumbs to such dictation.

Sex is a fundamental human need. Those who do not interfere with the rights of others and who pursue this need privately should be protected from interference.

Those people concerned with the meaning of America, longing to build a truly great society, will protest official sexual inspections and official approval of sexual desires and inclinations. They will realize that support of the Homophile Movement is an important way of curbing and stopping such tyranny.

August 1967

Washington Statement

North American Homophile Conference

The North American Homophile Conference convened at George Washington University in the District of Columbia from August 17 to 19, 1967. Among the items discussed was this statement of purpose for the North American Conference of Homophile Organizations (NACHO), which was agreed upon as one of the more notable results of the meeting. The text was originally printed in the September 1967 issue of *Vector.*

The purpose of the conference is for organizations and selected individuals dedicated primarily to the improvement of the status of the homosexual, to formulate, plan, discuss, coordinate, and implement strategy, tactics, ideologies, philosophies, and methodologies for the improvement of the status of the homosexual as a homosexual.

The conference will provide for the expression of contributions that may be made by individuals and organizations whose activities are, though not primarily involved with the problems of the homosexual, relevant to the crucial problems that face the homosexual community.

Understanding that only a free exchange of worthwhile ideas can eliminate inter-group strife, the conference will allow for open communication in the homosexual community. The conference will stimulate and encourage the formation of new homophile organizations with the ultimate goal of establishing a legitimate homophile movement on a national scale with an organizational code of ethics. Inter-group projects and co-operation will be encouraged on all possible levels.

Believing that the problems facing the homosexual are only one facet of North America's restrictive sexual ethics, this conference will recognize the study of sexuality in general with particular emphasis on homosexuality.

This conference will consistently work to expose the "sexual sickness" that pervades our society and offer meaningful answers to the wide range of problems forced on homosexuals. To be effective, this conference must articulate and respond to the needs of America's homosexual community. The conference, while presently consultative in nature and function, shall consider itself to be a duly constituted continuing body, having the power, with the concurrence of the delegates, to make rules and establish criteria necessary for the orderly transaction of business and the furtherance of its goals.

SECTION IV: THE 1970s

February 14-15, 1970

Western Homophile Conference Keynote Address

Harry Hay

This is the text of the speech given by Harry Hay, founder of the Mattachine Society, to the Western Homophile Conference, which met at the First Unitarian Church of Los Angeles in February 1970. It contains the introduction by historian and activist journalist Jim Kepner. DAR refers to the Daughters of the American Revolution.

INTRODUCTION BY JIM KEPNER

My chief function in speaking here is to make an introduction. So I hope my friend, whom I am about to introduce, won't mind if I am a bit perverse about it. My method is perverse, in a way. It is a little bit like introducing Troy Perry by first saying a few kind words for Mohammedanism.

I want to introduce one of those persons who has had a really revolutionary effect on the homophile community in the United States, and a person who isn't much a believer in reformism, so I want to say a few kind words for reformism first.

Without changing the system, without overthrowing the Establishment, whatever that is, we have made a hell of a lot of progress in the last twenty years. I don't think that those of you who are under thirty can begin to appreciate what it was like for homosexuals two decades ago, and some of you older ones have forgotten.

We had no organizations of our own. No publications of our own. Bars—we had plenty of them, and some just as wild as any are today, but the arrest rate in some of the liveliest ones was great enough that if the same thing were to happen today, we'd be storming City Hall in half an hour. We couldn't meet in Churches—the very idea was unthinkable. For that matter, we couldn't meet much of anyplace else either. I spoke in this Church, the most progressive Church in Los Angeles, just ten years ago, and the Church was pretty upset about it afterward. I could go on a long time, but I just wanted a quick reminder, before we start talking about throwing out the system, of how much progress we have made.

It took revolutionaries to get that progress rolling. Until the homosexual cause began to be a bit respectable, it was only the revolutionaries that had time for it. Everybody else was afraid of their shadow.

I was thinking about starting a magazine, or a defense organization, in 1942. But I didn't do it. I drew up some plans, talked to a few friends, but nothing came of it. Nothing at all.

One person was more persistent. In 1948, the dream became a bit more than a dream, and by 1950, the spirit became flesh and moved among us. The spirit, the hope, the dream that homosexuals had suppressed for centuries burst forth here in Los Angeles, and travelled to San Francisco and to San Diego within a few months. The first homosexual organization, the first mass homosexual organization was born twenty years ago—the first Gay Liberation Organization.

I would like to introduce you to my very dear friend, and mentor and antagonist, the man who first brought us out of Egypt, if not quite over the Jordan, the father of the Homophile Movement, Henry Hay.

KEYNOTE BY HAY

With all the members standing in a circle made suddenly transcendant through the fellowship-power of its crossed-hands couplings, the Moderator requests that each repeat after him the following:

> "Let us hereby resolve that no young person among us need ever take his first step out in the dark alone and afraid again"

Does that sound like some fragment of a Gay Liberation ritual? Well, it is! It is the concluding sentence of the New Member Welcoming Ritual of the *first* Gay Liberation Movement in the United States . . . the original Mattachine Society, 1950 to April 1953.

That first Movement called Homosexuals to a brotherhood of love and trust; it called Homosexuals to rediscover their collective—as well as personal—self-respect and integrity. It raised into consciousness, for the first time, the concept of the Homosexual Minority complete with its own subculture, with its own Life-styles. It struggled to perceive—however dimly, and with little language to help it—that, in some measure, the Homosexual Minority actually looked out upon the world through a somewhat different window than did their Heterosexual brothers and sisters. The Homosexual world-view surely deviated in dimensional values from that of its parent society . . . a world view neither better nor inferior—but *athwart.*

Rejecting the ultimately unexaminable assumptions of Heterosexual Psychiatry, mired as they were—and still are—in the obsolescent modes of Aristotelian thinking, the first Movement called to its own fellowship to search themselves and their several cultures to find out at last—"what WE are"—"WHO we are." It called to its membership to assemble these findings and then introduce to the Parent Society that widening dimension of spiritual consciousness our contributions would bring. And finally, upon the gift of such contributions, it postulated the integration of our Minority into the Parent Society AS A GROUP . . . *not* a "passing" assimilation by individual but integration by the *total* group . . . for this was 1950-53 and Montgomery and Birmingham and Selma still lay in the unpredictable future.

In the scant generation between that largely non-verbal THEN—and now, a host of new scientific modes of discourse have flooded us with resources, with language, and revelations, to firm up our early hesitant footings . . . Ethology, Etho-Ecology, Bio-Genetics, Cultural-Genetics, to name a few. Penetrating voices, speaking in these dimensions that presage new horizons of higher consciousness of the Spirit of Man, have caught the ear of the new generations who would be free . . . Konrad Lorenz, R.D. Laing, Herbert Marcuse. And within their contexts, WE ARE *THERE*—if we will but seek at last to define and disclose ourselves.

In the long years between the miscalculations of, and the headlong flight of brothers from, that first dream of Liberation—and its rebirth in Spring of 1969, the many elements of the earlier society . . . continually grouping and regrouping . . . devotedly attempted to retain such basic principles of the Mattachine Idea as were salvageable when the root think (the radicalism motivating and inspiring the original vision) had been precipitated out. Adjusting their sights to the more tried-and-true forms of the middle way the new groups sought respectability rather than self-respect, parliamentary individualism rather than the collective trust of brotherhood, law reform and quiet assimilation rather than a community of rich diversity within the Family of Man. One might say that they sought to be exactly the same as the D.A.R.—except in bed.

This is not to say that the long and futile struggle of the Homosexual Minority Movement to wear shoes that could never fit, did not have its gallant and contributive aspects. For it did—and a number of the consequences are far-reaching. Occasionally these managed momentarily to deodorize spots in our putrefying Society within which the Organizations wheel and deal. Also, in the larger healthier growing edges of social consciousness Homophile organizations have postulated several right questions . . . albeit mostly for the wrong reasons.

Yet—for all that—until now, the head count of the memberships throughout the United States was never able to equal the thousand who rallied, in California alone, to the original Mattachine Idea between 1950 and 1953. Why do the shoes of middle-class respectability and conformity never seem to fit? Why do our essays at right questions time and again bear witness that we postulated wrong reasons? Why is it that Homosexuals presumably high-principled and disciplined enough to join the and serve the Minority's Democratically-run Service Organizations comprise so small a percentage of the Minority? Why is it that non-organized Homosexuals—in their thousands over the years—opine smugly that Homosexuals kid themselves when they think they can effectively organize at all . . . because they really have nothing in common but their sex drives? Why? Why? WHY?

Because . . . when the Queens of closet rank chose to seek respectability by turning their backs resolutely on their brothers and sisters of the Street, they shut out from their purpose the first and primary task laid upon the Minority by the Original Mattachine Vision—the task of discovering "What ARE we?" "WHO are we?"

We Homosexuals know much about ourselves we've never talked about—even TO ourselves. History knows much about us that it doesn't know it knows . . . but WE could recognize it if we would look. Myth and Legend, Tradition and Folk-ways know much about us that has been deliberately obscured by endless politically minded Conspiracies of Silence . . . WHICH WE CAN EXPLODE IF WE WILL. As the Free Generation, and the Third World, have revealed beyond any possibility of longer denying it, our vain-hallowed culture is slowly sinking into a veritable kitchen-midden of obscenely generated *unexamined assumptions,* learned by rote, inherited without question, and having not one shred of a basis for possible justification in the modern world. That the three largest oppressed Minorities in the United States today are victims of politically-motivated unexamined false assumptions, sanctimoniously parading as religious *Revelations* of our Hallowed Western Civilization, should come as no surprise.

From the marriage of Hellenistic philosophy and Judaeo-Roman [*sic*] politics, projected to God-head and named Christianity, we proudly inherit through *REVELATION* the unassailable proof that *Women are inferior.* From the Divine Revelations of Renaissance Humanism, and the Reformational Elect, we inherit the unassailable proof that both *Women and non-Whites are inferior.* From the White Anglo-Saxon Protestant "Best of all possible Worlds" we inherit the unassailable proofs that *both non-Whites and Queers are inferior.*

Second-class citizens ALL . . . it should not be surprising that as oppressed and harried Minorities we three learned lessons and share certain levels of consciousness in common. As with the largest oppressed minority—Women—the Homosexual Minority knows the shape and substance of Male Chauvinism—we too have lived under its lash all our lives. As with the second largest oppressed Minority—the non-Whites, the Homosexual Minority knows the bitter harvest of being the Village Nigger!

Women know that no man has ever been able to describe or project what it means to be, and to feel like, a self-appreciating woman. Yet she does not need to be explained or defended. She is existential. She IS! Today Blacks are making it unmistakably clear that no *Whiteman* has ever been able to describe or project what it means, and feels like, to be a self-appreciating Black. Nor does he need to be explained or defended. He is existential. He IS! We Homosexuals know that *no Heterosexual man* has ever been able to describe, or to project, what it means to be, and feel like a self-appreciating Homosexual. To update Descartes, COGITO *ET SENTIO* ERGO SUM! And for each of our three minorities—*to know this is to make us free within ourselves*—requires us (whether we like it or not) to move to social consciousness, and foretells our several potentials as allies in the struggle for the new world a-coming.

What is it that we know of ourselves that no Heterosexual as yet has begun to perceive? It is that we Homosexuals have a psychic architecture in common, we have a Dream in common, man to man, woman to woman. For all of us, *and for each of us,* in the dream of Love's ecstacy [*sic*] . . . The God descends—the Goddess descends; and for each us the transcendance of that apotheosis is mirrored *in the answering glances of the lover's eyes.* FOR WE SHARE THE SAME VISION . . . Like to Like. Heterosexuals do not partake of such a communion of the spirit. Theirs is . . . other. And—in this mating of like to like—what is it we seek? Not the power and vanities of dynasty, not wealth or property, not social contract or security, not status, nor preferment, as does the Parent Society. We seek union, EACH WITH HIS SIMILAR—heart to mirroring heart—free spirit to free spirit!

We are a Minority of a common Spirituality, we are a Free People . . . and we have always been so—throughout the millennia, each in his generation! No allegiance, no sanctions, no taboos or prohibitions, no laws have ever been encompassing enough or powerful enough to stand between us and the pursuit of our Dream. It was no accident, no poetic stroke of whimsy, that translated our persons—in the King James Testament—as "Fools," nor translated our vision quests as "folly." Tradition knew us well—"Fools rush in where angels fear to tread!" Throughout our millennia we were, and are now, in the faithful service to the Great Mother-Earth-Nature, and in loyal service to her children—the people who preserved the Great Mother's ecological harmonies, both psychically and materially, in the ritual of their everyday lives. To those of her communities who granted us respect and acknowledged our integrity, we gave loyalty beyond ordinary measure of endurance, Les Societes Mattachines of both Feudal and Monarchical France give ample testimony to that BUT—to tyrants, and to alien usurping Gods, the clear unflagging flame of our Dream was—and remains still—heresy—treason—witchcraft—the unforgivable sin. Towards the expropriators of the Spirit of Man we Homosexuals are forever alien: in their eyes we are forever Anathema!

We Homosexuals are a Minority who share each other's Dream whether we speak the same language or not, who share a common psychic vision whether we share the same cultural make-up or not, all the days of our years. Though we are born with all the aggressive fighting instincts of our common humanity, the psychic architecture—characteristic to our Minority natures—begins to reshape and redirect these vital energies with almost the first stirrings in us of spiritual consciousness. The aggressive competitiveness, taken for granted as an eternal verity by our Heterosexual Parent Society, in us *Redirects,* under the guidance of the Blueprint of our Minority nature. In us, this genetic redirection transforms our perceptions of unconsciously inherited animal Maleness or Femaleness into appreciations of—nay even a life-long passion to call forth, to call into being, the grace and tenderness behind that territorial ruthlessness, in our fellow siblings of the Great Mother. For grace and tenderness, humility and compassion are revealed to *us* as being implicit in the *aspect* . . . the spirituality . . . of the Masculine Ideal, the Feminine Ideal. He who answers, she who answers, our call into being is our LIKE, our SIMILAR . . . *the one who finds in our aspect the ideal we find in his*—that ideal which we can understand in him, in her, and cherish in ourselves, because we share its outlook in common. This shared commonality of outlook is a world-view totally unfamiliar to the accrued experience of our Parent Society. It is a view of the life experience *through a different window.*

The Free Generation, the young Millions, now striving to perceive the dimensions of the Family of man, also seek to achieve that redirection of the fists of territorial aggression into the compassionate hand-clasp of the Community of Spirit. That capacity for redirection has characterized our Minority from the beginning. We were its proving-grounds in the process of natural selection. We carried—we carry, through the millennia of lives—experiences—the promise that one day all mankind might be able to learn to make that redirection manifest.

For three hundred years, our useful contributive past in Western Culture has been pulverized and effaced by deliberate politically motivated Conspiracies of Silence. In this hell of Anomie, we—of the Homosexual Minority—have been reduced to semi-conscious rudder-less wanderers, driven like sheep to conform to social patterns which atrophied our perceptions and shredded our souls, beset on every side by the bacilli of—to us—alien value-judgments which riddled the very sinews of our Dream. But now, even in this late hour, there is a light at the end of our long tunnel. There are voices on the wind giving dimensions to the freeing of the Spirit of Man. The time is *now* for our Minority to begin at last to comprehend what we have known for so long. The time is NOW for us to speak of, and to share, that which we have lived and preserved for so long. The reappearance of the "Gay Liberation Ideal" calls to each of us to stoke anew the passionate fires of our particular vision of the Community of Spirit. The breath-taking sweep of "Gay Liberation" challenges us to break loose from the lockstep expectations of Heterosexual life patterns so obliterating of our natures. Even the Free Generation, seeking a widened angle of worldview, challenges us to throw off the Dream-destroying shackles of alien thought that we may exhibit, at long last, the rich diversities of our deviant perceptions.

To liberate our Minority life-styles, we first must explode once and for all the obscene unexamined assumptions by which *we bind ourselves* into the obsolescent social conformities . . . as for instance our concern for the "Image" assumption. I conform to no Image: I define myself. WE DEFINE OURSELVES! To a people who would be free—images are irrelevancies. Again—we assume that to govern ourselves we must enact forcible restraints upon each other, and that the cumulative detriment will be negligible so long as these restraints are patently disguised as "Democratic" procedures. In this field the great unexamined assumption is the *Robert's Rules of Order* achieve a maximum of free expression within a minimum of collective restraints. To the competitive, to the territorialists, to the ego-ridden, to the status-seekers, of our decaying Society, the parliamentary coercions of "majority" votings . . . of special interest lobbyings . . . of cloak-room obligations cunningly connived . . . of filibusterings and steamrollerings . . . do appear to provide a set of minimal repressions whereby the random aggressions of delegates may be controlled. The sad truth is that, because of the failure of the Spirit of Man to surface into collective consciousness in our Western Society, these procedures serve only to assure the continued *domination of the pecking order.*

All of this is NOT of us! these are the shoes which never have fitted us; these are the shackles of alien thought that—brainwashing us to accept a worldview through the WRONG window—hold us to our bondage. Our Homosexual Liberation Movement *must* consist of far-ranging Communities of Free Spirits. What have Free Peoples to do with politely-masked repressions of one another? With coercions, or with claims-laying upon one another? What have Free Peoples to do with the voting principles that divide people from one another, or with the pretentious mounting of resolutions? Each of these restrictions seeks to shame and cajole the many to conform to the ego-mania or the wishful thinking of the few. Have we permitted our perceptions to become so atrophied that we can assume fellow Homosexuals, or ourselves for that matter, vulnerable to being shamed and cajoled by brainwashed sell-outs in our midst? Being shamed and cajoled by pressures inimical to our natures has been the ever-present bane of our Homosexual life-experience; we are past masters in the arts of dissembling, and/or vanishing under an invisible cloak, whenever such pressures threaten.

The Community of Free Spirits is not just a fantasy in the minds of woolgatherers such as I. It has a history of long-lasting and exceedingly viable Societies outside of Western Europe (and even smaller contained communities within Western Europe) to recommend it. Anthropologists who, in recent years, have learned to perceive societal systems as things-in-themselves wholly within the context of their own self-developed referants, confess that individual life-styles within such systems are more free than life-styles conceived in Western Civilization. Our Homosexual Liberation Ideal *mandates* such a community of Free Spirits. Not for us the constrictions of political parties, of leaders who presume to speak for us, of experts who conspire to think for us, of alliances that obligate us to act in the name of others or that permit others to expropriate the use of ours. We come together in a voluntary sharing of a spiritual outlook. We touch hearts. Together we grow in consciousness to generate issues, AND ACTIONS UPON THESE ISSUES, which make manifest the fleshing out of our shared world-vision. We consense, we affirm and re-affirm the Free Community of Spirit, we acknowledge a spokesman to voice our thinking when such voicings seem called for. Sometimes we may do a thing together and so we will act in the name of the Community. Other times we are, each or several, off on our own thing and here we act in the name of the self-liberated (or in the name of the group, depending entirely on the specific Group's feelings in the matter). BUT—within this Community—let the Spirit be betrayed, let coercion or opportunism attempt to bind any of us against our will, and PRESTO, like the Faeries of Folk-lore, suddenly we are no longer there. Shame me, call me names, resolve me to a position I do not share, couple me to an opinion I do not hold, vote my presence to an action against my grain . . . and I'm *long gone.* "Once bitten, twice shy!"

Our Faerie characteristic is our Homosexual Minority's central weakness . . . and, paradoxically, also the keystone of our enduring strength. For whether we are self-liberated, or still self-imprisoned within the territorial conformities of our oppressors, we Homosexuals are moved to answer ONLY when the call is to the special characteristics of our psychic natures. We Homosexuals are moved to act ONLY when the call—as heard in our hearts—is a Spirit call to freedom.

January 27, 1971

An Open Letter to Gay Activists Alliance

Arthur Bell

The book referred to by New York journalist Arthur Bell at the end of this open letter is *Dancing the Gay Lib Blues,* published by Simon & Schuster later in 1971.

Political reform must run concurrent with social change. Changing the laws means nothing if we can't change heads, too.

These past few weeks GAA has undergone tremendous eternal [*sic*] pressures resulting, once again, in its near collapse. One of the most important issues at stake, it seems, is the issue of control of GAA by the president and his friends. It is a problem of "letting go."

GAA was founded by a few people who had no idea of its future importance. They built a structure for a small organization, strong enough to last a few months. As GAA grew, the architects insisted that we follow that shallow structure. They had set up GAA as a political activist organization. Issues, functions, events, were meant to relate directly to the political core.

From the start, this posed a problem for a homosexual liberation group. Many liberationists are not into hard core politics. Many Blacks, transvestites, transexuals, street people, women, plain people and fancy people found they wanted to relate, yet the gifts they had to give were not accepted. Understandably, they deserted us. This fact had to be obvious to the people at the top of the family totem pole. But they set up GAA as a political reformist organization "according to the constitution." Period.

When the first big threat of change came during the summer months, three power heads flashed a warning. Their architecture was being tampered with and they would systematically destroy anyone in order to keep it going. They threatened Phil Raia's pleasure committee and loudly accused Phil of subverting the organization (a finger-pointing loud dogmatic attention getting scene in the courtyard outside the church by our most brilliant strategist to Phil Raia—"You're destroying GAA!"—say it often and loud in public and people will believe it, is the tactic. Phil stayed around for a few more meetings, but finally left GAA defeated and disgusted. He had both a political and social head; his social committee became too popular, thereby a political "threat" to the power people.

Two of the power heads also got involved in a political power brouhaha. In November, the Fair Employment Committee, a political reformist committee working splendidly within its own context, yet relating to the organization, came a cropper with these people who take this organization to be their own. The Committee struck back, however, and the issue of committee control and "just like that" arbitrary decisions by the power people came out on the floor. It was a nasty business.

Most everybody knows about the elections. Politicians were playing political chess with people as pawns. Some of the chess pieces this time refused to be moved around. I was one of them.

When our president came back after the New Year with offhand nepotistic committee appointments, some of the membership loudly protested. To coin a phrase, we wanted our rights, and we weren't getting them. We were accused of disrupting and plotting to break up the organization. We were also chastised for allowing our basic emotions to overrule parliamentary procedure.

There are a handful of people at GAA who behave like archetypical homosexual mothers. They have given birth to a baby whom they won't let go of. They will do anything in their power to protect that baby. Anything includes cheating, slandering, smearing, maneuvering, and screeching "liar" and "destroyer" to those people who ask questions, sometimes too loudly, sometimes too vigorously—questions that may shake that baby into mature development.

I am one of those question troublemakers. As such, I ask that the structure builders loosen up and let their baby go. I ask that they do it honestly. I ask that they stop the maniacal ego trips and the cover ups and the backroom dealings that we accuse politicians of. I ask that they treat the question askers, the disturbers of the peace as people, not as political threats, because they are people, people whose lives are being played with, and who have a right to question anything or anyone—publickly [*sic*] or privately. And I ask that every member open his eyes to the truth and demand that the overprotective mother honestly allow her baby to grow. Otherwise, the baby is a corpse.

Ask questions. Demand to participate in events that are now covered only by the chosen few. Respect and trust and love are hollow words until they are honestly earned. Truth, no matter how painful, is a starter. Shake GAA good and hard when it needs shaking. Don't try to be nice, and don't be afraid of destroying GAA. If it's good, it can only grow.

The patriarchal group, since the latest breakup threat (a threat, incidentally, of finances as well as ideology) has claimed that they see the light, that political reform must indeed run concurrent with social change. They claim that they are ready to institute new social groups. I hope that they are sincere, that this is more than just another political concession to save the organization, that they will not try to control whatever social or sociological committees may come from this change. If they do, they will kiss their baby goodbye.

I'm leaving GAA to concentrate on my book. After that, I'll be back as an active member of the gay community. I hope that GAA will become a more pertinent part of that community. It's time the baby grew up.

1971

Preamble to the Constitution and Bylaws of the Gay Activists Alliance, Inc.

Gay Activists Alliance

WE AS LIBERATED HOMOSEXUAL ACTIVISTS demand the freedom for expression of our dignity and value as human beings through confrontation with and disarmament of all mechanisms which unjustly inhibit us: economic, social and political. Before the public conscience, we demand an immediate end to all oppression of homosexuals and the immediate unconditional recognition of these basic rights:

THE RIGHT TO OUR OWN FEELINGS. This is the right to feel attracted to the beauty of members of our own sex and to embrace those feelings as truly our own, free from any question or challenge whatsoever by any other person, institution, or "moral authority."

THE RIGHT TO LOVE. This is the right to express our feelings in action, the right to make love with anyone, anyway, anytime, provided only that such action be freely chosen by the individuals concerned.

THE RIGHT TO OUR OWN BODIES. This is the right to treat and express our bodies as we will, to nurture, display and embellish them solely in the manner we ourselves determine, independent of any external control whatsoever.

THE RIGHT TO BE PERSONS. This is the right freely to express our own individuality under the governance of laws justly made and executed, and to be the bearers of social and political rights which are guaranteed by the Constitution of the United States and the Bill of Rights, enjoined upon all legislative bodies and courts, and grounded in the fact of our common humanity.

To secure these rights, we hereby institute the Gay Activists Alliance, which shall be completely and solely dedicated to their implementation and maintenance, repudiating, at the same time, violence (except for the right of self-defense) as unworthy of social protest, disdaining all ideologies, whether political or social, and forbearing alliance with any group except for those whose concrete actions are likewise so specifically dedicated.

It is finally to the imagination of oppressed homosexuals themselves that we commend the consideration of these rights, upon whose actions alone depends all hope for the prospect of their lasting procurement.

1971

The GAA Alternative

Gay Activists Alliance

This document was created by the Gay Activists Alliance in New York City within two years of the riot at the Stonewall Inn. It reflects much of the pioneering role played by the GAA, as an example to other, more fledgling gay liberation organizations of how successful organizing might be carried out.

The gay liberation movement is a movement for the right to be different, the right to be free. As new gay groups have sprung up across the nation, the diversity within the movement itself has become clear. Some groups focus primarily on social and cultural approaches to liberation. Others are involved in programs of consciousness-raising, helping gays to rise above society's oppressive attitudes. Gay churches have been formed to provide a new way for gays to relate to religion. Organizations have been formed to combat public hostility and ignorance about gays through educational programs.

Among the alternate approaches developed within the liberation movement, one is that of stressing gay political power and gay cultural identity. The Gay Activists Alliance (GAA) and a number of other groups have adopted this approach and found it highly successful. In the past months, various individuals and groups have contacted GAA and expressed an interest in organizing along similar lines.

GAA and groups similar to it consider themselves to be activist organizations. The basic principle underlying activism is the commitment to bring about change in the present, rather than theorize about change in the distant future. While our individual goals and beliefs about the nature of an ideal future society may differ widely, there are many concrete forms of oppression and discrimination which we can agree to struggle against together right now.

The heterosexual establishment would like nothing better than to see gays devote their energy, talent and strength to rambling debates over ideology and future social organization, for this effectively keeps us from confronting and abolishing the concrete facts of our daily oppression. This oppression is often disguised, since many gays, having found that things seem to have gotten slightly better in recent years, assume that the struggle is over. Rushing to accept a limited second-class citizenship, they fear that action will rock the boat, that even their few meagre rights will be taken from them. GAA and other groups like it have found that this is not the case. Active confrontation with the existing system quickly draws the oppressors out into the open. The gay community quickly learns where its real enemies have been hiding and how to deal with them.

The spirit of activism goes deeper than mere political tactics. Throughout our lives we have been forced to confine our behavior within the rules and roles of heterosexual society. Our feelings about ourselves, our ways of relating to one another, our understanding of our oppression have been limited and distorted by the games we have been forced to play. We can truly change ourselves as well as our society only by actively breaking through the patterns which have been forced upon us. We can raise our consciousness forever and yet never change our lives or heads if we do not put what we have learned into action. It is not enough to talk about being free, we must *start* being free.

As GAA has grown, we have found that a group which is politically and culturally active faces problems differing from those encountered by other types of groups. From our experience, we have found that five principles have been especially important in maintaining both group cohesion and political and cultural effectiveness.

We strongly hope that other groups which wish to adopt the name "Gay Activists Alliance" will also decide to adopt these five principles. They have been essential in making GAA what it is. They define a unique political and cultural alternative within the gay liberation movement. Although conditions vary from city to city and from state to state, we hope that other groups interested in developing a program of gay political activism and gay cultural identity will take these recommendations into consideration. They are as follows:

We recommend that the group subscribe to the purposes of GAA as stated in its Constitution's Preamble.

That the group have its own written constitution and democratically elected officers.

That the group be solely concerned with the issue of the liberation of homosexuals, and that the group not ally itself with any other group for any action which is not related to the homosexual liberation issue.

That the group not endorse political candidates or parties.

That membership not be refused to any person because of mode of dress or personal mannerisms.

THE PREAMBLE TO THE GAA CONSTITUTION

The preamble has served as the core of the GAA Constitution and the vehicle of the spirit of the Group. It is a statement of purpose, an explanation of why we are working together and for what. It is a militant statement of intent, as well as a basic bill of rights for all gay people.

The preamble is the core of the Constitution. While much of the Constitution has changed as GAA has grown, the preamble has remained unchanged. It has provided a way of evaluating proposed constitutional changes, a way of determining whether they match the spirit of GAA. Similarly, in times of conflict within the group, it has set the boundaries of argument by providing a common base of agreement. The preamble has provided a continuity of values and ideals for the group. The basic issues of policy tend to find solution in reference to the principles set forth in the preamble.

For example, when confronting politicians, should we dress to suit the establishment's tastes? The preamble states that we have the right to treat and express our bodies as we will, to nurture them, to display them, to embellish them solely in the manner we ourselves determine, independent of any external control whatsoever. We dress as *we* please, without any regard for "respectability." No member of the group can be asked to stay behind the scenes because of his or her style of dress.

As another example: a riot has broken out after a police raid on a gay bar. What is the organization's role? What should individual members do? The preamble repudiates violence, except for the right of self-defense. On the question of violence, the organization can adopt only a protective stance, which may range from providing medical facilities to training members in the art of self-defense. If individual members wish to initiate violent acts, they do so as individuals, not as GAA members, for the preamble makes it clear that initiating a violent offensive cannot be an official GAA action.

As a third example: a resolution is introduced on the floor at a general meeting, setting guidelines for members' behavior in public. To avoid possible arrest and the necessity for bail and legal fees, the resolution provides that members not engage in sexual solicitation in public. Can such a resolution pass? The preamble protects the right to love. This is the right to express our feelings in action, the right to make love with anyone, any way, any time, provided only that the action be freely chosen by all persons concerned. The resolution cannot be passed, for it abridges a principle of right.

The preamble thus has a double value. On the one hand, it makes explicit a set of core values to which all members subscribe and by which the basis policies of the organization are determined. On the other hand, the preamble separates these core values from the more mechanical aspects of the Constitution, the articles and by-laws, which may need to be revised from time to time as growth and emerging problems in the gay community require adaptive change.

The preamble is not sacred: it can be amended. But it provides a basic level of consensus without which it would be difficult to operate. We would hope that other groups adopting the name "Gay Activists Alliance" subscribe to the principles set forth in the GAA preamble.

A WRITTEN CONSTITUTION AND DEMOCRATICALLY ELECTED OFFICERS

A constitution provides any group with a basic structure within which to carry out its work. While non-structured organizations may be well suited to some areas of activity concerning gay liberation, a certain degree of structure is essential for political activism and systematic cultural development.

In GAA, general meetings are conducted in accordance with *Robert's Rules of Order*, but a certain amount of flexibility is retained so that parliamentary procedure does not become oppressive. Committee meetings, being much smaller, are generally conducted more informally, although formal votes are taken and the meetings are led by a chairperson.

Especially in large organizations, parliamentary procedure provides a greater deal of freedom than no structure at all. Personal fights or ideological diatribes are less likely to develop. Everyone has his or her say—not merely the loudest or most charismatic members. Everyone at the meeting is entitled to speak, present motions, and vote.

Much is gained in terms of efficiency. Debate is kept within the framework of rational argument. All points of view can be expressed. Decisions are not made on the basis of partial information. A vote is binding on the organization and sets its policy. No small group of members can undertake actions decided against by the whole organization and yet claim to be acting in its name.

In GAA, committees work within the framework of written mandates which have been voted upon by the general membership and which provide guidelines for the scope and nature of their actions. When a committee has a specific action to recommend or wishes to suggest the adoption of a new policy, these recommendations are brought to the floor during the committee's report at the general meeting and are voted on by the membership as a whole. In this way, committees are kept within the mainstream of the organization and do not become independent entities in themselves. This procedure helps to insure that different committees will not be working at cross purposes and that no committee will become involved in activities which would misrepresent the whole group or conflict with the will of the general membership.

Coordination and communication between committees is extremely important. Under the GAA Constitution, this coordination has been handled by holding weekly meetings of an executive committee, comprised of officers and committee chairpeople (or their representatives). These meetings are open to attendance by the general membership and often have been useful in solving disputes between committees which would otherwise hinder the conduct of business if brought to the floor during general meetings.

The practical value of democratic procedures should not be underestimated. The organization *is* its members. If the members do not have the right to choose who shall represent them in positions of leadership and authority, then cliques, factions, and a spirit of discontent will rapidly develop within the group, destroying its effectiveness. Under these conditions, the energy which should be turned outward against the oppressors of gay people will instead turn inward, and the group will be torn by internal strife. GAA has been through a few such crises, an experience which leads us strongly to recommend democratic procedures within a parliamentary framework to others, with each separate gay organization deciding for itself the exact details of this framework.

A ONE-ISSUE ORGANIZATION

Embodying the most central principle of GAA, this recommendation is nonetheless the most frequently misunderstood. GAA calls itself a "one-issue" organization. Bound by its constitution, the organization as such does not involve itself in other causes, issues, or actions beyond those directly related to the liberation of gay people. The fact that the organization finds reason to limit itself to this issue does not mean that its members—acting independently of the organization—must do so. Actually, most of the members of GAA have been and continue to be involved in actions related to other important social issues confronting our society, but they do so as private individuals or as members of other organizations.

One of the main reasons for this policy is this: from the start, GAA was conceived as an organization in which all gay people would be welcome and could make a contribution. By limiting itself solely to the gay liberation issue, GAA makes it possible for gay people of all political ideologies to work together for the common cause. Although our members range from conservative to revolutionary, we somehow manage to work together on concrete projects. No one need choose between gay liberation and the endorsement of a political objective with which he or she may not agree.

Restricted constitutionally to the issue of gay liberation, GAA is better able to focus and use the energy of its members. The need to adopt an ideological platform which is agreeable to every member is avoided, along with the argument and wrangling which this endeavor so often entails. Rather than be reduced to a mere clearing house which directs gays into support for other non-gay issues, GAA draws its members into the active work of gay liberation towards concrete actions that can make noticeable changes in their lives as *gays.*

The underlying assumption of this policy is that members can think for themselves, and that those who have strong commitments to other issues will act upon those commitments outside of the organization. In practice, gay activists tend to be activists in other areas as well. Thus, a large percentage of the GAA membership may become actively involved in a non-gay issue, but they do so as private individuals, not as GAA members. Where there is a special interest in a particular issue within the membership, individual members frequently organize ad hoc groups outside of GAA, which nevertheless enjoy the participation and organizational skills of a large number of GAA members.

What is a gay issue, and what is not? A gay issue is one that immediately affects gay people as gays. Many of the social and political problems in our society naturally affect homo-sexuals as much as they do non-homosexuals, but GAA does not relate to these as gay issues.

On the other hand, there are many policies which appear on the surface to affect all people, regardless of sexual orientation, but which actually are directed only at gays. Such things as selective application of the law and unofficial discriminatory practices would fall in this category. These are gay issues.

GAA neither allies itself nor supports actions of other groups that are not directly related to the gay liberation issue. Avoiding entangling alliances, GAA remains free to go about its work unhindered by commitments to other organizations for future support, and its members remain free to lend their support as individuals where *they* feel it will do the most good.

A one-issue commitment in a gay organization builds an intense sense of a common gay identity in its members. Unlike the members of many multi-issue gay organizations, we do not come to think of ourselves as primarily men or women, blacks or whites; we come to think of ourselves primarily as gays. Although involved in other issues outside the organization, when we come together in GAA we experience a heightened feeling of ourselves as brothers and sisters with positive personal characteristics that derive from our being gay.

The spirit of gay identity has inspired us to look for ways to encourage the development of a new gay culture, a liberated culture arising out of our experiences as one gay people, free of the oppressive role-playing of a hostile sexist society. GAA celebrates the idea of an indigenously gay culture, attempting to develop a gay sensibility in the arts and new forms of personal interaction through consciousness-raising sessions and actions.

We have discovered a gay solidarity because we are a one-issue organization. When an organization involves itself in many issues besides immediate gay oppression, its members display a very low sense of gay identity. As a result, the emergence of a uniquely gay culture under these conditions is severely impeded.

REFUSAL TO ENDORSE POLITICAL CANDIDATES OR POLITICAL PARTIES

Like the previous recommendation, this one seeks to guarantee that no part of the membership will be forced to endorse a particular type of politics on pain of leaving the organization. By refusing to endorse political candidates, platforms, or parties, the group protects the political freedom and diversity of its membership.

As we have developed contacts with politicians and political candidates, we are careful never to give endorsements, for an endorsement would preclude the possibility of effectively using office holders with a different party affiliation. We seek to be an independent political force, bound to no partisan labels. Our basic policy is this: if politicians, candidates, or political clubs are interested in working for gay rights, then we will use them with no strings attached. Whatever else they are interested in is their own business.

With candidates for major office we use militant tactics of confrontation politics. When they appear to address rallies, we are there. We shout out questions about gay rights, making our presence clearly felt. If the candidates refuse to speak to the issue of gay rights or give an unsatisfactory answer, they are shouted down, chased off the podium, or otherwise embarrassed.

Even avowed gay candidates are not endorsed, for a gay candidate is invariably forced into taking a position on many non-gay issues, some of which may be highly controversial. In addition, when the time comes (as it undoubtedly will) in which electoral races have more than one gay candidate, the decision between the two would have to be made on the basis of non-gay issues.

The political system is there. Some of us approve of it: others do not. We all agree, however, that we would be foolish not to exploit it. In many ways, the political system is corrupt and inefficient—it certainly does not operate in reality the way it is supposed to operate on paper—but it remains vulnerable to militant confrontation tactics.

Most of the gay population is still in the closet. Because gay issues have never been dealt with openly in the past, the gay population has tended to be apathetic and apolitical, rightly feeling that it made little difference in terms of gay rights which candidate or party came to power. Only by making gays visible and gay issues public can the gay vote be made into a credible threat. For this reason, GAA has adopted a policy of militant (though non-violent) public confrontation with the political system and other social institutions that contribute to the oppression of gay people.

Back-room deals and private agreements with political candidates and office holders are self-defeating. These people represent us only on paper. We demand representation openly in public. We demand that they acknowledge the existence of a gay constituency and speak out on gay issues. We demand a specific open commitment to work for gay rights.

We could not pursue this policy while at the same time endorsing candidates or parties. We would lose our flexibility as a credible voting threat with candidates or parties not endorsed. In addition, American politics is frequently a dirty game. Deals and political trade-offs are made behind the scenes. A public support for gay rights need not indicate a private commitment to work for their realization. Endorsements would hinder us from zapping any political figure we might choose—regardless of whether he or she had once or twice said something favorable about gay people in the past.

We must not fall into the trap of *owing* anybody anything. Our demand is not for favors, but for rights. If people support our goals, let them do so out of free choice, not out of the expectation of getting something in return. We can use the political system to our advantage only if gay power remains independent and selective. We can create gay political power only by bringing gay issues out into the open and putting ourselves on the line.

Gay political power means a great deal more than simply changing laws and influencing politicians. It strikes to the heart of the less visible, less obvious political relationships of our sexist society. In essence, gay political power means that no individual gay person stands alone, that he or she has a community of sisters and brothers who are prepared to put themselves on the line to defend their common rights. No gay person should be discriminated against in a public establishment or business, harassed or refused protection by the police, forced to undergo brutal psychiatric techniques, or the like, without the gay community rallying to show its support and anger. Gay political power means gay solidarity, the defense of the individual by the community.

OPEN MEMBERSHIP

The gay world is diverse. Gays with similar backgrounds, lifestyles, ways of dressing, behavioral mannerisms, and sexual tastes tend to stick together. Often this tendency manifests itself in the existence of separate subgroups within the gay community, sub-groups that have little communication with one another. This lack of communication can frequently lead to misunderstanding, stereotyped thinking about other gays, and sometimes even hostility. Nothing could be more damaging or dangerous to the gay liberation movement and the realization of its goals. We cannot fight an oppressive society if we allow ourselves to oppress one another. We must live by the principle that all gays are equal.

Gay people will not be free until a revolution in cultural values has occurred in our society. From the experience of other minority groups, we in GAA have concluded that such change can be brought about most rapidly by creating our own gay power and our own gay culture. Avoiding legal reform as an end in itself, we do believe that confrontation with the political system forces the system itself to promote social change. We do not basically care whether society likes or dislikes us because we are gay; we demand that society and its institutions recognize and respect our rights. This can only happen if we first respect ourselves.

We are a diverse people. We have been told that our gayness—the one thing we have in common—is evil. We have been told that we are men and women, blacks and whites, capitalists and communists first. The fact that we are sexual beings who love and are loved is considered to be secondary and, to some minds, unfortunate. We have been squeezed into oppressive social roles that serve the interest of heterosexual society. Our talent, our creativity, and joy in ourselves have been channeled into the narrow ravines of a labyrinthian underground life. In spite of this oppression, we have developed traditions and lifestyles of our own, a wide variety of sub-cultures.

Yet these sub-cultures have limitations. In part they are a reaction to the larger heterosexual culture and incorporate many of its roles, values and taboos. We remain stifled and held back from exploring our gayness on our own terms, from creating a positive gay culture, an alternative, a gay counter-culture based upon positive experiences as gay people.

The prejudices which some gay people hold against others are intrusions on our way of life from heterosexual society. They are based on the demands of heterosexual roles, values and morals; they are not *ours,* and we must reject them. With the opportunity now before us to create a way of life based on freedom and diversity, we would err tragically if we mirror the faults of straight society. We would be re-creating our oppression at the very moment when we first had a chance for liberation.

In GAA we have felt that gay power and gay culture are the prerequisites for that liberation. Gays must be strong enough as a people to prevent straight society from denying them the opportunity of being themselves and choosing their own way of life. We must have an identity and we must have pride in ourselves if we are to give birth to something that is truly ours. With every political gain we make as a people, we open up the possibility and the necessity for new forms of cultural expression that are inherently gay, inherently our own.

We believe that liberation means the right to be oneself. As gays, we are all brothers and sisters, with much to learn from one another and much to share with one another. We should not try to fit a common mold—we should be ourselves. Each and every one of us brings something new and valuable to the whole. We enter the future together.

June 25, 1971

Frieda Smith Tells It Like It Is

Frieda Smith

This speech was the last one given in Sacramento, California, at the end of the march on the California state capitol on June 25, 1971, led by Reverend Troy Perry to support the AB437, a state bill introduced by Willie Brown to legalize homosexual acts in private between consenting adults. Contemporary reportage by *The Advocate* describes this as one of the two most militant addresses given at the rally.

In New York Harbor, there is a large statue of a lady carrying the torch of freedom. This afternoon, I would like to ask that lady to turn around. I would like to shout across the three thousand miles between us. I would like to shout; "America . . . Your tired, your poor, your huddled masses yearning to breathe free are angry. The wretched refuse of your own teeming shore is ready to explode."

America's wretched refuse, her oppressed minority groups from shore to shore . . . the disenfranchised; black, Chicano, Indian, poor, women, and even homosexuals are getting it together with each other. Many of us are getting it together even in ourselves, for these classifications can overlap. As a woman, and a member of the world's largest minority group, I am aware also of the punitive legal oppression which has the power to imprison me for up to 15 years in this state for a single homosexual act, in addition to legally deny me (according to state business and professional code) licenses, credentials and public employment.

We are here today to urge the passage of AB#437, Willie Brown's consensual sex bill, as an opening step in the reforms which must be made. Homosexuality is not a problem which is out there. Every one of us came from a straight family. Most of you straight people [referring to the spectators at the rally] have someone near and dear to you who is struggling with the problem. To paraphrase the scripture: "Who is there among you, that if her child is hungry, will offer her a stone?"

A leading cause of teenage deaths in America is suicide . . . and many authorities believe that if you could untangle that broken, slender thread, you could unlock those lips which are forever silenced, you would find that the majority of these young people, these boys and girls, were wrestling with their sexual identity in a culture that legally, morally, religiously, socially, educationally and psychologically condemns them. What can we say to those young people out there fighting alone? The majority of homosexuals here today were aware of their homosexual nature before that first act . . . and it was a lonely knowledge. We are not the victims of seduction or rape by older experienced homosexuals which affected us as would the bite of the legendary vampire, sending us out to suck the blood and change the lives of the innocent. Rather, we are living as nearly as possible that life we were meant to live. Even though the world outside, and often the world inside, is trying to stop us.

Do not give a stone. What can I say to that young girl out there? Can I say . . . "hold on"?

All I can say is that as a single woman you will probably be living a life which borders on poverty. If you are a homosexual you will work, regardless of ability, at the lowest levels of employment if you should live openly. There are no civil service or "nice" jobs available to the declared homosexual. If you aspire to a managerial or professional position, you have two choices: a life devoid of love and sex (and if you are single, this often excludes heterosexual sex), or a life in the closet living in constant fear of detection and loss of the position regardless of the performance of your work. This, coupled to the fact, according to the latest Department of Labor statistics, that as a professional woman, college graduate, working in your field, already you will earn $2,900 per year LESS than your male counterpart. This time, according to a Department of Census report: A woman employed full time earns *60%,* a little over half of what the average fully employed man will earn. And 35% of all marriageable age women are unmarried. The percentage of these that are homosexual—open, closeted, or latent—is not known, but the single woman has the smallest income in the country, and shares with the single man the honor of paying the highest percentage of taxes.

Housing for the single woman is not easy to obtain. Apartment house owners discriminate against single women on the ground that they are not "nice." Many single women will never be able to obtain government financing to buy a house because their incomes are so low that they cannot qualify. And even though her tax rate is the highest, government programs are for families. Talking about the government brings to mind the G. I. Bill which brings to mind women in the armed services. Which brings to mind the American caste system of classification of ex-service personnel . . . the person with the "bad" discharge. The majority of "bad" discharges from the women's services are for homosexual acts committed by consenting adults in private. A vast amount of money is spent to spy, present evidence, and prosecute these cases . . . in a country where children go to bed hungry for lack of funds. The ex-servicewoman, ego shattered, can crawl back to civilian life, bearing the onus of her service career, to face the American myth that women in America are only working for extra money, or because they are bored . . . that they will quit to have babies and also they are not reliable because their families come first. Employers give lip service to this myth to justify the payment of a pauper's wage and the denying of advancement to women . . . even though study after study has shown that most women work out of *economic necessity*. And that the majority of poverty level families in this country are headed by women.

How can we face this? How can we fight it? Can we go up to our boss and say, "I am working in earnest. I am not supplementing my husband's ample salary. I do not, nor shall I have a husband. I will not have a family to come first. I am gay." Tomorrow you probably would not have a job.

There are many steps which must be taken to end discrimination. Today we are here to urge the taking of the first small one. We must hold these truths to be self evident: "That ALL men are created equal" and I use the word "men" in the androgenous [*sic*] dictionary sense to include ALL people, not just white, Anglo Saxon, male, Protestant, heterosexuals . . . but ALL human beings. And endowed by their creator with certain inalienable rights . . . and that to insure these rights governments are instituted among men, "and we must hold with Thomas Jefferson and with the framers of the Declaration of Independence . . ." that whenever any form of government becomes destructive to these ends, it is the right of the people to alter or abolish it. We are here today in an effort to alter it.

Peace.

August 28, 1971

We Demand

Gay Day Committee

The Gay Day of the title of the group issuing this manifesto refers to the demonstration of over 200 lesbians and gay men on Parliament Hill in Ottawa, Ontario, before the Canadian House of Parliament in support of this document, the text of which was presented to the federal government of Canada in August 1971. This was the first such demonstration in support of gay rights ever held in Canada.

In 1969 the Criminal Code was amended so as to make certain sexual acts between two consenting adults, in private, not illegal. This was widely misunderstood as "legalizing" homosexuality and thus putting homosexuals on an equal basis with other Canadians. In fact, this amendment was merely a recognition of the non-enforceable nature of the Criminal Code as it existed. Consequently, its effects have done but little to alleviate the oppression of homosexual men and women in Canada. In our daily lives we are still confronted with discrimination, police harassment, exploitation and pressures to conform which deny our sexuality. That prejudice against homosexual people pervades society is, in no small way, attributable to practices of the federal government. Therefore we, as homosexual citizens of Canada, present the following brief to our government as a means of redressing our grievances.

We demand:

1. *The removal of the nebulous terms "gross indecency" and "indecent act" from the Criminal Code and their replacement by a specific listing of offences, and the equalization penalties for all remaining homosexual and heterosexual acts; and defining "in private" in the Criminal Code to mean "a condition of privacy."*

   The terms "gross indecency" and "indecent act" in the Criminal Code remain largely undefined, thus leaving the degree of offensiveness of many sexual acts open to interpretation by enforcement officials according to their personal prejudices—which, by and large, are anti-homosexual. Therefore a specific listing of public offences is crucial in that only in this way can personal bias be eradicated and the legal intent of the law be preserved.

Sections 147 and 149 of the Criminal Code have been used to cover public homosexual acts, an offence which is punishable upon indictable conviction; similar public heterosexual acts have usually been dealt with under Section 158 of the Criminal Code, an offence which is punishable on summary conviction.

Moreover, indecent assault upon a female (Section 141) can result in a maximum penalty of five years imprisonment, while a person—in this case, always a male—convicted of indecent assault upon another male (Section 148) is liable to imprisonment for ten years. There is no reason for the continuation of this discrepancy in maximum penalties, since the relevant factor is assault, not the sex of the person assaulted.

"In private" when applied to homosexual acts means strictly in the confines of one's home or apartment. For heterosexual acts this interpretation of "in private" is less stringent, as the existence of "lovers' lanes" so well testifies. Persons engaged in sexual acts who have genuinely attempted to create a "condition of privacy" should not be arrested but—as now happens with most heterosexuals—be told to "move along."

2. *Removal of "gross indecency" and "buggery" as grounds for indictment as a "dangerous sexual offender" and for vagrancy.*

Since persons convicted of homosexual acts are usually charged under Sections 147 and 149 of the Criminal Code, they are liable to be labeled as "dangerous sexual offenders" and sentenced to "preventive detention" for an indefinite period under Section 661 of the Criminal Code.

Section 164 of the Criminal Code labels an individual as vagrant and subject to summary conviction if, *inter alia,* he or she has been convicted of an offence such as "gross indecency." Denying the right of an individual to frequent places (school grounds, playgrounds, public parks or bathing areas) on the basis of having been convicted of "gross indecency" is excessive, especially when the specific offence for which the individual was convicted may have been merely an indiscretion and in no way a harmful act.

3. *A uniform age of consent for all female and male homosexual and heterosexual acts.*

   Since the federal government of Canada does not recognize legal marriages between homosexual persons, the age of consent for their sexual contact, is twenty-one years of age. However, since heterosexual parties can be joined in a legally recognized marriage, their age of consent is dependent only upon the age at which they can legally enter a marriage contract. Further inequities result in that Sections 138, 143 and 144 of the Criminal Code specify various ages of consent for heterosexual acts between unmarried persons. We believe that the age of consent (twenty-one) for engaging in sexual acts is unrealistic and should be lowered. A number of provinces have reduced the age of majority. The effect of this is that individuals under the age of twenty-one can enter into contractual agreements, vote and drink alcoholic beverages, but cannot exercise their sexual preferences—no small part of one's life. The principle of maturity should be applied uniformly to all aspects of deciding individual prerogatives.

4. *The Immigration Act be amended so as to omit all references to homosexuals and "homosexualism."*

   Denying immigration to Canada for any individual merely on the basis of his or her "homosexualism" is inconsistent with the Criminal Code. Since "homosexualism" is not, in itself, an illegal practice between consenting adults in private, the Immigration Act thus discriminates against a minority group.

5. *The right of equal employment and promotion at all government levels for homosexuals.*

   The proposed implementation of Paragraph 100 of the Royal Commission on Security makes one's homosexuality an issue in the promotion and recruitment of civil servants. If an individual freely admits his or her homosexuality and is not afraid of disclosure and engages solely in legal acts, that person is hardly susceptible to blackmail. One cannot profitably threaten to broadcast to others what is already known. The effect of Paragraph 100 is to *force* homosexuals into a furtive situation in which they *might* become susceptible to coercion. Thus, Paragraph 100 becomes self-defeating.

If "homosexuals are special targets for attention from foreign intelligence services," this is evidently due to the threat of dismissal from employment, a situation which could be greatly improved by a more open policy on the part of the government.

6. *The Divorce Act be amended so as to omit sodomy and homosexual acts as grounds for divorce; moreover, in divorce cases homosexuality per se should not preclude the equal rights of child custody.*
7. *The right of homosexuals to serve in the Armed Forces and, therefore, the removal of provisions for convicting service personnel of conduct and/or acts legal under the Criminal Code; further, the rescinding of policy statements reflecting on the homosexual.*

Note (c) of Queen's Regulations and Orders (103.25: "Scandalous Conduct of Officers") and Note 9 (b) of 103.26 ("Cruel or Disgraceful Conduct") both suggest that homosexual acts between consenting adults may be considered punishable offences in the military. This effectively contravenes the Criminal Code and, thereby, the principle that military law should be subordinate to civil law.

Paragraph 6 of Canadian Forces Administrative Order 19-20 ("Sexual Deviation-Investigation, Medical Examination, and Disposal") reads: "Service policy does not allow retention of sexual deviates in the Forces" and specifies the manner of discharging persons convicted of homosexual acts while in military service.

8. *To know if it is a policy of the Royal Canadian Mounted Police to identify homosexuals within any area of government service and then question them concerning their sexuality and the sexuality of others; and if this is the policy we demand its immediate cessation and destruction of all records so obtained.*
9. *All legal rights for homosexuals which currently exist for heterosexuals.*

Although numerous instances of the injustices and discrimination embodied by this demand could be cited, the following are indicative of the inequities with which homosexuals must contend:

- because homosexuals cannot legally marry, they face economic discrimination in that the benefits of filing joint income tax returns and conferring pension rights are denied to them; likewise, homosexuals are unable to partake of the benefits of public housing;

- they are brought up under an education system which either through commission or omission fosters both a narrow and prejudicial view of homosexuality;
- again, owing to the fact that homosexuals cannot enter into legally recognized marriages, they are not permitted to adopt children except under the most unusual circumstances. (Although we recognize that adoption is an area of provincial jurisdiction, we feel that this does not completely remove all responsibility from the federal government.)
- too often in the private sector, once an individual's homosexuality has become known, he or she is discriminated against in employment, and exploited by unscrupulous landlords.

In known places frequented by homosexuals or in places where they gather, both direct and subtle harassment by police officers is too often commonplace;

Since sexuality is not covered under the Canadian Bill of Rights, homosexuals are excluded from protections which are guaranteed to other minority groups such as those of race, religion or national origin.

As a group, homosexuals are "second class citizens" in a democratic society which purports to recognize only one class of citizenship, based on equality.

10. *All public officials and law enforcement agents to employ the full force of their office to bring about changes in the negative attitudes and* de facto *expressions of discrimination and prejudice against homosexuals.*

The role of public officials must be twofold: (1) to serve as legislators formulating the letter of the law, and (2) to serve as representatives of the spirit of a system founded upon democratic principles. As such, holders of public office must transcend prejudicial attitudes (in this case against homosexuals) in favour of leading society to levels consistent with the principles of human rights.

We call upon government officials, as a show of good faith, to enter immediately into a dialogue with the various Canadian homophile groups regarding all the aforementioned demands and to respond publicly by supporting the purpose of this brief.

February 1972

The Lesbian and God-the-Father

Sally Gearhart

At the time this speech was delivered to a pastor's conference at the Pacific School of Religion at Berkeley, Sally Gearhart was a professor of speech communication at California State University, San Francisco. The speech is subtitled "All the Church Needs Is a Good Lay—on Its Side," which refers to the call for change and spiritual growth issued by Gearhart.

Of the host of things I'd like to share with you, a few at least bear mention.

I could speak with you about the twelve specific references to "homosexuality" in the Bible, about the misinterpretations that have been put upon them, about the fact that only one of those references includes any suggestion of female homosexuality.

Or, I might use a feature-article approach on "Lesbians I Have Known In The Church" (and still know). I doubt that many of you would be shocked at personal or experiential estimates of the number of lesbians in your congregations. I would, though, assure you that you don't find lesbians just among the single women of the church, nor, of course, are all single women lesbians. What may come as a bit of a surprise is that lesbians are to be found in significant numbers among heterosexually married women, women trapped by their commitment to families and to husbands, women who know deep in themselves that their most authentic love relationships have been and perhaps even now are with women.

Perhaps more important might be a recounting of the hundreds of lesbians I have met in the past year who have left the church. I could relate hair-raising stories of how the church attempted to dehumanize them, of how much pain they have suffered at its hands. I could tell you of the rage that erupts in some of them at the suggestion of anything Christian and of the tolerant laughter that springs from others at the mention of such devitalized concepts as "sin" or "salvation."

Or I could fall into the old trap of trying to define a lesbian by male standards, by the same philosophy that says. "All the lesbian needs is a good lay with a real man to make her normal." The male notion of the lesbian is the sexual one: she is a lesbian simply because she "has sex" with women. Nothing could be farther from the truth. But *if* we were talking in man-language about lesbianism, I'd want to point out that what lesbians and gay men do in bed is *technically* no different from what many of you do in bed with your wives or husbands (assuming that you have a healthy and vivid sexual relationship). The pain is that although heterosexual couples do "it" and marriage manuals even recommend "it" to buck up an otherwise tired and dull sexual life, still you give lip service to the notion that the "missionary position" is the only proper mode of sexual expression. You support a hypocritical morality that sanctions only the sex act that is potentially progenerative. By your silence on any other mode of sexual expression you continue to oppress gay people every minute of every day.

But the main thing I want to share with you is twofold.

First, I cannot separate the lesbian from the woman. This is not only because my oppression has been more as a woman than as a lesbian (though that of course is true), but also because to me being a lesbian is what really being a woman means. I like to think that the way politically conscious lesbians "are" in the world today is the way all women were before the tyranny of the patriarchy. To be a lesbian is to be identified not by men or by a society made by men but by me, by a woman. And the more I am identified by/for me, by/for my own experience, by/for my own values, the more a full woman I feel I become.

More and more woman-identified women are emerging everyday. More and more lesbians. It's not that more and more women are leaping into bed with each other. That may be your fantasy—certainly it is a common male fantasy—as to what lesbianism is all about. And indeed, my understanding is that astounding numbers of women are extending their love relationships with other women into sexual dimensions. But that's not the distinguishing characteristics of a lesbian. Lesbianism is a life-style, a mind-set, a body of experience. I would like to call any woman-identified woman a lesbian, and if she's really woman-identified, she'll feel good about being called a lesbian, whether or not she's had any sexual relationship with another woman.

The woman-identified women who are being reborn every day are those who are shaking off the chains forged by thousands of years of ecclesiastical propaganda. Shaking off their definition as male property, as male's helpmate, as the pure and empedestaled virtue-vessels that need chivalrous male protection. They are the unladylike women, the angry women, the ones who make you feel a little uneasy with their freedom of body, with the way they cross their legs or open their own car doors, or the way they look as though they'll give you a karate chop if you hassle them. They are the ones who reach a deep and threatening place inside every man's gut, the ones who can make your stomach turn over because they represent a truth that your own stomach has always secretly known. Particularly if you are a man, you both hate and admire their independence, their strength.

The women being reborn today (that's the real meaning of resurrection) are the ones marching for the rights to their own bodies at abortion demonstrations. Often they are women of witch-like appearance, women in jeans and boots who have laid away the girdles and garters that bound them into the profiteering system. They are women whose faces are honest, whose hair flies free, whose minds and bodies are growing supple and steady and sure in self-possession, whose love is growing deep and wide in the realities of newly discovered relationships with other women.

They don't need the church. The last thing they think about now is the church. They have within themselves what the church has claimed as its own and distorted so ironically for its own economic and psychological purposes these thousands of years.

Second, being a lesbian involves for me some growing political consciousness. That means I am committed to assessing institutions like the church, which, as far as women are concerned, takes the prize as the most insidiously oppressive institution in Western society. The matter of its influence needs no elaborating. Its insidiousness lies most obviously in the fact that it has made women (particularly white women) not only victims but murderers in a complex and exploitative economic system. One of the greatest marks of women's oppression is our conviction that we are not oppressed.

I look forward with great anticipation to the death of the church. The sooner it dies, the sooner we can go about the business of living the gospel. That living cannot take place in the church, and I suspect that most of us here have known that for a long time. But if we count on "renewal" or "reform" then we understand neither the depth of the church's crime nor the nature of the women's movement. If we count on "renewal" or "reform," then clearly we have not heard the voices of Third World peoples here and abroad.

Renewal and reform are not enough. Renewal and reform are more often sops, liberal cop-outs and tokenism in the face of real and harder tasks. For example, with gritted teeth some denominations offer to ordain women. They then expect me to rejoice in this, light bonfires on the hillside, and dance around the sacred flame. Far from rejoicing, I really feel sick, sick that woman energy shall now officially be made captive to the institutions, sick that in the very act of ordination a woman has separated herself from me and from others. She has played the church's game for good reason—in order to secure her survival. But in doing so, she hasn't challenged the church. She has only mounted another pedestal.

I am weary of the timid reassurances that "things are changing," or that "our congregation/pastor/district/seminary is different," or that you have to play the system's game to get into a power position so you can do some good. I mistrust with all my woman-heart the motive that keeps women committed to church renewal, i.e., "The church *needs* me." I am tired of hearing liberal churchpeople (both women and men) lay out transforming radical ideas in private and then collapse into meek submission in public when the chips are down. But I do understand why it happens: I know how important in this society it is to get a paycheck.

I long to hear voices *in public church gatherings* insisting not only upon the death of the institutional church but upon specific ways of carrying out that goal. In other words, I want to hear voices (so bold in private) insisting *in public* upon programs that affirm plural relationship, collective and communal living, same-sex love relationships, childhood sexuality, masturbating, and self-love. I want loud voices protesting sex-role socialization: that is, our practice of brainwashing people with outside plumbing to assume the role of strong-dominant-active-intelligent-conquering HE-MAN and those with inside plumbing to assume that of weak-submissive-receptive-dumb-conquered GIRL. Of course if such voices are heard, they are not likely to be heard again very often under the rafters of the institutional church. Such speakers have to be prepared to be ousted—and that, after all, may be the real point.

What is devastating and dehumanizing about the church is not its foundation of love, but the superstructure of patriarchal, theological claptrap that has been hoisted on that foundation. The superstructure shivers and quakes whenever the sanctity of the nuclear family or the traditional concepts of sexuality are called into question—and well it might shake, for it is these two concepts that are the bricks and mortar of the church.

The structure of the church (God over man, man over woman, father over family, clergy over laity, power over powerlessness) is vertical, hierarchical. The church's very identity depends on that hierarchy. This identity is dependent upon standards of success and failure, on authority, on competition.

It is dependent on who has power over whom. The idea is that God is at the top with power over all, and I as woman am at the bottom of the heap. Together with my children passivity is sanctified.

It will do no good to "renew" this church. If the gospel is to live, then vertical structure will have to be laid on its side—horizontalized—and that, to me, means the death of the institutional church.

Women who are being reborn these days do not want a man to step down from the pulpit so that a woman can step into it. They would do away with the pulpit altogether—do away with the physical setting apart of any person for purposes of "preaching" or "teaching."

Women of high consciousness do not want an equalization of the number of women and men on church councils. They would do away with councils themselves, with any body of people that is anything but voluntary and open to anyone concerned.

Women who are really getting it together don't want to be national presidents or bishops or pope. They don't want presidents, bishops, popes, and the like to exist at all, for the very definition of their office puts them above some and below others.

Woman-identified women don't want the Bible rewritten to talk about God-the-Mother or Jesus the Savioress. The women I have in mind believe that each person creates herself out of her own experience and that we must all work out in community our salvation from the repressive system we've grown up with.

Women who think of a revolution don't want just to have "ladies' Sunday" in the local congregation, where women run the show. They want to do away with the show altogether, because as it presently exists it is just that: a performance and not a participation. They do not want traditional worship, because that calls for craning their necks to look up or for bowing their heads in subjugation. They are only now learning what it means to look with love eyeball to eyeball with equals.

What can it mean to individuals in the church that they must begin to conduct the church's funeral, that they must themselves be the agents of the church's death? It must mean at least risks never taken before. It might mean, on an action level, throwing out the phallic pulpit that sets one person higher than and apart from another. Or it might mean tearing out puritanical pews and putting in comfortable chairs and pillows for being-with rather than being-under. Then the otherwise unused building can become a crash-pad or a refuge for transients—surely the church should be a refuge I use every hour of every week in the shelter and care of human beings.

It might be a good thing to use a generic "she" or "woman" or "womankind" in all our conversations for a decade or so instead of the masculine generic so men can begin to understand what it feels like to be made invisible.

You pastors can refuse to preach anymore, refuse to be the enlightened shepherds of a blind flock. You can also suggest some primitive Christianity in the form of pooled salaries and resources in your congregation—which would be divided according to need. All of this, of course, is with full knowledge that if you try any of it you're likely to be spewed out of the mouth of the church (ironically, because you are *not* lukewarm). Then perhaps you can come into the streets and ghettos of the secular world where the gospel is being discovered and lived.

But to make such changes—if you should succeed—is still to treat only the symptoms. We don't really get anywhere toward toppling the church structure until we articulate loud and clear some fundamental assumptions.

> That traditional Christian teaching is anti-life; it is antithetical to any liberation ideology, its enfleshment, Christian practice, is not enfleshment at all but one of the Western world's most eloquent expressions of the fascist mind-set.
>
> That traditional Christian concepts are the constructs of male thinking and depend for their perpetuation on the myth of male superiority.
>
> That because the submission of women is absolutely essential to the church's functioning, the church has a vested interest (economic and psychological) in perpetuating the institutions that most oppress women: the nuclear family and the sex-role socialization of children.

When we admit these things, then we can commit ourselves to one of only two paths: either toppling the hierarchy completely (which action would be the destruction of the church), or packing up whatever shred of personal worth we've got left and leaving the church entirely—hopefully in a hell-raising burst of glory that in itself may educate other Christians.

So, as a woman, as a lesbian, I invite you not to attempt reform of the church. I invite you either to destroy it or to desert it. Personal integrity allows no other alternatives.

February 13, 1972

Waffle

Jearld Moldenhauer

This speech was delivered in 1972 at the New Democratic Party Waffle Convention in Hamilton, Ontario. A note accompanying the text states that "This is the first time a gay liberation representative has addressed a political party conference." Moldenhauer was one of the two coordinators of the editorial collective in Toronto that produced Canada's popular gay newspaper, *The Body Politic.*

Perhaps there is real reason to be optimistic about the future of Canada. The struggles for autonomy—the national struggle against American control, the struggle of Quebec to achieve liberation from the forces which strangle the identity of the French-Canadian people and our efforts to establish an Independent Socialist Canada—are all indicative of the emergence of a new consciousness which seeks an end to the exploitative values and dehumanized lifestyles of advanced industrial capitalism. The struggle of workers, cultural minorities, women and gay people is the same in that we all, in some way, are working for freedom—for the autonomy of every individual and of our country in its relations with the rest of the world. We, as aspirants of a more humanistic society, of a society based on the autonomy of the individual which literally returns Power to the People, must concern ourselves about the quality of life in terms of interpersonal relations and environment. At last, our political consciousness might penetrate beyond the institutional superstructures and return to a full realization that politics begins on the interpersonal level. The basic patterns and rules of institutionalized political bodies are extensions of behavioural practices between individuals. Politics is power. When one person rules another, when in the interaction between any two persons—one imposes their mental or physical selves upon the other, the relationship is political. Accordingly, in the world we live in, where each is, from birth, conditioned to act out certain roles according to pre-established rules—every interaction is political. Until people stop attempting to give meaning to their lives in the roles of oppressed and oppressor there is no real personal autonomy. In this sense then, one must unfortunately conclude—to love is not our mode of being. Personal autonomy is still a long way off as long as an individual's experiential perimeter and choice are limited by the restrictions inherent in the prime socializing institutions of the nuclear family and the educational system.

Recent social evolution has seen the emergence of two significant popular movements: Women's Liberation and Gay Liberation. Together we compose the minorities of the sexist social order, together we speak about Sexual Politics, about the roles and rules which determine the power relations involved in interpersonal relations, and which in this culture, at this time in history, keep us subordinate to the heterosexual male ruling class. Sexual politics is bringing the revolution home—Marx challenged the economic status quo—Freud, Marcuse and Ronald Laing challenge the status quo of the individual. I hope that when you think and talk about social change you will not neglect the challenge to your own personal status quo implicit to sexual politics. The importance of women's lib and gay lib in social evolution cannot be underestimated.

The Canadian homosexual population, which sociologists have estimated to be no less than 10% of this country's population, will no longer tolerate the denial of our basic civil liberties. Through education and political activism we seek to change the sexist nature of Canadian society—including eliminating all inequalities and negative social attitudes.

Because we are still in the process of uniting our minority, we have not represented a strong voting block in political elections. In the United States, where gay liberation has been a growing socio-political force for one year longer than in Canada, politicians are beginning to realize that homophiles represent a significant voting block in national, state and city elections. Edward Kennedy and Eugene McCarthy have recently publicly announced their solidarity with the gay community in achieving full civil equality for homophiles.

For years now, political candidates of major political parties in Los Angeles, San Francisco and New York City, have addressed the gay minority. They are not blind to the reality that we do constitute a group with significant voting strength, a strength far outweighing any backlash vote from the bigots, who in the name of democracy, would deny us our basic rights and needs. With ever increasing strength, the Canadian gay community will make its opinions felt through the support of politicians and political parties which show their solidarity with our democratic struggle.

August 1972

Democrats, Nation, Hear Gay Delegates

Jim Foster

This is the text of the address given by Jim Foster, political chairman of San Francisco's homosexual activist group Society for Individual Rights, at the 1972 Democratic National Convention.

Mr. Chairman, Assembled Delegates. My name is Jim Foster. I am a delegate to the Democratic National Convention from the Fifth Congressional District of California.

I am also the Political Chairman of *The Society for Individual Rights,* the nation's largest gay rights organization. As such, I am here tonight, not only representing the 1,200 members of the Society or the thousands of gay men and women who live in the Fifth Congressional District, but the twenty million gay women and men who are looking for a political party that is responsive to their needs.

Due in large part to the reform of the Democrat [*sic*] Party, I and other members of the gay liberation movement are able to participate in the process of choosing those who will represent us all. But the issues associated with gay liberation are not partisan issues. They are not Democratic issues or Republican issues. They are not conservative or radical issues. They are HUMAN issues. As such they deserve support from all people, regardless of their political philosophy.

We, the representatives of the national gay community, are here to present you with a statement which concerns the rights of America's gay citizens . . . a statement, which if you affirm and include in the Democrat [*sic*] platform, will help to bring an end to the oppression that gay people have lived with for centuries.

We do not come here pleading for your understanding or begging for your tolerance. We come to you affirming our pride in our life style, affirming our right to speak and to maintain meaningful emotional relationships and affirming our rights to participate in the life of this country on an equal basis with every other citizen.

It is a basic assumption of many Americans that no citizen should have to fear oppression from society because he or she does not share the opinion of the minority [*sic*]. There is no minority in America today that can testify to this false assumption better than the gay minority. Our artists and poets have depicted what life is like for all oppressed people, perhaps because we realize how an oppressive society attempts to control those who are different from the white, affluent, male, heterosexual power structure.

There are many forms of oppression that gay people face in this country. Perhaps the worst forms of it are the real and imagined fears with which gay people live everyday. These fears stem from the knowledge that for a person to love another of the same sex is at variance with society's expectation.

Del Martin and Phyllis Lyon, in their book, *Lesbian/Woman,* list the fears that gay people must contend with every day: Fear of identification, fear of ridicule, fear of rejection, fear of group association, fear of the active gay community, fear of police, fear of family, fear of forming friendships, fear of loneliness, fear of losing one's job or career, fear of loss of respect, fear of displaying affection and, perhaps the most devastating fear of all—fear of self-acceptance.

Most of these fears are well-founded, for as members of an "out" group, gay people are subject to reprisals from all corners of society—friends, family, employers, police, government and the church—which has made of homosexual behavior a special kind of "sin" and of the homosexual, a special kind of "sinner." Let us look at these forms of reprisal more closely:

In practically all parts of the country, gay people are subject to arbitrary and discriminatory law enforcement on the part of the police and their agents. A display of any kind of affection between gay people can be cause for immediate arrest, humiliation and punishment—no matter where it is observed. Non-gay friends of mine are amazed to discover that even the simple act of taking another's hand in a gay bar is frowned upon by the management as it could cause the loss of their license and their livelihood.

The laws which prohibit adult, consensual behavior are enforced almost solely against gay people. In recent testimony in Sacramento, before the Criminal Procedure Committee of the legislature debating Assemblyman Brown's consensual sex bill, law enforcement officials from Los Angeles admitted that these laws were enforced against gay people only. They do not send undercover agents into bars frequented by heterosexuals in order to entice people into making solicitations. It would be too costly. Yet through some logic, known only to themselves, it is not too costly to use these same undercover agents in gay bars and businesses to effect arrests on charges. If they were uniformly enforced, there would not be jails large enough to hold us all.

A kind of harassment, enticement, entrapment, brutality, discrimination and injustice is perpetuated against gay people and is a shame to the concept of justice in this country.

On April 27, 1953, President Eisenhower signed Executive Order 10450 which effectively denies employment to gay people in the federal government. Many people believe that the order applies only to jobs in sensitive areas. The truth is that a gay person may not push a broom down the hall of the Smithsonian Institute or hang a picture on the wall of the National Gallery.

It is ironic, in view of its valiant efforts to eradicate prejudice, discrimination and abuse in the areas of race, creed and color that the government has itself become a major source and an active promoter of prejudice, discrimination and abuse that our society directs against gay women and men.

It should be of interest to all citizens to realize that the Civil Service Commission launches thorough investigations of every job applicant's private sex life. These investigations, conducted at the cost of some $12,000,000 a year, do not stop at the examination of arrest records. Persons have been followed, their neighbors and fellow employees interrogated and their mail intercepted. It should be emphatically made clear that these investigations are never related to one's competence but only to one's sexual preference.

In no area is federal employment carried out in a more brutal and ruthless manner than in the armed forces. Fortunately, for all of us, gay people are no longer willing to accept such patently foolish and immoral prejudice. We are citizens and we too are entitled to work in the federal system to the limit of our capabilities.

To this end we urge the Democrat [*sic*] Party to enact this gay rights plank. But, regardless [of] whether this convention passes this plank or not, to our millions of gay brothers and sisters as well as to the Democratic Party, we say "We are here. We will not be stilled. We will not go away until the ultimate goal of gay liberation is realized. That goal being that *all people* can live in the peace, freedom, and the dignity of what they are."

Thank you.

August 1972

Address to the Democratic National Convention

Madeline Davis

This speech was given to the 1972 convention of the Democratic Party by Madeline Davis of Buffalo, New York.

I am a woman and a lesbian, a minority of minorities.

Thank you for the opportunity to speak to you. Twenty million Americans are grateful and proud of the Democratic Party.

We are the minority of minorities. We belong to every race and creed, both sexes, every economic and social level, every nationality and religion. We live in large cities and small towns. But we are the untouchables in American society. We have suffered from oppression—from being totally ignored or ridiculed to having our heads smashed and our blood spilled in the streets.

Now we are coming out of our closets and on to the convention floor—to tell you, the delegates, and to tell all gay people throughout America that we are here to put an end to our fears. Our fears that people will know us for who we are, that they will shun and revile us, fire us from our jobs, reject us from our families, evict us from our homes, beat us and jail us. For what? Because we have chosen to love each other.

I am asking that you vote YES for the inclusion of this minority report into the Democratic platform for two major reasons:

First, we must speak to the basic civil rights of all human beings. It is inherent in the American tradition that the private life and life styles of citizens should be allowed and insured, so long as they do not infringe upon the rights of others. A government that interferes with the private lives of its people is a government that is alien to the American tradition and the American dream.

You have before you a chance to reaffirm that tradition, that dream. As a matter of practicality you also have the opportunity to gain the vote of 20,000,000 Americans that would help in November to put a Democrat in the White House.

Secondly, I say to you: I am someone's neighbor, someone's sister, someone's daughter. A vote for this plank is a vote not only for me but it is a vote for all homosexual women and men across the country to peaceably live their own lives.

I wish to remind you that a vote for this plank may now or someday be a vote for your neighbor, your sister, your daughter or your son.

We ask for your vote and we ask because our people have suffered long and hard. That you reaffirm for every human being the right to love.

August 1972

Speech to the American Bar Association

Richard Hongisto

This is the text of an address given to the 1972 convention of the American Bar Association meeting in San Francisco by Richard Hongisto, a professional criminologist and ten-year veteran of the San Francisco police force who had been elected sheriff of San Francisco in 1971. He was speaking at a hearing called by the Resolutions Committee in support of a proposed ABA resolution calling on all the states to pass "consensual sex" legislation. His presentation was one of two "pro" statements presented, the other being by Dr. Donald Lunde of Stanford's medical faculty. No opposing statements were given.

It would be wise for all of us in the interest of our communities, our state and our country, to recognize that there are some things we cannot do. Senator William Fulbright put it well in his book, *The Arrogance of Power,* when he pointed out what was happening to us in Vietnam and what the arrogance of power did to us as a country. It was a lesson that we learned and then forgot, when we became involved with Prohibition. I think we all know what happened there. We can't over-extend ourselves too far; we can't do too much or we end up doing nothing but getting egg on our face.

I think the same is true with our crime problem in the United States, in general, today. In 1969 the San Francisco Police Department could solve no more than 13% of our killings, forcible rapes, robberies, aggravated assaults, burglaries, larcenies, and other thefts in San Francisco. Not more than 13% were solved. But during this same year, over 50% of all arrests were for what we call non-victim crimes, which include drug abuse, homosexuality, prostitution and abortion.

I submit to you that it is fair for us to ask ourselves, in terms of cost analysis, what we are spending money for and what we are getting. I submit to you that behind every patrolman on the street, there is a sergeant who makes considerably more money, a lieutenant who makes more than that, detectives and supervising captains who make even more. Behind every building of criminal justice—the hall of justice, the youth guidance center, the jail, the probation department, and the patrol department—similar structures exist. The ground the building sits on has to be bought and paid for—then filled with clerks, janitors, utilities, and so forth . . . With all this machinery we can only solve 13% of our more serious crimes . . . I submit that we should take a very serious look at the priorities. I think that the argument in regard to non-victim crimes is a very strong argument.

The majority of unmarried young people between the ages of 20 and 25 are sexually active and hence "criminal" in 22 states in the union. Fornication statutes describe who may not be sexually active . . . in other words, anyone who is not married. This burdens many unmarried young people with feelings of guilt and the possibility of punishment at a time when, for biological reasons, they are most likely to be sexually active, and for cultural reasons, the least likely to be married . . . All of our current studies show that the earlier the age of marriage the more likelihood there is of divorce.

A similar example of unsound legislation is the law prohibiting oral copulation. Here we have a law describing what kind of foreplay not to perform in the privacy of the marital bedroom or between homosexuals.

Sexual problems are a major cause of marital conflict and divorce. Often a spouse feels, and rightfully so, that her partner is unduly brief in those activities preceding sexual intercourse. To advise a couple of common techniques for prolonging sexual activity, such as oral-genital sex, is to put the marriage counselor or clergyman in a position of advocating a crime in 41 of the 50 states.

The criminality of many sexual behaviors may also inject vindictiveness into divorce proceedings. Sexual activity is not only a common ground for divorce but provides the potential for blackmail in the negotiating for property settlement, etc. Oral copulation and sodomy statutes all provide for a means of incarceration and the coersive treatment of homosexuals.

The Freudian theory of homosexuality has never been scientifically substantiated. Even if it were true, the notion that the confinement of male homosexuals in an all-male prison or hospital is a means of rehabilitation makes as much sense as trying to treat obesity by locking a fat man in a candy shop. Furthermore, these laws allow for some of the most sadistic forms of treatment ever performed under the guise of rehabilitation.

I believe that the economic chaos that has resulted in this country from our excursion in Vietnam has its exact parallel for what is happening in criminal justice in this country. We can use tanks, mace, spy systems—the same kind of thing as focusing attention on non-victim crime and spending 50% of our time with that.

My second point is that I believe there is a very strong argument regarding what the law ought to be concerned about. Herbert Packer, a law professor at Stanford, wrote an excellent book on that—*The Limits of the Criminal Sanction*. He argues the case that the sexual conduct of people, in general, is not a fit matter for the law to be concerned with.

I believe that a law must have a basis for being written, that there must be a reason for criminal sanction. There is no reason for criminal sanction in the area of consenting adults, in private.

One of the main arguments in favor of criminal sanctions legislation has to do with the notion that they are necessary to maintain the health of society. But as we all know, in England, Sweden, and in many countries in Europe and even in several states in the United States, the health of society has not been impaired by consenting adults legislation.

Lastly, I would remind you, that the law is used as a model for our young people. Present laws in regard to non-victim crimes tend to propound and further vicious, unrealistic stereotypes about homosexual people, about prostitutes, about alcoholics, about drug users, all sorts of people. All of these areas of non-victim crimes and the people involved in them are loaded with gross distortions of reality.

For example, the idea that there are "homosexual" acts. What we are talking about is sexual legislation that affects heterosexual people just as well. There is no form of sodomy, oral copulation or genital manipulation that heterosexuals can't do and don't do with great regularity. So such laws are not just for homosexual people, it is for all people. I think such laws should be eliminated because the bedroom is a place where the police officer ought not to tread.

It must also be considered that homosexual people are not homosexual by choice: it is from something other than that. "We are what we are and we aren't what we aren't."

When alcoholics, drug addicts, prostitutes and homosexual people go to jail the evidence is very clear that they are neither deterred or rehabilitated by their stay. This is particularly true with alcoholics.

Arresting people for non-victim offenses is not a deterrent. It is a waste of money. It is not a solution. I am not saying that there is a problem in all these areas either. We must do something else that is positive, forward, constructive.

I would recommend that you read the Wolfenden Report and the San Francisco Crime Commission Report of Non-Victim Crime of 1970 and Herbert Packer's book, *The Limits of the Criminal Sanction.*

August 1972

Speech to the Resolutions Committee of the American Bar Association

Donald Lunde

This is the text of the presentation made to the Resolutions Committee of the ABA at its annual meeting in San Francisco by physician and medical professor Donald Lunde of Stanford, co-author of *Fundamentals of Human Sexuality,* in support of a proposed resolution calling on all states to pass "consensual sex" legislation. It was one of two "pro" statements given at this time, the other given by Sheriff Richard Hongisto of San Francisco. No opposing statements were aired at the committee hearing.

Sex laws clearly define what, when and where individuals may engage in sexual activity of any kind. Essentially, all sexual activity with the exception of kissing, caressing and vaginal intercourse with a lawful spouse is forbidden by law in most states of the union.

In light of this, consider the following data from the Kinsey studies of Americans in all walks of life: 85% of males have engaged in pre-marital intercourse, 59% have participated in oral-genital activity, 7% have had intercourse with prostitutes, 40% have had extramarital intercourse, 37% participated in homosexual activity at some time or other and an additional 10-15% of the population have been exclusively homosexual for prolonged periods of up to two years or longer. You add all that up, and the sex offenders in the United States number at least 95%.

It seems logical that laws that are violated with impunity, such as sex laws, by a majority of the population create disrespect for the law in the broadest sense. Furthermore, rarity of enforcement creates a problem of arbitrary police and propitorial discretion of these laws.

Much of the concern is for an examination of these laws in a psychological sense—not only for young people "living in sin" as some would have it, but, for instance, an elderly couple living together in an unmarried state to preserve their small estates and committing felony or misdemeanor by doing so.

My concern is not only for homosexuals who are susceptible to extortion and blackmail because they may have, in the words of the California penal code, "copulated the mouth of one person on the sex organ of another," but for the 60% of the heterosexual married who admittedly engage in the same activity as an expression of love in the privacy of the bedroom and who, by so doing, in California, risk a 15-year prison sentence.

Two of these laws, in particular, demonstrate the kinds of problems that are involved . . . namely, the fornication and oral copulation ("crimes against nature") statutes.

Fornication referred to sexual intercourse between unmarried adults. Illegitimate pregnancy is sufficient grounds for conviction under these laws. A 27-year-old woman in Paterson, New Jersey, recently went to court in order to obtain child support for her children. The judge, noting that she was presently pregnant and unmarried, referred her to the County Grand Jury where she was indicted and convicted of fornication. The branding of this mother of a yet unborn child as a criminal is hardly supportive of society's interest in providing a loving and wholesome environment for children—the kind of start that that child is getting by having the mother singled out and branded as a common criminal. A society which has any interest in illegitimate pregnancies should be more concerned with providing birth-control clinics, for instance. Note also that it is only the woman that is prosecuted for fornication as men are not bothered by the obviousness of pregnancy.

Most sex laws were written in another era and were based on assumptions that are no longer true today. For instance, 150 years ago when many of these were written (or there about) young people were married shortly after puberty and puberty occurred later in life. It is a biological fact, too complicated to go into at this time, that puberty is occurring about five years earlier than it was 100 years ago. For instance, today the average age for girls is 11-12 while years ago it was 16-17. Yet many young people are marrying *later* because of longer periods of education, military service, etc.

Let me mention two of these "treatments" that I personally witnessed here in California at Atascadero state hospital, a California facility that specializes in sex offenders. One, called "aversion therapy," employs painful electric shocks in conjunction with the showing of pictures of nude males. (It doesn't work, by the way, and is very unpleasant.) The second is a treatment wherein a drug is used which paralyzes all of the muscles, including the diaphragm, which induces a feeling of suffocation and impending death.

There is a strange cohersion [*sic*] in this country—to award medals to a man for killing a man in battle and to torture a man for loving another man in the privacy of his own home.

Let me close by reading the last few sentences of the Wolfenden Report which was published in Great Britain in 1957: "Unless a deliberate attempt is to be made by society, acting through the agency of the law, to equate the spirit of crime with that of sin, then there must remain an area of private morality and immorality which, in brief and crude terms, is none of the law's business. To say this is not to condone or encourage private immorality. On the contrary, it is to emphasize the personal and private nature of moral or immoral conduct, to emphasize the personal and private responsibility of the individual for his own actions and that is a responsibility which a mature agent can properly be expected to carry for himself without the threat of the punishment of the law."

1973

The Potential of Our Vision

Judy Quinlan

This presentation was given by writer Judy Quinlan to the students of a women's studies course at the University of Toronto in 1973.

I am a *lesbian.* Because I am a lesbian I can enjoy equal relationships with the people I love. I can devote my life to a career or a cause without suffering guilt for leaving a husband to cope without me. But, also because I am a lesbian, I can lose that job or alienate that cause because the people around me are threatened. I can be jailed, beaten and have my children taken away from me. I can be marked by society as a sexual deviant, as disturbed. I can be presented as a pornographic fantasy in the media of a sick society.

Because I am a *radical* lesbian, I am willing to risk ridicule, and comfort, and job and my personal freedom for the sake of my lesbian sisters. I am committed to fighting in the streets, on the job, in the courts, in the jails, in the mental institutions and in the bedrooms of the nation to free all of us who are cowering under the oppression of the heterosexual ethic.

I am a radical lesbian *feminist.* I believe in the power of groups of people, in the careful analysis and destruction of systems that oppress us. I believe that until all people are free no-one is free, that the victims of an oppressive system are those who will rise up to destroy that system, and create a just alternative.

None of the systems that oppress people are mutually exclusive. They are a complicated web of interlocking devices, which combine to form new systems and more insidious types of oppression. This is their power. They set us up against one another if we are too short-sighted to see their interrelationship. There is no gain in falling into the traps set for us where we see feminism and socialism as contradictory, or rationalism and anti-imperialism, or third world liberation and working class struggles.

Because I am a woman, I identify the first system of my oppression as the patriarchal system. This system is not primary in the oppression of all people; *there is no primary system.* How you are oppressed depends on who you are. I am a woman, I must fight the system that keeps me down for being a woman.

Patriarchy has developed in a clear historical progression since its birth six to eight thousand years ago. It is responsible for burning tens of thousands of women who dared to believe in their own power. It is responsible for veiling hundreds of thousands of women—deeming each of them the private property of some man. It is responsible for the rape of millions of women every year, and the beating and murder of countless others, because it deems all of them the public property of all men.

Patriarchy is the system responsible, and maintained by, the family, headed by the husband, mediated by the wife and controlling the children. It is responsible for stealing our sexuality and selling it back to us at a profit, for paying women half-time wages for two full-time jobs, for controlling our lives and our bodies, ignoring our health, suppressing our genius, stripping our pride, and then turning around and blaming us for our own weakness.

Another system that oppresses us is capitalism—a system whereby many people work to produce goods which are then sold for the profit of a few. Capitalism fits in very well with patriarchy. It uses patriarchal morality to keep the workers apart. It uses women as consumers, producers of goods, and reproducers of labour power. It manipulates women according to the needs of its own instabilities, so that we are a reserve to be pulled into the labour forces in time of boom or war, and pushed out in times of crisis.

What am I, as a radical lesbian feminist, doing here—and why do I identify myself as a radical lesbian feminist in the first place?

One of the basic assumptions of the patriarchy is that all women are attracted to all men by some basic biological urge. Think about it. What else would keep women in such a state of servitude? What else would explain the arrogance of patriarchy? How could it function except by assuming 1) that women need men to survive, so we'll do anything to keep them, and 2) that this is the natural order of all human societies.

So, with these assumptions, I, as a lesbian, am seen as a misfit—a genetic fault in a smoothly running biological reality. I must be abnormal, sick—I may or may not be curable. I may or may not be tolerable. But when I turn around and say *NO, I AM A STRONG PERSON,* then, my very existence challenges that order. When I say I am not a freak to be tolerated and simply given a few more civil rights and a few more psychiatric apologies; when I say that all women carry within themselves the potential of lesbianism and that this potential must be explored whether or not it is acted upon; when I say that any woman can live without men, and that women can build a movement for our own freedom without men—then I am questioning the patriarchy—*the roots of its existence.*

Before patriarchy can be changed the victims of patriarchy must rise up against it. Face it, identify it, seek it out in the recesses of our own minds and everywhere around us. The victims of patriarchy are women—that is why there is a women's movement.

To know your enemy, to understand your enemy, to want to destroy your enemy; this is not enough. When a group of people rises up to fight, the impetus comes from something more than recognizing oppression. It isn't hatred of men that will keep women fighting. It is self-pride, self-love and love of people. In the course of fighting, we discover the potential of our vision. Within the women's movement, the cry of "sisterhood is powerful" grew out of a real understanding of our capacity to love one another. We knew then, and we know even better now, what solidarity between women is all about. The strength of our struggle has been, and always will be, dependent on our capacity to believe in ourselves and each other.

January 8, 1973

Viewpoint

Bruce Voeller

This is the full text of the statement read by Dr. Bruce Voeller, then president of the Gay Activists Alliance, on New York City radio station WQXR on the program *Viewpoint,* broadcast at 6:30 p.m. on a Monday night. Copies of the statement were sent to New York officials Thomas Cuite and Saul Sharison, the Committee on Gay Rights of the Village Independent Democrats, Americans for Democratic Action, and the New York Civil Liberties Union.

How many of you know that many of the world's most famous people would be refused employment in the United States Government and armed services if they applied for jobs today?

Sappho, Gertrude Stein, Michelangelo and Leonardo
King James of England, after whom the celebrated edition of the Bible is named
Tchaikovski, Walt Whitman
Queen Christine of Sweden
James Baldwin, Jean Genet, Hermann Hesse
Kate Millett, Tennessee Williams

They would be refused jobs and apartments in many parts of New York City?

WHY?

Because of their homosexuality. Because they love someone of the same sex in a world where love is so rare.

Some 20 million Americans are homosexuals . . . nearly 1 million of us live here in NYC. We are just about the largest minority group in this city . . . but you don't know we are here because most of us look exactly like you. In fact, nearly everyone of you has a cousin, a sister or son or mother who is homosexual. Although you probably don't know it, many of your friends are gay, whether you or they are truck drivers, ministers, housewives, football players or bankers. We are an invisible minority, because you can't recognize most of us. But, if an employer wants to find out about us, he or she can, and many gay people who are very good at their jobs, lose those jobs each year, merely because of their private lives. Unlike other minorities, we are not protected by laws against unfair discrimination in employment and housing.

Senators Edward Kennedy and George McGovern have spoken out against such irrational discrimination, as have most civil rights organizations. Yet in NYC, a bill which would protect the jobs and homes of nearly a million New Yorkers, has languished for *two years* in the General Welfare Committee of the City Council. Most of the political leaders and civil rights organizations and all of the Gay organizations in this city support this bill, called Intro 475. Mayor Lindsay and Human Rights Commissioner Eleanor Norton endorse and support it. Indeed, enough of the members of the City Council have signed a petition committing their votes of support, that the bill will pass if permitted to come to a vote.

Despite this, the Committee's Chairperson, Saul Sharison, and the Majority Leader of the Council, Thomas Cuite, refuse to permit the Committee to meet so that it may vote favorably on the bill. The two men are blocking the democratic process of government. They are preventing the elected representatives of city government from meeting and voting on this bill. They are depriving nearly one million New Yorkers from the protection of laws against job discrimination. They are preventing New York from maintaining its long-standing national leadership as proud champion of the civil rights of its minority groups. Write or call your Councilman or Council woman and demand that New York catch up with such cities as San Francisco and Ann Arbor where laws similar to Intro 475 have been passed and are now in effect. Help to put an end to prejudice and irrational discrimination in New York City.

March 16, 1973

Walt Whitman: Poet of Comrades and Love

Jack Nichols

This address was given at the Twenty-Sixth Annual Conference on World Affairs at the University of Colorado; it was one of Nichols's early attempts to place Whitman as a source of gay and lesbian liberation philosophy.

I've been active in the gay liberation movement since I was in my early twenties. The intervening years have been exciting ones for me: the first picket line in front of the White House, TV and radio appearances, debates with old-fashioned psychiatrists and clergymen, confrontations with officials of the U.S. government, political campaigns, writing a book, editing a gay newspaper, and, more exciting than any of these, sharing, for the last nine years, the companionship of an extraordinary man!

This morning, in fact, is a strange sort of culmination for me. It's my 35th birthday today, and here I am far from my home on the East Coast. This is the first time I've seen the Rockies. It's a great birthday present. I'm honored to be here.

After all this time, I'm expected to be an expert of sorts on homosexuality, and on homosexually-inclined people. My work has taught me more about homosexuality than most people's jobs, I suppose.

You'd be surprised at the great changes I've seen in attitudes toward gay people in the last decade. I can remember the days when people asked me—as a public homosexual—if I had the sex organs of both sexes. Folks never tired of asking me who's the husband and who's the wife in my relationship. But all this sort of ignorance is starting to evaporate.

Now that I'm 35 I can afford to start relaxing a bit. There are thousands of younger gay liberationists and they're taking the reigns where I left off, just as I took them up when those in an earlier generation left them for me.

By yesterday's standards, gay liberation is new to the American public. It's new to media. But it's really a very old movement: one that extends back to the middle of the 19th century, or, if we were to peek into ancient times, we'd find plenty of famous homosexually-inclined poets and philosophers who let us know about their own integrity and who sang about the beauty of their homoerotic feelings.

I haven't left the gay liberation movement. I'm still interested in seeing the social reforms go full speed ahead. I think everyone will benefit—both straight and gay—when these reforms are further along the road to accomplishment. I'm still interested in civil liberties and social rights. But unless it is a special occasion, once or twice a year, I don't feel that it's necessary for me to do as much marching anymore. I'm dispensable.

Being an editor—particularly of a gay newspaper—makes me wonder if my job now isn't to introduce a sense of background and culture, of a developing community attitude—which has real roots in our history, bordering on the edge of something I might call—tenuously—gay culture. Other minority groups are seeking their roots—finding their cultural strains.

Since I've been learning to cultivate my own garden, I've unearthed cultural strains that certainly would not appeal to all homosexually-inclined people, but which *do* appeal to me, and which give me adequately, in fact, a satisfying perspective on my own sexual culture, and on that of others too. I've unearthed a giant—a cultural giant, and I'm intending to sound his name. He compliments my own vision as a homosexually-inclined man and compliments my own best sense of life.

No homosexual, no matter what his breadth of experience, can speak for all other homosexually-inclined people, just as no heterosexually-inclined person can speak for all folks with his preferences.

A friend of mine, a simplifier who likes categories, once told me that there were two types of homosexuals. He said there were Gideans—Protestant agonizers like André Gide—and there were Wildeans—after Oscar Wilde, the flamboyant. I told my friend that he'd left me out. I explained that I'm a Whitmanite. I see the American poet, Walt Whitman, as a great precursor and fountainhead of prophecies, visions and attitudes, both toward society and the self, that I feel are at the very basis of the movement I've been working to advance.

Some of you may have picked up Whitman for a moment or two. Others of you may have found his erotic love poetry difficult to comprehend. The great grandfather of British gay liberation was Edward Carpenter (who wrote *Love's Coming of Age*—the big sex revolution book of its day—1900). Carpenter was an avowed disciple of Walt Whitman. He realized long ago, as I'm now rediscovering—that Walt was talking to anyone whose sense of curiosity and whose appreciation extended to those of the same sex.

What did Walt Whitman write poems about? What was he saying? The truth is that he was not asking to be interpreted except by each individual who reads him—on an individual basis. Let me quote him:

Stop this day and night with me
and you shall possess the origin of all poems
You shall not take things at second or third hand, nor look
through the eyes of the dead,
Nor feed on spectres in books.
You shall not look through my eyes either,
nor take things from me.
You shall listen to all sides and filter them from yourself.

Walt Whitman said that with the love of comrades he would plant companionship thick as trees to make the continent indissoluble. He said that with such comrades he could make divine magnetic lands. He asked those who read his book, *Leaves of Grass,* to draw closer to one another irrespective of gender.

Now, I'm not here to argue that Walt Whitman was homosexually-inclined. It isn't necessary for a self-regulating, self-dependent person to claim any list of cultural heroes. But I would like to remind you of Whitman, to ask you to pick up *Leaves of Grass* and feel the strong strains at its core of the love of man for man. Walt Whitman, as I read him, speaks more powerfully than any writer I know about the beauty of love between those of the same sex.

Here, at the University of Colorado, it seems to me that a call for the re-examination of Walt Whitman's poems (in the light—not only of gay liberation—but of our whole changing sexual culture) is not at all out of place.

He was among the first women's liberationists. The opening lines of *Leaves of Grass* say this:

The Female equally with the Male I sing.

He was the first major writer in western literature who re-introduced a buoyant, healthy, positive celebration of sexuality in his poems. In another poem Whitman wrote:

And sexual organs and acts! Do you concentrate in me
for I am determined to tell you with courageous clear voice
to prove you illustrious.

Through me forbidden voices, voices of sexes and lusts,
voices veiled and I remove the veil, voices by me clarified
and transfigured.

My enthusiasm for *Leaves of Grass* would have been no surprise to Whitman himself. Many times in his poems he anticipated that the Leaves would be chanted by young men-loving comrades—and that centuries after his death he would still stir their hearts. He knew that men and women of the future would fall in love with him. He sings:

I will therefore let flame from me the burning fires
that were threatening to consume me.
I will lift what has too long kept down those smoldering fires.
I will give them complete abandonment.
I will write the evangel poem of comrades and love.
For who but I should understand love with all its sorrows
and joy?
And who but I should be the poet of comrades?

Whitman's hope to be understood and appreciated by his countrymen was not so misplaced as some critics ask us to believe. That he hasn't been understood is less his fault than the fault of the cultural conditioning—our lot—which has made understanding him more difficult.

But I think there are signs today that we in America are ripe for a Whitman revival.

He was a robust poet. He was totally affirmative. He said Yes to life.

Many critics have found this throbbing enthusiasm of his hard to relate to. But literary critics are seldom what one might call physical people. Too often their minds seek fulfillment while their bodies do not. Whitman was the poet of the body.

His contemporaries were still enclosed in 19th century puritanism. Emerson tried to talk Whitman out of incorporating his very frank sexual poems into *Leaves of Grass.* As perceptive a man as he was, Emerson lacked Whitman's robustness because he began from another starting point. He saw the material world—our bodies—as a manifestation of spirituality. Whitman's emphasis arrived from the opposite direction. He realized that it is through the material world—through our bodies—that we experience spiritual awareness. It was Whitman's sexual awareness that separated him from any other writer of his day, including Emerson, and gave his poems an earthy quality that the others lacked. Most writers have not yet caught up with him.

Twentieth Century poetry is full of intellectual complexity. It is concentrated, too much, I think, into cubicles of wit. It lacks physical joy. The New Puritanism, and that's where 20th Century poetry through its current traditions, has been going—is too dry, too lifeless.

No wonder Americans can't relate well to poetry. Where is the song, the incantation, the magic, the passion? Instead, 20th Century traditions are harsh, obscure, full of intellectual pride and a wry sort of despair.

But the Whitman tradition is well-suited to our rapidly growing American civilization. It throbs with a sense of magic, of primitive passion. It is a great barbaric chant. It steps over the labels: such as male and female, young and old, national and international, human and nature, and it fuses them in a magnificent harmony of rhythm, free and jubilant. It reaches out and embraces existence with a more positive joy than any other tradition of which I know.

I'm not saying that it is a specific homosexual tradition. But it includes homosexual inclinations without fear and with great love. Whitman was very much larger than his homosexuality and he simply used it as he used everything—to touch others and make them sing too! To make each person aware of his or her godlike nature.

His sexuality was blended with his whole feeling for life itself. He understood that what he felt inside himself was good—that his own body was a miracle. And in a very important sense, I think, he was a prophet of men's liberation too. Unlike many American men today, he was truly able to appreciate his own body and at the same time he could look without fear on the bodies—and into the souls—of other men and appreciate their great beauty too.

Whitman suggests a self-awareness which many beautiful men are starting to develop. Too many men, of course, are still afraid of their innate ability to appreciate their own unique beauty, and to see that other men can be beautiful too. "If I can appreciate my own beauty," they fear, "then I can see that same beauty in other men too, and that might make me queer." Fear of being thought homosexual makes many men turn away from their own selves.

But Walt Whitman was not afraid of any such implications. He was the precursor of a kind of self-awareness that almost bordered on bio-feedback. When he wrote, **"I celebrate and sing myself and what I assume you shall assume"** he meant that the great feelings for himself that he entertained are the natural property of every man and woman. I'd like to close by reading you a passage from *Leaves of Grass,* from its greatest mystical poem, "Song of Myself":

I believe in the flesh and the appetites,
Seeing, hearing, feeling are miracles, and each part and tag
of me is a miracle.

Divine I am, inside and out, and I make holy whatever I touch
or am touch'd from,
The scent of these armpits aroma finer than prayer,
This head more than churches, bibles, and all the creeds.

If I worship one thing more than another it shall be
the spread of my own body, or any part of it,
Translucent mould of me it shall be you!
Shaded ledges and rests it shall be you!
Firm masculine colter it shall be you!
Whatever goes to the tilth of me it shall be you!
You my rich blood! your milky stream pale strippings of my life!
Breast that presses against other breasts it shall be you!
My brain it shall be your occult convolutions!
Root of wash'd sweet flag! timorous pond snipe!
nest of guarded duplicate eggs! it shall be you!
Mix'd tasseled hay of head, beard, brawn it shall be you!
Sun so generous it shall be you!
Vapours lighting and shading my face it shall be you!
You sweaty brooks and dews it shall be you!
Winds whose salt-tickling genitals rub against me it shall be you!
Broad muscular fields, branches of live oak, loving lounger
in my winding paths, it shall be you!
Hands I have taken, face I have kiss'd,
mortal I have ever touch'd, it shall be you.

I dote on myself, there is that lot of me and all so luscious,
Each moment and whatever happens thrills me with joy,
I cannot tell how my ankles bend, nor whence the cause
of my faintest wish,
Nor the cause of the friendship I emit, nor the cause
of the friendship I take again.

That I walk up my stoop, I pause to consider if it really be,
A morning glory at my window satisfies me more
than the metaphysics of books.

April 14, 1973

Lesbianism and Feminism: Synonyms or Contradictions?

Robin Morgan

This is the keynote address given by Morgan at the West Coast Lesbian Feminist Conference, held in Los Angeles, California, in spring 1973.

Very Dear Sisters,

It seems important to begin by affirming who, how, and why, we are. We all know the male mass media stereotype of the Women's Movement: "If you've seen one Women's Libber—you've seen 'em all—they each have two heads, a pair of horns, and are fire-spouting, man-hating, neurotic, crazy, frigid, castrating-bitch, aggressive, Lesbian, broom-riding Witches." So I want to start by saying that this shocking stereotype is absolutely *true*. The days of women asking politely for a crumb of human dignity are over. Most men say, "But you've become so *hostile*," to which one good retort is a quote from a nineteenth century Feminist who said, "First men put us in chains, and then, when we writhe in agony, they deplore our not behaving prettily." Well, enough of that. We are the women that men have warned us about.

That settled, I want to talk about a number of difficult and dangerous themes relating to what others have variously called "The Lesbian-Straight Split." This is the first speech, talk, what-have-you, that I have ever written down and then read—and it may be the last. I have done so because the content can so easily be misunderstood or wilfully distorted, because misquoting is a common occurrence, because the risks I will take today are too vital for me to chance such misrepresentation. If there are disagreements with what I have to say, at least let them be based on what I *do* say, and not on some people's out-of-context mis-memory of what they thought I meant. So, for the record, one copy of this talk is lodged at the offices of *The Lesbian Tide,* another with sisters from *Amazon Quarterly,* and still another in a secret safe-deposit box guarded day and night by the spirits of Stanton and

Anthony, Joan and Haiviette, and a full collective of Labyris-wielding Amazons. I also want to add that the lack of a question-discussion session when I finish was decided upon not by me but by the conference organizers, for lack of time and in light of the necessity to get on with the Agenda.

Before I go any further, I feel it is also necessary to deal with who, how and why *I* am here. As far back as a month ago, I began hearing a few rumbles of confusion or criticism about my "keynoting" this conference—all from predictable people, and none, of course, expressed directly to my face. "Is she or isn't she?" was their main thrust. "Know anyone who's been to bed with her lately? Well, if we can't *prove* she's a Lesbian, then what right has she to address a Lesbian-Feminist conference?" Now, such charges hardly devastate me, having been straight-bated before. So. It is credential time once again.

I am a woman. I am a Feminist, a radical feminist, yea, a militant feminist. I am a Witch. I identify as a Lesbian because I love the People of Women and certain individual women with my life's blood. Yes, I live with a man—as my sister Kate Millett. Yes, I am a Mother—as is my sister Del Martin. The man is a Faggot-Effeminist, and we are together the biological as well as the nurturant parents of our child. This confuses a lot of people—it not infrequently confuses us. But there it is. Most of all, I am a Monster—and I am proud.

Now all of the above credentials qualify me, I feel, to speak from concrete experience on: Feminism, Lesbianism, Motherhood, "Gay Male Movements" versus Faggot-Effeminist consciousness about women, Tactics for the Women's Revolution, and a Vision of the Female Cosmos. I am an expert with the scars to prove it, having been, in my time, not only straight-bated, but also dyke-bated, red-bated, violence-bated, mother-bated, and artist-bated. As you can see, the above credentials further qualify me for being an excellent target, available not only to the male rulers but also to any woman just dying to practice—even on a sister.

But, finally, to the subject. In order to talk intelligently about the so-called "Split" it is necessary to recap history a little. In the early days of the current Women's Movement, many of us were a bit schizoid. The very first-consciousness raising session I ever went to, for example, gave me the warning. We were talking about sexuality, and I described myself as a bisexual (this was even before the birth of the first Gay Liberation Front, and long before bisexual became a naughty or cop-out word—besides, it did seem an accurate way of describing my situation). Every woman in the room moved, almost imperceptibly, an inch or so away from me. Wow, I thought. It was not the last time I was to have such an articulate reaction.

Later, with the creation of GLF, a few of us Jewish Mother types spent a lot of time running back and forth between the two movements, telling the straight women that the Lesbians weren't ogres and telling the Lesbians that the straight women weren't creeps. Simultaneously, the intense misogyny coming against Lesbians from gay men drove many women out of the "gay movement" and into the Women's Movement. There was a brief and glorious sisterhood-glazed honeymoon period among all women in our Movement. Then, those contradictions began. For example, a personal one: I had announced my Lesbian identification in *The New York Times* (which is a fairly public place, after all) in 1968, before the first GLF had been founded. Then, in 1970, one group of Radicalesbians in New York said to me, "Don't you dare call yourself a lesbian—you live with a man and have a child." Now, while I might (defensively) argue the low-consciousness logic of this, since statistically most Lesbians are married to men and have children, I had nonetheless learned one important thing from all my previous years in the Left: *guilt.* So all my knee-jerk reflexes went into action, and I obeyed. Six months later, another group of Radicalesbians confronted me. "We notice you've stopped calling yourself a Lesbian," they said, "What's the matter—you gone back in the closet? You afraid?" Meanwhile, the monosexual straight women were still inching away from my presence. Wow, I thought, repeatedly.

The lines began to be drawn, thick, heavy. Friedan trained her cannon "the Lesbian Menace." (In a show of consistent terror and hatred of Lesbians, and indeed of women, one might say, she only recently announced in *The New York Times* that the Lesbian and radical feminists in the Movement were CIA infiltrators. We met her attack with a firm political counterattack in the press, never descending to a level of personal vilification or giving the media the cat-fight which they were trying to foment.) In 1970, backlash began, starting in NOW and infecting radical feminist groups as well. The bigotry was intense and wore many faces: outright hatred and revulsion of Lesbian women; "experimentation"—using a Lesbian for an interesting experiment and then dumping her afterward: curiosity about the freaks, dismissal of another woman's particular pain if it did not fall within the "common" experience, and many other examples.

Meanwhile Lesbians, reeling from the hatred expressed by the gay male movement and the fear expressed by the Women's Liberation Movement, began to organize separately. Of course, a great many Lesbians had been in the Women's Movement since its beginning—a great many had, in fact, begun it. These included some women who were active in Daughters of Bilitis under other names, not only to keep jobs and homes and custody of their children, but also so as not to "embarrass" NOW, which they had built. In addition, a great many formerly heterosexual or asexual women were declaring themselves Lesbians, as they found the support to "Come Out" of their kitchens and communes as well as their closets. Some women *were* pressured, not necessarily, although certainly sometimes, by Lesbians. The pressure came mostly from confusion, contradictions, pulls in different directions, paths which each might have led to a united Feminism but which the Man exploited into warring factions; he was aided, of course, by the internecine hostility of any oppressed people—tearing at each other is painful, but it is after all safer than tearing at the real enemy. Oh, people *did* struggle sincerely, hour upon hour of struggle to understand and relate—but the flaw still widened to a crack and then to a split, created by our collective false consciousness. We are now teetering on the brink of an abyss but one very different from what we have been led to expect.

At present, there are supposedly two factions. On one side, those labeled heterosexual, bisexual, asexual, and celibate women. On the other, those labeled Lesbians. Not that the latter group is monolithic—far from it, although monosexual straight women can, in their fear, try to hide the bigotry behind such a belief. No, there are some Lesbians who work politically with gay men: some work politically with straight men; some work politically with other Lesbians; some work politically with only certain other Lesbians (age, race, class distinctions); some work politically with all Feminists (Lesbians, heterosexuals, etc.): and some, of course, don't work politically at all. As Laurel has pointed out in an incisive and witty article in the current *Amazon Quarterly,* there are sub-sub-sub-divisions, between gay women, Lesbians, Lesbian-Feminists, dykes, dyke-feminist, dyke-separatists, Old Dykes, butch dykes, bar dykes, and killer dykes. In New York, there were divisions between Political Lesbians and Real Lesbians and Nouveau Lesbians. Hera help the woman who is unaware of these fine political distinctions and who wanders into a meeting for the first time, thinking she maybe has a right to be there because she likes women.

Still, the same energy which created *The Ladder* almost twenty years ago (and we mourn its demise last year and we all hope for its resurrection this summer)—that same energy is now evident in the dynamism of *The Lesbian Tide,* the dedication to the fine points of struggle and contradiction in *Ain't I A Woman?,* in the analytical attempts of *The Furies,* and in the aesthetic excellence and serious political probings of the new *Amazon Quarterly,* to name only a few such publications. That energy, contorted into hiding and working under false pretenses for so long, has exploded in the beautiful and organized anger of groups like Lesbian Mothers (begun in San Francisco and now spreading across the country), to defend and protect the rights of the Lesbian and her children, and, by extension, to stand as guardian for all women who, the moment we embrace our own strength, rage and politics, face the danger of having our children seized from us physically by the patriarchy which daily attempts to kidnap their minds and souls. The development of this consciousness, so tied in with ancient Mother-Right, is, I think, of profound importance to Lesbian Mothers, all Mothers, indeed all women—it is one of the basic building blocks in our creation of a Feminist Revolution. And again, that energy, which drove my sister Ivy Bottini to almost single-handedly keep the New York NOW chapter afloat for several years (despite the ministrations of Betty Friedan) has now impelled her and other sisters to create Wollstonecraft, Inc. here in Los Angeles, the first major overground national Feminist publishing house; to say nothing of Shameless Hussy Press, Diana Press, Momma, and other small radical Lesbian-Feminist presses. That woman-loving-woman energy, freed into open expression and in fact into totally new forms of relationship *by the existence of the Feminist Movement,* has exploded in marches and demonstrations and dances and films and theater groups and crisis centers and so on and on—a whole affirmative new world within the world of women.

And yet.

A funny thing happened to me on the way to the Feminist Revolution: both Betty Friedan and Rita Mae Brown condemned me for being a "man-hater." Both *Ms.* magazine and *The Furies* began to call for alliances with men, The Furies at one point implying that Lesbians should band together with gay and straight males (preferably working-class) in a coalition against the enemy: straight women. Indeed, in one by now infamous statement, Rita Mae declared that Lesbians were the only women capable of really loving men. Now of course this did come as a shock to many a Lesbian who was obviously under the misguided impression that one had become a Lesbian because she in fact loved *women,* and was indifferent-to-enraged on the subject of men. But now that the "correct line" had fallen from heaven, one was supposed to penitently dismiss such counterrevolutionary attitudes, learning to look at them *and* other women who still clung to them with contempt. One was also supposed to place issues such as the Vietnam War, political coalition with men, warmed-over marxian class analyses, life-style differences, and other such un-lavender herrings in the path, in order to divide and polarize women. While doing all this, one was further supposed to hoist the new banner of the Vanguard. You know, the Vanguard—Lenin leading the schlemiels.

Before we get into Vanguarditis, we have to backtrack a little, take some dramamine for our nausea, and talk about men—and male influence, and male attempts to destroy the united Women's Movement. This is such an old subject that it bores and depresses me to once more have to wade through it. I feel that "man-hating" is an honorable and viable *political* act, that the oppressed have a right to a class-hatred against the *class* that is oppressing them. And although there are exceptions (in everything), i.e., men who are trying to be traitors to their own male class, most men cheerfully affirm their deadly class privileges and power. And I *hate* that *class.* I wrote my "Goodbye To All That" to the male left in 1970—and thought I was done with it. Del Martin wrote her now classic article "If That's All There Is" as a farewell to the male gay movement, soon after—and said it all again. We were both touchingly naïve if we thought that sufficient.

Because there is now upon us yet another massive wave of male interference, and it is coming, this time, from *both* gay men and their straight brothers. Boys will be boys, the old saying goes—and boys will indulge in that little thing called male bonding—and all boys in a patriarchal culture have more options and power than do any women.

Gay men first, since they were the ones we all thought were incipient allies with women, because of their own oppression under sexism. I won't go into the facts or the manners of the male-dominated Gay Liberation Movement, since Del did all that superbly and since most women have left the "Gay Movement" a long time ago. But I will, for the sake of those sisters still locked into indentured servitude there, run through a few more recent examples of the "new changing high consciousness about male supremacy" among gay organizations and gay male heavies. Are we to forgive and forget the Gay Activists Alliance dances only a few months ago (with, as usual, a token ten percent attendance by women), at which New York GAA showed stag movies of nude men raping women? Are we to forgive and forget the remark of gay leader and "martyr" Jim Fouratt, who told Susan Silverwoman, a founder of New York GLF, that she could not represent GLF at a press conference because she saw herself too much as a woman, as a Feminist? Are we to forgive the editors of the gay male issues of *Motive* magazine for deliberately setting women against women, deliberately attempting to exacerbate what they see as the Lesbian-Straight Split, deliberately attempting to divide and conquer—are we to forgive the following:

Once, when I was telling one of the Motive *editors, you Roy Eddy, about the estimated nine million Wicca (witches) who were burned to death during the Middle Ages—something that appeared to be news to you—you paused for a moment, and then asked me, "But how many of those nine million women were actually lesbians?" For a moment, I missed your meaning completely as a variety of sick jokes raced through my mind. "How many of the six million Jews were Zionists; how many of the napalmed Indochinese babies could be said to have lived outside the nuclear family?"*

Then it hit me: you had actually expressed a particle of your intense hatred for all women *by asking how many of the nine million were lesbians,* so that you would know how many of these victims to mourn, *because YOU DIDN'T OBJECT TO WHAT WAS DONE TO THE OTHER WOMEN! This is as close as I have ever heard a man come to saying in so many words that he didn't object to men torturing and incinerating millions of women (provided only that they met his standards for burnability).*

—this is a quote from the second issue of *Double-F, A Magazine of Effeminism,* in which even the faggot-effeminist males declare *their* Declaration of Independence from Gay Liberation and all other Male Ideologies.

Or are we, out of the compassion in which we have been positively forced to *drown* as women, are we yet again going to defend the male supremacist yes obscenity of male transvestitism? How many of us will try to explain away—or permit into our organizations, even, men who deliberately re-emphasize gender roles, and who parody female oppression and suffering as "camp"? Maybe it seems that we, in our "liberated" combat boots and jeans aren't being mocked. No? Then it is "merely" our mothers, and *their* mothers, who had no other choice, who wore hobbling dresses and torture-stiletto-heels to survive, to keep jobs, or to keep husbands because *they* themselves could *get* no jobs. No, I will not call a male "she;" thirty-two years of suffering in the androcentric society, and of surviving, have earned me the name "woman"; one walk down the street by a male transvestite, five minutes of his being hassled (which *he* may enjoy), and then he dares, he *dares* to think he understands our pain? No, in our mothers' names and in our own, we must not call him sister. We know what's at work when whites wear blackface; the same thing is at work when men wear drag.

And what of the straight men, the rulers, the rapists, the right-on radicals? What of the men of the Socialist Workers' Party, for example, who a short two years ago refused membership to all homosexual people on the grounds that homosexuality was a decadent sickness, an evil of capitalism, a perversion that must be rooted out in all "correct socialist thinking"—who now, upon opportunistically seeing a large movement out there with a lot of bodies to organize like pawns into their purposes, speedily change their official line (but not their central-committee attitude on homosexuality) and send "their" women out to teach these poor sheep some real politics? Are we to forgive, forget, ignore? Or struggle endlessly through precious energy-robbing hours with these women, because they are after all *women, sisters,* even if they're collaborating with a politics and a party based on straight white male rule? We must save our struggle for elsewhere. But it hurts—*because* they are women.

And this is the tragedy. That the straight men, the gay men, the transvestite men, the male *politics,* the male styles, the male attitudes toward sexuality are being arrayed once more against us, and they are, in fact, making new headway this time, using women as their standard-bearers.

Every woman here knows in her gut the vast differences between her sexuality and that of any patriarchally trained male's—gay or straight. That has, in fact, always been a source of *pride* to the Lesbian community, even in its greatest suffering. That the emphasis on genital sexuality, objectification, promiscuity, non-emotional involvement, and tough invulnerability, were the *male* style, and that we, as women, placed greater trust in love, sensuality, humor, tenderness, strength, commitment. Then what but male style is happening when we accept the male transvestite who chooses to wear women's dresses and make-up, but sneer at the female who is still forced to wear them for survival? What is happening when "Street Fighting Woman," a New York *all-woman* bar band, dresses in black leather and motorcycle chains, and sings and plays a lot of the Rolling Stones, including the high priest of sadistic cock-rock Jagger's racist, sexist song "Brown Sugar"—with lines like "Old slaver knows he's doin' all right/hear him whip the women just around midnight . . ." What is happening when, in a mid-west city with a strong Lesbian-Feminist community, men raped a woman in the university dormitory, and murdered her by the repeated ramming of a broom-handle into her vagina until she died of massive internal hemorrhage—and the Lesbian activists there can't relate to taking any political action pertaining to the crime because, according to one of them, there was no evidence that the victim was a Lesbian? But the same community can, at a women's dance less than a week later, proudly play Jagger's recorded voice singing "Midnight Rambler"—a song which glorifies the Boston Strangler?

What has happened when women, in escaping the patriarchally enforced role of noxious "femininity" adopt instead the patriarch's *own* style, to get drunk and swaggering just like one of the boys, to write of tits and ass as if a sister were no more than a collection of chicken parts, to spit at the lifetime commitment of other Lesbian couples, and refer to them contemptuously as "monogs?" For the record, the anti-monogamy line originated with men, Leftist men, Weathermen in particular, in order to guilt-trip the women in their "alternative culture" into being more available victims of a dominance-based gang-rape sexuality. And from where but the Left male "hip" culture have we been infected with the obsession to anti-intellectualism and downward mobility? Genuinely poor people see no romanticism in their poverty; those really forced into illiteracy hardly glorify their condition. The oppressed want *out* of that condition—and it is contemptuous of real people's real pain to parasitically imitate it, and hypocritical to play the more-oppressed-than-thou game instead of ordering our lives so as to try and meet our basic and just needs, so that we can get on with the more important but often forgotten business of making a Feminist Revolution.

What about the life-style cop-out? The one invented by two straight white young males, Jerry Rubin and Abbie Hoffman, for the benefit of other unoppressed straight white young males? What about the elite isolation, the incestuous preoccupation with one's own clique or group or commune, one's own bar/dance/tripping, which led one Lesbian to announce that the revolution has already been won, that she isn't compelled, like the rest of us, to live in a man's world anymore? As Jeanne Cordova has written in *The*

Lesbian Tide, "An example of these politics is Jill Johnston's calling for tribes of women capable of sustaining themselves independent of the male species. How very beautiful! Truth, justice, and the womanly way! How very unreal." And Cordova is right in pointing out that this is the "personal solution" error—the deadly trap into which so many heterosexual women have fallen. It should be obvious how painfully much everyone wants even a little happiness, peace, joy in her life—and should have that right. But to remain convinced that your own personal mirage is a real oasis while a sandstorm is rising in the desert is both selfish and suicidal. There is a war going on, sisters. Women are being killed. And the rapist doesn't stop to ask whether his victim is straight or Lesbian.

But the epidemic of male style among women doesn't stop there. No, it is driving its *reformist* wedge through our ranks as well: women breaking their backs working for McGovern (only to have him laugh in their faces): women in the Lesbian community especially breaking their backs to elect almost invariably *male* gay legislators, or lobbying to pass bills which will, in practice, primarily profit *men*. Myself, I have never been able to get excited over Tokenism, whether it was Margaret Chase Smith in the Senate or Bernardine Dohrn in the Weather Underground, let alone a few women to give GAA a good front (which women, by the way, are finally getting wise to and leaving), or to serve as periodic good niggers for the cheap porn reportage of *The Advocate, Gay, Gay Sunshine,* and the like.

Susan Silverwoman, a New York-based Lesbian Feminist active for years in the Women's Movement and at one time in GLF, has written a moving and courageous paper called "Finding Allies: The Lesbian Dilemma" which is available for 25 cents by writing to Labyris Books, 33 Barrow Street, New York City 10014. In it she writes, "Men have traditionally maintained power over women by keeping us separated. Gay men capitalized on the split between feminists and lesbians by suggesting and insisting that we [lesbians] were somehow, basically different from straight women . . . Gay men preferred to think of us not as women, but as female gay men." She goes on to say, "It is imperative that we identify with the total feminist issue . . . if we continue to define straight women as the enemy, rather than sisters . . . we rob from ourselves a movement which must be part of ourselves. We are choosing false allies when we align politically with gay men who can never understand the female experience and who, as men, have a great deal of privilege to lose by a complete liberation of women. Whether or not straight feminists come out, as potential lesbians they are far more likely to understand out experience."

Language itself is one powerful barometer of influence. More and more women use Lesbian proudly in self-description, calling on the history of that word, dating from an age and an island where women were great artists and political figures. Why do *any* of us still use "gay" to describe ourselves at all—that trivializing, male-invented, male defining term? If we are serious about our politics, then we must be responsible about the ways in which we communicate them to others, creating new language when necessary to express new concepts. But the sloppy thinking and lazy rhetoric of the straight and gay male movements pollutes our speech, and when Jill Johnston in one column claims Betty Friedan as a Lesbian and then, a few months later, after Friedan's attack in the *Times,* calls Friedan a man—I for one get confused. And angry. Because the soggy sentimentality of the first statement and the rank stupidity of the second *mean nothing politically.* The point is, very regrettably, that Friedan *is* a woman. And can stand as one of many examples of the insidious and devastating effect [of] male *politics.*

There *is* a war going on. And people get damaged in a war, badly damaged. Our casualties are rising. To say that any woman has escaped—or can escape—damage in this day on this planet is to march under the self-satisfied flags of smug false consciousness. And get gunned down anyway for her pains.

Personally, I detest "vanguarditis." I never liked it in the Left, and I find it especially distasteful weaseling its way into the Women's Movement. I think that if anything like a "vanguard" exists at all, it continually shifts and changes from group to group within a movement, depending on the specific strategies and contradictions that arise at given times, and on which groups are best equipped and placed to meet and deal with them—when and if called for [by] the movement *as a whole.* The responsibility of a vanguard, by the way, is to speak from, for, and to *all* of the people who gave it birth. Lesbian Nation cannot be the Feminist solution, much less a vanguard, when it ignores these facts. And it won't do to blame the straight women who wouldn't cooperate—after all, it is the *vanguard's* responsibility as leadership to hear messages in the silence or even the hostility of *all* its people, and to reply creatively, no matter how lengthy or painful that dialogue is. A willingness to do this—and then to *act* on the message—is what *makes* the vanguard the vanguard.

I don't like more-radical-than-thou games any better than more-oppressed-than-thou games. I don't like credentials games, intimidation-between-women games, or "you are who you sleep with" games. I don't like people being judged by their class background, their sexual preference, their race, choice of religion, marital status, motherhood or rejection of it, or any other vicious standard of categorization. I hate such judgments in the male power system, and I hate them in the Women's Movement. If there must be judgments at all, let them be not on where a woman is coming *from,* but on what she is moving *toward;* let them be based on her seriousness, her level of risk, her commitment, her endurance.

And by those standards, yes, there could be a Lesbian vanguard. I think it would be women like Barbara Grier and Phyllis Lyon and Del Martin and Sten Russell, and others like them who, at the height of the Fifties' McCarthyism, stood up and formed a Lesbian civil-rights movement, and whose courage, commitment and staying power are ignored by the vulgar minds of certain younger women, newly Lesbian from two months or two years back, who presume to dismiss such brave women as "oldies" or "life-style straights" or, again, "hopeless monogs."

There is a new smell of fear in the Women's Movement. It is in the air when groups calling themselves killer-dyke-separatists trash Lesbian Feminists who work with that anathema, straight women—trash these Lesbian Feminists as "pawns, dupes, and suckers-up to the enemy." It is in the air when Peggy Allegro writes in *Amazon Quarterly* that "at a certain point, flags can begin to dominate people." For instance, women are oppressed by the flag of the freak feminist dyke. There are all kinds of rules, shoulds and shouldn'ts, in this community, that result because of the image's power. We must beware the tendency to merely impose as new hierarchy . . . a new ideal ego image to persecute people. It is in the air when ultra-egalitarianism usurps organic collectivity, or when one woman is genuinely scared to confront another about the latter's use of "chick" to describe her lover. It was in the air when I trembled to wrench the Stones' record from the phonograph at a women's dance and when I was accused of being up-tight, a bring-down, puritanical, draggy, and of course, doubtless, a hung-up man-hating "straight" *for doing that.* The words are familiar, but the voices used to be male. And the smell of fear was in my gut, writing this talk, and is in my nostril now, risking the saying of these things, taking a crazy leap of faith that our own shared and potentially ecstatic womanhood will bind across all criticism—and that a lot more Feminists in the Lesbian Movement will come out of their closets today.

Because polarization does exist. Already. And when I first thought about this talk, I wanted to call for unity. But I cannot. I am struck dumb before the dead body of a broomhandle-raped and murdered woman, and anyway, my voice wouldn't dent the rape-sound of the Rolling Stones. So instead, my purpose in this talk here today is to call for further polarization, but on different grounds.

Not the Lesbian-Straight Split, nor the Lesbian-Feminist Split, but the Feminist-Collaborator Split.

The war outside, between women and male power, is getting murderous; they are trying to kill us, literally, spiritually, infiltratively. It is time, past time, we drew new lines and knew which women were serious, which women were really committed to loving women (whether that included sexual credentials or not), and, on the other side, which women thought Feminism meant pure fun, or a chance to bring back a body count to their male Trot party leaders, or those who saw Feminist Revolution as any particular life-style, correct class line, pacifist-change-your-head-love-daisy-chain, or easy lay. We know that the personal is political. But if the political is *solely* personal, then those of us at the barricades will be in big trouble. And if a woman isn't there when the crunch comes—and it is coming—then I for one won't give a damn whether she is at home in bed with a woman, a man, or her own wise fingers. If she's in bed at all at that moment, others of us are in our coffins. I'd appreciate the polarization now instead of then.

I am talking about the rise of attempted gynocide. I am talking about survival. Susan Stein, a Lesbian Feminist with a genius for coining aphorisms, has said, "Lesbianism is in danger of being co-opted by Lesbians." Lesbians are a minority. Women are a majority. And since it is awfully hard to be a Lesbian without being a woman first, the choice seems pretty clear to me.

There are a lot of women involved in that war out there, most of them not even active in the Women's Movement yet. They include the hundreds of thousands of housewives who created and sustained the meat boycott in the most formidable show of women's strength in recent years. Those women, Feminists or not, were moving *because* of Feminism—such a nationwide women's action would have been thought impossible five years ago. They are mostly housewives, and mothers, and heterosexuals. There are asexual and celibate women out there, too, who are tired of being told that they are sick. Because this society has said that everybody should fuck a lot, and too many people in the Women's Movement have echoed, "Yeah, fuck with women or even with men, but for god's sake *fuck* or you're *really* perverted." And there are also genuine functioning bisexuals out there. I'm not referring to people who have used the word as a coward's way to avoid dealing honestly with homosexuality, or to avoid commitment. We all know *that* ploy. I agree with Kate Millett when she says that she "believes that all people are inherently bisexual"—and I also know that to fight a system one must identify with the *most* vulnerable aspect of one's oppression—and women are put in prison for being Lesbians, not bisexuals or heterosexuals *per se.* So that is why I have identified myself as I have—in the *Times* in 1968 and here today. Although the Man will probably want to get *me* for hating *men* before he gets me for loving *women.*

We have enough trouble on our hands. Isn't it way past time we stopped *settling* for blaming each other, stopped blaming heterosexual women and middle-class women and married women and Lesbian women and white women and any woman for the structure of sexism, racism, classism, and ageism, that *no* woman is to blame for because we have none of us had the *power* to *create* those structures. They are patriarchal creations, not ours. And if we are collaborating with *any* of them for *any* reason, we must begin to stop. The time is short, and the self-indulgence is getting dangerous. We must stop settling for anything less than we deserve.

All women have a right to each other as women. All women have a right to our sense of ourselves as a People. All women have a right to live with and make love with *whom we choose when we choose.* We have a right to bear and raise children if we choose, and *not* to if we don't. We have a right to freedom and yes, power. Power to change our entire species into something that might for the first time approach being human. We have a right, each of us, to a Great Love.

And this is the final risk I will take here today. By the right to a great love I don't mean romanticism in the Hollywood sense, and I don't mean a cheap joke or cynical satire. *I mean a great love*—a committed, secure, nurturing, sensual, aesthetic, revolutionary, holy, ecstatic love. That need, *that right,* is at the heart of our revolution. It is in the heart of the woman stereotyped by others as being a butch bar dyke who cruises for a cute piece, however much she herself might laugh at the Lesbian couple who have lived together for decades. It is in their hearts too. It is in the heart of the woman who jet-sets from one desperate heterosexual affair to another. It is in the heart of a woman who wants to find—or stay with—a man she can love and be loved by in what she has a right to demand are non-oppressive ways. It is in the heart of every woman here today, if we dare admit it to ourselves and *recognize* it in each other, and in *all* women. It is each her right. Let no one, female or male, of whatever sexual or political choice, dare deny that, for to deny it is to *settle.* To deny it is to speak with the words of the real enemy.

If we can open ourselves *to* ourselves and each other, as women, only then can we begin to fight for and create, in fact *reclaim,* not Lesbian Nation or Amazon Nation—let alone some false State of equality—but a real Feminist Revolution, a proud gynocratic *world* that runs on the power of women. Not in the male sense of power, but in the sense of a power plant—producing energy. And to each, that longing for, the right to, great love, filled in reality, for all women, and children, and men and animals and trees and water and all life. An exquisite diversity in unity. That world breathed and exulted on this planet some twelve thousand years ago, before the patriarchy arose to crush it.

If we risk this task then, our pride, our history, our culture, our past, our future, all vibrate before us. Let those who will dare, begin.

In the spirit of that task, I want to end this talk in a strange and new, although time-out-of-mind-ancient manner. Earlier, I "came out" in this talk as a Witch, and I did not mean that as a solely political affiliation. I affirm the past and the present spirit of the Wicca (the anglo-saxon word for Witch, or wise woman), affirm it not only in the smoke of our nine million martyrs, but also in the thread of *real* woman-power and *real* Goddess-worship dating back beyond Crete to the dawn of the planet. In the ruling male culture, they have degraded our ritual by beginning conferences and conventions with a black-coated male, sometimes in full priestly drag, nasally droning his stultifying pronouncements to the assemblage. Let us reclaim our own for ourselves, then, and in that process, also extend an embrace to those Lesbians who, because they go to church, are held in disrepute by counterculture Lesbians. And to those women of *whatever* sexual identification who kneel in novenas or murmur in quiet moments to, oh irony, a male god for alleviation of the agony caused by male supremacy.

The short passage I am about to read is from "The Charge of the Goddess," still used reverently in living Wiccan Covens, usually spoken by the High Priestess at the initiation of a new member. I ask that each woman join hands with those next to her. I ask your respect for the oldest faith known to human beings, and for the ecstatic vision of freedom that lies hidden in each of your own precious, miraculous brains.

Listen to the words of the Great Mother. She says:

"Whenever ye have need of anything, once in the month, and better it be when the moon is full, then shall ye assemble in some secret place . . . to these I will teach things that are yet unknown. AND YE SHALL BE FREE FROM ALL SLAVERY . . . Keep pure your highest ideal; strive ever toward it. LET NAUGHT STOP YOU NOR TURN YOU ASIDE . . . *Mine is the cup of the wine of life and the cauldron of Ceridwen . . . I am the Mother of all living, and my love is poured out upon the earth . . . I am the beauty of the Green Earth, and the White Moon among the stars, and Mystery of the Waters, AND THE DESIRE IN THE HEART OF WOMAN . . . Before my face, let thine innermost self be enfolded in the raptures of the Infinite . . . Know the Mystery, that if that which thou seekest thou findest not within thee, thou wilt never find it without thee . . . For behold, I HAVE BEEN WITH THEE FROM THE BEGINNING. And I await you now."*

Dear Sisters,

As we in the Craft say, blessed be.

May 9, 1973

Stop It, You're Making Me Sick

Ronald Gold

This is the text of a paper presented by Gold, of the Gay Activists Alliance of New York City, to the convention of the American Psychiatric Association in Honolulu, Hawaii, on May 9, 1973.

At one point, we were "possessed by the devil." Somewhat later, we were "sinners" and "criminals." Now enlightenment is here. "Sick" is the epithet of choice for Gay men and women.

Just two years ago, I partly believed that epithet as applied to myself, or shunted it aside as irrelevant. But since I've joined the Gay Liberation Movement, I've taken the opportunity to read some of the theoretical works, and to study their application, and I've come to an unshakable conclusion: the illness theory of homosexuality is a pact of lies concocted out of the fundamentalist myths of a patriarchal society for the *political* purpose of perpetuating the current societal ethic.

To state it another way: Your profession of psychiatry—dedicated to making sick people well—is the cornerstone of a system of oppression that makes people sick.

I think I can prove these grandiose statements, and I'd like to begin by offering you a few facts.

In New York City, where I come from, the telephone company has an official policy: if you're Gay you're not hired, and if they find out you are, no matter how long or how well you've worked, you're fired. That's one among many. Just in the past few weeks, a young man was fired as an art teacher just for being Gay. A friend of mine revealed herself as a lesbian on *The David Susskind Show* and was fired from her long-term job as a counselor at a girl's club. She was good at her job.

That's New York, where attitudes are supposed to be liberal. Around the country there's hardly a private employer, landlord, bar owner, insurance company or bonding agency; hardly an agency of government (to which I pay taxes if I can find a job) which doesn't have an openly declared discriminatory policy. And the Federal Government is the worst, culminating in the military. I have a choice: stay out of the service and risk the chance that my file will be used against me for the rest of my life, or go into the service and face a triple risk. Dishonorable discharge. No veteran's rights. And the chance that my file will be used against me for the rest of my life.

Some discriminators do it covertly, like the employment agency that writes HCF for "High Class Fairy" on my application to make sure I don't get a job. Or the apartment complex which won't rent to two members of the same sex unless they're blood related.

They needn't bother to be devious. Everything they do is perfectly legal. Except for three places in the United States (Ann Arbor and East Lansing, Michigan; and San Francisco, where it applies to municipal employment only), there are no laws offering homosexuals the same civil rights as everybody else. Race. Creed. Color. Gender. Age. National Origin. Physical Handicap. Only sexual orientation is missing.

Why haven't our legislators passed such laws? One reason is that they've got other laws on the books, which only eight of our states have seen fit to repeal. These laws make it a crime for me, even in private, to perform what the law calls sodomy and I call acts of love. "Why," ask the legislators, "should we protect the civil rights of criminals?"

You'd think the courts would strike down the sodomy laws, as they did the abortion statutes, as violations of the right to privacy. You'd think that they'd rule that I'm entitled to equal protection under existing civil rights laws. But they haven't, and I'm not confident that they will, considering that judges are themselves discriminators; denying me the right to adopt children, to keep or even visit my own.

Just two quotes will give you the rationale for this sorry record. The Defense Department says that it revoked the security clearance of two long-term employees because "homosexuality is a mental illness." *The Wall Street Journal* isn't sure if a Gay lawyer should practice at the bar, because "We see every reason to believe that society generally and quite correctly continues to see homosexuality as a sexual aberration."

All that preamble, and that's all there is? No matter how sick I am (I can hear you saying) I ought to know that this isn't your position at all. I ought to know that you support my right to have any job. Or almost any. And that you favor repeal of the sodomy laws. You don't even have a problem about my working with kids. I could certainly visit my own, if I don't bring my lover along. All you do is say I'm gay and haven't taken the cure, and it's not your fault if others make sure that poor sick me doesn't get a chance to menace our youth by teaching algebra in junior high, or they make me go back twice a year for a "psychiatric evaluation" of whether it's safe for me to drive a New York City cab.

Almost right on for you. But ask yourselves some questions. If you were an employer, a landlord or a judge, would I get a job (apartment, child) if you thought I had "wild self-damaging tendencies" and "onslaughts of paranoid ideation" (Dr. Charles Socarides) or "grossly defective peer-group relatedness" and "rage reactions disproportionate to the provocation" (Dr. Irving Bieber)? If you were a legislator, would you vote for my full civil rights—or even let me alone in my bedroom—if you thought that my character was "a mixture of the following elements: masochistic provocation and injustice-collecting; defensive malice; flippancy covering depression and guilt; hypernarcissism and hyper superciliousness; refusal to acknowledge accepted standards in non-sexual matters; and general unreliability, of a more or less psychopathic nature" (Dr. Edmund Bergler)?

You're shaking your heads again. That must be because you realize that these descriptions are based entirely on studies of patients in treatment; that they don't apply to most of your homosexual patients, and do apply to many of the heterosexuals. You're probably aware that all non-patient studies of homosexuals show most of us to be free of such pathology. If you think I'm sick at all, you probably hold to some non-psychiatric theological construct like Dr. Bieber's extraordinary *assumption* that "heterosexuality is the biologic norm and that, unless interfered with, all individuals are heterosexuals." Or you just want to keep me listed under "Sexual Deviations" while you think it over for a while.

It doesn't matter *how* I'm described as sick. To be viewed as psychologically disturbed in our society is to be thought of, and treated, as a second-class citizen. And don't worry that nobody reads the "experts" books; there's no shortage of popularizers ready to spread the word.

Take advice-giver Ann Landers, who was asked by a Gay man why he wasn't allowed to hold hands or dance with his lover in public. She said, "Why can't members of the same sex proclaim their love as heterosexuals do? Because homosexuality is unnatural . . . a sickness, a dysfunction. For 18 years, I have been pleading for compassion and understanding and equal rights, and I will continue to do so. But I do not believe homosexual activity is normal behavior." So much for equal rights.

If the connection between my rights and your diagnosis still eludes you, I call your attention to the only speech at the last American Medical Association convention which received broad media coverage; psychiatrist Robert McDevitt's statement that political organizations like the Gay Activists Alliance are a threat to mental health. Only a few weeks later, Fordham University refused to recognize a campus Gay-rights group because "the expressed professional views of medical organizations" state that such groups are "not beneficial to the normal development of our students."

Yes, Fordham is a Church-connected school. But even the Church has borrowed your rhetoric. "A sexual relationship between two persons of the same sex is always seriously wrong." Says *New York Archdiocesan* newspaper, "A grave disorder which cannot be condoned." I think I'll repeat that: "A disorder which cannot be condoned."

If you still can't see that you're denying me my rights by labeling me with a pejorative term, you've got to admit that being a second-class citizen is not good for my mental health.

That's not the worst thing about your diagnosis. The worst is that Gay people believe it.

Imagine yourself at, let's say, 14. You already know that the kids on your block think that the love you feel is a dirty joke. Then you discover what the "experts" call it: "infantile sex"; "inevitable emotional bankruptcy"; "a masquerade of life, filled with destruction and self-deceit." That's what I found out, and it's even easier to do so today. All you have to do if you're beginning to discover you're Gay is to look yourself up in your high-school hygiene book. You're right there, along with the rapists, under "The Misuses of Sex."

I was leafing through the *American Handbook of Psychiatry* in preparation for my visit here, and I came upon a fascinating article, entitled "The Anxiety States," by Dr. Isadore Portnoy. What Dr. Portnoy says is that anxiety is "a discrepancy between the individual's capacities and the demands made on him which makes self-realization impossible." He says that a person experiences anxiety "when values essential to his existence, his sense of being, and his identity are threatened." And he adds that *Neurotic anxiety* in a particular individual stems "most particularly from his lack of feeling of wholeness, derived from his dissociation from, denial, repression, externalization of and active alienation from major aspects of his being, particularly the perceptual, sexual and organic."

What is more likely to alienate you from, let's say, the sexual part of yourself, than to be incessantly told that that part of you is sick? Nothing makes you sick like believing that you're sick. Nothing is more crippling than thinking that you're an emotional cripple, forever condemned to a personal status below those "whole" people who run the world.

Dr. Portnoy lists some of the characteristics of the person suffering from neurotic anxiety. Behavior dictated by compulsiveness. No firm sense of identity as expressed in compulsive needs for dependency and symbiosis, aggression and domination, attachment and isolation. An extreme undervaluation of one's own assets and possibilities, along with an equally extreme illusion of one's own perfection, superiority and invulnerability. All of which leads to intense self-hate.

Does the list sound familiar? It ought to. It's the "expert's" description of "the typical homosexual" (That is, the typical homosexual male in psychiatric treatment).

Dr. Bieber says, "it is a tribute to human adaptability that sexuality can be organized in such a way that arousal can occur in response to another man." I say it's a tribute to human adaptability that all of us who are Gay don't suffer from "the traits of victimization" that Dr. Evelyn Hooker identifies as those most characteristic of those homosexuals who are neurotic. I say it's a tribute to the love we feel for members of our own sex, and to the pleasure we derive from that love, that all of us haven't gone bats.

I didn't make it. And let me be the first to say that it wasn't entirely your fault. I just think you pushed me over the edge. I trace my first bouts with anxiety to the period when most of my gay friends had decided that the "playing around" we'd been doing together was "childish" and "unmanly"—and I didn't want it to stop. So I went to my older sister and said something like, "I think I'm a homosexual."

Now Dr. Socarides says "whenever an adolescent confides that 'I know I'm a homosexual, I just feel it', having acquired his identity through inner knowledge, this verbalization constitutes an immediate indicator for therapy." (Hear that, Dr. Portnoy—acquisition of identity is an immediate indicator for therapy.) So my sister sent me to a psychiatrist.

Dr. Portnoy says that the aim of therapy is "to help the individual become increasingly aware of and able to own, experience and be involved in his whole being." All I remember is that I was shot full of sodium pentathal [*sic*] and frightened out of my wits. If he'd told me that I was a homosexual, it might have come as a welcome relief. But welcome relief of this sort, says Dr. Socarides, is "a bad prognostic sign requiring treatment in adolescence."

So it took me bit longer to "come out"—that is to recognize myself as a member of an identifiable minority group. When I did, a year later at the age of 15, I was sent to another psychiatrist. He was a kindly man, and he gave me his diagnosis of my illness: homosexuality.

I switched to a school in California and a few good things happened to me there. I got into a "beat generation" atmosphere that made it possible for me to be open about my sexuality, and to avoid what Dr. Portnoy calls "the emphasis on living up to standards and being beyond criticism, not only for the sake of status advancement but also for the purpose of safety from the hostility of others." I met a number of young Gay men who, like myself and the vast majority of Gay people I've met since, hadn't the faintest desire to assume exclusively "active" or "passive" roles, either in public or in bed. I had a number of pleasurable heterosexual ones.

But having straight friends didn't help, not when my psychology text kept reminding me I was sick. I was sure about my gender, but that didn't help either; I still doubted whether homosexuals could compete in post-college society like "real men." Even making it with women didn't help, since I intuited then what I now state as a political reality; you can't be a little bit Gay in our society, no more than you can be a little bit Black.

Experts to the contrary once again, I know very few Gay men who hate or avoid women, or are "frightened of their genitals." I'm not at all frightened of women. Indeed, I'm struck by the small number of women here, and I would have liked to have seen a woman invited to represent half the people we're talking about. I'd like to see those of you whose vision of Gay people is two males fondling each other at a public urinal try to use that one to prove the pathology of Lesbians. I'd like to see the incredibly small amount of literature on gay women expanded, and purged of such drivel as "castration anxiety connected with the surrender of the body to union in the sexual act can prevent heterosexuality in either sex."

It's amazing to me now that I could have kept on reading such nonsense about homosexuality when so little of it had anything to do with my life. But something always seemed to ring true. At 19, I hadn't met any of the Gay couples I know now, who've lived together for years. The longest affair I'd had was with a woman, and the love I'd shared with other men was always brief. It seemed to me that this was just as the "experts" had described it, and I almost believed Dr. Bergler's notion that my persistence in going to bed with men was nothing but "self-created troublemaking" caused by my "unconscious wish to suffer." I began to think that my love *was* "childish" and "sick," and I asked myself, "How can I love someone who, if he loves me, must be just as sick?"

Like most of your Gay patients, that was the way I felt when I sought out a couple of new psychiatrists. I learned one thing from them; that a part of me didn't want to give up was something that needed to be excised. I was ready for what Dr. Portnoy calls "psychic annihilation," the choice "neither to fight nor to flee but rather to shrink, to vanish as a self."

If you're looking for a quick but expensive way to vanish as a self, try heroin. I did, with what I recall as near-deliberation, and I lived like a junkie, with periods off for hepatitis and jail, for about five years. Until I got worn out from psychic annihilation, and was faced with the choice between actual annihilation and another psychiatrist.

This time my sister came up with a man who decided I wasn't a "real junkie" because I was middle class and Gay (this was 20 years ago), and decided I was a likely candidate for the Menninger Clinic.

It was a good place, and I had a good therapist, Dr. Harvey Schloessner. I got out of the hospital and finished college. I stopped being frightened without the support of drugs. I learned to handle self-damaging impulses as they arose. I learned I could do a lot of simple, "masculine" things I'd thought I couldn't. I regained a sense of myself I hadn't had since grade school, that I could be "a leader of men." By the end of three years, I'd put back a lot of the missing pieces of my "whole" self.

But I hung around in treatment for two years more—and almost all we talked about was sex. I was convinced that an essential part of my "cure" would be a change in my sexual orientation, and Dr. Schloessner did nothing to dissuade me from that view.

He didn't take the unsubtle tack of Dr. Bieber, who informs his patients that he has "no judgmental bias" against homosexuality, merely that "homosexuality is incompatible with a reasonably happy life" and that "heterosexuality is desirable for many reasons to be elucidated as the analysis proceeds." Rather, he employed the behaviorist techniques of Dr. Lawrence Haterrer, your latest well-publicized "expert" in the field, who takes the pragmatic view that while homosexuality itself is not an illness, it "most certainly is a sickness when it makes the person feel sick." He tells his patients that the choice is up to them, and then proceeds to brainwash them with a series of rewards and punishments; encouragement for heterosexual responses and reinforcement of guilt for homosexual ones.

For instance, I had a brief and pleasant affair with a young woman who happened to be a social worker at the Clinic, and during the course of it, Dr. Schloessner's approval was tempered by only brief reference to the rule against staff-patient relationships. But a few months later, I had a similarly brief and equally pleasant involvement with a young man, also on the staff. This time the rule was staunchly invoked and my permission was asked to report the incident to the head of the hospital, for a decision on whether my friend should be fired.

I knew him to be one of the most competent, perceptive—and loving—people around, and I was certain that in his years on the staff, he'd never once made or accepted advances from a patient under his care. I'm happy to say I refused my permission. But I'm sorry to say that even after my friend was fired, a month or so later, I never told Dr. Schloessner (or myself) how angry I was, and I dropped back instead into a self-lacerating period of non-function. I wasn't able to perceive that respect for me as a man had been knocked down by disrespect for an important part of my bag. I wasn't able to see how directly your diagnosis is used to violate our civil rights.

At last I was told that there wasn't much more I could accomplish in treatment. I was ready to leave. Ordinarily, that would have meant that I was well. But it seemed to me that I'd done half a job; that one very important part, or symptom, of my illness hadn't been touched. I believed that I was doomed to a loveless, lonely life, and the best I hoped for was to sublimate my sick sexuality in some rewarding work.

I came back to New York, and I found work. But I also found that my idea of what was in store for me has been dead wrong; that all I'd needed was to like myself a little better, to believe that someone else could love me. I discovered, like many a heterosexual neurotic at the completion of successful treatment, that I didn't need to "test" my partner at the beginning of an affair. I discovered that I knew how to make the first move of reconciliation, and to generously accept my lover's first move. And I was lucky enough to meet a young man whose image of himself had never been corroded.

We lived together for 12 years, and we had a good, happy life for the most part. We fought, but not, as far as I can tell, appreciably more than our heterosexual friends. We stayed home mostly and stared at the tube; or we visited friends and family, took in a play or a movie. We loved each other, and I believe that we still love each other, though we see each other infrequently (and chastely).

I'm not altogether sure about the reasons for our breakup, except that in the last years of our life together, his job made it necessary for him to be away from me for months at a time. I do know that the thing that helped me to keep a sense of humor during an upsetting period, was that our conflicts were not adequately described in the psychiatric literature, but rather in those tales of heterosexual divorce that grace the pages of *Redbook Magazine.*

Both of us now live happily with other people, and I should mention that the person my former lover now lives with is a woman. I went to their wedding, and was happy for him just as I'd been happy for friends who'd found homosexual lovers after leading predominantly heterosexual lives. I was sure that he had made the right choice for himself, as I'd made for myself. He had found another person to love, who happened to be a woman, as I had found another person to love, a man.

The man I live with now is a warm, loving, open person, totally free of Bergler's "free-flowing malice." Once again, my life is centered around our home, though he's younger than I am, and he likes to go out dancing, which I've found I enjoy more than I thought I would. (It's only been a few years in New York that Gay men could dance with each other in public without fear of arrest.) For the past two years, we've been going through the joyful, troublesome process of discovering our similarities and respecting our differences. And together, both sexually and emotionally, we've been discovering the full repertory of *mutuality* which, anatomically and by virtue of social conditioning, seems to be easier for two members of the same sex.

Despite the observations of your "experts" that "the homosexual act symbolizes the heterosexual act in that one partner is conceived as feminine and the other as masculine," neither of us has ever fantasized ourselves or each other as anything but men and, odd as it may seem to those of you who insist that our love is a second-best parody, we wouldn't have it any other way. We like men.

Sexually, I've never thought of myself as anything but male. But I, and a lot of other gay men I know, have had a lot of trouble thinking of ourselves as "masculine" in a social context. When I left treatment, I'd pretty much resolved that fear-envy-hostility thing I had about authority figures (a neurotic trait I shared with a goodly number of heterosexuals), and I enjoyed my image as a really "tough" newspaper reporter. But it's only since I got into the Gay Liberation movement that I've begun to realize that it's absolutely okay for me, even though I'm Gay, to be just as aggressive and competent as the rest of you.

I don't think I've quite reached the top of that plateau yet, but what I'm hoping for when I get there is to be free enough of all the myths and hogwash to abandon my "macho" trip once and for all. You see, I've been listening carefully to my Gay brothers and sisters and to my sisters in the women's movement, and I no longer *believe* that I need to conform to the social stereotypes of what it means to be a "man," any more than I need to conform to the sexual ones. Indeed, I have a theory about the folks who get so wrought up about my life that (like Dr. Socarides) they call it "a serious disorder of tremendous social proportions." I don't, you'll be happy to learn, think of them as "latent homosexuals." I just think they're frightened to death of someone like me, who can calmly consider himself a man, without following all the rules they've so painfully been striving to obey.

I learned something else in the Gay movement; that I was oppressed. I learned that even though I'd never been hiding, I hadn't really "come out of the closet." I hadn't made the choice to identify myself as oppressed and do everything I could to cease being the accomplice in my own oppression.

Now I hold hands with my lover in Central Park, and kiss him goodby on the subway—just as heterosexual lovers do. I talk with my co-workers about my home life, and I contribute to family conversations from my own experience, not repressing my insights or avoiding the pronouns. I even had the *chutzpah* to go up to my editor and ask him to stop using the word "homo" in headlines, just as I'd done if the word had been "kike." I have had an immense sense of psychological growth through making those decisions. I've at last fought through to a sense of myself not as an incomplete person, that is, a flawed heterosexual, but as a whole person. A good, concerned, loving-fighting mad-homosexual.

Until I joined the movement, I was angry fairly often without knowing why, and I chalked it off as a bothersome hangover of neurosis. Now I know why and I'm angry in a different way. My anger is no longer diffuse or turned inward. It's focused and directed outward toward my oppressors—including those of you who think you have the *right* to decide that perfectly happy people, who don't do the slightest harm to themselves or anybody else, are sick.

Dr. Bergler described how a Gay patient came to him and said he didn't have much confidence in him, because he's read his books. And this was used to show the inherent pathology of homosexuals. "By no stretch of the imagination" said Bergler, "can a helping physician be construed as an enemy." But Bergler was not a helping physician, and he was my enemy, because he, and others like him, told bald-faced lies about me—lies that, out of respect for your profession, I was fool enough to believe.

I still have respect for your profession. And because I have, I must again part company from Dr. Bergler who says that "the normal person. If he fights, has only one aim, to punish the aggressor." I'm fighting now, to get you to stop torturing me and calling it my masochism. But I don't want to punish your profession. I don't want to see the Gay "consumer boycott" of psychiatry that Dr. Green has predicted (and is already in effect among those young people who won't have any truck with the oppressors). I don't want to punish you because I'm fighting not only for myself but for those young people who are struggling for an identity. I know it's possible to be helped by psychiatry. And I think you can help.

After our meeting with your Nomenclature Committee in New York last February, the committee chairman, Dr. Henry Brill, told *The New York Times* some right-on things. He said that he and his committee "agreed that whether a person prefers to have sexual relations with a member of the same or of the opposite sex was, in itself, not an indicator of a mental disorder." But he went on to ask, "What are we going to do about the homosexual who comes to us and says he's miserable, that he doesn't like the homosexual way of life and says he wants to change?" Such people, Dr. Brill said, often have "very clear psychiatric problems."

I couldn't agree more. They need help. But what is the nature of their problems, and what can you do to help? Is it their homosexuality that's doing them in? Or is it something which psychiatry has helped to create, their image of themselves as pitiable, incomplete freaks? Is it reinforcement of guilt that they need, or the awareness that at the root of their pathology is something they share with a great many heterosexuals—that irrational fear and hatred of homosexuality that Dr. George Weinberg has identified as "homophobia"?

Instead of acceding immediately to their request for brainwashing, what you can do first is to help these people realize that, as Dr. Brill put it, there are "many successful, well-adjusted people in various professions who are homosexual." And then you can help them to see that a successful sexual adjustment—homosexual or heterosexual—can't be achieved in a climate of guilt and fear.

When these patients begin to see themselves as people, not sets of stereotypical patterns, I suspect that most of them (about as many as you get with your current techniques) will go on being Gay. Only they'll be happy about it. Some, perhaps the same percentage you have now, will wind up predominantly heterosexual. And many of those who had been exclusively homosexual—many more than you now count as treatment "successes"—will discover the heterosexual component in themselves. We've found, to our surprise, that such things happen frequently as people discover themselves in the Gay Liberation movement.

To our surprise, I said, not to our chagrin. For unlike your "experts," we don't believe that homosexuality and heterosexuality are discrete entities. Contrary to what these "experts" tell you, we have no "megalomaniacal conviction about the superiority of our kind over all others." We think that heterosexuals are as good as we are.

Like other oppressed minorities, we know more about you than you know about us. We know a lot about heterosexual adjustment and behavior, and we're not frightened of it, because we know it covers the same range of joys and problems as our own.

We think we can save you the trouble of treating some presently unhappy people, and allow you to use your talents on people who need you more. But a false adversary situation has been drawn between psychiatry and Gay Liberation. We also know we can be a helpful adjunct for many of your patients, by pointing them along the road to self-esteem. Indeed, a growing number of psychiatrists are encouraging their patients to join us.

You can say it's all a sham. There'll be no stopping some of you. But if you don't believe me about other people, believe me about myself. I feel better since I've joined Gay Liberation. I work better. I'm happier in love. Would you rather have me the way I am? Or would you rather go on calling me sick ("Except it's so difficult for him to know it") and suggest that I go in for another round of therapy, so I can come out what Dr. Socarides calls "much improved: the abolition of the conscious homosexual impulse, without development of full extension of heterosexual impulse"?

The people in the Gay Activists Alliance took a risk in sending me here to talk to you. They know that some of you would hear me tell you about my history of drug addiction and consequent hospitalization, and would stop listening after that. They sent me nevertheless. They knew that some of you would take the convenient out of saying to yourselves, "He's sick" and discounting everything I've said as the delusions and confusions of yet another potential patient. But I'm not sick now, and I think you really know it.

I think you really know that my homosexuality is not a pathology I've failed to remove, but a part of me that, in the past, I was not allowed to accept. I believe you're prepared to think over the idea that I might not have been sick at all if the people who meant anything to me—including myself—hadn't believed that I was. I think you're prepared to agree that my illness, at least in part, was a direct result of the crimes perpetrated on me by a hostile society.

In the past your profession has been a willing accomplice to such crimes. But now, in the name of mental health, it is time for those of you who support the platform of "the concerned psychiatrist" to prevent such crimes. Now is the time to do what your Northern New England branch has already done:

> Take the damning label of sickness away from us. Vote resolution of this convention, to take us out of your nomenclature of psychiatric disorders.
>
> Vote here, and work in the community, for repeal of the insane sodomy laws, and for civil rights protections for Gay people.
>
> Most of all, speak out.

I suspect that for many of you, most of what I'm saying is not new, and that a growing majority of you don't agree with the self-styled "experts" in the field. But thus far you've allowed this handful of homophobes to tell the public what your profession thinks. These are the people the media always call on when they want something "official" about the fags and dykes. It's up to you to beat them at their game. You've got to get on the late-night talk shows and write for the newsweeklies as they do. And you've got to tell the world that you believe, as we do, that Gay is Good.

Just one last word to that substantial number of you in the psychiatric profession who are predominantly homosexual.

I know what you must be going through, and I understand how one of you, when we spoke some weeks ago, could tell me that "the time isn't ripe." I heard what you said about the man who'd been picked to head a hospital, and was dropped when they found out that he was Gay. And I remember that we compared notes about two straight psychiatrists who wouldn't speak out, because they might be "suspect."

But psychiatrists here today are speaking out, including Dr. Green and Dr. Judd Marmor, Vice President of the American Psychiatric Association. And the entire profession is now committed to the principle of Gay civil rights. I believe that the time *is* ripe: that if 10 or 15 of you came out now, all at once, you wouldn't lose your patients or your jobs. Instead, you'd provide your profession with just the shock therapy it needs. And the personal rewards, take it from me, will be great.

"Courage" says Dr. Portnoy, "is an expression of the healthy state, the process of self-realization which is the unfolding and developing of the constructive potentials of the real self." And he goes on to catalogue the conditions of self-realization. Wholeness, or the owning by the individual of all aspects of his being. A hierarchy of values arising out of genuine conviction rather than compulsive conformity or defiance. Good relationships to other human beings and to the community, expressed in the ability to move flexibly toward them in cooperation and love, against them in differing, opposing and fighting, and away from them in the ability to stand alone, separate but not isolated from others. And finally, the acceptance of struggle as an invariable component of living. "To the degree to which the individual can move in this direction," says Dr. Portnoy, "he will be able to have a sense of his own 'I' and be able to affirm 'I am.' "

I'm here with all of you today to that spirit of courage and self-realization, and I invite you to join me. Let me personally invite all of you to join the Gay Pride march in New York on June 24th. And for those of you who are Gay, a special invitation. Don't let yourself be like the man at last year's parade who stood quietly on the sideline, not daring to touch his lover's hand, while a friend of mine, one of his former patients, marched by, shouting Gay is Proud.

Come along with me, hold my hand as we march, and say with me, "I am."

January 18, 1974

Remarks for Integrity/Houston

Morty Manford

This address was taped by Manford, an officer of the Gay Activists Alliance in New York City, and sent to the Houston chapter of Integrity, the organization for gay Episcopalians, on the occasion of its second anniversary. This was done in response to a request received by the GAA from Integrity/Houston on January 12, 1974.

My sisters and brothers of Integrity/Houston:

Warmest congratulations from the Gay Activists Alliance on your second anniversary celebration. Your progress as an organization in reaching out to Gays all over the great state of Texas brings pride and inspiration to other Gays throughout the nation.

So often Gay women and men in places like New York and Los Angeles remark: "It will be years and years before Gay Liberation comes to Texas." The inroads Integrity has made into the Texas legislature, in helping to elect a State Representative and a mayor, with its social and educational programs inspiring Gays to come out and join the struggle for Gay Liberation prove how strong Integrity is and how unshakeable the merits of our cause.

I believe the success of Gay Liberation depends on our abilities as Gay Liberationists to fuse the political with the personal. We must be strong in the political arena to command responsiveness from our elected officials, that when discrimination exists in employment practices they will fulfill their obligations in representing our Constitutional right to equal protection under the law; at the same time the imaginations of sisters and brothers must be ignited to light the paths of creativity and pride so that from expression of our deeply felt needs and convictions, Gay strength may be forged. I know this direction is being pursued by Integrity because of your concrete successes and motivating spirits.

Gay Liberation is a process the success of which involves this fusion of personal and political needs. It is an ongoing process which achieves as you have done with great style awakening of Gay pride, exposure of prejudices and encouragement of kindness and love.

As you move into your third year may I say I'm proud of your unswerving commitment, your understanding, kindness, courage, tireless efforts and loving spirits. For 1974 I share with you the hope of grander strides to come.

With peace and Gay Love from New York City: Carry On.

May 4, 1974

Joint Statement

Ad Hoc Committee of Gay Organizations

At noon on May 4, 1974, a rally was held in New York City on Christopher Street near Sheridan Square, attended by both leaders of the gay liberation movement and members of New York's city council, along with prominent civic figures and entertainers. The object of the rally was to rouse support for Intro #2, the gay rights bill then before the city council. Representing the gay liberation movement at this rally were Jean O'Leary, former president of Lesbian Feminist Liberation, Morty Manford, president of the Gay Activists Alliance, Ginny Vida, of the Intro #2 Committee of Lesbian Feminist Liberation, and Jim Owles, president of the Gay Democratic Club. This text is the joint statement issued by them on this occasion. In addition to the four groups represented at this rally, the Ad Hoc Committee of Gay Organizations included the Gay Academic Union, the Gay Legal Caucus, the National Gay Task Force, Dignity, and the Mattachine Society.

Intro #2, the pending civil rights legislation, which would bar discrimination against gay women and men in employment, housing and public accommodations, was approved by the City Council's General Welfare Committee on April 18th by a vote of 7-1. A final vote by the full Council is expected within a few weeks.

The Archdiocese of New York and the Fire Officers Association have attempted to generate a massive fear and hate campaign to stir opposition to the passage of Intro #2. We derive great encouragement that the much heralded "mass rally" scheduled for this past Tuesday noon at City Hall by the Fire Officers, bolstered by a full-page ad in the Daily News and supporting ads in metropolitan area press—a rally they predicted would pull at least 5,000 opponents of Intro #2—mustered a grand total of 35 Fire Officers. The unorganized noontime passersby at City Hall, [who] spontaneously indicated their support for Gay rights, vastly outnumbered the Fire Officers.

We think that a great lesson is being learned and a great victory is being won today: that archaic, irrational prejudice, and distorted fears are being vanquished by pride, openness, love and reason. The facts are:

> Gay women and men are as capable as non-Gays to perform *any* job, public service or social function, and indeed today are working in the Fire and Police departments, teaching in our city schools and working compassionately and conscientiously with young people in every type of service organization.
>
> Gays are not sexually interested in children: child molesting is a category apart from sexual orientation, and in fact the only registered cases of child molestation in the New York City School system in the last two decades involved male teachers and female students.

We ask the people of New York to judge us on our merits—to give us the equal opportunity to work as productive members of society without being subject to abusive discrimination. Our civil rights must be protected in law the same as the civil rights of blacks, Puerto Ricans, women, Jews, Italo-Americans and all other minorities who have been denied the opportunity to demonstrate their creativity and ability by bigots.

Summer 1974

Sexual Liberation Through Revolution, not Reform!

Revolutionary Marxist Group

This is the text of a statement on gay liberation distributed at two gay political events in Toronto, Canada, in the summer of 1974 by members of the Revolutionary Marxist Group. The position taken here was rebutted in a letter from Maurice Flood of the Vancouver Gay Alliance Toward Equality, published along with this text in the September 10, 1974, issue of *The Body Politic.*

In a capitalist society such as we live in, all sexual relationships are crippled and distorted. Capitalism defines only one mode of sexuality, a rigid and oppressive heterosexuality as acceptable, and any other form is despised and attacked. Fundamentally, the definition of "acceptable" sexuality flows from the need to reinforce the nuclear family, the institution which acts as the major vehicle for the reproduction of the individuals who form the class society as a whole; workers and capitalists. In the family, sexual stereotypes are introduced. The deformation of personalities begun in the family is reinforced by the schools, the churches, the mass media, governments, and the laws. At the most extreme points of social control, capitalist sexual (as well as political) relations are maintained through the use of the police against individuals and groups. All these institutions carry on their functions of "socialisation" with respect to political ideology as well as sexuality. "Acceptable" sexuality rigidly relegates women to passive, secondary roles, and men to the playing out of the male aggression towards women which is considered the epitome of masculinity. The rise of women's and gay liberation struggles in the last few years is the expression of revolt against confining, dehumanizing sexual-social relations.

Gay relationships—in fact, sexual relationships in general which break out of the norms prescribed by the needs of the monogamous nuclear family—are threatening to the social stability of capitalist society as a whole. Homosexuality in particular tends to undermine the ideological foundations of the family. Homosexual relations generally occur outside of legal, reproductive and economic definitions and thus violate the basic assumptions of bourgeois notions of the family and marriage. Male chauvinism, the ideological mainstay of capitalist sexuality, is confronted directly by homosexuality, precisely because sexual roles are demonstrated to be learned, and indeed, imposed on us by society. The fierce resistance to homosexuality exhibited by the institutions of the society is a direct response to the threat the social order feels from sexual behaviours outside the prescribed boundaries of "normal sexuality."

Gays and Political Struggle

Because sexual oppression is endemic to capitalism, the road to liberation can lie only in its destruction. That revolution is already beginning in the actual struggles of the workers' movement around the world. More and more of the oppressed are finding that only these struggles express their own historic interests. To begin to acknowledge the need for the socialist revolution, one must begin to recognize the necessity for gays to adopt forms of struggle which lead toward the goal which contains the seeds of our liberation. The gay movement in Western Europe, where the class struggle as a whole is more advanced, has taken substantial steps towards this perspective, solidarizing with and intervening in working class struggles. Sectors of the GLF in Britain, the Gay Action Group in Germany, and the Anti-Norm/Sexpol (formerly FHAR) in France are examples.

For us, the road lies out of the gay ghetto, to independent initiatives and alliances with the left and the labour movement. The gay ghetto, through its manifold institutions, maintains the isolation of the gay subculture from the rest of society and allows it to be kept "under control." Operating in the general framework of capitalism, it is fertile ground for oppression, exploitative relationships, and sexism. Like the ghetto, a simple "civil rights" perspective is a trap in the long term, for as long as capitalist social relations remain, so will gay oppression. Campaigns for democratic rights can be useful, however, if carried out from a revolutionary perspective: dramatizing our oppression to others, aiding people in coming out, and putting pressure on the state by independent, militant initiatives. A perspective based on direct action (demonstrations, sit-ins, etc.) would not only bypass the ineffectiveness of petition campaigns, but could provide an alternative pole to the ghetto. We must also be prepared to defend ourselves (and, in this instance, there are most certainly other allies on the left) from attacks by bigots and fascists.

The Solution-Revolution

The understanding and resistance of the ruling class to homosexuality is not necessarily matched by the understanding gays have of their own situation. Whether gays will perceive their antipathy to the ruling class or not will be determined largely by how they begin to organize in defiance of it. Capitalism understands who its enemies—and potential enemies—are. For our part, we must understand as well. Our first task is to discover who our allies can be in the fight for sexual liberation. We believe that gays have nothing to gain by lining up with capitalism, the very system which oppresses us. Even attempts to ameliorate or reform conditions under capitalism contain the dangers of taking sides with the enemies of sexual liberation. We must seek our allies in struggle among other oppressed and exploited groups and classes. In capitalist society, there exists one class, the working class—male, female, gay and straight—which possesses the social weight and direct interest to reverse centuries of oppression, to defeat those who seek to preserve it and to transform society as a whole. Like racism, anti-semitism, and sexism in general, anti-gay prejudices are a form of prejudice which serves to divide workers and oppressed groups and fragment their unity. Sexism, like racism, exists within the working class. Gays must begin to examine how they can work to overcome the hold of this ideology within the workers' movement, just as they must begin to examine how they can help in the struggles of the working class. The workers movement and especially its political organizations must take up the struggle for human liberation. The news article in *The Body Politic* 14, describing the attack of the Chilean counter-revolution on homosexuals as part of the broader attack on the working class and oppressed, stands as a clear illustration of why this is true, not only in the case of Chile.

The Tasks Before Us

1. Campaigns for equal rights based on militant action and not only on petitioning and lobbying.
2. Defence against police and legal repression.
3. Self-defence in alliance with the left and the workers' movement.
4. Support for actions in the broader class struggle, strike support, and participation of gay organizations in international solidarity actions, such as that for Chile in September.
5. Clarification of the nature of our oppression and of how to achieve our own liberation.

ABOLITION OF AGE OF CONSENT LAWS
—— SEXUAL RIGHTS FOR YOUNG PEOPLE!

STATE-SUPPORTED ECONOMIC INDEPENDENCE
FROM PARENTS AVAILABLE TO ALL ADOLESCENTS!

FOR AN END TO EXCLUSIVELY PRO-HETEROSEXUAL
SEX EDUCATION IN THE SCHOOL SYSTEM!

FOR AN END TO AVERSION THERAPY TREATMENT!

END POLICE HARASSMENT!

ORGANIZE SELF-DEFENCE!

END SEXUAL ORIENTATION DOUBLE STANDARDS IN IMMIGRATION!

EQUAL RIGHTS FOR GAY PEOPLE!

ONLY ONE SOLUTION, REVOLUTION!

WORKERS OF THE WORLD, UNITE!

September 13, 1974

For My Granddaughters . . .

Valerie Taylor

This is the address given by author Valerie Taylor to the 1st Annual Lesbian Writers Conference in Chicago, Illinois, in September 1974. The "gentle and timorous creatures" she mentions were Sarah Ponsonby (1755-1831) and Lady Eleanor Butler (1739-1829), the "ladies of Llangollen." Socarides and Bieber are psychoanalysts. Dr. Charles Socarides wrote *The Overt Homosexual* (Modern Library, 1962) and Dr. Irving Bieber (and colleagues) wrote *Homosexuality: A Psychoanalytic Study* (Random House, 1962).

When *Lavender Woman* began to publish, it was a pleasant surprise to find in one of its early issues a page of letters from young women to their mothers—attempts to explain their viewpoint and lifestyle and find some way of bridging the age gap. It was also good to learn that a feminist press was called *Daughters*. To learn our origins is a first step in establishing identity; as Dan Berrigan says, "if you don't know where you come from, how do you know where you're going?" For women who are becoming liberated it's valuable to know who our mothers and grandmothers are.

Notice that I say "becoming" liberated. Liberation is an organic process and is always progressive and always incomplete. Nor are we the first women to work at it. In thinking about lesbian literature we must first take a look at our grandmothers—not our biological grandmothers necessarily, but our social and cultural ones. They began what today's writers and readers are carrying forward.

And what a crazy mixed-up bunch they were! One was a wealthy Englishwoman who probably had the worst literary style ever developed, but who had so much to say and said it with such passionate intensity that she became a one-woman revolution. One was an ex-medical student who claimed to be a genius and proved that she was by inventing an extremely new literary style. One was a sensitive woman who after several periods of insanity committed suicide because she felt unable to face another bout of madness in a world gone crazy with war. One was a clergyman's daughter who emigrated to Paris and devoted her life to discovering and publishing great books. One was the first woman to be admitted to the French Academy. In her need to earn a living she interspersed the writing of books with acting in vaudeville and running a cosmetics firm.

Two were gentle and timorous creatures who ran away from home together and lived to an old age on a secluded farm in Wales. One gave up her native language, English, to write distinctive poetry in French. And of course, if we go back far enough we find the great-great-grandmother of us all, the sweet singer of Lesbos whose name has come to be a synonym for lesbians even though only fragments of her work remain. Ours is a proud inheritance.

Let's begin with Sappho, the woman who wrote, "Love, like the mountain wind upon the oak, falling upon me, shakes me leaf and bough." Peter Green's book, *The Laughter of Aphrodite,* is a fictional, but imaginative and sympathetic reconstruction of her life and loves. For the poems themselves we have Mary Barnard's translation of and commentary on the bits and pieces attributed to Sappho. This book was published by the University of California Press in 1958 and is still a definitive work.

I know this is a forum on fiction, not poetry, but how do you tell where one ends and the other begins? Read Colette and you find that some of her best passages are really poems in prose form—their quality comes across even in translation—and God knows much of the so-called poetry read by any editor is extremely prosy.

Read Aphra Behn, the first woman to earn an independent living in the theatre in the male-dominated seventeenth century, and you'll understand the Family of Woman. We're all inheritors. Only the idiom changes.

Let's come up to our own day—that is, to the twentieth century. Let's begin with Radclyffe Hall. I suppose everyone here has read *The Well of Loneliness.* It's one of those great trailbreakers which open the way for thousands of others to follow.

A terrible book in many ways—the literary style is almost incredibly bad, the sentimentality is spread on so thickly that some of the most emotional passages tempt a modern reader to burst out laughing, and the theories of causation and homosexual development have been rejected by everyone except a few Neanderthals like Socarides and Bieber. The heroine, Stephen Gordon, thinks of herself as a man in a woman's body. That's a concept no self-respecting lesbian would accept today. In an Edwardian, upper middle class English context Hall's errors are understandable, perhaps inevitable. Still in the light of later work *The Well of Loneliness* is a bad book.

It is also a tremendously valuable book. Gertrude Stein, who was also an innovator, said something to the effect that when an artist creates something new it's never beautiful because it's still taking shape. Later it becomes beautiful—but then it's no longer new. She was talking about painting, but it's equally true of writers and social activists and we think of Hall as both. Being a pioneer is a lonely business. It's easy to move ahead with a thousand others supporting you. In 1924 Radclyffe Hall stood alone and appealed for the right of the lesbian to be accepted for what she was. We have to respect her.

In the 1950's when Jeannette Foster wrote her book, *Sex Variant Women in Literature,* no commercial publisher would accept it. Dr. Foster was an excellent writer; she had been one of Kinsey's librarians, with access to a huge body of material, much of it still unpublished. But she ended by having her book published at her own expense, after which it went out of print. This year (1974) her book has been honored by the Gay Task Force of the American Library Association and will be republished by a good press. Pioneers don't always live to see their experiments accepted—when they do it's a great thing.

In addition to reprints of primarily lesbian interest a number of books which dealt with lesbianism as a minor theme came to the attention of women readers in the fifties. Colette's work had been thought of as heterosexual, she was known in this country as the author of *Gigi* and *Cheri.* Now the Claudine series was translated, to be followed by *Earthly Paradise* and *The Pure and the Impure.* Mary Renault's two lesbian novels—*Promise of Love* and *The Middle Mist*—appeared in paperback and took their place on the shelves of many private libraries alongside her Greek stories. May Sarton's early work had included overtones of lesbianism, for example, *The Single Hound, A Shower of Summer Days* and later, *The Small Room.* In the fifties she began to publish poetry that was overtly lesbian in tone, *Mrs. Stevens Hears the Mermaids Singing* and her two recent autobiographical books, *Plant Dreaming Deep* and *Journal of a Solitude* were yet to come. The increasing frankness of this gifted writer has won her a small but devoted following; the progress of lesbian writing over the last three decades can be followed in her work.

Virginia Woolf's *Mrs. Dalloway* was reread for its lesbian implications, as were Katherine Mansfield's writings. When *Memoirs of a Woman of Pleasure* (sometimes called *Fanny Hill*) appeared in 1963 after 200 years of obscurity, readers enjoyed Fanny's initiation into prostitution by another girl in the house where she was to work and the implications of homosexuality that were scattered throughout the book. Tereska Torres' novel of the Free French women's army in London, *Woman's Barracks,* appeared in 1950 and included several lesbian and bisexual characters. In each of these books, and many others, lesbianism was not the main issue, but it does appear as a part of everyday life, more or less taken for granted by the author and without moral implications. The same is true of Josephine Tey's *Miss*

Pym Disposes and *To Love and Be Wise*. In the mid-sixties Sarah Kilpatrick's *Ladies Close* described the breakdown of a middle-aged teacher after an affair with a young pupil, her pursuit by another pupil whose advances she resisted and a handful of assorted love affairs on the part of her neighbors, most of them hetero. The cast includes a delightful homosexual actor who reminds one of Noel Coward. It's refreshing to discover so many books that take lesbianism for granted.

Of less literary value, *Diana,* published in 1939, and Nora Lofts' *Jassy,* from 1945, were reprinted in paperback during this time.

Alongside the revival of many books which have become classics, the fifties saw the appearance of many new titles, most of them paperback originals. Ann Bannon wrote the Beebo Brinker series, among the first paperbacks with which gay readers could identify. Paula Christian, who wrote under several other names, wrote *This Side of Love, The Far Side of Desire* and other gay stories whose characters grappled with social ostracism and their own guilt feelings more or less successfully, making it clear that the problems were not inherent in lesbianism but were forced on the main characters by bad social attitudes and institutions. It was a shock to many readers when Christian later repudiated her lesbian works. She later went to work as an editor in a porno publishing house, which she seemed to feel was morally superior to writing honest and realistic gay books.

A sensational journalist named Marijane Meeker adopted the name Ann Aldrich and wrote *We Walk Alone, We Too Must Love,* and *Carol in a Thousand Cities,* the last a putdown of *The Ladder,* which at that time was the only lesbian magazine in the United States. Aldrich's gambit was to pretend a sympathetic interest and then show lesbian life as frantic, promiscuous and tragic. Jess Stearn was to use much the same technique in *The Grapevine*.

Far different was Claire Morgan's *The Price of Salt,* published in 1951. Here two women in love eventually overcome all obstacles, including a resentful husband to make a lasting relationship.

Unfortunately, not all the paperbacks that appeared during this time were as good as Morgan's. Carol Hales wrote a sticky, drippy book called *Wind Woman,* in which a female psychiatrist draws out all the facts of her patient's frustrated lesbian life and ends by virtually seducing her. Edwina Marks' *My Sister, My Love* adds incest and violence to sex, as does Fletcher Flora's *Strange Sisters.*

These books were written more or less skillfully and some of the situations were believable. However, the market was soon flooded with hastily written and superficial titles that relied on sensationalism to make sales. Many were written by men writing under feminine pseudonyms. They follow the same pattern: a beautiful and insatiable lesbian goes through one affair after another, averaging one sex scene for every ten pages, and ends in the arms of a handsome and remarkably virile man. One Chicago hack named Paul Little claimed to have written five hundred of these, using the pen name of Sylvia Sharon. Around 1964 his publisher admitted to me that Little simply outlined his plots and turned then over to another hack on the publisher's staff who filled in the details. So the author's hardest job was signing his royalty checks. The women in the books were always voluptuous and bosomy, they all wore black lace underwear, they loved to seduce innocent straight women and they never did anything but have sex. Male readers got a double kick out of these books—first they satisfied the man's curiosity about lesbians and what they do together—never mind the information was all wrong—and their machismo was fed by the final triumph of the male. Readers must have got some strange ideas about women during this period. I remember one book about women in which a butch—size 44 bust and black underwear—snarls "I am the man!" and plunges her arm into her girl friend's vagina up to the elbow. Some of us are still looking for that femme.

Eventually the market for this sort of trash was saturated and as the market for hard-core porno became more open there was less and less of specifically lesbian interest. The sixties saw a few good books instead of a lot of bad ones—many of them in hardcover. Outstanding was Maureen Duffy's *The Microcosm,* a stream-of-conscious novel about four lesbians in widely different life styles and May Sarton's *Mrs. Stevens Hears the Mermaids Singing.* With the seventies we have had more non-fictional books on lesbianism and fewer novels. I think there's room for both and it is possible that some of you who are here tonight will fill a real need by writing some really good gay novels.

One book published here in paperback last year has an unusual and interesting history. *Patience and Sarah,* written by Isabel Miller (Alma Routsong), found no publisher here and was issued in England under the title *A Place for Us.* Based on the lives of two young women who lived in New York state around 1820, one of them a primitive painter whose works are still found here and there in collections of early Americana, it's a love story with fresh charm, a great deal of tenderness and some humor. It deserves mention not only for its own merits but as a possible indication of a new trend in lesbian fiction. Also making the transition from today's mood into tomorrow's are a few non-fiction works which ought to be read by everyone interested in lesbian liberation. Jill Johnston's *Lesbian Nation* is worth reading although it's repetitive, self-centered and written in an imitation of e.e. cummings' style. More important are Del Martin and Phyllis Lyon's *Lesbian/Woman* which won the ALA Gay Task Force award last year, and

Kate Millet's *Flying*. If you want to know what intelligent lesbian activists are doing and thinking, these books are required reading.

Let's not forget, either, that 1973 was marked by the reappearance after many years of Gertrude Stein's *Q.E.D.,* her only overtly lesbian work with the exception of certain poems.

What happens now? No one can say for sure, but we might guess at the future by looking at a few current trends. One possibility is that with the swing away from pornography, which seems to be killing itself with dullness and repetitiveness, there will be a return to Victorian prudery and hypocrisy. More hopefully, readers may demand more variety and a more realistic approach in the books they read. There's a practical argument against censorship as well as a moralistic one: if people are allowed to read anything they want to by the age of 15 or 16 they will be bored with the average dirty book, movie or what-not and ready for something more lifelike.

The young writers coming up will have something new to say and an informed readership to say it to. As gay liberation and feminist liberation proceed, as people try to find a meaningful way of life, a new freedom should open up for the lesbian author. She may even be able to treat lesbianism as one phase of a complex, fascinating and diverse world and not as an isolated phenomenon.

There will be less defensiveness as self-guilt and social pressures lessen. Think of a play like *The Children's Hour,* in which a sensitive and intelligent young woman kills herself when she realizes her own latent lesbian tendencies. Or a situation like that in *The Price of Salt,* in which a husband has his wife and her lover trailed by detectives so that he can get custody of their child. Today the wife would find a good feminist lawyer and win custody. In Lawrence's *The Fox* and *The Rainbow* the lesbian episodes are kept under cover as far as the women's families and friends are concerned. Both affairs are treated as not being very important—preludes to heterosexual marriage. I've always thought that if Lawrence had written a sequel to *The Fox,* the young wife would surely have been ready to leave her arrogant husband in a very short time and create a new life with another woman. Incidentally, Lawrence might have understood his own latent homosexuality better if he had written such a sequel. Certainly if *The Fox* were written today the conflict between the two kinds of love would have to come out into the open. There would be a confrontation between the two rivals for the younger woman's love and she would understand her own feelings better. We've made some headway since the 1920's.

One way to see what has happened in the last forty years is to compare two books about Vita Sackville-West. In 1928 Virginia Woolf, a longtime friend and sometime lover of Sackville-West, wrote *Orlando.* It's a bisexual fantasy in which the protagonist, based on Vita, lives for 300 years and changes sex every century. Forty-five years later Sackville-West's son, who plainly loved and admired both of his parents, wrote *Portrait of a Marriage,* an explicit account of his mother's and father's life together with the homosexual tendencies and experiences of both parents described with names, dates and places.

Perhaps tomorrow's lesbian books will go even farther. If we become civilized enough to realize that there are many viable life styles we can stop being defensive. The young woman who becomes aware of her primarily lesbian nature won't have to struggle against self-blame or social rejection. Even if she's subject to social and personal pressures—inner and outer conflicts—she won't have to cope with them alone. There will be supportive organizations and accepting friends, as well as a tremendous body of lesbian and feminist literature to help her find her place in life.

With all this clutter of blame and guilt swept away, there will be room for tomorrow's writers to develop interesting characters and situations. Today many young lesbians setting out to become writers feel that they have a moral obligation to write about nothing but lesbianism, just as many black writers over the last half century have felt that they must write only about black problems. That's a hang-up that won't trouble us when we become more free. Can you imagine a heterosexual author feeling that she must write only about heterosexuality and its problems, ignoring all the other aspects of human life? The world should be our subject matter—not just one small corner of it!

Colette and Sarton have already pointed the way to this universality of subject matter. Sarton writes about marriage, friendship, parent-child relationships, teachers and pupils, neighbors, rejected old people, the impact of love on art and many other things, as well as about women in love. Her books are full of complete human beings.

So all of us build on the lives of those who have gone before. Today we think in terms of sisterhood—and that's good, that's productive. But when a writer reaches sixty she also begins to look for daughters, for inheritors. We hope that our work too will help to make a foundation for those who come after us. We hope that young women coming up realize the challenge and the rich possibilities that are open to them . . . that they will go on where we leave off.

I'd like to attend a conference like this one in twenty years, when I'm eighty. Perhaps by that time we'll all be much farther along on the path to liberation. Perhaps the infinite variety of human life will be caught in our books—lesbianism just one important theme among many others. If that happens, it will be because you who have come to this conference, and others like you all over the world, have made it happen. You have tremendous power.

Some of my daughters are here tonight. Some will be reading their own work on Sunday—I am eager to hear what they have to say. We're planting a seed here. Unless male politicians and militarists manage to blow up the human race, I believe that some of you will still be around in the year 2000 to harvest what grows out of this weekend. That's your future—and I wish you luck with it!

March 25, 1975

Seeks Equal Protection

Bella S. Abzug

These remarks were made on the floor of the House of Representatives by Representative Abzug of New York and were entered into the *Congressional Record* for March 25, 1975. This was the first time that a bill had been introduced at the federal level explicitly to provide civil rights protection for gays and lesbians.

Mr. Speaker, I am today introducing, with 23 cosponsors, a bill to amend the Civil Rights Act of 1964 and related acts to prohibit discrimination on the basis of sexual or affectional preference. This bill would insure that gay individuals would be entitled to jobs, to housing, to education, to utilization of public accommodations, to participation in federally assisted programs, on the same basis as other Americans—and would be provided with a legal remedy if such rights and opportunities were denied to them. What is at issue here is equal rights for all Americans.

Equal protection of the laws and respect for the rights of individuals are fundamental principles of our Constitution. I have long been a proponent of measures which would insure that these principles are guaranteed for all individuals—women as well as men, married individuals as well as those who are unmarried, people of every nationality, ethnic group, race or religion. Likewise, sexual orientation should be no barrier to equal treatment under the law.

It has been estimated that there are 20 million homosexuals in the United States. But even if homosexuals were only a small minority, the considerations would be the same. These considerations are the right to privacy, and the right of a person to choose his or her own affectional or sexual preference without being denied other basic rights—principles which I firmly support.

A long list of national organizations has gone on record as opposing discrimination against individuals on the basis of sexual preference. These organizations include the American Bar Association, the American Psychiatric Association, the American Federation of Teachers, the National Education

Association, the American Civil Liberties Union, and the Young Women's Christian Association. Most recently, the National Council of Churches governing board adopted a resolution recommending that member churches work to pass laws to assure the civil rights of homosexuals. I hope that Congress will follow the lead of these prominent organizations by giving favorable consideration to the bill which my colleagues and I are introducing today.

August 10, 1975

British Theologian Speaks to Gays

W. Norman Pittenger

This address was given by the British theologian W. Norman Pittenger in Chicago to a special service hosted by the Good Shepherd Parish of the Metropolitan Community Church (MCC) at 615 West Wellington in August 1975. Pittenger had been guest preacher at the MCC conference in July 1975 and at the first national Integrity conference, also held in Chicago in August 1975. His remarks were prefaced by an introduction by Patrick Townson, Gay Pride chairman and head of the committee that planned the program. The poem quoted, "The Penalty of Love," is attributed to the Irish writer Sidney Royse Lysaght.

I think I ought to say, after what Mr. Townson has been saying to you that I am a little embarassed. I am not going to talk for four hours. God forbid! The best I can manage is half an hour, and by that time most of you would be dead!

As we came in this evening to that hymn, with words written by Henry Van Dyke, I recalled that a great many years ago, possible forty-five years ago, I was talking with Dr. Van Dyke, who I and my family knew, and who had kindly read some of the things I had written. In the course of the conversation, he said to me, somewhat ambiguously, "Well, Dr. Pittenger, you have preserved your literary chastity."

But I don't intend to talk about my chastity, literary or other wise. Instead, I want to think with you about some of the words which were found in the Lesson which we read a few minutes ago. These were words which had to do with love, and with God as Love, and with human love in response to God's love.

This is, I think, especially relevant to a community of gay Christians. Note that I almost said "grey" by accident. I suppose that almost everyone here now is gay, but not necessarily grey. If some of you are not gay, then I assume you are at least a straight person who understands, and sympathizes with gay people. No one here will think that to be gay is being abnormal, or deviant. It is simply to be different from the majority in our contemporary society.

To those people, that minority, I believe the words of St. John's letter speak with a direct significance. Why are gay people as they are? Quite apart from stupid questions concerning origin and development, to which no one really has the answer, any more than we have the answer about why 85 to 90 percent of the population appears to be heterosexual; quite apart from that question, there is something that was said to me by Anthony Grey, the director of the Albany Trust in England which tells us precisely why the words of the Lesson speak so directly to the heart and mind of gay people.

Tony Grey said to me one day, that after counseling some five thousand homosexuals in London over a two year period, he had yet to find one who did not want to love and be loved. An English theologian, whose name will be known to some of you here, has a wonderful sentence which we need to bear continually in mind; "The best way to find the heart of God is to trust our own deepest affections."

How scared we are! How unwilling to do just that. How unready we are to express those affections. During the past few days, down at the Episcopal Cathedral, the name of E.M. Forster, the English novelist, has been mentioned several times. I knew him well. I had dinner with him every night. We talked all the time. He said once, "The trouble with Englishmen is not that they have cold hearts, but that their hearts are undeveloped."

I suspect that is not true just of residents of the United Kingdom. It may even be true of Chicago. Undeveloped hearts, with fear and unreadiness to let one's deepest affections provide a way to the heart of God.

Do you remember, in James Baldwin's novel, *Another Country* the incident where Vivaldo and Eric are in bed together? Suddenly, and now I quote, "they found that love had entered that bed, and although they might never embrace again, they could be sure of one thing: That there was a man in the world who loved them. This gave them strength and meaning in all the uncertainties of life."

There is a man in the world who loves each of us. Christian faith is all about that man. That man, who once walked the ways of the world in Palestine, still exerts his power, even today. Nothing, or no one yet has been able to stop him. That man loves us. We may love him. In that heart's affection, there is opened a door to the secret of all existence.

Of course, we can put this sentimentally. When I was young, there was a song which said, "It's Love, and Love Alone the World Is Seeking." Sentimentality, but true. "It's Love That Makes The World Go Round" was still another song, which was sentimental, but true.

That man's affection gives us the assurance that behind all the puzzling and difficult things about life, there is a love that will not let us go. That is the first half of what I wanted to say to you tonight.

The second half has to do with our little, imperfect, human response to love like that. Can we dare to live in love with a little "l" because we know that we live in a love with a great big "L"? Can we venture to live with our heart's affection because we are sure that our lives have been caught up into the all embracing love that we name when we use the G-O-D?

I think that gay people have an opportunity both to understand and express this more deeply but more painfully than most straight people. Why? Because the deepest yearning of a gay boy or girl, man or woman, as Tony Grey said, is . . . for love. Their whole being cries out for love. When this is not known, received, and given all sorts of substitute ways of finding loneliness overcome by affection must be sought for and, as we all know quite well, will be sought for.

Second bests; not bad, mind you, but second bests then become the object of our search. I should be prepared to bet all the money I have, which at the moment wouldn't consist of much American money, and so wouldn't be of any worth to you: but I've got quite a lot of English money in my wallet, that there is not one person here tonight who will not say with me, "I want love, I want to be loved, I want to give love."

I want literally to give and receive love. Not in a shoddy furtive manner, [to] which our society so often drives the gay person, but with utter honesty and openness, and the emotional sincerity that is the real meaning of chastity. We must strive for the type of relationships where persons become better persons; where the relations between them become more personal; where more and more of life may be shared. You will never find that this is easily obtainable. You are likely to find the best intentions, promises and undertakings can go awry. We should be fools if we denied that! Nonetheless, what is being aimed at the best things possible, is an embracing of the whole of life, which includes our body, as well as our mind and spirit.

Yesterday, I proposed to those who were present at the Integrity meeting a question to be asked: When I, when you, leave the bed where sex has been had, are we leaving a body that has gratified us, or are we leaving a person with whom we have shared life?

It is Christendom: it is the quality of personal relationships, where people never become things that matter. I was terribly moved and enormously humbled many years ago, when a black boy who was a student of mine in New York, said to me, as he was leaving seminary after three years, "Father, you were the one member of the faculty who thought of us as people, and not as students."

That was not true, nor fair to my colleagues. But it does provide a key to our understanding of any and all human relationships. Above all, it speaks, I think, directly to those who are gay. No coercion, no possession, no control, no domination, but sharing life together, person with person. This is the goal: and this form of sex, as such, is very good indeed. But the best of all is when sex is set in the context of true love. I am almost finished with my sermon, you will be glad to hear.

What I am urging to gay people and straight people, in fact all people, is that it is indeed love which makes the world go 'round. Everybody wants to know and experience love. Tragically, it is not always possible. I cannot, I will not condemn, and I suspect none of you would either, the boy or girl who finds a sole source of fulfillment in the pickup, or the one night stand.

But I will say to that person that there is something better than that: although "that" isn't all bad. The thing that is better is to know in our limited, finite, defective fashion a love that binds us together with somebody else.

Or, as once I said, and Troy Perry tells me he likes to repeat, "Having sex is always fun . . . making love is an absolute joy." Usually I hate to end sermons, of which this is a poor example, by reading poetry at a long-suffering congregation. But tonight, I am going to do it anyway! I didn't write it! I have the name of the author, but who he was, I can't tell you. He wrote this bit of verse, a sonnet, some sixty years ago. It turned up in a book that my friend, the pastor of Trinity Church Boston, and I found one day when we were over in England. Here it is: I will read it, and then I will shut up.

If love should count you worthy, and should deign
One day to seek your door and be your guest,
Pause! ere you draw the bolt and bid him rest,
If in your old content you would remain,
For not alone he enters; in his train
Are angels of the mist, the lonely guest
Dreams of the unfulfilled and unpossessed,
And sorrow, and Life's immemorial pain.
He wakes desires you never may forget,
He shows you stars you never saw before,
He makes you share with him, for evermore,
The burden of the world's divine regret.
How wise you were to open not!—and yet,
How poor if you should turn him from the door!

September 19, 1975

The Possibilities Are Staggering

Barbara Grier

This address was given by Grier, founder of Naiad Press and longtime writer and editor of *The Ladder,* to the Second Annual Lesbian Writers Conference in Chicago, Illinois, in September 1975. The biography of Marion "Joe" Carstairs was written by Kate Summerscale and published in 1997 as *The Queen of Whale Cay.* The speech by Robin Morgan (included in this book) is "Lesbianism and Feminism: Synonyms or Contradictions?" and was given at the West Coast Lesbian Feminist Conference in Los Angeles on April 14, 1973. The bibliography referred to is Maria Kuda's 1974 compilation *Women Loving Women,* published in Chicago by Lavender Press.

"A great wave of sisterly love." All I can really hear or feel is my heart beating, because I am very frightened to be up here. Part of the price paid for being "Gene Damon" was living away from people for twenty years of my life. Collecting and reading books was about all I did while writing for *The Ladder.* This makes speaking to even a happy, good audience very difficult for me.

I have always been arrogant about *The Ladder* and our past. And because I spend all my time reading about what happened to all of us or all those lesbians who came before us, I've always assumed that everybody else knew all those things too. But, obviously, that's not so.

The Ladder was begun in 1956, ran until 1972 and stopped publishing. We hope someday that if it doesn't begin again some magazine will come along to do the things it began. There were other writers beyond those that Valerie Taylor mentioned. One early contributor of two lengthy letter-essays was Lorraine Hansberry. We published her in 1956, about a year before she became the first—let's see, I want to get this right—the first Black writer to win the New York Drama Critics Circle Award for her play *A Raisin In the Sun.* I am especially proud that she was among the very first contributors. Every fifth issue in those days we had to write a disclaimer telling our readers, "Your name is safe, we won't tell that you subscribed to *The*

Ladder." Our mail was almost evenly divided between women who were overjoyed that we existed and those who were so terrified that they wanted their names off the mailing list after seeing an issue or two.

That's very sad, and I'm glad that that's gone and over. There could have been no meeting like this one tonight then. Which brings me back to "Gene Damon" which has now become my albatross. By the time it was "all right" not to use a pseudonym, I was too well known as "Gene Damon" to become "Barbara Grier." At a speech Robin Morgan gave in Los Angeles a few years ago she said, "Among the women who founded the DOB and began *The Ladder*, were Del Martin and Phyllis Lyon and Barbara Grier." Two different friends wrote me to say they heard women in the audience say, "Who the hell is Barbara Grier?"

Hopefully, next year Diana Press will be bringing out a three-volume compilation of biography, fiction and essays from back issues of *The Ladder*. The information on the jacket of these books is going to say "Gene Damon" though I have insisted that "Barbara Grier" appear after it everywhere that the name comes up. I guess after twenty years I'm stuck with it.

On the subject of being an "up-front" lesbian, the pseudonym was not to keep people from finding out that Barbara Grier was and is a lesbian. I began telling people I was a lesbian when I was about twelve—which is when I discovered it. The very first person I told, I have since learned, is the last person most people tell. I went home and told my mother. I was very lucky she took it so well; it might have given her ideas because my next youngest sister is also a lesbian.

There seems to be a real demand for the women of our past. And that's really what I want to talk about tonight. I'm always expected to talk about literature and writers, but I don't have to do that by myself anymore because, as Marie pointed out, there's a marvelous book out which does a good job of talking about the more famous and open lesbian writers of our past, *Lesbian Images,* by Jane Rule. There are other books bearing on the subject; many women are interested in talking about lesbian writers—Marie's own bibliography is an excellent example. I said about all I needed to say in *The Lesbian in Literature,* which is a guide to help you find the books if you want to read on the subject.

We have a glorious past and much emphasis in the lesbian press in recent years has been placed on how lost our women have been, buried, more or less, in male history. Buried they may well have been, but we are here to dig them up, figuratively, to bring them to life for today. We need less commentary on our losses and more on our gains . . . and much more research and reportage for the women who will come after us, women hungry to know their heritage.

You out there in the audience are their hope. A year ago at one of the myriad conferences on the west coast dealing with lesbians, a packet of information distributed contained a series of interesting quotations from one of the developers of the meeting. She said in effect, that she was ignorant of her history as a lesbian and "not into a scholarly trip," that she hoped to learn from sisters willing to do the "hard research."

Hard is not a valid word for the work needed: most of it is exciting and the sources exist. Willingness to spend time reading and compiling is half the battle. The possibilities are staggering. I have card files overflowing with unworked information, notes on women I've personally not had time to research fully or even at all beyond the basics. And even the fifty or so women I've written about at length through the years need much more said about them.

I'd like to talk about a particular woman who is virtually unknown. The fascinating, almost movie script life of Marion Barbara Carstairs deserves a full-length book at the very least. And one of these days, possibly someone in this room will write it. "Joe" Carstairs was born in 1900 into a socially prominent family. As have so many women in such surroundings, she rebelled early. She ran away from Lowe-Heywood School in Connecticut when she was sixteen. She went to England, drove an ambulance in the First World War as did the heroine of *The Well of Loneliness* as well as its author, Radclyffe Hall. She raced boats, raced motorcycles and drove fast cars; she ran a gypsy caravan in Brighton. None of this would make her a candidate for biography, possibly, but her later life surely would. In 1933, the year I was born, Joe liquidated her personal fortune (by that time, despite having been disinherited by her family she was wealthy) and bought an island in the Bahamas called Whale Cay. She moved there at once, finding she'd become owner of 3000 acres of land, 8 miles long and virtually uninhabitable except for a lighthouse cared for by a lonely elderly couple. In the next eight years, she built that island into a paradise and a fortress. She put fifteen miles of paved road on it. She built forty-odd buildings, including a house that would make this church look small. She brought an almost-army of workers to it and gave them all jobs and training. Then she turned it into a vegetable-growing paradise. Which perhaps doesn't sound remarkable in Chicago this year, but it was remarkable on the soil available there. And that's just the bare bones of the things in her life. She really was a fabulous sister. She belongs to our past; somebody should dig her up and write about her.

There are many, many others just like her. I have probably three thousand cards, just single cards at home in files. Each one of them has just one or sometimes two—pairs of women are much nicer really—and every one of them should be looked into. Not all of them, probably, would be worthy of a book; but certainly all would be a chapter or at least a few lines, and they all need to be talked about because all the women out there are really waiting to hear about their past.

It's very, very difficult to feel that you were born when you came out and women are still doing that today. When you are close to a movement, as presumably all of you are, it's hard to realize that most of the women who come out come out alone. That's something I do know about, because through the years, the vast majority of women who were most interested in receiving *The Ladder* were isolated people who lived in small towns. They still exist; we still get mail constantly, from young women primarily, although not exclusively, between fifteen and twenty-five. They write saying: "I have just discovered myself; no one else in the world, no one else in my area is like me." They all love some kind of identity.

[Question from the audience: Do you try to put them in contact with one another?] No, I really don't have the facilities to do that; however, we do answer all the mail we get. Which brings me to another thing: the problem of responsibility in publishing, and it's something I have to mention tonight because it seems an important part of keeping everything going and everyone together. Probably most of you are familiar with *Ambitious Amazons' Lesbian Connection*—the lesbian newsletter that is coming out with lesbian information and going to people *free.* They are trying to keep a sort of tie with every group so that all lesbians can keep in touch with what is going on in their world wherever their world may be at the time.

We need a great deal more of that; but also, those of us who work with publications in any sense need to be responsible to people who write in to us or approach us in any way. It's still as difficult today as it was fifteen or eighteen years ago to get responses to mail inquiries. We are not even active in the sense that *The Ladder* has not been published since 1972, but *we do still answer inquiries.* Many, many publications are not answering their mail. Many of them do not have or do not *think* they have the time to do so. But we *have* to have the time to do so. We have to, even if it means less public activity or private time, because it's *extremely* important. The only way our ranks will swell the way they have to swell, the only way all the women will come out is if we help everybody who is in the process of coming out. Not just the people we know and greet happily as we did downstairs tonight—all fairly self-confident, all very happy to be here, all very unnervous about being here.

Most lesbians are still nervous. Yesterday afternoon in downtown Chicago, while going around a corner of a building, Donna and I passed a sister who isn't here tonight. She should be; she tried to crawl through the stone wall of the building just because she had seen us walking together down the street. There are still, for every one of us in this room, thousands out there who would react the way she did. I wish she were here tonight: I wish they all were. I'm sure you know what I mean, and the writers—lesbian writers—are the ones who can do this. We can with what we write, what we publish, what we put together and send out. For the isolated ones, the frightened ones, we're their only hope. The only place they have to go, for the most part.

Which brings me to publishing. More of it is needed; new presses, more newsletters and newspapers, all magazines that exist, and right now we're mourning the death of *Amazon Quarterly;* it has issued its last. I understand—and I won't name them (that sometimes is almost a death sign)—there are at least two other publications, one of which is exclusively lesbian and one of which is lesbian/feminist, that are definitely dying and dying almost immediately. Reasons given are usually time and money . . . but there is, I suspect, a far more dangerous reason, the malaise of overwork and the exhaustion of those willing to work. We need to support them and I don't necessarily mean support them with money, although that helps a great deal. We need to send them material. They still, all of them, suffer for material. All they get (and I've had this information from several) is coming-out stories or political analysis, and they cannot build whole issues on this material. Because eventually when the readers cannot stand to read any more political analysis, and don't care who came out, they'll stop reading.

About once every month, I am asked to write a biographical or historical article—right now I am not—I may be again—but there have to be a lot of women right here in this room who can do the necessary bare-bones research and write a biographical article for whatever local newsletter, newspaper—or one of the national ones; they all need material badly.

Most of the lesbian writers I know are interested in *individual publications,* which is understandable; to be a writer means to have an ego, it means to think that you have something to say that is important enough that at least one or two other people in the world will read what you have to say. So I can understand wanting to do individual publications. They're very, very important, but there's no money for that either. In a lot of cases, so many more cooperative enterprises need to happen. We need to put things together with the help of other people, pool the resources to get things out; once again, if we don't, they won't get out. Everything that gets out, brings out more people; the more resources, the more money. All of it is very important. All of it needs to be done.

So far almost none of our publishing ventures have been self-sustaining . . . and there is going to be a long period of time probably before that will happen. There are encouraging signs in the book creating publishing ventures. Daughters, Inc. of Vermont is flourishing; if I understand correctly, they have a great deal of money. They now deal entirely in fiction. Diana

Press is functioning well, though they struggle a good bit. They are doing non-fiction though and that is encouraging. Their next release is Jeannette Howard Foster's *Sex Variant Women in Literature,* due out on or about Thanksgiving Day this year. Next year, they hope to begin publishing a series of three anthologies gathered from the sixteen years of *The Ladder,* the late lamented lesbian journal to which I owe my life's allegiance. The first of these is to be biographical in nature, the second a collection of fiction and the last a collection of essays from *The Ladder*'s pages. Many other presses are dealing in poetry, which is a loving and needed, but very limited field. The Naiad Press which just began in 1973, has so far published only fiction, two novels out now and two scheduled for release in 1976. Chicago's own Lavender Press has published poetry and Womanpress *Women Loving Women,* an annotated bibliography. *The Ladder* has issued its own index and the new edition of *The Lesbian in Literature* (which title was supposed to be my talk tonight, but I fooled you!).

What to do next? Well, one thing is certain, those of us who fancy ourselves as writers for the lesbian movement have got to begin contributing well-worked out material to the existing newspapers. Most of them are in need of material and welcome it. Most of them will privately admit to getting a good many coming-out tales and a good deal of political analysis and little else. They can also use, where you are situated physically near enough to help, your presence as a laborer, and the writers of this movement have got to be laborers too.

There are many women to find, many lesbians to write about and for. We are the women to do this. We are leaders, whether we like that term or not. Not elitists, and maybe not even doers . . . we are the orators. We watch and record . . . that is our place and it is a good one. We have to go out on hills and listen for the fine wild sweet singing of our past and record it for our future.

January 10, 1976

The Gay Pagan's Manifesto

Tommi Avicolli

Although the text of this document as presented in the January 10, 1976, *Gay Community News (GCN)* lists Tommi Avicolli as the author, the accompanying note states "below a group of gay pagans centered in Philadelphia states their reasons why they do not support the Christian or Jewish faith." It is a useful view of the diversity of religious exploration in the gay and lesbian community in the 1970s and an aspect not often discussed.

The recently passed California bill legalizing gay sex has, of course, come under attack by fundamentalists organizing to oppose the bill in a referendum next year. It seems likely they will at least succeed in getting the signatures they need to promote such an action. In other states, other cities, everywhere, wherever gay rights or anti-sodomy statutes have risen so have the crazies—the religious fanatics with their bibles, self-righteousness and their tales of impending doom. It's all so confusing to me that in the midst of this, gay church people are still urging us to cling to Christianity. But to give them the benefit of the doubt, let me examine briefly the HIStory of the Christian church!

The Jewish nomads settled in the promised land, a land ripe with patriarchy and father-right. Whatever remained of the former matriarchies had been washed away by the onslaught of the male deities Zeus, Jehova, Rama, etc. Some matriarchal influence remained in the pagan cults which the good Jews protected themselves from through such ordinances as the ban on homosexuality, on idolatry, etc., attempts to purge themselves from their neighbor's lifestyles.

The Jews were a small people, yet Christianity was born out of their patriarchal roots. Jesus, whom we're not even sure existed (read *The Pagan Christ*) established a new order. His was to be a church of love, yet his teachings speak only of "brotherhood" and of men, not of women. His only dealing with women seems to be the forgiving of a prostitute. What did he do with her afterwards? Was it for his own "convenience" that he forgave her?

Christianity was strongly misogynistic from the start. Paul denies the right of women to teach: he further asserts that Adam was innocent of the first sin. Writings of the early Church fathers also try and deny maternity, but in theological terms, of course! I Corinthians 11: 8-9 said, "The man is not of the woman, but the woman is of the man." It's not much different than the attempt in Genesis to deny maternity by depicting Eve's creation from Adam's rib. Clement in the second century A.D. said: "every woman should be overwhelmed with shame at the thought that she is a woman" (Elizabeth Gould David, *The First Sex,* p. 231). Thus echoing an earlier Jewish prayer and completing a full circle.

Later Christians sought out the witches, females who revived earlier totemic practices, and together with the faggots, burned them on the altars of male supremacy. A woman could be persecuted for the most obvious "crimes": lesbianism, refusal to have sex with a priest, and/or even striking back a husband who had just beaten her. Heresy was a catch-all charge, loaded and convenient for the medieval patriarchs to use against any attempt on the part of women or faggots to break the chains of their oppression.

Modern Christians try to whitewash this tradition, apologizing for Paul and Clement, for the persecutions of the nine million women and countless faggots! Even the gay church apologists strive to make right the wrong of Christianity.

Christianity is based upon the belief that men are superior to women; witness Genesis. Witness the absence of any strong female deity. Mary is an impotent fertility figure probably robbed from the Egyptians. The main deities of the Christian faith are male. The basic creation myth of the Christians concerns a male god creating life, an impossible situation since only women biologically can give birth. Christianity is a good psychological study of *womb envy* on the part of the male sex, the envy to procreate.

Christianity punishes women for the first sin. Eve is told to bear children in pain as punishment, and to be subservient to her husband. In medieval times, women were denied use of the pain killer, belladonna, during childbirth because the church felt it was against God's will. After all, they said, women were meant to suffer in childbirth!

Christianity clearly declares gay love sick. The bible cannot be changed. Nowhere does it give us the freedom to love. All those vague passages about everything are of no use to any free-thinking gay person.

Christianity is a bigoted way of life. It segregates one person from others of different faiths, declaring them heretics and sinners: it promotes prejudice and male supremacy. In other times Christians waged holy wars against pagans and murdered millions of us. Today it wages these same wars in other ways, through political manipulations and economic control. Witness the defeat of Intro 554 at the hands of the Catholic church!

It has never been accurately determined just how much wealth the Vatican has. Millions (if not all) of the poor could be fed on what the Catholic Church owns. Yet the Pope chooses to live like an aristocrat and to appease the poor with phony encyclicals and ridiculous pomp and circumstance.

The poor have been deluded by centuries of queer-baiting and sex role re-enforcement done at the expense of their freedoms of choice to love and to be adequately fed and housed. The church helped the feudal lords oppress the masses, helped capitalism, and did nothing to stop Hitler in the '30s. The silence of the church during times of oppression only re-enforces my own concept of it as concerned with its own continued patriarchal existence.

Christianity has most of all created a network of co-optation that can incorporate any current trend back into itself. A few years ago the church complained of dwindling members; now recently they're rejoicing at their growing numbers. A clever propaganda campaign? Probably not. Economic recession sends people back to their security blankets and Christianity is an easy crutch to lean on.

Christianity can even absorb gay liberation. It can pretend to be accepting and loving to us while all the time greedy to snatch our co-operation. What will the church of the future be like? Will gays be worshipping a male deity, marrying and establishing nuclear family units (2.8 adopted kids) and supporting holy wars in new Vietnams? Will we be feeding the new popes and patriarchs? NO!

Christianity has attempted to co-opt feminism by setting up a token commission to study the status of women: and in some churches by ordaining women. Yet if it were truly feminist, it would burn the cathedrals and feed the poor, abolish male deities, obliterate the nuclear family and allow us to love and live in total freedom. I don't trust Christianity, not in its most tolerating, liberal streak. It's fool's gold. I don't understand why gays find it necessary to apologize for their homosexuality by asserting that God loves them, too. The Christian's patriarchal God doesn't love dykes and faggots and queens. He's all of our fathers, the strict disciplinarian who for years told us to be women and men in the finest tradition of the sex-role system. Little ladies and gentlemen, pooh!

We are queers in the eyes of this male God. We are perverted. But we shouldn't be ashamed of this fact. We should realize that in this fact we are most free. Free to challenge the millions of years of oppression and persecution against gays and women for their violation of a sexist and male supremist theology, a theology based upon the twisted logic of man creating life through *womb envy*. Man has never created life; his HIStory is one of wars, violence and persecutions.

This male god is my enemy. I do not ask any acceptance from him. I rejoice in my queerness. He is not my god, nor my savior. I await his destruction as I await the destruction of all homophobes.

There is no salvation in Christianity: only a continuation of our oppression as queers and as women. As free entities. As androgynes. As pagans and atheists. As goddess worshippers. As earth lovers, as matriarchy seekers. The goddess lives. Paganism now!

March 30, 1976

Privacy and Sexuality

Ed Koch

Given on the floor of the House of Representatives by Representative Koch of New York and entered in the *Congressional Record* for March 30, 1976.

Mr. Speaker, yesterday, the U.S. Supreme Court ruled by a vote of 6 to 3 that States may prosecute and imprison consenting adults for participating in homosexual acts. The decision of the Court affirmed without comment the 2 to 1 decision last fall of a Federal district court in Virginia which upheld a State law prohibiting sodomy.

Every person, without regard to his or her sexuality, heterosexual or homosexual, should be outraged by this decision. Outraged, first because the Court summarily ruled on this matter, without hearing arguments or issuing an opinion. This was an insensitive handling of an issue affecting the lives of millions. The fact that the Court closed its doors to arguments of law may suggest to some that the Court could not adequately justify its decision by law or reason.

And second, all citizens should be concerned with the failure of the Court to protect the privacy of citizens. In the future, other citizens will be affected by other questions of privacy in matters such as birth control, other sexual practices between husband and wife, or abortion. The failure of the Court to recognize the privacy issue surely undermines the groundwork of privacy protections handed down by the Court since 1965, beginning with *Griswold vs. Connecticut,* the decision forbidding a State to interfere in the decision of a couple to employ birth control devices.

Yesterday's decision affects a significant portion of the population. It is estimated that at least 10 percent of the population engages in homosexual acts, and Kinsey in his famous study found that an even larger percentage of the population has had at least one homosexual experience. Does the Court seriously intend to allow all such persons to be considered criminals?

The Court's decision will not convince homosexuals to become heterosexuals. But, it will make it more difficult for those who believe in individual freedom to change State laws to provide equal protection for homosexuals in housing, employment, and public accommodations, as well as to repeal the State sodomy laws. Some 13 States have already repealed sodomy prohibitions, and while these States will continue to be free of criminal sanctions for acts between consenting adults, the Court's decision will make it much more difficult to obtain repeal of existing criminal statutes in the other 37 States.

Civil libertarians had hoped that—in view of the Supreme Court's right-to-privacy rulings since 1965 striking down restrictions on the sale of contraceptives, allowing citizens to have pornographic literature in their own homes, and protecting a woman's right to have an abortion—the Court would in appropriate cases protect consenting adult sexual conduct in private as part of a person's right to privacy.

But now, not only must civil libertarians pursue changes in the criminal laws to overcome this horrendous failure to act by the U.S. Supreme Court, they must redouble their efforts to enact legislation on a Federal and State level to bar discrimination against homosexuals in the areas of employment, housing, public accommodations, and Federal programs. There is legislation now pending in the House, H.R. 166, of which I am a cosponsor, which would do exactly that. That legislation is sponsored by Ms. Abzug, Mr. Badillo, Mr. Bingham, Mr. Brown, Mr. John L. Burton, Mrs. Chisholm, Mr. Dellums, Mr. Fauntroy, Mr. Fraser, Mr. Harrington, Ms. Holtzman, Mr. Koch, Mr. McClosky, Mr. Mineta, Mr. Mitchell, Mr. Nix, Mr. Rangel, Mr. Richmond, Mr. Rosenthal, Ms. Schroeder, Mr. Solarz, Mr. Stark, Mr. Studds, and Mr. Waxman.

Sponsorship of controversial legislation is generally avoided by those running for election. But indeed, Mr. Speaker, that is the time when the public can ascertain which of their legislators have the courage to stand up and be counted in support of the rights of persecuted minorities. No one has ever improved upon the statement of Prime Minister of Canada Pierre Trudeau, who years ago stated:

> *The state has no business in the bedrooms of the Nation.*

Regrettably, the Supreme Court has allowed the Government to intrude into the bedrooms of our Nation, and that decision must be reversed judicially or by legislation.

July 11, 1976

Speech at NYSCGO Demonstration

David Thorstad

Thorstad was at this time one of the organizers of this demonstration, former president of New York City's Gay Activists Alliance, co-author of the book *The Early Homosexual Rights Movement, 1864-1935,* and plaintiff in a lawsuit filed by the Lambda Legal Defense and Education Fund challenging the constitutionality of New York State's sodomy law. The NYSCGO was the New York State Council of Gay Organizations.

Sisters and Brothers,

Let me share with you a few things that I know about gay.

I know that gay is good.

I know that gay is proud.

I know that gay is beautiful.

The gay liberation movement taught me that.

But I also know—and I feel it in my guts—that gay is angry! I did not know this at first. At first, I—like so many of us here—turned my anger inward on myself. But the gay liberation movement opened my eyes and taught me how to look around and see oppression where it was. It taught me how to recognize injustice. Now, I hate injustice. Now, I turn my anger outward, at the injustice of this society toward my millions of sisters and brothers. I have learned that the only way to correct injustice is to fight back against it. That's what we're doing today.

And we're fighting not only for ourselves, but also for those millions of homosexuals who have not yet opened their dark closets of fear.

It is sad, but true, that we still have few friends among other oppressed peoples willing to join us in this fight. But their numbers are growing. We know that we are the cutting edge of the revolution for a better world. We know something about oppression. And we know something about freedom too. Freedom is something we have never tasted.

We are here today to send a message to the world. That message is this: So long as one homosexual remains in bondage, no one—whether they be

Black, Indian, Puerto Rican, Chicano, women, or workers—will be free. There can be no revolution without us!

We're here today to demand basic rights that everybody else takes for granted. But we know, deep down, that we're struggling for much more too. We're not satisfied with merely being tolerated—though we're not even *that* yet. We're not satisfied with token gay planks in party platforms—though we did not even get *that* from the Democratic circus performers who will be showing off across the street. No. We want a new and better world, in which gay will be unchained and free. We want a world in which not only we, but everyone else too will know that gay is good and gay is beautiful! We want a society that will throw all the oppression and garbage of capitalism into the trashcan of history.

But we will never be free if we rely on others to free us. We must build our own struggle, as we are doing here today, and make no concessions to anyone. Kurt Hiller, a hero of the early homosexual rights movement in Germany, said it well in 1921: "The liberation of homosexuals can only be the work of homosexuals themselves!"

JUSTICE!

August 17, 1976

Statement on Sex and Violence on Television

Ginny Vida

This address was presented at a hearing on sex and violence on television held in Los Angeles, California, on August 17, 1976, by the Subcommittee on Communications of the House of Representatives Committee on Interstate and Foreign Commerce. Ginny Vida was at this time the media director of the National Gay Task Force. The full hearing text was reprinted as Y4.In4, 94-140, the committee's publication of its proceedings.

As I was thinking about what I might say here today, I was struck by a passage in E.L. Doctorow's *Ragtime.*

The novel takes place in the early 1900's, a time when, as Doctorow puts it, "There were no Negroes. There were no immigrants."

The big news of the period was the murder of architect Stanford White by the husband of his mistress, Evelyn Nesbit, who quickly became the sex symbol of her generation and part of America's fantasy world of riches. Doctorow imagines a meeting between Nesbit and "Emma Goldman, the revolutionary," at which Goldman attempts to raise Nesbit's social consciousness.

"Goldman," Doctorow says—and I quote—"lashed her with her tongue." Apparently, there were Negroes. There were immigrants. And though the newspapers called the shooting the crime of the century, Goldman knew "it was only 1906 and there were 94 years to go," unquote.

Seventy years have passed, and the families of America, who for half that time have been watching an unimaginably wonderful invention called television, have only in the past decade or so begun to be exposed, after dinner each evening, to Emma Goldman's truth. There are black Americans, people with the same capacity for laughter and tears as the rest of us. There were immigrants, and people with names like Arthur Fonzarelli and Gabriel

Kotter and Shirley Feeny and Abraham Rodriguez are part of our nation and part of our lives.

Seventy years have passed, and I, who left a career as a children's book editor to go public as media director for the National Gay Task Force, have come here to tell the distinguished members of this congressional subcommittee some more of the truth.

The truth is that there are gay people; millions of homosexual men and women in every city and town across America. The truth is that American families, yes, and American children, have the right to know that we exist.

Gay people are the only group in America which emerged from total media invisibility into total media abuse. Until just a couple of years ago, the only gay men to be found on network television were a breed of closet Stepin Fetchits, who traded on the hilarious potential of that great American hallucination, the "sissy." Then, the big breakthrough came, and gay men, labeled as such, were allowed to be not only comic sissies, but hysterical drunkards ridden with guilt, cowardly murderers who burst into tears on the witness stand, and rapers of teenage boys.

Until recently, on television, there definitely were no lesbians, and then the big breakthrough came. There were lesbians and it wasn't a joke. We were permitted to make our television debuts as the brutal rapists of pitiable young girls, as the heartless killers of dear, sweet ladies in an old-folks home.

Partly due to the efforts of organizations like the National Gay Task Force, things are looking up a bit. Dr. Newton Deiter, coordinator of the Gay Media Task Force, here in Los Angeles, can tell you a bit more about current and upcoming shows involving gay characters.

But, on programs directed to children, and in the so-called family viewing hours, there are still no gay people. Why is that? Because the people at the networks tell each other, parents think that gay people are synonymous with violence and with sex.

No wonder, we answer, that parents think we are violent, considering the stuff they have been served up in adult viewing hours.

But, what about the sex, they ask each other in the corridors at the networks? Surely, if it is called homosexuality, how can it not be sex?

Our answer, of course, is to ask the same question, about heterosexuality. The truth is that pictures of two homosexuals, two women or two men, kissing each other tenderly on the lips, are no more and no less about sex than what heterosexuals are seen doing every night in full view of everybody in family viewing time. The truth is that stories about two young women or men discovering love and regard for each other are not about explicit sex, and stories about lesbians or gay men coming out to their families are not about sex at all.

As for violence and sex, the National Gay Task Force takes no position on whether children are harmed by explicit depictions of these subjects.

We are opposed to violence, however, and we think that violence on television is a reflection of a male-dominated culture that squanders its energies in endless, violent attempts to prove its manhood.

We are not opposed to sex, but we believe that emphasis on sex, without love and caring, insofar as that is depicted on television, is the reflection of a heterosexual world which has just discovered that women are sexual beings, and is madly celebrating that awareness by imagining that women must now do what men in our culture traditionally have been programed to do: treat their partners, not as whole human beings, but as pieces of décor, sexual trophies to be used as false measures of personhood.

We, at the National Gay Task Force, believe that children have the right to learn the truth.

Gay women and men do care about children. I hope it doesn't surprise you to learn that many of us have children of our own, and all of us care about all of the children in America who are taught to believe, and dare not confess, that each one of them is the only one in the world to have loving feelings for members of their own sex.

Gay people do care about morality. We think, for instance, that just as it was immoral to foster prejudice and discrimination by pretending to the children of America that there were no black people, no real people who were Jews, Mexicans, or Poles, it is immoral to foster prejudice and discrimination by pretending to the children of America that there are no real people who are gay. We think that just as it was immoral to provide no models for America's black children to look at on television and say, "Yes. That is just like me," it is immoral to provide no models for the children that all of us millions of gay men and women once were, children who sit by their sets with their families and hope for a sign that there is someone about whom they can say, "Yes. That is just like me."

We think it is not only immoral, but illegal, for the industry, mandated to serve the needs of all the public, to fail to serve our needs.

We are not asking the Congress to pass a law requiring the networks to present only positive depictions of gay people at all viewing hours. We believe that the Congress is wisely restrained by the Constitution from such narrow restrictions on speech.

We do ask that this committee, as part of its oversight functions, request the Federal Communications Commission to use all of its existing powers to require the television industry to offer fair and accurate images of all Americans, including this country's second largest minority, the gay population.

We understand that congressional hearings, such as this, are often used not only as forums for public interest groups like ours, but as a means of acquainting the public with the views of the committee's members.

If we have persuaded any of the members of this subcommittee of the rightness of our position, we also ask that you speak out today to the public, the FCC, and the television industry and tell them that you believe public ownership of the airwaves is not being protected for a significant number of the owners: gay citizens who pay their taxes and vote for Congress people like everybody else.

You may hesitate to speak out. There are lots of other voters who are frightened of us, but, as you think it over, I would like you to recall Emma Goldman and 1906. Like the founders of this Nation, she was a revolutionary, and most of the revolutionary ideas she fought for—the right of workers to unionize and strike, the right of all citizens to equal treatment, regardless of their place of origin or color of skin—are believed in today, I hope, by every one of us here in this hearing room. Even the revolutionary ideas she went to prison for—an end to the military draft, the right of heterosexuals to practice birth control—are parts of our legal system today.

Other of Goldman's ideas have not been fully accepted, like the right of women, as Doctorow has Goldman say it, to, quote, "love whom they want, develop their minds and spirits, commit their lives to the spiritual adventure of life, and provide philosophical models for the betterment of mankind," unquote. But, I think we don't stamp ourselves as revolutionaries by saying that this idea is one that we at the National Gay Task Force believe in.

I am not Emma Goldman. I am not a revolutionary. I am simply a woman who respects the truth and tries to act with integrity, and I see no reason, at all, why my life is unsuitable for children.

But, I believe, with Emma Goldman, that there was no reason, at all, to wait 70 years, or a single moment, for blacks, or for Jewish, Italian, Mexican, Chinese, Polish, Puerto Rican immigrants, or for our only native American non-immigrants, to remain invisible as real people to other American families and children. I believe that neither I, nor any of my gay brothers and sisters of all ages, should be required to wait a single moment for fairness and visibility from this Nation's largest communications industry.

There is a great deal of hope today among the American people that integrity and loving regard for human needs can be put to work at the helm of Government. There is growing confidence that if that promise of integrity and humanity turns out to be a sham, we will be told about it by our communications media before it is too late.

We, at the National Gay Task Force, share the Nation's hope, but we cannot share its confidence. Not so long as the most influential of the communications media continues to defame us or deny we exist. Not so long as television fails to present us to America's families in all of our human variety. Not so long as the purveyors of mass entertainment refuse to realize that oftentimes, for children, as well as adults, there is nothing quite so entertaining as the truth.

August 17, 1976

Gay People on Television

Newton Deiter

This is the text of the statement made at a public hearing on sex and violence on television held in Los Angeles by the Subcommittee on Communication of the House Committee on Interstate and Foreign Commerce, and entered in the committee print of said hearing (Y4.In4, 94-140). Dr. Deiter was at this time a member of the Gay Media Task Force, formed in the early 1970s by members of the National Gay and Lesbian Task Force.

Mr. Chairman and members of the committee, my name is Newton Deiter, and I am here to make a statement on behalf of the Gay Media Task Force, an organization which was established to work on behalf of fair, impartial, and balanced treatment of the lifestyles of gay men and lesbians presented on television.

We, on the Gay Media Task Force, recognized that the approximately 20 million gay women and men in the United States, because they represent a cross section of Americans, are as concerned with presentation of sex and violence on television as are other Americans. We are, at the same time, concerned about first amendment rights guaranteed to all people, including, but not limited to, the writers, producers, directors and creators of television programming.

Some years ago, the Honorable Newton J. Minnow, former Chairman of the Federal Communications Commission, referred to television as a vast wasteland. Since that time, we have observed that television has ceased, in large part, to serve the American public a diet of sugar-coated pap. It has shown a willingness to deal with pressing social issues, and to provide the American public with a more realistic picture of the society in which they live and the problems which plague that society.

At first, this willingness manifested itself in documentaries, primarily limited to the Sunday "Ghetto Hour" programming. Programs of this nature were later moved into television prime time. More and more, the creators of television drama and comedy have dealt with issues of social relevancy in their material, and have, in our view, enormously increased the three-dimensional view of American life thus presented. It is our view that this sort of presentation should and must continue.

We base this statement on our belief that television has the potential for being the most important educational medium the world has ever known. It has the capacity to bring into the home a host of ideas, a view of the world which may lie outside the personal experience of its viewers. In doing so, it can provide its viewers with views of their fellow Americans as human beings, which they may not otherwise be able to obtain.

A farmer in Maine, for example, may better understand the problems of a ghetto dweller in the city, the problems faced by people who live in a world he has never seen, and will, in all likelihood, never have the chance to see; all through the common humanity which binds them both. In a simple, subliminal fashion, ideas of peace, friendship and acceptances of differences in people have been, and can continue to be, propagated by television creators.

There are those, today, who feel that the pendulum has swung too far, and that television has become far too graphic in its presentation of social issues which it brings into American homes. In certain regrettable instances, this may be so. We hold, however, that these occasional lapses of good taste and judgment should not be permitted to cause blanket condemnation of socially relevant programming and its creators.

There are those who feel that divorce, childhood pregnancy, prostitution, the hell that is our penal system, denial of educational opportunity, racial and religious prejudice, the moral question of abortion, the rights of women to determine their own destiny, and the rights of gay men and women to lead happy and productive lives, are not fit subjects to be brought into the American home. We do not agree with this contention.

We believe that social evils are born of ignorance of conditions; that many of these problems and situations do, in fact, exist in American homes, and that the American public has the right to receive a fair and honest presentation of the society around them. We believe that those, who would terminate social relevancy in television programming, are engaging in the same sort of specious reasoning which once banned sex education from schools and the books of Hemingway and Salinger from library shelves to protect American children from the vivid realities of the life for which they were being prepared.

It is our belief that television has the obligation to inform and to educate, and that those who have been granted a license in the public interest have, in fact, an obligation to present sensitive and emotionally charged material on that medium.

We believe that, up until a year ago, the television industry, on a national, regional and local level, was making dramatic efforts to live up to the responsibilities the Communications Act requires of them.

A little more than a year ago, the creators of television programming discovered that an evening time line has been drawn. Earlier hours were reserved for family viewing, a period of time, during which certain kinds of issues were banned from the airwaves. Prior to the time line, and afterward, the rules remained unchanged, and sensitive or controversial subjects could still be explored. All this despite the fact that children come home between the hours of 3 and 4 in the afternoon and are free to watch the evening news shows, which frequently carry subliminal messages about excesses of human behavior which social psychologists have discovered, frequently, have more negative effects on children than dramatic presentations.

Children, these professionals have found, draw a distinction between the real as represented by news programs and make-believe as represented by written dramas and comedies, and the effects of news accounts of murders, such as the Manson slayings, of riots, of political corruption, coverups, and sex scandals, and of the grim effects of war, because they are real events, have more capacity to engender violence in children than do programs which they recognize as mere representations of life.

The institution of family hour viewing created a problem for networks and suppliers of products as well. The networks recognized that the Federal Communications Commission could exercise a large degree of moral persuasion by their granting or withholding licenses to network-owned and operated stations, and was able to persuade the networks to self-censor the products they allowed on their airwaves.

Insofar as the sellers of program material—studios, production companies, and individual products—were concerned, they felt that they would now have to steer a safe course. They had to assure themselves that the product which was being sold for viewing before 9 P.M. would be safe and acceptable, instead of deciding whether a project had merit and was worth developing. Their thought processes had to change from, "Does the project have merit?" to "Does this project have merit before 9 P.M. or after 9 P.M.?"

Obviously, if they developed a product that was adult in its approach, they had 2 hours in which it could be presented. If, however, they developed a product that was safe for family hour, they then had the possibility of all three hours in which the product could be bought; therefore, the opportunities to sell safe products are greater due to more flexible programming scheduling.

The result was stultification. With few exceptions [writers] became cautious in the presentation of their product to their buyers, the networks. Packagers of shows already on the air assigned to the 8 and 9 P.M. hour became far less adventuresome in the development of scripts for production. Conversation all over Hollywood revolved around, "What is acceptable for family viewing?"

No one really had the answers. Not the networks, writers, producers, no one. One network executive said, "Oh, it was simple to solve the problem. We just told the producers to deliver just what they delivered before, except pitch it lower for the whole family." I don't know if the members of this subcommittee know what that means, but the producer to whom the remark was addressed confessed utter confusion.

Insofar as gay men and women were concerned, with the notable exception of one segment of producer Danny Arnold's *Barney Miller,* appearing on ABC, no presentation of gay people, in any way, appeared during the 8 to 9 hours all last year. The networks indicate that they had no blanket prohibition against the portrayal of gay people, or situations involving gay people during these hours, and that they would evaluate each request for clearance of this subject matter on a case-by-case basis.

On the surface, a fair standard; in actuality, producers selling product to all three networks have told me that before 9 P.M., the subject of homosexuality or lesbianism in any way, shape or form is taboo. Since their livelihood depends on delivering to the networks what they perceive the networks want, in effect, gay people disappeared from television during that hour, and from other time slots, as well. We believe this to be in direct contradiction to the obligation which television has to inform and educate its viewers. For the simple fact is that Americans of all ages, in all walks of life, come into contact with gay women and men every day of their lives.

Gay people teach in schools, work in offices, are manual laborers, and work in factories. Gay people are, in fact, born into families and participate in family life. Just as with Jews, blacks, Chicanos, and native Americans, prejudice practiced against gay people arises from ignorance of the common humanity which is shared with the other 180 million people who live in these United States.

We are very troubled by the fact that the existence of more than 20 million people, most of whom lead lives which are as productive and constructive as those of other Americans, has been eliminated from one-third of the hours available for network programming. This elimination, linked as it is with the entire matter of a blanket prohibition against sex and violence in the early evening, seems to us akin to using an atomic bomb to destroy a fly. It will certainly do the job, but the cost appears to be out of line with the desired outcome.

There is, built into the American free enterprise system, and in particular, television, a simple mechanism for showing one's displeasure with a product or service. If one is displeased, one ceases to buy or to patronize; and, if, in fact, the overwhelming majority of the American viewing public wants bland programming between 8 and 9 P.M., it will very quickly make the networks aware of the fact by not watching programming that they believe has an excessive display of violence, is blatantly sexually oriented, or is otherwise offensive.

Self-policing and the intelligent use of the airwaves is a responsibility incumbent upon the networks, and certainly, by law, upon the owners and operators of individual television stations.

These stations that persist in presenting programming not in the public interest, or offensive in subject matter or content, to a majority of their audiences, would soon find their licenses under assault from groups within their own communities. Sponsors who buy time in programming segments would find, we believe, that if this programming were offensive, they would hear from the consumers of their products, and would quickly remove commercials from these programs. Since networks are dependent on time sales for their income, the economic pressure would be quickly felt, and programming changes would be made.

We cannot believe that network personnel are unaware of this. They use these same tools to cancel programs which are not accepted by the public, and if they are able to do it very quickly, these tools can be used, also, to determine when viewers find programming content to be distasteful and unacceptable. To exclude subject matter by inaction and misdirection denies the creators of television programming their right to explore, in the public interest, all facets of American society in the last quarter of the 20th century.

As gay people, we do not ask that we be the recipient of special programming, or that our concerns be given special handling. Just the opposite. We ask, and, in fact, insist upon, fair presentation of our lives, lifestyle, existence as Americans, in the same manner as that of any other minority group or subcultural group.

I thank the subcommittee for its attention and am ready to respond to questions.

August 29, 1976

How Do You Define "Lesbianism"?

New Jersey Lesbian Caucus

This paper was reprinted in the Chicago newspaper *GayLife* on August 29, 1976. An accompanying note states that the document was produced "in an attempt to establish a definition of radical Lesbian/Feminist . . . as information and a source of discussion and self-definition." *The Furies* was a lesbian feminist collective formed in Washington, DC, in 1971. It sought to translate the lesbian feminist ethic into practice and focused on two main issues—the social and political bases of heterosexuality and homosexualty (defining lesbianism as a political choice) and the connection between class and heterosexuality.

In our sexist and sex-oriented society lesbians have generally been defined as women who have sexual relations with other women. We reject this identification on purely sexual terms, just as non-lesbian women hopefully reject their identification only and solely by their sexual activities.

Martin and Lyon in their book *Lesbian/Woman* define a lesbian as "a woman whose primary erotic, psychological and social interest is in a member of her own sex . . ." Rita Mae Brown in an article in the now defunct FURIES defined a lesbian as a woman who loves lesbians.

We feel that both of these definitions are only partly valid, and that lesbianism and lesbians are far more difficult to define.

Last year National NOW convened a taskforce on "Lesbianism and Sexuality." We of the Lesbian Caucus disagree with the combination of sexuality and lesbianism as if they were part of the same issue. They are not. Lesbianism is a way of being, while sexuality is basically an act.

When women—sometimes women-oriented women—try to tell us that the only difference between us and other women is what we do in bed, we need to ask these women several questions. For one, what about women who for shorter or longer periods decide to be celibate? Are these women "nothing"? Also, if lesbianism is only a sexual act, then, when a lesbian leaves her bedroom, does she cease being a lesbian? The absurdity of these statements is obvious: a celibate woman is either a lesbian or straight, and when I leave my bedroom I am still a lesbian. I do not suddenly become straight because I leave my bed and my bed-partner behind.

Another reason for a need to define who and what we are is the spread of the feminist movement causing women to learn to relate to each other as working partners, friends, and possibly more than that. When we work with people and form close relationships, we tend to develop feelings beyond "accepted" limits, including at times—sexual feelings. Some women become frightened when this happens, and leave the movement. Others less inhibited decide to explore their feelings and get emotionally and sometimes sexually involved with other women. While many of these women explore with other women in similar circumstances, some feel that only a "true" lesbian will do, putting many lesbian sisters in sticky situations where they are damned if they accede, and even more damned if they refuse the advances of the straight woman.

The question naturally arises whether these previously straight women are now "becoming lesbians," and the attending question is whether lesbianism is something one decides to "become," like joining a party or a club. Also, most if not all of these women undoubtedly will eventually return to their previous lifestyle, and men, and the question arises whether lesbianism is a "stage" in a woman's life.

These questions have become especially urgent in the past months, as we see movement "lesbians" return to a male-oriented lifestyle, such as Jill Johnston who has been exhibited as "Lesbian #1" to the American public by the media, and who has written books about her life as a "lesbian."

Those of us who have always been lesbians, have lived the lesbian lifestyle for many years, and who identify as radical lesbian/feminists, are understandably disturbed by these events, because they seriously threaten the credibility of our lifestyle. After all, if Jill Johnston after writing books and being so very public . . . is returning into the male-female fold, doesn't it prove that lesbianism is just a passing fancy . . . a man-hating phase which will go away as soon as the woman meets the "right" man? Doesn't it prove that "dykes" are sickies at worst, and poor women who cannot get a man at best? That lesbianism is not a valid and permanent lifestyle? Of course, we reject all such conclusions.

Then, who or what IS a lesbian, and what IS lesbianism? We are here trying to formulate some kind of a position, as best we can, because there is, of course, no pat answer to a way of living, relating and loving.

We feel that lesbianism is a "given": that a woman either IS, or IS NOT a lesbian, and that she has basically no choice in the matter. She DOES have a choice as to whether she will ACT upon her lesbianism. Or not. But she has NO choice in whether she is, or is not, emotionally basically oriented towards women in contrast to non-lesbians who are basically oriented towards men. This is where the difficulty arises: because in our society the emphasis is on the male-female relationship, and many lesbians marry men, have children, and try to live a conventional lifestyle. This does not, in our opinion, make these women "straight"—it simply means that these women have opted for a lifestyle not "natural" FOR THEM, but easier (in their opinion) in our society as it is. On the other hand, we see women who have been poorly treated by men ADOPT a same-sex lifestyle which is also not natural FOR THEM . . . adopt a preference for females out of an aversion to males. It is these women who eventually return to the male/female lifestyle, because it is natural for them to do so, and "playing" lesbian is not.

It must be emphasized that lesbianism is never hating men (negative) but rather that it is only and solely a positive attitude of loving women.

Lesbianism is then, basically, a head trip, and one that is developed early in a woman's life. We don't know how early, but we know some women who were aware of their total involvement with women early in life, at age 3 or 4. Others do not come to this realization until their "teens," and for others the assurance of where their heads and hearts are comes even later, often after some years of marriage and several children.

Many of these women have felt a vague uneasiness about themselves all of their lives. They never felt "right," but could not determine what was wrong. Sometimes when such women finally become aware of their lesbianism, the feeling of "wrong" disappears immediately. With others the realization is more gradual and the adjustment not so sudden.

We have so far mentioned sexuality only at the very beginning. What about sex and sexual orientation? Sexual orientation is, of course, mostly a matter of choice or *preference*. Most people are sexual, and can function at least to some degree with either or both sexes. Most people make a deliberate choice when they choose a sex partner. The lesbian, however, will never feel fulfilled with a male, as the non-lesbian woman will never be fully fulfilled with a female sex partner, meaning both emotionally and physically. Most of us can go through the motions, but true fulfillment is another matter.

We reject the sexual definition of "lesbian" mainly because we feel that lesbians relate sexually to other women *because* they are totally women-centered in their entire outlook. We do not feel that women are lesbians by virtue of relating sexually to other women. In other words, we feel that same-sex expression is a *consequence of,* rather than a *criterion for* being a lesbian.

March 1977

Neither Profit Nor Salvation

Barbara Grier

This address was given at San Jose State University by Grier as the keynote speech of Women Together Day during the university's Women's Week in March 1977.

In the last several months while I've prepared, or tried to prepare, to speak to you today, I've often thought—talking to myself in the bathroom mirror, riding back and forth to work—how extremely arrogant it is for anyone to get up in front of a group and pretend to be able to discuss in 15, 20, 40 minutes the subject of Lesbians and Lesbianism.

I'm 43 years old. I've spent virtually my entire life from age 14 studying the subject. (If I have 5 more lifetimes ahead of me, I'll barely begin to scratch the surface, even though I've specialized primarily in one tiny aspect of the panorama of our existence, the Lesbian in literature because, after all, there are millions of Lesbians.) There are millions of Lesbians in the United States. Not thousands nor hundreds of thousands, but millions of women who are Lesbians. We have many things in common, but we have many more things not in common with one another. What is true for one of us may not be true for hundreds of thousands of us in different personal circumstances.

Probably the Lesbians sitting in this room have a little higher sense of what we call "consciousness" but maybe not even that, because I'll bet there are some closeted Lesbians in this room too. In fact, there are probably quite a few secret Lesbians sitting out there listening to me now. And as I'm talking, you're beginning to shake inside or squirm a little. There's bound to be some of you out there. There are always some of you in any room where there are a few women, always. Every time you ride a bus and there are a handful of women on that bus, someone on that bus is probably a closet Lesbian, maybe several someones on that bus. In fact, the closet, that ridiculous place, may be just exactly the only other thing we have in common besides the basic one, that we are Lesbians.

I'm not even sure that I want to try to define the word Lesbian in front of a group like this. Those of you out there who know what the word means don't need any explanation, and those of you who do not, why are you here? But the closet, we all know about closets. We hang our coats, shirts, pants, shoes, lives in closets. In fact, not just some of us, not just a few of us, not half of us, or three quarters but more like 95% of us live our lives in closets.

Now, even the closet folk have differing levels of "closetism" . . . I guess we'll coin a word. Some of us live in closets part of the time, some of us live in closets, say 75% of the time and 25% we're out of the closet. We have select people to be out of the closet with. We're out of the closet with all of our gay friends, for example, and five select heterosexual individuals that we've chosen throughout our lives to decide to confer the great honor on them of telling them that we're Lesbians, and holding very still for a few moments and looking into their eyes for fear they'll flinch, back up, turn away, reject us outright, as if it mattered. As if it mattered a damn bit. It is the closet that is our sin and shame.

There's been a lot of talk since the late 1960's about coming out of the closet. There've been marches and speeches. There'll be many more speeches, at least, if not so many marches since marching doesn't seem to be this year's thing. There'll be some slogans:

"2,4,6,8, gay is just as good as straight"
"3,5,7,9, Lesbians are mighty fine"

The first slogan is an insult, and the second slogan is silly.

There will be speeches and more slogans. There will be another tiny percentile point rise at the end of the year in the number of visible Lesbians. This or that artist, this or that writer, this or that composer, this or that politician, this or that priest this or that minister. A few more of us will come out of the closet. Come out, come out, wherever you are. That will be very good for them and that will be very good for the handful of people whose lives they touch and it will probably even be somewhat beneficial for the Lesbians who have access to their public derring-do and take some comfort from their acts.

But coming out of the closet is getting to be less and less of an option and more and more of an obligation. It is not a matter of "you ought to because it's healthier to live like an open free person" or "you ought to because it's easier" because deception is difficult at best . . . you have to carry it forward and it keeps you busy looking over your shoulder on both sides. And you ought to because being in the closet is not necessary any longer. It's a moral obligation. It's not a matter of coming out of the closet because it's good for you. It's not a matter of coming out of the closet because it's good for your lover, because you're going to feel better, because it'll eventually loosen up your relationship with your neighbors or help at work. It has nothing to do with that. You need to come out of the closet because *you know* you're a Lesbian and every one of you who stays in the closet makes it harder for the woman down the street to come out of the closet. We help oppress each other, we are our own oppression. We even have a few women out there who are ashamed of being Lesbians. That's hard to imagine, I know, but it's true. There are still Lesbians out there who are ashamed of being Lesbians. Incomprehensible, illogical, of course, but it exists. Now, there are a few people who remain in the closet and enjoy being uncomfortable about being Lesbians, and I'm not sure if anything I say here today is going to have any effect on any of them. But there are some weird people everywhere, there are even some weird Lesbians, so if you're weird in this way, fine, stay in the closet, I'm not talking to you. I'm talking to the run-of-the-mill Lesbians out there, the women who do not belong in the closet, are not comfortable in the closet, don't really want to be in the closet, but think for some real or imagined reason . . . and imagined reasons are every bit as good as real reasons . . . that they must remain there because if they don't stay in the closet, if they come out, they're going to lose their jobs or no one will love them or people will point at them on the street and laugh or their co-workers will have nothing to do with them or well, make up your own reasons. I'm sure there are as many reasons as there are closet cases out there.

But it's not a matter of choice any longer. I'm not really asking you to come out of the closet, I'm telling you. You have to come out of the closet, you have to come out. Not only do you have to, but the time has come when those of us who are out of the closet need to put pressure on those who are in. And I don't mean unkind pressure but real pressure. We need to talk to the women we know who know that they are gay and that we know they're gay and that they know we know they're gay but who for one reason or another still remain in the closet. If there is a crusade in the future, the crusade is to strengthen our numbers publicly. I mean make those women who are Lesbians and know they are Lesbians stand up and be counted. It is time to do so. Once again, I am not advocating that you run around with sandwich boards, I am not saying you need to go out on the street and chalk it in front of your house. I am saying that you need to start acting like you really are. Don't lie, don't pretend. Behave as you are, you're a Lesbian, act like a Lesbian, be glad you're a Lesbian, tell the world you're a Lesbian, subtly, of course. But make sure that every thinking, intelligent person anywhere around you, that has any relationship with you, however casual, is aware or likely to be aware of your orientation. It's the least you can do for the cause, it's the least you can do for your own people. We have a terrible disadvantage . . . we aren't marked in some clear cut way. We can't be seen, we aren't visible. As others have suggested, I too wish we'd all wake up lavender some morning and solve that part of the problem. We cannot be seen and because we can't be seen, we can pretend, and in years past, perhaps there were reasons for it. Perhaps it was better, perhaps it was easier to pretend. But it's not good anymore, it's not healthy, it doesn't feel good, it's not good for you, and it's very bad for the movement. It's very bad for the future. It's extremely bad for the young Lesbians now, the 10-year-olds, the 15-year-olds, the ones who are 20 and looking to us as examples. Why not make this world a little easier for everyone who comes after us? It's really not too much to ask. Don't we owe the world that?

Shouldn't our passage through it enrich it? Shouldn't our having lived mean something good for those who come after us? And what about our own lives? There are an awful lot of young people in this world. Why should we reinforce in them fear for the safety of any job? Why should you for a minute imagine that you have to fear for your job? One of the reasons that women are having trouble in universities and in businesses on a professional level is the closet. Many women who would be active in the women's movement, women who have the knowledge and the wherewithal to do wonders are cautious in many cases because they fear that if they rock the boat about feminism, someone will come out with the fact that they're closet Lesbians and rock their boat back a little. I've heard that argument offered up so many times, I can't count it. The way to combat it is to come out first.

What it boils down to is this. When you start counting the women who have succeeded on an historical level, you find that virtually all famous women were Lesbians. Not all, but virtually all. Such enormous quantities of them, such a proportion far out of reasonable belief that you're forced to come up with one of two conclusions. Either almost every woman must be a Lesbian given the choice to be, which happens to be my personal opinion, or, if you can't accept that you must at least accept that those women who step out in the world and do something important in it are Lesbians. It is unrealistic to believe that some social body is going to turn upon all of the successful and creative women in the world and put them out of commission by some kind of mass genocide. I rather doubt that's going to happen. For one thing, there are far too many women for it to happen. If all the Lesbians come out of the closet, think how many famous women that's going to concern. Think for a minute in your head about every entertainer you can name who is gay, every movie star that you know is a Lesbian. Think about that for a few minutes. Then let's talk about all the women we learned about in school in literature. Let's take one relatively small group—American women poets. Let's name the famous American women poets we now have reasonable proof were Lesbians. There's Amy Lowell, and Emily Dickinson, Edna

St. Vincent Millay, Elinor Wylie and Sara Teasdale. Get the point? Did you ever hear of any of those women? Could you get through school without having heard of any of them? We can go on, there's quite a list more. Let's see, who's the latest one to come out publicly? Adrienne Rich was the winner of the National Book Award a couple of years back. She's just come out, and Olga Broumas has established her reputation on her lesbian poetry. In fact, I have trouble finding heterosexual women poets. Marianne Moore, as far as I know, is the only famous American one, but I'm sure there are others. There just aren't very many, for some reason, there just aren't very many. So when all these women come out, including all the women who work in factories and work on switchboards and run elevators and work for Macy's Department Store as I do, when all the women come out, how is it going to change the world? Well, for one thing, it's going to make it easier for all us to live in the world. It's going to make it impossible for people to be fired for being Lesbians because it is going to be extremely difficult to fire all the Lesbians and still run all the businesses, and all the schools, and all the universities, and all the churches because you cannot get rid of all your talent and keep everything moving forward properly. And an awful lot of talent would have to go. But I'm not really asking or cajoling or convincing, I'm trying to tell you in as kind a way as I can that it's time to come out of the closet and make sure everyone around you comes out of the closet too.

I'd like to tell you about my sister. My sister is five years younger than I am. Her name is Diane. She lives less than an eighth of a mile away from me in a valley in Missouri, forty miles east of Kansas City, Missouri. She lives with another woman. They consider themselves married. They have a number of closeted gay friends like themselves, both male couples and Lesbian couples. They're very open with them or at least as open as they are able to be open with anybody or anything. They've both worked at the same company for more than ten years and it's a company with a hundred or so employees. They've been together all of those years and in that length of time, owned two pieces of property together. They still think, and will tell you, that none of the people they work with know they're a Lesbian couple. I don't think all the people they work with are that stupid, but maybe they are. But when you ask them why they don't let the people they work with know, for sure, they say they don't fear for their jobs at all and they wouldn't mind if their bosses knew, but they'd hate for their co-workers to know they are Lesbians. Have you ever thought for a minute what people think of you if they don't think you're Lesbians? Think about that. Do you really want to be thought heterosexual? I personally do not. Think about it, just think about it.

I'd like to tell you about Donna, the woman I'm married to. She is head of several departments at the Kansas City Missouri Public Library. When we started living together over five years ago, I had been a patron of that library for 15 years or so. Needless to say, every librarian in the system had heard about the notorious Barbara Grier who collects those books, so there would have been no possible way that Donna could have remained in the closet in any sense. It's been a rich and rewarding experience for her in every way.

I think I can demonstrate using her as an example how seriously it can disadvantage you to be known as a Lesbian. When we began living together, she was an assistant in a department in the library, a professional librarian, simply one of many in a department. She's now head of several departments and she's doubled her salary, and she's very well thought of by everyone she works with, very well liked, and they know that she's a Lesbian. They know that we're a couple. They don't make a big point of it, they don't run around discussing it at great length, at least, not with Donna. But if it has caused her any inconvenience, she hasn't noticed it.

But there's another comparison between my sister Diane and her life, and the life Donna and I enjoy, and it's probably the most important one. There are young Lesbians in the library in various positions who are open, increasingly open, and they are using as their example the obvious, unstated but present-presence of Donna in their lives. It's okay to be open in the library. Not flamboyant, not troublesome, not obnoxious, but open, casual, obvious. After all, why not?

I don't know how the young Lesbians at Diane's company feel about her ludicrous behavior but I can guess. And if there are any shy and timid ones I hope they are not hurt by her bad example.

Now, coming out despite everything you ever heard or feared is not difficult. I came out when I was 12 years old. I have been out ever since and I have been out with all the people I've ever been around. And I'm not a special and not a privileged person. I worked in a nonprofessional position in a public library. I worked for a mutual fund called Hamilton Funds. I've worked in a whole bunch of miscellaneous offices, the Singer Sewing Machine Co., Pyramid Life Insurance, Macy's Department Store, where I now have a quasi-clerical job, but it's a perfectly ordinary punch-a-time-clock kind of job, but every person in Macy's knows who I am and what I do. There was an article about my life in *Christopher Street* magazine in October, 1976. There's a dog-eared, tattered copy of *Christopher Street* that went all over my department. Everybody in the place read it and everyone came and talked to me. My boss, who is a stereotype male-chauvinist-pig, oppressive person who dislikes everything that he doesn't particularly share an intimate acquaintance with, the kind of person who has a bumper sticker that reads "Take your boy hunting and you won't go hunting your boy." Even my boss finds somehow an obscure pride in my openness.

But I'm not asking you, I'm telling you that you have to come out of the closet. We have to, we all have to be out, we have to because there's nowhere else to go. We've done all we can do as a small, isolated, spotlighted public movement. It's not enough that every year a few thousand kids come out of high school and decided, boy, oh boy, I'm going to break with the enemy, my family, I'm going out and I'm going to live my life. That's one kind of coming out. They've got a long way to go. They're going to walk out of society and walk back into it, and walk out of it and back into it and go through a lot of changes, a lot of education processes, a lot of jobs, a lot of things. Right now, I want all of those women who have made their "place" in the world, I want all of those women over 25 or so who have jobs and responsibilities and obligations and functions to perform and a life of their own and don't-bother-me, I'll-call-you, and I-don't-see-why-I-should-do-that-because-I-did-it-all-myself, let-them-drag-themselves-up-by-their-bootstraps, I don't owe them anything. But you do. You owe them plenty. You owe them your wit and wisdom. You owe them all the suffering you went through, passed by, the right not to have to go through it all just like you did. It's not that it wouldn't make them stronger, perhaps, but it's just not necessary anymore. What is necessary is coming out. Coming out every day in every way. Neither for profit nor salvation, but because this is the time to come out.

June 8, 1977

Prayer Breakfast

Barbara Gittings

This brief speech was delivered by veteran lesbian activist Barbara Gittings at a prayer breakfast in Norfolk, Virginia, sponsored by that city's Coalition for Human Rights. The Save Our Children campaign referred to was the antihomosexual effort mounted by former beauty queen Anita Bryant against gay and lesbian rights in Florida and in particular against the employment of homosexual teachers.

The "Save Our Children" crusade is concerned about children. So are we. Who saved us when we were children growing up being taught that we were wrong and sick and sinful? Despite that cruel message from our parents and teachers and doctors and books and churches, we knew that our feelings were as natural and moral for us as left-handedness is natural and moral for people who are left-handed.

We owe it to ourselves, the gay children of yesterday, to make better conditions for gay people right now. We also owe it to the gay children of today and tomorrow, that hereafter every gay person can grow up feeling good and right and positive about being gay. Naturally, we need our own role models to look to—gay people as human beings who love and are loved—rather than distorted images of homosexuals as furtive and freakish.

Your presence here today is a clear message to those who would keep us hidden: we are here, we won't disappear, and we WILL be ourselves as God meant us to be!

The world needs more love. We want to contribute our share of love, openly and honestly. May your loving efforts toward this be blessed with success!

June 9, 1977

Tribute to Troy D. Perry

Henry Waxman

This address was given on the floor of the House of Representatives by Representative Waxman of California and entered into the *Congressional Record* for June 9, 1977.

Mr. Speaker, on June 26, the Metropolitan Community Church of Los Angeles will mark "Gay Pride Sunday" with a special service of celebration and the conferring of special honors on the denomination's founder, Rev. Troy D. Perry.

The denomination founded by Troy Perry, the Universal Fellowship of Metropolitan Community Churches, is one of the most unusual religious organizations in the world. It is dedicated to extending to members of the gay community the spiritual guidance and religious fellowship so often unavailable to them in the mainstream "straight" churches.

Reverend Perry, himself a gay, had to build his church in the face of tremendous hostility from other clergymen and deep doubts within the gay community as to whether such an unusual institution could succeed. Reverend Perry's first church was founded in Los Angeles with just a dozen courageous "charter members." I am proud that the church was founded and prospered in Los Angeles.

The Los Angeles church not only attracted gay Christians, it also attracted large numbers of straight people who admired the tremendous sincerity and dedication of Rev. Troy Perry. Reverend Perry's Christian church inspired the founding of a gay Reform Temple in Los Angeles. This temple, which Reverend Perry and his congregation assisted in every way they could, was the first of its kind to gain recognition and membership in the Union of American Hebrew Congregations.

Few people have done more than Rev. Troy Perry to give to gays a sense of self-worth and an ability to fulfill joyfully and without guilt or social rejection their most profound religious needs.

Reverend Perry's tiny band has grown into a mighty denomination of churches all over the world with a membership of over 17,000. In helping liberate individuals of his own sexual orientation, Rev. Troy Perry contributed to the liberation of all of us. I share Reverend Perry's belief that the humanity of any and each of us is diminished when the humanity of any of us is denied.

August 1977

A Lesbian Mother on the Abortion Issue

Joyce Kaufman

This speech was delivered at a rally outside the Massachusetts State House in August 1977 protesting a proposed piece of legislation which would have barred Medicaid funds from being used to pay for abortions for poor women. It had at this time passed both houses of the legislature and was expected to be vetoed by Governor Michael Dukakis, with an attempted override vote forecast as being very close. HEW refers to the Federal Department of Health, Education, and Welfare.

Some of you may be surprised that there is a lesbian speaker at this rally. There are several reasons why I feel that it is important, as a lesbian, to be here. The Gay Liberation Movement, like the Women's Movement, like any people's movement, centers around the issue of Power. The aspect of power we're concerned with today is control of our bodies. The Supreme Court has decided that individual states are not required to make Medicaid payments for abortion. HEW has cut off Federal funding of abortion. The Doyle-Flynn bill would enforce this in Massachusetts. This all-out attack on our right to abortion represents an enormous encroachment upon our power over the most intimate aspect of our lives. It is an attempt to define sexual interaction solely as reproductive interaction and to further narrow the definition of family as well as of sexuality. The Doyle-Flynn bill would legislate that some people must have children. This goes hand in hand with current efforts to say that some people must not have children. These efforts include forcing women (particularly Third World women) to be sterilized, attempting to withhold birth control and sex information from adolescents, forbidding adoption by homosexuals, and through stepped-up harassment of lesbian mothers. Over the last several years, both the Women's and Gay Liberation Movements have struggled for control over our bodies, our sexuality and our lives. It is vital that we remain vigilant in protecting the gains we have made. We understand that the reforms we have secured (and they are reforms) come from long and concerted struggle in the face of constant and growing opposition. The opposition we face will, whenever possible, continue its attempts to limit or reverse these reforms.

It is *crucial* that we work together towards building ourselves into a movement that is strong enough *not only* to retain these reforms, but also to be a force that is capable of working toward the restructuring of the basic institutions and attitudes of this society.

Having once won the right to abortion, we must not lose it. As lesbians, we see this attack against the right of all women to maintain and assert control of our bodies as a severe threat to our struggle. The Women's Movement and the Gay Liberation Movement are ultimately in the same struggle . . . we are demanding complete control over our lives—in the workplace, in our homes, in our bedrooms, and in society as a whole.

The recent attacks against our right to safe, free, legal abortion, against our rights as gay people, against Third World people, are evidence of an anti-life movement which is attempting to legislate its own narrow definition of morality, family and sexuality; a movement which seeks to enforce its notions of who is or is not an acceptable person and what is or is not an acceptable way to live. It is important, in our struggle, to remember that we *are* a threat. Our demands threaten the very foundation of this society. Control over our bodies, as well as control over our sexuality and its implications, is one step in the process of gaining control power over all the parts of our lives. What the anti-life forces are saying to us is this: "*We* will control your bodies. *We* will control your sexuality. *We* have the right to say who must and who must not bear and raise children in our society." What we, as women, gay people, Third World people, working people, say to them is this: "You will *not* control our bodies, *nor* our sexuality, *nor* our right to bear or not to bear children. *We* will control our lives. *We* will create a society in which *we* have power."

"We will defeat the Doyle-Flynn bill!"

August 24, 1977

Resolution on Anita Bryant

Libertarian Party

This is the official position paper of the Libertarian Party issued in response to Anita Bryant's antigay campaign of 1977 and the repeal of the Miami/Dade County gay and lesbian civil rights ordinance.

WHEREAS the Libertarian Party condemns the use of government power to promote racial, religious and other forms of discrimination, including those directed against homosexuals and women, and

WHEREAS the Libertarian Party deplores the calculated incitement to hatred against homosexuals which is likely to lead to the use of government power and private violence against them, and

WHEREAS the Libertarian Party recognizes the rights of anti-Gays, as well as Gays, to pursue their own peaceful lifestyles,

BE IT THEREFORE RESOLVED that the Libertarian Party condemns the efforts of Ms. Anita Bryant and her associates and followers to create a climate of hatred against homosexuals, to continue the present systematic state oppression of Gays, and to extend it, for instance by banning homosexual men and women from teaching in the public schools. While we did not, and do not now, support the principle of the Dade County anti-discrimination ordinance—clearly a violation of property rights and freedom of association—we unequivocally denounce the whipping up of anti-homosexual hysteria which is likely to lead to the infringement of the individual rights of homosexuals. We demand that homosexuals be accorded those rights in full and immediately.

January 1978

An Open Letter to Anita Bryant

Wages Due Lesbians, Toronto

Wages Due Lesbians was a feminist collective formed in Toronto in October 1974, with ties to the Wages for Housework group in the United States.

Dear Anita Bryant,

We are speaking out tonight as lesbian women because we want you and the rest of society to know who you are attacking. Though we number in the millions, we are forced to be invisible, and crusades like yours only fill us with more anguish and fury. We are not criminals, we are not depraved. We are women, like you.

Though you may think that lesbians are all single and childless, the truth is that many of us are mothers. When our children are taken away from us we fight back, just as you would.

We are school teachers, child care workers, nurses and social service workers. We give of ourselves to nurture society's children, but in return we risk losing our jobs if anyone discovers we are gay.

We are women on welfare struggling daily to feed and clothe our families on incomes far below official poverty levels.

We are immigrant women from the Third World. We work here scrubbing floors and cleaning toilets, thousands of miles from our children. For years we scrimp and save to bring them here, never knowing when we'll lose it all through arbitrary deportations.

We are prostitutes because it pays us enough to provide for our children, and live with whom we wish. When we are thrown in jail, we have to leave them behind, sometimes forever.

We are full-time housewives caring for our families' needs, with little time left for ourselves.

As mothers, we want our children to have better lives than we have had, with more freedom and less prejudice. And we are fighting harder than anyone else to protect them from the sexual coercion that we ourselves have suffered, as women. We stand with our children against all sexual assault by their fathers, uncles, friends, teachers or strangers, whether straight or gay. We want our children to be able to decide for themselves in everything that matters to them.

Because you also oppose abortion, we want you to know that many of us have been forced to abort because we can't afford to give our children the life we think they deserve. Until we can, we defend the right of all women to free, safe and legal abortions.

Our invisibility and isolation are coming to an end, because we are determined to lead our lives as we choose. Many straight women and a lot of men stand with us against your crusade, because they too want sexual choices, and a better future for all the children, whose fight begins with our moments of triumph.

April 30, 1978

Gay Rights Can Be Achieved

Alan Cranston

This address, given by Senator Alan Cranston in April 1978 at the Hollywood Palladium, was reprinted in the May 11, 1978, issue of the *Bay Area Reporter.*

I traveled 3,000 miles across the country from Washington to be here. I am proud to be here. I am proud to be here for the Gay Chapter of the American Civil Liberties Union.

In its 58 year history the A.C.L.U. has been involved, in one way or another, in just about every unpopular cause in America. Be it the cause of the suffragette or the black, the Nazi or the Ku Klux Klan, the feminists, or the war resisters—the A.C.L.U. has defended many, many thousands of individuals and causes. Many of them are long-forgotten. But all of them are important because of one unifying idea: Men and women must be free, must be free to express themselves and free from governmental and private oppression.

That idea is embodied in our Constitution and our Bill of Rights, in the Declaration of Independence and in the principles fought and died for in the American Revolution. You celebrate that idea in honoring Rev. Troy Perry.

As the founder and moderator of Metropolitan Community Churches, Rev. Perry has gained widespread admiration and respect. He has waged a tireless crusade for human rights and he has waged it well.

The tribute that you pay to Troy Perry has been earned through hard and selfless work to improve the lives of others, the lives of oppressed human beings. Having earned this tribute, one would think that Troy Perry would be standing in what Hubert Humphrey once called "the bright sunshine of human rights" which is the very promise of our democratic society—that Troy Perry's own human rights had not been violated. Far from it.

Because he is Gay and solely for that reason, he is subject to all sorts of discrimination and his rights in our society are severely limited. And there are those who would limit them further. This man that you are honoring, whose work has benefited so many is a second class citizen of a society that he nonetheless respects and serves.

Most public and nearly all private employers can refuse Troy Perry a job. Landlords can deny him an apartment or a house. All branches of the United States armed forces can refuse him a right to serve his country and refuse him the right to visit members of his church who are inmates.

Troy Perry can be barred from teaching, from practicing law, from being a doctor of medicine or even from driving a cab. He can have his application for credit denied. He can be refused insurance.

In the sovereign state of Virginia he can not go into a bar and buy a drink.

For Troy Perry—and for millions of others who share with him one characteristic—the bright sunshine of human rights is trapped behind clouds of ignorance, intolerance, bigotry and fear.

So I submit to you that although it is wonderful to pay tribute to him that is not enough. It is not enough to pay respect to him for acting on behalf of society in spite of society. Troy Perry is owed the full measure of civil and constitutional protection that is the fundamental right of every American.

The discrimination that Troy Perry and so many other Americans can be subjected to, and are subjected to, must be ended.

There has been great progress in recent years in reducing discrimination against women, Blacks, Hispanic, Asian, handicapped and many other minorities. There has been great progress in recent years in reducing discrimination against homosexuals, especially in California, and I am proud of that.

But now that progress is being challenged. Threatened. Halted in some communities. Reversed in others.

Many of us in public service are becoming increasingly concerned about the nature of the dialogue that has come to surround the issue of the civil and constitutional rights of gays to be free of discrimination, to share equally in the opportunity of our bountiful land, to enjoy the equal protection of our laws, and the right to privacy that is so fundamental in our society. Increasingly, it seems to me, the dialogue has been marked by apprehension, by lack of understanding, by misinformation and by the use of false stereotypes.

Securing and defending the basic human rights of *everyone* is a compelling course of action which a free society must understand. A commitment that it must keep if it is to remain free.

Those of us who comprehend this clearly, those of us who share this belief fully, must stand firm in our conviction in behalf of every individual and in behalf of every minority.

We must strongly and steadfastly serve the principle that every American—regardless of race, color, national origin, religion, sex or sexual orientation has a right to equal opportunity in employment, housing, and public service: a right to serve our country, a right to be free from fear and intimidation in his/her daily life.

These rights are fundamental in a just and free society. They are as difficult to achieve as they are essential. They are as hard to keep as they are to obtain.

The vote in St. Paul to repeal that city's anti-discrimination ordinance is a vivid illustration of the agony of the struggle for human rights generally and of the arduous nature of the battle by-and-for gay Americans specifically, and to end discrimination.

The St. Paul vote tells us much about the strong, sustained, relentless effort that must be made in the days—and yes, the years—ahead if rights not yet won are to be won and if those *now in hand* are to be held.

Know this. Mark this. Remember this. Throughout all history, throughout all of the world, the struggle for human rights has been a succession of victories and defeats. With setbacks often severe that are a blow to the human spirit. But the rights of individuals, and of minorities, are historically obtained in this painful, halting way. And a pain they are, at least in our society, all too slowly—but none the less surely.

The way toward achievement for full and equal rights for gay men and lesbians will unfortunately be no different. It will not come easily but come it will.

How will it be done? What will it take? . . . It will require a deep, personal commitment of gay Americans. It will take a commitment of *all* so-called minority groups. And it will take a certain personal commitment by the so-called majority, whether motivated by concern for others and devotion to the principle of equal rights or by an awareness of "for whom the bell tolls," recognizing the simple fact that the denial of the rights of one individual—one minority—is but a prelude to an assault on the rights of each and all.

The struggle demands—yes, demands—a careful, thoughtful, practical, persistent educational and political campaign. This process will have to precede any real progress toward the enactment of anti-discrimination legislation in Congress.

I listen—and I listen carefully—when my colleagues discussed from time to time the Miami crusade, the St. Paul vote, and the gay community's hope for legislation banning discrimination. I have engaged in these discussions and I know from these discussions how much work needs to be done.

The situation in Congress is different in its implications, its ramifications, its complexity, its difficulties from the state situation and that in the cities of our nation.

In Congress there are times to plan and prepare, and there are times to move, to strike. There are times when it is wise to provoke and engage in the first battle, even though defeat is inevitable. This is when there is reason to hope that, in a series of ensuing battles, new support, new allies will be won.

There are times when it is wise to pause, to prepare, to postpone the first fray. This is when there is reason to fear that not only is the first defeat inevitable, but it will be so overwhelming as to be fatal.

It is all, of course, a matter of judgment. It is my judgment that too early an effort to enact anti-discrimination legislation in Congress would put off by far—perhaps by decades—the achievement of the ultimate victory that will surely be won if the battle is waged with wisdom, courage and determination.

All too often, when a highly controversial bill is defeated in the House and Senate by an overwhelming margin, that bill—and others like it—are dead for years.

Having either body of Congress say no on gay rights legislation could, among many other effects, provide the basis for more negative rulings by the courts in the areas involving gays throughout the country.

There are no shortcuts. There are no evasions of the tough, methodical, thorough drive at the grassroots and at the level of community and national leadership that must pave the way for a movement for the right legislation at the right time. It is not solely a matter of demanding rights, as you know. It is a matter of also working to assure that those rights that now exist—and there are some that exist nationally such as the availability of legal services to gay Americans—are not wiped out.

You men and women who have been subjected to a scourge of discrimination, who have suffered the denial of human rights, who have perhaps been denied your own identity, know full well how difficult it is to secure laws to insure your rights, how difficult to enforce those laws, how difficult it is to keep them on the books. But I say to you, it can be done . . . and it *must* be done. It can and must be done to protect your rights and to protect the rights of every American.

In the Nazi holocaust which saw the murder of six million Jews it was less than four years before this horror of horrors was taking place, that this country had been deemed one of the most civilized in all of the world.

I was a young foreign correspondent in Hitler's Germany and Mussolini's Italy and I witnessed the crushing of civil rights in those countries where freedom had once flourished. I came home to America to do whatever I could do in my own country to prevent the horror of Holocaust.

The monster of discrimination and demi-fascism and then holocaust burst forth in a society while citizens looked the other way while someone else's rights were being violated. Hitler's goon-squads, the brown shirts and storm troopers, were attacking Jews in the streets and in their homes long before Hitler seized power. Too many Germans looked the other way. Once

Hitler was in office, the apparatus of the state was put to the task of assaulting Jews and communists and socialists and the likes of our own Republicans and Democrats. Too many Germans still looked the other way . . . so did too many elsewhere. Then it was Austrians who were dying . . . then Czechs, Poles, French, British, Russians and finally Americans.

I recite this tragic litany only to stress again a fundamental precept of the democratic society founded on constitutional rights: liberty and freedom indivisible.

One can be sure of enjoying human rights in a democratic society by assuring that everyone enjoys them.

If even one individual loses his/her rights or fails to gain rights then all are in danger. That is the heart of the A.C.L.U. philosophy.

We will enjoy all the civil liberties that we assert and fight for—and only those.

The civil rights movement of the 1960's broke the dam of discrimination against Blacks, whose rights were not secured even by the Civil War—and who today are still denied first-class citizenship. But that dam has been broken.

With the Civil Rights Act of 1964 and other legislation, and a broad range of court decisions, we have begun to move forward in other areas of discrimination . . . the women's struggle against discrimination and for the Equal Rights Amendment: the Chicano movement—La Raza, men and women who are often seen as aliens in the land that their ancestors settled long before pioneers made their way West; Third World immigrants who came here as refugees from Vietnam and Cambodia and other countries to escape oppression and poverty only to find doors closed and opportunities denied: the struggle for rights of the handicapped, civil rights by wheelchair, a new questioning of the rights of children—are they people? Do they have rights? My answer is yes—but there are those who deny it. What about the right to die?

These and countless other questions are posed now in our society . . . a society that is on the move. These and countless other crusades are being waged. Slowly the country is responding in the affirmative. The country will respond in the affirmative to the asking, the seeking, the demanding of the gay movement—a movement barely begun but establishing visibility and credibility for the bright sunshine of human rights.

I am an optimist about our ability to solve our human problems, both in our nation and in our world. But we, the people of the United States, and we, the people of our World, cannot make our common dreams come true unless we develop a higher sense of shared responsibility and our indivisible faith that each of us—all of us in America—remember our common bonds. It is a bond born of common men and women joined together in an uncommon way and united by the cherished belief that humans—working with the framework of social and governmental institutions based on principles of liberty, democracy, mutual concession and mutual respect for the maximum degree of free and individual choices—can together do what cannot be done alone.

If we will only act and approach with that belief—thoughtfully, charitably and prayerfully—we can surely overcome the ills that plague us at home.

Each and all of us in our world must unite in the pursuit of peace on earth—a peace that will never be secure until there is food and shelter for all; a peace that will never be secure until there are human rights for all; a peace that will never be secure until there is a respect for each nation and its individual people which transcends culture and nationalism, race, and religion; a peace that will never be secure until there is respect for all of the rich differences and diversities that distinguish each individual on the face of the earth for every other; a peace that must embrace the concept of the brotherhood and the sisterhood of humankind—living together as one family upon our small planet. A peace in the world based upon love and understanding that will, at long last, bring peace within ourselves.

May 12, 1978

A Union Leader Speaks for Gay Rights

David McDonald

On May 12, 1978, a rally sponsored by Bay Area Coalition Against the Briggs Initiative was held in San Francisco, California. Among the representatives of organized labor speaking was David McDonald, then newly elected president of the 17,000-member Local 2 of the Hotel and Restaurant Workers and Bartenders Union, the largest in the city.

Good evening. I am privileged to be here tonight as a representative of Local 2.

I am not here as a special favor. And I am not fulfilling any obligation other than representing the workers who elected me.

There's a slogan in the labor movement: "An injury to one is an injury to all." The Briggs Initiative is such an injury, and I am committed to fighting back.

I was elected to office because I represented the most oppressed and militant sectors of the hotel and restaurant industry. By that, I mean low-paid workers, women, minority people and gays. I ran with a slate of people from an opposition caucus called the Alliance of Rank and File—ARF. Throughout the campaign we called ourselves "watchdogs, not fat cats." We ran as workers first and foremost, not career-minded officials. Our program represented the fundamental necessities of trade-union democracy—shop stewards, workers councils and workshops, elected business reps, rank and file negotiating committees, and, an end to discrimination in hiring and promotion. ARF was and is a diverse group of people working together for change.

Lesbians and gay men have historically been invisible and unrepresented by the labor movement. Until very recently, homosexuality was not a fit topic for serious discussion. The truths about homosexuality were hidden behind repressive laws, taboos and myths. But I know that gay people have always been present in all sectors of society—including positions of support and leadership of mass movements for justice and equality.

With growing visibility over recent years, lesbians and gay men have become a social and political force to be reckoned with.

For instance, gays working in the labor movement have actively supported the on-going Coors boycott. That support—both from gay bar owners and patrons—is a major step toward improving conditions for workers. In turn, many unions supported the orange juice boycott during the Dade County campaign last year.

In our recent campaign, I worked alongside lesbian and gay culinary workers. These people played leading roles in the work, which led to victory for ARF. They have now formed a growing gay caucus within the union. This is a positive step toward active participation and representation for gay people in Local 2. I hope that gay workers in other unions will be encouraged to demand representation, and that non-unionized gays will demand protection as workers.

Protection of workers—this brings us back to the Briggs Initiative. Being a cook myself, I know what it means for people to be fed. Briggs feeds on ignorance and fear, and his appetite does not stop there. He sits at the head of the table with those who support capital punishment, and we all know that it is poor and black people who are on death row. People like Briggs are hungry for our rights. They have already bitten off a large chunk of the rights for which gay people have fought so hard—in Miami, St. Paul and Wichita. They are nibbling on abortion reform—while increasing forced sterilization on poor white and minority women.

But, can they swallow the Equal Rights Amendment? NO.

They are gnashing their teeth out of fear of racially integrated schools. Unless we stop them, they'll eat away the democratic rights of racial minorities and women—won through affirmative action. They are eating Labor's share too. Striking workers are still denied social services—the government still acts as a strike leader—as we've seen with the recent injunction of the Taft-Hartley against coal miners.

In the face of these attacks against labor, workers must remain united. Gay workers are isolated from each other and from straight workers on the job, making it hard to organize in their workplace. Queer-baiting is used by bosses to divide workers and isolate potential leaders. Many gays are pressured socially as well as economically to side with management against their co-workers. Making racial and sexual division between workers serves those in power. If the Briggs Initiative passes, this situation can only get worse. Fear and suspicion must be fought with mutual understanding and patience.

For my part, I pledge the resources of our union. Our newspaper and general meetings can reach out to our membership. We can promote the involvement of other labor leaders. We can encourage and establish dialogue with the gay community and gay workers in particular. A rank and file committee to work against the Briggs Initiative will be appointed in Local 2.

We all come from many different political, religious affiliations and lifestyles which affect how we see this issue.

We must not let these differences divide us, but use them to reach the many sectors of the voting public which we represent. Now that we are here together, let's unite against Briggs and the forces behind him. We need to get together at tomorrow's conference to affirm this commitment.

Let's establish a statewide organization that coordinates our many different struggles and then go back to our own committees and organize there. We need and must appreciate each other's help and involvement in this campaign.

I thank you.

June 17, 1978

Speech at Boston Lesbian and Gay Pride Rally

Kate Gyllensvird

Welcome, Sisters and Brothers. It's great to see so many people here. I'm going to start off with an announcement. Today is also Soweto Solidarity Day. On June 16, 1976, South African police fired on a demonstration of unarmed school children in the black township of Soweto, setting off a massive wave of protest. Within a few months, over 1000 blacks had been killed, many more wounded or detained. But the tide of South African history has turned with these events. The black majority is more determined than ever to free itself from racist oppression.

There is a demonstration this afternoon in Franklin Park to commemorate the second anniversary of the Soweto Uprising. The Soweto Day Solidarity Coalition is making an announcement in support of lesbian and gay pride at their demonstration. They have asked me to announce their rally and to extend to all of us here their support of our common struggle against right wing repression of all kinds.

A lot of you may think this has been a bad year for lesbian and gay rights. In terms of electoral politics, that's true. In the past couple of months gay rights bills have been defeated or repealed in St. Paul, Eugene, and Wichita. One reason is the growing right wing backlash in this country, led by people like Anita Bryant, Phyllis Schlafly, and Meldrim Thomson. The New Right attacks at the polls. It is successful within its own institutions because it manipulates and mobilizes the voting public through fear—fear of difference, fear of change, fear of any challenge, to the institutions of the state, the courts, the schools, the church.

How do these attacks and defeats affect us? They create a repressive mood which makes us feel paralyzed with fear of guilt, isolated from each other, and closeted. These attacks inhibit our ability to feel good about being different. They affect our pride in the lesbian and gay liberation movements and our desire to work for change. We respond with fear and cynicism. And no wonder—the consequences are increased violence and repression like police entrapment, beatings in the Fenway, and the Briggs Initiative.

If the Briggs Initiative passes in California, any teacher or school-related person who advocates homosexuality can be fired.

Can struggling for civil rights, fighting for gay rights legislation, really confront the growing homophobia, violence and repression in this country? There are some ways in which electoral politics have helped to strengthen our movements for lesbian and gay liberation. They have put the issues of lesbian and gay rights in the public eye. People have been made aware that we are everywhere in this society and that we demand equal recognition. People have been pushed to take a stand. Many non-gay individuals and groups have come out in support of lesbian and gay rights. And a lot of these people are here today.

But lesbian and gay rights are not won at the polls. We may win a referendum or an election. But as we have seen, these victories can be, and are, reversed. Our rights, anybody's rights, can be voted away, can be judged unconstitutional no matter how hard we campaign for them. Winning an election does not change people's homophobia, nor does it change people's sexism or racism. Most importantly, it does not challenge the irrational fear and hatred on which the institutions of racism, sexism, heterosexism, classism and anti-Semitism are built; it does not confront the ways in which these institutions are used in this society to divide people; it does not ask who benefits from this fear, hatred and division.

The New Right is strong but we shouldn't respond as victims. We should try to understand the basis of its strength and we should also know the basis of ours. The New Right didn't spring full grown out of the mind of Anita Bryant or Ronald Reagan or Richard Nixon. It is a reaction to people who have been demanding a qualitative change in this society for the past twenty years. The New Right is reacting to us, to our movement for lesbian and gay liberation, to our nine-year open attack on sex roles, sexual rigidity, and male supremacy.

How have the lesbian and gay movements grown in numbers and strength since the Stonewall uprising? We've grown from our internal victories—victories which the right can't go to the polls and vote away: victories like the creation and spread of lesbian and gay culture, like the film *Word Is Out*—a movie about real people like any of us here and not some trashy Hollywood hype—the proliferation of lesbian and gay music and poetry, some of which we're hearing today, the proud sharing of our lives through this culture. Victories like the growing awareness of gay health care, the existence of Fenway Community Health. Some of our most important victories are the expressions of support we show one another. When the gay rights bill was repealed in Eugene, there were massive demonstrations in San Francisco and other cities. At the Lesbian Mothers' day rally here in Boston there was an organized and supportive gay male presence. Lesbians have brought culture and support to women in Framingham Prison. People from all over the lesbian and gay communities are angered by the authorities' vigilante tactics in the Boston/Boise and Boston Public Library entrapment cases. And this march which we have every year is an example to the rest of Boston of our pride and our strength.

All of these victories, these expressions of solidarity, have added to the building of the lesbian and gay movements and to the strengthening of our communities. We have power in this movement. One reason is because we do support each other. We have learned to see our individual lives as part of a common struggle against a heterosexist society which has always taught us to hate ourselves and to put ourselves down. There is a growing pride and respect in our movement which affects how we relate to each other and to the rest of society. Lesbians and gay men question the accepted ways of relating. We question the assumption of heterosexuality, the tradition of marriage, the institution of male supremacy. Most importantly, we question the basic component of relationships in this society—that one person (a man, an adult, a white person, a boss) naturally has power over another (a woman, a child, a black, or third world person, a worker). We explore and experiment with new ways of relating, ways of developing and sharing power, ways of improving the quality of our lives.

Our questioning and experimenting is very much a threat to traditional institutions and those who uphold them. They are fighting back. And they are powerful because they have money, because they work within existing institutions, and because they play with people's insecurities about sexuality, about power, about realizing the American dream. We must use our strengths to contend with the forces of the right and to continue building our movement.

In confronting the right wing we must also look to other groups which are under attack. Organized groups of women who are fighting for our rights to control our bodies, to control our sexuality, to determine what it is to be a woman. Organized groups of Black and third world people who are fighting for the survival of their own cultures, for an end to racism and genocide. All these groups are under attack by anti-abortion, anti-ERA, anti-affirmative action right wing organizations. They are under attack because they confront the hierarchical structure of social relations in this society.

We have to go to the roots of oppression and repression in this society to understand the basis for homophobia and heterosexism and to figure out new ways to confront them. I work with Lavender Resistance—a group of lesbians and gay men who are socialist, feminist, anti-racist and anti-imperialist. We struggle as part of a larger movement for lesbian and gay liberation in the context of a total transformation of society. We support other groups who struggle to change society and we push them to deal with gay and sexual oppression.

The lesbian and gay movements have built up a great sense of pride and strength over the last several years. We must not allow the right wing attacks to stop us; we must always remember that they are reacting to our strength and not our weakness. We must continue to strengthen our community and defend our sexuality. It's a long struggle and we will win.

June 25, 1978

Speech at Gay and Lesbian Pride Rally, New York City

Kay Whitlock

Whitlock, at the time of this speech, was Chair of the National Organization for Women Lesbian Rights Committee in summer 1978 at the Gay and Lesbian Pride Rally in New York City. The quotation she uses is from the opening pages of Lillian Hellman's 1976 work on the McCarthy era, *Scoundrel Time.* Hellman herself was called before the House Un-American Activities Commitee in 1952, and *Scoundrel Time* conveys the atmosphere of ideological persecution of those days well.

Today I am here on behalf of the tens of thousand of NOW members in hundreds of NOW chapters across the nation.

I am here to say that the National Organization for Women—the largest feminist organization in the world—firm in its demand for full human rights for lesbians and gay men.

I am here to say that NOW is proud to be a visible, politically active witness against the cheap political opportunism of unprincipled demagogues—symbolized by California State Senator John Briggs—who foster and exploit the sexist fears and myths and stereotypes surrounding lesbians and gay men and our struggle for those rights.

I am here to say that NOW will continue to work ceaselessly, in every possible area, to counter the bigotry, the ignorance, the lies, being promoted by the hypocritical, prating, self-styled anti-lesbian/anti-gay "moralists" who would have this country repudiate the principles on which it was founded by making the granting or denial of basic civil liberties and Constitutional rights dependent upon a particularly repugnant, particularly vicious version of a popularity contest.

As I speak to you this weekend in New York, NOW President Eleanor Smeal is speaking in San Francisco, making sure that this country, that the world, knows that NOW believes unequivocally that human rights are indivisible; that NOW's determination to confront this neo-fascist anti-gay rights crusade has not wavered in the face of Dade County, Wichita, St. Paul, Eugene—or in anticipation of the struggles ahead.

If anything, we grow angrier, we grow stronger, we work harder to confront and expose the opposition; to continue long-term educational efforts; to do whatever is necessary to stop this present-day witch-hunt and to make certain that lesbian and gay rights are secured and guaranteed. NOW does not engage in struggles that we do not ultimately intend to win.

All of us here today have a common political enemy. It is that slick, well-funded, well-organized political machine of repression known as the New Right. The New Right is racist, it is sexist, it is anti-labor and pro-big business. It pursues its reactionary agenda aggressively, and we are among its targets.

The playwright Lillian Hellman once wrote of a time that is similar to today's climate—the "scoundrel time," she called it. Then it took the form and name of McCarthyism. But the dynamics of witch-hunts and of repression are always the same. And of that previous time of scoundrels, Hellman wrote:

> *It was not the first time in history that the confessions of honest people were picked up in space by cheap baddies who, hearing a few bars of popular notes, made them into an opera of public disorder, staged and sung, as much of the congressional testimony shows, in the words of an insane asylum . . .*
>
> *A theme is always necessary, a plain, simple unadorned theme to confuse the ignorant . . .*

These words haunt me today. They describe our present time so well.

But scoundrels prevail only when they have intimidated their opposition; not only when they have frightened their intended victims into submission.

Our opponents may not have the luxury of our silence.

The struggle will be difficult. "Truth," said Lillian Hellman, "made you a traitor, as it often does, in a time of scoundrels."

Yet you, by your presence here, do not fear speaking truth. We in NOW do not fear speaking truth. That voice of truth, the voice which speaks of justice, must thunder throughout the land.

And it must never stop.

July 1978

Lesbian Schoolworkers Stand Against Briggs

Lesbian Schoolworkers in San Francisco

Originally printed in the San Francisco lesbian periodical *Gibbous Rising,* this text is a formal response to the antigay initiative sponsored by California State Senator John Briggs, which called for "filing charges against schoolteachers, teacher's aides, school administrators or counselors for advocating, soliciting, imposing, encouraging or promoting private or public sexual acts defined in . . . the Penal Code between persons of the same sex." The Bakke decision was a 1978 ruling by the U.S. Supreme Court which overturned race-based affirmative action admissions policies at the University of California.

As gay schoolworkers, we are a potentially positive force in Education. The schools are one of the main places where children learn the differences between the roles of women and men in this society. Boys learn they are superior to girls. They learn to have more confidence in themselves and in their bodies. They learn to be unemotional and patronizing toward women who are "the weaker sex." They are given praise for assertive, aggressive behavior. And they are trained for jobs with higher status and higher pay than "women's work." They are trained to take positions of authority over women solely because they are men.

Girls learn that their first place is in the home—as mothers and housewives. Their jobs outside the home most often fit in the same category—clerical workers, waitress, teacher's aide, teacher, hospital worker—taking care of adults and children—nurturing, subservient, relatively powerless. Women are taught to accept these low paid, low status jobs solely because we are women. Most women in this country work two jobs. Because society teaches that women's role is primarily in the home, employers can get away with paying us less outside the home. This is obviously to their advantage. Women who demand women's rights are no longer accepting this inferior status.

As schoolworkers, we are supposed to play a major role in maintaining this system and its divisions. Groups of workers who don't conform are a threat to the system and are targeted by it. Third World schoolworkers and communities face repression when they attempt to right the racism of the school system. Now we are facing repression as gay schoolworkers.

Gay school employees do not conform to fixed sex roles for men and women. This challenges the division of labor between women and men which threatens the very structure of women' s oppression. As lesbians, we disprove the idea that women must be economically, emotionally and sexually dependent on men. This directly challenges the authority of men over women throughout U.S. society and is therefore dangerous to the government. The profits of the ruling class rely on the maintenance of men's authority over women. We know this threat to male supremacy is positive. As lesbian schoolworkers, we are committed to building a school system and a society that does not have these divisions based on race and sex. **BUT,** in order to be the best possible teachers for our students, we MUST have the freedom to be open about who we are.

It is no accident that the Briggs Initiative is happening now. The militant struggles of Third World people and women in the '60s won affirmative action, more equal education, abortion rights and other progressive demands. Gay women and men also fought back against our oppression and gained pride in our gayness. In the past few years, the government has been trying to take away these gains. The U.S. economy is in crisis. As nations around the world win their independence from the U.S., such as Vietnam and the African nations, the U.S. economic crisis grows. There are cutbacks, layoffs and rising unemployment. People are angry. People are frightened. The ruling class is trying to use this situation to build a right wing base within the white working class against the rights of Third World people, women and gay people. The living conditions of the working class in this country are atrocious. We suffer from inadequate housing, poor medical care and an inferior educational system. People are angry about all of this, and the government is trying to channel that anger against those who have the least control over the way things are run. The ruling class is trying to increase economic and social differences between white and Third World people, between women and men. They are trying to win public support for such actions as the Bakke decision, anti-abortion, forced sterilization, anti-busing and Save Our Children campaigns. THEY MUST BE STOPPED.

There is an organized alliance of conservative forces around the country, which is using local right wing groups to support the government's goals. The KKK, Nazi Party, American Labor Party and John Birch Society are increasing in numbers and becoming much more visible. They are united in their attacks against Third World people, women and gay people. The government is doing nothing publicly to stop these right wing groups while covertly encouraging them. The racism and sexism of these groups on a local level plays right into the hands of government strategy on a national level. Another aspect of this strategy is to give all these attacks the appearance of a grassroots campaign. In fact, they are directed and financed from the top.

Lesbian Schoolworkers has been working with the Bay Area Gay Teachers and Schoolworkers Coalition. We are building popular support against the Briggs Initiative. We have been speaking on radio and TV and to community groups. We are writing and distributing literature and a newsletter; and we are raising money to continue with our work.

As gay people in the schools, we want to fight for more than the rights of gay schoolworkers. We want to fight for the rights of students, parents and other school employees. We want to join in the struggle for quality, anti-racist, anti-sexist education, hiring of Third World staff, bilingual education, community control, and the many other demands of oppressed groups within the educational system.

September 19, 1978

A House Divided

Gay Community News

This editorial addresses and conveys some of the concerns regarding Anita Bryant's campaign.

We are tired.

Not from overwork. Not from overexpenditure of our energies.

We are tired of fear and senseless acts. We are tired of finding our offices once again forcibly entered and vandalized. We are tired of the lack of police interest in the break-ins. We are tired of listening to telephone harassments and death threats.

On Sunday, Sept. 3, the much discussed "violence" struck at a center of our community. A group of vandals battered through barred windows and ransacked the *GCN* office. Howard Phillips' "militant homosexuals" were being punished for their stand against the forces of oppression.

That our offices were vandalized is nothing new. It has happened before and it will happen again. Dissidents have never been safe from cowardly attacks.

That we receive anonymous death threats constantly goes without saying: it has become a matter of course. The fight for that in which one believes has never been without risks.

That our windows have, in the past year, been shattered by bullets may surprise you. It shouldn't. Human dignity has never been attained without sacrifice. There are those who would rather we cower than hold our heads high. We are prepared to confront the homophobia which threatens us daily.

But, as we get back to the business of running the paper, we are stunned: the long-standing fact that there is a lack of support from the gay community has finally hit home for us all.

When the 200 lesbians and gay men who formed the September 1 Coalition called upon all people committed to the struggle for human rights to demonstrate against Bryant's campaign, we saw it as our duty to publicize that call to action, and so produced an extra edition to fulfill this obligation to our community. Yet during Bryant's visit and resultant rally in Copley Square, we suffered through more negative feelings from sectors of the gay community than at any time in our history.

Instead of a much needed coming together and a necessary supportive effort, many politicians and gay businesses retreated to a stance of fear and non-activism masquerading as "respectability."

Some of us feel strongly that the planned activities will unnecessarily jeopardize the safety of a large number of lesbians, gay men and their supporters. Others hold that the strategizing meeting was hastily called, chaired and dominated by a particular philosophy and, despite rhetoric supporting "unity" within the gay community, was in itself the most divisive and insensitive gathering of gay people in Boston to date.

The above declaration was endorsed by a number of bars and other businesses in the Boston area. Many members of the Gay Business Association saw fit to lend their support to this statement rather than to those people working to battle our enemies: fear and ignorance.

One prominent business person brought a new meaning to our telephoned threats. He angrily labeled us "radicals" and began a campaign in the business community to boycott *GCN*.

Also distressing to *GCN* was the confusing decision by politicians to denounce this demonstration. Both State Reps. Barney Frank and Elaine Noble cited the divisive argument of "fear" of violence as they withdrew support at this vital time.

In the face of economic blackmail from within the community, lack of commitment from political allies, and violent homophobic terrorism, we must reiterate our mandate and the principles by which we abide. *Gay Community News* is committed to providing a forum for all of the diverse and opposed elements and perspectives within the gay community, and to maintaining open lines of communication between us all.

Elaine Noble and the Boston/Boise Committee, *Fag Rag* and Dignity, they belong to us, and we to them. And we will fight always, when faced with prejudice and hatred.

We challenge our elected officials Frank and Noble and others to answer for their fears.

We challenge the gay business community to support those who support them and stop their attempts to intimidate an open and free gay press.

We challenge the straight community to have the courage to respect and defend the basic rights of all people.

We ask all those who stepped back in fear and ignorance to raise their heads and join hands with us to battle injustice and hate.

We are tired.

We will not stop.

1979

Letter to the Pope

International Gay Association

The pontiff being addressed in this letter is John Paul II. The remarks referred to were made in Chicago on October 7, 1979, to a gathering of 300 Catholic bishops, where the pope endorsed a letter from them which said homosexual activity (as opposed to orientation) was morally wrong, and said that homosexuals should be dealt with "with clarity and great pastoral charity."

Your Holiness,

For the first time during Your papacy, You have made an explicit public statement about Homosexuality. In a speech delivered in Chicago on 5th October You stated that the moral viewpoint of the Church remains unchanged and that homosexual acts will continue to be prohibited.

We wish first of all to acknowledge how difficult it must be to break down barriers within the Roman Catholic Church against modern views on controversial matters like abortion, women's liberation, divorce, extramarital sexual relationships and homosexuality. We would however stress our belief in the notion of respect for each individual's right to self-determination over his/her own life and body. We sympathise with the fact that an all male priesthood may have lost touch with the experienced reality of its flock in sexual matters, by nature of its unnatural and statistically abnormal sexual status of celibacy. Nevertheless, because a priestly caste has voluntarily denied itself full expression in human relationships, this does not confer upon it a right to exact by force of law or spiritual blackmail, a similar involuntary denial of full human expression from the homosexual members of its church.

We do not, Your holiness, wish to enter into a discussion of theological niceties, but we do wish to emphasize the great social responsibility of the Roman Catholic Church and its leaders toward millions of homosexuals all over the world. Homosexuality is a fact of life involving 5-10% of the global population. It is therefore highly irresponsible to attempt to plaster over this reality with 2000 year old cliches that fail to take into account modern developments in human understanding.

We want to share with You knowledge of the Joy and Comfort we have as gay men and lesbian women, derived from the very fact of our sexual orientation, a fact you appear to treat with contempt. Homosexuality in itself is not a source of sorrow. The misery of gay people has sprung in the past from society's negative attitude toward its homosexual members, attitudes so unfortunately reinforced by Your adamant and uncharitable remarks in Chicago.

We would remind You that it was not only Jews who died at Auschwitz. The extermination camps of the Third Reich performed their grisly work on hundreds of thousand of homosexuals also. For gay people, the way to the gas chambers and medical experimentation units was paved with the pious platitudes of Church authorities. We take this opportunity to serve notice that the days when homosexuals allowed themselves to be led like lambs to the slaughter ended in 1969 with Stonewall. Your words may be translated by bigots and zealots as the words of Anita Bryant have been, into acts of brutality against the gay community. Despite this we put our trust in the liberating power of truth. In the interests of such truth we ask that You reexamine the ancient sources of prejudice with an open mind. It is no longer sufficient or intellectually justifiable to meet argument with the brute force of blanket condemnation.

If You have a real desire to be of relevance to homosexual men and women both within and without Your church, may we suggest that You act in a socially responsible way towards us. This is not done by imposing a burden of irrelevant guilt, or inviting us to betray or deny a necessary and good part of our make up as human beings. The rights of gay men and lesbian women are human rights. Their implementation is an integral part of the social justice for which You have so movingly called. We urge You to cease denying the right of homosexuals to live their own lives according to their own innermost needs and feelings.

David Norris
Edmund Lynch
International Gay Association
GCC
1469 Church Street, N.W.
Washington, D.C. 20005
202-134-6268

March 16, 1979

Farewell

Charles Brydon

This is the text of the farewell message issued to the gay and lesbian community of the state of Washington by veteran local activist Charles F. Brydon, cofounder of the Dorian Group (Washington State's statewide gay and lesbian rights organization), in the spring of 1979 upon his departure for New York City to become co-executive director of the National Gay Task Force (NGTF), succeeding Dr. Bruce Voeller in April 1979. Initiative 13 was a proposal made by a former police officer, David Estes, to repeal Seattle's ordinances banning discrimination in housing and employment on the basis of sexual orientation.

How does one say good-bye when he (in this instance) doesn't really want to and, paradoxically, does not feel that the imminent departure for the Big Apple signals the end to a long and familiar friendship? Such musings are for the philosophers and theoreticians. As a pragmatic man, deep thought gives me a headache. On to other matters.

Seattle is a great city for gay people. It was that in 1974 when I arrived from San Francisco. It remains so today as I prepare to leave for New York. The past four years have demonstrated clearly that given the chance to see gay people as human beings in contrast to angry, rage-filled and frightening people, the nongay majority will not reject us, even when given the chance. This does not mean that we are the most popular folks in town, but our existence as a rightful part of the body politic has been acknowledged. That is an enormous step forward. This is the message for gay people in the wonderfully lopsided vote against Initiative 13.

The credit for all this rests with every single gay man and women who did something for themselves not just during the campaign of '78 but in the years before when attending a Dorian function or visiting the YWCA Lesbian Resources center or whatever was considered risky business at the least. The fact is that we all did something wonderful for ourselves in the process and the November 7 vote was one of the rewards.

November 7 was not the end of the line, however. There are too many of us who remain afraid to acknowledge who we are to friends, associates, family. That fear is rooted in the pain of rejection. And we all know how God-awful it is to be rejected. The reality of acknowledging oneself to friends et al. is absolutely different from the fear fantasies that have crippled so many of us. My personal experience is but one example. There are thousands upon thousands of coming out stories that support and confirm my experience.

My sense is that the next phase of growth for Seattle's gay citizens is the area of wide-scale self-acceptance and acknowledgement. All of us, including myself, need to work on the anger and rage that so controls our perceptions of self and others like us. Once free of that burden, the opportunities of life will open to a degree that will please and delight each person who takes the risk.

And it is a risk. One thing we need to appreciate is that when we tell a friend or associate who we are, that person experiences his or her own "coming out," if you please. As we should know, that takes time. Don't be surprised or beat a retreat if the news takes a moment or months to be accepted. After all, our friends have been victimized by the same bullshit we have bought about ourselves. On the other hand, be not surprised by a "so what" response. That can be startling for someone who has worked up an enormous head of steam for the "Big Announcement." Yet it is more often the case than not. But sharing who we are is so freeing for the individual, a natural high.

While doing these things we must preserve and build further the institutions we have created to pursue our political, civic and social interests. Gay people have an exciting opportunity to really make a difference in the quality of life every person enjoys in our city while strengthening gay political gains in Seattle and extending these across the state. Getting involved makes a difference and only you can do that.

Your involvement on the national level as well as here in Seattle is equally important. Occasionally I hear comments to the effect that we cannot support concurrently local and national organizations. The truth is we cannot survive without both.

Gays are all in this together whether we live in Seattle, Indianapolis, Memphis, San Diego, or Portland, Maine. Those cities and the innumerable urban, suburban and rural settings in which gay people live, work and play together need one another's strength. Given Seattle's position as this country's most livable and integrated city for gays, we have a particular responsibility in this regard. A great way to involve yourself on the national level is through membership in the key national organization whose work supports us all, NGTF. Support the local group of your choice and NGTF as well. If you join or belong to Dorian, you can join NGTF for half price the first year through the piggyback membership arrangement. This arrangement is available to other groups which would like to offer it to their members as well.

I expect my work with NGTF will bring me back to Seattle from time to time. I look forward to those visits and perhaps someday will return permanently to this city and the people I have come to love who live here. For those of you who have an opportunity to visit New York, please stop by the National Gay Task Force offices at 80 Fifth Avenue (at 14th Street), Suite 1601. You will be welcomed as the special people you are and have an opportunity to meet the women and men of the staff who make things happen for all of us. Until then, thank you all. You are wonderful people.

June 20, 1979

Community and Power: Building Gay Services for the Next Ten Years

Susan Rosen

This speech was given at the Gay Town Meeting in Faneuil Hall in Boston on June 20, 1979. At this time, Susan Rosen was the executive director of the Homophile Community Health Service. She worked for thirty years in human services and higher education. Susan is now serving a church as an ordained United Church of Christ minister.

Ten years after Stonewall, two ideas—two realities—stand out as exceptionally important for the future of our people: community and power.

For a decade, we have been building our communities across the country. One of the ways we have done so has been by creating institutions through which we can express our love and concern for each other. Without these institutions—our service agencies, religious organizations, and political action groups—we would have no "community." A group only becomes a community when its members learn how to meet each other's human needs.

As a service provider, I have a particular interest in the forms of community which are expressed through service institutions. What I would like to focus on is how we can use our service institutions over the next 10 years to nourish our community and each other; and what might happen if we fail to do so.

No one has yet undertaken to assess the special needs that gay people have for community services. In Boston, our little institutions have grown up in a helter-skelter fashion as individuals have perceived the importance of providing specialized counseling, medical or alcoholism treatment services for lesbians and gay men. Most of these services are far too small and too underfunded to reach out to the hundreds of thousands of gay people who live in this state. Even if the existing services in the gay community could make outreach to all the lesbians and gay men in Massachusetts, many other needs would remain unmet. For example, there is currently no psychiatric emergency service for gay people, and one is very much needed. No vocational and rehabilitation services exist which are sensitive to the special problems gays face in the job market. There are no community residences for mentally ill or retarded gay adults, or for homeless gay adolescents.

We have the power as lesbians and gay men, and as knowledgeable service consumers, to assess the needs of our community and to provide for them. We can join together and plan services for the next decade. We haven't used our power in this way yet. But we can—if we are willing to commit ourselves to each other.

Service providers at the small institutions which now exist in the Boston area—places like the Gay Health Collective, the Homophile Community Health Service, Janus Counseling and others have the power to pool our energies, skills and staff. We could, if we wanted, greatly expand our ability to help our sisters and brothers by bringing together a range of services under one roof as a comprehensive program for the community. So far we haven't used our power to do this. We've been too busy trying to survive. But we could work together, and some of us have begun to talk about doing just this.

Lesbians and gay men compose some 10% of all the voters and taxpayers in the state, but we get very little in return for our votes and tax dollars. One reason for this is that we haven't asked for such a return. We have the power to insist that the interests of our community be recognized and served. We can confront the Massachusetts Department of Mental Health about the fact that only one-hundredth of one percent of its budget is expended to meet the specific mental health needs of gay people. We can demand that the special needs of lesbians and gay men be identified in the state's Health and Mental Health Plans—the documents which project needs and outline goals to be met through state and Federal funding. Should all our taxes be going to meet the needs of heterosexuals? As voters, we all have the power to make demands on behalf of our community. Some of us have started to do so. We will be much more effective if we have the community behind us.

We have the power to tell straight officeholders who court our votes—like the Mayor of Boston—that we want a tangible return for our community. We can ask for something very concrete: for example, that the city of Boston donate one of its dollar-a-year buildings—and a big one—to the gay community so we can house our services under one roof at minimal cost. If we don't make demands like these, we will never be taken seriously, because we are not taking *ourselves* seriously as a community. We haven't done this yet, but some of us are going to do this very soon.

We have the power to join with other gay people on a national level and seek to influence Federal policy so that some proportion of the immense Federal tax bill paid by 20 million gay people is returned to the gay community. Right now, the community gets almost no return on the gigantic chunk that comes out of our paychecks. We need to make the funding of specialized gay-controlled community services one of the demands of the March on Washington. And we need to utilize the power of our numbers so that we have an impact on Federal decision-making in health, mental health and other areas. That's why we organized the National Association of Gay Service Centers one month ago in New York, at the Second National Gay Health Conference. This group will provide a platform for us to come from, so that we will be in a position locally—through a Massachusetts chapter—and nationally to advocate and lobby for appropriate services to the gay community. We have the power of numbers, if we are willing to use it.

If we do not use the power we have as caring community members, as voters, taxpayers and activists to plan for the needs of gay people, what will happen over the next decade? The picture is clear. Straight institutions have a way of periodically getting interested in an issue or a minority, and they are starting to take note of us. They know that in a few years there may be affirmative action requirements demanding that gay people be served by their agencies. They suspect that there may be funds provided for such services. These traditional institutions have powerful political support. They are well placed to apply for funds to "serve" us, and to pay themselves for doing so with *our* tax dollars. This is already beginning to happen. Therapy groups for gay people have begun in several mental health clinics in Boston. A group for gay alcoholics is planned at the city's most prestigious hospital. And there are undoubtedly other such programs in the offing as traditional providers wake up to the existence of the gay minority.

Now, from a philosophical standpoint, it could be argued that it would be ideal if all conventional institutions made provision for the needs of lesbians and gay men. There are certainly enough gay people to go around. But, as someone who has been in the human services for the past 15 years, I can make some predictions as to the scenario from here on in. First, unless our community organizes itself rapidly and seeks political support for gay control of services to gay people, straight institutions will apply for government contracts to serve gays, and will be chosen in preference to institutions in our community. Second, since fads in service go in cycles, and there is no lasting commitment in our society to meet *anyone's* human needs, it is predictable that after a few years the straight institutions will lose interest and greatly reduce or drop their token programs for gays. When that happens, our community will have gone the way of every other minority over the past 10 years, Blacks, Hispanics, drug users—the list is long: all used by straight, white, male institutions for institutional survival, then dumped.

If our community permits this to happen, we will have lost several things which are very important. One is our self-respect. Just as an individual needs to be able to take care of herself or himself in order to feel good, so a community needs to empower itself to meet the needs of its members in order to feel healthy. We need to take care of our own business, because we are the ones who are affected when our human needs go unmet. If we let others strip us of the ability to do this, we lose our pride, our power, and ultimately our community.

We can make productive use of this tenth anniversary of gay pride and power to lay our plans for another decade of community-building. We can get together as service consumers and providers, citizens and activists, to take a good look at ourselves, assess our needs, and get down to work for our own gay-controlled community institutions. We have the power to do this. It is the power of our love for each other. We have the means: our own existing institutions, our new national service organization, our political action groups, our community media. Through these means we can join together and build power and cohesiveness in our community. Will we use the power within us to build a caring community and make it grow in the second decade after Stonewall? The decision is entirely up to us.

November 27, 1979

Speech at Harvey Milk's Memorial

Wayne Friday

This speech was given by Tavern Guild President Wayne Friday to a crowd of 25,000 on the first anniversary of Harvey Milk's assassination. The guild is an organization of San Francisco gay bars, founded in 1962.

When they asked me to speak tonight about Harvey, I wasn't quite sure what it was I could say about a man of whom so much has been said and written in the past year, but I recently took the opportunity to go through dozens of articles that Harvey had written over the past few years for the *Bay Area Reporter,* and I found that, not surprisingly, their message was simple.

Again and again Harvey pointed out who our enemies were—and why. Secondly, those we could trust—and why. A third theme was trying to make others see what we were seeing through our eyes. And finally, and most importantly—almost stridently—to get Gay men and women to take stock of their lives, to be proud of who and what they were, and to, most importantly, COME OUT OF THE CLOSET. Those who knew Harvey at all, knew he often spoke of coming out of that dreaded closet. For everyone who crossed that threshold, for Harvey Milk that was a singular victory. And, thanks to him, we have witnessed in the last five years hundreds of thousands of such victories.

The phrase itself—"in the closet" and "come out of the closet," a Gay expression if ever there was one—has passed into the general vocabulary. Battered wives, rape victims, child abusers, secret alcoholics, the incestuous parents—all of them have taken a leaf from the Gay book and have learned that fear and self-loathing are part of the problem—if not, indeed, the problem itself. And that, my friends and friends of Harvey, was the problem of Dan White—FEAR. Fear of exposure, fear of inadequacy, fear of an indictment, fear of the rejection by his friends and family—and, in the more vain attempt to cover up, to plunge deeper into the personal closet of the wreckage of his disordered personal and public life, he strapped on his revolver and, like the deer slayer, gunned down the two innocents who were nudging him out of his dreaded closet.

Harvey Milk was truly a free man and Dan White was a man in disgrace—enslaved by his fears and hatreds—and that is the fundamental difference between the two men. Harvey Milk was just beginning and Dan White was finished. Dan White was a failed, bankrupt human being. And ultimately, murder was the blackening proof of his depravity.

Harvey, in his writings and speeches (which were often one and the same) had an additional message for those he welcomed out of the closet. Once out, don't stand alone. Clasp hands with the Gay man or Lesbian nearest to you—turn the two into three, the three into a club, a panel, an organization, a caucus. Today—and not only in San Francisco, we have blocs of Gay doctors, Gay architects, Gay political clubs of every stripe, Gay business organizations, Gay church groups, Gay sports leagues, and on and on. And from these nuclei of personal and professional solidarity, the next stage was to stretch out our arms to every segment of society that was dirt swept under the rug by an elitist society. The Gay movement today has moved out to the minorities, the women's movement, the elderly, and the handicapped. And taken together, this nation can be re-established on grander interpretations of liberty and justice for every one of us.

See to it that Gay rights don't go down next year in Santa Clara County and San Jose.

See to it that Gay people aren't kept from visiting this country by either a homophobic Immigration Service or the State Department.

See to it that Gay men and Lesbians are included in every city department, every city commission, every agency, and every important board in the city service.

If, as many believe, we are indeed 20 to 25% of the citizenry of this city, then by the American political system we are entitled to 20 to 25% of the action. And I am not talking about a token Gay on a meaningless "window dressing" commission. And I am not talking about some closeted Gay on someone's back office staff. And I am not talking about some anonymous Gay man or Lesbian slipped under the circus tent in the police or fire department. What I am talking about is an across-the-board power representation—for the doors that are thrown wide open and a civic voice that says "Welcome . . ."

We have demonstrated our skills. We have proved ourselves capable and competent. THIS IS OUR CITY TOO!!! Manage it well, and together we will make a better life, a freer life, and a more meaningful life for us all.

THAT, my friends, was what Harvey Milk was all about—simple, clear, steadfast, and free. That was the dream that Harvey Milk dreamed for us—ALL OF US!!!

Those people who think that this building and this plaza and this city belong to them and them alone—those were the ones who blew off Harvey's head, my head, your head, our heads, a year ago this morning—but not our hearing, not our spirit, and NEVER our vision.

Harvey Milk was a patriot in the truest sense of the word. He loved this country. He loved this city, and he loved his people. And today, maybe only WE know that he can stand with the best of them—with the Martin Luther Kings, the brothers Kennedy, the Abraham Lincolns, and, yes, even the George Washingtons. WE know that, and someday the nation itself will so honor him. For, like those greats, Harvey Milk, too, was leading a people out of another kind of bondage—some of it self-inflicted, some of it inflicted by churches or public officials, and some of it by the Bryants, Briggses and Dan Whites of this country.

HARVEY DID NOT DIE IN VAIN—DAN WHITE KILLED IN VAIN! Harvey's death will have been in vain only if we allow that to be the case—and that will not happen, because in the 12 months since Harvey's death we have not faltered. TODAY there are more of us. TODAY we are stronger. TODAY we are better organized.

As Harvey would have said if he were here with us tonight at this memorial service: "Don't memorialize—ORGANIZE!!!"

And today we are organized. We are organized and armed with Harvey's own last will—when Harvey himself said: "Let the bullets that rip through my brain smash through every closet door in the country."

So, Harvey, until indeed every closet door has been opened, I pledge to you tonight that we shall not rest.

WE SHALL NOT REST!

Thank you.

SECTION V: THE 1980s

February 11, 1980

A Petition from the Netherlands Parliament

Henry Waxman

This speech was given on the floor of the House of Representatives by Representative Waxman of California and entered into the *Congressional Record* for February 11, 1980.

Mr. Speaker, two Members of the Netherlands Parliament presented to me on February 5 a petition, signed by 133 of the legislature's 150 members, urging the United States not to discriminate against foreign visitors on the basis of their sexual orientation. I applaud this overwhelming expression of concern by our colleagues at The Hague, and wish to bring their petition to the attention of the House.

The Immigration and Naturalization Service has recently decided to continue to enforce its antiquated policy of prohibiting suspected homosexuals from entering the country—despite the judgment of the Surgeon General that this restrictive policy should be ended. It is today generally accepted medical practice that homosexuality is not an illness or psychological disorder, and that the law should reflect this consensus. But under our immigration statutes, INS continues to deport and refuse to issue visas to suspected homosexuals. To end this discriminatory policy, I have joined with Representatives Beilenson and Dixon in introducing H.R. 6303 to repeal this law.

In their letter to Congress, our friends from the Netherlands contend that these legal impediments conflict with our obligations under the Helsinki accords to guarantee the free movement of people. Their letter states:

> We won't hide our feelings that to us a country which claims to value so dearly a respect for human rights all over the world, by acting in this way, is acting contradictory to that same necessary respect for human rights.

Their letter reinforces my longstanding concern that the issue of discrimination against homosexuals is a matter of basic human and civil rights, and must be judged accordingly.

The full letter from the Netherlands Parliament follows:

LETTER FROM THE DUTCH PARLIAMENT TO THE AMERICAN CONGRESS

The Hague, Binnenhof, 1a, January 1980

To the Chairman of the House of Representatives of the United States of America,
Hon. Thomas O'Neill, Jr.
Capitol Hill
Washington, D.C., U.S.A.

Dear Mr. Chairman,

We, the undersigned, all of us members of the Netherlands Parliament want to address ourselves with the following:

Information has reached us that your country's State Department has ordered visas should not be issued to non-Americans, who consider themselves to be homosexual. This would be a consequence of the law of 1917, whereas changes in the law by the American Congress in 1952 and 1962 did not alter this situation.

We beg to inform you that we find this deeply disturbing. We had thought up to now that such regulations could not arise in our times. Moreover we find it an unacceptable concept that Dutch and other non-American citizens would have to go through a humiliating procedure to determine their sexual orientation, even if such a thing were possible.

We won't hide our feelings that to us a country which claims to value so dearly a respect for human rights all over the world, by acting in this way, is acting contradictory to that same necessary respect for human rights.

We consider the right of each individual to experience his or her sexuality in his or her own way, as a matter which belongs to a person's private domain, and as such an undeniable right of every person. It follows from that, that the United States ought not to let the question of a foreign visitor's eligibility for a visa, depend among other things on his or her sexual orientation. Apart from that, in our opinion, the Immigration Law also clashes with the free traffic of persons. This is an international principle, which gained momentum from the Helsinki Agreement.

We are of the opinion that as champions of this agreement the United States ought to follow this principle also in this matter.

That is why we address an urgent appeal to the House of Representatives to bring about an end to this form of discrimination, for example by asking your country's Government to repeal the measures recently enacted.

In your capacity as the law-making authority of the United States we urge you most earnestly to enact legislation, which ensures a ban on this kind of grave discrimination.

While a few members of the Netherlands Parliament will visit the United States in the first week of February, we would appreciate your assistance in arranging a meeting on the matter with the appropriate Committee of the House of Representatives.

Sincerely yours.

The names of 133 members of the Dutch Parliament were appended to this text as signatories of said petition.

March 3, 1980

Carter Response to NGTF Survey

Robert Strauss

During the 1980 presidential campaign, the National Gay Task Force sent a survey to all candidates for the White House on gay rights issues. In response, the Carter White House replied to this survey with the following letter, written by Robert Strauss, Carter's campaign manager. The letter is addressed to Charles Brydon and Lucia Valeska, at that time codirectors of the NGTF, and was published in San Francisco's gay newspaper *The Sentinel* on March 7, 1980. HR-2074, referred to in the letter, was the gay civil rights bill then before Congress.

Dear Mr. Brydon and Ms. Valeska,

Thank you for the opportunity to respond to your letter and to state President Jimmy Carter's positions on matters of particular interest to the gay community.

As a candidate, the President was the first major presidential contender to openly discuss gay concerns. He stated his opposition to employment discrimination in the federal government because of sexual orientation. Three months after the inception of this Administration, senior White House advisors met with representatives of the National Gay Task Force to discuss matters of concern to the NGTF and its member organizations from around the country. That meeting provided the basis for a series of discussions at all levels of the federal government (including additional White House meetings) on a wide range of issues with your full participation.

These experiences are examples of the President's policy to expand the involvement of the American people, including the gay community, in their government. For too long, the doors of the federal government were closed to many Americans. Jimmy Carter has opened those doors and he intends to see that they remain open. In a similar vein, the President is committed to continuing his policy of appointing qualified individuals without discrimination based on race, color, sex, religion, national origin or sexual orientation.

Jimmy Carter campaigned on a promise to overhaul the country's outmoded civil service laws and lead a legislative effort to that end. As a result, one of President Jimmy Carter's major legislative successes occurred in 1978 when he signed into law the Civil Service Reform Act, the first comprehensive revision of civil service laws in over 100 years. One important provision of this new federal statute prohibits discrimination in federal personnel actions based on private, non-job related behavior such as sexual orientation. It has been estimated that this provision prohibits discrimination because of sexual orientation in approximately 95% of all federal jobs covered by the civil service system. The Administration is committed to fully enforcing this protection.

The legislative history of the Civil Service Reform Act and the relevant laws show that the vast majority of the jobs not protected by the Civil Service Reform Act were excluded by statute. Under these circumstances, an executive order would not resolve these statutory exemptions. Nonetheless, some exempted agencies have initiated aggressive personnel policy changes on a case by case basis. Both the Agency for International Development and the Peace Corps, in making their determination of suitability for foreign service, have made favorable rulings with regard to employees who are homosexuals.

With regard to your inquiry about supporting passage of HR 2074, the Administration's legislative policy requires that prior to the adoption of a position on specific legislation, the bill must be circulated to affected agencies and departments for review and comment. That process is normally initiated if the Administration has been invited to testify on the bill. However, as of this date, no hearing has been scheduled for HR 2074 and a decision on the bill will be made as the legislative process proceeds.

In the area of public policy decisions, gay concerns now have an equal opportunity to be heard and have been made part of the public process with demonstrable results. Gay organizations now qualify for both tax exempt and tax deductible status and those benefits are being used by groups throughout the country. At the Federal Communications Commission a new rule has been proposed that would require broadcasters to ascertain the needs of significant community groups, including gay organizations, to determine community broadcast needs.

The Bureau of Prisons will soon permit the receipt of non-pornographic gay literature in federal correctional institutions. This follows from the inquiry of the NGTF at its December meeting with White House officials.

In conjunction with the Congress, the President has established a Select Commission on Immigration and Refugee policy [*sic*] to review the need for changes in our immigration laws. The Commission held hearings recently in Boston on the effects of excluding homosexuals who seek to enter the country. Both of you accepted invitations to testify and, accompanied by Leon Castillo, you testified for the hearing record and proposed recommendations which will be reviewed by President Carter and the Congress. Representatives of the Justice Department and Immigration and Naturalization Service have been meeting regularly with the NGTF to review the department's immigration policies and to consult on enforcement procedures while the Select Commission's work continues. I believe that process has worked well.

In conclusion, the President's record shows that he has taken steps in his first three years in office, to address most of the public issues articulated historically within the gay community. I believe that this record warrants your continued support.

Sincerely,

Robert Strauss, Chairman

May 23, 1980

Presentation to the Temporary Committee on Resolutions

Timothy Drake

This is the full text of the testimony prepared by Timothy E. Drake, openly gay delegate to the Republican National Convention from the 9th District of Illinois, which he was not allowed to read but only to submit in written form to the Temporary Committee on Resolutions, meeting in Chicago, Illinois, on May 23, 1980. Drake was the first openly gay person ever to have won a delegate spot in the Republican Convention. This document was originally published on the front page of the June 6, 1980, issue of *GayLife,* Chicago's gay and lesbian community newspaper.

Members of the Committee. I stand before you today as the first admittedly homosexual ever elected as a delegate to a national convention of the Republican Party. Although the first, I am already not the only Gay Republican to win a delegate spot this year.

One of the principles establishing the Republican Party when it was founded 124 years ago here in the Midwest, was the protection of individual rights and individual equality. The first Republican president stated this principle very clearly when in his Gettysburg address he described America as a "new nation, conceived in liberty, and dedicated to the proposition that all men are created equal."

I speak here to call your attention to the fact that today in America, over a century since Abraham Lincoln, written policies of the United States government do not recognize this principle.

If the employment policies of the U.S. government are a fair indicator of recognizing if "all men are created equal," then the U.S. government, under both Democratic and Republican administrations, failed the test.

Since today's hearings in Chicago are to deal with Defense related issues I'll speak specifically to the personnel policies of the Department of Defense. Let me quote a letter from the Office of the Under Secretary of Defense dated October 26, 1979:

"With respect to entrance into military service, it is, in fact, the policy of the military services that homosexuals are not accepted for military services . . . Military members who are homosexuals are subject to discharge." L. Britt Snider.

This policy has been held as a violation of the First, Fifth, and Ninth amendments to the Constitution on several different occasions, yet it remains the policy practiced by the Department of Defense.

On May 20th, just three days ago, U.S. District Court Judge Terrence T. Evans, in ordering the reinstatement of a lesbian by the Army stated, "the court believes that constitutional privacy principles clearly protect one's sexual preferences in and of themselves from government regulation."

In the past few years, the Army has discharged Pfc. Roger Cutsinger. The Air Force has discharged Sergeant Leonard Matlovich, a winner of the Purple Heart and a Bronze Star. The Navy has discharged Ensign Vernon Berg. All three of these men had excellent military records and were discharged because they are gay.

The federal court system has overturned all three of those discharges on constitutional grounds. Yet, and I must repeat, the Department of Defense still continues to maintain this unconstitutional policy.

One solution for this paradox is an Executive Order by the President and Commander in Chief prohibiting discrimination on the basis of sexual orientation. I have attached a proposed plank for consideration by the 1980 Platform Committee calling for such.

This proposed plan embodies that founding principle of the Republican Party, the protection of individual rights and individual equality. This principle has the support of the leading Republican candidates for President.

Governor Reagan, in a position paper on Homosexual Rights, has stated that. "While I do not advocate the so-called gay life style, all citizens have equal rights before the law."

"I believe the government should not interfere with the private lives of Americans, nor should there be any place in our society for intolerance and discrimination."

"So long as a person's private life is private and does not interfere with his or her job performance, *it should have no bearing on private sector or government hiring*."

Ambassador George Bush has stated several times that, as President, he would be opposed to any legislation or rules which would single out Gay Americans for discrimination or other unequal treatment.

Congressman John B. Anderson, a co-sponsor of federal Gay Rights Bill H.B. 2074, has said that he is "opposed to discrimination on the basis of sexual preferences," and further stated that "if rights are to mean anything in our society, they ought to be codified."

In presenting for consideration this plank on Gay Rights I have sought to make sure that it is consistent with the founding principles of the Republican Party. I believe it is, and I sincerely hope that the 1980 Platform Committee will adopt it as a rededication of the principle of individual rights and individual equality.

GAY RIGHTS PLANK

We affirm the right of all lesbian and gay Americans to full participation in the social, political and economic life of the country, without fear of prejudice or reprisals based on sexual orientation.

To support this commitment and give life to this principle, we call for an executive order, prohibiting discrimination on the basis of sexual orientation in all government employment and government programs, and further we support the enactment of legislation to protect the civil rights of gay people and the repeal of all laws which are used to stigmatize persons on the basis of sexual orientation.

May 24, 1980

Building the Lavender Left

Joyce Levine

This speech was delivered at the Northeast Conference of Multinational Lesbian and Gay Male Feminist Socialists in Shirley, New Jersey, as the opening address.

My fondest desire at this moment is to be able to express the pride, the joy and the sense of strength that each of you reflects as I look upon you. This pride, this joy and this strength has been forged in our mutual struggle as lesbian and gay male socialists. It is a world historic moment: the first Northeast Conference of Multinational Lesbian and Gay Male Feminist Socialists. Our presence here is an affirmation of the dreams of those who struggled before us. We are the embodiment of their vision. Our struggle started millennia ago. Within each and every one of us there is stamped the memory of those lesbians and gay males whose history has been stolen from us.

We reclaim that history. We honor our sisters who were burned at the stake; our brothers who were used as the fuel; those who died at Dachau and Buchenwald, or were shot down in the streets of Pinochet's Chile, or in the hallowed halls of city government in San Francisco. And let us not forget those who can't be here today because they are incarcerated in the mental institutions and prisons of this society, or who still choose the prison of conformity. We carry the seeds of all our sisters and brothers—those who survived, those who were beaten down and those who died fighting.

Millions of names have been lost to history. We *know* some of the names; Magnus Hirschfeld, sexologist and homosexual emancipation leader; Deborah Sampson; Lucy Ann Lobdell, Marian West—lesbians who passed as men in order to survive—Del Martin, Phyllis Lyon—founders of Daughters of Bilitis; Henry Hay, socialist and founding member of the Mattachine Society.

All who dared to struggle in order to love *who* and *how* they wanted to are part of our proud history. And we cannot forget those courageous street people; the lesbians, gay males and transvestites, who eleven years ago fought the battle which gave birth to the modern-day lesbian and gay liberation movement—the Stonewall Rebellion, a battle so far-reaching that it made our movement a world movement.

Yes, we are survivors, and no force on earth has been able to wipe us out! Much work has been done by all who came before us and by many of us who are sitting here to make this conference possible. We are here because we recognize that much is still to be done. Many tasks lie before us.

As specially oppressed people we are unique. Our community embodies all the exploited and oppressed in society. We are members of national minorities, we are women, we are youth, older people, disabled, welfare mothers and fathers, students, workers, employed and unemployed. Because many of us are oppressed on many levels we know that we cannot separate our oppressions. We have learned that the same enemy who denies us our dignity and humanity as lesbians and gay males also robs us of all the richness of life and poisons us with the diseases of racism, sexism and heterosexism. All of us share the experience and the pain that fear of difference brings upon us. Our task is to take this fear of difference and turn it around. Our diversity can become our strength. We can lead the way in forging a unity based not only on our common oppression and class exploitation but on a respect for our differences. In order to do this we must recognize our priorities at this time. Racism is on the rise. The right wing is organizing to strike a blow at the progress that was made by the black liberation movement; the movement of all national minorities, the women's movement, the worker's movement and the lesbian/gay movement. As lesbians and gay males, we have a rich tradition of struggle. What makes us unique, however, is that we are socialists. This distinguishes us by virtue of the fact that we have an understanding and consciousness of the roots of our oppression which has been further illuminated by the insights and lessons of the women's liberation movement. We know that the struggle for our liberation can *only* succeed if there is a fundamental change in society. That our liberation is tied to the liberation of all the oppressed and exploited can never be stated too often. No one will be free until we are all free. The lies that divide us can only persist as long as the institutions that support them exist: big business, the military, the schools, the church, courts, prisons, news media, the medical and psychiatric professions. In 1917 a cataclysmic change took place in history when the Czarist government in Russia was overturned and the working class, led by the Bolshevik Party, took the future into their own hands. For the first time in history all laws against homosexuality were removed from the books, as well as the laws keeping women oppressed. Although the revolutionary leaders of the Russian revolution had far-reaching ideas to end sexual oppression and women's oppression, and passed very progressive laws to put an end to that oppression, Lenin knew that such laws alone would not bring about a change in the deeply rooted backwardness of the people on the questions of sexism and heterosexism. On the subject of the sexual role of the masses, Lenin felt that the sexual revolution had not yet been analyzed from the standpoint of dialectical materialism and that its mastery would require a tremendous experience. He felt that whoever would develop this analysis would do a necessary service to the revolution. This, too, is our historic role, for it is we who can make the greatest contributions in this area.

So, my brothers and sisters, we are gathered here because we have struggled and we have fought, each in her or his own way, each with a dream for the future, each contributing to the birth and creation of a movement with tremendous potential. With unity and organization, with the tools of scientific socialism, lesbians and gay males have the power to make our vision of the future of humankind the shared vision of the entire world working class.

May 30, 1980

25 Ways to Shaft the Gay Movement

J. F. Guthrie

This satirical text (the second to bear this title) is a revision and update by Guthrie (the national news editor for the *Philadelphia Gay News*) of a document originally written by Alice Ford and published in the New York City newspaper *Gay* in 1972.

Make sure that the most dedicated people in your group do every bit of work. This ensures that they will burn out quickly, so that there'll be a high turnover.

Maintain that it is never possible for lesbians and gay men to work together. All men should adopt the word "dyke" as a pejorative expression. All women should denounce gay men as "sexist."

Denounce all fundraising as a capitalist venture. Make sure that the movement does not have enough money to do its work.

Make sure that the movement is always so serious and so heavy that nobody ever has a good time. Especially denounce humor, social events and other non-political happenings.

Always fault groups for not meeting an ideologically pure stance on such issues as racism and sexism. Spend all your group's time arguing these matters instead of working for lesbian and gay rights.

Establish rules of procedure so complicated that no one is ever empowered to take any action at all. Make it easy for a handful of disgruntled individuals to halt proceedings completely.

If you are a person of means, never give financial support. Decide that you needn't give money because others will.

Make commitments and don't follow through. When an individual makes a commitment, but asks for additional resources or other help, ignore them.

Make sure that no one else in the community knows what your group is doing. Duplicate as much work as possible. Avoid working with the lesbian and gay press as much as possible to reach the community, especially if you don't like their editorial stance on one or more issues.

Force any group or committee that is working at top efficiency to give new members their say immediately. It is important to waste time rehashing old methods and ideas which have been found to be ineffective.

Underplay lesbian and gay professionals working in the movement. Fail to support lesbian and gay businesses. After all, our rights are their fight too.

Alienate as many other lesbian and gay groups as possible. Publicly criticize them and sabotage their work. If possible, bring your complaints before a straight government body.

Disparage all religious faiths, especially those within our community. Make sure lesbians and gays must choose between their god and their sexuality.

In the media, identify the movement for lesbian and gay rights with every other radical movement for social change. This will ensure that the public knows we stand for everything they find abhorrent.

Isolate all lesbians and gays who are not politically correct. Make sure that those who hold conservative right-wing views on other issues are not welcome in the movement.

Use the term "sexual preference" instead of "sexual orientation." Prove that being lesbian or gay is only a matter of free will, so that others will believe it's possible to make us into heterosexuals.

Always find fault with the media. Criticize every bit of coverage the movement gets. When invited on a talk show, denounce the host as a bigot, so that no lesbian or gay will ever be invited back.

Make sure that the public knows that child molesting is one of the aims of the movement. Demand that the age of consent laws be lowered to 10.

Denounce all militant action such as demonstrations and marches as counterproductive. Never participate in mass support for lesbian and gay rights.

Choose the worst public stereotypes to represent the movement in public. Make sure the ignorant, the indifferent and the irresponsible represent us before the public, especially the media.

Denounce all leaders of the movement as self seekers. Never allow any real leadership to emerge especially on a national scale.

Make no demands of members. Do not require them to show up at meetings unless they feel like it. When the indifferent do show up, always give them a free reign to criticize what the group has been doing in their absence.

Manipulate people for your own ego satisfaction. Having done so, make sure they know they've been manipulated so they won't ever want to work in the movement again.

Never take any action requested by any lesbian or gay group. Do not write letters to members of Congress, state legislators and other elected leaders in support of lesbian and gay rights. Especially refuse to give them support when they take a courageous action on your behalf.

Maintain that to impose an admission charge on any event is oppressive. Always make it optional for everyone, even the millionaires.

June 1980

Speech to the Democratic Party Platform Committee

Bill Kraus

This is the text of the speech delivered to the Platform Committee of the Democratic Party addressing a proposed amendment to the platform placing the party on record as opposing employment discrimination based on gay or lesbian identity. Kraus was at this time an openly gay delegate to the committee. A companion address on this matter was also made to the committee by Virginia Apuzzo. Both speeches were printed in San Francisco's gay newspaper *The San Francisco Sentinel* on June 27, 1980.

This is an amendment to end discriminatory practices by the government against gay people and to provide gay people with protection against job discrimination.

As some of you may know, there are six members of this Platform Committee, representing millions of our people in every state in this nation, who have a special interest in this amendment. We are gay men and women, representing both presidential candidates, and we come from the states of Texas, Minnesota, California, New York and Washington.

Some of us have worked with you since April on this platform. To my knowledge, no one has questioned our ability, our competence, or our right to be here.

But when we go outside of this Platform Committee, we find that today in areas under the authority of our federal government, we are denied the right to receive a security clearance, we are banned from service in the military, and—if we were citizens of a foreign country—we would, under current law—if we came to New York to visit the Statue of Liberty, be barred from entering this country as tourists, or we would be placed on probation for the duration of our visit to this nation. All solely because we are gay.

We are by law denied access to federal low-income housing and legal services. Under various state laws we are prevented by statute from obtaining jobs in occupational fields that range from teaching school to piloting airplanes. We are subject to a mind-boggling variety of legally-mandated discrimination. And in some states, it would be illegal for us to be served an alcoholic drink. All because we are gay.

Finally, we gay members of this Platform Committee and the millions of people we represent, can today in this country be refused employment or fired from our jobs—jobs we need as much as anyone else in this room—fired from our jobs, with *no legal recourse*. Solely because we are gay.

Fellow members of this Platform Committee, this is not a frivolous issue. Millions of us—the great majority of whom vote for the Democratic Party and support the programs of this party and its attempts to assure the rights of all other Americans—millions of us suffer because of this discrimination.

Like all discrimination, discrimination against gay people diminishes the lives of those who suffer from it.

Like all discrimination, discrimination against gay people is a violation of the fundamental principles of this nation and this party that *all* people are created equal and are entitled to equal justice under the law.

Fellow Platform Committee members, I have seen too many times the pain and the fear and the human suffering which discrimination against gay people causes and I have seen the hatred, the bigotry and the violence of many of those who inflict this discrimination upon us.

This amendment is a moderate, even conservative attempt to commit the Democratic Party to begin to rectify the situation in which the gay people of this country find ourselves.

It does not ask you to give us special privileges.

It does not ask anyone to like us.

It does not even ask that the Democratic Party give us many of the legal protections which are considered the rights of all other Americans.

Fellow members of the Platform Committee, what this amendment asks in a time when we hear much from prominent members of the Democratic Party about human rights is that the Democratic Party recognize that we, the gay people of this country, are also human.

June 1980

Speech to the Democratic Party Platform Committee

Virginia Apuzzo

These remarks were made by Apuzzo, one of six openly gay and lesbian members of the Democratic Party Platform Committee, addressing a proposed plank which would have set the Democratic Party on record as opposed to employment discrimination based on sexual orientation. It followed a companion speech by Bill Kraus which had set forth many of the legal strictures facing gays and lesbians in the United States at this time. The texts of both speeches were printed in San Francisco's gay and lesbian newspaper *The San Francisco Sentinel* on June 27, 1980.

Mister Chairman, I rise on a point of personal privilege.

Bill's excellent summary barely touches the heart of what is at issue here. Four years ago I lobbied many of you on the Platform on this and other issues—at that time I was told that Gay Rights was an "embarrassing issue." I ask you—what other group would be asked to accept their discriminated status because it would be embarrassing to take a stand *against* that discrimination.

This Party would not tolerate a move to legitimize prejudice and failure to act on existing prejudice can be no less indicting. I implore this committee to come to grips with the fact that discrimination against gay people is the *last accepted prejudice*. That *must* become unacceptable to you.

For the last three months we have listened together as Americans have come to express their concerns, their anguish, their hopes and in some instances their despair. These last couple of days those same concerns have come before this body and we have been put in the unenviable position of forging compromises. Many have been painfully arrived at. We in the gay community understand that. We have never achieved a single inch of progress without that pain.

This is not a struggle for the sprinters or the faint of heart.

It is a marathon. And we are prepared.

We are prepared to stay in this party.

We are prepared to work for victory in November.

And we are prepared to continue to press for one change at a time until we are *full* participants in this process.

With that firmly fixed, Mr. Chair, I move to withdraw this amendment.

June 22, 1980

The Cock of Basel

Rosalie Nichols

This speech was given at the Gay Freedom Day celebration in San Jose, California, on June 22, 1980. Quinn was the archbishop of San Francisco and resigned in December 1995. Nichols had been the editor of the California newspaper issued by the Sisters of Sappha, *Lesbian Voices,* for five years at the time this speech was given.

Freedom from religion is a heavy subject, and I can tell you're not in the mood for any speeches, so I would like to tell you a simple story. This is a true story.

Once upon a time back in 1474 at a place called Basel, a rooster—to everyone's shock and dismay—laid *an egg.* The rooster and his egg where subsequently put on trial, convicted, and burned at the stake. Now, why should a rooster be burned at the stake simply for laying an egg? Well, first of all, the Bible says, "Male and female created he them." So, any creature of nature that did not fall distinctly into the male or female category had to be the work of the devil, right?

But, in addition, the Church and the people of the Middle Ages believed in a monster known as the cockatrice, or basilisk, which is mentioned in the Bible. This fearful creature was produced if a cock's egg was set upon by a snake, bringing forth a **cockatrice,** with the body of a snake and the head of a cock with a treble comb on its forehead.

The cockatrice killed all living things. It burned up the grass with its hot and poisonous breath, and the fowls of the air fell down dead when they came near its nest. People, including the Church fathers and civil authorities, really believed this, however ridiculous it might sound to us in this age of science. So, when our unfortunate rooster laid his egg in 1474, the medieval Christians were alarmed. Not only might a cockatrice hatch from the egg, but it was also well known that cocks' eggs furnished the most active ingredients of witch ointment. Therefore, the rooster and his egg were duly put on trial:

Attended by a large concourse of people, the trial was held on a hill and conducted with a dignity appropriate to the occasion.

The prosecution proved that a sorcerer would rather possess a cock's egg than be master of the philosopher's stone. It was asserted, too, that in pagan lands Satan employed witches to hatch such eggs, from which proceeded animals most injurious to all of the Christian faith and race.

Counsel for the defence had no option but to admit the facts of the case, but asked what evil animus had been proved against his client. What injury to man or beast had it affected? Besides, the laying of the egg was an involuntary act, and as such, not punishable by law.

If the crime of sorcery were imputed, the cock was innocent; for there was no instance on record of Satan ever having made a compact with one of the brute creation.

The public prosecutor declared in reply that, though the devil did not make compacts with brutes, he sometimes entered into them. So much was sure from the scriptural account of the Gadarene swine which, possessed by devils, were involuntary agents. Nevertheless, these pigs were punished by being made to run down a steep place into the sea, and so they perished in the waters. So the cock of Basel was condemned to death, not as a cock, but as a sorcerer or devil in the form of a cock. With its egg, it was burned at the stake with all the due form and solemnity of a judicial punishment.

In the story of this trial in 1474, we can begin to understand how deep lie the roots of religious persecution of anyone who does not fit the Biblical concept of male and female. This includes hermaphrodites, transexuals, transvestites, asexuals, and homosexuals. If the Bible says "male and female created he them" and "be fruitful and multiply," then anything, any animal, or any human being who does not fit those simplistic beliefs must be evil, unnatural, or possessed by the devil.

We have made some progress since 1474, but we have not come far. In spite of all the scientific knowledge gained and all the modern technology produced, there are still people who believe *literally* in every word of the Bible and would turn the clock back to 1474 if they could. And they are *winning* now.

The attack on gay rights is just one sign of the times. These fundamentalists, with their medieval mentality, are working desperately to keep woman in the inferior position she has always held under their religion. Even Anita Bryant, now that she has filed for divorce, complains that the church pays too much attention to Biblical injunctions requiring wives to be submissive.

The fundamentalists also are attacking birth control, abortion, children's rights—anything they perceive as detrimental to the traditional Christian family of, as TV Evangelist Jerry Falwell would say, "one man and one woman for one lifetime"—with man as head and woman as helpmate and the children as property to be controlled, disciplined, abused, with no will of their own and no legal recourse.

Also, the fundamentalists are attacking what they perceive as "liberal education." We have all read of their attack on sex education, which they object to because it does not teach their religious views on chastity, marriage, monogamy and the traditional family. They want to put prayers back into public schools despite our constitutional principle of separation of church and state, and they have widespread public support for overturning the Supreme Court decision which eliminated religious exercises from our secular school system.

But more significantly, they have developed a strong drive to have the creation story of Genesis taught in schools—**not,** I wish to point out, as a religious exercise, but as **science!** In other words, they want their mystical *beliefs,* their religious views which they have accepted on *faith* taught in class side by side with scientific theories and scientific laws which have been established through meticulous *observation, experimentation* and **reason.** This makes as much sense as teaching about the "tooth fairy" in a course on dentistry. They wish to raise a whole new generation of schoolkids to not think, but to be brainwashed into accepting unsupported dogmas on faith and under the weight of Biblical authority.

Every advance that gay people have made has been made through science and reason. The work of anthropologists and psychologists has overturned much of the superstition and dogma against us. The work of modern philosophers and legal minds has cleared away some of the ancient theocratic laws against us. We cannot afford to let our friends, *science and reason,* be banished from the public schools and from public life and let our enemies, mythology and irrationality, be put in their places as standards for society.

We know that the Mormons and fundamentalists who opposed us this June 3rd operate under an authoritarian structure in their churches and in their homes. Now they want to bring authoritarianism back into the public schools, back into public life, back into our government. And they are *winning.*

Friends, we are in deep trouble. Every person here should become aware of what these religious powermongers are doing and the danger it presents to us. What can we do? We found out over the last two years of struggle, culminating on Black Tuesday, June 3rd [the day gay rights lost in San Jose] that straight people are very hard to reach with our concerns. On June 3rd, the public had a choice between civil rights and Biblical Morality, and they overwhelmingly chose Biblical Morality.

There was never any basis for our opponents' accusations against gay people. They resorted to lies, distortions, and gut level prejudice. They lied about us, they lied about the ordinances. Ministers of the Gospel and Attorneys at Law signed their names to lies and published them in the press, and one of them has now been elected a Municipal Court Judge.

All our efforts to stop the religious backlash failed, and there seems little hope of reaching the general public as long as they are caught up in the anxiety of inflation, recession, shortages, urban congestion, and the threat of war. We are facing hard times, and in hard times, it is easy to set up an unpopular group as a scapegoat, and it looks like *we are it.* Just as we were in Nazi Germany—and then the gypsies, and then the Jews, and then the mentally retarded, and on and on.

We did not succeed in achieving social freedom this June. But what we can do is preserve the freedom of our own minds and spirits. We can recognize that when our opponents accuse us of bringing about social decay and the Fall of the American Empire, the development of *their* minds has been arrested at the level of the Biblical story of Sodom and Gomorrah. When they accuse us of being immoral—or as Archbishop Quinn put it, "gravely evil"—we can recognize that *their* concept of morality has never progressed beyond the superstitions of the Middle Ages.

We are not immoral. Our morality is based on humanism, on love for each other and for life on this earth. We are not unnatural. We are the children of nature. And we are *truly* everywhere.

August 14, 1980

Speech to the Democratic National Convention

Mel Boozer

On August 14, 1980, at the Democratic National Convention in New York City, Bill Kraus and Virginia Apuzzo formally placed in nomination for the office of vice president of the United States the name of Mel Boozer, head of Washington, DC's Gay Activists Alliance. A petition with over 400 signatures had been submitted on his behalf, and he was awarded the usual fifteen minutes in which to address the assembled delegates. This was the first time that an openly gay person had been nominated for this high office.

Mr. Chairman,

I rise in grateful appreciation of more than 400 delegates at this convention who gladly signed a petition to place my name in nomination. And in appreciation of those who wanted to sign but were not able to, and for the 77 women and men in the Lesbian and Gay caucus who have worked day and night to circulate the petition.

I rise in proud recognition of the Mayor of the District of Columbia, Mr. Marion Barry, and the entire delegation of the District of Columbia, who have supported me and encouraged me in this effort. I rise in thankful recognition of the citizens of the District of Columbia who voted for me to come here knowing that I am Gay; and who continue to labor and live in a city which has no voice in determining how it shall be taxed and which has no power to affect the decisions which affect the quality of our lives.

And finally, Mr. Chairman, I rise in anguished recognition of more than 20 million Americans who love this country, and who long to serve this country in the same freedom that others take for granted! Twenty million Lesbian and Gay Americans whose lives are blighted by a veil of ignorance and misunderstanding.

For more than 200 years, a majority of Americans have waited to be admitted to the institutions of our nation on an equal footing. This struggle has led us successfully through the abolition of slavery, the movement of universal suffrage, the Civil Rights movement, the continuing movement to include the elderly, the physically challenged, and economically disadvantaged. And now the same vision which had guided the first two centuries of our existence compels us to pass the Equal Rights Amendment so that women and men can share equally in that vision, and in our continuing struggle to make that vision a reality for all Americans.

But this same struggle which has animated our greatest leaders and our most loyal citizens is far from over.

Mr. Chairman, today across our land more than 20 million Americans hide in the twilight of fear and oppression. Lesbians and Gay men throughout the country are daily forced to choose between a life of service and labor to their communities without identity or an identity which would deprive them of the opportunity to serve and work at all.

Mr. Chairman, we have come to the Democratic Party, as others have come before us, to appeal to the vision of equal justice, the belief in fair play, and the sense of compassion which are the bedrock upon which the greatness of our nation is founded. We believe that, now more than ever, fairness, equal justice, and compassion are under attack by the forces of the extreme right. But we also believe that the ideals embedded in our Constitution by the founders of our Republic are alive and well in the Democratic Party.

Mr. Chairman, we come from towns and cities where our friends are jailed and beaten on the slightest pretext. We come from churches which have been burned to the ground because they admit us to worship. We come from families which have been torn apart because our jobs have been lost and our names have been slandered by false accusations, myths, and lies.

Mr. Chairman, the leadership of the Democratic Party has called upon us to be responsive to the plight of all oppressed groups.

Governor Brown of California has declared that Lesbians and Gay men have a right to a job without reprisals and a right to serve in the highest capacities of civil government.

Representative Dellums of California has affirmed that Lesbians and Gay men are entitled to the same rights as all other Americans.

Senator Kennedy has declared that it is the responsibility of government to protect the rights of all American citizens including Lesbians and Gay men.

And President Carter, before he became president, declared that Lesbians and Gay citizens should not be subject to arbitrary discrimination.

Mr. Chairman, we are pleased that the charter of our party now bans discrimination on the basis of sexual orientation. We are pleased that the platform of our party calls for an end to this kind of discrimination. But today, the suffering continues. We are abused physically and morally by those who would offer us up as scapegoats to the right for all the ills which beset our society.

But why should so many men and women continue to suffer from arbitrary discrimination? Why must we be denied a fair chance to participate in the American life to which we have contributed as much as anyone else? Why must we be subject to harassment and intimidation and ridicule? When the Constitution of this great nation has already provided that all citizens shall enjoy the equal protection of law.

Mr. Chairman, there can be no justification, no defense, for social injustice. The Constitution does not make exceptions. We who waited so patiently to be admitted to the vision of the Constitution know the consequences of prejudice. We have felt the sting of ignorance. And we have come to the Democratic Party seeking "new hope" which this party has always represented.

Over and over again, the Democratic Party has insisted that in our society there can be no haven for discrimination. Is this not the same party which has championed the causes of every minority which has come before us? Is this not the same party which has sought to include women on an equal basis? Is this not the same party which has led the battle for civil rights for Black Americans?

Would you ask me how I dare to compare the civil rights struggle with the struggle for Lesbian and Gay rights.

I can compare them and I do compare them, because I know what it means to be called a nigger and I know what it means to be called a faggot, and I understand the difference in the marrow of my bones.

And I can sum up that difference in one word: NONE. Bigotry is bigotry. Discrimination is discrimination. It hurts just as much. It dishonors our way of life just as much. And it betrays a common lack of understanding, fairness, and compassion just as much.

Mr. Chairman, I know that I am an American. I know not because of my birth certificate but because when Old Glory is unfurled and the anthem is played, my heart is warmed and my eyes water. I love this country as much as anyone in this hall. I am thankful in my prayers for the privilege of being a citizen of this nation.

I believe that there is no power on this earth that can defeat the American people as long as we remain true to the values which have made us great. Equal justice, fair play, and compassion are the true sources of our greatness.

I shudder to contemplate how we waste the energy and devotion of more than 20 million Lesbian and Gay Americans who remain shackled by degradation and isolation.

And I am astonished by the longing and pleading of my Gay brothers and Lesbian sisters whose faith in this party, in this country, and the democratic process has not been defeated and will not be defeated by the falsehoods and fears of all those who would oppress them.

Like them, I have faith in this nation and in its people and in this party, and I believe that when the people and the nation have heard the facts, when they have seen us as we truly are, then they will surely not abandon us to the prejudices and caprices of the ignorant.

So, my fellow Democrats, I appeal to you to search your hearts and minds and recall that you too have wanted the right to work as long as you could work competently, and you have wanted the right to seek happiness as long as you could do so without interfering with the rights of others to do the same, and I beg you to recall that most of you who now take those same rights for granted have had to struggle to overcome suspicions and fears and prejudices in order to achieve them.

So, now, we too appeal to you to acknowledge for ourselves the same rights so that no American can ever again be subjected to abuse and harassment.

October 4, 1980

NOW Speech

Lucia Valeska

This address was given by Valeska, at that time coexecutive director of the National Gay Task Force, as the opening speech to the annual conference of the National Organization for Women in San Antonio, Texas, on October 4, 1980. She was the only lesbian speaker to appear at this event. This text is combined with remarks made by her a few weeks later in Portland, Oregon. The same address was given by Valeska to the Dorian Group at the Eastlake East tavern in Seattle on October 16, 1980, and reprinted in the January 2, 1981, and January 16, 1981, issues of *Seattle Gay News*. The quotation from Sally Gearhart is taken from an open letter sent to District Five on the relative qualifications for office of Harry Britt and Kay Pachtner, and was only one point in the larger discussion but was picked up and reprinted in the *Village Voice* and elsewhere. The "first manifesto" quoted is the 1970 essay "The Woman-Identifed Woman" written by the Radicalesbians, which helped start the lesbian-feminist movement.

Will there be a national gay agenda for the Eighties?

Five years ago—even two years ago—no one much questioned our fundamental ability to survive. But with the rise of the radical right and the election of Ronald Reagan, who has publicly endorsed the goals of the radical right, we are not so certain of our fate. Much will depend upon how lesbians and gay men across the country choose to conduct their political affairs in the next four years.

But first things first: from Stonewall in 1969 to the American Psychiatric Association's decision to remove homosexuality from its list of mental disorders in 1973, to the Lesbian and Gay March on Washington one year ago attended by 100,000, we have witnessed the phenomenal growth of a brand new political movement with concrete achievements measured across the land.

In California, the State Supreme Court has held that *coming out* on the job is a political act and to be protected by free speech.

In Oklahoma, we have just filed a complaint in Federal Court against the Helms Bill (prohibiting openly gay teachers from teaching in the public schools), which is likely to take the cause of gay teachers all the way to the Supreme Court.

In Wisconsin and California, a team of distinguished psychiatrists, psychologists, and social workers has completed a four-year investigation of lesbian mothers and their children. The positive verdict pronounced will serve gay custody cases by providing just the documentation that has been missing from the courtroom.

In Washington, D.C., the FCC has ruled that the needs and news of the gay community must be ascertained by broadcasters across the land. The Bureau of Prisons has agreed to admit gay publications into federal prisons in an out-of-court settlement after a three-year lawsuit. We are able to get the White House Conference on Families to listen to the needs and aspirations of gay families at conferences held throughout the country. The National Convention Project, with the help of gay and lesbian delegates from around the country, came away from the Democratic National Convention with the first gay rights plank in American history.

Other significant achievements include:

Tax exemption for gay organizations (Carter, mid-Seventies)
Teeth into Civil Service Reform Act (Carter, 1980)
Extension of job protection (e.g., Peace Corps, 1979)
Presidential Administration support of Cranston legislation
Directive from Attorney General's office that opened our borders
Cooperation of U.S. government in resettlement of gay Cuban refugees
Two openly gay Presidential appointments

In the past ten years, we have set down an institutionalized network of communications with ninety gay publications and twenty gay radio stations.

Let me talk for a moment about the National Gay Task Force, its resources, its membership, and some of its obstacles. At NGTF, there is a paid staff of eight, some fifty volunteers, and a national membership of 10,000. The annual budget is $350,000. The only other national gay civil rights organization is Gay Rights National Lobby (GRNL), which is a one-person operation with a board of directors that hasn't met in two years and an annual budget of $50,000.

There are two major obstacles which must be dealt with if we are to sustain ourselves through the crush of the next few years. First, the great problem internally is obviously a lack of support from the national lesbian and gay community for a national agenda. Ten thousand members is a meager showing from a population of twenty million. Think of what kind of an effect could be made by the National Gay Task Force with a budget of $600,000,000 compared to our $350,000.

The next greatest internal obstacle concerns the relationship between women and men, and the lack of adequate participation by lesbians in the gay rights movement.

Now I don't want to make the situation on this front seem more bleak than it is. There are a number of lesbians putting a tremendous amount of energy into the mixed movement. We are better off this year than last, and there is a growing sense on the part of lesbians that we have too much to gain (or lose, as the case may be) by not staking out our territory in the mixed movement.

As we try to pull this coalition between women and men together, I think we are going to have to build a whole new consciousness within both the lesbian and gay male communities. What I would like to briefly outline for you here are some of the elements which I think our new vision will contain.

First we must validate the assertion that there are two different communities. As such we are not creating a whole new entity; we are building a coalition.

We are not erasing the lines between women and men, but rather understanding them. And in a very pragmatic fashion, we are creating a well-defined agenda, which both women and men in the movement will support *over and above the differences.* But this cannot be done successfully *unless the differences are aired, listened to, and respected.*

We start from the premise that gay civil rights—basic protection under law and massive change in social attitudes toward same-sex love—is necessary, and neither of us—women or men—can win the battle alone.

Yet to the idea of working with gay men to achieve this goal, my gut level response has *often* been: "If men would just put their clothes on and come in from the bushes, we could get on with the real job."

Sally Gearhart expands the theme when she states flatly: "Weary lesbians have spent untold hours explaining to middle America that lesbians do not worry about venereal disease, do not have sex in public bathrooms . . . and do not want to go to the barricades fighting for the lowering of the age of consent for sexual acts . . . I will continue to defend my gay brother's right to his sexuality . . . though many of its dimensions embarrass and frighten me . . . I am frustrated and angry that many gay men remain totally oblivious to the effect on women of their objectification of each other, their obsession with youth and beauty, their camped-up consumerism, and their demand for freer sexual expression."

And, indeed, there are many things in the visible traditions of gay male culture that lesbians do not aspire to. But we must not forget that there are many things in traditional female culture that we do not aspire to either. The heritage in both cases is not created hormonally. Culture means human-made. One is not born sado-masochistic.

Gearhart and many lesbians now speak from developed feminist perspective—one that I think gay men as a whole will eventually accept and respect. In the interim, what holds back male approval of feminist principles and strategies is that the push for *understanding* has been made primarily in one direction: from female to male.

At the annual NOW conference, held in this year in San Antonio, I asked the audience (primarily made up of straight women and lesbians) to shout out *"I am a faggot!"*

It was not a popular request. But I believe the discomfort comes partly in direct proportion to the current level of ignorance about gay male life among women, straight and lesbian.

Why the ignorance? Why the one-way push for consciousness? There are a number of significant factors—all related to fundamental differences between gay and feminist movements and between lesbian and gay male experiences.

The gay movement is roughly a century behind the feminist movement. In terms of a political focus, the gay movement only began eleven years ago. Feminists were taking on the major social institutions of the church, the psychiatric profession, and the state long before gay people had any notion that they numbered more than a handful worldwide.

Yet feminists (lesbians and straights) expect this infant movement to be where they are right now. Feminists need to curb their self-righteousness. It must be realized that it took the blood, sweat, and tears of hundreds of thousands of women, numbers of years, to bring the feminist movement to where it is today. Think of the recent Democratic Convention and what was accomplished there by women! Women broke the Carter whip system on women's issues and in so doing radicalized the party platform on women' s concerns—over and above the firm opposition of Democratic Party leadership. *This victory was over one hundred and thirty years in the making.* It was not achieved by our mothers, but by us. Not because our mothers are stupid and we're so smart. It is because we've had help that our mothers did not have, hope that our mothers did not have, and resources that our mothers did not have. Most important, we've had years now on the battle front from which many hard lessons have been learned.

Gay men have not had this process. They have not yet taken on an analysis of sex roles and their relationship to it (with the exception perhaps of a few isolated academics, but certainly without a movement to articulate it).

Just because one angle has been articulated, does not mean the other angle doesn't exist.

It is my contention that many gay men are somewhat terrified by women's head start, super organization, vast in-depth social networking. Not because they hate women, although some surely do, but because they have been abused by people who have had control over their lives. And women, through feminism, have unprecedented control over the fate of gay men.

Past the fundamental historical lag between feminist and gay movements, there are a number of other primary differences.

One: the inevitable and unique trail of organizing an *invisible constituency.*

Two: this concerns the nature of gay existence and gay oppression. The church has never come out against being female. The state has never forbidden blackness or being born working class. There is a big difference between being inappropriate in certain places and being inappropriate altogether!

Now I realize that it is politically incorrect to accentuate the miseries of growing up a member of a despised, unmentionable, and untouchable minority. But in the gay movement's absolute, overnight insistence on defining gayness as the latest and greatest wonderful world event—in the process of attempting to literally replace a totally negative identity with a totally positive identity—some real people have gotten stuck in the middle. I'm sure you know a few.

In our enthusiasm, we have denied ourselves any kind of reasonable transition.

You can't just become *that* overnight when you're *that* bad to begin with.

Three: unlike women's culture, gay culture is an *outlaw* culture. At its core it thrives on breaking majority rule on disobedience. That gay men balk at the new set of rules that feminists present is the least we might expect. If gay men so readily picked up rules laid down for them, they probably wouldn't be gay in the first place. You can't force rules on a group which defies the rules by its very existence; not without a little preliminary havoc.

We know from history that gay men *ought* to be the first feminist men. For, like women, they suffer whole-heartedly the world over from a gross and inhuman application of sex role. I believe that when gay men are encouraged to better articulate the psychological and social components of their ill fate at the hands of traditional sex role, they will indeed come around.

Four: in the meantime, we know the need to mask one's core identity to survive takes an incredible toll on the human psyche.

Approval is the key to a solid sense of self-social approval. We can't mandate that key out of existence. The general social context for gay people is still infused with massive doses of negativity, contempt, fear, and disapproval. Even extremely liberal parents are alarmed to discover a gay child under their roof. Especially if that child is male. The alarm is real and so is its effect.

Five: another thing to consider seriously; people coming out of prisons, marriages, parental homes, long-term restraining situations of any kind—all of them experience a certain degree of trauma and *act it out.*

Sometimes the acting out provides nourishment; sometimes it is merely cute. On the other hand, it can be sad or destructive. Often it is simply boring. It is always irrational and it may be bizarre. Like the infamous Rollerena in New York City—conservative Wall Street broker by day, and on roller skates in a Victorian dress and bonnet by night.

We are witnessing the beginning throes of a long series of emotional and cultural shock waves, as we dismantle one of the fundamental building blocks of our entire world order—sex role. It won't be overnight. It will be generational. It will be hard. People do not let go of survival patterns easily.

Six: the final difference I would mention that severely affects the climate of gay-feminist coalition is the advent of lesbian-feminism.

Back in 1970, or before, around the time of the Stonewall riots, radical feminists ran into gay women who were just bursting out of their closets and a hybrid was born. Quite virulent in the beginning, it flatly asserted: "Feminism is the theory, lesbianism the practice." The first manifesto asserted: "A lesbian is the rage of all women condensed to the point of explosion." The idea promulgated in wide circles was that it is not only good to be gay, but it is superior to be lesbian. Organic feminism.

It's interesting that when straight society thinks of recruitment it still thinks of gay men going after young straight men, or worse, boys. Meanwhile, on the lesbian front there was indeed active recruiting of straight feminists. What's more, that recruitment was somewhat successful. Which is why, incidentally, all the feminist literature on the subject of gay rights still uses the term "sexual preference," denoting a clear choice in the matter. In any case, the effect was tremendous for both feminists and gay movements. Suffice to say for now that gay men have never had a full-blown political movement to complement their fight. It has been good to be a lesbian in a way it could never be for gay men. And this phenomenon in terms of women's art, culture and connectedness to one another has been the envy of men everywhere.

These are some of the fundamental differences and internal obstacles which cannot be ignored if we are to pull ourselves into a united front.

Next are the *external obstacles:* Christian Voice has at least 187,000 registered members and controls over 100 radio stations. It sponsored the Washington March for Jesus with a reported 200,000 in attendance. It endorsed Reagan for president and contributed $1 million to right wing campaigns during this past election, joining the Right to Life movement in ousting McGovern and Frank Church as well as a number of others.

The Praise the Lord Club is run by Jim Baker. His organization earned over $51 million last year primarily from many small donations by private citizens through media evangelism.

Then there is the Schlafly family: Phyllis, former president of Women for Goldwater and husband, Fred, who is an attorney for a John Birch front called *The Wake Up America Foundation.*

The Conservative Caucus this year organized the "I Love America" rally, featuring Senators John Warner (Liz Taylor's husband) and Harry Byrd of Virginia.

Anita Bryant's ministries managed to raise over nine million dollars this past year, in spite of her domestic strife. Of that amount, only $150 actually went into religious counseling. The rest went into a national hate campaign and major fund-raising effort.

The Protect American Children campaign raised another $1.3 million.

You know you can afford the luxury of sitting on your heels when it's just right wing religious fanatics who are coming after you. It's quite another when it's CBS News and the President of the United States. In Sodom we take too much for granted.

Ties between Christian Voice, Praise the Lord Club, One Nation Under God, and members of the House and Senate are so strong that the two groups become indecipherable.

As one black lesbian put it: "This is no longer a battle about attitudes but a struggle to change the very political assumptions upon which this system is currently functioning. Part of fighting the right is identifying it."

President-elect Ronald Reagan is one of the founders of the anti-gay Citizens for the Republic, an organization founded by strike-breaker Adolph Coors. Reagan is also connected with the conservative caucus, founded by Howard Phillips, formerly of Young Americans for Freedom and Nixon's last director of the Office of Economic Opportunity.

In 1978 Reagan publicly opposed Proposition 6 in California and defended the gay community.

In June of this year he came out with a new statement saying, "I oppose gay rights ordinances because they require employers to hire people solely on the basis of their sexual preference."

Patently false and he knows it, he is not just catering to a new mood in exchange for money and support. He is actively building it.

His latest public statement: "I don't think the American people can condone homosexuality, and neither can I."

The response of one gay activist speaks for us all: "The threat from the right must be treated as a battle for survival and it must be won."

In the past several minutes I have tried to describe the nature and strength of some of the primary obstacles standing between the gay movement and the kind of unification required for survival and growth in the 1980s.

Clearly we must look toward the concept and practice of *coalition* with a greater sense of urgency and a willingness to use our differences creatively. For the nature of gay oppression warns us that at this moment in history we cannot go it alone. However unfashionable, arrogance must submit to reality.

The final point I would make is this: Any movement that refuses to place itself at the center of the storm of what concerns most Americans in the next ten years will forfeit that concern. If the decade ahead is going to have a moral tone, we'd better provide one of our own.

December 4, 1980

Address to the Kennedy Institute for Politics, Harvard University

Virginia Apuzzo

There are only two groups in America who really believe that lesbians and gay men will force significant political changes—the New Christian Right and gays themselves. At this moment, they are both wrong.

The New Christian Right is wrong, but it doesn't matter, because it is working for them.

Gays are wrong and it does matter. We are wrong because we believe our success will come merely if we have more of what we have already—more money for our organizations, more volunteers, more support from within our own community.

More of what we have already is not going to bring us into political influence and power. At this point, the benefits we have earned over the past ten years are still overshadowed by the failures we refuse to acknowledge, and that is what will prevent us from becoming anything more than what we are now—an interesting new group with things to say—but ultimately not a serious movement.

For what we lack is the willingness within our movement to assess, to evaluate, and to demand accountability. Those are the tools used to take corrective steps, points on a compass used to pilot a course. Without those points, we can only become a machine turning out energy but not set to accomplish a purpose.

It is not that the past ten years have not brought us forward, for they have. It is that we must not mistake where they have brought us and confuse that sense of progress with a sense of direction, which we still lack.

The major difference between today and a decade ago is that gays and lesbians have become a community and not simply an issue. It is still a controversial community, to be sure, but increasingly it is an acknowledged community. Most important of all, we have acknowledged it to ourselves, through our community service programs, our newspapers, our churches, our literature.

Ten years ago we could not have gathered a panel who could speak of their particular experience in a gay community. They could speak of their own gayness, of their own beliefs about politics, but not of a community they participated in and which existed visibly.

It is that sense of community, carried in each individual, that has brought us most, if not all, of the way over the past ten years. It is our visibility as a community and as individuals that accounts for the increasing public acknowledgement that we are part of America's diversity, more than the resolutions passed in city councils, more than the proclamations by mayors.

Whether the gay rights movement can evolve from that, and can be taken seriously, will be determined in the next six months. The challenges before us, as a movement and a political force, are immediate and they are concrete; how we handle them, indeed, whether we address them or not, will not alter that. Within a very few months, the verdict will be in.

After ten years, there is an unbecoming amount of evidence that we have not found an agenda, that we have not forged tools to get us an agenda, and that we are in danger of failing in our commitment to our own community as well as to all others with an investment in our participation in social change.

At this moment, the national gay rights movement is less significant than gay and lesbian efforts in Houston or New Orleans, and has less concrete accomplishments than gays and lesbians in Pennsylvania have with state government to eradicate discrimination in all sectors. The gay rights movement taken as a whole is far less than the sum of its parts.

In our major cities, gays and lesbians have made some important gains but we have failed to grasp them as a national movement. At times, we have even contradicted their importance. Why is it, for example, that gays and lesbians in Washington, D.C. can win more city appointments and more complete guarantees of their rights than gays and lesbians in San Francisco? Why can gays in Los Angeles boast of a gay community service center with a staff of dozens and an annual budget of over a million dollars, when gays and lesbians in New York City can claim nothing? Why can gays in Minnesota field the largest percentage of gays in its delegation to the Democratic National Convention of any state, and gays in Massachusetts can't claim even one delegate?

Nor is it just our successes we are failing to learn from. We are also ignoring the lessons of our failures. We have yet, for example, to even assess the failure of our movement to gain from the Carter Administration what we needed and what was possible. We fail to even see it as a failure that as a movement we took no position on congressional proposals to repeal the Voting Rights Act and days later were forced to accept an anti-gay provision. Indeed, we fail to see the relationship between those events and the intent behind them.

The political game is being played around us, and we have yet to learn what cards are on the table and how to play them. What is even worse is that after the election, one increasingly hears that there is nothing wrong with this, and little is lost. The answer to the New Right's take-over of national politics, we are told, is to retreat to our cities and their local agendas, leaving behind a national effort before we can put it to the test.

There are local agendas, and they must be pursued: but they must be understood as part of a national effort, for that is what they truly are. There is no mistaking the fact that those who oppose us know and understand this. Time and again the New Christian Right has mustered its national strength to attack us on the local level, and they will continue to win as long as we abet them by standing alone. The victory in Oregon for a gay rights supporter opposed on that issue, is a victory that extends beyond the borders of the congressional district. The loss in Virginia Beach of a referendum against gay and lesbian publications in the public libraries is a loss that extends beyond that one city.

Our local groups must also grasp the fact that their agenda is national. The advances of the past four years were possible because local politicians, who knew the local gay and lesbian groups, took up national positions. More was not accomplished because our local groups did not continue their dialogue and maintain their access; because they took a limited view of their role and their agenda. Our national leadership partook of that failure as well, when it sought to usurp the role that our local groups had carved out with politicians who became national leaders.

We can no longer patronize the shortcomings of our national organizations as though they are beloved children who are incapable of reaching maturity. We must begin to demand accountability from them, and where they prove themselves incapable, we can no longer accept a shrug and a smile.

At the local level, we must dispense with the politics of tantrums. We do not need it, we cannot afford it, and it will not get us where we need to go. Slogans and street marches challenge policies, as well they should, but they do not rewrite them. That is the job for those committed to the tedium of details, for those who will understand the value of that work, for those who believe not just that the past is wrong but that the future can be right.

Now that the national power is in the hands of those who willfully misunderstand us and want the nation to believe that our goals are threatening, we can no longer afford to be ambiguous about these goals and how they are achieved. Nor can we accept the strategies of the past, that too often sneaked us into the agenda by the side door. That is the strategy that will be turned to sneak us right back out those side doors. What we win without public notice can be taken away from us without public notice. We must accept the strategy of the long run and not the end run.

The first issue we face is reform of the U.S. immigration laws, which for decades have declared that lesbians and gay men were unfit to enter this country.

For two years, our immigration laws have been reviewed by the Select Commission on Immigration and Refugee Policy. This week the first formal recommendations are being considered by that panel. Included is a proposal to admit gays and lesbians to our country without regard to sexual orientation. By March 1, the commission will formally submit these proposals to Congress.

It will be the first major debate on immigration policy since 1952, and it may well be twenty more years before we have another debate. The confrontation over the issue of admitting gays and lesbians is set, and it will be won or lost with or without us.

The question for us now is whether we can stitch together our partners and work effectively for that goal. Congressional approval of these recommendations is not the test; the test is how we play the game or if we play at all.

We have on our side the support of the American Psychiatric Association, the U.S. Public Health Service, and the major health profession organizations. This is a sharp reversal from the past, when they supported the provision to keep homosexuals out of this country. It is also crucial because, under the current law, *they* are charged with implementing this policy. This they are no longer willing to do. Instead, they are willing to stand with us and ask for a repeal of that provision altogether.

It is also a policy that has caused the United States intense international embarrassment. Foreign governments, such as the Dutch and the Swedes, have raised the issue and condemned our nation's law.

It is important to know that the Council of Europe also has condemned this law, because the Council of Europe is the very vehicle the United States uses in approaching human rights violations in Iran or Afghanistan. It has an undisputed reputation for substantive and serious participation in human rights as a foreign policy issue.

By the admission of our own government, this policy is a violation of the Helsinki Accords, the treaty which is our lever in witnessing and raising human rights violations in the Soviet Union. Last year, the U.S. State Department formally concluded that our nation was guilty of a human rights violation under this treaty because of our anti-gay immigration law.

Repeal of this anachronism has won the support of many at home as well. Newspapers from Des Moines to Miami have all editorialized for repeal, and national leaders in both parties have supported it.

At the Democratic National Convention last August, the Democratic Party went on formal record to call for repeal of this provision. John Anderson, in his presidential bid, took the same position.

We have worked to hold these cards, and while they may not win repeal, it is incumbent on us to play them purposefully and publicly. To be truly effective, we must bring all of our national components into play. Gays in Boston must strongly lobby Senator Edward Kennedy, as must gays in other cities who have worked closely with him on his campaigns. He will continue to be a member of the Judiciary Committee where the first consideration will take place; Gay and lesbian health professionals must use their access to see that their profession is joined solidly with us. We must reach across to the Dutch and other gay and lesbian organizations to insure that pressure continues from that quarter. Above all, we must show that we recognize the forces that can be marshalled on our side, and that we know how to marshall them in an impressive display.

In doing so, we must not lose sight of the people who are affected, particularly the Cuban refugees. We must be unwilling to let them be swept under the rug and unwilling to let others ignore the message of their arrival.

They are refugees from anti-gay and lesbian persecution, the scarred victims of a system that holds the life of homosexuals cheap and devalues their humanity.

Their gayness is not incidental, not an irrelevancy, but at the heart of their flight and our plight—the recognition of our right to participate and be visible as a legitimate community.

The recognition by our government and other governments of their humanity and their rights would pull away the curtain which makes the suffering of gays and lesbians invisible, whether they are in Iran, Cuba, the Soviet Union, or Oklahoma.

The question of violence against gays, painfully evident with the Cuban refugees, is the second major issue which will be acted upon at the national level very shortly.

That issue is at the forefront in nearly every city where gays and lesbians are organized and visible in this country.

But it is not just a local issue. Eighteen months ago, the U.S. Civil Rights Commission began considering the question of police abuse of minorities. For the first time, the commission ruled that it would take note of lesbians and gay men in one of their studies. Public hearings were held in Houston and Philadelphia, and lesbians and gay men testified about police problems in our community.

Now the U.S. Civil Rights Commission is considering a full range of proposals to correct the problems they found. They have already concurred with the testimony that gays and lesbians are subject to prejudice and abuse from the police, and are victims of both official and random violence as a specially targeted population.

It is in their power to recommend that police departments drop their ban on hiring gays as one step to better community relations. It is in their power to recommend that police review boards include gays and lesbians so that our voices are heard officially. And it is within their power to pressure the U.S. Justice Department to insure that the civil rights of gays and lesbians are not violated by the police of our cities.

Those were issues at the very heart of the Stonewall Rebellion that launched our coming together as a community. Those are the issues which remain at the heart of our community at every level. We must prepare ourselves to respond to those issues when the commission makes its public report.

We must also understand the opportunity we have been offered by this commission beyond the question of police problems. In effect, they have opened the door for an examination of all questions of legal justice. It can include review of regulations and ordinances that are used to prevent gays from receiving professional licenses, which say that we may not be served an alcoholic beverage in some states. It can reach to the very judicial temperament which holds that sexual orientation is a bar to child custody.

I have picked the examples of pending immigration and police issues because they touch on our standing in the nation, and on our daily lives.

But they are not the only issues immediately before us, and they are not the only issues which will decide the future of the gay rights movement.

In just a little over a month, Ronald Reagan will take office. Shortly after that he will send a legislative package and a budget proposal to Congress. When he does, it will surely raise issues of importance for gays and lesbians as well as for other groups who share our commitment to social change.

It is really only in the past four years that we have won national attention for our claim to be an important political movement. During those past four years, we have had an administration and a Congress that has valued to some degree the points of view of other social change advocates, those who spoke for the Equal Rights Amendment, for the right of women to control their own bodies, for the concerns of minorities to partake tangibly in the success of America.

During the past four years, we also have had the luxury of relying on lip-service commitment to participate in that coalition, just as those groups have had the luxury of standing with us in symbol rather than substance.

That period has come to an end. Whether we choose it or not, we are bound together because those who oppose us relate to all of us as if we were a single group, a single issue, and a single constituency. It is incumbent on us to acknowledge that mentality and respond to it where ever it is raised.

At this moment, one single example of that stands out. It is the Family Protection Act, sponsored by Sen. Paul Laxalt and endorsed by the Republican party platform this year. By its very name, it seeks to link the Equal Rights Amendment, gay rights, abortion, school busing, even public education, as threats to the American family.

Make no mistake. If we do not mature in our vision, and look beyond the one issue that is gay rights-related to address the mentality itself that opposes us where ever it exists, we will fail as a movement and be relegated to a nostalgic footnote.

That was why, when the Congress considered anti-busing and anti-civil rights amendments to an appropriations bill and we did not respond, we failed. That very same bill had been used as a vehicle against us only a month earlier, but we thought we had won, and so we turned aside from the others who would be hurt. And that is why, when the Congress then turned back and passed the anti-gay amendment to that same bill, our pleas for assistance were mere whimpers.

We can not afford that. If next year's version of the Family Protection Act were to drop or modify its anti-gay content, and one hears that is being considered, it does not mean that we can afford to turn away from the other provisions in that act, the other groups that would be hurt by its passage. That obvious fact, that clear lesson, is one that we have yet to take to heart and make a reality in our efforts and that will spell defeat for us.

The same thing is true for the coming budget proposals. If there should not be one line in the thousands of lines that says gays are to be denied one cent, it does not mean we are safe. We must learn to read those things for their implications for us, because today's implications will be tomorrow's realities. If CETA funds are cut, if social research funds are cut, if community health services funds are cut, we all bleed.

But we are going to continue making those mistakes, enjoying false security, even hearing false assurances from our own leaders, until we demand accountability.

We must consider what the implications were, over the past four years, of a national leadership that was only sporadic in its pressure on an Administration that had showed it could and would deliver to us. We must consider the implications of a national leadership that never once, in the past four years, asked a congressional gay rights bill sponsor to officially request an Administration position on the bill, that never once met with the Justice Department over that issue.

And above all, we must consider the implications of having a national leadership that is free of accountability to us on these questions, free to face us or not on these issues, and then still leave them free to speak for us.

Until we do those things, we will not have started to become a national political force. Until we demand that our gay newspapers give us honest and factual reporting, we will not be able to use them to assess reality. Until we focus on an agenda, a specific set of steps that can be accomplished, we will have no vehicle to participate in national political change, no way for us or others to evaluate our goals and our strategies.

Until we are willing to take the responsibility for assessing and evaluating, we will have no basis for holding our national leadership to a standard of accountability. Otherwise our willingness to contribute or a decision to deny support to them will be as random and yet as damaging to ourselves as is the violence done to us on the streets, or through the whimsical enforcement of the laws against us.

Above all, we must know that we do not have an unlimited span of time ahead of us to begin that process. We will be held accountable—all of us—in a very few months as we either exhibit the sophistication and power we claim, and that we ought to be able to claim, or pay the price of forfeiting.

It is not the decade ahead which holds the answers, or poses the questions, but we ourselves.

June 26, 1981

Speech at Daley Plaza

Jay Deacon

This speech was given at a rally on Daley Plaza in Chicago, Illinois, sponsored by the Illinois Gay and Lesbian Task Force on June 26, 1981, by F. Jay Deacon, at that time the pastor of Good Shepherd Parish of the Metropolitan Community Church in Chicago. Ernest Lefever was a neoconservative ethicist who viewed political and moral debate as degraded by a society estranged from basic Western values.

Polls show that most people in this country now favor the recognition of our rights. Legislation to protect our rights has been introduced in Congress, in the state legislature, and in this City Council. Yet few politicians show evidence of the basic courage, decency, civility or could it be intelligence, to vote for these bills and ordinances.

But let me tell you this: our rights do not begin the day somebody passes a piece of legislation recognizing those rights; they are ours as human beings of sacred worth, whether the politicians and bishops have the sense to recognize it or not.

Now we live in times of promise, but times also of perils to the liberties this nation is all about, and we'd better know it, and we'd better know that no one is going to fight for our rights if not *us*. As Martin Luther King once said, the powerful never voluntarily surrender the power by which they oppress or abridge the rights of others.

The U.S. House of Representatives has this past week, by a 281-124 vote, celebrated gay and lesbian pride by passing an amendment to the Legal Services Corporation funding bill, one proposed by Rep. Larry McDonald (D-Ga.) forbidding the use of the program to "promote, defend or protect homosexuality." The President's closest friend in Washington, Sen. Paul Laxalt (R.-Nev), is one of the earliest sponsors of a piece of violence known as the Family Protection Act, to be pushed when they've done abolishing social services, environmental protection, and other marks of a civilized society.

This so-called Family Protection Act will make it almost impossible to run a shelter for battered wives or children and very difficult to operate a day care center. It denies public funds to any school that refuses to establish religion by establishing prayer or buys books or provides instruction that "tend to diminish or deny the role differences between the sexes as it has been historically understood in the United States," which means reinforcing the rule of patriarchy. And a final section specifically states that Federal discrimination statutes shall not be construed to protect homosexuals from discrimination in employment.

The co-sponsor of that bill in the House used to be former Rep. Robert Bauman (R.-Md.) who denied his own sexual identity while serving as a chief mouthpiece for the nervous patriarchy now led by Ronald Reagan in its constant attacks on the rights and dignity of our people.

You've heard the rhetoric of those who would ration our rights. You've heard the downfall of society and the family blamed on—*you.* You have seen history rewritten before your eyes by bishops and politicians to show civilizations falling because of *you.* They warn of some cataclysm from which the family must be protected, and the cataclysm is *you and me.*

You have been made society's scapegoat, and your rights don't even seem to merit the recognition of members of this City Council. We have become grateful for small favors when our own alderman in the 44th Ward [Ald. John Merlo] says he's for our rights but regularly insults us with public statements that fail to acknowledge our immense contribution to our community while invoking the New Right's call for a return to only family businesses and nuclear family units in the ward—as though people only came in families!

What, in these perilous times, must we do, *can* we do?

The most important thing you can do is to *be,* unapologetically and defiantly, a free and sensuous person in the midst of a passionless, senseless society—a nation whose religious and political leaders have come to disclaim and deny passion, and have sought it out and found it elsewhere, projecting it onto *you* and then denouncing you.

The ultimate hangup for those threatened by gay and lesbian persons is that gay and lesbian sexuality is non-productive, non-justifying: there can be only pleasure, fun, sensuousness and love as a goal. You have become a symbol for the sensuality that others fear and deny. Well, if we're the alleged experts in sensuality, then in this sense-deadened society, we must never hide our light under a bushel.

That's why they're afraid of you. You are the scapegoats for the denied passions of bishops, TV evangelists, and politicians everywhere. That we who are gay or female have come to symbolize this dreaded sensuousness is in its way a tribute to us.

So I say that what we must do is to be here defiantly a free and, yes, sensuous people who love life passionately and intend to live it fully in the midst of an America now ruled by Reagan's gang of anti-sensual exploiters, patriarchs, moralizers, and freedom-stiflers, in a time when human rights means Ernest Lefever, where getting the government off our backs means getting the government into our bedrooms, when spiritual revival means inquisition, where morality means anti-sensualness, and where "truly needy" means absolutely nothing. In times like these, we're tempted to draw back and live a little less.

Gay and lesbian people are prophets just by being here, and we're better prophets if we are defiantly free and sensuous and life-affirming than if we're timid and boring. Don't, don't, for heaven's sake *don't* quench the Spirit, the breath of life which breathes through our senses and energizes us. If the Moral Majority wants to know where the Spirit is, the Spirit is *here.*

September 5, 1981

The Gay Tradition: Strategies for the Decades Ahead

Jack Nichols

Jack Nichols gave this keynote speech at the eighth Texas Gay Conference, held in Houston in 1981. The two texts of Walt Whitman quoted in the speech are, in their order of occurrence, the poem "A Woman Waits for Me" and the essay "Democratic Vistas." The quotation from Edward Carpenter is taken from his autobiography, *My Days and Dreams.*

While I am keenly aware (as my words show) of feminist aspirations, I am speaking primarily to gay men. The struggling men in today's Gay Liberation Movement will always need new vision to get done what needs doing. But what is vision's best approach for our movement? It is knowing of those points at which segments take their parts in the Whole, a Whole that thereafter steps over wastelands to green pastures, satisfying the aspirations of each segment as it goes.

This creates a harmony of ensemble. Coalescence. Unity. Vision takes our present and creates a future from it. It calls to us in apocalyptic tones: *Mount the barricades! Contend for your very lives!* (Walt Whitman)

Today's Gay Liberation Movement needs vision expansive enough to encompass multitudes—to reach them—to contain them. We also need to feel currents within ourselves, streams of self-liberating knowledge.

With the arrival of each new decade we'll have to re-evaluate our Movement priorities. Let's look again at what needs to be done. The arrival of Ronald Reagan and the cohorts of the "Moral Majority" has brought about a shift in circumstances facing the Movement. While it is not necessary to discard effective strategies used in the past, weatherbeaten though they may be, we must also devise new strategies, ways that offer more than habit, more than bureaucratic security, more than opportunities for ego-tripping through a political mish-mash, more than a few crumbs for the queers.

It is one thing to be an efficient gay liberation strategist responding to one crisis after another with makeshift Band-Aids, and it is another to feel confident enough to go on the offense, moving swiftly to neutralize or to call attention to bigotry's lieutenants, stepping into the midst of chaos calmly, aiming darts so that they go to the heart of the matter.

At the same time, the gay liberationists today must know how to create alliances, networks, friends, all of whom will be needed. Unfortunately, too much of what passes for gay liberation work today is myopic and culture-bound, doomed, I fear, to some very dismal failures.

Much of the talk I hear among those trying in vain to stay the forces of erosion since the Reaganites have taken office sounds like a conversation among straws before the onset of a great hurricane.

Is there some secret remedy for the resuscitation of our Movement? Has fate provided us with a method that can be used in times of emergency? I think so.

Little known, even to some who study the most recent trends of liberation-evolution, is the fact that there has evolved and been nurtured an amazing tradition—a truly gay tradition—during the last 100 years.

While this tradition has had a history made by visionaries, poets, mystics and seers, it also has a number of present-day supporters: a nucleus of thinkers and writers of whom I am one.

I will tell you about others and suggest to those who would expand gay liberation's ground of being, that you examine their work. In short, I'm from what some people might call a radical wing of the Gay Liberation Movement—a wing which can and will walk hand-in-hand with the established movement.

Our method is not to condemn but to woo. And this, we believe, must become characteristic of the Gay Liberation Movement itself when it deals with the Establishment or when it deals with local gay communities.

To condemn is to wax angry—and an angry person loses his or her audience. There are too many angry people clamoring for attention.

Wooing means smiling. Wooing walks with laughter. It doesn't complain incessantly about oppression. Neither does it wear a perpetual frown. The person who woos is at peace with life. He is happy. He has something more important to say than "please accept me and my kind." He has something to offer, something to give! He has reached a plateau where he can advise those he woos, "Please accept your self!"

One who woos well is not only looking at his own predicament—he's looking at the other person's too, and he seems to say, "Don't be afraid. You can embrace what will not hurt you without fear. Life offers promises of good times!" This is the kind of emotional confidence that hits its mark.

Now I can hear you asking, "What's he recommending? That we woo strait [*sic*] people?"

Yes. Not primarily in a sexual way—but if the sexual is one segment moving among others toward the satisfaction of aspirations—it must be welcomed too.

We must make clear to ourselves that we're not here to *defend* same sex relationships. Instead, we must begin to recommend them as necessary and as healthy for all men. We must encourage close relationships—emotional in tone—among men, relationships that are not stymied by homosexual fears and that can possibly find friendship's natural joys outside of sex as well as in its hearty, sensuous embrace.

The tradition of which I speak has a vision that sees beyond single issues like civil liberties and social rights for sexual minorities. It focuses on the evolutionary part this present-day stage of gay social development can play on the larger scales of human unfolding.

It sees that there is a narrowing of consciousness that takes place if gays and straits [*sic*] think themselves as separate camps of humanity. It says we must drop this dualistic approach to homosexuality and heterosexuality. There is no "them." There is only "us."

For far too long now we've regarded ourselves as a dumped-upon minority.

It is now time for us to point out that those who condemn same-sex relationships are condemning their own best potential. In a nuclear age men who are afraid to show their feelings for each other—who square off against each other competitively—and avoid one another because of a stupid taboo, isolate themselves and create a more tense and dangerous climate in the world.

Looked at in the larger framework of experience, the homosexual taboo is a great threat to human survival. It is a block to comradeship.

I predict that if we in the movement continue to regard ourselves as an isolated and nearly defenseless minority weathering hard times, we will lack the jaunty spirit we need to do our wooing. Instead, we will be going hat in hand, asking for some water with our slice of bread. We will suffer from a kind of inferiority complex that accompanies us because we tend to regard heterosexualism as monolithic and impregnable; as mighty and powerful; and as the dominant trend forever.

I say that this assessment of our situation is retrogressive and reactionary; a static view; a static perception. Homosexual feelings are the necessary soul property of every person, waiting to be discovered on levels other than the sexual—but including the sexual—expressions that can be exuberant and must be without shame.

How does such a way of seeing things work in a practical situation? It takes away our defensiveness and gives us questions of our own to ask when others ask why we aren't married, namely, "Where is Your most loving Friend? Do you have a close, loving relationship with one? Why not? Have you been prevented by the gay taboo? Are you afraid of what others will think?"

Here, at this juncture, we begin to see the connection between our movement and the larger world. We are reminders to humanity of its own outmoded, regressive repressions: those which put barriers between everybody, causing unnecessary anxieties, keeping everybody from rightful fulfillment with others.

Our message addresses not only our own self-assertions and self-fulfillments, it speaks to millions of others too whose lives have been stunted and maimed because of their same-sex fears.

The strait [*sic*] man who fears close contact with a member of his own sex is as much in need of liberation as any gay man who dislikes and treats women unfairly, or who hides fearfully in a closet.

A fountainhead of the tradition I'm speaking about is the poet Walt Whitman. His name appears prominently in every book I write. He practiced in his poems the theme of the androgynous psyche. Let me read you his poetic prophecy, what he says to the women of tomorrow.

They are not one jot less than I am,
They are tanned in the face by shining suns and blowing winds,
Their flesh has the old divine suppleness and strength,
They know how to swim, row, ride, wrestle, shoot, run, strike,
retreat, advance, resist, defend themselves
They are ultimate in their own right—
they are calm, clear, well-possessed of themselves.

Whitman summoned attitudes to use in ways he considered fundamental to the evolutionary processes. He must be read, as Oscar Wilde counseled, as a philosopher perhaps more so than a poet. His famous essay Democratic Vistas sees love among men as the very adhesive of society. He looked to the development of such love to counter our materialistic and vulgar American democracy, and for the spiritualization of America. I will read you another quote to show what this great visionary of the tradition says:

Many will say it is a dream, and will not follow my inferences: but I confidently expect a time when there will be seen, running like a half-hid warp through all the myriad audible and visible worldly

> **interests of America, threads of manly friendship, fond and loving, pure and sweet, strong and life-long, carried to degrees hitherto unknown—not only giving tone to individual character, and making it unprecedentedly emotional, muscular, heroic, and refined, but having its deepest relations to general politics. I say democracy infers such loving comradeship as its most inevitable twin or counterpart, without which it will be incomplete, in vain, and incapable of perpetuating itself.**

In other words, the man whom *The New York Times* has finally (and just recently) called "An American genius" after calling him "a pig rooting about in licentious garbage" during his lifetime, and of whom *LIFE* magazine recently said was "America's Greatest Poet"—this man who is known as the Poet of Democracy actually believed that democracy is in need of the development of love among men as its most inevitable twin or counterpart. Without such love, he says, democracy will be incomplete, in vain, and incapable of perpetuating itself.

This is not a defensive statement. Whitman does not defend love among men. He recommends it. He is on the offensive.

The poet lived until 1892.

Thereafter, until 1929, the tradition was carried aloft by a remarkable Englishman, a social scientist and poet, Edward Carpenter (1844-1929). Carpenter had visited Whitman twice. The power of his own affirmative vision he compared to the moon's, while he compared Whitman's to the sun.

Edward Carpenter's fame extended beyond England. His works on civilization, feminism, and socialist and anarchist views were read in many lands. He was the first gay liberationist essayist I read—at age 14. His essay I discovered had been written before the turn of the last century. Carpenter's thought integrated gay liberation, feminism, political awareness, and an understanding of how these must coalesce.

Listen as Carpenter celebrates the equality of the sexes, and Uranian love (the word used in his early works to denote homosexuality):

> **But as these sufferings of women, of one kind or another, have been the great inspiring cause and impetus of the Women's Movement—a movement which is already having a great influence in the reorganization of society; so I do not practically doubt that the major sufferings of the Uranian class of men are destined in their turn to lead to another wide-reaching social organization and forward movement in the direction of Art and human compassion.**

> **It is possible that the Uranian spirit may lead to something like a general enthusiasm of Humanity, and that Uranian people may be destined to form the advance guard of that great movement which will one day transform the common life by substituting the bond of personal affection and compassion for the monetary, legal and other external ties which now control and confine society.**
>
> **Such a part of course we cannot expect the Uranian to play unless the capacity for their kind of attachment also exists—though in a germinal and undeveloped state—in the breast of mankind at large. And modern thought and investigation are clearly tending that way—to confirm that it does so exist.**

In other words, Carpenter foresaw a future in which women and gay men would hold to the cutting edge of change.

What would be left for strait [*sic*] men to do? Would they have no part? Could they or would they understand? If they began to understand—the sufferings of women, the limitations of the conventional male role, their fear of showing feelings within themselves, and the homosexual taboo, it would mean a breakdown of the very base on which conventional masculinity stands.

It would mean a withering of machismo, sounding the death-knell of the macho man and, little by little, the emergence of a new esthetics and new kinds of social behavior. The new male would incorporate spiritual values: nurturing, empathy, tenderness, which were formally thought "feminine" but are, in fact, only human virtues.

The tradition I speak for calls for the emergence of such values, of such a kind of man. It calls too on the Gay Liberation Movement to help bring forth such a male—no matter his reputed orientation.

Undermining social norms of masculinity and instilling survival virtues like empathy will break down false divisions between gays and straits. Obsolete masculine warrior codes blindly move us toward violence and disruption, threatening continuance on the planet.

This gay tradition couldn't have been understood until now because the development of both women's and gay liberation had to pre-figure it, paving its way, laying groundwork, pointing to necessity.

Here we see the connection between our movement and the very needs of the planet: to resoundingly call for the birth of the new male, a call which is on the offense, not the defense, a call which seeks planetary health on the one hand and personal happiness on the other, a call which seeks the utter destruction of the gender system that divides labor into male and female camps—into the camps of violence and warfare on the one hand and childcare and the caring professions on the other. Warfare in these nuclear times—if humanity is to exist—becomes obsolete.

The male who was once trained to pursue warfare as his contribution to society is now obsolete. His threatening manner is obsolete. His toughness is obsolete. We all bleed—male and female—we are all delicate physical constructions, and we will all die if this threatening macho male is not laid to rest and soon.

Today, among men, orthodox social values are not passed on through religion, nor education, nor merely through parental training. None of these hits the mark anymore. Hellfire. Purgatory. Everlasting punishment after death—none of these scarecrows has the power to frighten a man into an assured acceptance of orthodox social behaviors.

But if the fires of Hell have cooled, what still remains to frighten men into becoming social robots for the status quo?

The male gender prescription, that's what. The fear of being called "unmanly." Our current social system, unable to perpetuate itself through religion or patriotism, can still count on a handing down of a prescription that divides men from women in the fields of labor.

Since the obsolete male stance is tied to warfare, the values at the base of the old-fashioned male-role find men often trying to prove masculinity, striking out, posing, boasting. Private boasts step out from the areas of the personal into social/political realms. Thus, the personal becomes political, and we get bullies and warmongers as well as heavy-duty control freaks for our leaders. Finally, if there's no change, we'll get death.

Perhaps our movement has more radical potential than we first assumed. The tradition, nurtured over the last 100 years has long been aware of its larger, more comprehensive role.

Thank you.

April 24, 1982

The Fem Question, or We Will Not Go Away

Joan Nestle

This speech was given at the conference on "The Scholar and the Feminist: Towards A Politics of Sexuality" at Barnard College in New York City in April 1982.

Voice One—1956: Yes, I am a fem and have been for over twenty years. Believe me, I know the reaction *that* gets. You know, we are the missing women from Lesbian history, but honey, we helped hold our world together: we poured more love and wetness on our bar stools and in our homes than a woman was supposed to have. I have no theories to explain how the love came, why the crushes on the lean dark women exploded in my guts, made me so shy. All I could do was look so hard they had to move away. But honey, I wasn't a piece of fluff and neither were the other fems I knew. We knew what we wanted and that was no mean feat for a growing girl of the 'fifties. Oh, we had our styles—our outfits, our perfumes, our performances—and we could lose ourselves in the world under the chin of our dancing partner who held us close enough to make the world safe, but we walked the night streets to get to that bar, and we came out bleary-eyed into the deserted early morning, facing a long week of dreary passing at the office or at the beauty parlor or the telephone company. I always knew our lives were a bewildering combination of romance and realism. Oh Honey, I could tell you stories. . . .

Like about the 23-year-old fem who carried her favorite dildo in a pink satin purse to the bar every Saturday night so her partner for the night would understand exactly what she wanted . . .

Or how at 17 I hung out at Pam Pam's on Sixth Avenue and Eighth Street with all the other fems who were too young to get into the bars and too scared to forge an ID . . .

Or how I finally entered my world, a bar on Abingdon Square, and learned that women had been doing it for years and how as a young fem I took on the Vice Squad, the plain clothes police women, the bathroom line, the Johns trying to hustle a woman for the night and the staring straights who saw us as entertainment. You see, my passions had taken me home, and not all the hating voices of the McCarthy 'fifties could keep me from being near my women.

Oh the stories I could tell if you would listen . . . if you would only listen . . .

Voice Two—1982: Every time I speak at a Lesbian feminist gathering, I introduce myself as a fem from the 'fifties. I do this because it is the truth, and therefore allows me to pay historical homage to my Lesbian time and place, as well as to the other fems who stand invisible beside me, the women who have slipped away, and yet whose voices I can still hear and whose V-neck sweaters and shiny loafers I can still see. I do it to call up the women I would see shopping with their lovers in the Lower East Side supermarkets, the fem partners of the butch women who worked as waiters in the Club 81. I remember how unflinchingly the fem absorbed the stares of the other customers as she gently held on to the arm of her lover. I do it in the name of wives of passing women whose faces look up at me from old newspaper clippings, the women who were always described as the deluded ones, and yet whose histories announce such clear choices, such courageous entries into the land of freaks. Butches were known by their appearance; fems by their choices. And if fems seemed to be the wives, it was so easy to slip over their lives the categories established for all women to lose the curiosity about what made them sexual heretics because they looked like women. If we are to piece together a profound Lesbian history, we must begin asking questions about the lives of these women that we have not asked before, and to do this, we will have to elevate curiosity into a much more exalted position than concepts of politically correct sexuality would ever allow us to do. Curiosity is not trivial; it is the respect one life pays to another. It is a largeness of mind and heart that refuses to be bounded by decorum or by desperation. It is hardest to keep alive in the times it is most needed, the times of hatred, of instability, of attack—and surely these are such times.

When I stand before a new generation of Lesbians and use the word *fem* I sometimes feel like an old relic from a long buried past that has burst through the earth, shaken the dust from off its mouth and started to speak. The first reaction is usually shock, and then laughter, and then confusion when my audience must confront their stereotyped understanding and yet face the fact that I am a damn powerful woman who has done some good in this brave new world of Lesbian feminism. But the audience is not the only one who is going through waves of reactions. A 1982 Lesbian activist who defines herself as a fem poses the problems of our plight as a colonized people in a most vivid way. We, both butches and fems, are a people who have a history of dedication to the creation of personal style. Yet, if I dress to please myself and my lover, I will be called a traitor by many of my own people because I seem to be wearing the clothes of the enemy. Fems are looked upon as the sexual Uncle Toms of the movement. If I wear movement clothes because I am afraid of the judgment of my own people, then once again I am a traitor; this time to my own fem sense of personal style, but my fem style represents what I have chosen to do with my womanness. I cannot hide it or exchange it without losing my passion, without losing my strength. Colonization and the battle against it always poses this contradiction—the need to throw the colonizer's image back at him and yet the need to keep alive what is a deep part of one's culture, even if it can be misunderstood by the oppressor because he thinks he knows what he is seeing. Thus, the fem is faced with the charge of passing, of trying to dissociate herself from the visible or androgynous Lesbian, and this is a terribly painful indictment. It twists my language of desire into the language of collaboration.

Last week, Deb, my lover, and I did the Lesbian Herstory slide show at the Stonybrook campus of SUNY. We were speaking to fifty women health workers, four of whom identified themselves as Lesbians. I wore a long lavender dress that made my body feel good, and black boots that made me feel powerful. Deb was dressed in pants, a shirt and a black leather jacket. I led a two-hour discussion, working with the women's honest expressions of homophobia, their fears of seeing their own bodies sexually and the different forms of tyranny they faced as women. Finally one of the straight women said how much easier it was to talk to me rather than to her, and she pointed a finger at Deb who was sitting on a chair at the side. I looked more like her, she said. Here my dress, which was really an erotic conversation between Deb and myself, was transformed into a boundary line between us. I walked over to Deb, put my arm around her, and drew her head into my breasts. "yes," I said, "but it is the two of us together that makes everything perfectly clear." Then I returned to the center of the room and lied. "You see," I said. "I wore this dress so you would listen to me but our real freedom is the day when I can wear a three-piece suit and a tie and you will still hear my words." I found myself faced with the paradox of having to fight for one freedom at the price of another. They felt more comfortable with me because I could pass; their view of my femness was betraying its deepest meaning.

The erotic clarity that for me is at the heart of a fem's style has never been clearly understood. One piece of sexologist's literature from around 1909 states that the "pure female invert feels like a man." The fem, a few years later, is described as an "effeminate tribadist." Thus, we were first perceived as inauthentic inverts. In the 'fifties, our pathology was explained in the following way: "The feminine type of Lesbian is one who seeks mother love, who enjoys being the recipient of much love and affection. She is often preoccupied with personal beauty and is somewhat narcissistic. She is the clinging vine type who is often thought and spoken of by her elders as a little fool without any realization of the warped sexuality which is prompting her actions" (Frank Caprio, *Female Homosexuality,* 1954). And the final blow: "She is more apt to be bisexual and also apt to respond favorably to treatment." Here the fem is stripped of all power, a foolish woman who can easily be beckoned over into the right camp. Historically we have been left disinherited, seen neither as true inverts nor grown women.

The feminist seventies and eighties have had their troubles with fems too. Why do some fems dress the way other women say is pornographic? Why do we walk the streets holding the arms of our butch lovers, reinforcing all the old stereotypes? Why do we talk about sex so much? Why don't we embrace androgyny as the true liberated image? And since the conference, I must add my questions: why are we perceived as unchanging stereotypes, as if our love is a dead thing? I am now a fem of the eighties, and my passion has the added force of my feminism behind it. Finally, why do some of you keep saying *roles* when we say *relationships*? But you see, we have a long history of surviving someone else's image of ourselves, and through it all we have forged our sexuality. We are powerful women. So many have refused to see us as real because of the contradictions of oppression. But if we let these contradictions take away our own territory, force betrayals of our deepest selves and turn curiosity into judgments and restrictions, then we will truly have only one history in which to live—the one they have created for us.

Afterward: For speaking these words, I have been labeled a "sex deviant" by some of my own people. I and three other women at the conference were considered too pornographic to be allowed to speak. This small talk will grow into a much larger work on the history of fems and to my comrades in the battle for sexual liberation, Dorothy, Pat, Gail and Amber, and to all those who spoke at the Politically Incorrect Sexuality Speakout on Sunday, I send my love and announce my dedication to fighting the new McCarthyites of the 1980s, those who label other women thought-criminals.

August 21, 1982

Harnessing Our Anger

Bob Nelson

This opinion piece was written by a member of the news staff following the firebombing of the offices of *Gay Community News* in Boston on July 7, 1982. On November 10, 1980, Ronald Crumpley opened fire with a machine gun on the patrons of the Ramrod, a bar in Greenwich Village. Although two men died, Crumpley was found "not responsible by means of a mental defect."

One of the biggest news stories *GCN* has ever reported was the burning of its own offices on July 7th. The national news media, of course, greeted that event with deafening silence, though the probable firebombing of one of only three nationally-distributed newspapers for gays and lesbians was surely a newsworthy event. Though our own community has been forthcoming with dollars and sympathy, much of the emotion that has been expressed has consisted of an unfocused anger or a helpless rage. While a sense of outrage is the only rational response to atrocity, if that outrage is maintained at too high a level over too long a time it can generate feelings of impotence, as we permit ourselves to be awed by this irrational act of violence. Then, the sense of community created by our anger will dissipate as surely as the smoke rising from the remnants of 22 Bromfield Street.

Rather, I think we must harness our anger, and many in the *GCN* community have done so by organizing benefits and helping to rebuild the paper. But that anger should also help us to raise our consciousness about the kinds of motivations that can lead to acts of antigay-violence. What follows is a brief analysis of some of those motivations.

Clearly, the national political scene plays a role in such acts. The cries of "Here's one for Anita!" shouted by the gang that beat Robert Hillsborough to death in San Francisco in June of 1977, indicates clearly enough that the killing did not take place in a political vacuum. Even Hillsborough's mother saw the connection, for she filed a $5 million civil suit against Anita Bryant and the "Save The Children" campaign, charging that Bryant "affirmatively mounted a campaign of hate, bigotry, ignorance, fear, intimidation and prejudice directed at homosexuals, including Robert Hillsborough." (The suit was later dismissed.) And surely there was more than coincidence at work in the slaying of Harvey Milk in November, 1978, less than a month after California voters defeated the homophobic Briggs Initiative.

Whether our enemies are emboldened by political attacks on gays and lesbians, or whether they react in vengeance to our victories, the results are the same—tragic. Probably the very fact that gay rights has become a controversial public issue creates an awareness of our vulnerability. Currently, the national atmosphere of homophobia and of questioning gay rights can be credited to the political machinations of New Right groups pressing for a return to traditional, patriarchal values—as the misnamed Family Protection Act states, "to preserve the integrity of the American family." The temporary failure to pass the ERA, the actions of conservative political action committees and assaults on abortion rights have been correctly assessed as contributing to the climate of fear in which we live.

The Moral Majority's hate campaign has legitimized homophobic attitudes in the public mind, but more importantly it has reinforced those attitudes among those who were already prejudiced against us. Here I'll recount an anecdote that some will find only amusing, others a horrifying portent of what is likely to come. A couple of days after the *GCN* fire, I called one of the chief arson investigators at the Boston Fire Department and identified myself as a reporter from the mainstream news organization for which I work. Asked if any of the rumors about a political basis to the fire might be true, the investigator told me, "you know, those gays are always fighting among themselves. I don't know how many of those newspapers there might be in Boston, but it could have been one of 'em up against the other." If there were any doubts about how the arson squad is conducting their investigation, or what its findings are likely to be, let them be dispelled.

Police attitudes, I've concluded, tend to mirror those of the teenaged gangs that perpetrate so much of the violence against us. What, exactly, are those attitudes and what is behind them? For while the broad concept of a link between the national police scene and anti-gay violence is certainly justified, it is not useful. Saying that homophobic violence occurs because of homophobic attitudes tells us nothing about why individuals *act.* The perpetrators of the *GCN* fire had no hotline to the offices of anti-abortion senators such as Jesse Helms and Paul Laxalt. The gangs in New York City's Chelsea district certainly haven't waited for the ERA to fail before beating up gays all along the West Side. And while presumably thousands of people have homophobic attitudes, what is it that brings a tiny minority of them to take the brutal step of acting on that homophobia?

When first thinking about the problem, I concluded that economics somehow had to be at the root of it. After all, we are in the midst of a depression deeper than any since the 1930's. Wouldn't gang violence abate if these kids had jobs and were off the streets? Isn't economic deprivation a basic cause of crime, wherever it occurs? What of the obvious link between economic decline and gang violence in Britain, where riots and looting swept across the country last year in response to Margaret Thatcher's version of Reaganomics? Aren't gays scapegoated in times of economic trouble because they're perceived as both rich and immoral, and thus envied?

While *The New York Times* certainly has done its best to portray us in that fashion ("Tapping the Homosexual Market," June 13, 1982) the Chelsea gangs and the Boston arsonists probably don't read *The New York Times*. On the economic question, it could just as well be argued that crime and violence increase in times of prosperity, since unemployed teenagers become relatively even more disadvantaged when the system is unable to provide them with jobs. While violent crime is no doubt related to economic deprivation, the links are tenuous and even more difficult to demonstrate in the specific case of violence against gays and lesbians.

More important is the unique place violence occupies in the American culture. Violence has almost always been perpetrated by groups of citizens against each other rather than against the state, which is part of the reason we have such a limited revolutionary tradition in this country. In Britain, the gang violence was directed against property, against racial minorities, against the economic situation and against the state, so it is difficult to single out the economic factor as the only one responsible. In the U.S., violence has usually been used by patriarchal and conservative whites against blacks, labor and women under a variety of circumstances, but usually because those groups were perceived as trying to change the traditional order of things. Blacks were lynched because they got "uppity," women were beaten and raped because they were "loose," and scabs were hired and strikes broken because labor was "too greedy."

Such violence in our national life has been legitimized by our gun culture, as illustrated by the Second Amendment to the Constitution, which holds that an armed citizenry is the surest guarantee of freedom, and by official (police, army) violence, notably our prolonged adventure against the rice farmers of Vietnam. While I'm not particularly impressed with use of the concept of a national character to analyze the motivations behind individual instances of violence, I think much of the American fascination with guns and bombs has to do with the uniquely repressive moral traditions we have inherited, which dictate a certain sublimation of sexual drives into violent acts. Though sexual repression is blamed for a whole variety of social ills, here is one case where the connection can be made to stick.

That sexual repression continues to operate in this society should not be a topic of debate, in spite of all the blather the straight press generates about "swinging singles" and "computer dating." I've been struck by the particularly vitriolic and sensationalist way in which the press reports on so-called "child prostitution rings" on the Congressional page sex scandal.

Thus by far the greatest portion of society is still firmly encased in a moral system that finds homosexuality an abhorrent transgression of family values. Yet as gays and lesbians have come out, we have by our very existence challenged the traditional moral system so precious to the Moral Majority, and have in fact become an example to certain segments of society. I think the root of much anti-gay violence must be traced to individuals who retain the burden of traditional morality, yet who are aware of the possibilities of greater sexual freedom presented by the sexual revolution. As Dennis Altman puts it:

> It is important to recognize just how threatening are the changes wrought by the "sexual revolution." Most people, particularly those who are older or who come from a more religious background, grew up committed to a high degree of sexual repression, albeit often unconsciously. The changes in the past decades seemed to mock their standards and the sacrifices they made for them . . . What is bearable when it seems inescapable becomes intolerable when others do not share it. (*The Homosexualization of America,* p. 99)

The New Right was correct in its prediction that the sexual revolution would undermine traditional family values, but as Altman says, "What is a decline in standards for some is a lessening of oppression for others." Young straight teenagers are sometimes the most sexually oppressed members of society, though their sexual desires are the greatest. They thus have a considerable need to sublimate or to redirect their sexual energy into other channels, and I think it is quite possible that they choose gays and the institutions that serve our community as objects of violence precisely because gays have something they want but can't have—not money, but sexual freedom. This is as much a motivation for the repressed Italian Catholics who beat up gays in Chelsea as it is for the repressed Irish Catholic cops on Boston's vice squad.

I would urge anyone who finds these ideas farfetched to read Wilhelm Reich's *The Mass Psychology of Fascism,* a book written during the first years of Hitler's rise to power in the early 1930's. Reich's thesis is that fascism, or what he calls "patriarchal authoritarian mysticism," is not only an organized political movement, but also an omnipresent character disorder created by the repression of sexual desire. "Fascist mysticism is organic yearning, restricted by mystic distortion and inhibition of natural sexuality," Reich tells us. Reich has quite a bit to say, and some of it is contradictory, but he does focus on the process by which sexuality is inhibited in children, citing fascist pamphlets on how "masturbation fouls the blood" and how "the ideal of the Virgin Mary should inspire young men." Through this process of repression, patriarchal society creates a psychic force in each individual which defends against genital sensuality by invoking nausea and disgust. And one source of that psychic force is the "sadistic conception of sexuality" imparted to children in patriarchic cultures, which seems to me to be at the base of violence rooted in misogyny, homophobia and perhaps racism.

We should thus realize that our sexuality in itself is probably the major factor in anti-gay attacks. We are more visible now than at any time in our history. That does not mean that visibility is the cause of the problem; it simply means that when Ronald Crumpley wanted to go out and murder a few gays in November of 1980, all he had to do was drive over to the Ramrod and start shooting—"because gays ruin everything," he explained. While we are caught up in the battle for formal gay civil rights, we also need to recognize that we will still be vulnerable to violent attacks no matter what laws are on the books as long as negative popular attitudes about us persist. While the Eagle Forum and the Moral Majority understand that abortion rights, equal rights for women, and civil rights for gays and lesbians are all part of the same struggle for sexual liberation, most of the rest of society, including many gays and women, don't understand this basic fact. Conservative gays and some elements of NOW dismiss this as political rhetoric or as an attempt by gays to take advantage of the power of the women's movement.

What these doubters need to experience is the immediate and visceral understanding of the political nature of anti-gay violence: just remember the feeling you got when you found out about the *GCN* fire. Think how obvious racism was to blacks when a black New York transit worker was pulled from his car in the Gravesend section of Brooklyn recently and beaten to death by a gang of Italian teenagers. Or think how you'd feel if your lover was killed by a street gang shouting "Here's one for Jerry!" Such attacks, in my view, will end only when society as a whole discards its moralist attitudes and permits all individuals, of whatever sexual preference, freely to experience their sexuality. We must therefore work for "liberation" writ large, not for the petty interests of one group or another.

October 13, 1982

Speech at the Human Rights Campaign Fund Banquet

Barbara Gittings

This address was given on October 13, 1982, in Philadelphia, Pennsylvania, at a fund-raising dinner of the Human Rights Campaign.

When I joined the gay rights movement 24 years ago, there were only half a dozen gay organizations in the entire U.S. The total number of us active in the movement was around 150: it was like a club, and we all knew each other even if we were 3,000 miles apart. Most people used false names to protect their jobs and their families. We were completely invisible on TV and we had just begun getting on radio talk shows—the ones late at night, after the kids were in bed.

It's very heartening for me to see so many people here tonight, for just one event for one of many, many organizations, because there's so much that still needs to be done, many bigotries and barriers to erase, and we need all hands and all hearts to help.

People often ask me, how come I haven't burned out, how come I'm still going strong after 24 years? I credit three factors.

One: sharing the work with me for the past 21 years is my nearest and dearest, Kay Lahusen. Among her own direct contributions to the cause, Kay was a founding member of Gay Activists Alliance in New York in 1970 and a co-founder of Gay Women's Alternative in New York in 1973. She is also co-author of the first book of biographies of activists in our movement, a book called *The Gay Crusaders,* published in 1972.

The second reason is the personal satisfaction I get. I'm a joiner by temperament, and it was a thrill to me to find groups of My Own People that I could join and work with. If it weren't for the gay movement, I'd probably be active in the wilderness conservation movement—but frankly the gay movement is a lot more fun!

The third key ingredient in the gasoline I run on is the response from gay people themselves. I'm lucky enough to get a lot of mail from gay people, because the gay group I head in the American Library Association has been listed in several books, and people pick up these books in libraries and bookstores and see us listed and reach out. Most of the letters are from people who are not part of the movement. There are thousands, hundreds of thousands, of them out there. They are, ultimately, the people we're doing all this for. Let me share with you messages from two of them.

From Lafayette, Indiana:

> I don't want to subscribe to any magazines or newspapers because if I started receiving material on gay people in the mail, my mother would take me straight to the shrink. I just want to tell you: I read about a gay women's group in Boston and it made me want to die. You see, I live in a very small Indiana town and I go to a very small school. Believe me, at 17 in a hick town, with a bunch of super-prejudiced people, being gay can just about bring out the 'suicidal person' in anybody. So please, if you feel discouraged about a lot of shit you're seeing hit the fan, or if you think the articles published by Gay Lib aren't doing any good, feel or think again. If it wasn't for the fact that I know someone else out there has gone through the same battles I'm fighting now, I'd be dead by my own hand. Don't give up, PLEASE! Because when I get out of this town, I'm gonna be right out there fighting with you. I need you! Keep those articles and editorials and programs coming. They keep me alive.
>
> A sister, Susie.

And this from a teacher in Massachusetts:

> Thank you for keeping us singing in a society that would stop our song completely if it could.

If Susie had given her full name and an address, I could have written to her: Hang in there, Susie, because those of us who are out are oiling the closet door hinges just as fast as we can!

Whether you are gay or not, out or not, your support of the Human Rights Campaign Fund and other movement organizations is the necessary oil for those closet door hinges. Thanks for your help in the work.

And I hope you've had a gay time tonight, whether you are or not!

November 27, 1982

Statement

Boston Lesbian Sadomasochist Group

The members of the Boston Lesbian Sadomasochist Group who put their names to this document were Sage Desertdyke, Claire Humphrey, ReaRae Sears, and Jude Van Dyke.

We believe that the society we live in is a patriarchy, with power concentrated in the hands of men. Wimmin are oppressed by being denied access to economic resources, political power, and control over our own bodies. The oppression is managed by several institutions, mainly family, religion and the state.

An essential part of the oppression of wimmin, as we see it, is control over sexual ideology, mythology and behavior. Since our training in conventional sexuality begins at birth, and the penalties for rebellion are so high, no individual or group is free from erotic tyranny, even within the womyn's community.

We are lesbians. We are feminists. We are talking about our sexuality, and we are taking control of our own bodies. We are lesbian feminist sadomasochists, who get sexual pleasure from a consensual exchange of power involving physical pleasure and eroticism. We are everywhere. We sit next to you at concerts. We work with you at womyn's centers and rape crisis centers, and every other feminist project, gathering and event that lesbians are involved in. We have always been here, and now we too are coming out.

Often worst fears are based on misconceptions and lack of information. Here's a partial list of what lesbian-feminist S/M is *NOT:* brutality, violence, rape, cruelty, power-over, beatings, coercion, non-consensual, unimportant, growth-blocking, a choice made lightly, boring. What lesbian S/M *is* to us: passionate, erotic, intense, growthful, consensual, trust-building, sometimes fearful, loving, unbelievably great sex, reclamation, often hilariously funny, creative, integrating, a development of lesbians' inner power, an art.

Consent and control of what happens to our own bodies, including how we define pleasure, is of primary importance to us as S/M dykes. In S/M sex, each lesbian retains full ultimate control over what happens to her body. As lesbian-feminists, we are all aware that our oppression has included patriarchal violence in all of our past herstories, which is in no way, shape or form related to consensual dyke S/M. We are as opposed to violence as you are. When will you trust us with ourselves?

S/M is accused of being a hostile or angry kind of sex as opposed to the gentle and loving kind of sex that feminists should strive for. In the last decade, the wimmin's movement has increasingly promoted romantic egalitarianism in relationships. Lesbians especially are prone to this trend, and planning a sexual encounter and using toys to produce specific feelings seems antithetical to romance. Romance, gentleness and tenderness are not antithetical to dyke S/M. Our question to you is whether living up to an ideal of romantic equalness is the reason we are lesbians or is it being able to experience our sexuality to the fullest? S/M violates taboos that preserve the mysticism of conventional, romantic sex and that's why so many "right-on feminists" deny us our existence.

Yes . . . we are exploring and taking our right to choose, give consent, and ask for what we want sexually. Our sexual preferences may be different from the side-by-side politically correct lesbian-feminist image you are used to. You may feel uncomfortable with us, even resent our visibility in this lesbian community—much like many straight feminists have resented the presence and visibility of lesbians in the feminist movement. But we are here to stay. We do have the right to meet and talk with each other in safe, public, feminist, womyn's space. To meet, network, and give each other much needed information and support.

As a minority within the feminist community, we are being objectified and made scapegoats within this community, because we are "perverts," because we talk openly about our dyke sexuality which, incidentally, happens within the feminist ideology of love and trust. That objectification is the same one lesbians were subjected to in the early years of the womyn's liberation movement. We ask you, when will you stop using patriarchal values on your sisters, lovers, friends, acquaintances, and the wimmin right next to you, just because of what we do in bed?

We, the authors of this statement, would like to thank Martha Equinox, whose article "If I Ask You to Tie Me Up, Will You Still Love Me?" appears in *Coming to Power,* a book published by Samois, a Bay-area lesbian-feminist S/M support group.

Also, our appreciation to Pat Califia, who wrote "S/M and Feminism" in *Heresies' Sex* Issue, #12. Without it, we couldn't have done it.

March 26, 1983

Who Belongs in the Gay Movement, Who Decides?

Chicago Stonewall Committee

The members of this committee were Michael Botkin, Laura Hathaway, Bill Leubrie, Sharon Page, Mary Kay Ryan, Richard Wilson, and Donna Wood. Their statement was first printed in *Gay Community News* on March 26, 1983.

We began working on this statement over a month ago, when we read about the separate controversies arising from the lesbian s/m group's request to meet at the Cambridge, MA, Women's Center, NAMBLA's conference at the Lesbian and Gay Community Center in Philadelphia, and NAMBLA speakers at a regional gay conference in Terre Haute, IN. Since then, there has been so much debate on these subjects that we can't begin to address all the questions that have been raised. But a common theme runs through these discussions: Who belongs in the gay movement, and who decides?

We think s/m lesbians and NAMBLA *do* belong. The gay movement is based on expanding people's options, in bed and out, not on setting some new sexual "party line." Not too long ago, the whole gay issue was too kinky to be taken seriously as a progressive social movement. In the particular cases mentioned above, NAMBLA and the s/m women were only seeking places to talk about *their* sexual preferences. We certainly support their right to act on them as well, but what does it mean when a section of the movement wants to write them off as just too disgusting to talk about?

All most people know about sexual minorities are the stereotypes: Lesbian s/m is the matron in some grade B "Hellcats Behind Bars" flick, made to titillate straight men. Sex between adult and underage males calls up images of John Wayne Gacy and Dean Corll. Nice people don't talk about those nasty things.

None of us can claim that we have a free, healthy sexuality. Our kinks are just closer to or further from the "norm" which is itself a product of sexual repression. S/m lesbians and gay men who cross the age line are where all lesbians and gay men were 15 years ago, where straight couples shacking up together were before that. Who are we to say that someone else's turn-on is too disgusting to mention in public? Freezing people out this way, keeping them in the closet, just stifles the whole movement. What we need is more discussion and diversity, not less.

There is also an ugly element of throwing our weakest to the wolves. The right wing is already trying to scapegoat gays, and repress sexuality in general, particularly women's and youth's. The drive to exclude our "kinkier" sisters and brothers has made them pariahs among the untouchables, and the Right knows it. It's clear from the straight media's coverage of the NAMBLA raids that they want to use the mainstream gay movement against the fringe, and some movement activists are letting themselves be used. One gay activist in Indiana reportedly suggested that the "good" gays join a Moral Majority picket against the Terre Haute conference where NAMBLA was speaking, to show that the "gay community" abhors that sort of thing.

But you can't bargain with bigots. You can't buy narrow civil rights by promising to respect "parents' rights." You can't maintain battered women's services by keeping out the s/m dykes. And how far would we go to clean our own house? Who would we offer up next? The Right is anti-woman and anti-gay. It wants to bring back that old-time morality in all its oppressive forms. Right now they are going after the weakest. They will be happy to use us against each other until we are whittled down to total invisibility. We mustn't kid ourselves that they want anything else.

Since we began working on this statement, the Cambridge Women's Center has excluded the lesbian s/m group by parliamentary maneuver (dressed up as "consensus"). According to the original *GCN* report, some of the staffers thought that letting s/m lesbians use the space would jeopardize working with battered women and rape victims, who would not be able to distinguish between consensual s/m and the real abuse they had suffered. "To a battered woman, a bruise is a bruise." The staffers themselves seem unwilling to distinguish between coercion and women seeking out what turns them on. The same confusion is promoted by cops, shrinks, and other sexists, who conclude that raped and battered women really wanted it, while genuine sexual masochists are crazy. S/m women and women fleeing abuse share the desire to have control over their own lives and bodies. Who decides what is "legitimate" in women's sexuality?

The NAMBLA controversy has grown by leaps and bounds. The Murdoch papers are making a fortune off of it. *TIME* has written up the "child molesters lobby" with quivering indignation. CBS has shown us the Pederast Papers. And Ginny Apuzzo of the NGTF has assured us that, "One principle is that the mainstream gay rights movement is essentially a movement to secure the rights of consenting adults, and I underscore adults." Where the hell does all this leave gay youth?

Young people of both sexes are raped and sexually exploited every day, most often by their fathers or other male relatives. We're not reading about that. The anti-NAMBLA crusade is not about protecting children. Besides being a wedge against the gay movement, it's part of the campaign to further repress young people's sexuality. It's in the same spirit as the new federal "squeal law," requiring clinics to tell parents of teenage women seeking birth control. All that Murdoch and Densen-Gerber and the cast of thousands want to protect is parent's control over their children. When we join the uproar, when we say that "responsible" gays abhor that sort of thing, we are hypocrites. We are supporting the very same assumptions and laws that keep youth in captivity. The only real way to stop the sexual abuse of children is to get rid of the legal, social and economic chains which keep them in a subhuman status.

We have nothing to gain by policing our movement. No lesbian or gay man is "decent" to the protectors of conventional morality. And none of us can say the last word on sexuality. All of us can learn from each other.

April 22, 1983

An Open Letter to Archbishop James Hickey

Larry Uhrig

Reverend Larry Uhrig at this time was a leading pastor at the Metropolitan Community Church in the Washington, DC, area. In 1984, the year after this letter was written, his guide to same-sex unions, *Two of Us,* was published by Alyson Press. Hickey was the conservative Catholic archbishop of Washington. In addition to the indicated recipients, the full text of the letter was printed in *The Washington Blade* on April 22, 1983.

Dear Archbishop Hickey,

I write to you as one pastor to another to express my grave concern as to the nature of the current relationship between the church and gay and lesbian Christians. On Friday, April 15, I was informed that the Gospel Choir of St. Augustine Church, a parish of your diocese, was forbidden to join in a scheduled concert with the choir of Metropolitan Community Church. After the choir accepted our invitation, St. Augustine's rector received significant political pressure. This resulted in his decision to forbid the concert.

I address you because your office embodies the full authority of the Catholic Church. You ultimately set the tone of ministry within the Archdiocese. And the climate created under your leadership is one in which fear and political expediency have become the motivating factors behind pastoral decisions. For too long, gay and lesbian Catholics, both laity and priests, have been compelled to lie and deny themselves for the sake of ecclesiastical advancement and security. Such conditions induced under your leadership cannot go unaddressed by the Christian community of our city.

I urge you, as a pastor and a servant of our Lord Jesus Christ, to open dialogue with the gay men and women who serve you and whom you serve. I wish to join with you in constructive efforts to heal past pain and to forge a future to enable the Church's embrace of its gay children. One more day of fear, rejection, and condemnation represents a continued denial of the Gospel we both claim to serve.

I urge you to listen to the wisdom and scholarship of Catholic theologians and Biblical scholars who have concurred with many of their Protestant colleagues, that the Gospel of Christ and the Scriptures do not offer condemnation to gay people.

Today, together, we can set a new direction consistent with our New Testament Faith. You are especially imbued with the unique power and authority to set at liberty a multitude of God's gay children. These are your own gay children, those who in obedience have called you Pastor, Father and Priest.

Join me now, for the sake of Christ Jesus.

Faithfully,

(The Rev.) Larry J. Uhrig
Pastor, Metropolitan Community Church

Cc: Archibishop Pio Laghi, Apostolic Delegate
The parishes of the Archdiocese of Washington.

May 5, 1983

The Boston Project Studies Queerbashing

Larry Goldsmith

This testimony was given at a panel held at Boston City Hall on May 5, 1983, on "Police and Gay/Lesbian Community Relations." It was part of The Boston Project, which the front matter of the original republication in *Gay Community News* on May 29, 1983, describes as "a comprehensive landmark study to identify and analyze the needs of gay and lesbian citizens and to develop a workable agenda to better meet those needs" (p. 5). Goldsmith was the local news reporter for *GCN* from 1982 to 1984.

Let me begin with a few examples.

On March 31, 1977, at 10:15 P.M., passers-by found Ralph Heaney, a 28-year-old gay man stabbed to death in the Fens. His murder remains unsolved to this day.

On June 22, 1980, at 3:50 A.M. passers-by found Charles Kimball, a 47-year-old gay man, shot to death in the Fens. Four days later, 1200 people marched with candles through the Fenway neighborhood to condemn the murder and to protest increased violence in the area. Kimball's case remains unsolved.

On April 9, 1981, at 1:45 A.M., Mel Horne, who once served as Promotions Manager for *Gay Community News,* was stabbed to death on Huntington Avenue, near the Prudential center. Robin MacCormack, Boston's mayoral liaison to the lesbian and gay community, told a *GCN* reporter that anti-gay violence in the neighborhood was on the rise. Horne's murder remains unsolved.

On July 15, 1981, at 4 A.M., five young men in a van pulled up alongside two men as they walked home along Providence Avenue near Park Square. The assailants beat them with a baseball bat, sending one to a local hospital for brain surgery. Two of the attackers were later arrested, making the incident an exception to the usual rule of police inaction. But this case stalled in court, and the attackers are back on the streets.

On November 1, 1982, around 11 P.M., three young men followed a Dorchester gay man home and beat him up. A police report was filed, but no arrests were made.

Three days later, on November 4, 1982, at 8:30 P.M., two young men assaulted a gay man on Atlantic Avenue as he walked toward his car. Police reported no arrests.

On July 7, 1982, at 5:20 A.M., an arsonist ignited the offices of *Gay Community News, Fag Rag,* the Glad Day Bookshop, and several artists' studios. The contents of the building were destroyed. Police say they have no leads, and have apparently given up on the investigation.

Not one of the cases in my thick file on anti-gay violence has been successfully prosecuted. Only a tiny minority, in fact, resulted in arrests.

I have been asked to give an overview of violent attacks on lesbians and gay men in the city of Boston and to comment on the conduct and performance of the Boston Police Department in investigating those attacks and preventing future violence. The purpose of this panel, as it has been related to me, is to establish the existence of homophobic violence in the city, define the patterns of such violence, and suggest investigative and enforcement methods to help the police keep the streets safe.

I have to say that I think that the nature of the problem is so patently obvious as to call into question the necessity of this study. Racial violence extends throughout the city. Parts of Boston—the majority of Boston's neighborhoods, in fact—are unsafe for people of color. Parts of the city are unsafe for white people. Women are not safe on the streets of Boston. Lesbians and gay men are not safe on the streets of Boston. Come to think of it, *no one* is safe on the streets of Boston, not in *any* neighborhood. I'm not basing this estimation on FBI statistics or articles in the *Boston Globe,* either; I'm basing it on personal experience and the experience of my friends, concrete and painful experience which brings home the point more realistically than any government arithmetic.

I hope it comes as no surprise to anyone here today that lesbians and gay men are most often the victims of violence in the parts of town where they live, work and socialize. In neighborhoods such as downtown, Beacon Hill, the back bay, the South End, the Fenway, Dorchester and Jamaica Plain, where the concentration of lesbians and gay men is higher than in other parts of the city, the incidence of homophobic violence is, not surprisingly, greater than in other areas.

Frequently, homophobic attacks occur in situations where the victims are clearly identifiable as lesbians and gay men. Attacks routinely take place near bars and cruising areas, where not just our presence but our physical appearance—the way we're dressed, for example—marks us as clear targets to our attackers, who more often than not are groups of young white men who have traveled into our neighborhoods specifically to beat up some queers—or anyone they think is queer. These attacks occur more frequently during warmer months. On weekends, and in the hours of late night and early morning, as cultural events wind up, the bars close, and people head for home.

It's more than likely that violence under any of these conditions I've described involves some homophobic element. And we can be sure, of course, that an attack is homophobic if the assailants, as they often do, yell something like "Fucking queers!" or "Faggots suck!"

I don't think I've ever read a story in the *Globe* or the *Herald* that reported something like "Two men were brutally beaten last night as they walked home from Chaps, a local bar. Witnesses reported seeing a group of men shout anti-gay epithets at the pair, then repeatedly beat them with baseball bats . . ."

I have never been told by the Informational Services Division of the Boston Police Department anything like "A man was stabbed last night in a possible queerbashing incident."

I have never been asked by a homicide detective anything like "John Doe was found dead last night a block from his apartment. We think he may have spent part of the evening at Sporter's. Would you mention in your article that we need to talk to anyone who may have seen him that evening?"

Often, however, I read stories in the *Globe* or the *Herald* that report something like "Two Boston men were listed in critical condition at Massachusetts General Hospital last night after a violent attack near the intersection of Exeter and Boylston Streets. Police report that witnesses saw a blue van speed away from the scene, but no arrests were made."

Reading between the lines of stories like these is often the starting point for investigating my own stories. The next step is to call Informational Services.

"Hello, I'm calling from *Gay Community News* about the assault on Exeter Street last night. Is there reason to suspect the attack might have been anti-gay?"

"Well, no, it doesn't say anything in the report about 'antigay,' and we don't keep statistics on people's sexual preference. Why don't you call Detective So-and-so? He filled out the report."

"Hello, Detective So-and-so? I'm calling from *Gay Community News* about the assault on Exeter Street last night."

"Oh yeah? What's it to you?"

"Well, from the details in the *Globe*, it sounded like it may have been an anti-gay attack."

"We can't comment on people's sexual preference. I mean, they don't want it all over the newspapers. And anyway, I can't comment on any investigation in progress. You'll have to call Informational Services."

You see the problem. There is the legitimate claim to privacy of the victims of anti-gay violence, a claim which the police have to make some effort to protect. I have a policy in my reporting not to use names or other identifying information pertaining to lesbians or gay men unless I have permission to do so. Most of the time it's not relevant anyway. For the journalistic intents and purposes of *GCN,* there's usually no necessity to report something like "John Doe was stabbed last night in the Fens" when "A gay man was stabbed last night in the Fens" will do just as well. Why should *GCN,* of all newspapers, want to destroy the privacy rights of lesbians and gay men? But I find it ironic that the same cops who furnish the names, addresses and places of employment of gay men arrested in undercover raids (remember—innocent until proven guilty) for front-page publication in the *Globe* or the *Herald* become masters of the "No Comment" when I try to find the particulars—even schematic, anonymous particulars—concerning a homophobic assault.

What angers me even more than this double standard of confidentiality is the failure of the police to recognize the most obvious telltale signs of homophobia as a motive for violent assault. Last summer I had to persist for several weeks before homicide detectives would consider the possibility that a late-night shooting in a known gay cruising area might have been premeditated queerbashing. Detectives seemed reluctant to hear my reasoning and when pressed seemed resentful at my suggestion that anyone sitting in a parked car on Atlantic Avenue was probably out for more than a breath of fresh air, and that anyone who went there at that time with a gun in hand probably knew that, and probably intended to shoot a queer.

I'm not trying to encourage the police to jump to conclusions, but I do want them to stop looking at violence as a set of random acts committed by "young punks" and "bad boys." There are patterns to the violence in this city, and it is important to note that the patterns of violence have some relation to other social patterns. Queers get beat up, not because they lead risky lives, but because there is a general assumption that queers are vulnerable, reluctant to fight back, and *deserve* to be beat up. And there's rarely much punishment for beating up queers. Dan White, who was neither a young punk nor a bad boy but a cop and a city supervisor, got only five years in prison for murdering a gay fellow supervisor and the mayor of San Francisco. He'll be out of jail, by the way, in July.

It's been suggested to me that one thing I should ask for here is a formal mechanism, similar to that now used by the Boston Police Department's Community Disorders Unit to monitor racial violence in the city. Police now have a formal investigative process to determine whether a given assault is a racial incident. Police statisticians keep a separate list of such incidents, and the addition of an incident to the list generally means that the incident will be given special investigative attention by the Community Disorders Unit. Why not have the police use a corresponding process to determine whether a given assault reflects homophobia? That way, we could prove to the police that anti-gay violence exists, that it falls into certain generally definable patterns, and that by recognizing anti-gay violence for what it is, police could better assist lesbian and gay victims of violence and learn ways to prevent such violence in the future.

I am opposed to this proposal on a number of grounds. First, if the Boston Police Department keeps a list of lesbians and gay men who are victims of anti-gay violence, it won't be long before the department finds itself with one of the largest gay mailing lists in the city. I don't trust the cops with a list of queers in Boston. Lesbian and gay victims of violence are reluctant enough as it is—and for very good reasons—to seek help from the police. I think the very existence of a special investigative process will discourage even more lesbians and gay men from going to the cops.

More important, I oppose this proposal because, as I said earlier, I think the problem is patently obvious, and I am frankly bewildered that I have to come here and explain it to you. The problem is not that lesbians and gay men lead unusual or risky lives and need special attention from the police—that's blaming the victim. The problem is that people are getting beat up and people are getting murdered. Such violence exists because it is encouraged, condoned or ignored in a city that has fostered bigotry and oppression based on racial differences, physical differences, class differences, political differences, and neighborhood differences.

I am insulted by the idea that I am being asked to prove that lesbian and gay men have been the victims of violence and will be again in the future. The burden of proof should be not on the victims, but on the aggressors, on the people who haven't bothered to notice the violence, and on the people who haven't raised their voices in objection.

We are not going to solve these problems by sitting here, in a closed hearing room at city hall, and talking to ourselves. We are not going to solve these problems with statistical analysis by a few appointed "experts" or "leaders." We are not going to solve these problems with an election-year embellishment of the city bureaucracy. We can, however, make progress by confronting these problems collectively, in forums open to all. We can make progress by having the courage to state the obvious: that lesbians and gay men exist in significant numbers and are but one of the many communities of people in this city who are objects of systematic violence. We *already* know who we are and where we are, and the various forms our oppression takes. I have no doubt that we could further refine our perceptions with a study such as the Boston Project. But everyone in this room knows of several lesbian and gay workers in city hall who are afraid to come out. We all probably know of several teachers in the Boston public schools who are afraid to come out. Some of us know of Boston police officers who are afraid to come out. All these people work in environments of institutionalized homophobia which force them to remain in the closet.

You've all probably noticed that everything I've said so far reflects a gross distrust of city government and the police department. Because of this distrust, which I want to emphasize is based on *experience,* I am *not* going to recommend hiring more city bureaucrats or police officers; that would simply give us more of what we've got. I would guess, however, that a city government and a police force which supported lesbian and gay workers and constituents, which supported *all* the people of the city of Boston, would function somewhat differently than what we have today. I would like to see our efforts put toward recognizing the presence and increasing the visibility of lesbians and gay men in our schools, in our communities, and in the operation and future planning of a city that will benefit and respect the people who live in its neighborhoods.

May 15, 1983

Testifying on AIDS Before Congress

Virginia Apuzzo

This is the text of the testimony given by Virginia Apuzzo, then executive director of the National Gay Task Force, in 1983 to the House Appropriations Subcommittee on Labor, Health and Human Services, and Education in support of increased funding for AIDS research at the National Institutes of Health and the Centers for Disease Control. Appearing with her were Dr. Roger Enslow of New York City's Office of Gay and Lesbian Health Concerns, and Dr. David Ostrow of the Howard Brown Memorial Clinic in Chicago. The full document was printed in the *Bay Area Reporter* on May 15, 1983.

Mr. Chairperson. Members of the Committee.

There are four factors concerning the AIDS epidemic and the type of response we are looking for from our representatives which I want to impress upon you. First, the response of the Gay/Lesbian community to the AIDS epidemic has been in the best spirit of American volunteerism. Second, the response of the government has thus far been a series of uncoordinated and inadequately funded gestures. Third, the scope of the problem demands a level of research and funding far beyond the resources of the private sector, however committed, a level which only the government has the resources to meet. And fourth, we are asking for a national agenda which is coordinated, adequately funded, respectful of confidentiality, public, and developed in consultation and cooperation with those segments of society most affected by AIDS.

Since the AIDS epidemic broke out, the Gay/Lesbian community in particular has responded with that magnanimity of spirit which is one of the finest characteristics of the American people when faced with a crisis. Existing local organizations have established counseling and referral centers. New organizations of volunteers have formed to provide accurate information, support groups, and services for those affected by AIDS. Volunteers have raised tens of thousands of dollars to support these services. Nationally, the

Gay press has provided the bulk of information on AIDS available to the public. The National Gay Task Force has established a Crisisline, the only national 800 number now providing information and referral information on AIDS to whomever asks for it.

I am proud of the way in which the Gay community has responded on behalf of all who are threatened by the AIDS crisis—and we are all threatened. Diseases tend not to limit themselves for long to just selected segments of society. At the same time, I am angry, frustrated and pained by the knowledge that gay people have had to be self-reliant if for no other reason than they are intentionally and systematically denied their rights. Additionally we are denied access by the media, by community agencies and by representatives in government who claim to—and ought to—represent all people, but who do not respond to their Gay constituents. Community agencies solicit our dollars, but refuse to fund our service, health and social agencies. Within the last two weeks over 17,600 people supported an AIDS benefit in New York, and not one newspaper printed a single line before or after the event. That's what I mean by being denied access. On an issue which threatens the health of every American, the Gay community alone cannot and should not be responsible for funding the level of research needed to meet the AIDS crisis.

I wish I could express as much pride in my government's response to this epidemic. While people die, a full year has passed since the first interagency meeting was called by the federal government to explore research directions for solving the AIDS crisis. During that year we have seen precious little action. While people die, the National Institutes of Health process research applications with a "business as usual" attitude. Over seven months into its fiscal year, only 25% of its funds for AIDS research have been allocated. While people die, the Centers for Disease Control are still struggling under a 20% budget cut imposed in 1981, the same year the AIDS epidemic was beginning to get attention. While people die, no detailed, comprehensive research plan of attack has been forth coming from the Assistant Secretary for Health.

The AIDS epidemic affects too many people, is too widespread, and the needed research too expensive to be handled solely by the private sector. Over 1,400 people have been diagnosed for AIDS so far and, with an estimated incubation period of from one to three years, we don't know how many cases may be developing right now. The number of patients afflicted is doubling every six months. The mortality rate is at least 50%, possibly as high as 75% to 100% according to the May 6 issue of the *Journal of the American Medical Association.* CDC has reported cases in thirty-four states. One out of every twenty people afflicted fits into none of the major groups affected—is not Gay, a Haitian immigrant, an IV drug user or a hemophiliac. It is a new disease with no known etiology. Patient care for 1,400 patients has already cost $100 million.

We are not dealing with a problem for which "business as usual" is adequate. We are not dealing with a problem which can be met by political gestures. We are not dealing with a problem which can be addressed only by volunteers from the private sector nor through an extra few million dollars for NIH or CDC.

Today I will call upon the Congress of the United States to appropriate at least $100 million for a comprehensive and coordinated program on AIDS in order to stop this frightful waste of lives and resources. This is an amount equal to what has already been spent privately for care. President Lincoln created the National Academy of Science to advise the nation of needs in science. I would suggest that it be charged with developing a comprehensive survey of the need and a plan of attack. I call upon the NIH to speed up the procedure for reviewing AIDS research grant requests and to release funds already available. I call upon the Assistant Secretary for Health to make public his agenda for dealing with this crisis. We need to know if the government has a plan, and what it is in order to coordinate private efforts and research, and to coordinate studies at other levels of government.

Members of the Committee, we are looking to you for nothing less than a crash program with the nation's finest minds and the funds to support their efforts. In view of the scope of this crisis, and in the name of those afflicted, the hundreds who have died and those who mourn, and the millions who are threatened we would be negligent to ask for less. You will be accountable for our government's negligence if you provide any less.

June 26, 1983

The Eyes of the World

Robert Gurdian

This address was given in San Francisco at the Gay Freedom Rally in summer 1983. Gurdian was a Nicaraguan gay man.

I am both happy and proud to be here with you today, and on behalf of revolutionary Nicaraguan gays I bring you a message of support in your struggle for gay liberation against the reactionary forces of the United States.

Gays in Nicaragua are actively participating in the creation of our new society without fears of persecution or harassment. We support our revolutionary leadership and we are committed to the defense of our country from the attacks sponsored by the same right wing forces that oppress gays and lesbians in the United States; the same forces that are blocking government funds for AIDS research and that also oppose the equality of women in this society.

The Reagan administration is reluctant to provide the money for research programs which are a matter of life and death for the gay community. However, there is never an end to the hundreds of millions of dollars being given by the United States government every year to Central American fascist dictatorships to oppress and murder our people, gay or straight, and to wage an undeclared war against the Nicaraguan Revolution.

Fifty thousand Nicaraguans have already sacrificed their lives to make our revolutionary dream a reality which is a source of inspiration for all the oppressed people of Latin America and the World. But our enemies, who are also your enemies, do not want to see an emancipated world of free men and women, gay and straight, enjoying the rightful fruits of their labor and sharing their love equally.

The Reagans, the Goldwaters, the Falwells and so many others want to keep gays and lesbians in their closets and also want to ensure that the fascist dictatorships of Central America keep on providing a cheap pool of labor for the United States multinational corporations.

The help that progressive North American gays and lesbians can give to our struggle is very crucial in this moment. We need to stop the United States war machinery and intervention in Central America. We need you to side with us and make your voices heard through the United States solidarity groups with the Nicaraguan Revolution and with the struggles of the people from El Salvador and Guatemala.

The eyes of the world are fixed upon us, and gay men and lesbians in this country have to be aware that through their actions and participation they will also be helping to change in a positive way the image that our revolutionary leaders and officials have of gays in general.

How many more Nicaraguans, Salvadoreans, or Guatemalans have to be murdered with United States Government help for you to take a stand and say loudly and clearly, enough!

Viva Nicaragua Libre!
Si Nicaragua vencio El Salvadaor vencista!

June 26, 1983

Militarism, Feminism, and Homophobia

Diane Warnock

This speech was given at the Lesbian/Gay Freedom Day rally in San Francisco on June 26, 1983. The Livermore Laboratory is located in the tri-valley region east of San Francisco.

Sisters and brothers, I want to talk about a major threat to lesbians and gay men. Right now we could be just twenty minutes from nuclear annihilation. By the end of this year the United States plans to place in Europe first strike nuclear missiles, called Cruise and Pershing. These new weapons will make the Nuclear Freeze we voted for hopeless. That's why there are now 840 people, many lesbians and gay men, in jail for civil disobedience at the Lawrence Livermore Lab. Today in jail they're holding their own Lesbian/Gay Freedom Day Parade!

If you're trying to decide whether to take action for disarmament while the threat of nuclear war hangs over our heads I can only say "Don't die wondering!" Lesbians and gay men are organizing for disarmament for the same reasons we march today: We want our love to survive.

Militarism and homophobia both stem from the fear of loving one's own kind. Lesbians and gay men intuitively understand that the same fear produces both queer bashing and the MX missile. This fear builds borders and creates enemies. We know how it feels to be treated as enemies.

There are many reasons why lesbians and gay men are naturals at peace politics. We know how to defy sanctions about who we should and should not love. We're uniquely able to hear the double message in the statement, "Make America a man again!" Because violence has been used against us, we're wary of violence. We seek more constructive solutions when people are divided.

By our loving, lesbians and gay men challenge not only homophobia. By our loving we also challenge the fear that causes militarism. By our very lives we prove it's possible to love beyond the imposed barriers. Our example teaches the world to reach across political borders, to befriend the Russians. In challenging homophobia we're building peace, for the heart of peacemaking is about extending the possibilities for love.

We have to continue to cross the borders. When faced with homophobia we organize: We talk to friends, we wear buttons, we raise the issue in organizations not used to dealing with it, we build coalitions. We come out as lesbians and gay men. Now we're faced with the threat of nuclear war, and we must come out as peacemakers too. We have to make it perfectly clear today, and every day, wherever we are that we are gay and proud and we are determined to survive! We are determined to disarm. If we're to have *any* future we must strengthen the ties, we must break the chains, we can and must dismantle the bombs.

October 9, 1983

Jericho: A Call for Activism in the Black Gay Community

Michelle Parkerson

This address was the keynote address at the Washington, DC, Black Gay Men's and Women's Community Conference, given on Sunday, October 9, 1983. The Jewel Box Revue was America's first integrated female impersonator show; it played on the black theater circuit from the 1940s to the 1960s.

To all Conference organizers, staff and Committee volunteers:

> I offer my deepest thanks and congratulations
> Your boundless energies have realized
> this historic celebration of the Black
> Gay community in Washington, D.C.

To Workshop panelists and leaders, Conference guests, and Conference participants:

> I offer a mandate to continue the vital
> efforts of eliminating all walls that
> separate us. Our immediate survival
> is contingent upon it.

Trumpets sound. It will take every voice hurled against each brick of racism, sexism/every hand rallied against classism and human oppression to topple this deadly maze. It divides us from one another. In these dangerous times, we cannot afford not to heed the call.

My single voice joins the many that comprise a unique presence in this city. The Black Gay community of Washington, D.C. thrives in unprecedented circumstances. Living and working in a city with a Black and female majority, we view national and world events from a multi-layered perspective. Yet our community suffers internal struggles. We reside in a city which pioneered Gay and equal opportunity legislation, but we exist in a white, male-focused society that defaces us as niggers, cunts, dykes, and faggots. We cannot afford not to heed the call.

This conference has addressed the burdens and bounty existing in our community. In "getting together, being together, and staying together," we recognize diversity as our greatest strength.

As Black Gay men and women, we confront sexual oppression with the same outrage with which we confront discrimination in this country. We take a stand against racism in the Gay and women's movements, but still grapple with homophobia in the Black community. Black Gays must challenge bigotry against race and sexual preference as passionately as we court lovers. We do not have the luxury of choice.

The health of our community hinges on a defiant self-worth and this D.C. Black Gay Community Conference heralds that the barriers between us must come down.

Getting Together

Shared experiences should lay the groundwork for a Black Gay community agenda. As with other coalitions for social change, one pitfall is not relating our struggle to the struggles of others.

We pay little attention to U.S. aggression in Nicaragua or the atrocities of apartheid in South Africa, but we are irate when "carded" at a local white Gay bar. There are Lesbians who are apathetic about AIDS; there are homosexuals who are misogynists, while both are potential victims of job discrimination. Some Gay men despise drag queens. Some Gay women are more chauvenistic than men. But all of us live under the precarious threat of nuclear holocaust, sexual terror, and homosexual murders.

What we do with our lives, our bodies, our money and time, how we treat each other on a daily basis are the ultimate political acts. In recognizing the Divine Source within each other, the first steps toward dialogue, toward mobilization are taken. It is a wholistic approach to the problems we face.

When we lay claim to our rich traditions as an African people, as Gay people, we establish [a] firm foundation. Self-determination is the force that motivates those of us who make our way in the world Black and gay. We have decided to be ourselves, witnessing our particular beauty. Others join us.

Being Together . . .

. . . has never been an easy task. It requires flexibility, respect and trust in the differences we each invest in a common goal. Agreeing to disagree is the essence of struggle and this principle will be tested many times as we move toward forging a unified community. But it is a risk we cannot afford not to undertake.

Risk-taking is a necessary step for any Gay person "coming out." For Black people, risk-taking has historically been a matter of course, a matter of freedom at any cost. As challenges unfold and test the resilience of the Black Gay community, our commitment to being together must grow.

We who are Lesbian mothers, transpersons, Gay youth, amazons, and senior Gays/We who call ourselves Gay women, homosexuals, good girlfriends, Gay men, butch or feminists/We who take the name androgyne or Miss Thing must remain conscious of our collective concerns.

Being together is a process that empowers. Through it, we redefine our image in this world and shape our relationships. Through it, we can build upon the African tradition of extended family to form networks that accommodate our gayness. We can develop positive approaches to Gay parenting. We will find a support base from which to deal with our immediate families around the issue of homosexuality.

Being together as a community of Black Gay people means we must be visible and vocal. We must dispel the stigmas of our Gayness as an open threat to "the Black family." While seeing ourselves as part and parcel of the larger Black world, being together as Gay people will equip us with the ability to combat conservatism and inertia which sustain the homophobic attitudes in our community.

Being together—Black and Gay—brings about affirmation: naming ourselves, exercising a collective strength, defining our destinies as we see fit.

Staying Together

Over the past five years in Washington, several Black Gay organizations have emerged which function as social and consciousness-raising groups. Among them: Sapphire Sapphos, The Coalition of Black Gays, and Black and White Men Together. These organizations join the list of established clubs and bars servicing the growing population of Black Gays in this city.

Our increased visibility has sparked new financial ventures, fresh artistic exchange, and developed a base of Black Gay political clout in local government.

The long-range business of staying together requires consistency and participation. A framework should be organized before this conference ends to carry out the objectives of this event and improve upon its weaknesses. The D.C. Black Gay Community Conference should become an annual celebration involving the whole spectrum of our community. It must utilize our multiplicity of talents and not merely depend upon the herculean endeavors of a dedicated few.

The staying power of our Black Gay community in D.C. depends upon the degree to which we educate ourselves about Black contributions to gay history. We must read about and document the achievements, the bravery of those Black people who shaped their own survival despite social and racial ostracism. We must know about Mabel Hampton, James Baldwin, Audre Lorde, The Jewel Box Revue . . . As Black people who are Gay, we must salvage that history before it too is lost, stolen or strayed. When we seek positive reinforcement for our Black Gay lives, we need look no further than ourselves.

Mobilization and resistance require stamina. As a community, we should consciously concern ourselves with maintaining good physical health—so that the quality of our lives improves with our capacity to love and struggle.

How Black women choose to love each other, how Black men allow themselves to love Black men are the real measures of liberation. Black men and women who are Gay have come together at this conference, exploring our possibilities and diversity. Ultimately, our concept of community must expand to include all people of color, the physically-different, and progressive people with whom we can work in solidarity. At this conference, we have come together to insure a future of promise and dignity for generations of Black homosexual women and men who will survive us.

At the close of the D.C. Black Gay Community Conference, we face the beginning of an immense task. Our community is armed with the knowledge that our anger at racial and sexual injustice must fuel our faith. That faith cannot be taken from us. It can move mountains. It can shatter any obstacle, any oppression that blocks our way.

Just like Jericho
Let these walls come tumblin' down.

October 22, 1983

Speech at the Philadelphia Gay Walk-A-Thon

Barbara Gittings

This speech was given at the Gay Walk-A-Thon in Philadelphia, Pennsylvania, sponsored by the Philadelphia Lesbian and Gay Task Force.

For today, the West River Drive and East River Drive are Lavender Lane.

We're walking for gay rights. Oh, you thought we got gay rights with the passing of City Council Bill 1358 last year? Not by a long walk! That bill gives us a legal leg to stand on to challenge a few kinds of discrimination against us—but only a few, and the bill does not by itself do away with the prejudice behind discrimination.

Gay rights means much more than getting good laws and rules, and changing bad ones, though that is a key step. We have to change all the bad messages that still come from doctors and churches and books and public officials. Progress on paper is fine, but we can't stop there. The struggle for equal treatment has to be won in people's heads and hearts where it counts.

We want relief from the pain of wearing the mask. We want freedom from the big and small compromises that pinch the spirit. We want to be judged as individuals on our own merits. We want the right to live and love and work and play, without being penalized for being ourselves.

Here we are in the very city where long ago our country's leaders declared for us all an equal chance at life, liberty and the pursuit of happiness. They didn't say it was for heterosexuals only. Yet for us lesbians and gay men, our life is limited, our liberty is limited, our pursuit of happiness is limited.

Yes, we need gay rights because that's fair play, in the best American tradition. We owe it to ourselves, the gay children of yesterday, to make better conditions for gay people right now. We also owe it to the gay children of today, and those of tomorrow, that hereafter every lesbian and gay male can grow up feeling good and right and positive about being gay.

Heterosexuals also need gay rights, because every non-gay person knows at least one gay person. It may be someone at the next desk, or the next counter, or the next pew in church, or the next chair at the family dinner table. When a gay person suffers discrimination for being gay, the non-gays who are close to her or him are bound to be affected.

So for all our sakes, we need to keep working for gay rights. There are still so many barriers to overcome, so many bigotries to erase.

I think we have no energy shortage for our walk today. But if you do begin to feel a bit tired, just take 100 more steps for a lesbian or gay man friend who can't be here today. And then take another 100 steps for your favorite enemy of gay rights. And another 100 steps for gay pride—your pride.

If people along the way ask us who we are, tell them: We're an army of lovers! Join us and share the love!

So let's go. Naturally, not straight ahead—gayly forward!

November 19, 1983

Gays, Politicking, and Republicans

Bill Green

This address was given by Representative Bill Green (R-NY) at a Human Rights Campaign Fund banquet in Dallas on November 19, 1983.

It is rare for a Republican to speak before major Gay organizations. Over the years, as a congressman and earlier as a state assemblyman, I have met many times with individuals or small groups concerned with Gay rights. But recently I received my first invitations to address large gatherings of Gay men and Lesbians.

In September, I had the honor to speak at a Human Rights Campaign Fund dinner in New York City and to present an award to the Gay Men's Health Crisis, a grassroots group that raised and distributed funds for public education and medical research on AIDS and, of equal importance, provided physical and emotional support for those who had contracted AIDS.

It was important for me to present that award because I had been made aware of the incredible savageness of AIDS and so, as a member of the House Appropriations Committee, had lobbied to increase federal funds for research into AIDS.

Thus I am also aware of the importance of the November 19 dinner sponsored by the Human Rights Campaign Fund which will benefit the National AIDS Fund. There is no more humanitarian goal than saving lives. But I am not going to give an emotional speech on that, on the tragedy impacting so many lives. You know it, you do not need me to say the obvious.

I think it would be of more value for me to address the matter of advancing Gay rights issues . . .

Lobbying and educating, while being sensitive to the political realities, are important in advancing the cause of Gay rights. In my case it was easy as I have been dealing with the issue since the mid 1960s. At that time it was a very unpopular issue. In 1966, John Lindsay, who previously had held my seat in Congress and then moved on to be Mayor of New York, appointed Harold Brown as Commissioner of Health for New York City. Years later,

Brown would write an autobiography, *Familiar Faces, Hidden Lives,* in which he described his fear of being "discovered" as a homosexual and his great sadness at not being able to openly celebrate his appointment with his housemate.

In 1965, when I served in the New York State legislature, only 19 of us out of 150 voted for legislation aimed at changing a law that had made homosexual activity between consenting adults a crime.

19 out of 150. I *know* more legislators believed the law to be wrong or at the least unfair. But many of them felt they could not "go out on a limb" because of the political ramifications back home in their districts. Some of them would have voted differently if there had been a chance of success, but they were not willing to accept damage for a lost cause, they said. Were they being selfish? Perhaps. But remember every public official has to make some enemies with each vote he or she casts and, in some cases, in order to do your job, you anger a lot of people.

The task before us is to work in the real political world—in that way we will succeed. How do we get more people to accept whatever risk lies in supporting Gay rights and how do we reduce the risk so that more officials will be free to support our view?

First, we all must understand, and explain to others, that Gay rights are actually Human Rights—with capital letters. A government that permits discrimination against gays is denying human rights and endangering the rights of all. At the time that New York State prohibited certain physical acts between homosexuals, the state also prohibited certain acts between heterosexuals. To my mind, the State had no right to legislate in the bedroom—in anyone's bedroom—no matter what the sexual preference of the people involved. To my mind, this position should be supported not only by "liberal" or "progressive" public officials but also philosophical conservatives who say they want less governmental interference and greater individual freedoms.

Second, when you lobby, use reason and logic. Speak of fairness and equality of rights. And as you lobby the officials, also educate the officials' constituencies. Push and pull. Have supporters in the officials' home towns write letters of support. Have them stop by the district office to say hello and express support. Try to garner the support of—or at least neutralize—civic, fraternal and social organizations. I know that is not easy. I know there are and will continue to be rebuffs, rudeness. I know there is a lot of prejudice and misunderstanding among the citizens that have to be overcome.

Probably, you will have a more difficult time with many Republicans for the simple reason that, by reason of the districts from which they are elected, they are likely to have more conservative constituents and, as a lobbyist for Gay rights in Washington said, "They can find themselves facing a challenge from the right in a primary." I would guess that would also be the situation for a conservative Democrat. But don't give up on the Republican Party. We have a tradition of progressive legislation that would shock most conservatives.

Allow me to digress for a moment on that point. Take as an example, civil rights. The Republican Party was born as an anti-slavery party. The Emancipation Proclamation: Articles XIII, XIV and XV of the Constitution are all Republican documents. And a higher proportion of Republicans than Democrats voted for the 1960 Civil Rights Act.

The Republican Party preceded the Democratic Party in endorsing the Equal Rights Amendment. The year was 1940. In 1980 the conservatives in the party knocked it out. Some of us are going to try to reverse that at the next convention. It was a Republican administration that created the Environmental Protection Administration and the Consumer Product Safety Commission. When progressive Republicans were in powerful roles in the party they promoted social legislation. Today, progressive Republicans are a small minority in Congress. I recently started a PAC, called MODRN PAC, to raise funds to help progressive Republicans get elected. I can't tell you every such Republican will support the Gay rights bill in Congress. But we will get more votes from them than we will from the Moral Majority types.

I understand that the Human Rights Campaign Fund is becoming one of the most powerful PACS in the country. When you do approach potential supporters, let them know that when they help you, you will help them in return. Activate people in their districts to help in their campaign or take other action to counter whatever negatives may result from their vote. This is what other lobbying groups in our society do with some success. And that is important. I have had good support from Gay and Lesbian groups myself, but there have been other public interest groups that have come to me time and time again in Washington, and then turned around and said that, despite that relationship and despite my votes in their favor, they would support my opponent because I was in the *wrong* political party. No major changes can be made in this country, in this political system, without support within both major parties.

And in our battle to gain Gay rights legislation, we cannot afford to ignore potential supporters. We need them all. Even if we cannot get an official on the Gay rights bill, perhaps we can get his or her support to end discrimination against Gays and Lesbians in areas such as immigration or perhaps we can convince them of the dangers in a so-called Family Protection Act which sought to institutionalize the 1950s image of the traditional nuclear family.

Perhaps this is well known to many of you, as you are sophisticated and educated. We need to raise the sophistication and education of the general public and of public officials. We need the people to understand that issues affecting Gays do not constitute a "them" vs. "us" situation. That a lawyer who is Gay is still a lawyer. That there is no more to be concerned about when dealing with a co-worker who is Gay than with a co-worker who is tall.

There is a lot of misinformation and misunderstanding to be cleared up. There are a lot of wrongs to be corrected. But the tide's direction is clear. America is learning. And as we do whatever we can to end the most immediate and important problem, the terrible ordeal of AIDS, we must also help America learn about the need to grant *all* of its citizens, including all Gay men and Lesbians, their Human Rights.

November 19, 1983

Sexual Politics of "Crime": Inside and Out

Mike Riegle

This talk was prepared for and given at the Conference on Sexual and Criminal Justice, held in Boston, Massachusetts, on November 19, 1983. Riegle was the coordinator of the Prisoner Project, run by *Gay Community News.*

The *Gay Community News* gets about 30-40 letters a week from lesbian and gay prisoners all over the country. They range from simple requests for penpal ads to screams of anger and frustration, and desperate pleas for legal and morale-type support.

And now and then, on the other hand, there'll be a story of a couple of people, or a group, that have managed to put together some pretty strong ties with each other.

I'd like to read from a pair of letters that we got recently at *GCN* to give you the flavor of the issues gay prisoners have to deal with: and then say something about what we're able to do, and what more needs doing.

By the way, I'm reading these letters from a packet of materials written for *GCN* by lesbians and gay men behind bars. If you're interested in receiving one, please write Mike Riegle, c/o GCN 167 Tremont St., Boston, MA 02111 and enclose $1.50 to cover printing and mailing costs. [Free to prisoners]

The first letter is from two women in Idaho;

> *Dear* GCN,
>
> *We are lesbian women who are presently incarcerated in the North Idaho Correctional Institution for three years. We are in a continual battle for our rights to sexual preference, and for our rights to be human as a black and white lesbian couple. Things are rough here since we are the only out lesbians out of 40 women.*

We are singled out for meetings by other heterosexual women, approved by the superintendent, to gripe about us as lesbians. They are trying to change us, to pick our brains and force their beliefs on us. It is out and out abuse.

We are trying to pursue a lawsuit for racial discrimination, and for discrimination because of our sexual preference. The NAACP has asked the director of corrections for an investigation, however, we haven't heard any more about it and fear that it won't be followed up as soon as the NAACP finds out that Jackie is a lesbian.

Another strike against us is the majority of white, heterosexual Mormons in this state. Not only have we endured discrimination here in the prison, but in the whole justice process in this state.

Any help and suggestions from our gay brothers and sisters would be appreciated from this isolated prison camp. We need some contacts: lawyers, organizations, or people who are concerned enough to help. We are two desolate, suppressed lesbians! We are seeking help from anyone who will help us fight for our rights.

In sisterhood and gay pride

Lorrie Ong 18301 and Jackie Jackson 18300
NICI Star Rt 3, PO Box 147
Cottonwood, ID 83522

The second letter is from a gay man in a New York prison.

Dear GCN,

I can remember lying naked on a bare concrete floor, no bedding, water or clothes, and it was cold. I remember the cold so well. It was in February 1980 and I'd been beaten by guards and called a "little fag" and thrown into a strip cell and left there for days, cold.

I am one of society's misfits, thrown into one of the largest successful businesses in America, the Prison System. I am not by any standards a writer but I very much want to express how I feel.

As I understand it, when people are sent to prison, **that's** *the punishment, we're not sent there to be abused. But we are, daily. I was 19 when I arrived in the Federal Bureau of Prisons system. As happens to many young men, I was raped. But what was really the rape was a guard who allowed it to happen and when I asked for help told me that it wasn't possible for a homosexual to be raped. After protesting I was classified as a "management problem" and transferred. Since that time I've been transferred six times.*

They will do anything to keep someone quiet. One method, as prisoners call it, is the "merry-go-round," where they put you on a Federal Prisons bus and you tour all the prisons in the U.S. as they try to keep you from making contact with the courts (when filing suits against them) or the media or your family and friends. Sometimes you get "lost" in transit and can be very hard to find for a while.

If they don't break your spirit the first time, they'll do it again. And if you refuse to get on the bus, they'll take a hypodermic needle and hit you with 100mg of thorazine. Then you won't even realize what's going on until it's too late.

I only hope the day will come when the American people stop preparing for and fighting wars long enough to see their folly and realize that everyone should be fighting to survive, to keep everyone warm and fed, or better yet, to make it possible for everyone to keep themselves warm and fed!

James Sipes 39790-066
Box 1000
Otisville, NY 10963

I've often found myself saying inwardly after reading some of these letters about life inside: "Well, sounds familiar, not entirely different in some ways from life out here for some of us." And there's a good reason for that. The old proverb, "What's above is below" could easily be adapted here to say "What's outside is inside too."

Some of what's happening in these letters isn't limited to gay men and lesbians, of course:

Keeping the prisoners divided against each other, often on the basis of race or sexuality;
Keeping everything that goes on behind the walls as much a secret as possible; any judge can tell you that the prison wardens are more afraid of the press than they are of the law;
Keeping the right people's pockets lined with big bucks from drugs, both recreational and sedative, available to, or administered to, prisoners as required by their "rehabilitation," as they call it;
Inhibiting resistance to all this by putting people on buses to somewhere else, where they can't talk so easily to friends or get legal help, or putting them in so-called "protective custody"—another form of blaming the victim, and encouraging the aggressors.

But lesbians and gay men have additional problems where "justice" is concerned, starting with the attitudes of the people on the streets, and with the cops, lawyers and judges, and moving right along through the prison hierarchy and parole system, and finally back to the people on the streets and trying to "come out" (and stay out).

I mean, we have to remember that what's going on inside is only an exaggeration and a distortion of what's happening right out here, in what some of my prisoner friends call "minimum custody." It's been one of the strongest organizing points of this conference, I feel, that we have to encourage people to resist sloughing off their responsibility (and power) for dealing with social conflicts to the police and prisons. The lack of solidarity on the inside is a reflection of our own lack of solidarity out here.

It would be ridiculous, for example, to try to create racist and heterosexist divisions inside if these weren't already so strong outside. The phrase "homosexual rape" is a good example of how attitudes inside mirror those outside. First of all, there's nothing homosexual about it (in the sense of gay or lesbian), they aren't doing it because they are attracted, or like someone. And second, and more importantly, it's not a matter of sex at all. Rape is *never* a sexual act, it's an act of violence and of desperation. And it's misleading to call it "sexual" on the streets or inside prison. A lie like this can only happen in a sex-negative society like ours where we have such a close association in our minds between sex and violence. It's one of the main selling points of the prison business; that they keep the sexually non-conformist or "deviant" out of sight of the respectable citizenry, especially to "protect" the children.

And if the children get a heavy dose of abuse from the parents, that's none of anybody's business; after all, the children *belong* to them, don't they? They're an important "investment."

As for secretiveness, again for the "protection" of prison "security" (or national security, as the case may be) it can only happen in a society like ours where most of the people have given up so much of their sense of community into the hands of the state and the police, "our finest." (We *have* to believe they're our finest, otherwise we'd have some more responsibility for checking out how they're doing their job.)

In all these cases, "protection" is a euphemism for control. This is amazingly clear when sexuality is involved. The victimless "crimes" that our finest spend so much of their time on have put a lot of gay people in jail; all to "protect" the nation's moral fiber. In the packet of materials I mentioned earlier, there's an excellent story about the Bridgewater Treatment Center for so-called "sexually dangerous persons," many of whom are in there for sentences of a "day-to-life" for having had consensual, non-violent, but nevertheless illegal, sex.

The Prisoner Project is hardly in a position to make major changes by itself in these prejudices. *GCN,* however, is a nationally distributed paper that has been giving itself away to gay and lesbian prisoners for about 7 years now, so word is out on the prison circuits, and the letters arrive in a regular flow, asking any of a number of things. Some of the more common ones are:

a chance to write to another lesbian or gay man, to let out some of the personal things that it's a little too dangerous to deal with in a closed, heavily anti-gay system;

a free subscription to the paper, because part of anyone's identity lies in their sense of the community they belong to, and *GCN* gives them some sense of what's happening among us;

requests for some of the donated books that we have to send out (when postage is available);

requests for support in their protests of something (in our case, these are usually denials of their right to receive the paper; often on grounds that it will interfere with their "rehabilitation;")

or just looking for some moral support, something all of us faggots and dykes can understand; some kind of reassurance that they're not the only ones, and they're not alone, even though they've often been rejected by both family and so-called friends, if their being gay has somehow come out in the justice process.

What's particularly mind-boggling, and discouraging from my point of view, is how little response gay men and lesbians on the outside give to this intensified version of what we *all* have gone through, this isolation; at least when we were young, and in some cases are still going through.

It's a powerful statement about how effective the propaganda and the secrecy surrounding the prison business are; put together with the self-hatred we've all had laid on us ever since we were kids and had our first queer feelings of attraction, and you've got a powerful deterrent to solidarity. So even we, who've never had the privilege of taking respect and acceptance for granted out in the straight world, often don't seem able to imagine how much these people need our support, how close their situation is to our own, and how much we can learn from them; and so don't show much solidarity with them, or among ourselves out here, for that matter. It's a social disease that's not limited to gay people, of course, and that we all need to think about. The *GCN* Prisoner Project is strong on this point; that we are not aimed simply at "helping" or "protecting" lesbians and gay men behind bars. *All* of our lives are profoundly affected by the pressure of a legal code and a justice system and social attitudes that push us hard in the direction of conformity, in sexual things especially.

Something as simple as holding hands in public is considered provocative, or at least "flaunting it" by most of our respectable citizenry. You can imagine what a kiss could bring down, inside or out. In fact, there's a good story in the packet about what a photo of two men kissing, that appeared on the pages of *GCN* one week, did to officials of two prisons where we are usually admitted.

If we had more labor power we'd like to set up a jailhouse lawyer network to share legal research on things like harassment and the misuse of "protective custody" to punish those who are openly gay; we'd set up halfway houses to help with the "coming out" process, with job referrals and housing information. We'd do a lot of little things like these. But I think the root matter that all of us need to deal with is the fear and ignorance around sexuality (and the racism and sexism and the rest of the bigotry) *among ourselves,* out here, where prisoners come from.

I'd like to finish by reading a few lines from another letter by a gay prisoner; something to show that in spite of all this ignorance and indifference, some of us (both inside and out) manage to put together some pretty fabulous relationships. He says:

> All along I've closed myself off to people and feeling. I've tried to reach out to certain ones now and then but no one was ever there. But recently I met a Cuban refugee and we became close. At first it could have been merely a sexual thing, but as it turned out, one night we were talking about his family in Cuba, who he would never see again, and he stopped in mid-sentence and turned to me and as I sat there he began to shake and he grabbed me and hugged me, and began to cry as I've never seen a man cry before. We both cried. I hadn't for so many years. I am 24 and for the first time I felt love for someone. As soon as they discovered our friendship, they separated us and sent me to another prison. I miss him so much and they won't let us write to each other, but he and my mother write to one another, so we're able to know each other is well and contact has not been completely lost. They could as well stop the rain as stop my loving him.

November 28, 1983

Police Brutality: The Continual Erosion of Our Most Basic Rights

James Credle

These remarks were presented at the congressional hearings on police brutality in Brooklyn, New York on November 28, 1983.

Chairman Conyers, distinguished members of the subcommittee, participants, observers, and people in the communities of Brooklyn, greater New York and other cities throughout the U.S.—for indeed, the issues we are attempting to address here are issues affecting us all, and indeed must therefore be of concern to everyone.

I come to you as a black gay man, an assistant dean of students at Rutgers University, an active member of my community, a Vietnam veteran, and a member of Black and White Men Together. BWMT is an interracial gay male, anti-racist organization. Our statement of purpose reads: the effects of racism are all too evident in the gay community. We, as black and white gay men, are concerned that racism affects our personal lives as well. To open up channels of communication between black and white gay men, to provide a forum for discussing and confronting issues of racism in our community and in our lives, and to create a supportive environment for less oppressive interracial relating among gay men, Black and White Men Together, New York was formed in June 1980.

We in BWMT recognize that as we personally struggle against racism in the gay community, racism in society at large is at the heart of this struggle. BWMT also realizes the importance of police brutality as an issue on which we must speak on behalf of our gay brothers and lesbian sisters. For while we are often stereotyped as members of a single community, our roots emerge from and encompass multiple ethnic and racial identities. We have suffered, and continue to suffer, brutality as blacks, hispanics, Asians and Native Americans, in addition to our third-class status as lesbians and gay men. All of us who have been maimed, physically and emotionally abused, unlawfully arrested—yes, even tortured and killed—have yet to receive any note of recognition or acknowledgement that we too are victims of police harassment and brutality. If we are serious about the eradication of such brutality from our community, then we must acknowledge the widespread abuses which occur daily against lesbians and gay males. Such acts of harassment and brutality occur in Brooklyn, in Manhattan, throughout New York City, other cities, and across the United States.

These daily acts of police harassment and brutality begin with the yelling of anti-gay and racist epithets at us. We are then stopped and questioned in a further attempt to humiliate and ridicule us. Often, regardless of our answers, we are detained, arrested and/or kicked and beaten with nightsticks, fists, gun butts and any other weapons in policemen's possessions. Given that we survive this heinous behavior—and many of us do not—we are then fined and imprisoned, where we are further subjected to brutality and rape.

But this process of hostility and violence against lesbians and gay men does not begin at the moment a police officer perceives a stereotypical faggot or dyke—either alone or in the company of others. Like racism, homophobia—the hatred of lesbians and gay men—pervades American society and can lead to our annihilation at the hands of police. These racist and anti-gay attitudes are constantly reinforced by the same society which bestows upon the police the job of "protecting the citizenry." The point is, that as a black gay man, I often ask "From whom do I need protection?" And more often than not, the answer is "I need to be protected from the police!"

We have come today to speak not only as victims of police brutality but also as a concerned community determined to break the yoke of oppressive behavior committed against us, while many in our society stand by allowing these acts of violence to happen.

Today, I am here to inform you about our history of and current struggles against police brutality. I have talked about acts of police abuse against the gay and lesbian community as something which occurs daily. Most of these acts are never heard about nor seen by the general public. However, at least one incident of police brutality against the lesbian and gay community was heard around the world.

In June 1969, after suffering years of police harassment, abuse and brutality, gays and lesbians fought back against yet another police raid at the Stonewall Bar [*sic*]. For three days, with hands, feet, bottles, sticks and whatever else was available, we sent the police a clear message: "We're fired up, we won't take it no more! We won't be your victims! We won't suffer your brutality! We won't allow our brothers and sisters to be arrested, beaten and killed! We demand our rights as citizens!"

It was not accident that our community's most vulnerable members—lesbians and gay men of color, and transvestites—were at the forefront of this battle.

Dykes, fags, butch, fem, women, men, blacks, whites. Hispanics, other people of color, transvestites—we were all at Stonewall, standing together to say to the police: "I have pride! I have dignity! I have respect! I will not allow you to destroy nor change me!"

This outbreak of gay pride—this "Stonewall Rebellion"—became the catalyst for the gay and lesbian rights movement. It triggered a reaction to police brutality felt around the world. When you hear, "Remember Stonewall," you should all remember that it was because of police brutality against our gay community that Stonewall is celebrated today, tomorrow and will be forever!

Despite the uprising at Stonewall, and because homophobia is so deeply rooted within the fabric of this society, daily acts of police brutality continue—sometimes reaching such blatant proportions that they seem unreal. On September 29, 1982, by all accounts currently a matter of public record, 30 to 40 of "New York City's Finest" stormed into Blues Bar, a gay bar located at West 43rd Street in Manhattan, patronized primarily by black and hispanic gays and lesbians. These police officers locked the door and proceeded, without provocation or justification, to line up the patrons and employees against the wall and brutally beat them. Heads, faces and bodies were hit, groins were kicked, requiring many to seek medical care afterward.

These officers, supposedly responding to a call that there was a fight in the bar, went on a bloody rampage, shouting anti-gay and racist epithets. They threw bullets on the floor and called them "gay suppositories," which next time they'd shoot "up gay asses." They battered a disabled man on a barstool because he couldn't walk to the back wall fast enough. They destroyed the interior of the bar.

The sad truth is that no arrests were made, either of any patrons who were alleged to have been involved in a fight nor any of the police officers who engaged in these acts of violence. The sad truth is that no one, including Mayor Ed Koch and those in his administration, feel compelled to address this issue, although tomorrow it will be exactly one year and two months since this brutal incident occurred.

I entered Blues Bar around 5 PM on September 30th, the day following the police raid. I have never seen such total destruction since my days in the jungles of Vietnam. It was as if a powerful, deadly tornado had wreaked total havoc within the frame of the building while allowing the outer structure to stand. Broken bottles, glasses and mirrors were spewed about the floor. The pool and games tables overturned, bashed in and strewn across the floor. The DJ booth was dismantled, with records broken, turntables busted and speakers destroyed. Blood was everywhere—spattered on the floor, on the walls, on equipment—a total wasteland. Some patron, the bartender and bouncer were there to tell us about what happened.

Their story is one in which a police force because of its racist, sexist and homophobic attitudes can, on pretense, raid a bar in the heart of Manhattan—virtually next door to *The New York Times*—lock the patrons in the bar; beat and kick them about the body with nightsticks, clubs and boots, shout racist, sexist, homophobic epithets; wreak total havoc and destroy a place of public accommodations—and return again and again without fear of punishment from the people who are responsible for the general safety, security and protection of all citizens in New York.

This violent raid was ignored by the straight media. Even the *Times* refused to report this total violation of civil and human rights. We in the lesbian and gay male community ask why, but already know the answer. As this society's most vulnerable members, gays and lesbians of color, are too often rejected by our ethnic and racial communities and excluded from the white-dominated lesbian and gay community. Consequently, the police believed they could act with impunity and feared no reprisal.

More than a year has passed, and we have not received any action which would identify those 30 to 40 officers who participated in the Blues raid. Nor has police commissioner Murphy (the commissioner at the time of the raid) done anything which assures us that a serious response will be forthcoming. Nor have any measures been taken to prevent any reoccurrences of violent police raids.

Therefore, I present to this subcommittee my statement, plus copies of newspaper accounts and pictures of the bar. I urge you to be serious about your inquiries. The spectres of racism, sexism and homophobia area inextricably linked.

And while the Blues raid is certainly the most vicious attack on our community, it is not an isolated incident. It reflects a pattern which, though unrecorded, pervades our society. When racism and homophobia in the police force interact for lesbians and gay males—and particularly the patrons of Blues Bar—the results are devastating and deadly. If we don't find ways to stop all forms of police brutality, and particularly its most blatant forms directed against the lesbian and gay male community, be assured it will continue to occur in society at large. And you, as elected representatives of society, have a responsibility to ensure that all the citizenry are protected—be they black, hispanic, asian, native american, white, female, gay or straight.

As gays and lesbians, we are here to ask: what is your response, when the police officer swings his nightstick a few more times because the target is gay or lesbian? What is your response, when the police shout racist and anti-gay epithets as they harass, beat up, throw into jail and further violate the rights of lesbians and gay men?

What is your response, when the bullet is fired and another lies dying because the cop believes that this act "protects" this society from undesirable elements—us, lesbians and gay men.

Nobody keeps statistics on the deaths and injuries to people who are suspected of being or actually are lesbians or gay men. Indeed, we can be and are subjected to additional abuse solely because we are largely invisible and deemed more expendable.

A concerted effort must be made to educate and instruct the police of this city that gays and lesbians are not expendable targets. That third world people are entitled to all the rights and protections afforded white citizens. Unless immediate affirmative action is taken by officers in the police department and the elected officers who supervise and establish this policy—we can anticipate a reoccurrence of incidents like the Blues raid, and a continued erosion of our most basic rights as citizens.

Finally, we are ready to work with you to ensure that the rampant police brutality is abated. However, we, as members of the lesbian, gay male, and third world communities, stand ready to make certain that police officers are held accountable for instances of brutality, abuse and harassment.

We see our presentation here today as the beginning of the kind of support and communication which must be established if the horror of police brutality is to stopped once and for all.

December 9, 1983

Being Who We Are

Gary Hirshberg

This address was given at the St. Louis Gay and Lesbian Community Services Banquet on December 9, 1983. John Stoltenberg is an American playwright and writer who cofounded Men Against Pornography in 1983. Stoltenberg's address to NOW is reprinted from "Refusing to Be a Man" in *For Men Against Sexism,* edited by Jon Snodgrass (Albion, CA: Times Change Press, 1977), by permission of John Stoltenberg.

I quote from John Stoltenberg, in his address to the National Organization for Women, 1974:

> I would be angry if anyone carelessly called me a bisexual, a heterosexual, or a homosexual. Those are not merely inexact words. They are bad words. Those are words of a masculinist culture. They are the vocabulary of male domination. They come from a language devised by men in order to perpetuate a system in which men are conditioned to be the pursuer, the possessor, and the fucker.
>
> I renounce being that kind of man. I reject any use of language which in any way defines me as that kind of man. And I abhore [*sic*] the language which indicates gender when that language would be used to objectify the bodies of the persons with whom my body has felt intimacy, sharing, mutual respect, and trust. The language which objectifies those partnerships objectifies both partners in the relationship. I am not an object; I reject anyone's erotic objectification of me. And I do not make love with objects, nor with people who clamor for objectifying attention. Not anymore. I no longer want to "be a man" in any conventional sense of the word—and here I refer specifically to masculinist genital functioning.
>
> The truth of my body and the sexual ethics of my life have nothing in common with the lies of the culture in which I live. I would like to say of myself: I intend to live as a moral androgyne. I am genitally male but I endeavor with all my heart to rid my life of male sexual be-

havior programming. My body never accepted that programming in the first place. I used to think there was something wrong with me. Now I'm dead certain there's something wrong with the program.

My body doesn't lie. The truth of my body contradicts cultural masculinist expectations.

Tonight I would like to take a few moments to talk to you. To speak to you, whom by your presence here have, in some manner, made a commitment. We have made a commitment to challenge ourselves, to challenge this society, we have made a statement of war—yes, war with sexism, with racism, with agism, with heterosexism. We who are gathered here tonight are perhaps the most important force in St. Louis today, we have each made a beginning to renounce the shackles of white male power dominated society.

Let's look, for a moment, at what that says. White is a color, and in this country it is *the* color, male is a biological sex label, and in this country it is *the* sex label. Power is a tool, it is valueless in and of itself, and can be used for any cause. Dominated, this indicates what is done with the power, this says the power is used to subjugate. Society, it is us, it is you, and me, and all the other haves and have nots. It is important to look at these words, it is essential that we realize who the enemy is—the enemy is anyone white, the enemy is anyone male, the enemy is anyone who uses their power to dominate. Each of us lives with the enemy inside of us. We all come here tonight sharing in a quest. We share the quest of freedom. Freeing ourselves not only from their shackles, but far more importantly from our own shackles.

Being gay or being lesbian is not a shackle, it is not a problem, it is not a biological certainty or a genetic endowment or an environmental causation. That is homosexuality. Being gay or lesbian is a choice. Take the power, your power. Choose to be who you are. Say to yourself every day "I choose to be gay, I choose to be lesbian." It is a choice of freedom, it is a choice of throwing off the shackles, it is a choice to challenge a society hopelessly bogged down in white male power dominated ethics and values. Being gay or lesbian is a way of life. It is not who we fuck, it is how we make love; it is not an orientation, it is a choice to challenge and to be challenged.

Throughout recorded history, there have been those people who raised up and cried out for greater truth, for greater equality, for liberty and justice for all. We are those people. Those of us assembled here tonight have raised up and are crying out—we will not be quietly raped any longer, neither physically nor psychically. We are forging ahead and are creating a new and more egalitarian existence for ourselves. We have questioned the roles and the realities that bind us and not just in who we make love to but in how we relate everyday to everyone. The most profound, powerful, spiritually freeing choice that one can make in the 20th century is not choosing to be gay or lesbian, it is renouncing masculinist social structure: this is where the freedom lies—not in what we are but in who we are. We must all take pride in ourselves and in each other, we must look to where we have come from and toward where we are going. None of us can afford the luxury of satisfaction, for to be satisfied is to commit spiritual suicide. We must continue to strive, continue to challenge, continue to dig within ourselves and root out centuries of white male power dominating ethos. We are gay and we are lesbian; but more importantly we must strive to be human beings—in the deepest and broadest sense of the word.

From John Stoltenberg—"Finally, I feel at liberty to say: I intend to do what I can to renounce—and to overthrow—the culture we live in with its masculinist lies. And to discover and to speak, with my own words and with my own body, some other truths instead."

December 17, 1983

United We Stand

Steve Endean

At this time, Steve Endean was the former executive director of the Gay Rights National Lobby (GRNL), and made these remarks at a membership meeting of that organization on December 17, 1983. He died in 1993.

A short time ago, I read two articles which I found of relevance and interest to this nation's gay and lesbian community.

The first was in *The Washington Post* and was about rival labor union activists in Iowa who had long histories of competition and hostility but are putting aside their past differences for a common goal: in this case, the campaign of former Vice President Walter Mondale.

The other article was by noted columnist and good friend Brian McNaught. In his column about support for past and present community leaders, he concludes with a plea, "I suggest a cease fire among warring factions within the gay community." It is a plea which I want to take this opportunity to vigorously support.

During much of this past year, our community has been divided over the leadership strategies, directions and structures of the lesbian and gay civil rights movement. Emotions ran strong as people who should have been working together fell into opposing camps.

While some at the state and local levels avoided this largely national fight, others analyzed the information they had and joined the battle on one side or the other. Sniping, character assassination and hostility on all sides became too commonplace. And certainly my own role with the Gay Rights National Lobby and the Human Rights Campaign Fund was one of the focal points of the acrimony.

When I announced my resignation as executive director of the Lobby, I did so not only with the intention of no longer participating in negative intra-community fights, but also with the hope that the community and its leaders could put aside their hostility and bitterness and get on with the task of fighting for civil rights, human dignity and equal justice for lesbians and gay men. As I said in my resignation statement, "Our purpose and the programs we use to accomplish it—not personalities—must be our focus."

I had hoped my resignation would bring to a close a very unpleasant period for our movement. Unfortunately, it doesn't seem to have been so. On the one hand, my former foes have remained mistrustful. On the other hand, I've become aware of a number of my own friends, allies or those who have supported and believed in me, who now have a "bad taste in their mouths" about our national movement because of this unpleasant period and therefore do not intend to participate or contribute to the national gay movement.

Although it is perhaps natural for it to take some time for the polarization to end and the wounds to heal, the last thing I would want to see happen is for those who supported and believed in me to remain alienated from our common struggle. 1984 could well pose a great challenge to our movement. It seems to me to be essential that we all put aside our internal community battles.

I believe that one of our community's greatest strengths is our diversity—of organizations, leaders, strategies and approaches. But that diversity and the differences of opinion among us become not an asset but a liability when they become the occasion for bitter internal wrangling. Unity is certainly important, but realistically there will continue to be differences of opinion on both major and minor matters. I hope that in the future, these legitimate differences can be dealt with without the hostility and recriminations that now seem so common.

Much has recently been said and written about restructuring the institutions that serve our community. While I anticipate the dialogue on this matter to continue, I believe that the respective leaders of our organizations are best positioned to judge these matters. I only hope that whatever structure our institutions take, a stronger sense of cooperation and mutual respect can be maintained.

In a community that has grown increasingly cynical, I feel compelled to even explain my motives for issuing this call for unity. The first is self-evident—my strong feeling that our community must put aside past differences and any bitterness that remain if we are to most effectively move forward on our agenda. The second motive is a more personal one. The past year has been one of the most difficult and painful years of my life. Initially, I felt a great deal of bitterness at the outcome. However, whether bitterness is justified or unjustified, it is clearly unproductive.

I hope that in issuing this call for reconciliation and unity I can, in some small way, now serve as a catalyst for the healing that needs to occur. I believe that we must all put aside past bitterness and divisions to make maximum progress in our common cause, which I joined 13 years ago. In my remaining time I will devote my time and attention to work for this reconciliation, some remaining legislative goals and the transition to the leadership of GRNL's new Executive Director, who will of course have my enthusiastic support.

February 16, 1984

In Support of Gay Rights

David Roberti

This speech was delivered on the floor of the California State Senate by Senator David Roberti on February 16, 1984, supporting passage of AB-1, which banned employment discrimination based on sexual orientation.

Thank you, Mr. President. This is a very important piece of legislation. It's often easy to preface a bill that you carry by saying it's an important piece of legislation but this one is. This one is because, quite frankly—it might shock some to hear me say this—this is the most important civil rights issue that we have before us in 1984. It's the most important civil rights issue because of the process of elimination. We have to this day eliminated discrimination against people because of race, religion, age, sex, disability, and today we have a large group of Californians who are petitioning us to eliminate job discrimination against them because of sexual preference.

In his book *Of Human Bondage* W. Somerset Maugham stated, "There is nothing so degrading as the constant anxiety about one's means of livelihood." That's what this bill is all about—"the constant anxiety about one's means of livelihood." This bill is not about anybody's individual attitudes on homosexuality, on sexual orientation. It's about fairness on one's means of livelihood.

Our Constitution, our Declaration of Independence, our Civil Rights Act, our Equal Employment Opportunity Act, numerous other bills that have passed in this legislature and by Congress, all specify that various kinds of discrimination have to be eliminated, because every individual is entitled broadly to life, to liberty, and to property. And a part of an individual's property is the salary and the means of livelihood that he or she can earn on the job. This legislation allows all individuals, irrespective of their sexual orientation, the right to feel free on the job, without the constant fear and the constant anxiety that they might lose that job because they could be found out, because of their sexual orientation.

Fear of losing your job, fear of getting found out for something you may have absolutely no control over, is a terrible kind of lifestyle to have to live through. And it's one which we impose upon people simply because we don't have the ability—have not had the ability to this point—to eliminate that last vestige of discrimination against people because of their sexual orientation.

Now, somebody can say, well, a gay person can still keep his job. Sure, they can still keep their job, if the employer doesn't want to hire gays, if they hide their orientation, if they live a life of hiding it, denying their nature, a life of constant fear, a life of having to prove to be something you are not. Sure, under those conditions you can keep your job. But it's no different, no different in degree from those people who were early immigrants to this country who found that to keep their job they had to change their names. Fortunately, they were able to change their names, and fortunately for many, they could get away with it, meld into the great melting pot of the United States and people would just not know who they were.

But we had to start passing laws when we realized that everyone couldn't change his name. Some people were just too dark. Some people were minorities. Women can't do anything about looking like a man and wouldn't want to. Some people just can't change the way they are, and more important, people shouldn't have to change the way they are.

Our slogan, right up there under George Washington [pointing to the lettering on the wall above the Senate podium] states the Senators are the guardians of the people's liberty. Liberty is what it's all about. The liberty to do and to be and to act as you feel free to do and to be and to act. Liberty is not about coercion, liberty is not about forcing somebody to be what he is not, liberty is not about forcing a person to change his name or change his identity or pretend to be something that he isn't. Liberty is not forcing a person to live in constant fear of being found out. We are the guardians of the people's liberty. Now, how do we guard the people's liberty? Do we guard the people's liberty only on easy questions submitted at easy times on easy matters that we feel comfortable about and that we agree with? That has nothing to do with liberty and liberty was never defined that way. Liberty is defended on tough issues at tough times that we feel very uncomfortable about. That's what liberty is all about and that's what our charge is—to be the guardians of the people's liberty. And there is nothing so basic to a person's liberty than his right to a livelihood, his right to a job and his right to feel free, to feel that he is not going to lose that job for being found out to be something over which he or she has absolutely no control.

Now, gays can still get jobs, no doubt about it, but it's a funny thing when you're discriminated against, and when there's no laws to protect you, you are forced to obtain those jobs in areas where the stereotype prevails. We do that sometimes because I guess people feel very comfortable with certain types of stereotypes. Generally, people in our society don't feel uncomfortable in thinking that gays can be employed, maybe as long as it's an interior decorator or designer. But the day wasn't so long ago that people didn't feel uncomfortable that Jews could get jobs as long as they were pawnbrokers, or Blacks could get jobs as long as they were only domestic servants, or Japanese could get jobs only as long as they were gardeners, or Chinese as launderers or Armenians as garbage collectors, or women as waitresses and Italians as singers. We feel comfortable as long as people can get jobs in the stereotypes that are assigned to them. So, gays still have jobs available to them, but all of us know about the great diversity of human nature and the stereotype never prevails. People have abilities that go far beyond the stereotype. People have a right to expand upon their abilities. People have a right to produce for society the very best in them and we shouldn't deny them that right.

So I get back to what I opened with and that is that this is the most important civil rights issue of this year and it is by a process of elimination. We have finally mustered the courage in this state and in this nation to eliminate discrimination because of race, religion, national origin, sex or handicap, and there is not this one lingering diversity. It's not a crime for a person to be gay. It's something that I believe a person is born with or is conditioned to at a very early age and we shouldn't punish people for being different from ourselves. That is what our whole list of legislation in protecting individuals from discrimination has been all about. We are the guardians of the people's liberty and as the guardians, we have to guard the liberties of those we disagree with, those we don't like, and those who are not like us at all. That is what liberty is about and that is what our slogan is all about, too. Guard the people's liberties even at uncomfortable times and uncomfortable questions and we will be doing our duty as Senators.

I urge an "Aye" vote on AB-1.

May 1984

Victory Speech

Merle Woo

When I was forced to "pack my bags" and leave Asian American Studies (AAS), University of California, Berkeley in June 1982, I tacked a big note over my desk which read "I shall return." I had been fired for criticizing undemocratic management policies in AAS and for speaking out as an Asian American socialist feminist lesbian and trade unionist. UC terminated me to censor me, and I fought back.

I am jubilant to announce that after nearly two years of waging a free speech battle, we have emerged victorious. We filed suits in both state and federal courts charging violation of First Amendment rights—free speech and association—and discrimination based on race, sex, sexuality, and political ideology. As we approached our federal trial set for early March, UC offered a settlement to which I have agreed.

I am returning to teach at UC Berkeley. The terms include a two-year, full-time contract as a Visiting Lecturer; $48,584 as a settlement sum, and $25,000 in attorney's fees.

I was fired because UC, no longer the liberal bastion of free speech, has been accelerating its right wing activities. The Reaganizing of UC is marked by attacks on Ethnic Studies, Women's Studies, Gay Studies, affirmative action, student democracy, union organizing and, of course, academic freedom.

My Defense Committee and I won because we were UC's most organized and committed opposition, representing the majority of people on campus: people of color, women, lesbians and gays, staff and low-paid teachers.

We were ready for trial with strong witnesses and unshakeable evidence. By this time we were receiving national and international media coverage.

UC, erecting legal roadblocks at every turn, tried to conceal the political issues and drain our resources. UC had three attorneys assigned to the case and huge financial resources. We had one attorney, a volunteer staff and community contributions. But we covered every legal avenue: we pursued the case in court and, with the American Federation of Teachers (AFT) through Public Employment Relations Board (PERB) and an internal grievance procedure.

My reinstatement, combined with a settlement sum and attorney's fees, is precedent-setting. UC has been extremely resistant to reinstating faculty after they have been dismissed.

This victory is a tremendous vindication for all of us who have worked so hard on the case. We showed that management must be governed by constitutional principles and that free speech for teachers, staff and students does not stop at the "schoolhouse gate."

Because I am a socialist feminist and member of Radical Women and the Freedom Socialist Party, I was discriminated against. But I am returning to campus as an open revolutionary Marxist who believes in building a socialist society dedicated to human liberation and who has a right to say it.

Personally, I am overjoyed to be teaching again. I have taught for 13 years focusing on people of color and women' s issues. I'm sorry not to be returning to AAS, and a two-year contract is no substitute for UC's original promises to me of permanent employment. If we had gone to court, I'm sure we could have gotten more; however, litigation is prohibitively expensive and I have been out of teaching for too long already! I just hope my classes in the Department of Education are as rewarding as those in AAS.

I owe my return to work primarily to the Merle Woo Defense Committee (MWDC) and its national coordinator Karen Brodine. The committee is a broad-based student and community group who believed my case affected them and the communities they represent.

Mary C. Dunlap, our attorney, worked steadily with us, because she believed that ours was a crucial civil rights case of the Eighties.

I also want to thank Radical Women, the Freedom Socialist Party and the hundreds of other supporters of various political backgrounds.

My victory comes in a wave of workers organizing against UC's union-busting tactics. The American Federations of State, County and Municipal Employees and AFT, among other unions, have won representation. Employees have recently won a sexual orientation non-discrimination clause in hiring, and PERB ruled that the four year limitation on lecturers teaching time is an unfair labor practice.

Examples of free speech battles on campus and at work multiply: Nancy Shaw, denied tenure, UC Santa Cruz; Mitsue Takahashi, fired 8th grade teacher, Merced; Kathryn Wan [*sic*] Wormer, fired from Kent State, with women at Cal State Long Beach and Medgar Evers College, New York fighting to retain Women's Studies and Black Studies; Henry Noble, socialist feminist labor organizer, fighting against retaliatory harassment at Hutchinson Cancer Research Center, Seattle.

As a unionist at UC, I see our connections to the Greyhound and Oil, Chemical and Atomic Workers strikes, the killing of the Amalgamated Transit Union and OCAW picketers is the most extreme form of censorship. But we can stop all attempts to silence us.

I am proud to be part of the explosive resistance movement of workers in the Eighties. One of the many teachers, student-workers and staff who are banding together against the Reaganizing of UC. One of the many workers mobilizing against cut-backs, forced concession, discriminatory findings.

Clara Fraser, a veteran socialist feminist who won a 7-year free speech battle against Seattle City Light advises:

"If you think you have a just cause; keep fighting. Don't let reversals crush your morale. Even the lowest paid workers have rights. Don't let the bullies kick you around."

I hope all U.S. workers will be heartened by our accelerating momentum and continue to fight for themselves and the entire working class.

The freedom to speak your mind is not a luxury, but a constitutional right, and if we don't use it, we'll lose it.

May 12, 1984

The Limitations of the Legal Fight

Susan Ritter

This speech was given at the Northhampton Lesbian and Gay Liberation Rally, May 12, 1984. GLAD is Gay and Lesbian Advocates and Defenders, New England's public interest gay and lesbian legal organization.

They [the Northhampton city officials] tried to silence us—but we didn't let them. They said "You have to do it our way." The march organizers said "let's compromise."

They said: "No way. You'll do it our way or not at all."

It was important to march on Saturday—to make our presence felt, our voices known. This is Northhampton, Massachusetts—we are known and watched all over the country as a large and vocal lesbian and gay community which is also subject to harassment in many violent and nonviolent ways.

We must be proud that we fight on, remain visible, keep working and struggling and making alliances to fight injustice and oppression on all fronts, recognizing that, as we say at Passover, none are free until all are free.

When they tried to silence us, we went to the courts for justice.

It was hard work, a real team effort. There was the law Committee of GALA (Gay and Lesbian Activists) which spent hours in the police station combing through old parade permits, hours going up and down the streets and more hours on the phone, gathering support from store owners and city councillors. There were the lawyers named on the Complaint—Nancy Shilepsky and me for GLAD, and Arch Battista of the ACLU.

And there were others, including a closeted lawyer who gave us much inspiration, and who I hope will be out next year.

I am so proud to be a lesbian and a lesbian lawyer in a large and visible lesbian and gay community, and it is especially joyful to work with GALA, who decided to go to court not only for themselves, but for all those voices which might be silenced by people in power who don't want to hear what we have to say.

And we won!

The fight to change the law, in the courts and legislatures, is good work. We must keep on fighting the legal fight to insure for ourselves and others the right to march, demonstrate, and speak.

But the legal battle has its limitations and is not an end in itself, but only a way which sometimes permits us to do what we have to do to achieve liberation. When we go to the law for what we need, sometimes they give it to us—but anything they give, they can always take away.

What we achieve through taking what is ours by political and social activism is ours for good. Political and social activists change people's lives, minds and hearts—this can provide the climate for changing the law, but it also provides more lasting change.

It wasn't the law which sparked the lesbian and gay liberation movement. Our struggle for freedom was given life by people in the streets—saying to others in the closet "You can be free, free to be visible, to be who you are."

This is *lasting* change, taken by us collectively and individually.

And it provides a political context for everything else we need to do in the courts, in the streets, in the meetings, at the dances and in our minds and hearts.

May 30, 1984

Lesbians Oppose the Klan

LIPS

This is the full text of a leaflet that was distributed by members of the lesbian activist groups LIPS when they picketed the U.S. Department of Justice on May 30, 1984.

We as lesbians, with our gay male and straight supporters, have called for this picket line in front of the Justice Department to express our outrage. We protest the denial of justice and the continuing complicity on the part of the Reagan Administration and the Justice Department in the acquittal of nine Klansmen and Nazis for the murder of five Communist Workers Party members in Greensboro, NC in November 1979.

At this time the Reagan administration is naming any groups who oppose its policies "terrorist," and denying the civil rights of dissenters or those of us who are not white, conservative, middle-class, heterosexual and at least nominally Christian. They intend to scapegoat, blame and silence us.

Today we hold this memorial before the doors of Justice, we make this statement of fact, we invoke the power of memory and say that we have not forgotten these murders. We have not forgotten that five men and women—Jewish, Hispanic and Anglo men, a Black woman, union organizers, Communists—were shot down in broad daylight by Klansmen and Nazis, who drove into a public rally shouting "Nigger!" "Kike!" "commmie bastards!" as they fired pistols, shotguns and rifles to wound and kill.

We have not forgotten that the murderers were acquitted in a criminal trial a year later (11/18/80) by an all-white jury, some of whom believed "it's less of a crime to kill communists," some of whom had been threatened with violent Klan reprisals if they voted for conviction. We have not forgotten that local police, the FBI, and the Federal Bureau of Alcohol, Tobacco and Firearms were implicated in planning this slaughter through the activities of their Klan/Nazi informants; nor that the US Justice Department intervened legally to protect the informants from having to give testimony and from being prosecuted. Nor have we forgotten how the US Justice department Community Advocates subverted public outrage at these murders in the Greensboro community. We are not willing to ignore the deliberate illogic of blaming the victims for the crime.

The Klan/Nazi attackers were acquitted of all charges a second time on April 15 of this year, when they were tried in federal court for violating the civil rights of the demonstrators they murdered. Why did the Justice Department choose to prosecute them under the wrong section of the US Criminal Code, thereby allowing them the defense that the people they killed were enemies of America? Their lawyer argued. "You're going to hear an awful lot about . . . the Nazi party, but . . . The Germans gambled everything and lost all in opposition to communism . . . These defendants are patriotic citizens like the Germans were."

We have not forgotten that it was in the name of patriotism that Nazis in Germany murdered 13 million people: 9 million Jews, hundreds of thousands of political opponents, homosexuals, members of minority ethnic groups, and others. Today in Klan paramilitary training camps in the US, the targets are labeled "Jew," "Queer," "Black" and "Commie."

We protest the injustice of the Greensboro verdicts. We protest the failure of the Reagan administration to actively pursue justice, not only in this case, but in its daily workings, nationally and internationally. We protest because this administration condones and encourages hatred in the name of patriotism.

The alliance between the Klan and the Nazis has given strength to the so-called New Right/Moral Majority and its Reagan-supported agenda. The KKK's racist, anti-communist, anti-semitic, anti-gay, and union, anti-feminist and fundamentalist Christian bigotry are hallmarks of the Reagan administration as well. It is no wonder the Klan endorsed Reagan for president in 1980, as they have again in 1984.

Two weeks after the nine Klansmen and Nazis were acquitted for the second time with the tacit approval of the Department of Justice, a DC Superior Court court judge in the Washington area acquitted two white, middle-class heterosexual young men of a brutal assault on a gay man. The implication was that their violent attack was excusable because they were drunk, and because they said they thought they were being propositioned! Acceptance of violence by white, heterosexual men on the grounds of the character of the victim is outrageous; the two acquittals are clearly identical in spirit.

By naming groups who oppose administration policies "terrorist," by denying the civil rights of dissenters, this administration wants to frighten us into silence. If we will not forget, they want us to shut up, to be afraid for our jobs, our homes, our relationships, our organizations, and our lives. They want to put every progressive, every political activist in this country back into a closet. They want us to be afraid to protest; they want to make it illegal and dangerous for us to demonstrate that we will not forget and we will not be silent. They label us terrorists, perverts, traitors, subversives.

Let us be very clear: it is *their* bigotry, *their* fear, *their* violence and *their* oppressive dehumanization of us that is outrageous.

We will not and cannot go back, be silenced or forget. In marching in this Memorial Day picket, we remember and we protest!

We call for Congressional field hearings in North Carolina on the Greensboro murders.

We hold the conservative Right, the Moral Majority, and the Reagan administration directly responsible through their policies for the increases in Klan organizing and acts of violence motivated by racist and anti-Semitic hatred over the past four years.

We encourage everyone to contribute money and support for the Greensboro Civil Rights Fund in their struggle with the judicial system.

We urge everyone here to speak out publicly against racist, homophobic, anti-feminist, anti-Semitic and anti-communist bigotry in their workplace and in their day to day relationships.

We also remember all of those lesbians and gay men who could not be here today, because they feared that their very presence at a Lesbian and Gay demonstration would risk their jobs, their homes or their relationships. Enormous gains have been made for Gay Rights in the last fifteen years, but until we can all stand in the streets without fear of reprisals, we have not come far enough!

We Oppose Klan Violence, We Protest Injustice, and We Will Not Be Silent!

June 24, 1984

Passion Is Our Politics

Joan Nestle

This speech was given at New York City's gay and lesbian pride celebration by the cofounder of the Lesbian Herstory Archives.

Today we are a people who once again have taken our anger and our courage into the streets because we once again have been told that our desire, that our sexual celebration, is our sin. This week we have been told by Mayor Koch, while he stood in front of the Lesbian and Gay Community Center, that he would not march in our commemorative parade because we desecrate the steps of a church, because religious bigotry is the right of the powerful but the outrage of queers is an insult to the divine being. The irony of all this is heightened by the congratulatory messages we give each other on this day—we have come a long way, we have political clout, but in this fifteenth year of our taking to the streets when the slogan is "Unity and More in '84" I find myself needing to remember certain small things.

I need to remember that the resistance of lesbians and gay men did not start with the courage of Stonewall, that gay pride did not start with marches in the street but in the collective steps of courage that were taken by thousands of gay men and women when they did such things as go to drag balls in Harlem in the late '30s; when they walked hand in hand down the hate filled streets of the McCarthy period; when they left small towns all around this country and came to cities like this one, determined to survive their own desires; when they organized homophile groups like DOB and the Mattachine Society: when they danced close together in lesbian bars under the intruding eye of the red light that would signal police surveillance.

I need to remember how in 1958 I endured and played on the bathroom line in the Sea Colony, a working class lesbian bar, where we were carefully given out our allotted amount of toilet paper, abiding by the guideline for bathroom use by deviants that had carefully been set down by the vice squad. I need to remember how we endured and survived the police raids, and the paddy wagons filled with our friends, how the policemen thrust their hands down the pants of our butch women to humiliate them in front of their lovers, and how we nursed battered faces after street assaults. I need to remember the Women's House of Detention where poor black lesbians bore the brunt of deviant punishment, the hot summer nights when women called to women, their assertions of love piercing through the red brick walls and the small narrow windows. Before Stonewall, we fought for the right to our love in a hundred different ways, and always this battle took its strength from our need to be part of a sexual community.

Our history is the history of desire and all the wonders that desire can give birth to—out of fragments and out of fear, out of shame and out of judgment, we have built a history of resistance: we have told the tale of loving and then worked hard to give our passion a place in this world. We have built institutions around it, we have become attractive to political candidates because of it, we now talk of a million dollars needed for a gay center, but the deepest memory I want to keep alive is the image of a frightened 18-year-old lesbian, who in 1958, knowing that the world scorned her both as a woman and as a bulldyke, found the places she needed and the women she loved on the so-called dangerous streets of this city. It is the courage to be different because of a passion and then a conviction about the right to that passion that is at the heart of our history.

This affirmation of the dignity of desire is also our gift to the world's history, and it is one of the ways that we become part of the human struggle against governmental oppression. Desire begins as a personal voice but when we as a people assemble in the name of that desire, we are a political community forcing a new understanding of the complexities of human choice. It is no accident that times of governmental oppression set up a legacy of sexual repression for decades to come. Our government is now mobilizing this country for further assaults on other governments it deems deviant. I believe that as celebrants of passion we must become vocal anti-Reagan activists. When American rifles bring down the chosen governments of other countries, when bodies hit the earth never to rise again, what also dies with each one is their history of desire. In Grenada, in Central America, in South Africa, in the Middle East, on our own streets, desire is murdered every day. If we do not battle as open sexual radicals fighting the forces of death by judgment, all the small freedoms we have won will disappear or exist only for a small group of us—a group selected out because of its connections to power and privilege. But these freedoms, this announcement that a people's sexual identity is part of all the battles for the liberation of the human spirit, are crucial not only for this country but for all the countries of the world.

When we march in the streets, hundreds of thousands strong, we carry with us the more lonely courage of those who risked all because they said to someone of their own sex "touch me here." This small voice is still enough to rule us out of heaven, but whatever power comes to us in 1984 and beyond we must not forget that for us passion is our politics.

June 30, 1984

Unity and More in '84

Harry Hay

This piece originally appeared in *Gay Community News*. The title was the slogan chosen for gay and lesbian pride parades for 1984. The address was given at Boston's Gay Pride Day Rally on June 30, 1984. Galatea was a statue brought to life in Greek mythology, and Pinocchio was the famous wooden puppet who wanted to be a real boy.

If any of you come to Los Angeles for the Olympics next month, some Gay person, taking you on a tour of gay Los Angeles, might drive you to the brow of a hill overlooking the east side of a quiet, silvery lake. On a windy November afternoon, 34 years ago, five politically radical Gay Brothers sat down together on that hill, under a Live Oak which is gone now, to contemplate the vision for a novel type of Gay organizing I was working on—I had conceived of developing "consciousness-raising raps" which we thought of simply as discussion groups in those years. And we began to dream of a Gay Family Collective which one day might stretch from sea to shining sea.

The five of us were committing ourselves to inventing a new Minority . . . quoting THE MATTACHINE MISSIONS & PURPOSES collectively written by five and then by seven of us as of April 1951, "paralleling the emerging cultures of our Fellow Minorities . . . the Negro, Mexican, and Jewish people." (Negro was the racially approved word then—Black came later.) Alike with Galatea and Pinocchio, the moment the New Minority was cut out, pasted together, and stood up on its teetery feet, it took off like a feather in the wind on a life of its own, inviting us to seek cracks and crevices in the heretofore impregnable walls of prejudice imprisoning us, through which our pent-up energies . . . now suddenly illuminated by political thought and direction . . . might at last begin to flow.

As spokesperson for that newly-invented but already impatient Minority, we five projected three immediate needs:

- to discover, or re-discover, who we Gay People were, where we had been over the millennia, and what we were for;
- to find ways and means of communicating our discoveries as to who we were, and what we were all about, to the Hetero Society surrounding us;
- to negotiate "free and equal" social and political spaces for our Minority—as a group—within that plurality of diverse Minority groups which comprises the American Community—wherein we could demonstrate what we were all about, wherein we could exercise and share the significant contributions we wished to make, the capacities for which we had been carrying and safeguarding down the many millennia of our refugee underground journeys.

Putting those right-brain feelings we had been secretly carrying within us—for many thousands of years—into left-brain words and phrases which could be written down and duplicated was one thing, to get any action started around them would prove to be quite something else.

When the committed five of us swelled to a sphere of influence of possible [*sic*] 5000 in the State of California by the Spring of 1953, even in the teeth of the McCarthy witch-hunt, we were in trouble. The majority—now middle class in outlook—swamped our radical perceptions and opted for the notion that we were the same as everybody else except in bed. With the advent of *Robert's Rules of Order,* the bright dreams of rediscovering ourselves died; as the dreams died our sphere of influence plummeted from 5000 to 500. And though we laid little powder trains here and there, and began to win favorable decisions in court cases—including one in the United States Supreme Court—here and there; and occasionally we radicals were able to squirrel up chances to present positive Gay images on National Public Radio or on major TV here and there, the middle class cop-out remained largely the Movement's policy and outlook until Stonewall. The Stonewall eruption ignited the powder trains we radicals had been laying in many parts of the country. The combined explosions shattered the door-locks of the Hetero Society's closets and attics to reveal that we Gay and Lesbian folk were indeed everywhere. Gay lifestyles and Gay-positive ways of being ourselves suddenly became visible all over the place.

But the ways and means of communicating to the Hetero Society around us as to how we wished to be seen in terms of this new visibility, to be heard, were still not forthcoming. Such communications, which would have started to explain to them our startling new visibilities which—right from the first—were running athwart the long traditions of Hetero conformities, and threatening many a Hetero male's self-confidence, did not accompany our visibility presentations. The ways and means of communicating to the Hetero Society surrounding us about who we really were—and where we might be coming from or about how Great Mother Nature might have in mind for us to develop and contribute new dimensions of perceiving which Society desperately needs but for which discoveries Hetero Society was itself in no way equipped—all these powerful and even painful sharings which the Mattachine had projected as requiring to be our first priorities 20 years earlier, did not materialize any more after Stonewall than they had before Stonewall.

A month from now, over June 12 to June 13 in San Francisco, we may collectively face a national showdown instead of the merely state and local trouncing as of heretofore. Jerry Falwell, Phyllis Schlafly, the rabid Homophobic Catholic Priest Father Enrique Rueda, and the Reagan Administration in the persons of Surgeon-General Koop, as well as the chairman of the National Endowment for the Humanities, and the Director of the Justice Department's Office of Juvenile Justice, are admittedly presenting a pro-Family conference at which THE THREAT OF HOMOSEXUALITY will be a major topic.

In the face of the long-announced plan of the Gay Movement Nationally to stage a giant march and rally on June 15th, to present to the Democratic Convention our determination to win first-class Citizenship;

- it has to be obvious that Falwell's single intention (as it is also of the massed forces of the New Right complete with official representation from the Reagan Administration) to taunt and goad the Gay Movement into dangerous inadvertencies of bitter and violent counteractions.
- it has to be obvious that the massed forces of the New Right, together with the Reagan Administration, wish to embarrass the Gay Movement in the eyes of the world and so jeopardize their campaign to impress the Democratic Convention with the justice and the *human rightness* of their petitions;
- it has to be obvious that the New Right, through this "Pro-Family" conference, this FAMILY FORUM III being mounted by the Moral Majority Foundation and the Committee for the Survival of a Free Congress, is attempting to stampede the integrity of the Convention itself by shaming it into repudiating all those who would presumably undermine the sacred foundations of the Traditional American Family—Apple pie—Home and Mother!

Falwell, as a person and a citizen, is far too clever and intelligent to be in ignorance of who Gay people really are and of what the Gay Movement really consists. We are dealing with a hidden agenda here (and make no mistake!) a sinister and even dreadful "hidden agenda" in which the real victims are the American People themselves. The New Right, with Falwell as its principal spokesman, is deliberately and calculatingly laying the basis for the BIG LIE and creating, in consequence, the scapegoat classification necessary to support it—exactly as did National Socialism, with Hitler as its spokesperson, in Germany 44 years ago. The BIG LIE, for Americans in 1984, is the Moral Majority version of the *Traditional American Family*, the family with the consciousness of Cotton Mather, the family where the roles have retrogressed to the menial servitudes for the women and children of families 100 years ago. The American People must be informed that Falwell's Family is the one in which Father is the autocrat solely responsible for, and therefore in charge of, all of its affairs, where the differences in the sexes have reverted to those laid out for all time in the Bible "as they have been understood historically in the U.S."—to quote the FAMILY PROTECTION ACT of the Hansen Bill HR#311, and the Laxalt-Jepson Bill S#1378, of 1981-82.

And we Gay and Lesbian folks, in the Moral Majority's eyes, are the prime threat to this noble Family Institution. It is by our ever-increasing visibility not only in new applications of law and social custom but indeed also in the Arts that we seduce and recruit the children. But because we have never shared with our friends and well-wishers in the grass-roots consensus of the American Community *our vision* as to who we are and what we might really be about, that usually kindly-disposed American Consensus has now no bottom line of informed opinion or shared experience concerning us by which to fend off this barrage of evil and scurrilous deceit parading as religion and holy writ.

However, this time round, in this particular juncture of the upcoming San Francisco convention, we may still have a legitimate way out. We Lesbians and Gays can point out, and rightly so, that PRO-FAMILY III is but one segment of the National Community demanding audience of other segments of that same National Community . . . it is not yet a United National Community confronting us as a commonly-perceived *Scapegoat*. The Moral Majority's irresponsible behavior should be reprehended by sober and responsible heads from other segments of that same National Community. I would propose that the combined forces of Gary Hart, a Senator of the 97th Congress who studied and shelved the FAMILY PROTECTION ACT, and of Jesse Jackson, a courageous innovator in our National Religious community, together should proceed to expose and reveal the BIG LIE in the true measure of Falwell's Traditional American Family. I propose that Hart and Jackson reveal for all to see that the Moral Majority, to defend the authority of this American Family, are demanding through the FAMILY PROTECTION ACT—Federal law changes that would cut off all federal funds from any state or local agency who maintained shelters or provided assistance for battered women.

The MORAL MAJORITY, though the Family Protection Act, demand federal law changes so that child abuse would no longer be deemed to include corporal punishment when applied "reasonably" by a "responsible" parent or substitute, such substitutes being, among others, school teachers. They demand that all federal funds be cut off from any state or local agency who maintained shelters or provided assistance programs for child-victims of parental abuse or family abuse. Gary Hart and Jesse Jackson, as political leaders who seek to chart new paths for the American Community, are precisely the right spokespersons to examine whether Falwell's and Schlafly's and Reagan's Family, wherein women and children can be battered and abused without recourse are indeed the Family role models for a New American Consensus. Hart and Jackson can easily expose the wicked fraud of *this* Traditional American Family . . . and so stop this BIG LIE dead in its tracks while there is still time.

I propose that in the very beginning of our evaluative sharing circles we begin to catalog these differences as sharply and as precisely as we are able. For in the so doing we may simultaneously begin to discern a focus by which to appreciate the unexpected wealth and resources which the width and breadth of these vision—differences between the Lesbians and the Gays can afford us.

These are some of the ways, I think, that we might use to teach one another who we are and what we might really be about. Out of a true unity between the Lesbians and Gay men based upon a strong and mutual respect for each other's differences, we will be finally in a place to confront the necessity of demonstrating to the Hetero Community what we are really all about. When we begin to do this, incidently, and—here and there—manage to create a revelation whereby they suddenly comprehend who we are and how we have been contributing to their cultural and political well-being all these many millennia . . . and whereby they also catch wise to the suspicion that their laws and prejudices already are impeding us from making further contributions, we'll begin to see the Heteros moving to eliminate those repressive laws and customs *to their advantage* in order to keep our creative and inventive goodies flowing their way. And it is here—when they change the Laws not to our advantage but rather to their advantage—i.e., so that it conforms to the Consensus of the Whole—where our real security as a People resides.

So let us begin!

November 14, 1984

Why Aren't More Gay Men Feminists?

Aubrey Wertheim

Given at a forum on "Men and Feminism" hosted by the New York University Women's Center. Wertheim was a playwright active in the Cleveland area who later wrote the 1993 play *Make Way for Dyklings.* He passed away on January 9, 2003.

When first asked to speak tonight on gay men and feminism, I was at a loss as to where to hang my theme. The first idea that sprang to mind was a sort of Roger Corman marquee: "The Return of the Lavender Menace." For those belonging to the post-60s generation (most of you), "The Lavender Menace" was the term affixed to lesbians for the threat they posed to the women's movement that re-emerged in the 1960s. Untraditionally, though, after considerable struggle, feminists refused to dissociate their cause from that of their lesbian sisters and, confronting their own homophobia, began the commitment to lesbian concerns and struggles which is now an established and substantial part of modern feminist agenda. A revival of this trial-by-fire could clearly singe the men's movement as it struggles to its feet and deals with similar accusations and dauntingly stronger internalized homophobia; but the issue has been addressed in the Organization for Changing Men Conferences as well as by other speakers tonight—so "Lavender Menace II" though not yet bagged is definitely being grappled with.

Another choice of topic came with the suggestion I deal with Misogyny in Gay Men, which is, I believe, a more modern recycling of the myth that gay-men-hate-women-because-deep-down-inside-we-want-to-be-women-and-if-we-can't-nobody-should. Right. I didn't address this, because basically I don't buy it. Misogyny is a very deliberate and ambitious irrationale thriving on the conflict of interests in a system required to make women objects of attraction and detraction simultaneously. It's hardly surprising any number of hostilities and phobias result, but gay men being often on the receiving end of that antagonism can hardly be indicted as its main perpetrators or champions. While sexism in gay men is clearly a debilitating and divisive force in our community, it's more directly linked to issues of separatism and self-interest which, though no less deplorable, are more easily recognized and addressed.

But taking a harder look at that second proposition, a more intriguing query arises and makes sounds indicating considerable potential. This being, why aren't more gay men feminists? And why aren't our organizations—which sadly remain for the most part still strongly male-dominated in agenda and membership—as influenced by feminism as the feminist movement has been by our cause? The second question finds its answer more readily. The women's movement, preceding ours, created an environment that is immeasurably more supportive of lesbian needs, both personal and political, and created what continues to be a greatly frustrating Catch-22 of the gay/lesbian movement: the failure to address lesbian needs profoundly and persuasively/the lack of broad-based lesbian support and involvement to sponsor the required sensitivity and sophistication.

But what about your average gay-man-on-the-street, why is he so rarely feminist identified? It's curious. So many factors predispose us towards feminism. The same tactics invariably are used against us both.

Discrimination. From the ever-popular "Crimes Against Nature" to the more abstract "Voluntary Deviate Sexual Intercourse" to the good old Puritan standby, "Bugger," 23 states still make gay activity an imprisonable felony or misdemeanor. These laws in turn taint policy in housing, employment, education—and one state alone has gone so far as to articulate state-wide protection of gays in all areas of potential discrimination.

Sexual harassment. Continuous from seemingly before one can differentiate between the sexes much less sexualities. Listen to how early boys master the language of gay baiting not even knowing exactly what a faggot is, yet totally hooked into its authority as the ultimate insult. Listen to how often men punctuate their conversations with verbal victimization of effeminacy and gayness, how they police each other's actions and self-expression with constant homophobic gesture and slur, yet the idea of a gay man registering a grievance regarding sexual harassment or going so far as to take legal action surely strikes them as patently absurd.

Religious persecution. Both historic—we've burned together—and present-day. And we needn't be so coy as to call it "traditional historical bias," whether it's most established religions in all their high-drag pomp or the more outrageous vaudeville of televangelism and the fundamentalists, the message is the same: in the name (though hardly in the spirit) of spirituality, distortion and stereotype are used to dehumanize, stigmatize and ostracize us from our faiths, the families we all belong to, the regions we grew up in. Talk to gay people and see how many of us were driven from homes and biological families due to religiously-sponsored intolerance. Any term but "persecution" is an insult to them and their exile.

Last, violence. Gay men are more visible in the past ten years than ever before in our history. Through gay-identified fashions, neighborhoods, businesses and socializing environments, the target has moved sharply into focus, thus fagbashing arises as a popular sport. You only have to listen to the response of victims—"I shouldn't have been there," "I shouldn't have worn that," "I can't go to the police—they'd say it was my fault"—to see how quickly parallels can be drawn to women. Add to this arson, prison assault, police brutality, medical neglect or malpractice, child abuse of the effeminate. The incredible potential of infliction rarely ventures far from consciousness once we're out in the world.

What then, given all these points of intersection between women and gay men, prevents so many of us from realizing feminism fully, realizing it at all? Perhaps the answer lies in examining that point where gay men and all women part company—which is that we can pass. This physiological quandary which separates gays from so many other minorities also plays a divisive role within our own ranks. A lesbian assumed a "regular woman" still holds a secondary status in this society, but a gay man assumed to and processed as straight discovers all the attendant preferential treatment afforded the party in power. This dual citizenship—this being of one country yet for most residing in, trading with and practicing the customs of another—produces a unique and exacting conflict whereby in the momentary perjury of a pronoun, a gay man can gain entrée to all the glittering prizes; not just the cliched High Gothic ones of mastery in one's chosen profession and great financial plunder, but the more pedestrian comforts of traditional church involvement, biological family acceptance (and the fathering of one's own family), military service, etc., etc.

It takes no sociologist to observe what toll this takes on gay men whether the package is bought wholeheartedly—becoming one with one's oppressor—or in pieces—merely customizing straight male biases, fetishes and failures: the voice of the embittered, the gesture of self-destruction so often witnessed among our number. If we look at the number of men who are truly, profoundly out of the closet, then compare it to even the most conservative figures of the gay male population, we could say as high as 95 percent of gay men straight-identify themselves to the world and personally pursue no great commitment to our community. Is it so surprising then how slowly we incorporate feminist perspective and aspiration?

But not to paint myself and all gay men into a black hole with no hope of redemption, I think despite all the factors impeding new allegiances, despite the current conservatism which endorses the closet for so many—most disturbingly our new generations—more and more men are coming out courageously, emphatically, on all fronts. And more are in touch enough to define themselves as feminists. But even those who don't, look to their lives;

gay men in social work, public education and community action careers working for recognition of gay/lesbian issues,
gay men working with lesbians to create the network of support services in practically every state,
the rise of the gay fathers movement to a place of national prominence,
the thousands of gay men who've volunteered in the health crisis to befriend, care for and bury their stricken brothers.

All this bespeaks a tremendous consciousness of nurturance which knows little correspondence in traditional male roles. If some are not feminists by name, this is surely feminism in action. Our liberation is still in its infancy. Self-determination does not come overnight. But, please, stand by us: gay men and feminists will come to terms.

1985

An Open Letter to the Gay Community

Vic Basile

At the time this document was sent out to the gay and lesbian press, Basile was the executive director of the Human Rights Campaign Fund, a national organization working for gay and lesbian rights. His comments illustrate the difficulties of mobilizing community support for continuing civil rights work in the early years of the AIDS pandemic.

Dear Editor,

We all remember playing hide and seek when we were children. It was a fun game and, as frustrating as it sometimes got when we were "it" and couldn't manage to find our friends anywhere, we knew our frustration was short-lived.

As soon as we shouted the familiar "come out, come out, wherever you are," the game would be over, and we'd laugh at the clever hiding places our friends had found.

Unfortunately, some of us are still playing, and we don't seem to have any immediate plans to stop. And for those of us assigned the ongoing role of being "it," that's a very frustrating state of affairs.

The Human Rights Campaign Fund (HRCF) has just finished compiling the results of a survey we've taken of our constituency. I use the term "constituency" very loosely because, now that the survey is in, I'm not sure how to define that word as it applies to us at the HRCF. Our survey has pointed out loud and clear that the people within the Gay and Lesbian community who are our contributors by no means reflect our community at large.

Here at HRCF we're struggling to champion the cause we all believe in: basic civil rights for Gays and Lesbians. In that regard, we feel we represent virtually the entire Gay community. But we are an organization kept alive by our contributors, and the portrait our survey paints of those contributors looks mighty different from the real-life canvas of the Gay community we see on a daily basis.

To look at our contributors, you'd think the gay community was 93% male. You'd think half of us were between the ages of 35-49. You'd think we all lived in New York and Washington. You'd think we were all liberal. You'd think fewer than 3% of us were registered Republicans. You'd be wrong on all counts.

To look at our contributors, you'd think Lesbians in Chicago didn't exist, let alone believe in Gay rights. You'd think the 25-year-old Gay yuppie in Houston was a rarity. You'd think barely a handful of Gays in San Francisco voted for Ronald Reagan. You'd be wrong again.

To look at our contributors, you'd think that nobody in New Orleans cared about the judges who send convicted "fagbashers" home with barely a slap on the wrist. You'd think there wasn't a single Gay person in Denver who felt threatened by the fact that Gays all over the country lose their jobs and their homes because of who they are. You'd think there weren't any young men in St. Louis who were frightened at the idea of how little money the government is spending on AIDS research and treatment. Once more, you'd be wrong.

What you'd be right about is that these people—and "these people" include just about every one of you reading this column—don't believe, don't care, don't feel threatened, frightened or discriminated against *enough* to do something tangible to alter the legal and social realities that place their very own civil rights in jeopardy.

This sad fact has at least two dangerous consequences. First, it prevents the Campaign Fund, as well as all other Gay organizations, from truly representing the needs and the wishes of the Gay community. As we find ourselves responding more and more to the people whose contributions keep us going, we risk becoming increasingly remote from those of you we have, so far, been unable to reach.

Second, and more important, the fledgling status of national Gay organizations does not go unnoticed by lawmakers in Washington or our opponents across the country. The Gay community—to a large, dangerous extent—remains elusive, remains silent, remains vulnerable.

There is no such thing as a "homogeneous homosexual community." But we do have two things in common; 1) our civil rights are either ignored or specifically outlawed; 2) potentially—as a community we have the power to change that.

So you hide, and we seek. We're not asking you to come out of the closet, we just want you to come out of the woodwork. We need to know that you're out there, and we need to know what you think. We need your monetary contributions, but we also need your ideological support. There are groups of retired railroad conductors who outnumber and outspend us in Washington. There are coalitions one-tenth our size who have amassed twenty times our level of influence. There is perhaps no other constituency whose numbers, commitment and potential power is as underdeveloped as that of our community.

The game of hide and seek must come to an end. Somehow, we in the Gay and Lesbian community must find each other because, if we allow those hostile to us to find us first, they may force us to remain in hiding forever.

So come out, come out, wherever you are.

1985

Black Men Loving Black Men: The Revolutionary Act of the Eighties

Joseph Beam

This opinion piece originally appeared in *Gay Community News* on April 20, 1985. Joseph Beam at that time was a writer and the editor of the first collection of black gay male literature, *In the Life: A Black Gay Anthology* (1986), founding editor of the newspaper *Black/Out,* and a contributing editor to the magazine *Blacklight.* He died of AIDS on December 27, 1988, three days before his thirty-fourth birthday, in Philadelphia.

Black men loving Black men is the revolutionary act of the Eighties.

At 18, David could have been a dancer: legs grown strong from daily walks from his remote neighborhood to downtown in search of employment that would free him from his abusive family situation. David, soft-spoken and articulate, could have been a waiter gliding gracefully among the tables of a three-star restaurant. David could have performed numerous jobs, but lacking the connections that come with age and/or race, the Army seemed a reasonable choice. His grace and demeanor will not be important in Nicaragua.

Earl is always a good time. His appearance at parties, whether it's a smart cocktail sip or basement gig, is mandatory. He wakes with coffee and speed, enjoys three joint lunches, and chases his bedtime Valium with Johnnie Walker Red. None of his friends, of which he has many, suggest that he needs help. His substance abuse is ignored by all.

Stacy is a delirious queen, a concoction of current pop stars, bound eclectically in thrift store threads. His sharp and witty tongue can transform the most boring, listless evenings. In private, minus the dangles and bangles, he appears solemn and pensive, and speaks of the paucity of role models, mentors and possibilities.

Maurice has a propensity for white men, which is more than preference—it's policy. He dismisses potential Black partners as quickly as he switches off rap music and discredits progressive movements. He consistently votes Republican. At night he dreams of razors cutting away thin slivers of his Black skin.

Bubba and Ray had been lovers for so long that neighbors presumed them to be brothers or widowers. For decades their socializing had been done among an intimate circle of gay couples, so when Ray died Bubba felt he was too old to venture the new gay scene. Occasionally he has visitors, an equally old friend or a much younger cousin or nephew. But mostly he sits, weather permitting, on the front porch where with a can of beer over ice, he silently weaves marvelous tales of "the life" in the Thirties and Forties. Yet there isn't anyone who listens.

Bobbi, a former drag queen, has plenty of time to write poetry. Gone are his makeup and high heels since he began serving his two-to-five year sentence. He had not wanted to kick that bouncer's ass; however, he, not unlike the more macho sissies clad in leather and denim, rightfully deserved admittance to that bar. Although he has had no visitors and just a couple of letters, he maintains a sense of humor typified by the title of a recent set of poems: *Where can a decent drag queen get a decent drink?*

Paul is hospitalized with AIDS. The severity of his illness is not known to his family or friends. They cannot know that he is gay: it is his secret and he will expire with it. Living a lie is one thing, but it is quite another to die within its confines.

Ty and Reggie have been lovers since they met in the service seventeen years ago. They both perform dull and menial jobs for spiteful employers, but plan to help each other through college. Ty will attend first. Their two-room apartment, which is neither fashionably appointed nor in a fashionable neighborhood, is clearly home and a respite from the madness that awaits outside their door. They would never imagine themselves as revolutionaries.

Black men loving Black men is the revolutionary act of the Eighties, not only because Sixties revolutionaries Bobby Seale, Huey Newton and Eldridge Cleaver dare not speak our name; but, because as Black men we were never meant to be together—not as father and son, brother and brother—and certainly not as lovers. At every turn we are pitted, one against the other, as permanent adversaries.

It is no accident that 100 applicants apply for 10 jobs, or that loan programs for higher education are being defunded, or that Black youth perceive the Armed Forces as viable employment. It is not a chance occurrence that the rate of Black male imprisonment remains disproportionately high or that drugs are so easily accessible in Black neighborhoods. We are not meant to be together. If one is fortunate enough to locate a crumb from the table draped in white linen, he scurries away to savor it—alone.

Black men loving Black men is an autonomous agenda for the Eighties, which is not rooted in any particular sexual, political or class affiliation, but in our mutual survival. The ways in which we manifest that love are as myriad as the issues we must address. Unemployment, substance abuse, self-hatred, and positive images are but some of the barriers to our loving.

It is my pain I see reflected in your eyes. Our angers ricochet between us like the bullets we fire in battles which are not our own nor with each other.

Black men loving Black men is a call to action, an acknowledgment of responsibility. We take care of our own kind when the night grows cold and silent. These days the nights are cold-blooded and the silence echoes with complicity.

May 23, 1985

We Are Everywhere, and We Have Children

Louise Rice

This speech was delivered at the May 23, 1985, demonstration protesting the removal of two foster children from their two gay male foster parents, Don Babets and David Jean. Rice was a member of the board of directors of Boston's newspaper *Gay Community News* (which originally printed the speech), an activist of many years standing, and a lesbian mother.

I am a lesbian parent of two teenage sons. They have either the same or fewer problems than most teenagers who live in this country. Most of the task of raising them has not had anything to do with lesbianism. The media's attempt to mix sex with childrearing is totally ludicrous to any of us who have spent the past 15 years mopping up vomit, attending parent-teacher meetings, doing laundry, washing dishes, and picking up underwear on the bathroom floor. But that's another story—all I can say to the *Globe,* to Dukakis, to DSS, is: they haven't been there and they don't know what they're talking about.

As far as gender identification is concerned, my sons weren't raised in a vacuum. Exposure to the media, to U.S. schools and culture has given them more gender identification than they know what to do with.

But ignorance on the part of the state is nothing new. This new decision scares me because Massachusetts is supposed to be more up to date than the rest of the country. When they start scapegoating gays here, it is because they are bowing to a wave of right-wing pressure. The past few years we've had one onslaught after another against us for whatever differences we might have, whether of race, or class, or sexual preference. But I don't want to defend myself for being different. I think that my kids don't just have a set of parents who are different. They have an improvement on some of the tired old models I grew up with! I don't think we'd be under attack the way we are except that our difference is meaningful. As lesbians and gay men we question the validity of what's normal. Kids who grow up with differences grow up with the ability to ask questions. I have been impressed with my kids' ability to identify with and stick up for other kids who are so-called different. And I think that comes from learning firsthand that the concept of "normal" is bullshit. I'm not interested in being considered normal. What's normal around here is racism, sexism, "covert" war on Central America, and not least of all, homophobia.

We're seeing a breakdown of rigid definitions of what men and women should be. Those changes, which benefit all people, didn't happen on their own. Gay men and lesbians have been leading the way—leading it—and the part we play is vital to the changes in men and women's lives. So DSS doesn't just have to *accept* us as parents. They can *learn* things from us. Because we have some of the answers they're looking for.

Finally, I want to say something about the importance of being out. These two men lost their children because they were out about their gayness. That takes a lot of guts. We've all had our experiences of fear and isolation in relation to our jobs or our families and friends. I have a pretty low profile at my own job. But we have to stand and be counted now. We have to let DSS and the State of Massachusetts and our closeted brothers and sisters know that we're here and we're everywhere and we have children. My own kids feel supported by the existence of other out gay parents and teachers at their schools. There are lots of gay parents in precarious situations who can't be out, because it would mean losing their children as these men have. Our strength is in our numbers and our pride. We are as diverse as those numbers. DSS and the legislature have a lot to learn from us. And before this is over, they'll hear it all.

June 11, 1985

Building Alliances for a Stronger Community

Henry C. Chinn

This speech was given at the Human Rights Rally sponsored by the Boston Lesbian and Gay Political Association on June 11, 1985. Chinn was at this time the president of the Black Men's Association, Inc., based in Boston, and a member of the law faculty of Northeastern University. The "recent action" against MOVE (an antitechnology collective advocating a "back-to-nature" lifestyle) that he refers to is the destruction, on May 13, 1985, of the group's communal house in Philadelphia by the city's police force, which caused eleven deaths.

My recent involvement in the gay rights movement has forced me to question my own values and motivations. I would like to share with you some thoughts, observations, and perceptions.

As a Black man, who happens to be homosexual, I am weary of many things. Racism, sexism, economic inequalities, homophobia and at the root of all these problems, ignorance and intolerance and the general purposelessness of life in this society, whose by products for many people have been loneliness, isolation and fear.

I find myself constantly mentally wrestling with these issues. How did humanity arrive at this abyss? Why are most people so insensitive to everything other than themselves? This insensitivity of which I speak has infected every aspect of our society. Boston is heavily populated by people of this type and the gay community is not exempt from this infection. Admittedly, there are individuals who are sensitive, caring and concerned—men and women who reach out and try to make constructive contributions. Yet the quality of life for many people is not what it could be. Human beings have developed many things to make life easier and last longer, but they have not conquered the problems I have mentioned. These problems all involve how people interact and perceive each other.

"Human rights" to me involves more than legal rights. It involves having the kind of environment in which people grow to be constructive, contributing participants in helping to make life better for *everyone.* At this juncture in our movement it is important that we channel our energies into trying to correct the inequities present amongst our own—that is, if we are truly to have a community that communes. The ideal community for me would be one made up of people who are able to exchange thoughts and feelings and be caring and sensitive to all its members regardless of sex, race, economic status or lifestyle. It is the only way we will ever find true peace, happiness and a real sense of community.

The recent comedy of errors (the DSS decision) and the general public's reaction to it only reinforces my concern. It was a reaction based on fear and political expediency. The recent action in Philadelphia against MOVE is another example of insensitivity, fear and political expediency.

The majority of the population is ignorant on the subject of homosexuality. Many people see members of our community only in stereotypes; narcissists, egotists, sexually depraved and perverts. Partly because of these perceptions, we are judged unfit by a hypocritical, dishonest and fearful society led by politicians who have neither courage nor vision.

There is much work to do in the community on these concerns. The focus of most of the larger organized groups in the Boston gay community is political and I think they perform a necessary function. But we also need groups to encourage and create a dialogue to help people become more tolerant, caring and involved in making this community a prototype of what a community should be.

Changing attitudes and perceptions must start with individuals if any real change is to take place. We can try to ignite this desire. We can be the catalyst to correct a situation that presently benefits none of us. We need to rethink our strategies and become more involved with helping each other, as well as involving ourselves in other's concerns. We need to build alliances if we are to succeed. Educating and sensitizing this community is vital.

We can begin by fighting racism in establishments the community patronizes. We can encourage gay businesses to employ people of color—especially when these establishments are located in communities like the South End where many people of color reside. Ignoring others and refusing to relate and understand their problems only creates tensions that would not exist if people were more aware. It only creates the climate we presently live in, giving politicians carte blanche to do whatever they want in order to appease people's fears. The differences between gay men and women must end. Our fear of each other must be eradicated.

We have to be bigger than those who oppose us. We can show others how it can be and should be. The effort must be made. We are no better than those who fear us if we don't rise to the occasion and change the negative, separative and destructive things we see in what is called "our community." It is a major task but not an impossible one if only enough of us will believe it is possible.

In closing I would like to quote a well known leader of Black people, W.E.B. Du Bois:

> So long as the world consists of the fortunate and the unfortunate, the weaker and the stronger, the rich and the poor, true human service will involve ideal and renunciation. If you really have at heart the good of the world, you simply cannot give your whole time and energy to the self seeking of your personal good. You cannot make accumulation of wealth for yourself the sole object of your education and your life. The object of St. Francis of Assisi's work was not to make the world poorer but richer. No doctrine of universal selfishness will ever reform society and lift men to the highest plane, simply because the world is too full of careless unfortunates and incompetent, vicious souls. While you are confining yourself to the work so selfishly raising yourself, these forces are dragging down a dozen of your neighbors and children. You must be your brother's keeper as well as your own, or your brother will drag you and yours down to his ruin.

June 15, 1985

No Regrets

Don Babets
David Jean

This speech was delivered at Boston's Lesbian and Gay Pride March on June 15, 1985. Babets and Jean were gay partners whose two foster sons recently had been removed from their care by the Massachusetts Department of Social Services on grounds of unfitness, triggering a national protest.

Since the very beginning of our ordeal, we have known and trusted that our community would be there to help us through the rough times. We have not been disappointed. Thank you for your outpouring of support and love.

We would like to especially thank the lawyers from the Gay & Lesbian Advocates & Defenders for the work they have done to protect all of our freedoms. We want to say a special thanks to Kevin Cathcart, Sandy Smales and Dr. Nancy Coleman for being not only our attorneys, but also our source of strength, our sounding board and sometimes even our dartboard. But more importantly, we want to say thanks to the folks from GLAD for being our friends. We are very proud to be members of a community that has a legal team like GLAD: strong, affirming and professional. Thank you, GLAD.

We know that the recent actions of the state government have caused a pain in all our souls that will not soon go away. A pain that gnaws at our very hearts and our efforts to build a more just society. We stand together today, all of us, with our dignity and our pride intact. No matter what they take from us they cannot and will not strip us of our dignity.

Caryl Rivers and Alan Lupo recently wrote in *The Boston Globe*—that newspaper we *won't* be buying on June 23—that there is a meanness in the air that does not bode well for any minority in this country or outside its boundaries. As a community, we must continue to press for economic and social justice for the people of South Africa, Central America and the children of Ethiopia. We must always remember that while the state legislators were decreeing our community to be a threat to the well-being of children, members of the Asian and Black communities were being attacked by unelected thugs and hoodlums: that women are still being attacked for demanding the right to control their own bodies.

We cannot strongly enough condemn the forces of hatred and bigotry being mobilized by the agents of ignorance and narrow-mindedness in our State House and in the White House.

It is time for the professional politicians to cease their victimization of innocent women, men and children. We must demand that the backs of lesbians and gay men cease being used as the stepping stone to power for third rate, intellectually dishonest, so-called liberal politicians. We must use all of our resources, our media, our institutions and our votes, to rid this state of politicians who claim to know what is best for our community, as they try to oppress us in their very traditional fashion.

In the past few weeks we have benefited from the strength and solidarity of a proud and determined people. A community we are very proud to be members of. We have no regrets that we tried to ease the pain of two young children caught in the battlefield of the traditional family setting, nor do we have any regrets that we are now "out" to our most distant cousins. Our struggle for an equal standing in the world-at-large will continue, and all of us will prove to the fools on the hill that we are a people of hope, dreams and visions.

We have already proven that we are nurturing, caring and loving. And we have proven that our community, more than the homophobic bigots in the straight community, truly has the best interest of the children in mind when we stand up and say "we too are the world: we too are the children."

June 15, 1985

The Need to Refight Stonewall

Angela Bowen

This address was given by black lesbian activist Angela Bowen at Boston's Gay and Lesbian Pride March on June 15, 1985. She later wrote a doctoral dissertation on Audre Lorde's contributions to three U.S. liberation movements (one being lesbian feminism) and in 1989 received the Fannie Lou Hamer Award for her work for women of color and against racism.

Hello, I'm Angela Bowen, a mother and a writer, and I'm really happy to be here today, and I'd like to tell you a story.

When I was a young, married woman with a year-old baby, I moved with my husband to Connecticut to open a dancing school. One day a social worker called to ask if I could find something for a 14-year-old to do in exchange for dancing lessons. We met, she started babysitting for our son and eventually began staying late for dinner, and later into the evening, obviously hating to return to her foster home at night. When I finally won her confidence enough to find out she was being physically abused by the woman, who used to beat her with a broom handle, and sexually abused at night by the 55-year-old man of the house (an elder in his church, by the way), I told the social worker, who asked us to take her. After persuading a very reluctant husband, I did. She lived with us till she was grown. She's now a 35-year-old mother of two, and says I gave her love and the first respect she had ever had.

Two years after we got her, my husband's first wife died and we acquired his 11-year-old daughter. I legally adopted her, and raised her until she was grown. She's 30 now, with one child.

Now, I was always the main parent of all the children in our house—but when I took in that foster daughter, I was a new mother with an infant, and I was 27 years old, only 12 and a half years older than the teenager I was raising. But that was okay with the state of Connecticut. They pestered, called and kept pressing for the placement all the while I was trying to convince my husband, and looking for a new apartment so she could have a room. I don't recall any examination, but the social worker was extremely impressed with us: The ideal heterosexual couple with a little baby, and just beginning a business. No experience with raising children but—no problem—we'd learn.

The judge who awarded the adoption decree for my stepdaughter also thought we were pretty ideal. He especially commented on my strong character. No problem. You see, I was clearly straight, so I had to be okay.

But now, five children later (and after a few thousand that I've taught as well) if I applied to the Department of Social Services of Massachusetts, I couldn't get a foster child. I'm unfit, says the State. Everything's changed because now I'm aware that I love women. So all the experience I've gained would be as nothing next to that of a young woman just starting out, as long as she had the shadow of a man beside her—whatever his character—willing or unwilling to open his heart to a child, or lying in wait to assault a child, with his cover of heterosexual respectability saving him from the slightest scrutiny. That's how this homophobic society wastes its resources, by throwing us away and wiping out our lives.

That's how they're trying now to wipe out the lives of two good men. Don and David have lived in a steady and loving relationship for nine years, about five times as long as I'd lived in such circumstances, when the state of Connecticut put a child's life in my hands—a child with a very troubled background, who just happened to trust me enough to allow me to help her. But two little boys who were beginning to build that same trust with two men were snatched away by political cynicism.

Much has already been said about the homophobic action of one particular man and the unprincipled reporter who began this witchhunt. So I won't repeat that. What I want to talk about is the potential solidarity this awful incident offers to us all. If some of us have felt alienated from one another, for whatever reasons, all the various factions of the gay and lesbian community can feel solidarity on this one issue, at least. As can all our principled straight friends, families and political allies.

It's a blessing in a way. Because it's made us remember that we'd better be ever-vigilant—no rest for the weary, you know. Just as pro-choice folks have to refight now the abortion battle we thought we were turning around in the 1973 *Roe v. Wade* victory—*we've got to refight Stonewall.* We've just got to pick our weapons carefully.

Just as Blacks are still waging the war on unequal education we thought was on its way [*sic*] when we won the *Brown v. Board of Education* case, *we've still got to refight Stonewall.*

Just as Mary Francis Berry is scrapping to hold the Reagan-revamped U.S. Civil Rights Commission to some measure of accountability as they deliberately chip away at our hardwon gains, *we've got to refight Stonewall.*

And look at Philadelphia—look at Wilson Goode. He's a perfect example of the need for eternal vigilance! The color of his skin lulled the LOVE people into not maintaining their vigilance. They knew what they were dealing with when they had Frank Rizzo. But they forgot that a person who craves to be accepted by the purported "right" people will go to incredible lengths to be included in their game. *Well, we won't. We won't be Wilson Goode* turning our backs on our own humanness! *We won't be Wilson Goode,* turning our backs on our own kind, either—because it's suicide to believe that they'll leave any of us alone.

I can stand up here now because I'm not endangered in the sense that my children are biologically and legally mine. Yeah, I've got my kids now, but they could decide to legislate on biological children being endangered by their own parents. Let's face it, if they come for you tonight and I don't stand with you, they'll be back for me tomorrow. Not one of us is safe, in or out of our closets, until each one of us is legally protected.

We were proud enough to come out today to honor ourselves and our own choices. Some of us barely out, scared, but here. Some stepping a bit more firmly each year, and some of us waaaay out there. For myself, I've been sticking my head further out each year, but I feel daring and proud today because I'm speaking for the first time as an openly lesbian woman.

Yes, we're gay and we're proud, and I'm so happy for all of us smart enough to have figured our way past all the obstacles thrown up to prevent us from finding our natural partners in our own particular order of the universe. But let's also be smart enough to get together and *fight, dammit—fight.* We've got to enlist support. And we *fight.* And we're fighting not only for ourselves, but for all those children waiting hopefully for loving homes that we've already proven we can provide.

Fighting was a way of life in the various Roxbury neighborhoods where I grew up. And the kids in my family were not allowed to start a fight. But we weren't allowed to run away from one either. You could lose one, that was okay, *but your adversaries had better know they'd been in one with you.*

Look at the numbers of us here. Now, we didn't start this fight—but we can let them know they've been in one, right? And the first step is to get registered and be ready for action. Because there is going to be some action!

Before I finish, let me just say that revolutionary movements pass strength to one another, over distance and over time. So I share with you the words and the spirit of a Black transplanted Jamaican poet named Claude McKay. It was written in 1922 and it's called "If We Must Die." Those of us who grew up with these words know that they refer to all who would fight back. And revolutionary that he was, I like to think that if McKay were around today, he would be—like his predecessor, Frederick Douglass—a feminist. So I automatically include women in his exhortations:

If we must die, let it not be like hogs,
Hunted and penned in an inglorious spot.
While round us bark the mad and hungry dogs
Making their mock at our accursed lot.
If we must die, O let us nobly die,
So that our precious blood may not be shed
In vain; then even the monsters we defy
Shall be constrained to honor us though dead!
Oh, kinsmen! We must meet the common foe!
Though far outnumbered let us show us brave,
And for their thousand blows deal one deathblow!
What though before us lies the open grave?
Like men we'll face the murderous, cowardly pack,
Pressed to the wall, dying, but fighting back!

June 15, 1985

Fifteen Years of Pride

Gil Gerald

This address was given at Boston's Lesbian and Gay Pride March on June 15, 1985. At this time, Gerald was the director of the National Coalition of Black Gays.

Happy Lesbian and Gay Pride Day, Boston! It is great to be here—to share with you this festive occasion—as we celebrate fifteen years of Pride.

In these times of mean spiritedness directed at those of us who are poor, lesbian, gay, women, Black, Latino/Latina, Asian, Native American, peace-loving, freedom-loving, all of us who yearn for equality of opportunity for all the groupings of people, yes, all of us, we can derive strength and comfort in the accomplishments of the Lesbian and Gay struggle over the past fifteen years. Ours is not so much a struggle to pass civil rights laws, but more of a struggle to create a community where one did not previously exist. Yes, we have much farther to go as a community of "gentle loving people," but after fifteen years of pride they cannot stop us and we are moving forward.

After fifteen years of many triumphs and some setbacks, we have some measure of our strengths and should therefore be assured that we can confront the difficulties of the moment and the challenges of the next few years. The issue of whether there can be lesbian or gay foster parents will not be laid to rest until the answer is Yes, here in Boston and everywhere.

Here in the city of Boston and in the state of Massachusetts, you have elected such distinguished pacesetters as Elaine Noble, David Scondras, Barney Frank and Gerry Studds. You came as close as anyone to the real thing, as far as coalitions go, in the Mel King Campaign for Mayor. Let us not forget our friends.

By taking stock of our victories, we can begin to define our mission and our goals for the next fifteen years, at the end of which, we will be in the twenty-first century. We should now also acknowledge the shortcomings of our struggle, and continue building a community that is far more responsive to the concept that we can derive greater strength because of our diversity.

Because of our diversity—Black, Brown, Latino/Latina, White, Male, Female—and the fact that we are everywhere, they cannot stop us, Boston!

Looking forward over the next fifteen years, what do we want our community to reflect in the year 2000? For one, we want to see ten times as many people gathered to celebrate Gay Pride, ten times as many of us out of the closet: we want to see not one of us fearing the possibility of losing our jobs, our homes, or having our children taken away from us. We want to see ten times as many people, whether they be lesbian, gay, straight, Black, White or Brown, who have found meaning and relevance in the progress of this struggle . . . and we want our encounter with AIDS to be part of the history books. No, with these goals in mind, they cannot stop us, Boston!

We want to become known as a "Different People"—a people who spurned the conservative, rightward move of the 1980's—who stuck to a progressive course of dismantling institutionalized racism, sexism and classism in our own community and in our society at large. With these goals in mind, Boston, they cannot stop us.

Yes, over the next fifteen years let us accept the challenge of being a "Different People."

A "Different People" because we refuse to be mean spirited in an era when it is being officially sanctioned by our government, a different people because we denied that rising poverty was a measure of progress and prosperity.

A "Different People" because the work of molding our community has only just begun, and we have a unique opportunity to fashion our community in such a way that we have even more reasons to express and feel pride.

A "Different People" because it is the principled and the only viable political course which will make our movement meaningful to the greatest number of lesbians and gays, here and everywhere—to women, who make up more than fifty percent of our community and who seek equal pay and reproductive freedom among other goals, to people of color who make up twenty-five percent of our community nationally and who number thirty-six percent of the community here in Boston, and who wish to end displacement from our neighborhoods by class- and race-conscious economic forces and attitudes. Let us incorporate these goals of women and people of color as the goals of the lesbian and gay community.

Let us become a "Different People" because it offers us the opportunity to seize and be a part of the leadership for a different course in our nation's history. A Different People because we need to rekindle the spirit of Martin Luther King, for whom the dream of a better world could never die. A Different People because as an organized struggle we choose not to deny or neglect our interest in the progress of the struggles for equality for African-

Americans and for women, for the end of apartheid in South Africa, and for decent and affordable housing and health care.

Let us choose to be a Different People—a different community—who will make an indelible mark on history over the next fifteen years, because we did not accommodate our ideological adversaries by marching to the more conservative and militaristic beat of the present times.

Happy Lesbian and Gay Pride Day, Boston!

June 15, 1985

Speaking for Our Lives

David Summers

This speech was given at the Gay Men's Health Crisis AIDS Conference, held at Hunter College in New York City on June 15, 1985. Its text also served as the basis for a second address made by Summers at the Candlelight Vigil on Christopher Street on June 29, 1985, on the eve of New York's 1985 Gay Pride Day celebration. Summers died in 1986. Phil Lanzaratta, who was New York City's first publicly identified PWA (person with AIDS), gave a number of interviews for the media and wrote an account of living with the disease for *Christopher Street* magazine.

When I was asked to make these closing plenary remarks, I had to ask, "What is a closing plenary remark?" Once that was explained to me, I began thinking of a title. I still like my first choice—"You're Gonna Like Us, PWA"—but I think that it's just a little too glib for a serious conference. "Speaking for Our Lives" is more to the point.

I have asked several others to speak to you today. I will tell you about my specific symptoms and their ramifications on my life and those around me, but I would also like to share some observations. I was diagnosed 16 months ago with Kaposi's sarcoma and, fortunately for me, it is not very aggressive right now. I have had Herpes Zoster and I presently have swollen glands, thrush and nightsweats. I am very lucky. I lead a fairly normal life.

As you know, the condition of someone with AIDS can change radically in a very short time. I sometimes feel like a time bomb on a battlefield. As I bury my friends and watch so many deteriorate around me, I wonder "Am I next?" I joined a KS support group at Gay Men's Health Crisis a year ago last March, with eight other men. I am the only original member left.

I do not pretend to have any answers about surviving with AIDS. I will tell you that I am doing everything possible to extend my life and to enrich the quality of my life. The support system I have is quite remarkable. My psychiatrist, Dr. Bertram Schaffner, is a loving and gentle older gay man who is very wise. My chiropractor, Dr. Janiz Minshew, is also my nutritionist, and my KS support group is led lovingly and professionally by Ms. Dixie Beckham.

Vitamins, wheat grass juice, acupuncture, gym workouts, meditation and solitary prayer are all a part of my weekly routine. But it is the love, care and support from my friends and my gay family that really give me the spirit to want to fight for my life. My beautiful lover, Sal Licata, has stood next to me through all of this. The courage of my own convictions is strengthened by his life-giving love for me. I am indeed a lucky man.

AIDS has empowered me in a very odd way. Standing here before you today is one part of my effort to turn a negative situation into a positive one. If you saw the Phil Donahue show last month, you heard me correct him when he referred to me as a "victim." One friend of mine said to me later "You are wasting your time with semantics." I am not wasting my time. Not buying into the victim mindset is keeping me alive. To me "victim" implies helplessness and passivity. At this time in my illness, I am not helpless and I am anything but passive in dealing with it. I can look around and I see incredibly courageous men who inspire me with their strength, men such as Horatio Benegas and Philip Lanzaratta. These men continue to defy the odds and say no to AIDS. They give me hope. They give me strength.

Never has there been a disease more political than AIDS, and while the Koch, Cuomo and Reagan administrations play politics, people continue to die. I recently attended Gov. Cuomo's press conference to declare April as AIDS Awareness Month. The press conference was held on April 21. Why did the governor wait three weeks into the month to announce it? Have you ever noticed that press conferences dealing with gay issues within our governments often take place on Fridays at 3 P.M., such as this one did? There was no press there, with the exception of the *Native* and *The Advocate*. All the city and state AIDS mucky-mucks were there. But where was *The New York Times*? And this was supposed to be AIDS Awareness Month.

I am critical of Gov. Cuomo, and he is the best of the lot. He has put money where his compassion lies. As for Margaret Heckler [U.S. Secretary] of Health and Human Services, she would make a great P.R. woman for Tupperware or Mary Kay Cosmetics. Her artificial sense of a managed crisis shows her concern for the public relations of the disease, but lacks any real compassion for the thousands who are dead and for the thousands who are dying. The federal government's approach has been vaccine, not treatment. Medical infighting and the race for Nobel Prize have caused many Americans to seek treatment in France, Sweden and Mexico. When is the last time you heard President Reagan discuss "America's number one health priority?" He has never once said a word about AIDS.

[Novelist] Bernard Malamud has said "It is not madness that turns the world upside down, it is conscience." Our first priorities here in New York must be education and housing. As long as there are people afraid to touch me, and as long as there are people with AIDS forced to live in YMCAs and welfare hotels, we have much work to do. The heroic work that is being done by Gay Men's Health Crisis, AIDS Resource Center, and the AIDS Medical Foundation, is simply not enough if we are to believe the numbers from the Atlanta Conference. I hesitate to draw this parallel, but our gay brothers and sisters in San Francisco are way ahead of us in many respects. The gay community there has reached out to people with AIDS with generosity and creativity. The AIDS Ward 5B at San Francisco General Hospital was decorated by gay decorators. It doesn't even look like a hospital. As one friend who is a patient there said to me "When we lose our ability to decorate, we have lost everything." In San Francisco, they have a clothing bank, a food bank, Meals on Wheels, free cable TV for all disabled people, weekend trips to the country, massage, Shiatsu. These are just a few of the services available to PWAs there that we don't have here.

You may be asking yourself "What does free cable TV have to do with any of this?" I will share a little secret of my survival with you—quite simply: hope. Having something to look forward to. Having people unselfishly give of themselves, that enables us to feel loved, supported, wanted. These powerful feelings can help us reach the understanding that we are not helpless, that we can help ourselves, that we can heal ourselves. We must have a say in our therapies. The assertion that we do not have to die from AIDS is very, very important. We have the ability to extend our lives and to enrich the quality of our lives, but this is difficult to do alone. We need help. I need help to focus on living with AIDS, not dying with dignity.

It is absolutely necessary to lead as normal a life as possible, to say no to this disease. To exorcise negative feelings, to forgive, to explore meditation, creative visualization, the power of affirmations, nutrition, and most importantly, to love ourselves. Every day I say the same prayer "The Living Spirit is right where I am. Within, around and through me."

The call I want to make to the gay community has already been heard by many of you here today. But, for every one of you here, there are a hundred people who are not, and they are the ones we need to reach. Every act of withholding ourselves is an act of denial that a crisis exists, and there is denial everywhere—not surprising, because gay people have been reluctant even to acknowledge and embrace the cultural heritage that is ours. Some of the brightest and most creative people of the century are gay people living right here in Manhattan in 1985. We must show the world that we care for each other and that we are not defined just by our bodies. We can give each other approval and raise our own self-esteem. I believe this is happening now.

The call I am making today is to gay people in this city who have something to offer and are doing nothing but burying their heads in the sand and saying "AIDS can never happen to me." If you can help, you damn well better get off your ass and help fight the greatest challenge we've faced since Hitler tried to exterminate us. All our lives depend on it.

If you own a gay business, please provide health insurance for your employees. Too many gay men today are facing a health crisis with no health plan or financial resources, and this in the only industrialized society besides South Africa that does not offer its citizens a guaranteed health plan. AIDS has made those of us without health insurance reliant on charity at a time when our dignity is most assaulted.

There are so many ways that healthy gay people can help those of us with AIDS. If you own a restaurant, why not open your establishment one afternoon a week to feed people with AIDS? If you are a clothing manufacturer, an aerobics instructor, a computer analyst, a lawyer, a waiter—it doesn't matter—you have something to offer, and right now is the time to step forward. What is important is to reach out and share.

We must also get beyond our embarrassment and seriously explore healthy sex. The truth is, we are killing each other and it is of primary importance to do everything we can to eliminate the risk of contracting AIDS.

In a few minutes, you will hear a patient bill of rights. For now, I would like to speak to those of you who are well and worried. All that we have is each other. We are all afraid. As I look into your faces, I see sorrow and pain. There is sickness and death all around us. But I also see hope. And it is that hope that inspires me daily to continue our fight—for understanding, equality, justice.

Robert Kennedy's words in Cape Town, South Africa in 1966, apply to us here today in 1985:

> Let no one be discouraged by the belief that there is nothing one man or woman can do against the enormous array of the world's ills—against misery and ignorance, injustice and violence. . . . Few will have the greatness to bend history itself; but each of us can work to change a small portion of events, and in the total of all those acts will be written the history of this generation.

It is from numberless diverse acts of courage and belief that human history is shaped. Each time a man stands up for an ideal, or acts to improve the lot of others, or strikes out against injustice, he sends out a tiny ripple of hope, and crossing each other from a million different centers of energy and daring, those ripples build a current which can sweep down the mightiest walls of oppression and resistance.

If we come away today with anything from this conference—from the speeches, the workshops, the forums—I hope it is the theme of the day. Together, we can make a difference.

1985

Remarks to the Democratic National Committee

David Scondras

At the time he made these remarks, David Scondras was serving as an openly gay member of the city council of Boston, Massachusetts.

I see a party which is lost, attempting to chase after the 24 percent of the American people who voted for Ronald Reagan, rather than address the needs of the 74 percent of the people do not support the mentality of the moral minority. The rules you will fashion ultimately reflect the philosophy we espouse, so I want to address the political philosophy rather than the rules which you are more than competent to fashion.

I speak to you today as an elected public official, a Democrat, and a gay person.

We are here today to discuss fairness, to talk of what our party is about, or what it should be about.

We have a problem, a fundamental problem which is moving our party further from the people, further from its roots, and further from any chance of capturing elections, much less the imagination and vision of a nation.

In an effort to out-Republican the Republicans, the Democratic party has abandoned traditional groups who have looked to them to correct injustice, groups the party now calls "special interests." Today, the cynical reasoning that these groups have nowhere else to turn, no other party to work for, is openly heard. This approach is misguided on two counts:

First, justice is not a peripheral issue; it is the soul of our party. Justice is not political baggage; it is the best way to achieve real power, and the only way to keep it. To repudiate that historic commitment to justice is to repudiate ourselves. To reject our commitment to justice for all, in hopes of short term political gain, is to invite not only ultimate defeat, but also deserved contempt.

Second, the smug taking for granted of a heretofore loyal constituency is plain stupid. When Democrats act like Republicans they force the groups they have abused and ignored to seek other independent channels to seek basic justice.

As gay people, we are sick and tired of "leaders" who want our time, our money, our creativity, our commitment, our work and our votes, but reject us.

When the national party says 25 million Americans do not deserve a caucus within the party; when the state party says one of its most loyal but under-represented groups does not merit party outreach; when the state leadership in effect labels all gay and lesbian people "unfit parents"; when the party remains virtually silent in the face of this nation's number one health crisis; how can we ask gay people to support the party?

How can any group trust a party so willing to dump its commitment to justice for all?

September 15, 1985

Text of the Harvey Milk Memorial Plaque

This piece of gay and lesbian public rhetoric is inscribed on the bronze plaque set up at Harvey Milk Plaza in the Castro Street area of San Francisco and was dedicated on September 15, 1985.

HARVEY MILK
May 22, 1930-November 27, 1978

Harvey Milk Plaza is named in honor of San Francisco Supervisor Harvey Milk, California's first elected official to be openly gay.

In 1973, Harvey Milk opened Castro Camera at 575 Castro Street and moved in to the apartment upstairs. Harvey' s store soon became a center for political meetings and voter registration drives. Through his involvement in neighborhood issues, Harvey earned the title "The Mayor of Castro Street."

As the influx of gay men and lesbians revitalized the neighborhood, Harvey assumed leadership of the Castro Merchants Association. In 1974 he organized the original Castro Street Fair.

In January 1976, Mayor George Moscone appointed Harvey to the Board of Permit Appeals as San Francisco's first openly gay Commissioner. In the 1977 District Election of Supervisors, Harvey was elected to the Board from this District.

Harvey Milk was a representative of a despised minority, yet his lasting triumph is that he championed the rights of all people. In his tragically short term as Supervisor, Harvey authored San Francisco's Gay Rights Ordinance and fought for the causes of women, the elderly, ethnic minorities, renters, environmentalists, union members and neighborhood residents. He also worked to establish district elections and improve public transit. Muni riders remembered him as the first city official to use a Muni Fast Pass every day.

Harvey Milk and George Moscone were assassinated on November 27, 1978. That night 40,000 San Franciscans gathered at this site and proceeded to City Hall in a candlelight march.

Harvey Milk Plaza was dedicated on September 15, 1985 by Mayor Dianne Feinstein, Board of Supervisors President John L. Molinari and Harvey's successor, Supervisor Harry Britt.

"I am all of us!"———Harvey Milk

November 14, 1985

No More Lies!

Darrell Yates Rist

This speech was the final address given at the town meeting called by the Gay and Lesbian Anti-Defamation League (subsequently renamed the Gay and Lesbian Alliance Against Defamation) at the Metropolitan Duane Methodist Church in Greenwich Village, with over 700 in attendance.

In the 50s, when I was a child, I was fascinated with a woman whose name was Sophie. Sophie wasn't like the other ladies whom I knew. She had very short-cropped hair, more akin to dad's than mom's. She never—that I saw—put on lipstick or rouge. She didn't paint her nails, which she kept very short. And, though I don't remember that she ever smelled *bad,* she never smelled exactly sweet, like my mother and her friends, like an overripe perfume.

Sophie didn't decorate herself with jewels. She chose the "no-frills" look. When she dressed up, she wore a shirt and pants that looked like men's, something like the ones my dad wore with his suit. Her shoes were strong, work shoes, shoes to drop a hammer on without an injury.

Sophie liked to hammer. She spent her summers on a ladder in her overalls, fixing up the roof, or gutter, or the siding on her house. And while she worked, the lady whom she lived with brought her snacks and things to drink. Anna. Her hair was long: she put lipstick on. She put red polish on her fine, long nails. Anna draped her neck with strands of pearls. She wore dresses.

The summer I was five, I took to spending afternoons in Anna and Sophie's yard talking, watching. *Wondering,* curious that they seemed married, these two ladies, just like mom and dad. And they seemed *right.* And they made me feel right too. They didn't scold me, like several of the other "couples" on the block. They never warned me not to play with dolls or girls. And, unlike the neighbor men she seemed to me to be like, Sophie *never* called me a sissy.

I liked them. I liked them a lot. That is, until the day my grandma, who lived with mom and dad and me, found out that I'd been hanging out at their place. She was swiftly angry. "Those two old women don't know who they are," she yelled at me. "That Sophie tries to be a man." Grandma pulled me to her knee, now wooing me with kindness. "God didn't mean for women to live together the way they do" she purred seductively, as only grandma could when some ungodly thing had put her in a rage. "They'll have to pay for that in hell. Do you understand?" "Yes, Grandma." "Now you'll stay away from them," she whispered. "*You* see the way those women live. That's sinful and disgusting."

That was a lie, and I believed it.

Some years later, when I'd just turned twelve, a new man joined our little church. He was middle-aged and somewhat fey. He was friendly, but too much. He talked to everyone. He talked to me. He liked to read, and I did too. He told me names of books. And *once,* he bought me one. Mom and dad were livid. "Don't you ever take another thing from that old queer," my father bellowed after we got home. "He'll try to make you just like him. Queers like boys. He'll touch you, treat you like a girl. And once you're touched like that, your life is over. You may as well be dead."

That was a lie, and I believed it.

When I was in college, *LOOK* or *LIFE* or some such magazine did a feature story: "Homosexuality in America." It took pictures at a leather bar—I think the Gold Coast in Chicago. The men looked cold and hard. As they were portrayed, they had no friends. These men were desperate, ruthless sorts whose sexual addiction killed.

For *LOOK* or *LIFE*—or whatever magazine it was—this portrait summed up homosexual leather men, and it summed up homosexuals. The *press,* too had lied, and I, like many others in this room tonight, believed such lies. We spent agonizing years believing lies about ourselves, hideous lies that fed self-hate, that ate away at us until we feared that any minute we would be destroyed. These lies sneered that we are sinful, we are moral blights, we are sick, we are desperate, we're violent, and, more than "normal" people, prone to heinous crime. *Lies* that we recruit young children—and innocent adults, that we cannot love, that we're unlovable; we're sexually obsessed: that we're all promiscuous; that our relationships don't last, that we spread disease, emotional and physical; that good, clean folks can catch perversion or a deadly germ by simply being near us in a room. *Lies.* That we cannot control our genitals, as heterosexuals can. That therefore straight folks must control us that, otherwise, we won't stop copulating as we wish, without a conscience, without precaution, without responsibility, until we've killed ourselves—for we are suicidal—*and* killed others for we are homicidal too. All of these are lies and *we are sick of lies.*

On June 28, 1969, a bunch of drag queens sipping cocktails at the Stonewall in the Village got raided. Not for liquor violations, not for drugs, not for lifting up their skirts to frolic in a back room of the bar, but for congregating. Back then in New York State, homosexuality was illegal as it is in 25 states today. And this was not the first time New York City exercised selectively the enforcement of the law, invading gay bars on a whim. It was just the first time anyone fought back. Barstools, glasses, fists and though I wasn't there, I must imagine purses and high heels, began to fly. The riot went into the streets and lasted three full days, until gay people had a starting point for truth.

More and more of us stepped from our closets, learning everything we could about ourselves, teaching straights, asking insistently that they listen as we, who had known nothing of ourselves but ugly myths, started to discover who we were. We were exuberant. We began exploring homosexuality. Many of us who'd denied ourselves through adolescence, who'd waited until 25 or 35 or older just to admit who we were, many of us who had married in a frightened bid to change, exploded. Our stymied puberties blew out. Many gay men, more than lesbians whose energies were siphoned for the battle with political misogyny—enjoyed an anarchy of passion. Sex, which had been suffocated, now was often unrestrained. The '60s and the '70s were excited days of strait [*sic*] sex liberation. Frantically we rode the crest to find our own.

We learned politics. And, if not all politicians liked us, they soon found out that we were loud, insistent. And in many places we began to get our way—that is, gays and lesbians weren't seeking special treatment, just our share of justice and protection by the law. Not that all the vulgar lies about us ceased, but they *seemed* at times to be contained. Things appeared to change—slowly, haltingly—and then our progress, more and more, took on a steady pace. Those were heady days—gay and lesbian pride from San Francisco to New York, and countless places, we thought, in between. And if we didn't beat Anita in Miami, we fought proudly and we gained respect. *It seemed sometimes that we were free.*

Then, AIDS.

How soon the bigots made the issue theirs, manipulating tragedy with hate. "GRID" they jumped to call it—*Gay* Related Immune Deficiency—as though just what they'd always said was true, that we were not like other human beings and this was proof—our very own disease. Or, more spiteful still, that we were damned because of who we are to suffer tortured, early deaths, a godly retribution. And from the very time this illness was identified, the air has swarmed with lies—in the street, in the press, and in the legislative halls.

Listen to the lies:

AIDS is a gay disease, when in the world-wide epidemic it is straight, striking men and women equally, wherever it occurs in Africa and, as *The New York Times* wrote just last week, spread through "conventional sexual intercourse." *AIDS is not now gay, nor has it ever been.*

Listen to the lies:

Gays, getting buggered by infected boys in Haiti, brought AIDS here. But, as the Centers for Disease Control *too* quietly announced, the first AIDS case was not a gay man in 1979—the mythic epidemic's starting point—but a San Francisco woman in 1976—heterosexual, and IV-drug abuser, three years before a case of "homosexual" AIDS was diagnosed. But addicts often die in slums or in the street, their deaths conveniently and callously ascribed to overdose, whether that's what it *really* was or not. And, as some epidemiologists, even some inside the CDC, confess, if there was one IV-drug related case in 1976, when no one had yet put a name on AIDS, there were many others, maybe hundreds, before one gay man got sick. *However AIDS arrived, gay men didn't start it in their rectums.*

Listen to the lies:

AIDS-infected gay men poisoned the U.S. blood supply. But it was American pharmaceutical companies which in the '70s were buying plasma from Africa, the Caribbean and Central America—from some of the very countries where AIDS is killing rampantly. And, as late as 1982, some of these companies purchased plasma from U.S. prisoners who, according to investigators, had tracks of needle marks running up their arms from recent drug abuse. This was plasma which became the Clotting Factors used by hemophiliacs, whose AIDS infections, and whose deaths, were wholly blamed on homosexuals. But *Gay men will not submit to lies and bear the wretched burden of this guilt.*

Listen to the lies:

That this country cares about our lives, that it is looking for a cure for AIDS as feverishly as it would if the victims of this horror were all straight.

Listen to the lies:

That the U.S. government, the CDC, the medical establishment *grieve* that some 10,000 of us have been stricken, mourn our dead—now more than 5,000—pray that not one more of us will die.

Listen to the lies:

That our sorrow has torn this nation, wrenched it just as horribly as it would if the epidemic were destroying, not gay men, but husbands and their wives.

Listen to the lies:

That this society has any value for our sexuality, our love relationships, our community. That it gives a damn about our civil rights.

Listen to the lies:

That official plans to battle AIDS are not in fact a way to punish us, abrogate our liberties, frighten and control us, take our sexuality away and make us eunuchs, terrify us back into the closet, make us once again invisible as we were before the drag queens started fighting back at Stonewall, make us once again the helpless targets of their lies. And we are saying *no* to all their hateful dreams. We are saying *no* to all their lies.

If we ever doubted what the government and its minions have been up to, within the last few weeks they've dropped their screen and we have glimpsed the reign of terror they have planned. Mario Cuomo and his health commissioner Dr. David Axelrod have unveiled the most insidious of clues. An amendment to the State Health Law which defines "high risk sexual activity" for contracting AIDS as anal intercourse, and flying in the face of all the epidemiology, throws in blow jobs too. A fine sweep. A sodomy statute hiding in a sheep's skin in the health code—and a peculiar bit of homophobic science. Nowhere has a case of AIDS been linked directly to fellatio. But AIDS in women, from Africa to Europe to America has been contracted vaginally. But Dr. Axelrod cannot be moved, for his law was never meant to be good public medicine. If it were, he'd be compelled to regulate vaginas, too. And that won't play politically. So the ploy is to *appear* to fight against this epidemic hard, and to score a couple of points in bashing fags.

But to do this, Mr. Cuomo and Dr. Axelrod had to tell just *half* the truth—the half that vitiates gay sexuality. But we are here tonight to warn the governor and the health commissioner that half a truth is just another lie. *And we are sick of lies.*

Perhaps the government believes that we've been weakened in this epidemic, that our suffering and fear has made us mild. That's not so. And if the bigots and those feeble souls whom they've intimidated think that they can trample on us now while we are mourning for our friends—and many of us for ourselves—they are wrong. For AIDS, while it has made us cry, has made us strong. It has taught us how to fight.

Let this be fair warning. To the ruthless politicians for whom gay men and lesbians have been convenient pawns. To doctors and to epidemiologists whose medicine has grown lethargically and hatefully from seeds of prejudice. To many of the press, who have exploited AIDS and homosexuality to sell their stories, caring nothing for the truth or for the violence they breed against gay men and lesbians. We have not forgotten that *The New York Times* cared very little very late. We do not forget that the *Daily News* still likes to paint gay sex as scandal—as in its headline screaming "Gov Would Ban Risky Gay Sex" and the *New York Post*—we will not be satisfied until this nasty piece of lunacy has folded. There is no place for journalistic filth like that in any sane society.

Tonight is the final notice to the bigots. Many of us had to live a lie too long. But in these years since Stonewall brought us out, we have learned the truth about ourselves, and it is good. *We will not go back*—not to closets, not to shame, nor to fear, *nor to celibacy,* nor to letting heterosexual lies about us rule our lives. Our tolerance is ended. We are no longer begging, *asking.* In the name of all our friends whom AIDS has killed, for the sake of all of us who live, we're demanding: *No more lies. Never again* will we be slaves to lies.

November 27, 1985

San Francisco City Hall Speech

Cleve Jones

This speech was delivered on the steps of San Francisco's City Hall on Thursday, November 27, 1985, the seventh anniversary of the murders of Mayor George Moscone and Supervisor Harvey Milk, following a memorial march. Cleve Jones cofounded the San Francisco AIDS Foundation in 1982 and originated the idea of the NAMES Project AIDS Memorial Quilt.

Seven years ago tonight, San Francisco Mayor George Moscone and Supervisor Harvey Milk were murdered in their City hall offices by former Supervisor, former police officer Dan White. That night we marched, forty thousand of us, from Castro Street to City Hall and the flames of our candles filled this plaza with light. We would return six months later, on May 21, 1979 when Dan White was convicted of manslaughter and sentenced to just five years in prison. But that night we did not march in silence and the light that filled this plaza came not from candles but from burning and exploding police cars.

All that is history now. The players are dead, we remain.

The candlelight march is an annual opportunity for us to face our community's loss together in a spirit of strength, love and hope. Above all else, this march is a symbol of hope.

I stood on these steps the night Harvey and George died.

Like you, I cried.

Like you, I have cried a lot in the seven years that have passed since November 27, 1978.

I cried for Bobbi Campbell.

I cried for Gary Walsh.

I cried for Jon Sims.

I cried for Tod Coleman.

I cried for Frank Cook.

I cried for Joe Schmall.

I cried for Nick Paris.

I cried for Allen Estes.
I cried for Mark Feldman.
I cried for Paul Castro.
I live in San Francisco and I can't cry anymore.

Now I fear it is your turn to cry, America. Now it's your turn to pace the hospital corridors, now it's your turn to wait up all night, now it's your turn to count the days, now it's your turn to wonder why.

And though I cannot cry for you, my heart grieves for you—for your mothers and fathers, your lovers, husbands, wives and children. For now you will know what we have known for the past four years. And you're going to wonder why.

Well, you need not wonder long, for the simple truth of this tragedy is as clear to me as the sun shining up at dawn. It's so simple even the smallest children dying from transfused blood in the Midwest can understand it easily: "LET THEM DIE."

That was the decision in Washington and Atlanta.

Those are the words whispered in the cloakrooms of Congress.

Those are the words emblazoned in the silence over the White House today.

Those are the words screaming behind the smiling face of the Secretary of Health and Human Services.

Those are the words echoing through the closets and hallways of Governor George Deukmejian's administration: "LET THEM DIE."

But let's not talk about tomorrow, America. This is what we want:

We want to live, without fear of violence, without need for deceit.
We want decent jobs, free from discrimination.
We want homes to live in.
We want our families.
We want to be healthy, and cared for if ill or dying.
We want to live.
That is all we want, America, are we so different from you?

And now our numbers have been diminished and many here among us have been already condemned to an early and painful death. But we are pledged to the memory of those who have fallen and those who will follow—to see this struggle through to the end.

And if the day should come when only one here tonight remains—one person with a voice, a heart and two strong arms—then even on that sad day the fight will continue.

We are the lesbians and gay men of San Francisco. For two decades we have been on the forefront of an international struggle to liberate homosexual people from intolerable prosecution, part of a movement that has profoundly transformed the lives of millions of gay men and lesbian women throughout the world.

Tonight we remember Harvey Milk and George Moscone.

Tonight we renew our pledge to Harvey's dream: a dream of a time and a place when lesbians and gay men of every age, race and background would stand together, taking their rightful place among the ranks of decent people everywhere who seek a world of peace and justice and freedom.

We are these people.

We send this message and we send out love to all people with AIDS everywhere: gay and straight, black and white; and to all our gay brothers and sisters who remain isolated and powerless; and most especially we send this message and our love to all the small children who are even now growing up gay in a land of sorrow and fear.

We send this message to America: We are the lesbians and gay men of San Francisco, and though we are again surrounded by uncertainty and death, we are survivors, we shall survive again, and we shall be the strongest and most gentle people on this earth.

1985

A Challenge to Gay and Lesbian Leadership

Rosemary Dunn Dalton

These remarks were made by Dalton, former chair of the Boston Lesbian and Gay Political Alliance, at its last quarterly meeting of 1985.

For the last year I have served as a facilitator for the discussions and actions taken by the Alliance and I am pleased to share my findings with you regarding the year's activities and my conclusions regarding leadership.

As you know, this past year it was our desire to open up the organization. This had more to do with the way the Alliance was perceived than with numbers or geographics. When I took office the main criticism had been that the organization was elitist and had made decisions that were generally not supported in the community at large. I'm not sure how accurate some of those criticisms were because in policy the organization did not shut others out, but may have done so in practice. It had been a very turbulent time around the Scondras and Mel King campaigns and the net result was that many people came away hurt and alienated—*including* those who were in leadership. I have wanted to continue to acknowledge their work even though we have deliberately said that we represented a change from some of those previous decisions.

As for our successes this year, we too have enjoyed a limited amount of success, simply because it takes longer than a year to develop trust in our community. Last year at this time, Holly Ladd, Mark Johnston and David Scondras spoke on behalf of real coalition-building and many of their suggestions were implemented. We have been working more closely with the progressive organizations, especially during convention time and in response to the foster care policy. We are seen as an organization that supports a progressive agenda because of our attempts to develop an awareness of the concerns of dispossessed people, especially on behalf of those gays and lesbians who are disenfranchised by inequities of sex, race, class, culture and disability. We need to continue in this work.

As for the coming years as they relate to leadership in our community, I feel the openly gay and lesbian elected officials said it well in their ideological statement issued to the press regarding the need to work on behalf of basic human rights for all.

A Need for Gay Officials

At their first conference for openly gay and lesbian elected officials, it became clear that our community needs to better develop a vision of the way we want life to be and we need to insure that our leadership carries that message to all places of power. This was reinforced when Sue Lovell, President of the Houston Gay Political Caucus, spoke about how the lack of openly gay and lesbian officials hurt them many times during the past year as they lost a referendum and were eventually eliminated from the Human Rights Ordinance as a protected class. She iterated over and over the strong relationship between their defeats and the fact that there were no openly gay and/or lesbian elected officials there to defend them. The liberal coalition with straights collapsed.

In addition, when we applied some of the Houston lessons to Boston, it became apparent again that we need to do more to encourage our own people to run for office; we need to pave the way for them to do that. People like Fred Mandel, Tim McFeeley, Ray Gottwald, Connie Apple, Mark Johnston, Kevin McFadden, Peg Lorenz, Arlene Isaacson. We must put into motion organizations that will insure that our own are given a real chance to succeed. We need a Political Action Committee to finance campaigns and lobbying efforts.

This year we must anticipate that the Dukakis people may try to block us from being elected as ward delegates to the Democratic convention. We need to make sure first that our people do in fact run for ward positions and go to the convention. This means we must begin now to examine our wards and precincts to see who is there and encourage them to get a slot at the convention. We also need to do something very visible at the convention to highlight our presence there; perhaps hold a press conference as a Lesbian and Democratic Club, stating our positions.

A Stronger Lesbian Presence

We must continually reach out to lesbians in a specialized way to insure their participation in electoral politics. It may mean *paying their way.* I was impressed this year whenever I was approached to make sure I could *afford* to chair the Alliance; and by David Scondras who actually insisted he put up the front money to pay my way to the West Coast conference. Lesbians who are political or grass roots organizers like the women of the Gay and Lesbian Defense Committee or former lobbyist Peg Lorenz do not have the financial resources and need subsidy. This should be *openly* discussed to root out the sexism within our own community that often assumes that women do not need affirmative action to insure their participation. Lesbians must be part of setting the agenda. There needs to be stronger lesbian presence in all of the campaigns, in all of the offices of those who say they support gay and lesbian rights. As suggested at our lesbian caucus open house, politicians should be polled to see what they are doing to increase lesbian participation.

Lesbians and gay men who are parenting bring a very important quality to political life and we can institute ways in which to encourage more to join us in the political arena. They have the experience of loving another unconditionally (a child) and often this has taught them to give up their egos at crucial times for the sake of others—a quality that is sometimes lacking in our movement. We need leaders who are committed and are less self-seeking. Mothers and fathers often demonstrate that ability.

We need the sense of community that people of color bring—a consciousness born out of a common oppressor, white institutionalized power. They bring to us a perspective of understanding the oppression that accompanies power in whatever form it takes; and also a compassion that runs deep.

Hopefully, it will be this year that our community activists and leadership will begin to discuss the realities of the financial crisis we are experiencing on a local and a national level. Our national organizations are deeply in debt and when we look to our elected officials to help, they reply that they have their own campaigns to finance.

The Needs of Our Community

It is time our Boston community representatives engage in a round table discussion to figure out a way to finance our health center, counseling services, and political organizations, in conjunction with the tremendous drain resulting from the AIDS crisis. Ideally, all aspects of our community can be tied together inextricably so that we understand that we cannot succeed if AIDS is seen as separate from the political, from the election of openly gay and lesbian candidates and the placement of key appointments at the political level. AIDS phobia is a crucial civil rights issue as more and more people are isolated from the loss of friends, free medical care, insurance, employment, housing and other services.

Our national and local newspapers need funding; without an organ in our movement we cannot reach the less privileged, the remotely closeted, the disenfranchised. It provides for us a place to debate what it means to be gay and lesbian in the world; we need our newspapers to facilitate open criticisms of power and how we use it; and mostly, how to get it.

It is time we acknowledge the need for a community center that is well staffed and well financed. To continue this drivel about the impossibilities of a gay and lesbian community center is divisive and self-serving. When I visited the Los Angeles Service Center and saw that it had programs for vets, handicapped, youth, counseling, lesbians, employment, outreach and a AIDS Committee arm, it was clear that we have models from which to draw. There is another in Baltimore, in Seattle and one being established in Alabama. To deny this need for our own community insinuates that we cannot work together and this is a need that transcends personalities and power turfs. Hopefully, we will instigate a planning committee to begin to organize such a center. It is time to stop belittling our abilities and, instead, enhance our potentiality as a community.

Learning from the Past

My impression of the community, locally and nationally, is that we have engaged in the process of criticism, self-criticism before we established a real foundation of support from which to spring. We can learn from the past and now work to empower only those who can envision a future of embellishing our abilities and strengths, even while we engage in a debate about our different approaches to change. We must acknowledge that like any other group of people we can and will make mistakes; we are not perfect and it is in making mistakes that we develop and grow.

Personally, I feel it is time that we *insist* that our leadership be able to extend to others—some people do not even speak or acknowledge others in public; this is totally unacceptable as a model for leadership. Development of those who are younger, less empowered, economically disadvantaged, and who want to work is the key to our success. Gay and lesbian activists, appointments and elected officials must openly and willingly share information, extend to others, and be models for the community that politics does not mean developing a personal power base for only the chosen few but that power can be shared among many.

For me, the motto "don't get mad, get even" represents a vision that has for too long been perpetuated by a destructive straight male ideology and something we do not need to emulate. Part of reaching out to others to expand our community and political base is to share our vulnerabilities and face our fears, not to cover them up or to punish others for showing theirs. One of our strengths as lesbian and gay people is that we are different: we dare to love others of the same sex.

A Delicate Balance

The Municipal Elections Committee of Los Angeles (MECLA), a gay organization, recommended that gay bath houses be closed. This was a very controversial decision. (Boston settles things differently; here the gay bath house was burned out last year.) It may, indeed, be necessary to monitor ourselves as illustrated, for example, in the safe sex campaigns, etc. However, we must not lose sight of the delicate balance required to maintain our civil liberties and to also act responsibly. Asexuality need not be the imperative; rather, new expressions of sexuality may transform us.

There is a sense of powerlessness that emerges whenever decisions are made in a vacuum in our community, when our input is not solicited. The Mayor's office is the key to many of our neighborhood and community successes. While we can congratulate our former and present liaisons for their work on behalf of the Mayor' s office; personally, I would like to see more concrete and visible outreach instituted by the office of the liaison. A program that would insure the diversity of input and one that facilitates a two-way communications system. Perhaps quarterly receptions, neighborhood gatherings, a newsletter and/or a regular column in our newspapers, a question and answer forum of sorts, would help alleviate the communication gaps.

There is presently a movement to establish state-wide contact with gays and lesbians in Massachusetts communities. Combined with a Political Action Committee, this would provide a path to untapped funds that are often directed to campaigns for candidates that do not return the favor at voting or advocacy time.

Governor Dukakis has been consistently rude to the Boston area lesbian and gay political leadership. Both he and/or his staff have repeatedly acted irresponsibly with people like myself, Ray Gottwald, Dermot Meagher, Fred Mandel, Helaine Simmonds. All of these representatives have emerged in good faith in attempts to gain access to the Dukakis administration. A strategy needs to be developed. The question is: How do we make a statement to an administration that will be around for another five years, a statement that will be understood as significant? In what ways can we compromise without compromising ourselves? Dukakis supports AIDS funding; will he support an executive order that insures the rights of AIDS survivors?

BL/GPA Goals

As for BL/GPA, hopefully this will be the year when we can pay our Chair a stipend that will enable him or her to establish a real funding base of salaries, support staff, a computer and an office. A fundraiser needs to be on board and membership dues and contributions increased. With the energies in this room, we can accomplish anything, but there must be a funding base.

In conclusion, our greatest challenge is the impact of AIDS and AIDS phobia. It is imperative that mandatory reporting of HTLV-3 testing not be instituted (as it is now in Colorado). We also need to prepare ourselves for the possibility of introduction of quarantine legislation being introduced by the Massachusetts legislators. In the meantime, as a movement we must continue to engage in the present system but begin to have less investment in the present power structure, as we know it. We are about the business of changing the nature of power. We are building a new majority, a new base, one that involves urban coalition-building. We are developing a new set of relationships just by our very presence in the political community. It is not one that is based on male dominance over the vulnerable, but one that removes the barriers to communication between people. We are shedding the invisibility that has prevented our full participation and the opportunity to humanize the culture.

1986

Remarks by 1985 Mr. Leather to the Courts

Richard Hennigh

The "courts" referred to in this address are the organizations of men who performed in drag, whose annual shows served as fund-raisers for designated charities. Hennigh won third place in the International Mr. Leather contest for 1985. He died of AIDS on April 20, 1987.

I wish to speak to you tonight not as a representative of one community to another, but simply as a gay man who has been living with AIDS for the past seven months. I want to tell you that my experience has been powerful and enlightening.

I am sure you are all aware that the AIDS crisis has generated an atmosphere of fear, hate and distrust, both inside and outside our community. I am here to tell you the opposite is also true. I have personally experienced love and support from individuals and groups of people from all over the country, indeed from all over the world.

It is my belief that the present health crisis has provided us with the tools we need to truly live and love together. The door to our destiny is now open before us. We now have the keys to our new life: ONENESS. I believe that we should bring all of our efforts together to work for unity and that we should take every opportunity to affirm togetherness, family and community. None of us can move any more rapidly than all of us, for now that we understand our unity as a family we can accept the joy and the suffering of all humanity as our own and thus unify our people.

I ask you to evaluate all of your plans and actions in terms of unity. We can proceed no further until we learn to move as a whole. Recent political and cultural events have forced us to gather together. To share. It has become very advantageous to share living quarters, transportation, fuel and food. I don't believe these events are accidental.

The lessons of the world are now directed towards coming together. We have become accustomed to living in isolation and separation. Separation exists not in the physical world, **but in the mind.** The lessons of this time are given to correct these false notions of boundaries. We are **not** apart from others, nor could we ever be.

Act united, feel integrated and practice oneness, for union is the truth that heals. I believe that the healing it can accomplish will go far beyond any individual such as myself.

Whether one believes that he or she has forty years in which to live or four months, I encourage you all to find value in life **in the present.**

Stop and smell the roses.

Listen to the music.

Learn to love yourself and in turn learn to love each other . . . for life is truly precious and a positive experience.

I feel like a very lucky man and my gratitude goes far beyond anything I could say to you tonight.

Together we will realize the vision we share—to ease the painful effects of this disease while efforts continue to find a cure.

Together we will continue to care, support and fight until we win.

Take care of each other, "play safe" and be of good cheer.

God bless you all—I love all of you.

I thank you all from the bottom of my heart—for being a part of my life.

April 29, 1986

Address to the Dorian Group

Jeff Levi

This is the speech given by Jeff Levi, at that time director of the National Gay Task Force, to the Dorian Group, Washington State's gay and lesbian advocacy organization, on April 29, 1986. The two referenda referred to here are Referendum 7 and Initiative 490. The first would have repealed Seattle's Fair Housing Ordinance of 1985; the second declared homosexuals "deviants" and denied them jobs at any level of local government.

Talks like this are supposed to have themes. As I was thinking about the political situation you face here—and more generally the state of the lesbian and gay movement—I thought the most appropriate description of where we are is the old saying—Just because you're paranoid doesn't mean people aren't out to get you. This should have a special meaning to a community that faces two referenda in the same election cycle. Election campaigns are not cheaper by the dozen.

We in Washington D.C. often think we are at the center of the universe. We are perhaps second only to New Yorkers in our self-centered view of the world. (As someone who grew up in NY, I can get away with saying that—but it makes for a fairly schizophrenic ego, I suppose.) But Washington State—as opposed to D.C.—is probably all the proof you need that more and more of the battle for gay and lesbian civil rights is occurring at the state and local level. We who are working at the national level can have a major impact on that struggle—I wouldn't be with the TF [Task Force] if I felt otherwise—but little will ultimately be won or preserved unless our state and local groups are strong and successful.

When you're in the middle of a campaign such as ours here, it is often hard to see all the good that can emerge from so much pain. I'd like tonight to try to offer some of that perspective—both in terms of your initiative campaigns and the impact of AIDS on our community and our movement. In the process, I hope to tell you something about the TF and how it does its work.

WSJ [The Wall Street Journal] last week—article impact of AIDS on gay polls—Conservative stand publication, reached the conclusion that:

> *Despite widespread public concern about the AIDS epidemic and pressure by some elements of the New Right, political experts see little evidence of erosion in the gains gay people have made in politics and public tolerance over the past two decades.*

The article goes on to quote a Republican campaign consultant who said:

> "Gays are one more thing we've accepted about our political landscape, like long hair and feminists."

How many here thought their real responsibility in the referenda campaign was to prove accurate the *WSJ* and a Republican campaign consultant? Well, it is.

This referendum campaign you're in-—and it's all of our fight, not just yours—provides, believe it or not, a tremendous political opportunity for the community. Win or lose—you will emerge better organized with more people involved in politics than ever before. One of the banes of our existence as political activists is convincing our gay brothers and sisters that politics is relevant to their lives. This is not the best way to be proven correct, but it certainly wakes people up.

In a campaign such as this there is room for everyone—from the street organizer to the number cruncher. Everyone can be given a sense of purpose, a sense of being part of a community or a battle. This is a fight for our rights—we must not disempower individuals in the process of improving a community.

But the opportunity this campaign offers you—that no other political effort can—is the chance to bring the lives of gay people—the real live thing—into the homes of every citizen of Seattle and Washington. There is a certain irony in the fact that in fighting for civil rights legislation we are asking to make our sexual orientation irrelevant—but in order to achieve that end, we must first make our sexual orientation relevant. But we shouldn't be afraid of that. This referendum gives us a chance—a motivation—for us to come out to our friends and families and neighbors—something that often frightens us for fear of rejection—but it shouldn't. There's polling data that shows that irrespective of any other demography—Open vs. Suspect.

One of the things we [do] at the TF each time we lobby is give a homo 101 course to those we are meeting with—about our legal, social, economic vulnerability in American society. It never ceases to amaze me how effective straight society has been in closing their eyes to our oppression. This campaign gives you the chance to give the homo 101 course to thousands of your neighbors. If you believe in our cause, then you can't help but conclude that this will help, not hurt us—especially in a city and state that, unlike Houston, for example, has a history of tolerance.

From a broader perspective, there is another significant political opportunity that if seized will outlast this campaign. One of the things that changed San Francisco politics—not gay politics but city politics after the Briggs Initiative was the permanent coalitions that were built by the gay community with labor, with feminists, with other minorities, with the Democratic Party. If seen as a threat to mutual interests, then this campaign can give the gay and lesbian community the chance to become an equal partner in the political culture.

If the *WSJ* is right—and if your victories in September and November are indicative—if gays (and lesbians—*WSJ* has not found gay women just yet) can become just part of the political landscape—then we've seen a very dramatic and positive change that is a reflection of the successful hard work of so many of us—nationally and locally.

I would like to think that the work of the NGLTF has had something to do with it. And so, for a moment, I'd like to give you a sense of the role the TF plays in the community and in representing the community to the world at large.

We are a civil rights advocacy organization—someone has perhaps more aptly described us as a barking dog, but we must elevate that notion to a somewhat higher status, a more academic plan, and say that we advocate for the gay and lesbian community everywhere: with the government, with the private sector, at the national level, and in the assistance we provide state and local groups, at the state and local level as well. Let me briefly tell you how this has played out in terms of the AIDS crisis.

Since the beginning, TF has been there—representing the interests of the gay community before the government or the media really knew who the gay community was, that it might even have representatives. From the first meeting on blood donor screening to the fight over mass testing now, we've been there. Over the years we've established a level of access and credibility that is unmatched by any other group. It has been our consistent professional representation to the government that now makes it impossible for the Public Health service to make major policy on AIDS without consulting with—though not always listening to—the TF. It has been our knowledge of the issues that has made us a resource to many of the key congressional offices working on AIDS and has made even conservative Republicans feel that if they are to understand the meaning of the AIDS crisis, they must consult with the representatives of the gay community.

This credibility carries over to the private sector as well. We have successfully taught a number of organizations involved with AIDS and AIDS policy making that they can benefit from the experience of the gay community with this crisis.

Our work with the media over the last few years, I would submit, has been instrumental in assuring for the most part a positive portrayal of our community in this crisis. The TF, through its media program, has become a resource for reporters and producers who are still trying to find their way to understanding an important story, the subjects of which seem such a mystery to them.

We are attempting to use our access at the national level to empower the entire community-led fight for dollars to locals for education groups—not just because they're the most qualified and competent, but because this could be used to build our local institutions. Let me shift gears slightly again, and talk in a broader sense of the impact AIDS has had on our community and our movement. In talking about the irony of having to first make our sexual orientation relevant in order to render it irrelevant in government and social policy I was reflecting one of the original precepts of the traditional gay/lesbian civil rights struggle: that we want to get the government out of our lives. AIDS has transformed that and certainly made our relationship with the government more complicated: we have gone from asking the government to stay out of our lives to demanding that it step in and save our lives. That requires a very different political strategy—one that all political groups have been grappling with at every level.

We can—and should—look at our community's response to AIDS as a model of volunteerism, of a community gearing up and helping its own.

But the AIDS crisis, unfortunately, also provides a model for the failure of the American political and public health system—a failure to respond to the needs of a significant minority group, in part because of who we are—not always out of willful homophobia, but certainly out of willful ignorance. By the 1988 election more Americans will have been diagnosed than died in the Vietnam war. When you look at it in such stark terms—the failure of the system to respond becomes clearer. When you think of the social dislocation associated with the Vietnam War—and then realize that we, as ten percent of the population, are absorbing most of that dislocation—our community's strength in coping with this crisis becomes more impressive.

AIDS has brought into our active community far more people than we old-time politicos were able to inspire. They are responding to a health crisis. We have a responsibility to make sure that they come to understand the connection between our being in a health crisis and our status—legal, political and social as gay men and lesbians—a connection between our status—and the government's failed response to AIDS.

There was a time when SSA, NIH, etc. have not been issues young, white middle class gay men have thought part of their agenda, Now it is—it is a golden opportunity to bring them into a broader political agenda—one that includes health issues, women's issues, economic issues, minority issues. If we do not help our brothers make that connection, we will have missed a tremendous political opportunity and will have weakened our efforts in the future to a point that would allow another crisis of this magnitude to occur.

It is with this in mind, then, that I think we must realize the degree to which AIDS has become a metaphor for all the oppression that gays and lesbians face and that therefore, devoting so much attention to AIDS has not diminished our strength in carrying on other aspects of our struggle. AIDS has come to pervade every aspect of our struggle—whether in fighting sodomy laws or fighting for the custody of our children. And it brings into focus all the issues we have been raising over the last fifteen years. The homophobia that is being fueled somewhat by AIDS does not distinguish by gender or by antibody status. The lives of gay men are at stake—and the rights of all gay people, men and women, are in jeopardy because of this crisis.

We are often told, in raising civil liberties concerns, in the context of AIDS that we must not place civil liberties above public health. I would respond—and hope we never waver in this regard—that good public health requires a healthy respect for civil liberties. To control any disease, especially a disease like AIDS, requires the cooperation of those who are at risk. If policies are initiated that threaten their liberties, the disease and efforts to control it will be driven underground. That is bad public health policy and will exacerbate, not improve the situation. We cannot and must not be embarrassed by raising these issues—because whether others appreciate it or not, we are the ones who are providing the greatest insights into how to solve this problem. We must remind our critics in the strongest possible terms that we as a community know better than any other could possibly imagine—the horror and toll that AIDS exacts from us; this is not some abstract discussion of public policy we are participating in—which it is for many who attack us—it is our lives that are at stake and how dare they suggest that we would oppose measures that might save lives. And frankly, when this disease becomes more a problem in the heterosexual community, there will be many who will be glad that we were at the cutting edge in fighting to protect the rights of those who are at risk to AIDS.

It is probably not necessary to go into the substance of the threats that arise in the name of public health: mass testing—pressuring people into taking a test without full regard to the consequences that taking this test might have in employment, insurance, and other areas; pressuring us when this should be a very individual decision—particularly since there is no medical intervention for those who test positive and there is no proven correlation between knowing antibody status and changing behavior. The push for mass testing I think is indicative of the hysteria that exists even in the public health community. Public officials feel a tremendous pressure to be doing something about this disease—even if our options are, in fact, limited. We as a community know that education works in changing behavior and thus reducing transmission of the virus. But that is too amorphous an approach to appease a nervous public. Testing is measurable; we can count the number of people tested—though just as with education we cannot count the exact number of people who have changed their behavior as a result of the test, the only outcome that matters. We cannot allow public health officials to deceive themselves and the public into thinking that something is being done about a problem when in fact they are diverting resources from approaches that work—even if safe sex education makes them nervous. It's our lives that are on the line: they'll just have to cope with a little nervous tension.

The irony is that those advocating mass testing often follow this up with proposals for reporting of test results to state officials and contact tracing—and even quarantine—all suggestions that make individuals less likely to be tested because the negative consequences become higher and higher. Logic has never been the strong point of public officials, it seems.

In fighting these initiatives, we must also never underestimate our strength. As you may recall, the health commissioner in Texas withdrew a quarantine proposal because, he said, the opposition from the gay community was so strong that he could not afford to lose their cooperation in the larger fight against AIDS. Texas is hardly a state where gays have control of the political system. We have the added strength of knowing more about the government than they know about us. We've been watching them for some time—you tend to learn a lot about your oppressor. But they are just discovering us—so they underestimate us and are generally ignorant about where we are coming from. We must never forget that the government needs us as much as we need them to control this disease—and when the chips are down we must not be afraid to play that card.

There is one chip that the government has that we must not allow ourselves to be seduced by. For the first time, our community institutions are going to be getting significant amounts of money for AIDS services—ultimately, every state will be providing them, if not of their own doing then as pass throughs for federal funds. That is a change that, as I said, improves our relationship with government that is ultimately for the better—but we cannot allow the government to use the carrot of funding to procure a compromise on fundamental civil rights issues affecting our community. Those organizations or leaders who play into the game of using government money to divide and conquer are not truly our organizations or our leaders.

In every community across the country, we are fighting for our lives. One of the tragedies of this struggle is that others are forcing us to divert our attention and scarce resources from saving lives to protecting our rights. And yet, those rights must be protected in order to save lives. If that combination does not make us angry—nothing will. But we must translate that anger into effective political action—action that will finally end the New Right's efforts to prevent us from being equal partners in the American society. You will do that in September and again in November. With those victories in hand, I hope you will join in spreading that good fortune elsewhere. Gay men and women across the country are counting on you to give our cause the shot in the arm we need so much.

May 3, 1986

Lesbians and Children: The Community We Create

Cindy Rizzo

The conference referred to is the Lesbians and Children Conference held in Boston in May 1986 and sponsored by the Lesbians Choosing Children Network, a Boston-area community group.

As we planned this conference, we became involved in the detailed work of putting together this day—who could we get to speak at a certain workshop, how many flyers to print, and whether or not to make t-shirts (we decided not to). In the back of our minds, and often more directly, we knew that there were larger issues we wanted to raise, issues that deal with the global impact about what we as lesbians, who have included children in our lives, are doing, and what are our visions for our community and for the world.

We hope that the information sharing and the networking that takes place today, will lead to future discussions about these larger issues. For surely that fact that lesbians are having and raising children in increasing numbers is a political phenomenon. Some fear that our growing involvement with kids will somehow depoliticize us and that the choice to raise a child is a "personal solution" that is being made in the larger context of the rightward shift in this country. Others feel that raising children can't help *but* politicize us, as many of us must begin to deal with issues of childcare, education, child safety, and the economics of either single motherhood or coparenting arrangements that have little or no legal recognition.

There are a variety of ways that we have and are including children in our lives: as mother, aunt, grandmother, big sister, teacher and friend. Each of these families and new arrangements are political since as outsiders in this society, we must continually assert the fact that *we are here* and we will follow our feelings and visions holding onto what we need and throwing out the rest. As we teach children, we are changing the world, passing on our feminist, antiracist, class conscious, and antiwar values. And as we have seen from the frightening world events taking place these last few weeks, our common sense and caring approach is desperately needed. Finally, we can point to the fact that our day to day lives and struggles are political. We do not have and raise children in a vacuum. We must deal with a world that pays us less, thinks of us as "other" (especially if we are not white or middle class) and often despises our very existence. This is our reality as lesbians generally, and especially as lesbians with children.

We need a place for those of us with kids and those of us now choosing to have children to be able to bond together on issues of common interest and begin as well to understand our great diversity. We also need a place for women who choose not to include children in their lives to dialogue with those of us who do. Can we bridge the fear and mistrust and exist as one community? Can we pause long enough to listen to one another's stories?

Some of us have experienced the pain felt by lesbian mothers who came out before and since Stonewall when our community did not open up to include them and their children. It is time to turn that situation around and to open our community to mothers and to children. In fact, it is embarrassingly long overdue. What new institutions can we create to nurture children of lesbians? What community rituals can we create to pass on feminist values? What kind of impact can we make on the next generation in order to build on the work we have done and to make the world a safer and more compassionate place? These are the questions we are beginning to ask. The answers are as rich and diverse as our varied backgrounds and experiences.

No matter when we came out and when we had our children, we are all pioneers. It is an exciting time, because, like our young children, many of us are taking our first steps into all sorts of new places, having to struggle about every part of the process. There are few if any lesbian herstory books we can turn to and only a handful of resources that are available. We ourselves are the only resources we have. And, so, we will keep talking at conferences, in support groups, in schools and day care centers. Our lesbian identity is our strength and our community is a lifeline. Together, with our children, we can make profound changes.

May 12, 1986

Answering the Call

Richard C. Failla

This address was given by Failla, at that time an openly gay criminal court judge of the city of New York, at the awards banquet held at the Plaza Hotel by the Fund for Human Dignity. He was awarded the Howard Brown Memorial Award. Howard Brown was the physician who was appointed by Mayor John Lindsay as New York City's first health services administrator. The story of his coming out in 1973 is told in his autobiography, *Familiar Faces, Hidden Lives*. WNET is New York City's public television station.

When the people from the Fund for Human Dignity called to tell me that I would be receiving this award, they also told me that I would be expected to address you. Over the past number of weeks, I have felt very conflicted about what I would say to you. These events are supposed to be celebratory in nature, and the people at the fund have worked hard to make this an enjoyable evening. Yet in thinking about my remarks and the theme of the evening, "Answering The Call," my feelings were more of anger and frustration than of joy. From my perspective, these are just not joyous times.

I am, therefore, going to ask you to indulge me as I address these feelings of anger. Let me hasten to add that these feelings in no way lessen the value I place on receiving this award. And to put you somewhat at ease, let me inform you that I am to be followed by a very talented and exuberant performer who will lift all of our spirits.

But back to the things that are making me feel angry. I will list only a few, but as I do so, I feel confident that each of you could add to this list your own grievances, and that, collectively, it could go on *ad infinitum.*

State Senator Marchi and his treatment of the memory of Peter Vogel *makes me angry!*

Bathhouse regulations that are homophobic rather than truly aimed at disease prevention *make me angry!*

Insurance companies that are doing their damnedest to redline gay men *make me angry*!

A bishop in Brooklyn who has done a sudden reversal in his public attitude towards our community and a Cardinal in Manhattan who probably had much to do with this reversal in attitude *make me angry!*

The constant reiteration by the nation's media of the ideas of quarantine and "scarlet letter" tattooing so that the public will not be shocked if and when the government moves in that direction *makes me angry!*

A gay rights bill which, after a 15 year struggle and much accommodation in the wording is then sought to be turned into a bill which actually legislates discrimination *makes me angry!*

And, along with this, the defection in the City Council of some of those who said they were our friends, and the deafening silence concerning the abortive amendment to the bill of those elected officials outside of the council who have also claimed to be our friends *makes me angry!*

But, getting angry, while a natural reaction, is not very productive. What we must do is be realistic and pragmatic. We must recognize that we cannot depend on others to secure and protect our rights. We must acknowledge that our fate is in our own hands. What that fate will be depends on us and us alone.

At first blush, it would appear that this is certainly not the audience to whom I should be giving this talk. This room probably contains 500 of New York's most generous and committed people. But, that is why you are the very people to help ensure that we as an entire community reach out for and take control of our own lives. To help us think about doing that, I would like to make a comparison. Comparisons are often odious, but they need not be, and this one is certainly not meant to be. We can learn from them, so please allow me to give you one as an example.

According to the American Jewish Congress, 2.5% of the American population is Jewish. Yet, in light of this relatively small proportion of our population, many cultural organizations shy away from underwriting or collaborating in a production of Shakespeare's *The Merchant of Venice* and its stereotypical portrayal of a Jewish merchant. This is so because American Jews have never denied who they are and have been unified on all of the issues that affect the quality of their lives as full citizens of this country.

Now, make the comparison. By all generally accepted estimates, lesbians and gay men make up 10% of the American population. There are four times as many gay men and women in this country as there are persons of Jewish extraction. Yet, PBS nationally, and Channel 13 locally, brushed us aside when we strongly objected in advance to their airing of a *Frontline* program that dealt with the life of a person with AIDS in an entirely inappropriate and negative manner.

In making this comparison, I mentioned the sensitivity of cultural institutions. Well, let's look at just one example of how sensitive such corporate cultural institutions are to our needs. The head of one such institution's departments agreed to bring together members of the non-elected power structure of this city—the David Rockefeller and Felix Rohaytan types—with people from the Gay Men's Health Crisis to discuss the many facets of the AIDS crisis and how they might be better addressed. This was to take place over dinner in a private dining room at the institution. This very important meeting had to be canceled and rescheduled because a certain segment of the board of the institution objected to it taking place on its property. Can you imagine such a meeting being canceled if the topic had been the freeing of Soviet Jews?

And let me ask you this: Do you know how many Jewish community centers there are in this city alone? Can we not have just one gay community center? Of course we can, if we learn from our Jewish brothers and sisters. We can, if we as an entire community stop denying who we are and take charge of our own lives. Doing so may take some courage, but that is what we are here for tonight—to celebrate and reinforce such courage. Has anyone ever read to you what these awards say: "For the beauty of courage which sustains lesbians and gay men in their struggle for dignity. To: Sergeant Perry Watkins; Gerry Studds; Charles Cochran; Dan Bradley; Virginia Apuzzo; Peter Vogel; Richard Failla—by whose example, freedom is a step closer." It is an example of these people that we must all follow.

Earlier, I compared the strength and influence of 2.5% of our population to that of 10% of the population. But, if we have the courage, we can enlist far more than the 10% of the population in our struggle for dignity. If we put aside what I consider the unrealistic fear of rejection and the flimsy excuse that we do not want to hurt them, we can surely enlist the support of our families.

They say that the worst thing that can happen to a parent is to lose a child. We readily believe this, except when it comes to our own parents. Those who gave us life will not abandon us. And they will fight like demons to protect us, just as they always have, if we will only ask them. And the same goes for our brothers and our sisters, and our nieces and our nephews, to say nothing of our friends.

We must also be open about our sexual orientation in our everyday lives, just as heterosexuals are. As long as the vast majority of us stay hidden, we are whatever our enemies say we are, for there is no one to refute what they say.

You do not accept or reject people on the basis of their sexual orientation. You have all known gay people who, because of their attributes, or lack of them, you have chosen not to associate with. And you also make the same judgments about heterosexuals without factoring in their sexual orientation.

Given the chance, the vast majority of the people we know will judge us in the same manner.

We who have received the Howard Brown Award have been open about our sexual orientation, both in our social and professional lives. I dare say that that is why we have received this award. Being open not only debunks the myths about us, it can have the ripple effect of raising people's consciousness. My colleagues on the bench are, for the most part, an intelligent and sensitive group of human beings. They have accepted me among them as a gay man just as they have in the past accepted women, Hispanics, and blacks. But homophobia runs deep into the subconscious and we must be there to root it out. Let me give you just two examples.

Not too long ago, a number of judges were in an administrative judge's office discussing a proposed change in court procedure. Most of the judges were skeptical about this change and the administrative judge said that the procedure had been implemented in California, to which a female judge responded, "Well, what would you expect from the land of fruits and nuts?" I did not want to embarrass this woman, any more than she intended to insult me, but I did ask her what kind of fruit she had in mind when she made that statement. She apologized and said she wasn't really thinking when she made the remark. This gave everyone in the room food for thought.

On another occasion, when a group of judges was attending an educational seminar in Buffalo, we met after dinner in the hotel cocktail lounge, to socialize. During the course of a very pleasant and exuberant conversation, a judge, a black man, was relating an experience that he said had made him "as happy as a fag in a boy scout camp." What he had said was so offensive, in both language and thought content, that I did not say anything to him in front of the others, feeling it would make everyone too uncomfortable. A few moments later, I did take him aside and ask him how he would feel if I said something has made me "as happy as a nigger in a watermelon patch."

It is only if enough of us do this every time the occasion arises that words like "fruit," "pansy," "queer" and "fag" will take on the same social taboo as words like "nigger" and "kike."

I asked earlier if we could not afford to have a gay community center. To many gay people, a number of whom might be in this room, the answer might seem to be no. I have often heard lately that the community is beginning to feel tapped out. I think that is because it is the same relatively small group of people who go to all of these dinners and give to all the gay causes. But, in truth, we haven't even scratched the surface of the giving potential of our community. It is our responsibility to talk to our so-called "non-involved" friends. We must convince them of what is at stake, and that they must participate in all ways, including, but not limited to, funding all of our organizations. And we must also convince them that they must convince others, and so on and so on. If we must, then we must make it fashionable to talk about and participate in gay and lesbian activism.

American Jews have only one-quarter our number and not only are multiple Jewish organizations strong and healthy in this country, there is money left over to support the state of Israel. Just think of what we could accomplish if we only *half* tried and only *one-fourth* succeeded.

And, for those of us who are feeling a little pinched as we get the momentum rolling, let me make some selfish recommendations. Review your giving habits. Give only to those organizations that directly or at least indirectly support us.

Take PBS and WNET, in particular. They do absolutely nothing for us as a community. Their programming has no regular content that addresses us or our issues. They run the same old tired programs once a year during Gay Pride Week, and if there is any new programming it has to be paid for out of the pocket of the gay community. I used to give to Channel 13 on a regular basis and when I stopped giving they wrote and asked me why. I wrote back and told them and I never heard from them again. If enough of us stopped giving and enough of us told them why, their production and programming habits just might change.

WNET is just one example. There are many other civic, charitable, and cultural organizations which I suggest will survive without our direct contributions. If they want our money, let them do something directly for us as a community. In the meantime, I suggest that we will not be full members of this society unless we devote all of our giving to our own organizations.

I am not suggesting that we stop going to the ballet or the symphony or to museums. We should continue to grow and enjoy ourselves by partaking in the cultural riches of this city. But, we should only pay for what we get and we should reserve our giving for our own institutions. This may sound radical or even barbaric to some of you, but I say it sounds better than second-class citizenship. If you truly believe in what this award stands for, you will "answer the call" and convince our brothers and sisters that they must do so also.

May 31, 1986

Speech to the Southern Christian Leadership Conference Women's Conference on AIDS

Gil Gerald

This address was given by Gilberto Gerald, at that time the executive director of the National Coalition of Black Lesbians and Gays. *An Early Frost* was a made-for-television film issued in 1985 about the impact of AIDS on an American family.

I am indeed honored to be able to address this SCLC Women's Conference on AIDS as a representative of an at-risk community—sexually active black gay men—and as a representative of the National Coalition of Black Gays and Lesbians. Once again the claim to leadership implied in the name Southern Christian Leadership Conference is upheld. Your actions come at a time when there are other prominent black organizations who will not touch the subject of AIDS because of its association with the taboo topic of homosexuality, which is often viewed as some sort of white disease, and therefore alien to the black community.

On behalf of the National Coalition of Black Lesbians and Gays, I wish to reciprocate your welcome by extending to all of you an invitation to come to the National Conference on AIDS in the Black Community which we are sponsoring in DC at the Washington Convention Center this coming July 18.

Today, some five years into the AIDS crisis, it is becoming more widely understood in the black community that AIDS is having a far more devastating effect on those of us who are black, This should not come as a surprise. Because of inequities in the health care delivery system and the disparities in education, diet, and economic well-being between blacks and whites, we are always struck harder by disease. One only need look at the continuing incidence of cancer, high blood pressure, heart disease, infant mortality, and other health indicators to recognize this fact.

More of us now know that 25 percent of all 20,000 U.S. AIDS cases are black individuals. This compares with the fact that the black community only makes up about 12 percent of the population. We also know that three out of every five children with AIDS are black, and that one out of every two women with AIDS is a black woman. We also know that four out of every 10 people with AIDS are non-white people—about 8,000 of the 20,000 cases in the U.S.

With all due respect to those of you who disagree, I believe that the proposition that this disease is God's punishment on a class or category of people is as racist a proposition as it is homophobic, in view of the facts—not the myths—about AIDS. Indeed racism and homophobia, as well as classism, are key impediments to AIDS prevention and the care of people with AIDS in the black community. Let's deal with racism and homophobia as an impediment to health care delivery.

Jeff Levi, executive director of the National Gay and Lesbian Task Force, informs me that over the past five years the gay and lesbian community has raised, matched, or exceeded the $500-$600 million the government has poured into the AIDS health crisis. It is a veritable example of what people can do for themselves in a society that spurns them.

This effort by mostly white organizations had its limitations. Racism and social divisions or separateness transcend sexual orientation.

A study of black gay men in the San Francisco area by black psychologist Julius Johnson explores the fact that black homosexuals have identity concerns which we resolve in a variety of ways. We often are made to feel we must choose between an emphasis on our identity as gays and our identity as blacks, and that these identities are mutually exclusive. By contrast, the organization I represent is founded on the proposition that we can be whole—we need not choose—we can be both black and gay, proud of both. Our current theme, "Black Pride and Solidarity: the New Movement of Black Lesbians and Gays" restates the political and social implications of that consciousness.

Blacks, who emphasized their gay identity, have adjusted to their personal encounter with gay oppression by socializing and adjusting to life in the white gay ghetto. His or her black-identified gay brother and sister, on the other hand, remain physically "closeted" in the black community and its institutions. Either option is a compromise. In the first case racism is accommodated, and in the second, homophobia is accommodated. Both options represent complicity with a system of oppression that denies our very existence. You cannot provide services, health or otherwise, to a community that does not exist.

These facts have great repercussions. The networks and institutions of the gay community, created to deal with the AIDS crisis, cannot have much effect beyond those black individuals who are already accessible to them. This represents a minority of us black gays, and practically none of the I.V.

drug users. The language we use, our socializing patterns, as well as our numbers, are very much still a mystery to the white gay community as a whole.

The racism that permeates many gay establishments is a documented fact that has necessitated the enactment of anti-discrimination legislation in cities like Washington, D.C. This fact of alienation and separation in the gay community would not be as devastating if our political institutions—like the National Coalition of Black Lesbians and Gays—were far more developed at this time in history. Black Lesbian and Gay organizing is still largely centered around our socializing needs and our need to remain hidden. We are less likely to risk alienation from our home community—the black community—by politicizing the gay issue.

This brings us to the issue of homophobia in the black community. We have been too eager to buy into the myths of AIDS and homosexuality that is perpetuated by the mass media—that these are white concerns. We have seen *An Early Frost* on TV and can empathize with the difficulties of the family. However, the all-white cast of characters contributes to the distortion of the truth about the demographics of AIDS. We read *Newsweek* magazine, and for the last 15 years we see depicted a distorted picture of who lesbian and gay people are. We somehow remove ourselves from lesbian and gay people and then dare to celebrate the lives and contributions of James Baldwin, Audre Lorde, Langston Hughes, Bayard Rustin, Alain Locke, Countee Cullen, Bessie Smith, Porter Grainger, Lorraine Hansberry, Wallace Thurmond, Bruce Nugent, and Sylvester—all people we love and appreciate for their contributions to community life.

Effective programs for the prevention of AIDS in the black community will require some frank and open dialogue that acknowledges the transmission modes of this disease and the existence of black lesbians and gays among us, who lead and have always led both exemplary and ordinary lives. Examination of the statistics indicate that intravenous drug use and sexual transmission contribute equally to the incidence of AIDS among blacks. The issue of AIDS cannot be tackled without acknowledging both of these facts.

If we are to make some headway in stopping the spread of AIDS and AIDS hysteria, we must recognize the social, political and economic implications of the crisis.

People with AIDS—by the way, they prefer this terminology to the term "AIDS victims"—require support services and love, like any other individual who is ill. It can be an extremely difficult time for persons afflicted with AIDS and for their families. It is likely to be the time when the individual must confront his or her family with the truth of his or her lifestyle, whether it be that of one of a myriad of gay lifestyles or that of an intravenous drug user.

PWAs are likely to encounter more discrimination than they already experience, and at a time when they are more likely than not to be within three years of their death at an early age. Persons with AIDS often have a reduced capacity for providing for themselves because they have been unfairly terminated from their regular jobs or are too ill to work. The insurance companies, under the guise of protecting everyone's insurance rates from going up, are beginning to deny insurance to people who are AIDS antibody positive. Fortunately the black leadership in DC, just this past week, passed comprehensive legislation barring this kind of insurance abuse.

One million people are believed now to be AIDS antibody positive, many of them black and poor. Only a small portion of them are expected to develop ARC or full-blown AIDS. Yet, the insurance industry proposes to deny all of them insurance. While most of these people will not develop AIDS, they will need health insurance to cover other ailments. It would be folly for us, as a community, to not understand and support the need for legislation of this kind all over the country.

Blacks with AIDS are dying quicker than their white counterparts. Diagnosis is likely to come at more advanced stages of the disease and we have less access to the best available medical care. It is the ultimate tragedy that those of us who come down with AIDS might need to seek refuge among strangers in our hour of need.

In conclusion, it is the position of the National Coalition of Black Lesbians and Gays that black institutions need to get involved more aggressively in pursuing funding for our own programs in AIDS prevention and information. Furthermore, we need to provide AIDS-related support services for people with AIDS and for the families of people with AIDS in the community. The most effective programs will be those that refrain from being judgmental, involve members of the at-risk communities as well as PWAs and focus on providing useful medical information and caring services to those afflicted with and at risk for AIDS.

1986

Speech for Gay and Lesbian Pride Day 1986

Chuck Harbaugh

Harbaugh was a clinician in private practice in Seattle, an investigator with the Washington State Human Rights Commission, and the facilitator for the Gay Men's Health/Support Group. Initiative 490 would have declared all homosexuals "deviants" and denied them any job in local government; Referendum 7 was a move to repeal the 1985 Fair Housing Ordinance in Seattle.

Let us remember how we got here today. Twenty years ago Carl Whitman authored a major document of what we now know as gay liberation. It is called *The Gay Manifesto.* Earlier this year Carl Whitman died of AIDS. Carl worked toward a singular purpose of liberation—liberation both as freedom from sexual oppression and freedom toward responsible sexuality. Carl Whitman's theme is still our own today: To Let Go!

Let go of homophobia.

Let go of the fear of loving, the fear of grieving, the fear of dying.

Let go of personal differences, the judgments that we make against our neighbors for a failure to look and behave—as we do.

Let go of hidden pride, the personal embarrassment that prevents us from standing tall as lesbians and gay men.

Let go of racial and sexual prejudices; the belief that AIDS is the disease of "Gay White Boys" is as racist as the belief that only men's lives are touched by AIDS is sexist.

Twenty years ago, in the context of gay liberation, we gays and lesbians taught straight America the value, the meaning, the very acts of unconditionally liberated loving. Today, in the context of gay pride and in the context of AIDS, we again become liberators, teaching the world about death with dignity, about community support of the dying and the disabled, about safe sex as an expression of this same unconditionally liberated loving.

We have learned to **let go** of bigotry, that other cancer afflicting so many Americans.

With our straight friends—and **because** of gay liberation we have many straight friends—we have built a community that spawns friendships, loyalties, trust and pride.

There is much about which we have yet to **let go:** The frightful hysteria of religious and political fundamentalists, who would quarantine persons with AIDS—*Will they* let go *of their opposition to the civil rights of racial minorities and women?*

The patronizing immorality of citizens who could deny human housing and medical services to persons with AIDS—*Will they* let go *of their irrational stance which would deny abortion rights to women*?

The politicians and business people who would deny substantial monies for researching a cure and a vaccine for AIDS—*Will they* let go *of their legal maneuvers that would narrow the scope of rights of the disabled?* Including persons with ARC? Including persons who are HTLV-III positive?

I challenge the so-called "pro-life" people, the frightened, unthinking fundamentalists—*and what is more fundamental than respect and life nurturing love*—When are you going to let go of your bigotry, your hatred, your ignorance? And when do you accept AIDS as an illness, without respect to sexual orientation? And when do you stand with us for the life, liberty and pursuit of happiness promised to us in our birthrights?

I embrace a "Unite to Fight for Human Rights" campaign.

I embrace my sisters and brothers who have AIDS.

I embrace their lovers, their friends, their families.

I embrace the struggle to fight AIDS, to educate myself and others about safe sex, and I commit to practice not only this safety of my body, but also to approach with honor, with a clean and an awakened spirit of love, with tenderness and pride, any partner, any friend, any member of my community.

I embrace the noble grief that surrounds my memories of Terry, Larry, Alex, Bill, Joe Carl Peter . . . all the men who enriched my life with the gifts of their forthrightness, their humility, their hope and love.

I embrace the struggle to die with dignity, openly as a gay person, to live with that same dignity, with the respect I unconditionally give my brothers and sisters, the respect that I want from them.

I embrace the involvement of volunteers during this epidemic and I recognize the pain we touch together in serving persons with AIDS—and only when I touch my own center, the self within myself that pushes into this pain, do I discover with others my fears, my joys, my growth.

I remember with pride the support given to persons with AIDS by the *Seattle Gay News,* the Gay Men's Health/Support Group, Shanti/Seattle, the Seattle AIDS Support Group, Blood Sisters, Mobilization Against AIDS.

I remember with this same pride in the involvement of persons with AIDS by the Dorian Group, the Greater Seattle Business Association, and today, the Freedom Day Committee.

Freedom! The power to enjoin against the incipient discrimination against persons with AIDS in the workplace, in housing, in insurance, in public accommodations.

Freedom! The power to demand governmental systems to appropriate substantial monies—and our governments have not yet done this—for services to persons with AIDS, for education in our community—indeed, in every community and in every language.

Freedom! The power to establish for ourselves the life, liberty and pursuit of happiness that otherwise would be denied us by the pernicious hatred of an Initiative 490, by Referenda 7, and then 10, to end fair employment and open housing.

I celebrate with you today, and everyday, a united fight for human rights.

I celebrate with you that however awful AIDS is and becomes, it does not overcome our love and care for each other.

I celebrate with you a special pride, a gay pride, the pride of our nobility as lesbians and gay men to whom persons with AIDS are forever connected in our spiritually gifted, stable, functioning family.

Let go with your feelings!

Let go with your love!

Let go and live!

Thank you.

July 18, 1986

An Open Letter to the Chicago City Council, Mayor Harold Washington, Cardinal Joseph Bernardin, Gay and Lesbian Communities, and the People of Chicago

This text was carried in the July 24, 1986, issue of *Windy City Times* as a paid political advertisement engaging the issues involved in the struggle for amendment of Chicago's gay and lesbian civil rights law to include sexual orientation. It was signed by twenty-six activists.

Awaiting the action of the Chicago City Council is a bill amending the city human rights law. The bill adds "sexual orientation" to the classes protected from discrimination in employment, public accommodations and housing.

After languishing for seven years, the Council was supposed to call the bill for a vote on July 9, 1986. Once again the vote was postponed. This time, the excuse was the statement released on the eve of the vote by the Roman Catholic Archdiocese, in fear of the loss of their rights to discriminate against Gay Men, Lesbians and Bisexuals and in which the bill was incorrectly labeled "too vague." We uphold the right of Cardinal Bernardin, or any other religious leader to express opinions on this or any other legislation, no matter how vehemently we may disagree. However, we are justifiably saddened, disappointed and angered at those who earlier proclaimed their support for our rights but, by intimidation, now cannot be counted on. We strongly urge Mayor Washington and all Aldermen to take the principled stand for human rights and support non-discrimination for Chicagoans of all sexualities.

The language of the bill is clear and simple. It makes no implicit or explicit moral statement about the behavior of all sexualities or any particular sexuality. Rather, the bill forbids discrimination against Homosexuals, Bisexuals, Heterosexuals and Asexuals of every color, race, national origin, sex, marital status, age, disability or religion. That means it protects everyone.

Many Gay Men, Lesbians and Bisexuals have worked hard for the passage of this bill. Some of them now would compromise our collective human dignity by capitulation to the Roman Catholic Church and those Aldermen who oppose us, based on alledged [*sic*] moral grounds. To justify their willingness to compromise, these leaders point to the compromises made with the Archdioceses of New York and Brooklyn and the New York City Council to assure passage of a similar bill there.

But to compare the two bills is like comparing apples and oranges. Both the New York and the Chicago bills would amend their respective human rights law to include "sexual orientation" as a protected category. That's where the similarity ends.

New York's compromise is a statement of an intention not to "endorse any particular behavior or way of life." It then refers to an already existing religious exclusion provision which applies to all protected classes, speaking in neutral language as to sex and sexuality. On the other hand, at the time this statement was prepared, the suggested compromise language to the Chicago bill significantly altered the nature and effect of the entire law. The Archdiocese insists on an extremely broad religious exclusion provision which, unlike the New York laws, would apply only to Gay Men, Lesbians and Bisexuals. According to Barry Adkins, Associate Editor of the *New York Native,* this would "single out gays and elevate every other protected class above gays and lesbians in Chicago." It is dangerous for us to set such a precedent for us and other oppressed peoples.

If a change is necessary for passage of the bill, the only change we can support is the use of neutral language as to sex and sexuality, used in such a manner as to avoid any negative impact on other classes and groups of people. We would borrow the following language from the New York law:

> The Council wishes to make clear that it is not the function of this civil rights statute to promote a particular group or community. Its principle is rather to insure that individuals who live in our society will have the opportunity to pursue their own beliefs and conduct their lives as they see fit within the limits of the law.

We share the pain and frustration of our brothers and sisters who would begrudgingly compromise their dignity in the mistaken belief that it would somehow move our civil rights bill forward. We disagree that a compromise, regardless of language, would make much of a difference in the City Council vote.

Regardless of our differences on compromise language, all of us in the Gay, Lesbian and Bisexual communities have come together with a new resolve. We demand a vote on our civil rights bill on July 29th. We will not accept any excuses for no vote or a vote of no from our representatives. We will carry our pain, frustration and resolve into the voting booth and we will make a difference!

1986

The Injury of Living Unawarely

Lorry Sorgman

This address by Sorgman was given to the 1986 board of directors meetings of the World Congress of Gay and Lesbian Jewish Organizations in Boston, Massachusetts.

The World Congress is comprised of 25 organizations located throughout the United States, Israel and Europe. Its existence was fueled by the 1975 United Nations resolution, implying that Zionism was synonymous with racism. In direct response to that resolution, Lesbian and Gay Jewish groups which had not been previously affiliated with one another met at the invitation of Congregation Beth Simchat Torah of New York. This began annual conferences and an exchange of ideas, which would ultimately be a mechanism for breaking down the isolation which had kept us separate from each other. I believe its true that if our adversaries can keep us isolated, they succeed in keeping us invisible and thereby powerless.

We began outreach through annual International Conferences, with the sharing of information and common experiences.

In 1979, an International Conference held in Israel attracted responses from gay and lesbian Jews of Australia, Bermuda, Canada, England, France, Germany, Holland, Israel, Mexico, Portugal, South Africa, and the United States. The 1987 International Conference of Gay and Lesbian Jews will be held in Amsterdam. It is hoped that once again we will attract a greater diversity of registrants.

We had a vision in 1980 when the World Congress was actually named. It included creating solidarity among member groups, appreciating our cultural diversity, promoting leadership to our member organizations and providing information to the public, as in the Speakers Bureau and Public Education Campaign, which we are currently undertaking. Our newsletter, the *Digest,* is a forum for dialog on issues facing Lesbian, Gay and Jewish people.

From its onset the Congress has been concerned with Universal issues. Whether we are struggling for the liberation of blacks of South Africa, the immigration of Soviet Jews or concerning ourselves with foster care equality in Massachusetts; our vision has been in harmony with, and sustained by, our belief in a rich Jewish tradition. Given our history of oppression, it is no accident that many gay and lesbian Jews are in the vanguard of social change.

It has been over nine years since that first meeting, yet the enthusiasm and need for solidarity and coalition building has never been greater. We are confronted with a rise in conservatism which threatens our freedom in the most fundamental of ways—what we do in the privacy of our own bedrooms. God only knows what's next.

A decade is nearly gone and the realization that building alliances is essential to the survival of all of us occurs to many. Consistent with our desire to educate and inform the public, last year the World Congress created a new status of membership. It is called "Friend of the World Congress."

Regardless of who we are in this room, we share a common enemy. It is known to me as the injury of living unawarely . . . I firmly believe that the correct sharing of information can rip away the barriers of ignorance. "Friend of the World Congress" status entitles you to a one-year subscription to the *World Congress Digest,* and helps support programs of public education in the fight against prejudice, sexism and homophobia throughout the world.

Please join us in liberating the world from oppression.
Thank you for joining us.

November 11, 1986

Remembering David Summers

Wayne Steinman

This speech was delivered as a eulogy to AIDS activist David Summers at Judson Memorial Church in New York City. Steinman was at that time a staff assistant to the New York City comptroller.

How do I even begin to reflect on the life of a friend? It is a truly difficult task for me, especially when that person has made such an impact on my own life.

I have to say that our friendship was the machination of Bea Roman, who was a friend of both David's and mine, and of many others here today. Bea was moving to California, to work with the Shanti Project and people with AIDS (PWAs). She had been working with PWAs here in New York and had developed an especially close friendship with David. She has a soothing spirit and a way about her which, if she allowed, develops into a deep, caring love. She knew already, from David, how much he would miss her. I was going through the same feelings about Bea's departure. In her inimitable way, Bea knew that David and I would hit it off, and gave me his phone number. She said we should look after each other.

I knew all about David through the gay media and Bea, and was excited that I would finally meet him. I called David soon after Bea left and we made a date to meet at his apartment. As it turned out, I got to meet David over a bowl of chicken soup. As many of you know, David always felt that a lot could be accomplished while sharing a meal. Sitting there at David's, I realized that I had seen David as the New Kid in Town in *The Faggot,* which was produced right here at Judson.

David had a special way about him. You knew right away whether he liked you or not. He had the admirable ability of truly being a friend to literally hundreds of people—and he really demonstrated that he cared for each and every one. David and I felt a kindred spirit, maybe because of Bea, maybe because of our fervent belief on our activism in the gay rights movement and the movement advocating for more AIDS services. By the time I left David's apartment, I knew I had a new friend.

I am honored that David chose to share part of his life with me. Our friendship was expanded to include David's life partner and lover, Sal, and my life partner and lover Sal. (I guess that's another thing we had in common—fondness for hot Italians named Sal.) The times the four of us spent together were special, times to get away from it all, to socialize and retreat from the stresses and strains of everyday living, to share some good times with good food and good friends. They were special moments which we will always remember.

I would like to share with you my reflections of this incredible man. A man filled with love and joy. A spirit that moved people. An anger that propelled him into political activism. Most importantly, a role model for other people with AIDS, whether gay or not, to be responsible for their own lives.

David was a founding member of the People With AIDS Coalition. He loved the Coalition and that love was returned to him. The energy and time devoted to his brothers and sisters with AIDS was limitless. He traveled the country on behalf of PWAs, whether to Washington, D.C. to a health conference where he was elected vice president of the National Association of People With AIDS, or to New Orleans, to speak at a convention and help a newly formed support group for PWAs get off the ground. I would be less than honest if I didn't say that David had a wanderlust that was fed by all this travel. "Hi, Wayne," he would say, "I'm off to San Francisco for a PWA meeting"—or to Connecticut or the Midwest or to New Mexico or Paris or . . . Part of David was buoyed by all this travel. Frankly, this is another trait that David and I had in common, and I was quite envious of all his travel.

That first day I met David, he was preparing a speech for a conference on AIDS which Gay Men's Health Crisis was sponsoring at Hunter College. He asked me to listen, and also to suggest any changes I might think necessary. Listening to David in his apartment, it was obvious no changes were necessary. He moved me to tears, tears that would come again and again as I would hear him speak at other events—at an AIDS vigil on Christopher Street, at hearings in City Hall for the gay rights bill. He spoke in interviews, whether it was on *Donahue* or on television news segments about AIDS. So many times, he clearly stated his feelings so that others would understand the full impact of the AIDS epidemic, in such a way as to personalize the generalities. "Here I am," he would say, "a person with AIDS," with feelings, emotions, pain—and also love and tenderness. David understood the need to be a public person to effect change.

Tears would also come to me when David sang a Sondheim song, wonderful tears of love and admiration as David sang "Our Time." Tears when my Sal and I saw David at Jan Wallman's, and when I would see him with his Sal, so much in love, sharing a life together. Tears of happiness, for David and Sal's happiness, and tears of sadness, knowing that, inevitably, this day would come when we would be honoring the memory of David after his death.

David always injected humor into life, and what I affectionately call a gay sensibility. In his last weeks, as his condition deteriorated, David continued to hold on to his dignity, his gay sensibility, his humor. During the last meal the four of us shared, David remarked on how uncomfortable he'd been feeling. He'd had a masseur come to the house and give him a massage. David commented on how much better he felt afterwards and how worthwhile it was, even though the massage was painful for him at times. Then, as was his style, David commented, "But it was worth it. The masseur was gorgeous, a very handsome 23-year-old who is muscular and hot." David never lost his taste for attractive men.

David liked to dish. I remember numerous phone calls in which David and I would chat about this or that personality in the community. David always kept up with who was sleeping with whom, who had what personality trait worth ripping to shreds. But always with love. He had the ability to comment on the entire gay community with humor. One of the comments I remember most was that, however devastated by the tragedy of AIDS, the gay community would never lose its ability to decorate. I am sure he would look around this room today and make some comment about us dizzy queens, who in the midst of our grief, had to decorate a church with a 40-foot rainbow flag.

That gay sensibility translated into a strong sense of community. Knowingly or not, David became a role model. I recall one instance David was especially pleased about, when he spoke before Gay and Lesbian Youth of New York, a peer-run, peer-support group comprised mostly of minority youths. He spoke candidly about having AIDS, showing them his Kaposi's sarcoma lesions, answering intimate questions about safer sex, risk reduction, and sex after being diagnosed with AIDS. He came out of that Saturday afternoon rap session so energized by the youths, and they learned more about AIDS that day than ever before.

David's energy also brought him before the City Council of New York, where he eloquently spoke as a gay man and a person with AIDS. David was arrested that day, attempting to get into City Hall: the police would not listen to him as he explained that he was scheduled to testify in behalf of the gay rights bill. A large gathering of people from the community witnessed his arrest and began chanting "Free David Summers," over and over, as the police escorted him away in handcuffs. Thankfully, he was later released and spoke for the rights of every individual to be free from discrimination.

I remember David's excitement each Gay Pride day. A day to celebrate our love and who you are with pride and dignity—that is what David lived every day of his life! You could feel his energy level soar at these times. This past June, even when he was losing some of his stamina, David marched most of the length of Fifth Avenue behind the People With AIDS Coalition banner, "Fighting For Our Lives." David and Sal marched together, with pride. My life partner Sal and I were also there, marching and driving with the PWA Coalition, providing our car for those who could not march the whole way. We had cold refreshments for those who needed it during the course of the parade. It was especially poignant, and David's feelings became most evident as we passed St. Patrick's Cathedral. The cardinal's recent anti-gay statements brought out the emotion in all of us. David's face tensed: his anger mounted. David (and Sal, too) chanted, again and again, "Justice! Justice! Justice!" On the next corner, the police had allowed anti-gay protestors to gather. Many of them carried placards with virulent anti-gay and anti-AIDS statements. It was apparent that we were all angered, especially the People With AIDS contingent. Once again, chants of "Justice! Justice! Justice!" Later, David mounted the Stamp Out AIDS float along with Harvey Fierstein. David was out there yet again, making his public statement for our community and the citizens of New York City. How proud I was of him.

There were serene moments for David, private times. One of the special moments I had the privilege to share was when David and Sal and my Sal and I went upstate to a place called Smitty's near New Paltz. It's located near the Mohonk Mountain forest preserve. David and Sal needed a day away from the city, time to unwind. Smitty's was just what the doctor ordered. We lay on our blankets on some rocks, on top of a 40-foot waterfall, shed our clothes and basked in the warm sun. How marvelous it was to play in the fresh, cold stream, to climb over rocks and wooded hills. One of those special moments was watching David roaming through the woods, touching some moss or a leaf on a tree, completely alone in his thoughts and feelings. He seemed so in touch with nature, experiencing his most basic, primal feelings, very much at peace with himself and his world.

David is at peace again, now. He died at peace with himself, his family, and his world. All of us are very thankful that we had the opportunity to share in his special warmth, friendship, and love. It hurts us now. We feel the emptiness and the hurt caused by his absence. But he lives on. There is an old Native American saying that goes something like, "To live in the hearts we leave behind is not to die." David will never leave our memories or our hearts. Our love for David will always be there. He was a special individual whom we cherished. We must go on, filled with his love.

The recent television documentary in which David was featured, *Hero of My Own Life,* was a special tribute to David, one in which he shared his innermost thoughts with the world on what it is like to be a person with AIDS. David was truly a hero—a hero of his own life and a hero for others. We all remember certain segments of that half hour that are special to us. His description of his feelings upon learning of his diagnosis of Kaposi's sarcoma and AIDS. What he experienced with his family and friends. The segment most memorable to me was also, it seems, the most important to David. In it, David read a quote from Robert Kennedy on how we all can leave our mark on this world. David became a hero to me all the more when he spoke Kennedy's words in the documentary. Other than Kennedy himself, no one could give more meaning to these words right now than David. [Kennedy's words, recorded by Summers, were then heard on tape.]

> Let no one be discouraged by the belief that there is nothing one man or one woman can do against the enormous array of the world's ills—against misery and ignorance, injustice and violence . . . Few will have the greatness to bend history itself; but each of us can work to change a small portion of events, and in the total of all those acts will be written the history of this generation.
>
> It is from numberless diverse acts of courage and belief that human history is shaped. Each time a man stands up for an ideal, or acts to improve the lot of others, or strikes out against injustice, he sends a tiny ripple of hope, and, crossing each other from a million different centers of energy and daring, those ripples build a current which can sweep down the mightiest walls of oppression and resistance.

1986

A Seat at the Banquet: Remarks to the Conference on International Human Rights

Will Hutchinson

The case of *Bowers v. Hardwick* was resolved in June 1986 with a decision rendered by the U.S. Supreme Court that upheld the constitutionality of the sodomy law of the state of Georgia, effectively denying gays and lesbians privacy even in their own bedrooms.

In December, 1986, gay men and lesbians can be, on the whole, thankful that they live in Boston, but much less sanguine about living in Massachusetts, and downright uneasy about living in Ronald Reagan's and William Rehnquist's America. It's a mixed bag.

In Boston Mayor Flynn has set the tone and has created a positive personal record in the field of human rights. It is significant that in 1984 openly gay Boston City Councilor David Scondras, the Boston Lesbian and Gay Political Alliance (BLGPA) and Mayor Flynn succeeded in passing the Boston Human Rights Ordinance, which bans discrimination in employment, insurance, and public accommodations. (Boston's Fair Housing Commission has existed for some time to protect individuals in that area of potential discrimination). It is equally important to note that the first (and current) Executive Director of the Boston Human Rights Commission is Fred Mandel, an openly gay, and highly qualified, young man.

On the other hand the Commonwealth of Massachusetts has much to answer for in its (at best) uneven record on human rights, particularly as it pertains to gay men and lesbians. In May of 1984 Governor Dukakis removed two small children from the loving and stable foster home of two gay men, setting off two years of anguish and anger within this state's social service agencies and the lesbian and gay community. Whether for reasons of political expediency or personal bigotry, the state's Chief Executive overturned long-standing Department of Social Services policy of determining placement in foster homes on a case-by-case basis, on a local level, and with the best interest of the children the major criterion. In its place the Governor substituted an anti-scientific set of regulations which effectively relegated the Commonwealth's gay and lesbian population to second-class citizenship and barred them from giving their love to the state's unwanted, battered and neglected foster children. In an orgy of AIDSphobia and legislative queer-bashing, the state legislature then passed the Governor's foster care policy and, for the thirteenth straight year, defeated a state-wide gay rights bill.

Yet we are now encouraged to believe that a change is in the air. Stung by the large numbers of blank ballots in the recent gubernatorial race, by Judge Morse's decision that *de facto* exclusion of gay men and lesbians as foster parents is inherently discriminatory, and chastened by the prospect of a national gay and lesbian opposition to his presidential ambitions, a state commission is currently reviewing the Governor's homophobic policy. Still, the Governor refuses to sign an executive order banning discrimination against homosexuals, so there remains a crying need to pass a state-wide gay rights bill affording gay men and lesbians equal protection under the law.

Nationally, the disgrace of a president unwilling and unable to act forcefully on AIDS funding, the tardiness of Congressional action on a national gay rights bill and immigration reform, the frightfully Orwellian Supreme Court decision on *Hardwick v. Bowers* (the Georgia sodomy case) have caused both anger and a demonstrably increased activism in the national gay and lesbian community, and an increasing uneasiness among civil libertarians everywhere.

For us, the Supreme Court's decision to invade the privacy of every American's bedroom has given governmental sanction to the harassment of this country's homosexual citizens, conservatively estimated at one voter in every ten. In turn, this judicial queer-bashing has led to increased verbal and physical attacks—including murder—on gay men and lesbians around the country. (In Boston, BLGPA is documenting increased instances of violence, and will continue to press for compliance with—and enforcement of—existing human rights laws, repeal of antiquated sodomy laws, and the enactment of a state-wide human rights bill.)

In the end, for the gay and lesbian community, the solution is *not* to return to the self-hatred and isolation of the closet, but to participate openly and actively in the full range of economic, social, and political arenas of life. The best and surest way to ensure our rights is to elect to public office our own openly gay men and lesbians. There is no substitute for a seat at the banquet table of life. Living openly and actively within our neighborhoods and places of employment, working within the system where it is possible, and actively opposing injustices in that system when they denigrate our value as human beings, we seek the support of all men and women everywhere who commit their lives to the cause of human rights and dignity.

For in the end the struggle for that cause is indivisible. So long as one of us suffers oppression, our lives threatened and demeaned by society, by executive, legislative, judicial, and law enforcement establishments, then the whole of humankind is threatened.

Internationally, until the West German government recognizes homosexuals as victims of Nazi persecution and declares us eligible for compensation, no one can pretend that the complete Holocaust story has been told and justice served. Unless and until other victims of the Third Reich admit the suffering and extermination of the men and women who wore the pink triangle, the awful story of twentieth-century genocide is incomplete. Let me be blunt: Until those who have suffered at the hands of totalitarianism of the left and right recognize gay men and lesbians as their brothers and sisters, until you see us as having lives worth fighting and dying for, you, too, are oppressors, and the stories of your own oppression are demeaned. And unless and until such international organizations as Amnesty International document and publicize world-wide violations of the human rights of gay men and lesbians, we feel free to charge them with the crime of hypocrisy.

We gay men and lesbians are a proud and gentle people, chosen by God to be who we are, wherever we are. We, too, are endowed by our Creator with certain inalienable rights, and among these are Life, Liberty and the Pursuit of Happiness. We are your friends and neighbors, your brothers and sisters, your aunts and uncles, and yes, even your mothers and fathers. In the end, we have a right to be here, to be free.

January 8, 1987

Goodbye to Wisconsin Governor Anthony Earl

Earl Bricker

Originally addressed to "Members and friends of Wisconsin's gay and lesbian community," this letter was written by Bricker, former liaison for Governor Anthony Earl, to that state's Council on Lesbian and Gay Issues, following Earl's loss of the gubernatorial election of November 1986 to Tommy Thompson. It was printed in *Windy City Times* in Chicago on January 8, 1987.

There's not much use in rehashing the election results. Everyone has had a chance to come to their own conclusions as to why it happened the way it happened. And, every community has its self-appointed experts who are more than happy to offer reasons for Tony Earl's loss to Tommy Thompson. All you need to do now is determine exactly how that will affect you.

First of all, the obvious: there will no longer be a resident of the Executive Office who is responsive to and supportive of the particular needs of lesbians and gay men. There likely will not be a Chief Executive who will appoint people who are openly gay or lesbian. However, we can assume that Gov. Thompson will have staff who are homosexuals since it would be difficult to do otherwise. After all, we are everywhere. Tony Earl has been great, and I personally admire him like I've never admired anyone before. I see no obvious future candidate for governor with even a *smidgen* of his principles. That saddens me, but that's reality.

The departure of Tony Earl means the departure of Ron McCrea and myself, which means different things to different people. Even so, there are not many governors in the country who would hire anyone who is open about his or her homosexual orientation. It has been quite an experience working in an office such as this, not having to hide anything. And Tony was open to appointing more gay men and lesbians to the many councils and commissions that exist. There will still be such appointments made by Thompson, but I suspect they'll be made only if those seeking appointment aren't open about their private life. Thompson has made no effort to conceal his "pro-family" stance, a way of looking at issues that transcends gay and lesbian concerns, but it certainly does not bode well for us. Tony Earl was an almost certain veto for legislation that would harm civil liberties of individuals. Tommy Thompson is on record as an opponent of the anti-discrimination law and a proponent of Rawhide's efforts to gut that very law by providing a special exemption for that operation.

On another level, the Governor's Council on Lesbian and Gay Issues, created by Gov. Earl in April 1983, will cease to exist, one way or another, upon the inauguration of Gov. Thompson. As the Council was formed through Executive Order, it will go with the person who created it. Governor-elect Thompson said several times during the campaign that the Council would be among the first to go, saying he would abolish it. Such a statement was made either through ignorance or in an attempt to woo votes of homophobic voters since, as I've mentioned, the Council goes with its creator. It remains to be seen whether or not Tommy Thompson wishes to make another grandstand appeal to anti-gay sentiments by holding a press conference or issuing a statement around the non-renewal of the Council. As a matter of fact, the present 13 members of the Council are contemplating action rather than reaction by resigning before being "fired."

The Council has been successful, and the men and women who have served upon it deserve more appreciation than they will probably ever receive. It is a tribute of sorts to those men and women who have served on the Council since 1983 that they have been more interested in results than in blowing their collective horn. It must be remembered that the Council was created to serve as an advisory body. The most important work of the Council, in my opinion, has been their outreach and informal educational efforts in so many communities across the state.

In addition to extensive travel and the resulting media exposure, which was almost always positive, the Council was responsible for a survey measuring the extent of anti-gay and lesbian violence in Wisconsin. The summary of the data resulting from the surveys returned was recently submitted to a U.S. Congressional hearing on the topic of violence against gay men and lesbians. A former member of the Council personally experienced such violence, having been raped and told by her assailant that the reason for the attack was her participation on the Council.

More subtly, the Council has a direct impact on issues being debated in the State Capitol. The Public Health Task Force on AIDS, which recently completed its charge to develop guidelines and recommendations, would not have had an openly gay man, Will Handy, as a member had no one suggested him to Gov. Earl as a logical inclusion. The final recommendations might have been much different without his input. The Council on Lesbian and Gay Issues was the first to come out strongly against the concept of contact tracing of the sexual partners of people testing positive for the HIV antibody.

Because of their early position and lobbying efforts, the final product was tied to the continuation of the alternative testing sites, where people can have the test administered anonymously, and the contact notification program will be voluntary. Wisconsin is still one of only two states that forbids insurance companies to request applicants to take the HIV antibody test.

Summarizing the work of the Council will be difficult because so much was done by phone and in meetings, but a Final Report is one of my chief tasks before leaving.

I know that many people in many areas of the state are beginning to organize. There is an immediate threat from Rawhide's efforts to alter the antidiscrimination laws to allow them and other non-profit groups to discriminate against a person because of his or her sexual orientation. If this is allowed, it might be only a matter of time before the entire law is repealed. My hope is that once individual communities have their own houses in order, an effort to first begin and then maintain contact be initiated.

1987

Greater Seattle Business Association Address

Barbara Roberts

Roberts was the state secretary of Oregon at the time of her speech. The full text was printed in the *Seattle Gay News* issue for February 6, 1987.

Susan B. Anthony, in her struggle for women's rights, made a very short but significant statement many, many years ago and its application seems very appropriate here tonight.

I sometimes wear a medallion that bears her words "Never another season of silence."

In January of 1985, I invited the Portland Gay Men's Chorus to sing in the State Capitol rotunda for my swearing-in ceremony as Oregon's new Secretary of State.

That day was the proudest, most public day of my life, and I wanted to say something important about my commitment to civil rights and human rights.

I knew that if I was not silent on the first day, I would not be tempted to be silent when I grew used to the office and the title.

But Secretary of State in my state is a four-year office, and there is a possibility, slim though it may be, that some of those offended Oregonians may forget that the first day ceremony that occurred in January of 1985 may have slipped their mind by November of 1988.

Well, remember the medallion?

Never another season of silence.

Thursday night as I was leaving Salem on my way to Olympia, I made a stop in Portland at the Metropolitan Community Church.

Now, it may be understandable that one would stop for spiritual guidance on the way to the Washington State Legislature for a day.

But that was not my reason for stopping.

Portland's Metropolitan Community Church was the scene of a major rally to kick off the introduction of an omnibus Gay Rights Bill in the Oregon Legislature.

I spoke Thursday night as the keynote for that big rally, and there is little chance that that will be forgotten by November, 1988.

But let me make clear, I am neither politically kamikaze, nor politically courageous.

I simply realize that if any group of Americans faces the loss of their civil rights, their dignity, their privacy, their freedom to assemble, their job or their housing, that I might be in the group that is chosen next by those who judge by self-appointment.

The rally Thursday night was an exciting, energizing, up-beat, positive, warm happening.

Our new legislative bill, introduced by the interim judiciary committee, has the printed endorsements of 27 organizations on the face of the bill, including the American Civil Liberties Union, the Ecumenical Ministries of Oregon, the Oregon Public Employee's Association, the Oregon Education Association, the Oregon Women's Political Caucus, and many many others.

The rally raised over $8000 in one pass of the hat, to help fund a full-time lobbyist to shepherd the bill through the legislative session.

I'd like to share part of the remarks I made Thursday evening with you tonight because they reflect some of my pride about what's happened in Oregon, and what I hope will soon happen across this nation.

And when my remarks refer to "Oregonians," I hope you'll sort of insert the word "Washingtonians" in the same spirit.

Never another season of silence.

We cannot stand silently by while any Oregonian faces the loss of their civil rights. We cannot stand silently by while any Oregonian faces the loss of their dignity and their privacy.

We will not stand silently by and watch organized bigotry and hatred demean any Oregonian.

We cannot stand silently by and witness tyranny, because this is America, and freedom has always been purchased with bravery and never with silence.

When the Portland Gay Men's Chorus performed in Schnitzer Hall last year, raising their voices in song, that was certainly not silence.

And when they sang again last week in the Oregon State Senate and the Oregon House of Representatives, we heard freedom ring.

And when Gay Pride week happens each year in Oregon, silence takes a back seat.

When the entertainment community in California spoke out loud and clear, with music and money, after Rock Hudson's illness became public, they said clearly that their friend would not die silently alone.

They spoke volumes for compassion.

When Oregon's two candidates for governor were both endorsed by the Right To Privacy Political Action Committee, our state's gay rights PAC, Oregon's voice for human rights was heard loud and clear across this country.

And tonight we celebrate another milestone in Oregon's quest for civil rights, human dignity and personal freedom.

House Bill 2325 (and please note that number, you'll be hearing from us) ends four years of silence in the Oregon Legislature on the subject of sexual orientation.

House Bill 2325, and its impressive list of sponsoring organizations, is a **hallelujah chorus** *for personal liberty and private choices in Oregon.*

Never another season of silence.

We are consistently challenged to defend the rights involved in economic independence against those who wish to deny employment.

We are consistently confronted to defend the right to privacy to keep government out of America's bedrooms.

We are constantly challenged by the fear and ignorance and hysteria and anger created by judgment and withheld understanding.

And we accept the challenge to right those wrongs.

We have gained some ground, but the road ahead is still longer than the road behind.

The journey will be easier because we travel together.

Our destination is civil rights and dignity for every American.

Over 200 years of American history should remind us of the power that is possible when we stand together, when we stand up for our rights and are willing to face even hatred and violence to make words mean something in this democracy.

We have stood together and spoken up for racial equality, women's rights, religious freedom and rights for the handicapped.

And our message tonight is no different from any of those.

When we all realize that if any group of Americans faces the loss of their civil rights, their dignity, their freedom to assemble, their job or their housing, that we might be in the next group that is chosen.

So we cannot afford to be silent.

It will not always be easy.

We will not always be surrounded by supporters when it is time to speak out.

Some will be offended, but that is a small price to pay for doing what is right.

I hope that my voice on this important human issue will make it easier for even one legislature to cast the vote that morally right and politically difficult.

We stand together for real democracy.

I want to tell you, when that rally was over, nobody was silent.

But communication is not just to speak, it is also to listen.

For example, millions of Americans recite the nation's pledge: **With liberty and justice for all** *and do not hear the words, do not understand the meaning, and do not live the oath.*

Groups whose names denote the right of liberty and justice—the Freedom Foundation, the Moral Majority, the Truth Crusade—they demand their brand of constitutional adherence.

They usually care about the so-called gold standard, but not the standard of living for America's poor and elderly and disabled.

They care about the right to bear arms, but often fight a woman's right to choose if she will bear children.

They want prayer in the schools, women in the kitchen and government in your bedroom.

They want schools without sex education; neighborhoods without minorities; a Constitution without an Equal Rights Amendment; and a workplace without gays and lesbians.

And we have justifiable difficulty communicating with those who rave about their constitutional rights, but would eliminate those rights for so many other Americans.

The words of our democracy can be powerful, and they can be a powerful tool. We must make their meaning and their strength clear to those who would spread hate and fear and violence in our land.

We, *we in this room, and others like us, must define the words, and not leave the interpretation to those who misunderstand, mis-inform, mis-interpret and mis-lead.*

Let me tell you a personal story about defining the words, about standing up, and not remaining silent, and about making a difference.

The words were: Free-Public-Education.

The time was 1969.

The child was mine. My older son Mike is handicapped. He's autistic.

Back in the late 60's, Mike had just returned home after three years in private institutional care. He was in a federally-funded experimental special education grant program in my local school district.

But the federal funding for the program was threatened and other school districts were constantly turning away children like my son.

I decided that the Oregon law needed to be changed, to provide public education for emotionally handicapped children.

There were hundreds of children across my state, and across other states, who were being turned away from our public schools, even though their parents pay taxes to those schools.

At that time, there were no federal laws, no federal programs, requiring handicapped education in our schools. In fact, the law had not even yet been introduced in Congress in 1969.

I knew this special education could make an incredible difference in these children. I had seen it in my own son.

And I thought that my son had a right to public education. I believed he deserved the same chance as other children, and so, I stood up.

I had seen the words: Free-Public-Education, and I would no longer let others interpret those words for me. I knew their meaning and I knew their meaning for my son.

Six months later, this then-divorced mother of two, working as a part-time, unpaid citizen lobbyist, while supporting my two sons by myself, had passed a bill unanimously through the Oregon House and Senate to require education for emotionally handicapped children in the public schools of Oregon.

Oregon had a new law. The words—my words—were in the Oregon law books, and they still are. And in my very first political experience, I had done it.

I understood then that the mountain of government was moveable . . . because I had moved the mountain.

And I had learned that one person could make a difference.

I could not stand silently by while my son's rights were ignored.

And I will not stand silently by while your rights are abused.

In the words of Robert Frost: "Two roads diverged in a wood, and I—/I took the one less traveled by/And that has made all the difference."

We travel together: our destination is human rights. And our guidebook is the United States Constitution, and the Bill of Rights.

We will not be silent.

We will make a difference.

Both politicians and homosexuals understand that there is risk to *come out of the closet* on this important human issue.

But there is no sunshine in the closet.

And we cannot see the road without the light.

Never another season of silence.

Thank you, very much.

[After long applause in the form of a standing ovation, Barbara Roberts returned to the podium.]

Let me share a line that wasn't in the speech tonight. I'd like to share it with you.

Thirty years ago, when my son was born, I did not know who he was, or what he would become.

Thirty years ago, when my son was born, I did not know who I was, or what I would become.

I thank my son, and you, for making me stand for something important.

Thank you!

March 27, 1987

National AIDS Network Conference Speech

Tony Coelho

This is the text of the address given to the National AIDS Network (NAN) Conference in Los Angeles, California on March 27, 1987, by Representative Tony Coelho (D-CA), at that time House Majority Whip. The legal case mentioned is *School Board of Nassau County v. Arline,* decided in 1987 by the U.S. Supreme Court, which held that a person with a contagious disease (in the original case, tuberculosis) could be considered disabled and therefore entitled to legal protection under the Rehabilitation Act of 1973. C. Everett Koop was the surgeon general of the United States at this time.

I'm really grateful that NAN asked me to speak today, because it gave me the opportunity to learn how vital the AIDS network truly is.

As local providers at AIDS service organizations, you're meeting the challenges presented by AIDS on the front lines and you're doing this despite scarce resources and minimal support from the federal government.

When I started to prepare my remarks I thought I knew a lot about the issue. It didn't take me long to realize how much I didn't know. Part of the problem is that this issue is hard to keep up with: AZT, self-inoculation, the Arline case—every day it seems there's another development and often another breakthrough.

We've learned in recent days that AIDS has replaced heart disease in the public mind as the second most serious health problem facing the country, with cancer still no. 1. And we've learned that your group forced the FDA's quick approval of AZT, but also that the drug comes at a high price: $10,000 per person per year.

Indeed there's a wealth of information out there and the situation's changing almost daily. That's good, but it's also intimidating, and I think you need to consider that when you lobby the Hill. But before getting into that, I want to acknowledge and thank my many friends with NAN and also the AIDS Action Council, the Human Rights Campaign and the National Gay and Lesbian Task Force.

You should be very proud of the job you're doing—I know I am—and I'm also very grateful for your help over the past several years electing enlightened people to the House of Representatives, especially since most of them turn out to be Democrats.

I know you'll all be glad to hear that I'm not going to spend too much time today telling you things you already know. You didn't come all the way to L.A. to hear another politician reel off the latest facts and figures. Instead I'll try to concentrate on how the AIDS issue is developing politically and legislatively, and then I'll close with a few thoughts on how you might gain more allies in Congress.

One thing I won't spend any time doing is congratulating the President of the United States for using his bully pulpit to mobilize public support to fight the AIDS epidemic. He hasn't done that, and given the overwhelming evidence that AIDS could destroy the social fabric of this country in the not too distant future, I think it's disgraceful.

As my good friend Henry Waxman [D-CA, chairman, House subcommittee on health] said recently, "If the 60s are remembered as the decade of war and protest, the 80s will be remembered for the epidemic." And the Reagan Administration, for all its sweeping policy changes, will not be remembered for its space shield, its secret wars or even, I think, its destruction of U.S. credibility abroad.

"The Reagan Administration will be remembered for its failure to deal with AIDS."

I agree with that. And I think it's appropriate at this time to say that this audience doesn't have a better friend or a bigger supporter than Henry Waxman. Henry's been trying to focus attention on this issue for some time now and it's about time the rest of us in Congress caught up with him. But back to his point.

We will in fact look back on this decade and remember with regret saving a few dollars but losing thousands of lives.

We will remember and regret shying away from education and turning instead to short-sighted non-solutions like mandatory testing.

We will remember and regret aiming discrimination at people with AIDS rather than devoting enough public resources to finding treatments for their problems.

We will remember and regret electing a President who loves to declare war—war on the Sandinistas, war on the so-called welfare cheats, war on the elderly and most vulnerable in society—but who ignores the most awesome threat to public safety in generations.

It's been said that no Hollywood script writer could have dreamed up the Iran-Contra affair, Swiss Bank accounts, real live Rambos, tragic suicide attempts—you name it. But to quote Congressman Waxman again, "Not even the Greek gods could have created a drama more tragic and more ironic than this disease at this time during this administration."

We have a nation under the reign of a budget-slashing President and under siege by a budget-busting epidemic.
We have an administration that finds it difficult to tell heterosexuals about contraception but must now support efforts to tell homosexuals about safe sex.
We have a Justice Department that claims to be pro-life but whose censorship of Dr. Koop is causing death by ignorance.
We have anti-gay ideologues and evangelists, who when they aren't paying hush money to cover up their own hypocrisy, are arming themselves with the new rhetorical weapon of AIDS.
We have a press corps that just six years ago would not use the words gay or lesbian but must now explain how bodily fluids are exchanged.
And we have gay people themselves, who wanted only for government to leave them alone but who now have a real need for protection and assistance from governments they fear more than ever.

I must say it was absolutely appalling for me to watch the *CBS News* Tuesday night and see a man with AIDS tell the reporter he was so afraid of our government that one day soon he thought somebody would come pick him up, take him to a clinic and tattoo his arm, just like the Nazis did to the Jews 45 years ago.

So this epidemic is tragic. And it is ironic. And in many ways it's only beginning. I don't have to tell you that a vaccine, a successful treatment and certainly a cure are perhaps decades away.

In the meantime, it will fall to groups like this one to convince the American people and of course the politicians that AIDS is too serious a matter to be dealt with through fear and ignorance.

Fortunately, I think the new 100th Congress is headed in the right direction.

As you know, AIDS funding nearly doubled from fiscal year 1986 to '87, from $233 million to $417 million. This year the President requested $534 million, but much of his request came at the expense of other health programs.

Congressman Waxman and Senator Kennedy have made it clear that the administration's proposals are inadequate. And I can assure you the House

Leadership agrees. Not only will we approve higher funding than the President wants, but we don't intend to displace other necessary programs.

We'll take it out of Star Wars or contra aid instead. Or if need be we should have the guts to raise taxes to pay for it.

In addition to funding, there's bipartisan support for a non-political national commission—a "Manhattan Project" on AIDS if you will—that would coordinate Federal research, education and prevention activities, and also override existing bureaucratic roadblocks.

The Senate is considering a bill dealing with liability problems that drug manufacturers fear could delay a future vaccine, and the House committees are concentrating on education, protecting civil liberties and financing the tremendous cost to those who've contracted the disease.

In all there are almost 20 separate bills being considered, and I would expect a comprehensive package to pass soon, although it's too early to say exactly when or in what form. This is not to suggest, however, that we're doing enough—we're not—or that everything being considered is constructive.

Indeed on the bleak side there are several bills that would violate civil rights and postpone medical progress.

One would make it a crime for persons with AIDS to donate blood or vital organs; another would put people in jail if they have AIDS and engage in sex or intravenous drug use; and of course some are advocating mandatory testing, job discrimination and quarantine.

But partly because of the work you've done, I think most Members of Congress understand that what we know about this disease, we know because people with AIDS have cooperated with the medical community. And we also know that when civil liberties are threatened, the only recourse will be that the disease is driven further underground. We will know less and the time we stop the epidemic will grow more distant.

We know that job discrimination is not the answer, either. If it is agreed that people who have the virus present no danger to their fellow workers—and it is—then they should have the right to keep working if they can perform their jobs. Fortunately, the Supreme Court, even this one, agrees.

But that does not mean there's no threat from the right or that everyone in Congress fully understands this issue and its potential consequences. Which leads us to my next point, which is political.

Next year, of course, is an election year, a president election year. And without question "what-to-do-about AIDS?" is going to be a major issue for all the candidates and for both parties generally. We've already felt some tremors, but I believe AIDS will set records on the political Richter Scale in 1988. Every candidate will have to deal with it—as they should.

If, as the experts now predict, AIDS will claim more lives by the time President Reagan leaves office than were killed in the Vietnam War; and if, as the economists now tell us, AIDS will consume billions and billions of our GNP; and if, as we all know, the Reagan administration has failed miserably, then AIDS should be debated in the campaign. It should be a major issue. And we should be aggressively taking it on, not just playing defense.

It would be my hope that the AIDS issues not degenerate into another debate between science and morality. And it was encouraging last week to hear Bob Dole say the government should spend $100 million or $2 billion—whatever it takes—to stop AIDS. Of course, he wasn't very specific.

Did he mean, as some conservatives are suggesting, that we should isolate people with AIDS? Did he mean the government should spend millions to conduct involuntary tests for the AIDS virus? Or did he mean we should spend whatever it takes to conduct the necessary research and education and otherwise deal sensibly with this epidemic?

I'm worried, because Bob Dole would probably agree with us privately. And he may still do so publicly. But we all know who controls the Republican Party these days.

And it's not surprising in the least to hear the right-wingers say they've already decided to make opposition to the Surgeon General's recommendations their major litmus test for GOP candidates in 1988.

They'll try to frighten the American people. They'll pit the San Francisco Democrats against the rest of the country. They'll ask voters to look at AIDS and make a choice: Should we protect civil liberties or protect public health?

You and I know the two aren't mutually exclusive. But we need to tell that to the American people. And I would urge you to use the campaign—it's not like you have any choice—as an opportunity to educate the public and members of Congress and to calm their irrational fears.

I know what motivates members of Congress and I know how to count votes. That's my job. And right now there's not enough support for any of what the radical right is proposing.

But let me tell you: there's nothing more dangerous than a group of panicked politicians.

And there's a political element in this country that plans to do whatever it can over the next several months to panic voters and thereby their elected representatives.

I would suggest several things; First, as with any issue that has broad social implications, you shouldn't spend too much time worrying about the left or the right. You've already got the Tony Coelhos behind you and you can forget about the Pat Buchanans.

Instead you should reach out to the broad, moderate middle, the people who lack enough information but are generally sympathetic. These folks want to be helpful but you've got to educate them.

I know you know this, but I've talked to them, and while there's a general sense the situation is getting worse, they still don't know the extent of the threat. For example:

You and I know that by the year 1991 over 5 million, perhaps as many as 10 million Americans will be infected with the AIDS virus—but most members of Congress don't know that.

You and I know AIDS is the leading cause of death for heterosexual women between the ages of 25 and 29 in New York City: and like most social problems, that this one is attacking the minority community disproportionately—but most members of Congress don't know that.

You and I know that AIDS will permanently reshape the health care system in America, and that by the mid 90s half—50 percent—of all hospital beds will be occupied by people with AIDS—but most Members of Congress don't know that.

And you and I know that we're "running scared," as the director of the World Health Organization said recently, because as many as 100 million people worldwide could be infected within five years—but most members of Congress don't know that. So we've got a lot of educating to do.

But keep in mind that what I call the fear factor is at work here. Politicians are often motivated by fear. And there's a fine line between making people understand the urgency of a particular problem and creating momentum for policy options none of us wants to see. Indeed, what we need above all else is to calm the right-wing hysteria surrounding this issue.

You do that the same way the right wing tries to instill fear: you go to the grassroots, you broaden your base. Reach out, as I know you're doing, to the business community. That's a powerful constituency. Stress the economic impact of AIDS with local business and industry leaders. Continue to coordinate your lobbying efforts with respected non-gay health organizations like the AMA and the nurses.

I want you know that I'm personally committed to doing whatever I can to help. We can start working on specific members as soon as you like. I also want you to understand that I appreciate the need for action now. We can't wait until 1988, we're years behind already. Congress needs to protect your jobs, your housing and your access to insurance from the threats that exist today. And most importantly we've got to pressure the President to get the bureaucracy moving. This is the message I pledge to take back to Washington and to the Speaker of the House.

Before he was killed in this city 19 years ago, Bobby Kennedy said history is changed by the isolated acts of individuals, people whose small actions seem lost but when taken together can change events. You are those individuals. Each day you're taking small steps of courage that will eventually move our nation and the world.

Summer 1987

We the People, We the 25 Million

David Fair

This text is part of an address given by Fair at the seventh annual convention of the National Association of Black and White Men Together, meeting in Milwaukee, Wisconsin, in the summer of 1987. Alyn Hess was a prominent gay activist in Milwaukee, founder of the local Gay People's Union of Milwaukee in 1970, and a cofounder of Black and White Men Together. He died in 1989 of AIDS.

The neighborhood I work in, around 13th and Locust Streets in Philadelphia, is known for its wide-open, "anything goes" kind of atmosphere. There's a lot of hustling and prostitution, drug selling and buying, and homosexuality.

About eighteen months ago, two black drag queens who worked that particular block were kidnapped. I knew them because they used to use the ladies room in my union hall. They were found a few weeks after the kidnapping, chopped up into little pieces and stuffed into GLAD bags in Cherry Hill, New Jersey.

What's interesting about this incident is not so much that it happened—a number of black drag queens have disappeared in Philadelphia over the past 24 months without a trace—but the organized lesbian and gay community has been totally silent.

Meanwhile, a white gay man walking about a block away from my union hall was chased by a group of fag-bashers into the lobby of a hotel right across the street. They started to beat him, right there in the lobby. He was eventually rescued when hotel security decided to break things up.

This story was on the front page of the city's daily newspapers the next day. The Philadelphia Lesbian and Gay Task Force and other gay organizations demanded—and got—immediate meetings with the police commissioner.

There were editorials not only in the gay papers, but in the mainstream press and on TV and the radio.

The way the movement responded to these two incidents says something very serious about the kind of movement we have.

Last Saturday morning one of my union members at Hahnemann Hospital stopped by to tell me that a patient with AIDS had jumped out of a window on the 18th floor of the hospital the night before. I didn't know this man or the special pain that must have led him across that window sill, but as I thought about what happened, it struck me for maybe the thousandth time that AIDS kills in all sorts of ways, and that gay people suffer in all sorts of ways different from the experience of everybody else.

What kind of person was the man who died? We know that because he had AIDS, he was an undesirable, a burden, unacceptable to the mainstream. If he was also a drug addict, or if he was gay, then he was also considered defective, suspect, immoral, sinful, and, in most states, illegal.

And if, god forbid, in addition to all the above, he was poor, black or Puerto Rican, then it's no wonder he would lose faith and seek a quicker end. Being poor, or non-white, or gay or addicted—they all add up to the price of a ticket to oblivion in America in 1987.

When I say "oblivion," I mean to say that we too, the mainstream of the gay and lesbian movement, cast such people out. We have no room for them. They have little to do with the community and movement we have built in *our* image, except at those times (increasingly rare) when our liberal guilt needs comforting.

So far, there's only one gay and lesbian *movement* in our society, but there are at least *two* gay *Americas*.

There's a gay America that has not been cast into oblivion, but only shunted to the side, the one made up of individuals dedicated to seeking compensation for their insulted self-esteem, the one that demands an equal chance to make money the way things are, *regardless of their sexual preference,* able to take for granted education, professional connections, upper-class affectations.

It's the gay America of *Advocate* Men and capital P capital C Politically Correct W-I-M-M-I-N.

It's the gay America of Provincetown summers and women's festival weekends, of disposable income and conspicuous consumption, of the latest style in clothes and haircuts, of materialism, consumerism, youthism and slimnessism, workoutism and tanning salonism.

And it's the gay America "community" organizations.

We have organizations for men, for women, for older gays and even older gays, for dyke-ettes and fag-ettes, for queens and bikers, for lesbians and gay women, for bisexuals who are married and others who are just confused, for blacks, for whites (but only one for blacks *and* whites), for fathers and mothers who are gay and *their* fathers and mothers, who claim they're not, for the politically-correct and the politically-unsure, for those who merely seek tolerance of gay and lesbian lifestyles and those who believe that same-sex behavior is the revolutionary-feminist-vanguard-that-will-overturn-capitalist-oppression-and-bring-about-peace-and-justice-for-all-humankind.

When Alyn Hess wrote to me about appearing here today he asked me to address what he called "the need for economic justice as well as civil rights."

"I get the feeling," he wrote, "that not enough members understand how economic inequality impinges upon their personal relationships . . . what I see going on in America today is peasantization, the creation of a new peasant or under class."

I'll be happy to address those questions. But the real question I want to address is how economic inequality impinges, not only on our personal relationships, but on our movement, on our identity as a community, on our ability to protect and advance the interests of the lesbian and gay community in all its diversity and with all its needs.

Because there is, after all, another gay America, one we're trained not to think about when the GWM's publish their so-called "gay community" newspapers and write their so-called "gay" plays and send out their stylish press releases about what's hot and trendy in the so-called gay and lesbian lifestyle.

In Philadelphia this year we're celebrating the 200th anniversary of the U.S. Constitution—you know, the one the U.S. Supreme Court says doesn't apply to us—and the official name of the celebration is "We the People." The people who call themselves the gay and lesbian community in Philadelphia are organizing a counter-demonstration under the slogan "We the 25 Million," basing their message on the old Kinsey statistic that 10% of any given population is probably homosexual.

Now, I don't know if that 10% figure really makes sense, but since we all seem to put such stock into it, let's think about what it means.

If 10% of the U.S. population is gay or lesbian, then it's true that there 25 million Americans with some kind of homosexual preference today.

Think about that for a minute. 25 million! That's a lot of people. It's a real lot of people.

And it's obvious that the people who we most easily see as the gay and lesbian community, the gay America I just described, don't add up to anywhere near 25 million people.

So that means that somebody else out there is gay besides the people we're used to calling "the gay and lesbian community." And a lot of those somebody elses belong to a different sort of gay America.

There are over 33 million people in this country who live below the Reagan Administration's definition of the poverty line. And, following our movement logic, almost three-and-a-half million of them are gay.

There are over 40 million people in this country who go to bed every night malnourished—many of them children who have to do with a Pepsi and a bag of potato chips as their evening meal. And 4 million of those hungry people are gay.

There are 4 million homeless people in this country today, without jobs, without shelter, in most cases without much hope and with very few advocates—and over 400,000 of them are gay.

Think about that, too. 400,000 homeless gay men and women, living on streets and subways, shelters and doorways, many selling their bodies and their self-respect for a warm meal and a warm corner.

4 million hungry gay men and women, unable to dine in faggot splendor in the fine gay establishments we so dearly want to "be seen" at.

3 1/2 million under-or-un-employed, uninsured, unwanted and outcast gay people, living in the kind of *real* poverty that makes our movement's leaders grasp their gold lambda medallions when one of us looks at them funny on their way to the grocery stores in their gentrified neighborhoods.

It is now time to build a new concept of "unity" among gay and lesbian people, a unity built around the genuine needs and demands of "We the 25 Million."

Unity demands full employment of our people at a living wage.

Unity demands affordable housing for our homeless people.

Unity demands a national health system that guarantees quality health care regardless of one's ability to pay.

Unity demands economic justice and an end to racial practices in American society as a whole and the gay community in particular.

"The worst sin toward our fellow creatures is not to hate them," George Bernard Shaw once wrote, "but to be indifferent to them. That's the essence of inhumanity."

August 1987

A Letter from South Africa

Simon Nkoli

This letter was originally published in *Gay Community News,* and was sent by the South African gay activist Tseko Simon Nkoli, who was on trial with eighteen other defendants charged with treason against the apartheid government of South Africa. Although his original protest had been to oppose rent hikes in the black townships surrounding Johannesburg, his trial (begun in June of 1984 and not completed as of the writing of this letter) drew global attention from the gay and lesbian community, and the Gay and Lesbian Association of South Africa (at that time white dominated) was expelled from the International Gay and Lesbian Association for failing to support Nkoli. U.S. groups supporting him included the National Coalition of Black Lesbians and Gays and Men of All Colors Together of New York. Stephanie Poggi, cited in the text, was *GCN*'s features editor. The letter seems to have been written on August 17, 1987, from a date inserted in the *GCN* text. Nkoli died in 1998.

Greetings to all fellow gay brothers and sisters in Boston and everywhere in the United States of America.

I wish to thank *GCN* for publishing an article on our trial, in which I as an individual gay activist and 18 other "straights" are appearing in a Pretoria Supreme Court to answer the charges put against us. I am also grateful to Tim McCaskell who contributed [the story] to *GCN*. I therefore make a request that although my English is not so good, publish this letter of mine in one of your issues to come.

I spoke to a comrade lady, [features editor] Stephanie Poggi. I was so excited to hear from her and it was also a privilege for a prisoner like me to talk to someone from another country. But what made me more thrilled was the idea of knowing that I'm not the only one who opposes apartheid. I have gay brothers and lesbian sisters who shared the suffering I went through when I was in jail. Not that I am not suffering at the moment. In fact I do suffer more at the moment since I am not in a position to work for myself. I depend on the R100 that the SACC is donating for me every month. Because that is too little, I am now looking for a Saturday job. Life must go on.

All right, let me tell you more about my going to the witness stand since it was the main issue in Tim's article. Brothers and dear sisters, it was not easy at all. The thought of going into the witness box gave me nightmares months before I [was to] go in there. I worked so hard trying to figure out how I would answer the unknown questions. How I would react if the state Prosecution [shouted at me].

Most of my co-accused thought I'd be a bad witness so they suggested I not go to the box. Why did they think I'd be bad? I don't know, but I guess it's because they were afraid that I was going to be confronted about being a gay. So what? I was not going to deny that I'm gay, but I was going to argue that the case has got nothing to do with my gayness. GASA [Gay South African Association], the organization that I belonged to when I was a free man, was not part of organizations alleged to have conspired with the UDF [United Democratic Front] and the ANC [African National Congress] to overthrow South Africa by means of violence. Saturday Group [subgroup of GASA organized by Nkoli] was not mentioned in the indictment.

But I know that the state and the police know that I'm gay and they might have tried to use my gayness to discredit me and my fellow co-accused. Hang on, let me just tell you that not all of my co-accused accepted me as a gay person. That was an extra burden for me. I was advised several times by some of them that I should not bring the subject of gayness up.

. . . I told them I was not going to volunteer to bring the subject up; I would only be directed by the Prosecutor's questions. If, for example, the Prosecutor has asked me, "Mr. Nkoli, are you a homosexual?" I would have answered, "Yes, my Lord" . . . I am what I am and I will remain what I am until the end of the day.

On the 24th of June 1987 at 12:35 [p.m.], the senior defense counsel—Mr. George Bizos—a very understanding person, a gentleman indeed—announced, "My Lord, we will call our shortest witness, Mr. Simon Nkoli, accused no. 13 in this matter." I couldn't hear the rest of what he said. I saw myself walking tensely to the witness box. Some guys were wishing me good luck, shaking my hands. Bad and terrible looks from the state side. I couldn't go back, I was going in the witness box.

"Your full name," the court orderly asked.

"Tseko Simon Nkoli."

"Raise your right hand and take an oath and say, So help me God."

I did as I was told, trying all my best to hide my trembling. I put my left hand in my pocket. I couldn't face the audience. I was rather too nervous, too shy. I had not addressed so many people for ages. The last time I addressed a meeting of such a number was at school when I was a member of GASA. That was a commemoration service of June 16, 1980. I was assigned to speak at that meeting . . . Of course, from 1982 to '84 I had been addressing gay meetings mainly in Johannesburg, Vaal Triangle and in Pretoria.

But this was not a meeting nor was it a gay get-together. It was Delmas Court and one had to talk about legal matters. But I was also in the witness box to depend on myself and to demonstrate to those who thought I'd be a bad witness that they were all wrong. I could be as good as they are. In fact, I did well. I got used to the witness box within ten minutes. I took my hand out of my pocket. I looked the judge in the eyes. I looked at those frowning faces of the state prosecutors and at the members of the public. I was no longer shivering or trembling. I was a smiling Simon. What was there to be afraid of if I said "God help me" while taking an oath?

Among other questions, I was asked, "What kind of freedom do you want?" I said, "I want a freedom where I will move free with who I want to. I want a freedom where our children will get equal education. Freedom where people of all races will be provided with equal standard of living. Freedom of speech. Freedom where all people will be treated equal before the law."

[They asked], "Do you regard Nelson Mandela as your leader?" I said, "Yes, in a sense that he is regarded by many people as leader of Black people. For what he has sacrificed, yes I do. I may not know what he is convicted of. But I have heard lots of people talking about him as one person who was fighting for freedom."

They asked, "Do you support the ANC?" I said, "No, I don't. There is no ANC in this country: it is banned. I do agree with them in fighting for freedom in this country, but I differ with them because I am opposed to violence. All the same, I think if the ANC is allowed in this country and allowed to negotiate, they will stop using violence."

These are some of the many questions that I was asked. As for the murder charge, I was asked no questions concerning this. Not a single state witness had said any of the accused had committed murder . . . There was little evidence against me and there were only two allegations in the indictment. That is why I spent only seven hours in the witness box. And I am now confident that many of us, if not all, will be acquitted at the end of the trial.

At the moment, Popo Simon Molefe is giving evidence. Today [August 17, 1987] is his 11th day in the witness box. He is one of the three who refused bail. Popo is a member of the UDF. It seems he is going to spend some time in the box. After Popo, there are three more people among the accused to testify. This may last until the end of the year. Then the defense is going to call lots of witnesses from members of the public. These will be ordinary people who attended meetings of the UDF and of organizations affiliated with the UDF. This process will take some time. That is why we are thinking that the case will go on for more than 18 months.

What are gay organizations in South Africa saying? Let me tell you without hesitation, GASA is doing nothing except that I heard that they are losing members. Kevin Botha, who represented GASA at the International Lesbian and Gay Association conference last year, is nowhere to be seen. I doubt that he is still a member of GASA. He has not contacted me since my release. I am not going to contact him either. No one from GASA's executive committee has welcomed me back, or wished me good luck. In fact, I don't even know who is in GASA. I met one guy who is an ordinary member of GASA. He didn't tell me what GASA is saying about me. In any event, I am not interested.

. . . I also believe that the Rand Gay Association [RGO] has about 600 members. That is great—and much better than Saturday Group, Saturday Group had only 124 members when I was arrested.

LAGO and AGA are two gay organizations from Cape Town, and I wish to inform you that they have been so supportive of me. Although they are so far away from Johannesburg, they managed to send people to the hearing while I was in Delmas. When I was in the witness box, they sent me lots of messages of support. I thank them so much for the support that they gave to me. I am going to make an application to court that I should be allowed to go there [Cape Town] for two weeks in December. They may refuse so I am not sure whether I will go. I will let you know.

As you know, I was the coordinator of Saturday Group in Johannesburg, a non-racial interest group within GASA. It was not a political organization, but most members believed in non-racialism. And although I am personally politically involved, I was not discriminating about who could be members of Saturday Group based on their politics. So our main aim was to bring gays of all races together. To help them solve their own personal problems. To counsel those who were depressed, because among South African gays, there are those who . . . pick or get picked up by strangers who happen to be thugs and at the end they are beaten up or mugged. Or you get those who think they are old, ugly, short, or too fat or too thin, those who believe that they are too rich or too poor, those who think that they are uneducated, those who think that they are unable to take part in any kind of sports. All these people are very lonely and they need to be helped, and that is what I was doing and that is what I am going to do.

The Saturday Group members feel that we should revive it again, but my view is that they should join RGO. At the moment, I am not allowed to attend any political meetings, so whatever I do for gay people in Johannesburg will be quite moderate. On Saturday the 22nd of August, 1987, about 15 of us are meeting to discuss what we can do for gays in this country . . . I do hope it will be something and we shall keep you informed.

Brothers and sisters, let me say goodbye for today. Hoping to hear from you.

With lots of love

Simon Nkoli
Johannesburg, South Africa

October 2, 1987

Chicago March on Washington Day Proclamation

Harold Washington

Harold Washington was the first African American to be elected mayor of the city of Chicago. During his time in office, he was supportive of civil rights efforts made by the gay and lesbian community and addressed one of the Gay Pride rallies in Lincoln Park. This proclamation is an example of the political responses made at the local level paralleling the mass demonstration of the March on Washington in October 1987.

Office of the Mayor
City of Chicago
Harold Washington, Mayor

PROCLAMATION

WHEREAS, there will be a National March on Washington for Lesbian and Gay Rights on October 11, 1987, in Washington, D.C.; and

WHEREAS, it is important that the nation understand that it is not gay and lesbian people, but rather the threats to their rights, that endanger the entire nation and its values; and

WHEREAS, the AIDS crisis has intensified discrimination against those who are perceived to be at high risk for AIDS, such discrimination being directed against lesbians and gays and also against minorities; and

WHEREAS, The March on Washington for Lesbian and Gay Rights will make an emphatic statement for the urgency of escalating the war against AIDS, not against people with AIDS; and

WHEREAS, participants and supporters of the March on Washington will be making an emphatic statement as well against the inhumanity of discrimination based on race, both in the United States and in apartheid-bound South Africa; and

WHEREAS, many lesbian and gay residents of Chicago will go to Washington to participate in the March, and many more will participate in spirit; and

WHEREAS, Chicago's gay and lesbian residents and their contributions are an important element in the fabric of the City of Chicago and should be supported by all residents:

NOW, THEREFORE, I, Harold Washington, Mayor of the City of Chicago, do hereby proclaim October 11, 1987, to be CHICAGO MARCH ON WASHINGTON FOR LESBIAN AND GAY RIGHTS DAY and urge all interested citizens to be cognizant of the events arranged for this time.

Dated this 2nd day of October, 1987.

Harold Washington
Mayor.

October 11, 1987

Our Demands

March on Washington for Lesbian and Gay Rights

The National March on Washington for Lesbian and Gay Rights, held October 8 through 13, 1987, attended by over one-half million people, was the second such event, the first occurring in 1979. Issues of anger were the federal government's slow response to the AIDS pandemic and the 1986 *Bowers v. Hardwick* decision upholding Georgia's sodomy law. The march was also the occasion of the first display of the NAMES Project AIDS Memorial Quilt. A mass civil disobedience action at the Supreme Court on October 13, 1987, resulted in the arrest of some 800 people.

OUR DEMANDS

Chosen Family and Relationships

Recognizing and celebrating the diversity in family relationships, we demand legal recognition of lesbian and gay male domestic partnerships with all the benefits and entitlements that flow from marriage. These include, but are not limited to, rights of inheritance, extended medical benefits, visitation and custody rights, insurance rights, parenting, foster care and adoption and immigration, etc.

- Since gay and lesbian youth are often without societal and familial support, we demand funding for a broad range of social services targeted to them, including, but not limited to: alternative housing, foster care, counseling services, legal aid, etc. All such programs must have significant representation of lesbians and gay men on all levels of policy and implementation.
- We demand safe sex information and health services for gay and lesbian youth, sexuality and anti-homophobia curriculum in the schools, access to and the freedom to organize and participate in all school and related social activities.

Sodomy Laws

Because the sodomy and related laws form the cornerstone of discrimination against lesbians and gay men, the lesbian and gay community of this nation demands a repeal, through federal and local action, of all laws that violate the right to privacy by criminalizing consensual sex between individuals above the age of consent; that the term "sexual orientation" be added to the Federal Civil Rights Act to prohibit discrimination against lesbians and gay men in employment; that Congress, through any means available to it, prohibit states from regulating private adult consensual activities and that education be done on the definition of sodomy to show that sodomy laws prohibit the majority of consensual sexual activity.

Presidential Action/Executive Order

We demand use of the full presidential authority to eliminate all discrimination based on sexual orientation in all aspects of executive branch employment, programs and policies. Specifically, we demand:

- Issuing of a presidential executive order banning discrimination based on sexual orientation in federal employment, the military, federally-contracted private employment, the granting of security clearances and all federally funded programs.
- Inasmuch as the exclusion of gays and lesbians is not medically or scientifically valid, the public health service shall resume its policy of non-enforcement of the gay/lesbian medical exclusion under the immigration law.
- Repeal of all military regulations discriminating against lesbians and gays, including sodomy regulations, upgrade of all less than honorable military discharges for reasons of homosexuality with full restoration of benefits, including retirement with no statute of limitations.
- A presidential order banning use of HIV testing or AIDS-related discrimination in federal employment or by federal contractors.
- A presidential order guaranteeing uncensored access to information for gay/lesbian prisoners, equality of visitation rights and protection from discrimination based on AIDS and/or sexual orientation.
- The Justice Department shall cease and desist from the interpretation of laws in manners which are oppressive and destructive to the civil rights of lesbians and gay men and all other people; including repeal of their interpretation discriminating against workers associated with AIDS.

Discrimination Against People with AIDS and People with ARC

- End discrimination against people with AIDS/ARC, those testing positive for the AIDS virus or those perceived to be in any of those categories.
- End the special discrimination suffered by people of color, prisoners, persons on active military duty, veterans and IV drug users.
- Stop discrimination in the delivery of health care, insurance, social services, housing, employment, public accommodations and education.
- End discrimination in immigration related areas.
- Criminalize discrimination by any corporate or governmental entity.
- End federal funding for organizations (or corporate tax breaks) for governmental bodies which practice discrimination.
- We demand compassionate, comprehensive health care services: both in- and out-patient services without regard to ability to pay, based on the San Francisco model. We must give special attention to health care services for people of color and those in low income areas.
- We demand the federal government immediately implement legislation which would prohibit any individual from invading the privacy of any person that has tested positive for HIV or has been diagnosed as having AIDS/ARC by revealing said information to employers, landlords, educational institutions, governmental agencies, or any other individual without the written informed consent of said person with AIDS/ARC.
- We demand that education be provided at the government's expense specifically geared to gay and lesbian youth.

Funding for AIDS

- We demand complete federal funding of all health and social services for all people with AIDS/ARC: that the federal government underwrite and insure all research for a cure and a vaccine; that the federal government fund a massive AIDS education and prevention program that is explicit, culturally sensitive, lesbian/gay affirming and sex positive.
- That funding come from the military budget, not already existing appropriations in the social services budget.

Other Demands

- Lesbian and gay people shall be included in the National Holocaust Commission and its administration.
- We demand the right to control our bodies and practice our sexuality freely. This includes an expansion of reproductive rights, an end to sterilization abuse and free abortions and contraceptives on demand to persons of all ages.
- We demand that the Federal Government fund a nation-wide educational campaign to counter the wave of hatred, violence and misinformation being directed against lesbians, gay men and youth. This fund is to administered by the lesbian and gay community.
- The lesbian and gay community shall support the ERA (This demand, we feel, may be either a demand or an incorporated principle).
- The system of apartheid in South America [*sic*] is racist and violates all human rights. We demand the freedom of black activist Simon Nkoli, facing treason charges, and all South African political prisoners. We support the South African freedom struggle and demand an end to U.S. Governmental and corporate support of South African Apartheid.

October 11, 1987

From the Stage

Barbara Smith

The full text of this address, planned to be given at the March on Washington, was not read due to lack of time.

My name is Barbara Smith. I am proud to tell you that I am an African American, a woman, I was born into a working class family in 1946, and I am a lesbian.

With only five minutes I will be leaving a whole lot out, but there are three things I need to talk to you about today. Number one is the issue of homophobia in the Black community. Number two is the problem of racism in our lesbian and gay movement. And number three is the question of our freedom and how to get it.

My life as an activist began when I was a teenager in the Black Civil Rights movement of the 1960s, growing up in Cleveland, Ohio. I am grateful to come from the race of people who have defined the parameters of struggle against oppression in this country. Yet there are some Black people who would deny my right to be respected, to raise my children, to keep my job, to have equal access to housing, to be free from verbal harassment and from violent physical attack, who in short would deny my right to exist because I am a Black person who is also a lesbian.

I want to take this opportunity to deliver a message to my people, to African Americans all across this country. It is time for us to throw out, once and for all, our old tired attitudes about lesbians and gay men. It is time for all of us to stand up completely for justice, for freedom.

Homosexuality is not a white disease. And AIDS is not even a white gay male disease, not when 25 percent of people with AIDS are Black, and 14 percent of people with AIDS are Latinos, and 52 percent of all women with AIDS are Black, and 80 percent of all the pediatric cases are babies and children of color.

Homosexuality is not what is breaking up the Black family—homophobia is. My Black gay brothers and my Black lesbian sisters are members of

Black families, both the ones we were born into and the ones we create. Quiet as it's kept, we have always been here in the Black community and long before that in the motherland on the African continent. We have always been here and we always will be here. Langston Hughes has been here. James Baldwin has been here. Bayard Rustin has been here. R. Bruce Nugent has been here. Jackie "Moms" Mabley has been here. Lorraine Hansberry has been here. Mabel Hampton has been here. Ann Allen Shockley has been here. Pat Parker has been here. Audre Lorde has been here. And if you don't know who these people are, please go tomorrow morning and find out, because they are just a few of our Black lesbian and gay ancestors, elders and warriors.

I am not raising this challenge because Black people are more homophobic than anybody else. In fact, I believe we may be less so and because of our position in the society more individually tolerant of differences and diversity. It is just that as members of a racially oppressed group, trying to survive in the poisonous and racist climate of the Reagan years, we cannot afford to be divided from each other. We cannot afford to lose any of our strengths, our gifts, and our capacity to love. For us as Black lesbians and gays, nothing devastates us more than being cut cold by our own.

I am completely confident that this challenge will be met, because in my life I have seen the Black community go through so much remarkable and positive change. I tell you, when Jesse Jackson stands with us, as he is today, the leading Democratic candidate for President of the United States, a Baptist minister, and a Black man, something real good is happening for us. I know that we can change.

The second challenge I have to deliver is to the white members of the lesbian and gay movement. I challenge you to grapple seriously with the reality of racism and to understand the disastrous impact it has upon the lives of people of color, including lesbians and gay men of color. Again, since I came out in 1974, I have seen great progress in the lesbian, gay and especially the feminist movements, in our ability to bridge our differences and in our capacity to build fierce and effective coalitions. But we still have a long, long way to go.

This country's racial history is far too complex for me to analyze or even to describe in all of its ramifications here. But there are two things I would like you to think about. First, you cannot only work on the issue of racism *inside* of the gay and lesbian movement. You have got to challenge and eradicate racial, and also sexual, and economic oppression in the society as a whole. We have got to apply our unique capacity to love and to work tirelessly for justice to every single struggle against oppression and exploitation in this country and on the entire globe.

I heard something very beautiful yesterday at our National Coalition of Black Lesbians and Gays meeting. Our executive director, Renee McCoy, who is also an ordained minister in the Metropolitan Community Church, told us that when the Reverend Allen Boesak and the Reverend Bishop Tutu had the opportunity to meet with members of the American lesbian and gay movement and to learn about our work and struggles, each of these men said "You must continue your work." If these Black leaders against apartheid in South Africa who live under constant state-imposed terrorism simply because of the color of their skin can support our movement, I think we can support theirs.

The second thing you must understand is that principled white people do not work against racism in order to be politically correct or to do a favor for people of color. You all have got to do this in order to save yourselves. Lillian Smith, the white Southern anti-racist writer and activist who also lived a life committed to women, said it best. She wrote "Back door treatment leaves scars on the soul," and she was referring to the damage racism does to the oppressor as well as the oppressed. The coalitions we've worked on for months to create this march are not just for today. They have to be for a lifetime, for many lifetimes.

Building viable and lasting coalitions brings me to my last topic, which is freedom and how to get it. As a radical and a member of this country's Left, I have never been satisfied with the goal of merely acquiring gay and lesbian rights. A strategy that relies solely on passing laws, or securing executive orders, or begging the straight world for grudging tolerance is much too limited, is totally unacceptable. What I am marching for and what we should all be marching for is not mere rights, but genuine liberation—for freedom.

In order to achieve that degree of freedom this very system will have to be transformed. We will need to build a new society where a viable basis for actually abolishing homophobia, sexism, racism, anti-Semitism, ageism and all the other isms exists because we have abolished the fundamental, economically imposed inequality of capitalism.

Ultimately our freedom is not going to come issuing from any of these white marble buildings in Washington, D.C., although we must continue to push the system for reforms at the very same time we work for revolutionary change. Marches like this one, movements like this one are built from the ground up, are built because of day in, day out grassroots activism. If we remember Stonewall and what it taught us about a spontaneous response to oppression and violation carried out by primarily working class, Black and Puerto Rican gays and drag queens, we know the most profound change comes when people empower themselves and refuse to bow to oppression. It does not come when we beg the powers that be for a tiny sliver of their pie or for a few crumbs from their moldy old pie, but when with our principles and committed activism we bake an entirely new pie, our own pie, and demonstrate what actual freedom looks like by challenging oppression at the root.

I want to end by honoring the people who have sustained me and kept me alive to do this work. Those people are all of you, but especially my doubly and triply courageous gay brothers and lesbian sisters of color. There are a lot of people who should be up here speaking to you today, who are not here. And unfortunately, one reason we are not up here in all of our diversity is that as hard as people of color have worked in coalition to build today's march, we ultimately did not have the autonomy and the power to determine as equal partners the march's agenda. There's a lot of frustration in always being tokens.

It is impossible for me to speak for all of us as people of color, but I *can* honor all of us: American Indians, Asian Americans, Latinos, East Indians, Palestinians, Africans, Pacific Islanders, Aborigines and many, many more lesbians and gay men of color. We have so much to be proud of, and although it usually goes unacknowledged, we have transformed every social and political movement we have touched. We have brought this country's painful and absolutely necessary dialogue about what it means to be of color, and female, and poor, and queer to a much higher level. We have left our mark on this part of the twentieth century. Today we have left an indelible mark on history. Thank you.

November 7, 1987

Being Open Is Best

John Maddux

This speech was given at the fifth Awards Dinner of the Greater Cincinnati Gay/Lesbian Coalition. Dr. John Maddux was at this time the state coordinator for GALA Ohio.

When I was invited to speak here tonight, I was asked to talk about the joys of being out of the closet and openly Gay. At first I considered the topic easy, given that being out and open, all I had to do was draw upon personal experience. But the more I thought about it, the more I realized that the topic wasn't as easy to address as it first seemed—not because there aren't any joys associated with being out for there certainly are; but rather because for each person, the benefits of being out are specific to that individual. And unfortunately, the perceived negative aspects of being out too often seem to outweigh the positive.

Need we be reminded that we live in a society that remains opposed to what I condescendingly referred to as the "homosexual alternative lifestyle." We function as a part of a social system that still regards homosexuality as unnatural, perverted, disgusting, and a sin against nature and God. We are led to believe by our oppressors that our very existence is offensive.

We are told that by living openly and without apology, we are doing little more than flaunting our perverted sexual behavior. As children, we learn that there isn't anything joyous or positive about being Gay or Lesbian. That by being open we bring shame and disgrace to our family. That we embarrass our friends. That we are destined for a life of failure, depression and loneliness. And that if we would just remain quiet and stay hidden away in our closets, everything would be all right—for them.

We have even been told to be satisfied with the social and legal progress we've made during the past few years. And indeed, although we have made progress, we are still denied our civil rights, we are still refused equal justice under the law. And we are still put in the position of believing that being out and open is radical, dangerous, and certainly less than desirable.

However, if any one of us cares to believe that progress has set us free, or has brought us all closer to living openly and proudly, outside the closet door; consider the media censorship that regularly accompanies the reporting of Gay and Lesbian events. Consider the dearth of factual information reported by the straight media during the March on Washington in October.

Consider that virtually every straight news report inaccurately reported the size of the crowd in Washington. Consider the virtual blackout of information concerning the March by publications such as *Newsweek* and *TIME* magazines. Consider how the largest civil rights demonstration in the history of this country was conveniently ignored by the straight news media. And consider that these misrepresentations were perpetrated by the same media that pride themselves for honesty, accuracy and investigative reporting.

And then consider the effect these distortions have, not only upon the public, but also upon the Gay and Lesbian community. They reflect a heterosexist bias that permeates even the most progressive straight news media and emphasize the negative aspects of coming out by demonstrating this society's almost total lack of empathy for our cause.

For if, indeed, the press cannot report the largest human rights demonstration in the history of this country honestly and accurately, what message does it send the person who questions the benefits of being out of the closet and open?

The joys of being open are individual realities that are experienced in a very special way. For each of us, being open means something different. For some, it means confronting his or her sexual identity with friends, family, peers, co-workers and employers. For others, it means deciding upon a life of openness and honesty. While for still others it means committing individual resources and energy to political activism. But for each of us, the decision to come out and to be open is one that must be personally decided, based upon individual circumstances and situation.

Certainly no one has the right to tell another to what extent he or she should be out. Not only does such an assumption prevail upon individual situation, but also presupposes a dangerous moral arrogance that fosters resentment and encourages self-righteousness.

Nevertheless, despite the negativity that surrounds homosexuality in this culture, and to those among us who remain dubious about the joys of being out and open, I'd like to suggest some of the joyous benefits of living openly, outside the closet door.

First, I must admit that without doubt being out and open, and being exposed to ridicule and violence can be dangerous: physically, emotionally, psychologically and financially. However, there are some very special joys that are exhilarating. Consider:

Never again having to experience the fear of being discovered.
Never again living in the shadowy corners of a dark and lonely closet.
Never again wondering when, and how, or if your friends and family will figure out the elaborate web of deceit designed to hide and protect your true identity.
Never again worrying about the way you walk or talk, the way you sound or act, the way you conduct yourself in day to day living.
Never again having to lie and deceive; or live a falsified life simply to satisfy the whims of a society that devalues individuality.

Being out and openly Gay or Lesbian brings the joy of rebirth and frees us to:

Experience the exhilaration of personal identity.
Allows us to relate with people honestly, openly, and with sincerity and confidence.
Makes us proud and strong.
Unites us in a common bond with our Gay brothers and sisters in a family of people who love and care about each other's needs and concerns.
Eliminates the last vestiges of internalized homophobia that somehow manage to creep into the core of our lives.
And once and for all, permits us to accept who we are, and to love ourselves and each other with unqualified acceptance.

We Also Have a Dream

Since returning to Cincinnati from the March on Washington, I have been struck by a variety of comments that in effect constitute a list of wishes that echo the joys of being out and open. I have heard people say in reference to that magical weekend:

"It was wonderful being with so many Lesbians and Gays, together, in one city."
"I've never seen so many Gays and Lesbians holding hands and openly showing affection in public."
"It was tremendous, the whole city belonged to us for that one weekend."
"I didn't want to come home. It was so beautiful. I felt so free and so alive."

Those comments, those statements, those wishes echoed by so many different people epitomize what the joy of being openly gay is all about.

It is the taste of freedom!

The reality of liberation!

The realization of the dreams we have harbored for so many years. Dreams we have hidden for far too long. Dreams of being free, Dreams of being emotionally reborn.

In 1963, Martin Luther King, Jr. stood on the Capitol Mall in Washington, D.C., telling the world of a dream he had, that someday his children and the children of his white brothers and sisters would walk hand in hand in equality.

In 1987, 24 years later, 600,000 Gay men and Lesbians gathered in the same city, stood on the same mall, and told a watching nation and a listening world that we too have a dream.

A dream that someday we will knock down the doors of our dark closets and burst into the sunlight of liberation

A dream that someday we will no longer be forced into hiding; afraid to be ourselves, afraid to be the good people that we truly are.

A dream that someday Gay men and Lesbians will walk down the streets of any city, anywhere in this country, hand in hand with their lovers—free, liberated and no longer fearing the retribution of violence and hatred.

A dream that someday the national disgraces of bigotry, discrimination and Gay bashing will be remembered as only footnotes to history; necessary reminders of the persecution that accompanies heterosexist paranoia.

A dream that someday, at long last our elected officials will awaken to the nightmare of a disease that is killing too many thousands of our brothers and sisters, and will accept their responsibility for funding research, patient care and education.

A dream that someday we will share in the same inalienable rights guaranteed other citizens of this nation.

A dream that someday we will stand in equal justice under the law.

A dream that someday we will no longer have to demonstrate and march, protest and civilly disobey, simply to gain our civil rights.

A dream that someday, all of us will be able to escape the denigration of third class citizenship and take our rightful place beside our straight brothers and sisters.

How? By Coming Out

But not until we all come out of the closets. Not until we all live openly. Not until we all demonstrate that we are indeed many people and everywhere, and that we are out and outraged and are not going back, will we be totally and absolutely free.

The joys of being out and openly Gay are available to us all. The reality of openness is more positive, more rewarding and more personally satisfying than is the fear we so often associate with coming out of the closet. As was said by Franklin Roosevelt "We have nothing to fear but fear itself," and indeed, the negatives we attribute to coming out are psychological fears dwarfed by the realities of personal satisfaction and integrity.

Being out and open means being free. Never again to relinquish our dignity. Never again permitting anyone else to hold power over our lives. Never again surrendering our destiny to a prejudice that selectively discriminates. Never again being controlled by fate, but rather, controlling the dimensions of our own choices.

Many people would just as soon we remain silent and closeted. Many people would wish us to simply go away.

But we won't remain closeted. We will not keep silent. And we most certainly will never go away. We will make love to whom we want in the privacy of our own bedrooms. We will walk hand in hand with our lovers down the streets of our cities. We will proclaim our sexuality openly and proudly. We will accept the risks that come with our visibility. And we will someday all share in the benefits of freedom.

The joy of being out is very basic. It can best be summed up with the word "liberation"—total, unequivocal, absolute liberation. That is what being out and openly Gay is all about. That is what joy truly is.

And believe me, it feels good . . .

April 14, 1988

The Hour of the Rooster, the Hour of the Owl

Catherine Lohr

This address was delivered at the Yom HaShoah service (an annual commemoration of the Warsaw Ghetto uprising and memorial to the six million Jews slain in the Holocaust) held on April 14, 1988, in Boston, Massachusetts, by Am Tikva, the city's gay and lesbian synagogue, at the Massachusetts Institute of Technology. Lohr was a founding member of the Jewish Lesbian Daughters of Holocaust Survivors. The Austrian election Lohr refers to is that of former Nazi officer Kurt Waldheim as prime minister in 1986. Terms not capitalized are as in the original text.

On Yom HaShoah I expected to be safe at the podium of this great university, this liberal institution at which many liberal events take place. But on Yom HaShoah, even while I stand before you, I am not here. Maybe I was assimilated, maybe I was underground, maybe I was outspoken. It didn't matter. I was a Jew.

I was murdered in 1933 because I was considered mentally defective. Maybe I was retarded or maybe I was mentally ill. Maybe I was psychiatrized against my will. It didn't matter—I was useless to the state. Maybe I was also a Jew.

I was murdered in 1934 because I was considered handicapped. I was in a wheelchair and although I was mentally fine, it didn't matter—I was useless to the state. Maybe I was also a Jew.

I was murdered in 1935. I was an activist who bore witness to atrocities against the Jews. I spoke against the government or had anti-Nazi newspapers printed. It didn't matter. Maybe I was also a Jew.

I was murdered in 1936. I was frightened and hungry and tried to leave for a safer place. It didn't matter. Maybe I was also Jewish.

I was murdered in 1937. I thought I would be safe if I pretended to like the Nazis. I agreed publicly with all their Jew-hating policies but privately spoke with outrage against the atrocities suffered upon the Jews. It didn't matter. Maybe I was also a Jew.

I was murdered in 1938. While my family waited outside, I bought cigarettes in a Jewish store. It didn't matter. Maybe I was also a Jew.

I was murdered in 1940. I was a communist. I was a Gypsy. I was considered misshapen, or deformed. I was too fat to work the way the Nazis wanted. I talked with an accent. I said maybe the Jews didn't deserve what was happening to them. I was gay. I didn't have a passport. I was circumcised. I was a transient. I was penniless. It didn't matter. Maybe I was Jew, anyway.

I was murdered in 1942. I hid in the cellar of my good friend who had been given all my jewelry to pay for the trouble I caused. It didn't matter. Maybe I was a Jew, anyway.

I was murdered in 1943. With my mate, my elderly grandparents and young siblings, I was caught trying to escape the country. Forbidden to travel, I believed my blue eyes and blond looks would save me from torture and violent death. It didn't matter. I was a Jew.

I was murdered in 1944. Along with women and men of every physical age and description. Of every ethical, moral, religious and cultural investiture. Of every financial status—rich as well as poor. Of every lifestyle—lesbian, gay, celibate, prostitute. Of every level of religious observance. Those who were good Germans, those who never lit the sabbath lights, those for whom the yarmulke was critical, those who had not yet known bat or bar mitzva. Those who were outspoken, those who were silent. Those who were strong, born destined for longevity, those who were frail. Those who wore their six-pointed star, those who refused. Those who smashed windows, those who passed among the Nazis for a time. Smart ones, educated ones, university graduated ones, land-owning and rabbinical ones. Rebellious ones, rousing, scheming, threatening, no longer mild ones, plotting and planning and willing to kill ones. It didn't matter. I was a Jew. We were all Jews.

I was murdered in 1945. Along with one of my siblings, along with three from the village close to ours, along with the girls whose bodies were assaulted by the Nazi guards, along with those who stole an extra bread crust to pass to a dying friend's hand, along with those whose last rebellion was to refuse to go quietly, along with those who raised their eyes equal to their captors, along with those who gave aid to a fallen friend. A Jew helped a Jew and was murdered.

In 1945 I was murdered early in the year, on New Year's eve, on New Year's day, on the Sabbath, on Sunday, in the hour of the rooster, in the hour of the owl. I was murdered as the snow fell and again as the first bud on the few wild flowers promised hope. I was murdered while I slept, while I worked into the 11th hour of my day. I was murdered by the calculated scheme of starvation, by the master plan of annihilation, by the merest misstep, by the cruelest of fates, by the unalterable destiny of the past, by the whim of chance, by luck gone awry. By the good church standing silently by, by the refusal of others to believe, to comprehend, by the silence, by the silence, by the long and murderous silence. By those abroad who knew, by those who were glad, by those who wanted proof, who wanted pictures, who didn't care, who remained silent, who had other things to do, who had important jobs, who thought they were safe who thought . . . thought it didn't matter. We were Jews.

I was murdered in 1945. During my liberation from the death camps, I was sent marching to nowhere. I weighed under 75 pounds. I had rags wrapped around my feet for cover. I wore the striped cloth of the prisoner—of the Jewish prisoner, of the prisoner promised to death. I had tuberculosis. I had the many diseases of starvation, I had lost my sibling, my neighbors from the nearby village. I had no eyeglasses, no hearing aid, no walking stick for the pain of my hip. I was bereft of worldly goods, of jewelry, of property, of convenience, of health, promise, pride, pleasure. Maybe I had will. Maybe I had faith. Maybe I had my covenant with God. Maybe today I had hoped for the quixotic maybe of a tomorrow.

I have been murdered many times since 1945. By the catholic [*sic*] church that aided nazis to relocate. By the american government who brought nazis here to recommence life, yet offered fewer than 1000 refugees sanctuary. By the austrian nation who elected, then consciously reconfirmed a nazi criminal as their leader. By governments and individuals who were silent. By governments and individuals who continue a tradition of intolerance for those different from themselves. Upon them I bestow the mantle of shame, which is bequeathed in mourning and rage.

Today I mourn four times.

Today, I mourn for those, Jewish or not, who were also murdered and whose names are not remembered by anyone here. I pray that somewhere a candle is lit in their memory.

Today I mourn for members of the lesbian and gay community, who think that they, Jewish or not, are safe, and keep silent in the false hope of preserving that safety. I pray that there will be someone who will light a candle for the lesbians and gay men who are silent.

Today I mourn for RU 20653, a genuine nazi-given number, preceded by a genuine nazi pink triangle. A real person who was murdered for a commonplace life choice among members of today's audience. Today I might look out in this audience and see Jewish lesbians and gays wearing this symbol. But many women and men in the lesbian and gay community wear the pink triangle with no comprehension of its origin. In the understanding that women always have a level of invisibility, I believe that this number belonged to a man. It might have belonged to a wealthy man. It might have belonged to a wealthy man, one who had position and power and maybe authority while the state allowed him to. Today, in the Auschwitz Exhibit, his number is traveling in a display of patches worn by non-Jews whom the nazis say committed crimes against the state. I pray this is the last time the death of a lesbian or gay person is remembered by a dehumanized number.

Today as I look out among the mourners here, I do not see my parents. But I join them in the bottomless sorrow of their loss. I cherish even in mourning, the names of my paternal grandparents, Joseph and Ida, and my maternal grandparents, Alice and Jacob. All murdered sometime between 1933 and 1945. For my mother's family, I carry one sister's—my unknown aunt's—name. Shy and comfortable between my first and last names, Odette survives where the only record I can have of her is kept safe. For my father's family I carry the Lohr name, never given in marriage, never altered. For both families I carry the physique of heredity. How many diabetics would there have been? How many would have had breast cancer? How many would have lived to see 80? 90? How many cousins would I have had? How many tall, short, bald, buxom, swarthy, smart, loud, quiet, nearsighted, proud, fat . . . how many cousins would I have had? How many lesbians, doctors, scholars, teachers, mothers, authors, artists, tailors, gays . . . how many cousins would I have had?

I remember in some depthless grief, those whose names I have never heard, and probably will never know. I mourn with all Jews, in any station of life and in any world setting, for the loss of the 6 million Jews, who remain nameless at ceremonies like today's. Today I mourn for the millions more who lived, but did not survive. Today I mourn for the lives of Jews and Jews and Jews . . . and Jews.

April 30, 1988

We Gather in Dubuque

Sue Hyde

At the time she gave this address at the Second Annual Gay and Lesbian Pride March in Dubuque, Iowa, Sue Hyde was the director of the Privacy Project of the National Gay and Lesbian Task Force.

My trip to Dubuque started me thinking about my own lesbian childhood and adolescence in a small town in Illinois. I grew up in Beardstown, Illinois, about 150 miles from where we stand today. I grew up in a town in which there were no black people, no Jewish people, and no openly lesbian and gay people, at least that I knew. Although, I am living testimony to the fact that we were there and still are, I'm sure.

The only time I ever saw black people was on the annual trip to St. Louis, Missouri to watch professional baseball games. I knew that the black people I saw were different from me. And in my child's mind, my white family, white friends, and white neighbors lived apart from these different-looking people because that was just the way the world was. Later I learned truths about the world: truths conveyed by these ugly words: racism, segregation and discrimination. Later I learned that my friendly, safe little white town had, through the 1930s and 1940s, posted signs at the city limits which read "Nigger, don't let the sun set on you here." Later I learned that the differentness of black people made them targets of white people's unaccountable suspicion and rage. But in my 11-year-old's mind, white people did not have black neighbors and that was just the way the world was. And that lie informed my thinking and shaped my consciousness.

I suspect many of us here today grew up with that same lie. And, as we discovered our sexualities, we knew we had been duped again. Duped into believing that our gay and lesbian sexuality necessarily sentenced us to a lifetime of unhappiness, proscribed by our shame and fear. We gather here in Dubuque to name those lies and to speak our own truths so that this community and this world will be forever changed.

We gather in Dubuque today so that none of us will ever feel afraid to walk this city's streets. Freedom of movement is such a basic right that we assume it for ourselves, especially if we are white and male. Thus, last Sept. 19, 30 lesbian and gay citizens took to these streets in a first ever Dubuque lesbian and gay pride march, only to be met by some 300 angry counter-demonstrators. The marchers were pelted with eggs while the police stood by and watched.

The march was cut short that day. But its organizers vowed to return this year because they would not simply bow down to the way Dubuque is. They did not agonize: they organized. And a wonderful thing happened. Ginny Lyons and Stacy Neldaughter, with their spark of courage, lit a fire of resistance and fueled a movement of gay men and lesbians to travel across the state, across the Midwest, and even across the country to stand with them today.

We have come to Dubuque to challenge it to be the best city it can be and to recognize and welcome its lesbian and gay citizens and to acknowledge their contributions to the quality of life here.

We challenge the Dubuque Human Relations Commission and the Dubuque City Council to amend the city's civil rights code to include sexual orientation. And if the events of last year's march are not evidence enough of the need for this, some people in this city have their eyes closed to reality. We challenge the city's police chief to open his mind to a proposal for sensitivity training for the members of his force.

And we challenge Mayor James Brady to realize that our sexuality is not simply a private matter, especially when he himself is quoted in the paper as saying "I wouldn't want to live next door to one." Mayor Brady, we want you to know that there is nothing private about your public declarations of bigotry and hate.

Mayor Brady and others no doubt feel uncomfortable about this demonstration. They no doubt feel unsettled by our challenge. They no doubt will breathe a sigh of relief when our buses and cars and trains pull out of town. But each man, woman and child in Dubuque has a responsibility to treat every other citizen with respect. And to the lesbian and gay citizens of Dubuque—the women and men who live, work and love here—Dubuque has a special responsibility to make this city safe for them, and to make last year's disgrace this year's triumph.

No more harassment. No more eggs or rocks or ugly words. No more governmental neglect and malevolence. No more fear. No more hate. No more silence. We choke on your hatred. We smother under your fear. We die of your red tape. And we cannot wait any longer to live.

With one voice, as one people, as a single wave inevitably crashes onto the shore, we say to you that our time for freedom has arrived. We promise to return to Dubuque each year until we no longer need to.

We invoke the spirits of Mahatma Gandhi, Fannie Lou Hamer, Martin Luther King and Barbara Deming, all of whom devoted their lives to freedom and justice. We call on them to guide us, walk with us, and join our one voice as we say:

We won't give up. We won't shut up. We won't go away.

And we will change this world.

June 1988

You Can't Build a Movement on Anger: Feeling Our Way Toward Failure, Thinking Our Way Toward Success

John D'Emilio

This editorial, by the author of Sexual Politics, Sexual Communities: The Making of a Homosexual Minority in the United States, 1940-1970 *(University Press of Chicago, 1983), first appeared in the June 19-25, 1988, issue of* Gay Community News.

At the "War Conference" that was held last February near Washington, D.C., 200 lesbian and gay leaders from around the country put our heads together to assess the state of our movement and look to the future. The conference has been criticized, and rightly so, for its inadequate outreach to people of color and to women. Still, whenever that many sharp, experienced and committed activists get together, good things are bound to happen. The energy level was high, the tone was by and large cooperative and optimistic, and lots of fine thinking was done.

Over the weekend, I noticed a recurring motif, one that's stayed with me since then. The motif wasn't new or startling but I heard it in a new way. Again and again, in the midst of working groups or strategy sessions, someone would say "But where's our anger? They're out there killing us—through disease, violence or neglect—and we're sitting here talking politely about strategy and thinking of 'nice' things to do. Where's our anger? Where's our rage?" As I said, it's not a brand new idea. It's been said many times before, including by me. But this time when I heard it, I realized that I couldn't disagree more. I'm convinced that political strategies based on anger—or any other kind of emotion—are recipes for failure.

My reasons for saying this may become clearer if we think for a minute about some of the feelings other than rage that are common to our lives. Take grief and sadness for instance. For the last few years, tidal waves of grief have swept over our community as lovers, friends, neighbors, co-workers, and acquaintances have died of AIDS. Grief has become a pervasive part of our lives. We are learning all sorts of creative ways to acknowledge and express it, from bereavement groups and community memorial services to the NAMES Project, and we need to keep doing this in order not to sink under the weight of our own sadness. But do we want to base our movement on it? Do we want to develop a political strategy for liberation that is based on grief? Of what use would a strategy, distorted by the overwhelming despair that death engenders, be? Not very useful, I suspect.

What about fear and terror? Terror entered my life the moment I became aware that I was gay, and it has remained a more or less prominent feature of my consciousness ever since. Fear, as a teenager, that I'd be arrested, blackmailed, or in some way publicly humiliated or exposed. Fear, in college and right after, that somehow my life would be ruined if word got out. Despite the fact that I have been publicly visible for the last 15 years, I still experience fear when I come out in new situations, or when I take the time to notice just how visible I am. Where would I be if I let gay terror serve as my guide for action? How much progress would the movement have made if we let it be shaped by the numbing fear that life in a violently oppressive society generates?

At first glance, anger appears different. It's healthy. It's not an emotion based on victimization, but a sign of life, strength, and a determination to fight back—right? I'm not so sure. I think rage is as much a sign of how much we've been hurt as is grief and terror. Were there not wrongs done to us and those we love, we'd have nothing to be angry about. And just as sadness and fear are not reliable guides to political strategizing, neither is anger.

The experiences of the Black movement in the 1960s and the feminist movement in the 1970s have a lot to tell us about the political dangers of mobilizing around rage. In the early 1960s, Blacks built an extraordinarily broad-based movement. Sit-ins, freedom rides, mass marches, community-wide mobilizations, national boycotts, court litigation, and legislative lobbying made racial justice, for a time, the central issue in American life. Careful, thoughtful, reasoned strategizing lay behind it all.

The resistance was intense. Especially in the deep South, Blacks faced police brutality, Klan nightriders, beatings, bombings and shootings. Eventually, the violence reshaped the movement as some Black activists began to mobilize on the basis of rage.

That may have been emotionally satisfying for some, but it was also politically suicidal. Militants in SNCC (the Student Nonviolent Coordinating Committee) and the Black Panthers found themselves cut off from the rest of the movement. The rhetoric of rage alienated many former supporters and immobilized others. Angry, impassioned calls to pick up the gun in self-defense lost for the cause the mantle of moral superiority that had been so potent a force in the early 1960s. Violence directed at Black activists mounted, but now, instead of provoking public outrage, the violence could be justified as necessary for restoring order. Strategies and tactics that evolved out of unthinking rage badly weakened a movement that only a few years before had been on the offensive.

Rage also reshaped the women's movement in the late 1970s. After the initial upsurge of feminism, many women took on issues of sexual violence—rape, battering, abuse, incest. Laws were changed, public consciousness raised, and institutions such as shelters were created. But daily immersion in the issue of sexual violence took its toll. Many feminists active in the anti-violence movement were living in a state of constant rage, and it began to affect their thinking about issues and strategy. From a campaign against violence came the feminist campaigns against pornography, with an overarching and simplistic analysis that defined porn as the source of the problem. The pornography wars gave sustenance to the Christian New Right, spawned internecine warfare among feminists and created their own kind of political casualties.

To me the lesson seems clear. A politics of rage weakens and destroys its proponents and their cause more effectively than it weakens and destroys an oppressive system. Movements for social justice cannot be based on painful emotion, whether it be grief, terror or rage. Yes, we have to feel these things. The feelings have real causes. And yes, we need to find ways to support one another through it all. But a movement that mobilizes a constituency on the basis of pain will end up feeling its way to despair, disillusionment and, ultimately, failure. I would much prefer that we think our way to success.

January 1989

Time Is Not Right to March on Washington

Cathy Woolard

This editorial appeared in Atlanta's gay and lesbian newspaper, *Southern Voice,* on January 5, 1989. Woolard was the president of the Lesbian and Gay Rights chapter of the Georgia ACLU and had served as coordinator for the Atlanta March Committee for the 1987 March on Washington.

There has been much gossip, suggestion and general anticipation of late concerning the possibility of another March on Washington in October, 1989. At a meeting in Chicago this fall, Names Project founder Cleve Jones issued a challenge to national lesbian and gay organizations to fund and staff the effort to re-organize an event similar to the undeniably successful week of activities held in 1987. As a board member of the National Gay and Lesbian Task Force and a Steering Committee member of the last March on Washington, I'd like to offer my opinion on this call to march.

The 1987 March on Washington took fifteen months of organizing by a grassroots network of individuals and groups around the country. In the course of that time, meetings were held in various locations to create a highly representative steering committee (despite criticism to the contrary), to closely explore the issues that would be presented to the nation and our government in what we knew would be an historic occasion. We also had to iron out all of the logistics and financial issues before an extremely large, diverse and frequently contentious supervisory body. We can all offer suggestions, with hindsight, as to what could have made the task easier or performed the job better. But I will always contend that we did the best possible job at pleasing and including the most people we could at the largest civil rights demonstration in the history of this country.

With all of this in mind, it is my opinion that to attempt to duplicate this effort in less than one year's time is a foolish attempt to create a sequel to an unduplicatible [*sic*] experience. The March on Washington Steering Committee and its creation was what gave the unique flavor of that March. And we did not empower ourselves (or anyone else) to continue that process on a permanent basis. To eliminate that process would be to eliminate the inclusion and input that we struggled so hard to create. And experience should point out that a hastily conceived sequel is never equal to the primary event.

Our greatest hope for the March was to begin a grassroots network of newly empowered activists who could carry the enthusiasm home, and begin work in their own communities in the same way that we created our ad hoc national community. That new activity is just beginning to come into its own power and local recognition. Witness the outburst of activity right here in Atlanta. Many of our groups are now known nationally and respected as organizations that can get the job done. To build another March would require an outpouring of local energy and finances that these fledgling organizations can ill afford and which would be detrimental to our local political goals. It is better to spend our tens of thousands of dollars at home to educate city and state politicians about local issues than to spend it on a weekend in Washington.

Suggestions have been made regarding a tie-in to the next Presidential election that I consider constructive. Perhaps a March in the fall of 1992, a month prior to the election with a goal of a million participants, all of whom have been registered to vote in the past four years. That would be a show of power with some teeth behind it!

If we cannot come to the planning table with an attainable and desirable political outcome, a colossal Gay and Lesbian Pride Parade is not a suitable alternative nor is it in order at this time. I challenge our community to stop looking wistfully behind at what was a brilliant piece of organizing and instead, to look ahead at what we can do to surpass that ideal and take ourselves to the next level of political power in the struggle for civil rights for all people.

June 8, 1989

A Love Letter to the Movement

Robin Tyler

Robin Tyler was at this time the producer of the Southern Womyn's Music and Comedy Festival and the West Coast Women's Festival, and was nationally recognized as one of the leading creative spirits in contemporary lesbian culture.

The 20th Anniversary of Stonewall will be celebrated this year.

I would like to congratulate you for being so dedicated, and for working so hard to keep our movement active, alive and growing.

Although we have gone through devastating times, especially since the AIDS crisis, the past 20 years have also been an era of great achievements. We have formed organizations, alliances and our own institutions, ranging from the Lesbian/Gay centers, to the Harvey Milk School . . . to scores of other institutions . . . and major organizations.

We began to discuss classicism, racism, anti-semitism, ageism, discrimination against the differently abled and fat oppression. We no longer thought the "12 Step program" was a dance lesson. We were no longer dancing our way to isolation through a disco beat.

Religion called us sick, so we formed our own places of worship, and Gay and Lesbian Christians and Jews could finally return openly to their beliefs—minus the shame and guilt. Many women started re-embracing Matriarchal Religions. Many of us even considered ourselves our own higher power.

We have been the first generation in which millions of us have come out of the closet. From dykes on bikes to lesbians in limos, from the Radical Fairies to ACT UP, in the streets, and in the suites we emerged. We refused to be invisible. We began to be concerned about our youth . . . knowing that when a community starts to take care of its young, it takes care of its future. 10-12% of the children today will grow up to be lesbian or gay, and we finally took the steps and the responsibility to help "save our children," so they wouldn't have to be called faggot, or dyke, or sissy, or queer.

We contributed on every level, and finally, we who were the back bone of theatre and the arts, had the courage to come out of the closet, and produce major works, such as *Torch Song Trilogy*. The lesbian movement culturally grew through its singers, and musicians, and comics, and poets, and writers, and record companies and festivals.

We achieved . . . and we started to communicate with each other. Our newspapers and literary works grew.

We participated in the largest demonstration in the history of the United States, the National March on Washington for Lesbian and Gay Rights. We were a community who knew how to live, and in the 80s, used our compassion and caring to help fight a devastating and deadly illness. With the founding of the "AIDS Quilt," a monumental achievement in our history, we brought ourselves together, through our fears and through our tears, to support each other in mourning and memories.

Oh yes, we have come a long way . . . from high camp to high anger, and civil rights demonstrations. We wore the triangle "lest we forget" the Holocaust and then, to remind us of the Holocaust perpetuated by our governments refusing to deal with AIDS. We were no longer talking about our "lifestyles," we were talking about our lives!

We are a civil rights movement based on fighting for the right to love . . . and in the past 20 years, we began to love ourselves.

Let us now look forward to the vision of the next decade . . . "The Gay 90s." (We are the only civil rights movement to have an entire decade named after them!)

I WOULD LIKE TO PROPOSE THAT WE EMBRACE THE SYMBOL OF THE PHOENIX AS THE NATIONAL SYMBOL OF THE LESBIAN/GAY PRIDE MOVEMENT, and then approach our sisters and brothers in other countries to take it under consideration as a possible International Symbol. It does not have to replace the Lambda or the Labrys . . . and can even be superimposed over the Rainbow or the Triangle. But the time has come to look ahead to positive images. Our courage, our will to live, and our strength through the struggles, while still maintaining our humor and our ability to love, has made us extraordinary . . . not just as a movement, but as individuals. For like the Phoenix, against all odds, we have risen again and again. I would like the Lesbian and Gay Pride Organizers to consider using the PHOENIX as the 1990 Gay Pride Symbol. Here is the *Random House Dictionary of English Language* definition. (The Phoenix's colors were scarlet, blue, purple and gold.)

PHOENIX

A mythical bird of great beauty fabled to live 500-600 years in the Arabian wilderness, to burn itself on a funeral pyre and to rise from its ashes in the freshness of youth and live through another cycle of years. Often an emblem of immortality or of reborn idealism or hope.

A person or thing of peerless beauty or excellence.

A person or thing that has become renewed or restored after suffering calamity or apparent annihilation.

I hope to attend the International Lesbian/Gay Pride meeting in October, 1989 in Vancouver to present this. This year I will be speaking at the Parades in Boston and in San Francisco, and calling for the Phoenix to become the National Symbol.

I hope for your support, and once again congratulate you on all of your efforts on behalf of Lesbian/Gay Rights. We were the generation who finally found each other. Perhaps, this was our greatest achievement.

June 14, 1989

The 20th Anniversary of the Stonewall Rebellion

Ted Weiss

Given on the floor of the House of Representatives by Representative Weiss of New York and entered into the *Congressional Record* for June 14, 1989.

Mr. Speaker, I want to draw the attention of my colleagues to the many events taking place this June as part Gay and Lesbian Pride and History Month in New York City. An annual event, the celebration will this year also honor the 20th Anniversary of the Stonewall Rebellion, widely recognized as the beginning of the movement to ensure civil rights for lesbians and gay men.

Events at the Stonewall Inn in New York City in June, 1969, created a new commitment in the lesbian and gay community to work for equal rights. Organizations were formed to promote education about gay and lesbian rights and to fight for the passage of laws to ensure nondiscrimination on the basis of sexual orientation.

In 1971, I was an original cosponsor of the first New York City gay rights bill introduced into the city council. It was not until 1986 that a local law was finally passed and signed into law protecting lesbians and gay men against discrimination for sexual orientation. In addition, there are several executive orders in place in New York City that seek to protect lesbians and gay men from discrimination. Executive order No. 4 (1978) prohibits discrimination against city employees because of sexual orientation; executive order No. 94 (1986, formerly No. 50—1980) prohibits the city from entering into contracts with companies that discriminate on the basis of sexual orientation and executive order No. 69 (1983) prohibits city employees from doing business in private clubs that engage in discriminatory membership practices.

Several other States and localities have passed laws, or issued executive orders, protecting lesbians and gay men from discrimination, but until a

Federal gay rights bill is enacted, most gay men and lesbians will have no recourse if they become the target of this type of discrimination.

Legislation now pending in the Congress would amend the Civil Rights Act of 1964 by adding affectional or sexual orientation to the list of forms of discrimination now prohibited in housing, employment, education, and public facilities. I am proud to be a prime sponsor of this important piece of civil rights legislation and prouder still that with each new Congress the list of cosponsors grows. In the 101st Congress, H.R. 655, the Civil Rights Act Amendments of 1989, is being cosponsored by 70 Members of this House who share the belief that a person's sexual orientation cannot be legitimate grounds for bias, any more than skin color or religious expression.

During this year's Gay and Lesbian Pride and History Month, events are scheduled honoring the many contributions to society made by lesbians and gay men throughout history. The new National Museum of Lesbian and Gay History located at the Lesbian and Gay Community Services Center will preserve for future generations the triumphs celebrated and struggles endured during the gay rights movement. In addition, the renaming of a portion of Christopher Street to Stonewall Place serves as an important reminder of the events that sparked a crucial civil rights movement.

Finally, at the end of June, Heritage of Pride will once again host the largest lesbian and gay pride march in the country. The first march in July, 1969 drew 500 participants. Last year, over 100,000 individuals marched down Fifth Avenue to the cheers of thousands of New Yorkers lining the street in support of their lesbian and gay friends. The theme of this year's march, "Stonewall 20: A Generation of Pride," indicates that this community's spirit will not be broken until they can live their lives with dignity and in peace.

During a time when the gay and lesbian community has seen a disturbing increase in bias-related violence and continues to lead our Nation in responding to one of this country's most devastating health crises, it is crucial for all of us to show our support for gay and lesbian concerns. Only when all of the citizens of this country have obtained equal rights will ours be a truly just society. Mr. Speaker, I ask my colleagues to join me in supporting the Civil Rights Act Amendments of 1989 and in saluting New York City's Gay and Lesbian Pride Month.

October 6-8, 1989

It Is We Who Are Kind

Cleve Jones

This text was delivered by Cleve Jones, the executive director of the NAMES Project, at the final display of the AIDS Memorial Quilt in Washington, DC. The title refers to a slogan of then-President George H.W. Bush, who purposed to make the United States "a kinder, gentler nation" under his administration.

I want to speak to the one who is not here . . .

Mr. President,

It is the tenth month of your administration, the tenth year of the AIDS pandemic. Time is running out, Mr. President, and it ran out long ago for those tens of thousands who we remember here tonight. The time has come, Mr. President, for you to see, and understand, and act. And the time has come for you to see us. Ten months ago, you shared with the American people your vision of a thousand points of light. Yet when we come to our Nation's Capitol, we bring with us a thousand points of light times ten, times ten again, and *still* you cannot see us. And though our nation seems not kinder, and not gentler, we have moved past hatred, past despair to stand here tonight with hearts that are full of love and hope. We are not here to tear down or destroy, we are here to build. We are not here to relive the mistakes of the past, but to fight for our future. We want to speak with you, Mr. President. We are people with AIDS: we are children, women and men living with AIDS, and we want to speak with you, Mr. President. We are the caregivers, families and lovers of people with AIDS. We are Gay and Straight, and Bisexual. We are Black and Brown and White. We are volunteers, activists, scientists and researchers and we want to speak with you, Mr. President. We are teachers, and we are students and doctors and nurses and administrators. We are the people who every day, every hour in every city and town of America are leading a war against an epidemic, and we *must* speak with you. Mr. President, our country today possesses the knowledge, the resources and the institutions to defeat AIDS. We are asking you to lead the way. We appeal to you to speak with us, to learn from the painful facts of the challenges before us. Speak with us, Mr. President; address the American people. Tell us of your plans to defeat AIDS as you have shared with us your plans for other wars. Tell us that your war on drugs includes rehabilitation and prevention. Tell us that you will build treatment centers as well as prison cells. Tell us that a cure for AIDS will be found, Mr. President, and that it will be accessible to all, regardless of ability to pay, and found in time to save the millions of us who are already infected. Tell us, Mr. President, that in America we will find the money to care for all who fall ill with compassion and love. Tell us that crimes of violence and discrimination against people with AIDS and other minorities will be resisted and prosecuted by the federal government; that profiteers will be restrained, and that the economic burden of this epidemic will not fall only on the backs of those least able to bear it. Mr. President, tell us that the American people, and your administration, will work together to meet the challenges of AIDS; that we will not be divided by race, gender, class and sexual orientation. Tell us, Mr. President, that you will speak with us; tell us that you will see us, Mr. President. Mr. President, we know that you cannot meet individually with each of us. You can't visit us in our homes and our hospital wards, for we are hundreds of thousands in this country alone, and millions across the globe. But speak with us, Mr. President—again we stand here seeking that appointment—and we will return, Mr. President, on a day when millions of people in many lands on every continent will stand in global solidarity against the AIDS pandemic. Will you stand with us *then,* Mr. President? The day is Friday, December 1, 1989: World AIDS Day. A good day, Mr. President, to meet with people with AIDS; a good day to address the American people. And those of us who cannot afford to again travel to our Nation's Capitol, we will gather in our cities, and our towns, and we will educate our people, and we will care for our sick, and we will remember our dead, and we will wait for you, Mr. President. Mr. President, you could have visited us today upon the Quilt; you would not have been harmed, Mr. President, though many would doubtless clamor to gain your attention. You and your family could stand among us on the Quilt, and fear no harm at all. For in all truth, Mr. President, it is we who are kind, it is we who are gentle, and it is our light that will lead the way to victory and to life.

Thank you all for being here: be with us on World AIDS Day.

Autumn 1989

Concession Speech

Harry Britt

This speech was delivered in San Francisco by Supervisor Harry Britt in the late autumn of 1989, and was addressed to supporters of a measure known as Proposition S, which had been successfully passed. The earthquake mentioned is the Loma Prieta event of October 17, 1989, centered south of San Francisco.

Tonight we've had to deal with a different kind of reality, that there are still in this town, 80,000 people or so, whom, when we ask them if they are ready to treat our relationships with respect, will leave their houses and walk down to the polling place and say "no."

Let's allow ourselves to feel that in this city there are still 80,000—maybe more people—who are not yet ready to say "Yes" to lesbian and gay relationships. And be aware when we feel that, that's the normal experience for lesbian and gay people in virtually every city in this country and in this world. Tonight, for just this little while, we're feeling some of those things that we have felt before in other places that other people in other places are still feeling. It's OK to feel that. We don't have to say this is an illusion, it's real.

A lot of people voted against us tonight. Now, that does not mean that those people are evil people and we are going to wait for them to go away. It means we've got some more work to do. Those people who voted No on S, that's because they don't know us yet and they've got a treat in store for them, because we're going to let them get to know us, and they're going to like us a lot.

It's OK to be disappointed and hurt—a lot of us have worked on this legislation for 10 years and we're not through with it yet. Let's be clear with every word that we speak that that is not the spirit of San Francisco. There is nothing in this election that says that this city does not respect gay men and lesbians as first class citizens whose love is just as good as anybody else's love, whose relationships are just as valuable as anybody else's.

The only thing that bothers me about this election is that I don't want one person in Kansas or Missouri or Texas or anywhere to think that somehow San Francisco is not the great city that it was yesterday or the day before that. Maybe what we need to do tomorrow is get on the phone as we did after the earthquake when everybody said San Francisco is gone, and tell people in other parts of the country San Francisco is not gone—that the lesbian and gay community in this town is alive and well, that human rights are alive and well in this city, that the people in San Francisco are never, ever going to go back from their appreciation of us. Because they know us too well for that, and that San Francisco is still the greatest city in the world in which to live.

SECTION VI: THE 1990s

1990

Song to My Master

John Eric Larsen

Songs to My Master is a two-volume cycle of lyric poetry (accompanied by original music) composed in 1990 by the gifted writer and composer John Eric Larsen (1965-2001) and performed by him at many venues within the leather community of the Midwest, including the Metropolitan Community Church service held during the International Mr. Leather contest in Chicago in 1998. The composition (viewed by its creator as an evolving work) had reached the sixth edition by 1996, with several successive versions of the primary texts of *Shadowlands* and *Outlander* printed by Larsen through his publishing company, Golden Bear Productions. Its themes of spiritual growth, courage, and self-exploration achieved through the rituals of leather sexuality make this work a unique voice in the realm of gay performance art. A third envisioned volume was never completed. Larsen died on April 2, 2001, in a hospital in Jackson, Michigan, of AIDS. He was a member of the residential leather family Household Keppeler.

This selection from *Shadowlands* is both the voice of the seeker, Jim, and the call of the writer himself to others through his personal vision of his journey of spiritual growth.

"Song to My Master"

Jim: My goal in this life has been to fight the odds
To fight for my rights and for all that I have wanted
But it all becomes misty in the games of give and take
And there is something in your voice that tells me I am wrong
And somewhere in the silence, I believe you. . . . So

Capture me, and take me where you want to
And take from me all I have and all I am
Enrapture me, and teach me what you want to
And I pray you I'll be worthy of the things you have in store

I have fought for so long that I don't know if I am winning
Or if I am losing as I try to keep my ground
And I hear you're calling me to a life that I must lose
But it's hard to give control when that's all you've ever known
And somewhere in the silence I believe you. . . . So

Capture me, and take me where you want to
And take from me all I have and all I am
Enrapture me, and teach me what you want to
And I'll learn that I'll be worthy of the things you have in store

I know that I must lose it all to find you
And that's the hardest choice I'll have to make
But I sense that living for you is the only road ahead
And maybe it's the only chance for me to take. . . . So

Capture me, and take me where you want to
And take from me all I have and all I am
Enrapture me, and teach me what you want to
And I'll learn that I'll be worthy of the things you have in store

January 9, 1990

Into the Light or into the Darkness?

Jim Thomas

This address was given as part of the rally and press conference held on January 9, 1990, in Jefferson City, the state capital of Missouri, calling for the repeal of subsection 3 of Missouri's Sexual Misconduct Law. Said section prohibited private, consenting sexual activity between adults of the same gender and had been targeted for repeal by the Privacy Rights Education Project, which organized a lobby day on January 9. Thomas was at this time the editor of the *Lesbian and Gay News-Telegraph,* the principal gay newspaper in Missouri.

Friends, members of the press, members of our legislature, Governor Ashcroft, we are here today with a clear and simple purpose. As freedom sweeps across the world, it is time for us to claim our own freedom here at home.

Our message is simple: Where it deals with Gays, Missouri's sexual misconduct law is against the very spirit of our country.

Yes, the legislative process is complex. Yes, there will be difficulties to surmount. Yes, we may have set-backs.

The battle will not be easily won, but we are committing ourselves to work for the day when all of Missouri's citizens, not just Lesbians and Gays, will live with the greater assurance that government will not be a Peeping Tom to their lives.

For the last decade, conservative religious fanatics have risen to the highest offices of the land, proclaiming they would get government off our backs. But the reality is far different. For any who disagreed with their narrow view of life, there was to be no freedom. Instead there is a sleazy, voyeuristic impulse to gaze into the most personal decisions and actions of others and to smother those who don't make the grade of their fanatical standards.

For Lesbians and Gays, for women, for workers, for African-Americans, the time has come to say "Enough."

We have been witness during the last weeks and months to great struggles for freedom in Eastern Europe. All of us have been moved by the resurgence of freedom, yet here in our own state, a legislator—a legislator!—leads the battle against freedom and a courageous young man leading the fight for freedom loses his home to arson. What sort of world is this for Missouri?

Well, I can tell you today, it is a world we are going to change. We have no illusions, freedom does not come easily. It does not come to those who do not work for it, strive for it, believe in it and live their lives for it.

Our opponents are fierce and unrelenting, driven by the desire to interfere in the lives of others. But these false judges, who set themselves up as the moral arbiter of others, will not win. These false gods, who clothe themselves in piety, cannot win. Though they hide themselves behind gilded words, they will be exposed.

The United States of America has ever been a bright beacon to the world, of hope for a better life. Our standard, though we sometimes fall short, has been a higher one, a standard of freedom and justice for all. For all, not just those who pass some ideological or religious test of morality.

We work, we pay our taxes, and we vote. Hear me now—we, too, are Americans. We, too, grew up saying the pledge of allegiance, believing "liberty and justice for all" mattered, born to the hope of freedom and born to the hope of justice.

We have come today, to Jefferson City, to stake a claim on our birthright of liberty. And to those who don't believe in freedom and justice, we say: We are here. For a time perhaps, you may hold us back, but we are here, we will not turn back. We will win because we believe in the ideals of our foremothers and forefathers, strengthened by the dreams and faith of so many before us, and for which too many—yes, Lesbians and Gays, too—have fought and died. Fought and died not just in war, but in the deep social struggles of African-Americans, Asian-Americans, Native Americans, Hispanic-Americans and American women. Like theirs, our faces will be looking towards the American ideal.

The United States of America has a great destiny, changing as its people change, but always growing, forever renewed. Like an awesome vista, it stretches before us, in our own lives and in the lives of those to follow. Let's not cloud the vista with the darkness and storm of prejudice and bigotry. No, let us suffuse it with bright light, a light of lives, lived fully and freely.

I ask today of each citizen, of each legislator, that you think clearly and carefully, that you remember the principles and ideals for which this nation's citizens have struggled and died, that you reflect upon the deeper meaning of our nation and its purpose. And I ask you: To what destiny would you deliver us? Which way will you face—into the darkness or into the light?

June 1990

I Hate Straights

During the New York City Gay and Lesbian Pride celebrations in the summer of 1990, a group of gay men and lesbians distributed a number of anonymous essays with the collective title, "I Hate Straights." Although such pamphleteering had long been a feature of local gay and lesbian protests, in this case *OutWeek* magazine, at that time a New York-based weekly for lesbians and gay men, reprinted the text of the main essay, which subsequently appeared in gay community newspapers as far afield as Madison, Wisconsin, and the Twin Cities. This wider distribution of the text transformed it into a part of the general rhetoric of the American gay and lesbian movement. Its provocative argument reflects both anger and a number of then-current areas of political activism. The main essay of this collection follows.

I have friends. Some of them are straight.

Year after year, I see my straight friends. I want to see them, to see how they are doing, to add newness to our long and complicated history, to experience some continuity.

Year after year I continue to realize that the facts of my life are irrelevant to them and that I am only half listened to, that I am an appendage to the doings of a greater world, a world of power and privilege, of the laws of installation, a world of exclusion. "That's not true," argue my straight friends. There is the one certainty in the politics of power: those left out of it beg for inclusion, while the insiders claim that they already are. Men do it to women, whites do it to blacks, and everyone does it to queers.

The main dividing line, both conscious and unconscious, is procreation . . . and that magic word "Family." Frequently, the ones we were born into disown us when they find out who we really are, and to make matters worse, we are prevented from having our own. We are punished, insulted, cut off, and treated like seditionaries in terms of child rearing, both damned if we try and damned if we abstain. It's as if the propagation of the species is such a fragile directive that without enforcing it as if it were an agenda, humankind would melt back into the primeval ooze.

I hate having to convince straight people that gays and lesbians live in a war zone, that we're surrounded by bomb blasts only we seem to hear, that our bodies and souls are heaped high, dead from fright or bashed or raped, dying of grief or disease, stripped of our personhood.

I hate straight people who can't listen to queer anger without saying "hey, all straight people aren't like that. I'm straight too, you know," as if their egos don't get enough stroking or protection in this arrogant, heterosexist world. Why must we take care of them, in the midst of our just anger brought on by their fucked up society? Why add the reassurance of "Of course, I don't mean you. You don't act that way." Let them figure out for themselves whether they deserve to be included in our anger.

But of course that would mean listening to our anger, which they almost never do. They deflect it by saying "I'm not like that" or "now look who's generalizing" or "you'll catch more flies with honey . . ." or "If you focus on the negative you just give out more power" or "you're not the only one in the world who's suffering." They say "Don't yell at me, I'm on your side" or "I think you're overreacting" or "BOY, YOU'RE BITTER."

They've taught us that good queers don't get mad. They've taught us so well that we not only hide our anger from them, we hide it from each other. WE EVEN HIDE IT FROM OURSELVES. We hide it with substance abuse and suicide and overachieving in the hope of proving our worth. They bash us and stab us and shoot us and bomb us in ever increasing numbers and still we freak out when angry queers carry banners or signs that say BASH BACK. For the last decade they let us die in droves and still we thank President Bush for planting a fucking tree, applaud him for likening PWAs to car accident victims who refuse to wear seatbelts.

LET YOURSELF BE ANGRY. Let yourself be angry that the price of our visibility is the constant threat of violence, anti-queer violence to which practically every segment of this society contributes. Let yourself feel angry that THERE IS NO PLACE IN THIS COUNTRY WHERE WE ARE SAFE, no place where we are not targeted for hatred and attack, the self-hatred, the suicide of the closet.

The next time some straight person comes down on you for being angry, tell them that until things change, you don't need any more evidence that the world turns at your expense. You don't need to see only hetero couples grocery shopping on your TV . . . You don't want any more baby pictures shoved in your face until you can have or keep your own. No more weddings, showers, anniversaries, please, unless they are our own brothers and sisters celebrating. And tell them not to dismiss you by saying "You have rights," "You have privileges," "You're overreacting" or "You have a victim's mentality." Tell them "GO AWAY FROM ME until YOU can change." Go away and try on a world without the brave, strong queers that are its back bone, that are its guts and brains and souls. Go tell them go away until they have spent a month walking hand in hand in public with someone of the same sex. After they survive that, then you'll hear what they have to say about queer anger. Otherwise, tell them to shut up and listen.

June 2, 1990

Philadelphia Gay and Lesbian Pride Parade Speech

Barbara Gittings

This is the address given by veteran activist Gittings when she served as grand marshal of the Philadelphia Gay and Lesbian Pride Parade on June 2, 1990.

This is the biggest closet airing Philadelphia has ever had!

We're here to celebrate gay pride, gay love, gay identity, and gay rights. Oh, you thought we got gay rights when City Council passed a bill in 1982? Not by a long parade. A law on paper gives us a legal leg to stand on to fight some cases of discrimination against us—but only the most blatant kinds of discrimination. And the law doesn't automatically end the personal prejudice behind discrimination.

Gay rights means much more than getting good laws and rules, and changing bad ones, though that is a key step. Progress on paper is fine but we can't stop there. The struggle for equal treatment has to be won in people's hearts and minds where it counts.

We want the right to live and love and work and play without being penalized for being ourselves. One way to secure that right is to live and love and work and play as ourselves whenever we can, to exercise our right, to let our city know that we are here and we *will* be ourselves.

Remember this is the city where long ago our country's leaders declared for us all the right to "life, liberty and the pursuit of happiness." They didn't say it was for heterosexuals only!

So today we play a little. And we meet in unity to enjoy our diversity.

We are a special people—and we always will be, even after all our rights are proved and all the bigotries and barriers are gone. Thank you for being yourselves!

And our fun today will boost the gay pride of our sisters and brothers who can't yet afford to be seen here but who will see us on TV and in the newspapers: Hang in there, folks, because those of us who are out are oiling the closet door hinges just as fast as we can!

Have a gay time today, whether you are or not!

June 15, 1990

Toasting Troy Perry

Barbara Gittings

This is the text of a speech given on June 15, 1990, at a dinner sponsored by the Philadelphia Metropolitan Community Church (MCC) congregation honoring Reverend Troy Perry, founder of the denomination.

My lover Kay Lahusen met Troy Perry before I did. She met him at the baths in New York City.

Kay at the baths? Troy at the baths?

You see, Kay was a co-founder of Gay Activists Alliance in New York in 1970, and GAA members sometimes did political leafletting in the baths. Troy happened to be in New York at one such time and he joined in the leafletting.

Then Kay and I both met Troy in Washington, D.C. in the spring of 1971. Troy and lots of us were there to help gay activist Frank Kameny in his campaign for Congress. The District of Columbia had just been given a non-voting seat in the House of Representatives, and Frank Kameny was running as the first openly-gay candidate for Congress. He came in fourth among six candidates.

At some point I took Kay and Troy Perry to the Washington airport for a flight to Los Angeles. Troy was going home, and Kay was going along to interview him for a book she was writing about gay activists who had solid track records of accomplishment for the gay cause. At that time, almost 20 years ago, there were only a handful of such activists.

Kay interviewed Troy in the plane all the way across the country, and she interviewed him for a few days at his home while his mother and his lover treated her to Southern hospitality and home cooking.

Here's Kay's book *The Gay Crusaders,* published in 1972. Troy Perry's is the first interview, and it opens quoting him, "When people call me the gay Billy Graham, I say—No, he's the straight Troy Perry."

A few years later, when Troy and I were both serving on the board of directors of the National Gay Task Force, several of us went to a meeting with top executives at NBC to complain about the lack of gay programming.

You know how such meetings go. We're polite, they're polite. We explain, they explain. We ask, they demur. We push, they postpone.

Then Troy spoke up. He said—and I'm sorry. I can't do the accent: "I've just come back from a trip to Australia, and one of their TV soap operas has a gay male couple who are having problems in their relationship. And do you know, every afternoon 13 million Australians are on the edge of their chairs to see if Jack and Tom can work it out!"

You should have seen their eyes. Troy hit the NBC people right where it mattered—hooking an audience. In two sentences Troy got through to them after all our rational negotiation rolled off their backs.

I think most gay movement people outside MCC have been slow to appreciate the power of Troy's direct appeal.

For instance, there was the crisis in 1976 when Christian singer Anita Bryant launched her national crusade against gay rights. She called her campaign "Save Our Children" and hoped it would roll back job-protection laws and undo other gains we'd made toward equality. Anita Bryant and others who hopped on her bandwagon were vocal and fiery and Bible-thumping.

Sometimes you need fire to fight fire. But whom did top honchos in our gay movement send to Florida to lead the counter-campaign against Anita Bryant? They sent northern liberal ideologues who could explain a hundred reasons why gays were entitled to be teachers.

What we really needed was Troy Perry to pound the pulpit right back at our opponents and proclaim, "We're all God's children and I double-checked it with God just half an hour ago and He said, Yes, and keep spreading my love."

Now I come to my own moment of embarrassment with Troy Perry. I don't remember the date. The Philadelphia MCC was in trouble: it had been through three pastors in two years, Troy came here to mend the trouble. I recall that his viewpoint, his solution, weren't acceptable to the members of the congregation. But I don't remember what the exact issue was. Anyway, I found myself siding with my friends in the church here.

There was a meeting with Troy Perry at the Joseph Priestly Chapel here at First Unitarian. I attended to give support to my friends in the congregation. The atmosphere was very tense. In the middle of one heated exchange, I piped up and called Troy a neanderthal.

You could have heard the hairpins drop.

The sequel is even more embarrassing. After Rev. Joseph Gilbert came to this MCC church, he once asked me, "What's this I hear about your calling Troy Perry a neanderthal?" I denied it. "Oh, I never said that," I claimed.

Later Joe came at me another way. "Say, Barbara, about that time you called Troy a neanderthal. Was the meeting in this room or that one?" "Oh, it was that one."

Back to that moment in the chapel. Troy is a real Christian. He forgave me, at least I think he forgave me. What's more, he converted me. I have had only good to say about him since.

What I think of Troy today is what I've known all these twenty years (except for that one mad moment): Troy is a national gay treasure who is underappreciated. And we're going to need him more than ever if Anita Bryant's comeback picks up any steam.

July 13, 1990

Chicago Speech

Tim McFeeley

This is the text of the address given by Tim McFeeley, at that time the executive director of the Human Rights Campaign Fund, to a fund-raising dinner held in Chicago, Illinois, on July 13, 1990.

Thank you. I'm very proud and happy to be here with you in Chicago on this historic occasion. Many people deserve credit, but I want to especially thank the dinner committee and its great co-chairs, Jeanne Branson and David Pence. I'd also like to acknowledge and thank the members of our Federal Club, whose generous contributions began our successful fundraising efforts here in Chicago. And I certainly want to introduce our hardworking Chicago staff member, Laurie Dittman for all her service to HRCF and to the Chicago community.

In this room tonight, we can see the Wave of the future. The Human Rights Campaign Fund has already experienced this year—the first in the decade of the 1990s—several significant successes in all three areas in which HRCF is engaged; political, lobbying, and constituent mobilization. On the Political side, Harvey Gantt—the former Mayor of Charlotte, and a candidate we supported early and heavily with a maximum $15,000 contribution—won a decisive primary victory on June 5th and is now ready to send North Carolina Senator Jesse Helms into the retirement he so richly deserves.

On the legislative front, the Hate Crimes Statistics Act is now law—and without a nasty Helms amendment, which was defeated February 8th on a 79-17 vote. The $600 million CARE Bill is close to final passage. It will authorize $9 million for AIDS care in Illinois. Again, all Helms amendments—and there were several—failed. And just today—July 13, 1990—the Americans With Disabilities Act which protects forty-three million Americans, including people with HIV disease, from discrimination passed the US Senate, and without the Chapman-Helms Amendment, which would have permitted discrimination against food handlers with HIV, as a result of Wednesday's Senate vote of 69-31 rejecting the Chapman-Helms amendment.

The Human Rights Campaign Fund spent hundreds of staff hours and over $25,000 to defeat this amendment.

We share these successes with many, and I want to publicly thank the Illinois Gay and Lesbian Task Force for their extraordinary help with both the Hate Crimes Statistics Act and the food handlers amendment.

And neither the Hate Crimes Act nor the deletion of the Chapman-Helms Amendment would have happened without the leadership of your Senator and our good friend, Paul Simon. He was with us earlier in the evening, but had to return to Washington. Senator Simon is in a tough race for re-election. His opponent, by the way, voted in favor of the Chapman-Helms amendment. He's been there for us, and we damn well better be there for him. I'm delighted to report that the Human Rights Campaign Fund has contributed the maximum allowed by law—$10,000—to Senator Simons's campaign.

In the third area of HRCF activity, we have also had great success. So far this year, we have signed up over 32,000 people in our Speak-Out program. We have distributed Speak-Out literature, and I urge you to join tonight. In one weekend alone, we signed up 16,000 people at Pride Celebrations from the Bay Area to Birmingham and from Boston to Boise. In Chicago we enlisted 1,800 subscribers. And this week, just before Wednesdays' critical Senate vote on food workers, we delivered our 100,000th message to Congress.

So we see the outlines of the Wave of the Future. This is a new decade and a time of change. Our community realizes that being Right is not enough—we need Power. We have been powerless too long and have wallowed in cynicism. Bertrand Russell defined cynicism as "the combination of comfort and powerlessness."

Whether in the streets waving banners or in the banquet halls writing checks, we have resolved never to be powerless again! We have a choice, and we choose change over cynicism. We at the Human Rights Campaign Fund—and all of you here tonight—live for change. We create change. We embrace and celebrate change.

In our lifetimes—yours and mine—we will see attitudes about lesbians and gay men change 180 degrees. We are privileged to be alive now, to see and be part of this change. We are not going to whine, we are going to win. We are not just surviving, we are going to soar.

We will see the day when:

The sixteen-year-old suicide, who could contribute so much to this country, finally understands that being gay is an asset, not a liability;

The twenty-year-old marine who wants to serve her country can do so *and* be open about her sexuality;

The fifty-year-old teacher who has devoted her life to teaching students the value of the Bill of Rights, can herself enjoy the freedom to hold her lover's hand in public;
The two hundred Americans diagnosed today with AIDS will have a safe, effective, and totally accessible cure.

We are going to see all of it and more—we are riding the Wave of the Future.

F. Scott Fitzgerald wrote: "America is a willingness of the Heart." No community has bigger hearts or stronger wills than the gay and lesbian community in America. You're all great Americans. I salute you and thank you.

April 27, 1991

The National Lesbian Agenda

Urvashi Vaid

This is the text of the address given by Vaid to the National Lesbian Conference meeting in Atlanta, Georgia, on April 27, 1991. Karen Thompson fought for eight years to become the legal guardian of her injured lover, Sharon Kowalski, finally achieving this in 1991.

Good evening. Thank you. I was asked to speak tonight on what the national lesbian agenda is; on where it is at: and what the obstacles are to its implementation. I hope to do that—but I want to begin very simply by asking us all to remember *why* we are are here at this conference asking this question?

We are here at the National Lesbian Conference because of the passion, love, excitement and desire we feel for women.

We are here because spectacular forces of evil and prejudice threaten our very existence as lesbians.

It is this evil present in Judge Campbell's decision denying Karen Thompson guardianship of Sharon Kowalski.

It is this evil that murdered Rebecca Wight, and wounded her lover, Claudia Brenner as they were camping in the mountains of Pennsylvania.

It is this evil found in the cowardly silence of all politicians who will not stand up to defend lesbians, will not pass laws to end the daily, massive relentless mountain of prejudice we face.

What brings us together tonight are the realities of discrimination we face as lesbians and our commitment to changing these realities.

Let us never forget the social context we gather in:

To be lesbian today means to face loss of our jobs, loss of housing, denial of public accommodation, loss of custody, loss of visitation simply because of our sexual orientation.

To be lesbian today means to face violence as a queer and violence as a woman.

To be lesbian today means to have no safety for the families we have created, to face the loss of our children and our loved ones, to have no status for our committed relationships.

To be lesbian means to be invisible, as Kate Clinton says, like the stealth bomber, low-flying, undetectable—to be a stealth lesbian, hidden from a world whose sight is monochromatic and patriarchal; hidden even when we are out and powerful, by a world that is obsessed with the relationships between men.

To be lesbian means to work in social change movements, in gay and lesbian organizations, in civil rights and feminist organizations that still ghettoize the multiple issues of discrimination that we face and that still tokenize us or put our concerns and voices on the back burner.

To be lesbian is to have, until very recently, absolutely no images in mainstream culture of out, proud, powerful, strong independent women.

To be lesbian today is to live in a society that identifies and defines us only through our relation (or lack thereof) to men—lesbians are masculine, man haters, the sexual fantasies of straight men.

To be lesbian today is to face multiple systems of oppression—to face homophobia, sexism, racism, ageism, ableism, economic injustice—to face a variety of systems of oppression *all at once,* with the type of oppression changing depending on who we are, but the fact of oppression remaining constant.

We gather here at this conference in Atlanta in 1991, not 1951, not 1971, not 1981, but today. And the context of this time is ominous. The world is which we strive to live as openly lesbian has taken off its ugly white hood to show its sexist, anti-gay, racist, and capitalist face as never before.

When a Ku Klux Klansman can run for the U.S. Senate and get 44% of the vote—the Hood is off.

When the President of the United States is elected on the heels of an orchestrated racist campaign—the Hood is off.

When he campaigns for Helms in North Carolina, when he vetoes the Civil Rights Act of 1990, when he introduces a Crime Bill that will strip our civil liberties, when he speaks in strong support of the anti-choice, anti-woman, anti-abortion movement, when he opposes equal rights for women, when he lets our brothers and sisters with HIV die from negligence, when he engineers a war to win re-election—the Hood of evil is off.

A second piece of the context in which we gather is more hopeful:

We meet at this lesbian conference at an historic moment in the lesbian and gay movement's history. Today tens of thousands of lesbians are actively engaged in the movement for lesbian liberation. At the workshops and caucuses I have attended it is clear that the 2 thousand of us at the conference are deeply and intimately involved in our movement for freedom.

Today, we are a truly mixed movement through the involvement of lesbians. And through our involvement, we are changing the face, the politics, and the content of our gay and lesbian organizations.

There is a revolution underway in the lesbian and gay liberation movement. The fact that organizations are developing multicultural plans and dealing with racism on their staffs, boards and in their programs—is a direct result of lesbian feminist organizing and politics. The fact that the gay and lesbian movement has begun to be multi-issue, that it is pro-choice, that it dares to speak out on the broad social issues of the day (like the war)—is a direct result of lesbian leadership. The fact that the feminist health agenda of the 1970's—the agenda of disability rights, insurance reform, health care access for all, welfare reform, etc.—the fact that these issues are now on the central burner of the gay and lesbian movement is in part a function of the painful experience of the AIDS crisis—and in part a result of lesbian feminist analysis and organizing.

The parallel contexts of great danger and great change frame our meeting together tonight as lesbians.

And as we have seen in this week together, the work we must do—our *agenda for action* is large and quite specific!

There are two big pieces to our national lesbian agenda: 1) is movement building; and 2) is public policy. Put another way, I believe that our lesbian agenda for the 1990's is about organizing and power; it is about taking and making as Audre Lorde said "power out of hatred and destruction."

These are not easy agenda items to move.

Movement Building

The experience of this conference suggests to me that we do not in fact have a national lesbian movement. We have a vital cultural movement, we have a huge amount of talent, we have a lot of grassroots leadership, we have lesbians active in a million projects—but the locus of lesbian community in our cities and towns remains the same as it was in the 1950's—it remains the Bar—augmented by women's cultural events, the Festival network and local feminist and lesbian bookstores.

We have no national movement, no national newspaper, no national annual gathering place for lesbian activists to meet and talk politics, we have one annual state conference I am aware of—in Texas—and for all the talk of a national lesbian organization let me remind everyone that we have a national lesbian organization that struggles for its daily existence—the National Center for Lesbian Rights. How many of us here support this ten-year old pillar of lesbian advocacy?

The centerpiece of our national lesbian agenda must be the recreation of a lively, open, organized and unafraid lesbian movement. It existed once.

The challenges to the recreation of this lesbian movement are manifest throughout this, our National Lesbian Conference. The NLC is a mirror to the current state of the movement. And the mirror shows us several harsh truths:

Truth: That we are not one lesbian community but a series of very splintered communities who have in fact not been working with each other at home or at this conference.

Truth: In this conference we have demonstrated that we do not trust each other at all; that we refuse to claim the cloak of leadership even when we have it—perhaps because we rightly fear the backlash or ostracism all lesbians who dare say the word leadership fear; we have shown that we do not understand that diversity politics is not about kneejerk or paying lip service but about action and internalizing the message, not about making sure that we have one of each—but learning and accepting that we have each in one—that we respect and carry the commitment to act in ourselves.

Truth: In this conference 2000 have gathered. I have met so many fierce, powerful, seasoned, interesting lesbians, and it pains me that any of us might leave this place feeling dejected and hurt, angry and excluded. Let us not do that. Remember—we will never feel included entirely, because the big social context is what excludes us completely.

Truth: That developing alternative decision making processes are wonderful and radical, but that all processes must be accountable and take responsibility for their actions.

Truth: That we can get so intense and focused on criticizing each other and focused on ourselves that we forget that we are in this together, that we are in this to change the fucked up world outside.

We must begin in our own house to put it in order. We must begin by taking a deep collective breath and looking around at the fierce, powerful women that we are. Look around at the skills we bring and let us let go of perfectionism and a purity politics based in fear; Let us enact instead a courageous and honest politics based in lesbian pride.

It is time for lesbians like me and you to bring our energies back home into our own movement and our own communities. It is time for us to mobilize on the grassroots level FIRST.

Every state must have a lesbian conference to encourage involvement by lesbians.

Every city and town should have lesbian activist networking breakfasts or potlucks to reconnect us to each other.

Let us certainly do our organizing on our particular and separate piece of the social change pie—but let us not forget that we are allies as lesbians—we are not the enemy.

Let us encourage and promote lesbianism! Let us link up across age to talk political vision. Let us not be afraid of doing the wrong thing—let us just do some thing!

Public Policy/Politics

On a political level, in the two years of planning for this conference, I have sat through many discussions of what is the lesbian political agenda. Lesbians have tried to define lesbian-specific issues—well, that is not my vision of my lesbian movement's political agenda.

My vision is to claim quite simply the fact that the lesbian agenda is (as it has always been) radical social change.

It is the reconstruction of family, it is the re-imagining and claiming of power, it is the reorganization of the economic system, it is the reinforcement of civil rights for all peoples. It is the enactment of laws and the creation of a society that affirms choice. It is the end to the oppression of women, the end to racism, the end to sexism, ableism, homophobia, the protection of our environment.

I have no problem claiming all these issues as the lesbian agenda for social change—because that is the truth. Lesbians have a radical social vision—we are the bearers of a truly new world order, not the stench of the same old world odor.

This large agenda does not overwhelm me, it tells me how far I must go until we all win.

It tells me who my allies really are.

How do we enact our agenda? We enact it by continuing to do what we are doing in each of our communities. We enact it by involving more of our sisters, the thousands of lesbians who do not interact with us or with our movement for social change.

We enact our lesbian agenda by building a movement for POWER. What are we afraid of? Why are we afraid of power—we surely will not make things more fucked up than they already are.

I am not suggesting that all of us drop the work we are doing to focus on this new exclusively lesbian thing called lesbian agenda—I am suggesting that we continue to do what we are doing, but that we do it as OUT lesbians. That we claim our work as lesbian work, that we be out about who and why we are how we are.

I proudly claim our unique multi-issue perspective. I am proud of my lesbian community's politics of inclusion. I am engaged in my people's liberation. Let us just do it.

June 25, 1991

Gay Pride Month

Ted Weiss

This address was given by Representative Weiss on the floor of the House of Representatives and entered in the *Congressional Record* for June 25, 1991.

Mr. Speaker, 22 years ago, following a riot at a bar named Stonewall, a tradition was born. This tradition has evolved into a yearly proclamation by the mayor of New York City declaring the month of June Gay and Lesbian Pride and History Month. This month of events culminates on the final Sunday, Gay Pride Day, when tens of thousands of gay men and lesbians, joined by their friends and families, fill the streets in celebration.

I am pleased to note that in the past 22 years the gay and lesbian community has made significant strides. As gays and lesbians have come out of the closet and organized, they have emerged as a formidable political force. Their lobbying efforts were instrumental in securing passage of the Ryan White AIDS Care bill and the Hate Crimes Statistics Act of 1990. Their diligent work also has been pivotal in garnering broad support for H.R. 1430, the Civil Rights Amendments Act of 1991, which amends the Civil Rights Act of 1964 and the Fair Housing Act to prohibit discrimination on the basis of affectional or sexual orientation. As lead sponsor of H.R. 1430, I particularly am proud to announce that this legislation has an all time high 91 House cosponsors in the 102d Congress.

Sadly, though, the AIDS epidemic has led to increased discrimination against homosexuals and those who are perceived to be homosexual. As violence against this community rises dramatically and many States, including New York, grapple to pass hate crimes laws, it is ironic that this celebration of gay and lesbian dignity arose from an incident of bias-related violence.

As gays and lesbians across the country commemorate this symbolic month of pride, it is time for Congress to join that celebration by finally extending civil rights protections to the approximately 25 million Americans which our Government has systematically overlooked.

August 19, 1991

Memorial to A. Damien Martin

Barbara Gittings

This is the full text of remarks made by Gittings in August 1991 at the memorial service for A. Damien Martin, cofounder with his partner of the Hetrick-Martin Institute for the Protection of Lesbian and Gay Youth in New York City.

In the printed program for the 1989 Emery Awards sponsored by the Hetrick-Martin Institute, there's an unsigned ad with the simple message: "If only you'd been around when I was a kid."

If only Damien had been around when *I* was a kid! When I was in high school in the late 1940's, I was clearly showing my homosexual interests—I was too naïve to conceal them. Also I was confused and I desperately needed someone to talk to, someone who could tell me what it meant to be the way I was and how I could live as a homosexual.

Of course I know now that there must have been gay teachers in my school. But at that time, 45 years ago, none of them dared to reach out a friendly ear much less a helping hand to the likes of me. I'm sure Damien would have done so.

It's been great knowing Damien for 15 years, enjoying him as a friend—oh the bubbly warmth and the sense of humor!—and admiring his work.

With Emery, he built an organization that was meant to last and not just rise atop a wave of popular interest. They brought a new high level of professionalism to social services in our movement. And they attracted such wonderful talent.

Damien has also left us a body of fine writings that are outstanding for their lucidity, including articles in *ETC Journal* on homosexuals as a minority group and on anti-gay prejudice, and a carefully reasoned article on man/boy love in a New York City gay paper that's now defunct.

When I last talked with Damien, he was planning to work up some notes into a full article on horizontal hostility within the gay rights movement. How badly we need his clear thinking and common sense and persuasiveness on such a messy topic!

Damien was generous-minded and always eager to honor others for their contributions—not forgetting Emery. Let me tell you of an incident which figures large in my memories of Damien.

In 1978 I prepared and ran a gay exhibit at the annual meeting of the American Psychiatric Association which was held in Atlanta that year. It was the third such exhibit I'd done for APA, the others being in 1976 and 1972. For 1978 I decided we had done enough to display "us" to "them." It was time to show that we are them and they are us.

I needed gay psychiatrists to come out in their own profession—and I began with Emery Hetrick. He thought about it, but not for long, and when he said Yes the dominos began falling—four other gay psychiatrists also agreed. So the front part of that exhibit, the part that everyone passing in the aisle couldn't help seeing, featured Emery and the other four, with pictures and biographies with all their professional credentials. It was a marvelous breakthrough. It stirred up a lot of talk in the APA, and it spurred the efforts of the gay caucus which was getting formally established in the association.

Emery was thrilled with what he'd accomplished. But he was even more thrilled when Damien, on the spur of the moment, hopped a plane to Atlanta to share the triumph with him!

Incidentally, the title of that particular exhibit at the American Psychiatric Association was "Gay Love Is Good Medicine."

Damien, thank you. You were good medicine for me. I'll always love you!

November 4, 1991

Tribute to Steve Endean

Olav Sabo

These remarks were made by Representative Sabo of Minnesota on the floor of the House of Representatives and were entered into the *Congressional Record* of November 4, 1991.

Mr. Speaker, I wish today to honor one of the leaders in the fight for fairness for lesbian, gay, and bisexual Americans—Steve Endean. Steve Endean became a gay activist in my home State of Minnesota more than 20 years ago, when the organized movement for gay civil rights was in its infancy. Steve was the first lobbyist for lesbian, gay, and bisexual rights at the Minnesota State Capitol in St. Paul, when I was Speaker of the Minnesota House, and he was a leader in efforts to pass the Minneapolis city ordinance on gay rights.

In 1978, after working at the local level for several years, Steve Endean moved to Washington, D.C. and founded the Gay Rights National Lobby, one of the first national political organizations in Washington working to outlaw discrimination on the basis of sexual orientation.

Steven Endean was a founder of the Human Rights Campaign Fund. Later he became the field director of the expanded Human Rights Campaign Fund and helped build its renowned grassroots network. Today, thanks largely to Steve Endean, the Human Rights Campaign Fund is the Nation's largest lesbian, gay and bisexual civil rights organization and one of the country's largest political action committees.

Steve Endean left the Human Rights Campaign last Friday, but that will not stop his work for equal opportunity for all Americans regardless of their sexual orientation. "A lot of elected officials, even if they don't oppose fairness for lesbians and gay men, choose to duck this issue," said Endean recently to the *Minnesota Star Tribune,* "They are misjudging the prevailing winds." He cited a 1991 Penn and Schoen poll that showed over 75 percent of the respondents supported protection from job discrimination for lesbian, gay and bisexual Americans.

Never one to rest, Steve Endean has embarked on a new campaign to ask prominent Minnesotans to support laws barring discrimination against gays, lesbians and bisexuals. The first leaders to take this stand include: Joan Mondale, wife of the former vice president; Alan Page, an attorney and former Vikings football player; Wheelock Whitney, a former Republican gubernatorial candidate, and Beverly McKinnell, president of the League of Women Voters of Minnesota.

Steve Endean has been a pioneer in the movement to provide fair treatment for all people regardless of their sexual orientation. I am proud to recognize him today and thank him for all the good work he has done.

November 22, 1991

In Honor of Roman Kalinin

Nancy Pelosi

These remarks were made on the floor of the House of Representatives by Representative Pelosi of New York and entered in the *Congressional Record* for November 22, 1991.

Mr. Speaker, the attempted Soviet coup in August 1991 was the back drop for a remarkable demonstration of courage and dedication to the cause of freedom. Roman Kalinin, publisher of Russia's first gay and lesbian newspaper, together with a group of gay men and lesbians worked to fight the coup by printing and distributing President Boris Yeltsin's decrees.

Roman Kalinin first learned of the coup from friends in San Francisco. From late in the evening of August 18, until the coup was defeated on August 21, Kalinin established a telephone link through Finland to San Francisco. A plan was developed to communicate with people in the Soviet Union who would have immediately become targets for intimidation and possibly death because of their sexual preference and work in the democratic movement. Fear and panic were rampant as reports surfaced of the possibility of waves of arrests. On August 20, an official demand was made for lists of people with AIDS and HIV from the Moscow AIDS clinic.

Kalinin is the publisher of *TEMA,* the first gay/lesbian newspaper in the Soviet Union. His publishing system and copy machine became virtually the only method available to print and distribute information against the coups leaders. For almost 60 hours, gay men and lesbians in Moscow marshaled their forces in an incredible display of courage.

Russian President Boris Yeltsin issued a list of decrees which became the document of resistance against the forces of oppression. Gay men and lesbians at the *TEMA* offices processed the information on the computer. Around the clock the copy machine printed the Yeltsin decrees with the logo of the well known gay newspaper on the bottom. Kalinin wanted the public to know that the gay community was working to fight the coup, even though he risked his own arrest by publicly claiming the work.

These heroes then took the printed decrees into the streets of Moscow, working with other leaders of the prodemocracy movement. The decrees were distributed throughout the city and appeared at every metro stop for confused Muscovites to read. The decrees were even handed to soldiers in the tanks aimed at the Russian Parliament building. This heroism represents an ongoing commitment to fight oppression and discrimination in the Soviet Union. They have for several years, led the fight to reduce the discrimination which is faced by gay men and lesbians throughout the Soviet Union.

They have also joined with others from around the world to provide information and educational material for the Russian people to fight the ever increasing threat of AIDS and infection from the HIV virus. Their efforts have been supported through the International Gay and Lesbian Human Rights Commission, an organization that has become in just one year, an international gay consulate to the world. Victory in the Soviet Union provided the opportunity to open doors for lesbian/gay freedom never before dreamed of in that country.

The courage and commitment to freedom and democracy of Roman Kalinin is being honored in December 1991 when he will be named the "Man of the Year" by *The Advocate,* the largest national publication in America serving lesbians and gay men.

May 28, 1992

African-American Community Celebrates Black Gay Pride Day

Eleanor Holmes Norton

These remarks were made by Representative Norton, of the District of Columbia, on the floor of the House of Representatives and entered into the *Congressional Record* for May 28, 1992.

Mr. Speaker, on Sunday, May 24, the African-American lesbian and gay community celebrated Black Gay Pride Day in Washington, D.C., culminating a month-long series of fundraising entertainment and religious events that both celebrate gay pride and raise desperately needed funds for AIDS services in the African-American community. With a theme of "Pride in ourselves and our ability to accomplish what we want and need for ourselves," the celebration started with the dream of three Washingtonians, Dr. Ernest Hopkins, Mr. Theodore Kirkland, and Dr. Welmore Alfred Cook, whom many have called the father of Washington's African-American gay community.

This year's Black Lesbian and Gay Pride Day is a tribute to Welmore Cook, a person of great conviction with a dream of raising significant sums of money for African-Americans living with HIV/AIDS. Welmore Cook died of AIDS on April 22, but not before acting on his dream of increasing funds for community-based African-American AIDS service organizations and instilling a new sense of dignity in the African-American gay community.

For much of my adult life, I have been in the battle to secure and maintain fundamental rights for gays and lesbians as part of my efforts to foster civil rights that should be guaranteed to all Americans. We can all learn lessons from the African-American gay and lesbian community of Washington, which, while bearing the burden of double discrimination, can celebrate their individuality within their own community and the diversity of all Americans.

The AIDS virus is spreading among African-Americans in Washington at a rate far higher than in other communities. The sense of responsibility the participants in Black Lesbian and Gay Pride Day bring to other persons who are struggling with AIDS is an example for us all to emulate.

Mr. Speaker, I ask you and my colleagues to join me in congratulating the organizers of this important celebration and in commending the African-American gay and lesbian community of the District of Columbia for their vital leadership on eradicating AIDS and eliminating discrimination.

April 21, 1993

Remembering Gay Victims of the Holocaust

Gerry Studds

This text was delivered on the floor of the House of Representatives by Representative Studds of Massachusetts, an openly gay member of Congress, on April 21, 1993, and was entered in the *Congressional Record* for that day.

Mr. Speaker, on the occasion of the formal dedication of the U.S. Holocaust Memorial Museum, I rise to pay tribute to those victims of the Nazi terror who were persecuted because of their sexual orientation.

In the decades before Adolf Hitler's rise to power, Germany was home to the world's first homosexual rights movement. The Nazis responded with a vicious campaign against "homosexual degeneracy" during the 1930s. Some 50,000 to 63,000 men were convicted of homosexual offenses in Nazi courts from 1933 to 1944; 10,000 to 12,000 homosexuals—most of them men—were imprisoned in the concentration camps. They were often singled out for the harshest treatment, and more than half of them died.

Gay prisoners in the camps wore uniforms that bore a pink triangle—an insignia that has since been adopted as a symbol of the modern lesbian and gay rights movement.

According to materials compiled by the Holocaust Memorial, gay survivors were subjected to continued persecution after the collapse of the Nazi regime. The Allied Military Government of Germany refused to release those who had been imprisoned for homosexuality, and the Nazi law criminalizing homosexuality remained in effect until 1969.

For too long, the Nazi victimization of gay people has remained a secret little known and seldom mentioned. The curators of the U.S. Holocaust Memorial Museum have taken an important step in redressing this neglect by including among the displays a poignant collection of artifacts documenting the persecution of homosexuals.

Visitors to the museum are issued an identity card that tells the story of a person of the visitor's age and gender who lived during the Holocaust. During my visit last Monday evening with some of my congressional colleagues, I received a card describing the life of Willem Arondeus, born in Amsterdam, Netherlands, in 1895. This is his story:

One of seven children, Willem grew up in Amsterdam where his parents were theater costume designers. When Willem was 18, he fought with his parents about his homosexuality. He left home and severed contact with his family. He began writing and painting, and in the 1920's was commissioned to do a mural for the Rotterdam town hall. In 1932 he moved to the countryside near Apeldoorn.

1933-39: When he was 38, he met Jan, the son of a greengrocer, and they lived together for the next seven years. As a struggling painter, Willem was forced to go on welfare. In 1938 Willem began writing the biography of the Dutch painter Matthijs Maris, and after the book was published, Willem's financial situation improved.

1940-44: The Germans invaded the Netherlands in May 1940. Soon after the occupation, Willem joined the resistance. His unit's main task was to falsify identity papers for Dutch Jews. On March 27, 1943, Willem's unit attacked the registry building and set it on fire. They were attempting to destroy records against which false identity papers could be checked. Thousands of files were destroyed. Five days later the unit was betrayed and arrested. That July, Willem and 11 others were executed.

Before his execution, Willem asked his lawyer to testify after the war that "homosexuals are not cowards." In 1945 Willem was posthumously awarded a medal by the Dutch government.

There is a special poignancy in our remembrance of gay Holocaust victims like Willem Arondeus. Unlike those who could marry and have children, many gay people perished with no one but us to remember them. We are their family, and we will never forget them.

Mr. Speaker, I am struck by the remarkable fact that the dedication of the U.S. Holocaust Memorial Museum coincides with what will be one of the largest civil rights demonstrations in U.S. history. The march on Washington for lesbian and gay civil rights, scheduled for Sunday, April 25, 1993, is expected to draw hundreds of thousands from throughout the United States. These people are coming to Washington to bear witness to the continuing discrimination visited upon lesbian, gay and bisexual Americans. Like Willem Arondeus, these American are murdered, assaulted, and denied basic civil rights simply because of who they are. Those who have the moral and physical courage of Arondeus are told they are unfit to serve their country.

This situation represents a tragic failure of our society to learn the lessons of history. We must never forget, nor allow the world to forget, that the degradation and dehumanization of any member of the human family endangers the life and liberty of us all.

April 22, 1993

Report of the National Gay and Lesbian Task Force on Anti-Gay Violence

Paul Simon

This address was given on the floor of the U.S. Senate by Senator Paul Simon of Illinois and entered into the *Congressional Record* for April 22, 1993.

Mr. President, I applaud the efforts of the National Gay and Lesbian Task Force [NGLTF] Policy Institute in its fight against antigay violence. For the past 8 years, the NGLTF has compiled data on antigay attacks, including harassment, threats, physical assaults, police abuse, and murder, in their annual Anti-Gay/Lesbian Violence, Victimization and Defamation Report. NGLTF's efforts in collecting these data and in working with Federal, State and Local government and nongovernment agencies has been instrumental in developing programs that combat antigay bias and violence. I commend their efforts to expose and eliminate hate crimes and would like to share with my colleagues some of the NGLTF's recent findings.

I was saddened to learn that reports to NGLTF of hate crimes against gays reached record high levels in 1992. Victim service agencies in Boston, Chicago, Minneapolis-St.Paul, New York City, and San Francisco recorded 1,898 incidents, including harassment, attacks on property, physical assaults, and murder. The incidents in 1992 represent a 172-percent increase over the 697 bias incidents reported 5 years ago by these agencies.

I am also disturbed by events in Oregon and Colorado, States where gay civil rights initiatives were placed on ballots last November. In 1992, the Portland, OR, victim assistance agency documented 968 bias incidents, more than any other gay agency in the United States. After the passage of Colorado's amendment 2, Denver victim advocates reported antigay episodes tripled during November and December. Forty percent of the 204 incidents recorded by victim advocates in Colorado in 1992 were reported during the last 2 months of the year, after amendment 2 had passed.

Clearly, data collected by local antiviolence programs and by the police account for only a fraction of the hate crimes against gays that actually occur. Studies which question individuals directly about antigay incidents are even more revealing. Such studies in 1991 added to the already substantial body of research suggesting the depth of antigay bias. In a study conducted by the Philadelphia Lesbian and Gay Task Force, 20 percent of the homosexual men and women surveyed reported that they had been threatened, chased, or assaulted in 1992. Perhaps most startling, however, is that AIDS bias continues to be a factor in antigay hate crimes. Among the incidents documented in 1992, 168, or 9 percent, involved AIDS-related epithets or were directed toward people with AIDS or people perceived to have AIDS. Equally troubling, a survey conducted by the National Association of People with AIDS found that 21 percent of those surveyed had been the victims of discrimination outside of their homes as a result of their disease.

The NGLTF Policy Institute and the NGLTF, in conjunction with other civil rights organizations, have been instrumental in drawing attention to hate crimes and proposing solutions to intolerance. While there is obviously much more work to be done, their efforts to date should be commended.

I urge my colleagues to carefully examine the Anti-Gay/Lesbian Violence, Victimization and Defamation in 1992 Report.

April 1993

Letter to the March on Washington

William Jefferson Clinton

This is the text of the official letter sent to the 1993 March on Washington by President Clinton in his first year of office, in lieu of the in-person appearance many activists had been hoping for. He was the first president of the United States to send such a document and the first to meet directly with representatives of the gay and lesbian community. The executive order referred to in the letter was never issued.

Welcome to Washington, D.C., your nation's capital.

During my campaign and since my election, I have said that America does not have a person to waste. Today, I want you to know that I am still committed to that principle.

I stand with you in the struggle of equality for all Americans, including gay men and lesbians. In this great country, founded on the principle that all people are created equal, we must learn to put aside what divides us and focus on what we share. We all want the chance to excel in our work. We all want to be safe in our communities. We all want the support of our friends and families.

Last November, the American people sent a message to make government more accountable to all its citizens, regardless of race, class, gender, disability, or sexual orientation. I am proud of the strides that we are making in that direction.

The Pentagon has stopped asking recruits about their sexual orientation, and I have asked the secretary of defense to determine how to implement an executive order lifting the ban on gays and lesbians in the military by July 15.

My 1994 budget increases funding for AIDS research, and my economic plan will fully fund the Ryan White Act. Soon I will announce a new AIDS coordinator to implement the recommendations of the AIDS commission reports.

I met nine days ago with leaders of the gay and lesbian community in the Oval Office at the White house. I am told that this meeting marks the first time in history that the president of the United States has held such a meeting. In addition, members of my staff have been and will continue to be in regular communication with the gay and lesbian community.

I still believe every American who works hard and plays by the rules ought to be a part of the national community. Let us work together to make this vision real.

Thank you.

April 25, 1993

Unashamed, We Embrace the Traditions of the Broad Civil Rights Movement in America

Eric Rofes

This address was given by longtime activist and educator Eric Rofes in Washington, DC, on April 25, 1993, during that year's March on Washington.

O beautiful for spacious skies, for amber waves of grain;
For purple mountain majesties above the fruited plain!

These words of Katherine Lee Bates describe a vision of America the Beautiful. I speak to you about the side of America which is not beautiful: the link between all oppressions and how the bigot's mind aflame in our nation does not care if we're queer, or we're Black, or we're Jewish. From sea to shining sea they have an agenda which is establishing a fascist theocracy in the land we call home.

You may have come here to demand justice for lesbian mothers, people with AIDS, gay and bisexual soldiers. But we stand at one of those times when Franklin Roosevelt said that we must speak the truth, the *whole* truth, frankly and boldly. *The truth is there is one movement with liberty and justice for all people, and there are many tribes in this movement.* It includes the gay movement and the women's movement and the Black movement, but we must see it as essentially *one* movement, because our enemies do.

O beautiful for pilgrim feet, whose stern impassioned stress
A thoroughfare for freedom beat across the wilderness!

The same feet which trudged for freedom across that wilderness marched to demand justice for Sacco and Vanzetti, kicked as we were torn away from blockading nuclear labs, and stormed the concentration camps at Guantanamo Bay.

The same black leather boots I wear today walked to free Angela Davis, support Cesar Chavez, protect Susan Saxe, avenge Harvey Milk, and celebrate Doris Fish.
Those red stilettos you're wearing are the same high heels which stomped the toes of neo-Nazis in Colorado Springs and kicked the shins of the Ku Klux Klan in Little Rock.

O beautiful for heroes proved in liberating strife.
Who more than self their country loved and mercy more than life!

Lesbians, gay men, bisexual and transgenders are no longer the unwanted stepchildren of the freedom movement. We are not freaks; our issues are not trivial; and *this is not a parade or a public spectacle.* We are part of a serious movement struggling to preserve some semblance of democracy in America as the Right Wing strengthens its foundations. And we demand the respect and dignity merited by every part of the movement for social change.

The suffragettes at the turn of the century—we share their dignity and pride.
The union organizers of the great depression—we share their determination and perseverance.
The Black Civil Rights Movement of the 60s—we share the weight of moral justice which they seized along the Freedom Trail.

We have couched the language of our movement in words that have failed to be powerful or specific enough to link us to core values in American democracy. Instead of framing the debate around "anti-discrimination," "human rights," or "freedom of choice," we need to state our struggles boldly for what they are: *a fight for freedom, justice and democracy in the purest sense of the terms.* This is about who participates in democracy in America.

When we articulate our efforts under the limited category of "gay rights," we play into a strategy that considers this a movement for "special rights." Let's not be afraid to say that we are fighting for civil rights generally and for the civil rights of bisexuals, lesbians and gay men specifically. The Christofascists are not only homophobes or bigots, they are the enemies of democracy, determined to reign in the "life, liberty and pursuit of happiness" promised to the citizens of this nation. We must make these connections through our organizing and must be unashamed to embrace the history, traditions and rhetoric of the broad civil rights movement in this nation.

The Christofascists say we have an agenda. You bet we do! We have an agenda and it is explicit, radical and uncompromising. We want your children. We want them freed from your bigotry and allowed to grow into gentle human beings, capable of critical thinking and grace with kindness. We want them to control their bodies and respect the autonomy of others. Yes, we want your children and your husbands and your wives to become part of our movement to reclaim democracy in America. And we won't stop until we succeed.

A powerful churning river has cut a swath across this century and it is *one* big river with liberty and justice for all. It is fed by the large tributaries of women's liberation and gay liberation and the Black Panthers and the peace movements of every decade of this century. Less acknowledged streams feed the river—movements for the liberation of children and old people, transgender activists and the leather community, movements fighting anti-Semitism and anti-Arab bigotry.

I say this not to list a litany of liberal causes to irk your conscience. It is the simple truth contained in Katherine Lee Bates' "America the Beautiful" and sung throughout this nation. While she didn't use gender-neutral language and believed in God, she wrote this anthem 70 years ago based on a vision of social justice which understands the freedom movement of this century. Katherine Lee Bates' spirit is with us today in our march to save democracy in America. She lived for 30 years in a home in Massachusetts with her female lover Katherine Coman. With all of us, she jumped into that great river of liberty and swam against the threatening currents of this century and in her final verse, captured our movement's grand vision for social justice:

> O beautiful for patriot dream, that sees beyond the years
> Thine alabaster cities gleam, undimmed by human tears!
> America! America! God shed his grace on thee.
> And crown thy good with brotherhood and sisterhood,
> From sea to shining sea. *From sea to shining sea.*

April 25, 1993

Speech at the March on Washington

Urvashi Vaid

This speech was delivered by lesbian activist lawyer Urvashi Vaid to the crowd attending the second March on Washington in support of gay and lesbian rights issues on the Mall in Washington, DC.

Hello lesbian and gay Americans. I am proud to stand before you as a lesbian today. With hearts full of love and the abiding faith in justice, we have come to Washington to speak to America. We have come to speak the truth of our lives and silence the liars. We have come to challenge the cowardly Congress to end its paralysis and exercise moral leadership. We have come to defend our honor and win our equality. But most of all we gave come in peace and with courage to say, "America, this day marks the return from exile of the gay and lesbian people. We are banished no more. We wander the wilderness of despair no more. We are afraid no more. For on this day, with love in our hearts, we have come out, and we have come out across America to build a bridge of understanding, a bridge of progress, a bridge as solid as steel, a bridge to a land where no one suffers prejudice because of their sexual orientation, their race, their gender, their religion, or their human difference."

I have been asked by the March organizers to speak in five minutes about the far right, the far right which threatens the construction of that bridge. The extreme right which has targeted every one of you and me for extinction. The supremacist right which seeks to redefine the very meaning of democracy. Language itself fails in this task, my friends, for to call our opponents "The Right" states a profound untruth. They are wrong—they are wrong morally, they are wrong spiritually, and they are wrong politically.

The Christian supremacists are wrong spiritually when they demonize us. They are wrong when they reduce the complexity and beauty of our spirit into a freak show. They are wrong spiritually, because, if we are the untouchables of America—if we are the untouchables—then we are, as Mahatma Gandhi said, children of God. And as God's children, we know that the gods of our understanding, the gods of goodness and love and righteousness, march right here with us today.

The supremacists who lead the anti-gay crusade are wrong morally. They are wrong because justice is moral, and prejudice is evil; because truth is moral and the lie of the closet is the real sin; because the claim of morality is a subtle sort of subterfuge, a strategem which hides the real aim which is much more secular. Christian supremacist leaders like Bill Bennett and Pat Robertson, Lou Sheldon and Pat Buchanan, supremacists like Phyllis Schlafly, Ralph Reed, Bill Bristol, R.J. Rushoodie—these supremacists don't care about morality, they care about power. They care about social control. And their goal, my friends, is the reconstruction of American Democracy into American Theocracy.

We who are gathered here today must prove the religious right wrong politically and we can do it. That is our challenge. You know they have made us into the communists of the nineties. And they say they have declared cultural war against us. It's war all right. It's a war about values. On one side are the values that everyone here stands for. Do you know what those values are? Traditional American values of democracy and pluralism. On the other side are those who want to turn the Christian church into government, those whose value is monotheism.

We believe in democracy, in many voices co-existing in peace, and people of all faiths living together in harmony under a common civil framework known as the United States Constitution. Our opponents believe in monotheism. One way, theirs. One god, theirs. One law, the Old Testament. One nation supreme, the Christian Right. Let's name it. Democracy battles theism in Oregon, in Colorado, in Florida, in Maine, in Arizona, in Michigan, in Ohio, in Idaho, in Washington, in Montana, in every state where we, my brothers and sisters, are leading the fight to oppose the Right and to defend the United States Constitution. We won the anti-gay measure in Oregon, but today 33 counties—33 counties and municipalities face local versions of that ordinance today. The fight has just begun. We lost the big fight in Colorado, but, thanks to the hard work of all the people of Colorado, the Boycott Colorado movement is working and we are strong. And we are going to win our freedom there eventually.

To defeat the Right politically, my friends, is our challenge when we leave this March. How can we do it? We've got to march from Washington into action at home. I challenge every one of you, straight or gay, who can hear my voice, to join the national gay and lesbian movement. I challenge you to join NGLTF to fight the Right. We have got to match the power of the Christian supremacists, member for member, vote for vote, dollar for dollar. I challenge each of you, not just to buy a T-shirt, but get into your movement. Get involved! Volunteer! Volunteer! Every local organization in this country needs you. Every clinic, every hotline, every youth program needs you, needs your time and your love.

And I also challenge our straight liberal allies, liberals and libertarians, independent and conservative, republican or radical. I challenge and invite you to open your eyes and embrace us without fear. The gay rights movement is not a party. It is not a lifestyle. It is not a hair style. It is not a fad or a fringe or a sickness. It is not about sin or salvation. The gay rights movement is an integral part of the American promise of freedom.

We, you and I, each of us, are the descendants of a proud tradition of people asserting our dignity. It is fitting that the Holocaust Museum was dedicated the same weekend as this march, for not only were gay people persecuted by the Nazi state, but gay people are indebted to the struggle of the Jewish people against bigotry and intolerance. It is fitting that the NAACP marches with us, that feminist leaders march with us, because we are indebted to those movements.

When all of us who believe in freedom and diversity see this gathering, we see beauty and power. When our enemies see this gathering, they see the millennium. Perhaps the Right is right about something. We call for the end of the world as we know it. We call for the end of racism and sexism and bigotry as we know it. For the end of violence and discrimination and homophobia as we know it. For the end of sexism as we know it. We stand for freedom as we have yet to know it, and we will not be denied.

September 18, 1993

Dallas/Fort Worth Speech

Tim McFeeley

This address was given at a fund-raising dinner for the Human Rights Campaign Fund in the Dallas/Fort Worth area by McFeeley, at that time the executive director of the fund. Sharon Bottoms was a Virginia lesbian who lost custody of her biological son to her mother under the state's "crimes against nature" law. Joseph Steffan was a midshipman discharged in 1987 from the Naval Academy. Cheryl Summerville was fired by an Atlanta Cracker Barrel store in 1991 due to the chain's new policy of refusing to employ gay or lesbian people.

I want to thank Cheryl Berman and Jack Pettit and our great black tie dinner committee for all their hard work in planning tonight's dinner, and all 2400 of you for attending this evening. This is the largest Human Rights Campaign Fund dinner ever held in the civilized world and once again Dallas/Fort Worth has led the way!

Dallas/Fort Worth not only has the largest dinner in the country, but it also has our largest and most active Federal Club with over 200 members who each donate $1200 or more every year to sustain the ongoing work of the Campaign Fund in lobbying Congress, mobilizing the grassroots and making us one of the largest federal PACs—in the top 1%, with $750,000 contributed in the last election cycle to over 150 federal campaigns.

I am accompanied by several members of our staff and the entire Board of Directors and Governors of the Campaign Fund who are having their semi-annual meeting at the Anatole this weekend, in order to witness and participate in tonight's festivities. Please join me in thanking these wonderful Board members from all over the United States, especially those members who represent Dallas/Fort Worth on our Boards: Mike Grossman, Lory Masters, Don McCleary, Candy Marcum and Worth Ross.

All of our directors, governors, volunteers, generous federal club members and each and every one of you are part of a small, but growing, army of people who will no longer be content with living in the shadows, on the fringes, or in the closet. Lying and hiding is not the way God intends for any of us to live, and we respect ourselves enough to finally fight for the civil rights, respect, and recognition we deserve.

As parents, like Sharon Bottoms, we will defeat Judge Parson of Virginia, so that we can love and nurture our children without hiding.

As patriots, like Joe Steffan, we will fight Sam Nunn, so that we can serve our country without lying.

As workers, like Cheryl Summerville, we will challenge the bigots until we have passed a national civil rights bill that insures we will not lose our jobs because of who we love.

As taxpayers, we refuse to accept the inadequate resources that the government provides to fight HIV and to get serious about ending the tragic loss of young lives from AIDS and breast cancer.

And as gentle loving and spiritual people, we resist the government's intrusive efforts to criminalize our love, to control our reproductive freedom, and to deny us the right to marry.

There is no one here asking for anything special from our government. In the words of Langston Hughes, we want "America to be America" for us. We want to raise our children, keep our jobs, love our partners, serve our country and stop the hate crimes, suicide and death from AIDS, and we will not pay the unhealthy and immoral price of hiding and lying in order to live and love in this country.

We learned a lot in the past 8 months in the struggle to be allowed to serve openly in the Armed Services.

We learned that being right—and we *won* the substantive debate on this issue hands down—but we learned that being right and winning the support of editorial boards was not enough.

We learned that most Americans don't know us—they only know the stereotypes proclaimed by our radical right-wing opponents—and that when Americans do know lesbians and gay men, they respect us and support our civil rights.

We also learned how incredibly powerful one honest person can be. Who can deny the power of Greta Cammermeyer over Strom Thurmond or the power of Tracy Thorne over Bob Dornan?

We learned that we have allies everywhere—from our civil rights allies like Coretta Scott King to conservative columnist Ken Adelman. Just two months ago, I attended a lesbian and gay dinner in Phoenix and sat at the same table with Senator Barry Goldwater. We are *not* alone!

We also learned that we do not have what our opponents do have, and used against us—an army of grassroots supporters, disciplined, dedicated and driven to act.

Most importantly, I believe we learned that we lost this political battle because President Clinton, just like our parents, friends, political allies, and co-workers, does not understand the closet—and this goes for many gay people as well—they don't understand the difference between the "all-American" belief in choosing privacy, and the devastation of the enforced privacy of the closet. For heterosexuals, being honest about love is so natural, and for us it is so hard. And this is the crux of our problem going forward. We gay and lesbian people need to talk about the closet, about our lives, and mostly, not about sex, but about love.

Think of the men and women who fought in Desert Storm who had to postpone their happy, tearful reunions until they were out of sight of the rest of their colleagues. We need to talk about these human, real needs and feelings.

Another aspect of our failure to overcome the closet came home to me at a Democratic National Committee Dinner which was attended by the President, the Vice president, and about 4000 of their "best friends." We saw an opportunity and had some of our staff and our gay and lesbian veterans outside handing out "Stop The Ban" buttons, while several of us inside were doing the same. I approached several attendees whom I knew to be gay and offered them a button. They'd take it, but not put it on. As we continued to talk, they would try to slip it, unnoticed, into their pocket. But I was watching and waiting and asked them to give it back! While lesbian and gay service members were sacrificing their careers, these politically connected, closeted gay people would not even wear a button to help them. **AND THAT'S WHY WE LOST!**

How can we expect Bill Clinton to understand or to convince Colin Powell that the closet is bad, when most of us stay in it? It's been accurately stated that the Clinton Closet policy reflects how most gay and lesbian Americans live their lives. How do we continue to live closeted lives and get the military to move beyond the closet?

To move forward, to meet the challenge of change, we need to change ourselves. We can change our circumstances by changing our attitudes. It is first and foremost our responsibility to change the political realities. It would have been nice to have had some leadership from the President—and let's not forget that Clinton is the first President in American history to even contemplate equality for gay and lesbian people—but even his leadership, without our will to win and commitment to change, would not have been sufficient. In my view, we will meet this challenge if, and only if and only to the extent that, we *all* do three things:

First, *come out.* The most important political act any of us can take is to come out, taking the next step every day. It's more important than street demonstrations, or lobbying, or increasing our PAC one hundred fold. Come Out! In the words of Audre Lorde, "Your silence will not protect you!" We must stop feeling shame and casting blame, and take responsibility for the fact that the rest of America does not know us.

Second, we must all *connect*—connect with other gay and lesbian people in our communities, in our workplaces, in our churches and nationwide. And just as important, we gay and lesbian people must connect with others who face discrimination in America—women, African-Americans, people with disabilities, and all other oppressed groups. We must connect and forge those alliances that will empower us all.

Third, and to me most importantly, we must all *believe in change.* Too often we choose not to come out and not to connect with each other because fundamentally we do not believe people can change. But they can and they do. Who here has not changed in her or his own attitudes about gay equality and gay marriage in the past five years? We all know the story of people who come out to their brothers and sisters and cousins, and find universal acceptance, love and support. And when our siblings and friends tell us that our being gay or lesbian will not affect their affection for us, they admonish: "But Don't Tell Mother!" What's wrong with mother? Why do we all believe we can change, but our mothers cannot—especially because in most cases our mothers knew about us long before anyone else? We must believe in change.

And if we do these three things: come out, connect with each other and others facing discrimination, and believe in change, we will change the world. The power of change lies within each of us.

Thank you all very much.

November 16, 1993

Lesbian, Gay, and Bisexual Rights in the Universal Declaration of Human Rights

Jerrold Nadler

These remarks were made before of the House of Representatives by Represesentative Nadler of New York and entered in the *Congressional Record* for November 16, 1992.

Mr. Speaker, I rise today to express my support for the inclusion of protections for the human rights of lesbians, gay men, and bisexuals in the United Nations Declaration of Human Rights. I would also like to recognize the work of Stonewall 25, a group that has formed to organize a march and rally at the United Nations to commemorate the 25th anniversary of the Stonewall Rebellion, and to call for recognition of lesbians, gay men and bisexuals in the Universal Declaration of Human Rights.

While we have certainly begun to make strides toward the recognition of the rights of lesbians and gay men in this country, we still have a long way to go. Although it has been 25 years since the Stonewall Rebellion in Greenwich Village, in which lesbians and gay men asserted their right publicly at a time when such assertions were rare, we still have not established in law the rights of lesbians and gay men.

The Civil Rights Act of 1993, of which I am an original cosponsor, still languishes in committee, and there is little chance that it will be brought to a vote this year. Lesbians and gay men cannot divulge their sexual orientation openly if they want to serve in the armed services. And lesbians and gay men still must live in fear that they may be assaulted, hurt, or killed at any time simply because of who they are.

While we, as a nation, have made progress, we have a long way to go. We have always been proud of our tradition of tolerance. Yet, if we do not act soon to codify the rights of lesbians, gay men and bisexuals, our faithfulness to our tradition of tolerance will be put to a test. The international community is being asked to add lesbians, gay men, and bisexuals to the list of those protected by the Universal Declaration of Human Rights. Let us not be left behind as a nation while the rest of the world makes progress in the fight for equal rights for all people.

February 11, 1994

Abraham Lincoln Award Acceptance Speech

Barbara Gittings

This address was given to the Log Cabin Club of Philadelphia at the Union League in Philadelphia on February 11, 1994. Gittings was awarded that organization's Abraham Lincoln Award.

Thank you for your recognition of my work. And thank you for your contributions of money and dedication and effort for our cause. I'm delighted that gay Republicans are shining out from the rich tapestry that is the gay and lesbian rights movement.

I'd like to pay tribute to a particular Republican gay activist who would thoroughly enjoy being here tonight if he could.

Before there was a Stonewall uprising, there were more orderly protests in Washington, New York, San Francisco, and Philadelphia. These were our early picket lines. As you may have heard, we had a dress code—women wore skirts, men wore suits and ties—according to the business dress standards of that time. And no matter how casually or unconventionally some of us dressed otherwise, when we got on the gay picket lines we put our egos in our hip pockets and put on our picketing drag.

But there was one picketer in the mid-1960s for whom the prescribed attire was natural and usual: Foster Gunnison, Jr. Foster regularly wore Brooks Brothers suits—*rumpled* Brooks Brothers suits—and bow ties. He had a nondescript crew cut. He smoked good cigars. He had a master's degree in philosophy. He loved trains and especially loved riding in an elegant parlor car. He read *The Wall Street Journal.* And he lived, with exquisite symbolism, at #1 Gold Street in Hartford, CT.

Foster was a bit of a puzzle even to those of us who liked him and worked well with him. At first some people even thought he was an FBI plant inside our movement. But after watching him, the suspicious eventually decided that Foster was just another eccentric in our movement—a different sort of eccentric.

From the time he joined the cause thirty years ago, Foster did a lot of good work. He walked in our picket lines. He helped Craig Rodwell plan the first gay pride march in New York in 1970 on the first anniversary of Stonewall. He loved trying to bring order and discipline to our chaotic groups and he was active in our regional and national alliances that had begun in the early 1960s. He set up his own organization with a cryptic name, The Institute of Social Ethics, and under its cover did such things as sending me to spy on the psychiatrists' convention in 1968.

Eventually Foster threw up his hands over the unruly and chaotic nature of our movement. He spent more time on his other interests, including the national association of barbershop quartets. He remained a registered Republican but he hedged his bets and also supported the Conservative Party and the Libertarian Party.

Foster Gunnison died suddenly last month. I wanted to remember him in this setting especially. He would relish being in this gathering, at this unique establishment. Thanks, Foster, for being a pioneer.

And again my thanks to you who are here and to your friends for your support for gay and lesbian rights. We gay people need our rights because that is fair play, in the best American tradition. Heterosexuals also need gay rights, because every non-gay person knows at least one gay man or lesbian. That may be someone at the next desk or the next counter at work, or the next pew in church or temple, or the next chair at the family dinner table. When a gay person suffers discrimination for being gay, the non-gays who are close to him or her are bound to be hurt too.

With so many bigotries and barriers still to erase, we need all hands and all hearts to help. Keep up the good work!

April 11, 1994

A Moment of Great Crisis, Great Potential, and Great Danger

Margaret Cerullo

This address was given by Margaret Cerullo, a member of the Department of Sociology at Hampshire College, to the Gay, Lesbian, and Straight Teachers Network of Massachusetts. The reference to "Walta" in the opening line is to poet Walta Borawski, whose poem "Cheers, Cheers for Old Cha Cha Ass" recounts the pain of school homophobia.

What has shifted since Walta was at Patchogue High living out his pre-Stonewall queer childhood? A few of the following stories (email missives) capture the confusing and contradictory moment we find ourselves in. In November in a small town in Virginia, outside DC two teenage women held hands and danced together during the slow dance at an ice-skating rink, and the owners promptly asked them to leave. Instead of a swift and jeering ejection, 60 other teenagers spontaneously intervened to try to prevent their departure; and a week later local Lesbian Avengers held (same sex) dance-ins at the rink. A second story: a young man was recently arrested in his school for wearing a dress. Again, instead of meeting broad approval, the board has split on the decision and students, parents and teachers alike are avidly debating whether he has a right to wear a dress to school. And the examples proliferate.

I don't have to emphasize to any of you that homophobia is alive and well, that it is being rekindled and continually reinvents itself—but it is contested. It does not have the same free reign that Walta's tormentors had at Patchogue High School. Yet, lest we get too optimistic, I was recently reading the "Queer Supplement" to the school newspaper at my alma mater, the University of Pennsylvania, and I was actually surprised by it. It was full of stories from students 19 and 20 years old, saying things like I grew up thinking I was the only queer on Long Island; or I grew up convinced there was no such thing as a Black lesbian; or in a high school of 500 people I sat for days in the library at lunch time, trying to find out something about myself, convinced there had to be another *one* in a school of 500.

I suspect that great numbers of us are still engaged in keeping faith with the promises we made to ourselves as children—promises that no other kid would have to suffer the terrors of isolation, invisibility, and erasure that we did. A promise that with the relative freedom of adults, we would confront directly those forces that constricted our space to breathe, that terrorized us into numbness, that shamed us into self-loathing, that sought to eradicate anything queer from our worlds in pursuit of the desperate project of right living.

I want to keep jumping back and forth between our personal pasts and our present, and also our historical pasts and our present, because it is in this way that we begin to assemble the materials from which we can imagine and project the kind of future we want to live in. I want to survey the ground from which we do create our visions.

Remembering Stonewall

Historically I want to go back to the moment of Stonewall as we approach its 25th anniversary, that moment that promised us gay and lesbian liberation, and to remind you that Stonewall was part of a youth movement. Now it wasn't about youth, but remember that Stonewall took place a month before *Woodstock,* to create a memory or an image of its time and its counter-cultural context. If Stonewall wasn't directly about youth, it did project a youthful future—unencumbered by rigid notions of gender, of sexuality, of normality, of right living. A future that we would invent rather than one that had already invented us, pre-assigned us to ready made social categories, job categories, gender categories and sexual categories. A future in which the marketplace would not determine our value or our values. A future in which we could live in more open and less segregated communities than many of us had grown up in. A time whose slogan was "All Power to the Imagination." A time when we dreamed about what we wanted, not what we thought we could get. If all we are allowed to think about is what we can get, we are first afraid and then no longer able to imagine what we want.

The Weakened Status of Civil Rights

I have been arguing for a long time that our movement is in danger of making a terrible mistake, and here I am borrowing from Norman Birnbaum who has critiqued the Jewish leadership in this country for what I think also applies to our movement—and that mistake is to confuse the prosperity, influence and access of some of us with the security and safety of all of us. The latter, he underlined, can only be bought by dissipating hatred in society. And that, of course, is our task. What kinds of challenges does it entail?

Last week after Joe Kennedy (D-MA) voted for the Hancock Amendment which would have banned federal funds to schools that "encourage or support homosexuality as a positive alternative life style," he said in defense of his vote, "I don't think they should be encouraging homosexuality in the schools" and then issued a press release affirming his support for a federal gay civil rights bill—as if the one cancelled the other. I think it is about time that we raise the stakes, raise the ante on what we expect from liberal politicians like Joe Kennedy who always begins by saying, "I do not condone or promote or believe the schools should encourage their 'lifestyle,' but I do support their right to breathe the same air as we normal people do and to hold a job without reprisals." Perhaps it is time for us to ask, for how long will they continue to condone and promote and fund the schools to encourage a lifestyle that has done so much damage and violence to the lesbian and gay youth in its families, to the lesbian and gay parents and children in its neighborhoods and schools, to the gay men and lesbians on the streets of our cities and towns, in the corridors of our schools. How long will they condone a way of life that remains content to see gay men die because AIDS didn't affect the general population, will they continue to promote a way of life—heterosexuality—that cannot seem to exist as one among many but can only exist as the one with all the power, which won't allow itself to be seen as *a* truth, but must parade as *the* truth under its various pseudonyms and impersonations: family, romance, commitment and love. How long?

I raise all of this because I think it would be a terrible mistake to see federal civil rights legislation as the ultimate goal of our movement. To do so would fail to understand the significant weakening of the meaning of civil rights after 12 years of Reagan/Bush assaults. The stripping of civil rights protection from the goal that underwrote it, the goal of empowerment—the deliberately and necessarily *open* goal of cultural, political, social and economic empowerment. That is the split we have to confront: achieving the goal of civil rights protection is not the same as empowerment. That is the message we should have learned from the gays in the military debacle. Those of us who have come to claim our place at the table, to claim our full cultural, intellectual, social citizenship are told that we are welcome on these terms—they won't ask as long as we agree not to tell who we are and how we live and love. Or as Lani Guinier found out, we're welcome as long as we agree not to tell what we understand about how exclusionary power continues to operate even after civil rights legislation has been passed. We must not accept the terms of that bargain. To equate our security and safety again with the passage of civil rights legislation—the answer to that I think can be given by any gay or lesbian teacher in Massachusetts who, despite the passage of the State Gay and Lesbian Civil Rights Bill is still unable or afraid to come out in their schools because of the fear of reprisals and discrimination that they face. So we have to begin to address what stands in that gap between the passage of formal legislation that recognizes our equality, and the full recognition of our humanity and dignity.

The Urban Crisis

To address that gap I would like to start by asking, *What is Clintonism?*—that much hoped for and promised sea change. What does it promise us? We are one and a half years into the new administration and as far as I can tell the central issue for our community remains fighting the Right. Even though the Rightwing is out of power, it has been dislodged from the presidency, it is still setting the terms of political debate on most of the issues that are being debated in this country—on race, on crime, on welfare, on foreign policy, on urban policy and on sexuality. Clinton recently underlined his commitment to "family values," agreeing that after all, Dan Quayle had a point in his condemnation of Murphy Brown. It is hard to see what's left that Clinton hasn't conceded on.

I want to spend a moment on an issue that is perhaps not the most obvious, but I do believe it is one of the most critical for our communities. That is the issue of urban policy where Clintonism has been continuous with the 12 years of Reagan/Bush assaults on the cities. Years that saw the intensifying segregation of our society, its resegregation, the wholesale disinvestment in our cities, the withdrawal of federal funds, white straight suburban flight, the immense suburbanization of resources, of jobs, of economic growth. This resulted in a significant reduction of entitlements to health, to education and to welfare; and in the process of that reduction, a devaluation of citizenship, of the citizenship of those who live in the "inner city," itself a code for race, for people of color. That is, the meaning of our formal equality and our formal citizenship depends upon what is going on in civil society, in social life and on whether our fellow citizens can recognize and respond to our need.

Now it is my argument that we can understand how that withdrawal of resources has been possible only if we look at how the cities are figured, symbolically, in our political discourse. The cities are seen as places of immorality, decadence, and vice—as the home of the expendables. I'm thinking here of Pete Wilson, Governor of California, "Welfare mothers and new immigrants are multiplying faster than taxpayers." Goaded on by Rush Limbaugh and Howard Stern, white middle class suburban "breadwinners" see themselves as under siege. The deeper they withdraw into the self-enclosed world of suburban housing tract isolation, the more they fear the outside world. I believe that that's the ground on which Ross Perot was able to be so successful in getting masses of Americans waking up every day thinking about the deficit rather than the plight of the inner cities and the abandonment of the poor. And in furthering a rhetoric about the cities, such that spending on the cities becomes "pandering to special interests" and "tough choices" means more austerity for those who live there.

So far, what I've been offering is a pretty straightforward familiar progressive critique of the failure of urban policy. But what is too often missing from these analyses, from urban sociology, urban cultural studies, is the recognition that the city is also where gay people live and where we are known to live. Part of the symbolic representation of the city as the home of the expendables is connected to that recognition. The failure of an urban policy to develop combined with the rhetoric of hard choices and austerity—that means the abandonment of AIDS funding which we are seeing being played out in New York City right now with the Giuliani cutbacks. I believe it is in the interest of community, it should be a central priority of our movement to demand an urban policy; that is, a commitment of our national resources to ensuring the health, the education, and the welfare of those who live in our cities. As far as I can tell, the only person out there demanding that is Jesse Jackson and this is a time when we ought to be seeking links with him. Also I would argue that the future of schooling, of public education, the future of our children also rests with the development of urban policy. What we are seeing is the complete abandonment of the future generations of children who live in the cities. Their citizenship, their entitlement to education is significantly less than their parents'. New immigrants have significantly less entitlements than earlier generations of immigrants. This is a very serious issue and place where our movement needs to mobilize, if it is going to think about and advocate around education, AIDS and families.

The Relentless Rightwing

The Right is mobilizing in this context of austerity-talk, deficit cutting, and the symbolic discourse of urban decadence. They are relentless, depleting and exhausting; full of resources, of motivation and energy. They are currently fighting seven statewide anti-gay initiatives with seven more up and coming.

They are not only active on the state level, but one of their major arenas has been library censorship, so that the most censored book last year was *Daddy's Roommate* beating out Madonna's *Sex*. Homosexuality was the major reason for library censorship according to the American Library Association. As Ralph Reed, head of the Christian Coalition—Pat Robertson's political arm—has announced, "the real battles of concern to Christians are in neighborhoods, school boards, city councils and state legislatures." What are these issues "of concern to Christians" at the local, city and state levels? I think their agenda can be summarized: to forbid school districts from teaching tolerance or acceptance of lesbian and gay people; to make it illegal for cities and states to adopt and enforce civil rights protections; force AIDS educators and AIDS educational materials to make moral judgments about homosexuality; and—to summarize it all—to permanently institutionalize homophobia at the grassroots level (again thanks to the Internet for this helpful summary). It is that momentum we have to counter, at the grassroots level, if we are going to ensure the safety and security of all of us.

The interesting thing is that the Right does not seem to care if it loses these statewide initiatives in the courts. If they lose one in the courts, as they did in Colorado, they see that as an occasion to devise the next initiative in a way that can withstand legal scrutiny. But more important, in fighting these state by state initiatives, they get a platform to go house to house, church to church, school to school to talk about homosexuality. We on the other hand have been relying on the courts and too often do not put our resources into going house to house, school to school, and church to church to enter the conversation. We rely instead on distant, slick (and expensive) media strategies. And despite what all the highly paid consultants will tell you, I think this is a losing strategy.

I do believe we are in a moment of great crisis, great potential and great danger, and must ask what is in place in our movement, and in the kinds of alliances that we are trying to build, to confront the challenge from the Right? If we ask that question we have to address several crucial questions, of which I will name three. The first is the polarization between race and sexuality. The second is the need to disentangle the many strands of what we too often view as a homophobic monolith, and characterize as "Rightwing," and the third is the inability of our movement to take up the issue of youth as its central and leading priority.

Polarization Between Race and Sexuality

The struggle over the Rainbow Curriculum in NYC points to the success of the Right in activating and mobilizing a polarization between "parents of color" (assumed to be straight) on the one hand; and "rich, white gay men" on the other hand.

I would argue to you that that polarization between "rich, white gay men" and "people of color" has been aided and abetted by our movement—in its representation of our movement as rich, white and male. How have we come to represent ourselves as rich, white and male? I think two things have fuelled that representation—the one I call the politics of respectability and the other the politics of mimicry. When we feel endangered we think our safety lies in putting our most respectable, that is, least threatening face forward. We think we can appeal to the powerful, calm their fears and keep our own painful histories at bay, by representing ourselves as really not so different from them. That is part of what fuels the strategy that confuses our safety with access to power; a strategy that I would argue is one of the sites that perpetuates racism in our movement. That strategy forgets that we are not just speaking to the powerful, we're speaking to ourselves and everyone else in this society about who we are.

The other thing that fuels this strategy is what I call the gay consumer movement, the politics of mimicry. We are *almost* the same as you, but not quite. The difference is that we have higher disposable income—we're 13.7 times more likely to be frequent flyers, 4.7 times more likely to take overseas vacations—we consume more. Or as Queer Nation puts it, we're the profit margins.

I think the way we fought the gays in the military campaign fuelled the polarization between race and sexuality. We said over and over again—we represent the *last chapter* in the civil rights struggle, the last governmentally sanctioned discrimination. We represent *the* civil rights movement of the 90s, implying that the issues of racial injustice have been (re) solved and we were ready to move on. It is that kind of assumption that was operating in New York City around issues of curricula, and one that we must challenge. Many gay people, and I include myself from afar, thought that multicultural curricula had been achieved in New York. I had followed the debates in *The New York Times,* I thought that Black and Latin parents had succeeded in gaining curricula in which their histories were represented, in which their children could find themselves recognized. Indeed, the only thing that had to happen was for queers to be added on. Now that was nowhere near true, in fact the struggle for multicultural curricula has met resistance and roadblocks all along the way. White queers moved in there with a kind of arrogance and ignorance, a privilege, assuming that we could lead the struggle for all of us without spending any time trying to learn what others had experienced, what they had encountered, without seeing others as resources from whom we could learn something. We cannot continue to move as a white movement.

Disentangling Homophobia

As we work to understand what fosters homophobia, I think there is a serious danger in overemphasizing the role of the Right. That is in representing homophobia as "rightwing" and representing our movement as crucially about "fighting the Right." Homophobia isn't a thing, it's not an essence, that exists for all time. It is a production, a constantly shifting and renewed production, Usually, it mobilizes the fear of sex, the violent disavowal of terrifying desire; sometimes, in some communities, the fear of racist associations of Blackness, immorality and disease; often, the fear of children and sex, most crucially the fear that my kid might think it is OK to be gay. That is the one that we have yet to put on the table, address, and not let slide under. That is the unspoken fear that galvanizes so many liberals behind a homophobic agenda. We have to disentangle these strands, decode these appeals. But unfortunately that has not been the strategy of our movement as we have fought rightwing initiatives. Just look at the commercials used in Cincinnati to fight the anti-gay momentum. What we tried to do was appeal to people to understand that the Rightwing was a dangerous movement. The commercials had images of Nazi book-burnings, hooded Ku Klux Klan members—saying that if you support this initiative, this is what will happen in Cincinnati. People didn't buy it. And, all we were asking people to do was to disidentify from the Right, not that they should understand anything about us. That is the danger in seeing homophobia as this monolithic rightwing production.

Making Youth a Priority

Lastly, is our failure to move youth to the center of our agenda. I have a utopian vision that the gay and lesbian movements come to lead a movement to save our children. That we should put that issue right in the center; not sideline it, not push it under the table, not rush to say that we don't have anything to do with NAMBLA. It is there. It is there in all that subtle language. They used to say I don't want anyone to condone homosexuality, now they say I don't want anyone to promote or encourage it. Now you know what that language is coding. It's coding that what gay people do is—promote, encourage, recruit—it is seldom absent, subtly coded into all the political language and we're not going to get rid of it by running away from it. We need to lead a movement that is about saving all our children. "Whose Kids? Our Kids!" was the slogan in NYC. I understand that confronts a lot in us as once queer children, our own painful memories of our childhood which can block us. One of the most radical things we could do in this country is try to articulate a vision in which we see all our children as all our national resources. Try to break through this horrible individual solutions response. One image someone suggested was to see our schools as a reservoir, you can't pollute one part of it without affecting all of it. We have to begin to figure out ways for people to see what happens to our children and in our schools as something of concern to all of us, not just to individual parents.

Many people have called for the abandonment of identity politics. I think that's a terrible mistake. I don't believe it's desirable in this moment to surrender the definition of our identity to the homophobes in the Congress and the courts, to allow their ignorant ravings and rantings about not encouraging "the homosexual lifestyle" to go uncontested. We inherit identity politics, identity politics inherits us, it's the politics that we have to take up. But, that does not mean that we have to project a unified gay identity. Rather, it seems to me, that the politics of our community right now must be a contest over the meaning of that identity, a multiplying of the possible meanings of that identity; and that has got to be seen as a strength of our movement, not as a weakness. That great contest, *who am I and who are we?* is the one that propels our movement, and when the argument stops so does our history and so does our movement.

June 30, 1994

Gay Rights

Major R. Owens

This is the text of the remarks made by Representative Owens on the floor of the House of Representatives and entered in the *Congressional Record* on June 30, 1994.

Mr. Speaker, 25 years ago this week, police in New York raided a gay establishment, The Stonewall Inn. This was not an uncommon occurrence, as police frequently moved to close down places where gay people congregated. But what made the Stonewall experience unique, was that for the first time the patrons fought back. For 3 days thousands of gay men, lesbians, and their supporters took to the streets of Greenwich Village and gave birth to the present-day gay rights movement. This weekend over a hundred thousand people, joined in spirit by millions more who will not be able to attend, will gather to commemorate this important event in gay history.

We should use this time to appreciate the quest of gay people for equal, not special, protection under the law. Who would have imagined 25 years ago that openly gay men and women could work as doctors, lawyers, college professors, professional athletes, and performers, as well as serve on corporate boards, at the White House, and even as Members of Congress. The importance of this new visibility can not be underestimated.

We must never forget though, how much farther there is still to go. Two recent major victories for gay people only emphasize this distance. A lesbian mother was recently re-awarded custody of her young son, after he had been removed from her home simply because she was carrying on a committed relationship with a woman. There were no other reasons—no parental neglect, no abuse of any kind.

A higher court overturned the previous court's ruling, and gave her back her child. Another court recently ruled that Margarethe Cammermeyer had been unjustly kicked out of the U.S. Armed Forces. Cammermeyer, an Army nurse, was awarded the Bronze Star for her service in Vietnam and was voted Army Nurse of the Year in 1985. During an interview she did not deny being a lesbian, and her exemplary career abruptly came to an end. I laud the court's opinion and the country should be grateful to have back the service of Colonel Cammermeyer. While I stress these are victories, it is a shame they are matters the high courts must decide. Isn't it a basic right for a loving mother to have possession of her son or for a patriotic American to serve his or her country? We still have a long way to go.

As chairman of the House Subcommittee on Select Education and Civil Rights which oversees the Equal Employment Opportunity Commission, I am all too aware of the rampant discrimination gay men and lesbians face in the work place. Last week I presided over hearings on gay discrimination and heard firsthand testimony from those suffering its effects. These men and women lost employment not because of job performance or company cutbacks, but simply because of their sexual orientation. We cannot tolerate discrimination of anyone be they women, black, Christian, Moslem, disabled, or gay. I also must commend such New York City companies as Montefiore Hospital, Showtime, Time-Warner, Planned Parenthood, and others, who have undertaken strong antidiscrimination policies and extended the same benefits to all of their employees.

We should all applaud and respect the gay and lesbian activists for many reasons. They have sowed political acumen, extreme creativity, and racial inclusiveness in their fight. On the anniversary of Stonewall, I especially commend them on their spirit. Like Rosa Parks, they have refused to sit in the back of America's bus anymore, and have stood up for what is right. It is also important that we not underestimate the extreme courage it takes to come out of the closet in a hostile world. Even though the gay community has suffered tremendous losses, especially in this time of plague, they have never given up the fight. Their unfailing commitment to fight for what is just is exactly what this country was founded on, and I extend my best wishes to these very patriotic Americans.

August 19, 1994

Asian-American and Lesbian/Gay Communities

Nancy Pelosi

These remarks were given on the floor of the House of Representatives by Representative Pelosi of New York and entered into the *Congressional Record* for August 19, 1994.

Mr. Speaker, the Japanese American Citizens league met last week in Salt Lake City and voted to uphold a resolution supporting lesbian and gay rights. This historic meeting marks a milestone in coalition building between the Asian-American community and the lesbian and gay community. The success of the effort is largely due to the work of two of our most esteemed colleagues—Congressman Norman Mineta and Congressman Barney Frank.

At the Salt Lake City convention, Congressman Mineta gave a compelling speech in support of the resolution. In that speech he recounted the leadership role played by Congressman Frank in passing the Civil Liberties Act of 1988, the decade-long struggle for redress by Japanese Americans interned during the Second World War. Mineta recalled that when Frank became the chair of the Subcommittee on Administrative Law, after years of futility with trying to move this legislation, he sought out Mineta—Mineta did not seek him out—to tell him that he would make redress his top priority.

By the end of that Congress, the Civil Liberties Act was written into the laws of the country. A gay Member of Congress, with very few Asian-American constituents, made redress his top priority. Now, a few years later, an Asian-American Member of Congress traveled to Salt Lake City to deliver a stirring speech in support of lesbian and gay rights. There should be nothing unusual about this when two champions of civil rights—Norman Mineta and Barney Frank—are involved. Both understand that human rights are an indivisible liberty, not subject to race, color, creed or sexual orientation. And both understand that unity and coalition building amplifies the strength and power of each community's struggle for freedom and justice in America. As a Representative of a city with substantial gay and lesbian and Asian-American populations, I commend their work, their courage and their commitment to the cause of civil rights for all Americans.

December 28, 1994

Welcoming Speech at the ILGA Opening Plenary

Hannele Lehtikuusi

This address was given by the chairperson of SETA, the national human rights organization of Finland concerned with the legal rights and equality of gays, lesbians, bisexuals, and transgendered people, at the opening plenary session of the ILGA meeting in Helsinki, Finland, in December 1994. ILGA is the International Lesbian and Gay Association.

It is a historical moment for SETA to have the ILGA conference held here: it is 10 years since the last conference of ILGA took place in Helsinki—that time ILGA only was called IGA. We are also very pleased to have you here since this year—1994—is an anniversary year for us. SETA was founded twenty years ago.

This is also a historical moment since Finland is joining the European Union in January. And as Lesbian and Gay rights activists, we are—here in Helsinki—strengthening old and creating new forms of co-operation in Europe.

Finland is a strange country: during this past year the discussion of lesbian and gay marriages and on lesbian and gay parenthood has been very much alive. Still it seems that even catholic [*sic*] Spain will have a law on lesbian and gay partnership before Finland. We are also here on the verge to have anti-discrimination law. Finland has also granted refugee status on the basis of homosexuality. The State of Finland granted money to SETA to produce information on the situation of lesbians and gays in the European Community.

On the other hand the Mayor of Helsinki has not seen [it as] important to honor ILGA's work on human rights, but has refused the traditional city reception from ILGA conference. Dismissal in this country is very subtle. We are often facing the problems of how to combat and point this out.

This is also a historical conference since so many friends and fellow gay and lesbian activists from the former Soviet Union and Eastern European area are here with us. Things are changing on the map—during this conference we will hear how the reality in these countries is changing. ILGA's conferences have always been vital forums for information exchange. Cooperation and lobbying, actions and projects. So be it also this time!

March 1, 1995

Prix EGALITÉ 1995 Speech

Claudia Roth

Claudia Roth was a member of the German Green Party and a member of the European Parliament at the time this speech was delivered. EGALITÉ (Equality for Gays and Lesbians in the European Institutions) was a group of European Union staff working to promote gay and lesbian equality in European institutions. Roth's name was associated with the "Equal Rights for Homosexuals and Lesbians in the EU" report, popularly known as the "Roth Report."

Dear Friends,

It is hard to know quite what to say. I am very moved and it is an incredible honour. At the same time, I feel rather guilty about being given an award for doing my job as a Member of the European Parliament. I want you to know that I am very grateful and that I see the award as both a challenge and a call to keep on fighting for respect, for fundamental human rights, for civil rights and freedom.

Politicians and governments love talking about human rights—when it is politically expedient—and yet they are violated every day in every part of the globe—East and West, North and South and here in the European Union.

I find it particularly regrettable, not to say shameful, that the human rights report was postponed yet again at yesterday's plenary. Human rights are inalienable: this basic principle is fundamental to the political and moral credibility of any democratic system. Human rights are not optional and no state can claim that human rights violations are an internal affair. The way a society treats its minorities is a good indication of just how humane, liberal and democratic it really is. In a society which does more than just talk about tolerance and is genuinely and actively accepting, there is no room for discrimination on grounds of colour, religion, nationality, ethnic origin or sexual identity. That is why I am fighting for equal rights for gay men and lesbians.

I would like to share this award—with everyone who has helped me prepare the "resolution rose" and get it adopted, with everyone who put in so much work, like Hein Verkerk and our friends from ILGA, with people from EGALITÉ, like Sussie Jolly, who lobbied so hard for the decision, and with all my colleagues who supported it, even if it meant swimming against the mainstream of their group or party—the ones who showed they had the courage of their convictions, especially in the run-up to the elections.

I also want to share it with my parents down in true blue, Catholic Bavaria. Despite having been ostracized on account of their Green daughter and inundated with phone calls and bibles when the report was adopted, they are still proud of me for doing what I think is right, as they always taught me.

So, what has happened since the report was passed?

The most important thing from my point of view—and indeed the most remarkable and unusual thing—is that the decision has sparked off an enormous public debate. It is amazing to think that people all over Europe and beyond are arguing thinking about the European Parliament's demand for recognition of the validity of all lifestyles, including gay and lesbian partnerships.

I think it is fantastic that demands for adoption rights for gay men and lesbians are at least being discussed and that we have succeeded in showing how real discrimination on grounds of sexual identity is, in all its different forms. But perhaps the best thing of all is that we have helped to bring the subject into the open, out of the closet where it is often locked away, to free people from the fear of being turned into social outcasts and to give them power to say, "I am proud to be out."

The very many reactions to the decision have convinced me and made me proud that the European Parliament has helped break down taboos and supported the work of gay and lesbian organizations at grassroots level.

The decision caused a sensation, especially in the Catholic Church. In Rome, the Pope himself mentioned in it a speech in Peter's Square, saying that the European Parliament had heralded the collapse of the family and the decline of humanity. The support the decision received from the gay clergy is an indication of what a burning issue this is in the church. And the need to attack hypocrisy, fundamentalism and persecution in whatever form they take is becoming increasingly apparent.

With the current resurgence of racist ideology and right-wing extremism, we must not forget that homosexuals were one of the groups slaughtered in the German concentration camps—as a German living fifty years after the end of the holocaust I have a historic duty not to forget.

At a time when there are calls for people suffering from AIDS, people with HIV and gay men and lesbians to be locked up away from the rest of society, it is clear just how important it is for us to work and fight for equal rights for gay men and lesbians across the board—we cannot settle for anything less.

There have been improvements in some Member States, which are definitely linked to our report. In Germany, the infamous paragraph 175 has been repealed, in the Netherlands an anti-discrimination law has been passed and in Sweden gay marriages are now legally recognized. Here in the EU institutions, now that the elections are over and the new Commission has been appointed, we have to get back down to work and make sure that our demands are met.

Rest assured: we will be demanding human rights for gays and lesbians from Anita Gradin: anti-discrimination measures and a new Commission task force from Padraig Flynn and genuine freedom of movement from Mario Monti.

WE NEED YOUR SUPPORT.

April 3, 1995

A Victory for Common Sense

Gerry Studds

This address was given on the floor of the House of Representatives by Representative Studds, an openly gay member of Congress, and entered into the *Congressional Record* for April 3, 1995.

Mr. Speaker, some 18 months ago this House enacted legislation to codify the so-called "Don't Ask, Don't Tell" policy barring gay and lesbian Americans from serving openly in the Armed Forces. The law thus placed on the statute books was an unprecedented exercise in overt, state-sanctioned discrimination. It was, from first to last, an irrational policy supported by nothing more than naked prejudice.

I stated at the time that I did not believe such a policy could survive constitutional scrutiny, and that the day would come when the courts would say so. On Thursday, March 30, 1995, Federal District Judge Eugene H. Nickerson fulfilled that prediction. In a 39-page opinion that is a triumph of decency and common sense, Judge Nickerson ruled in favor of six service members who challenged this cruel and unjust policy.

In striking down the law, the district court found it demeaning and unworthy of a great nation to base a policy on pretense rather than truth. "It also accurately characterized the scholastic distinctions on which the law relies as 'Byzantine' and 'Orwellian.'"

Since the decision was handed down, the court's conclusions have been echoed on editorial pages across the country. Few could surpass the editorial published on March 31, 1995 in the *Cape Cod Times,* which I am proud to insert in the Record.

It took a federal judge to tell President Clinton what a great many people have known for years to be true—his "Don't ask, don't tell" policy on gays in the military was a compromise full of flaws right from the start. Basically, the policy allows gays and lesbians to serve as long as they don't admit their sexuality to anyone. If they do, they will be handed an honorable discharge and booted through the gate.

Yesterday, U.S. District Court Judge Eugene Nickerson ruled that the policy is discriminatory, a violation of free speech and it forces people to lie. In short, he said, the policy is "inherently deceptive." The ruling involves, and applies to, only the six service personnel who filed the suit. The Defense Department will appeal.

This is the latest twist in a three-year debate that began when then-candidate Clinton made a rock-solid promise that if elected he would lift the ban entirely. That lit the fires, and the waffling started.

His first full year in office, 1993, was not a good one for The Pledge or the president. In January, the Pentagon and its supporters in Congress went on the offensive. The Joint Chiefs of Staff met with the Commander in Chief behind closed doors. When they emerged their only word was that it was a "constructive" meeting.

Two months later, in the semantic equivalent of jogging backwards, Clinton told his first televised press conference that he was now considering segregating homosexuals, which surprised even the military. Clinton fumbled that one, because it soon became clear he hadn't a clue as to how segregation could be done or whether it would even work (it wouldn't have—gays and lesbians aren't lepers).

As was inevitable, the gays struck back in a most telling manner. At the same time in May, 1993, that Sam Nunn, chairman of the Senate Armed Services Committee, was on the road collecting comments from military and naval bases about gays in the military, Sgt. Jose Zuniga, the Sixth Army's 1992 "Soldier of the Year" was packing his bags at the Presidio in San Francisco. The richly honored Sergeant Zuniga had "come out" earlier in the month during a gay rights march in Washington, D.C. He did so to prove to anyone who happened to care that gays and lesbians can be as good servicemen and women as any of their straight peers—and in Zuniga's case, much better than most.

The argument that Senator Nunn and so many others believe—homosexuals are a danger to morale, are incapable of doing battle, are born molesters who can't resist putting the make on their God-fearing mates in uniform and all the other stuff—is dead wrong.

Sergeant Zuniga, who could have stayed in the closet until retirement and remained a role model for his troops, is proof of that. So are two Medal of Honor recipients and an Army nurse with the rank of colonel. She served with distinction in Vietnam and has a medal to prove it, but she was later cashiered by the National Guard stateside because of her sexual orientation.

So are many others, who fought in wars or served in peace, all the while keeping their secret because of the fear of discharge or worse, should the straights find out.

One particularly egregious example of the mindset against gays resulted from the April 1989 explosion inside a gun turret aboard the battleship USS Iowa that killed 47 sailors. Looking for somebody to blame, the Navy settled on a young seaman who was killed, and put forth a story that he had caused the blast because he had been jilted by one of the victims.

Better that, they reasoned, than the truth, which emerged anyway, several months later: One of the propellant bags contained unstable explosive that went off when it was shoved into the breech. The story about the sailor was a crock, pure and simple.

As far back as October 1991, in a speech at Harvard, then-Governor Clinton made his position clear—at least, he thought he did—on permitting homosexuals to serve as equals in the military: It will be done. Thirteen months later came slippage. The then-president-elect said he would form a group to study the problem, "but I am not going to change my mind on it." So much for his pledge.

The frustration among gays and their sense of having been betrayed by the president is understandable. There is so much anger against them from society in general and the military in particular that it's truly a wonder that any of their orientation even dare enter the service.

But the fear of gays is largely based on an ignorance that breeds intolerance and is to be found not only in government institutions but among religious conservatives, who have become a political force now and will certainly have an effect in the 1996 election.

Judge Nickerson's ruling is a victory for gays and common sense, though in context of the war over equality, this—alas—was but a skirmish.

Mr. Chairman, the six plaintiffs and their attorneys have won an important victory, not only for themselves but for all who have served and still serve with honor and distinction. It is a victory shared most of all by those who challenged earlier versions of the ban in years past only to have their pleas fall on deaf ears.

I fully expect that the Government will appeal this decision, and that the constitutionality of the ban will ultimately be revisited by higher courts. But whatever may happen in the months to come, today's ruling is the beginning of the end for a policy that is unworthy of our country and the brave service members who offer their lives in its service.

October 19, 1995

Honoring an American Hero

Gerry Studds

These remarks were made on the floor of the House of Representatives by Representative Studds of Massachusetts, an openly gay member of Congress, and were entered in the *Congressional Record* for October 19, 1995.

Mr. Speaker, I rise to pay tribute to Tom Stoddard, one of our Nation's most eloquent and respected advocates for the civil rights of lesbians and gay men. On Friday, October 27, Mr. Stoddard will be honored by the New York University School of Law, which has established the Tom Stoddard Fellowship under the aegis of the school's Arthur Garfield Hayes civil liberties program.

Each year, one second-year law student will be selected to spend a year as the Stoddard Fellow, working with leading public interest organizations on gay and lesbian rights cases and other civil liberties matters.

I am told that this is the first fellowship at any law school in the world to be dedicated to securing and advancing the cause of lesbian and gay rights. It is hard to imagine a more fitting tribute to one who has done so much to reshape the law in this area from a sword of persecution into a shield of justice. Tom served as counsel and, later, as legislative director, of the New York Civil Liberties Union, where he came into contact with most of the major civil rights causes of our time. He left the ACLU to devote his full attention to the rights of lesbians and gay men and the rights of people with HIV as head of the Lambda Legal Defense and Education Fund. Under his stewardship, the organization grew from a staff of 6 and an annual budget of $300,000 to a staff of 22 and a budget of $2.2 million. Although he retired from that position in 1991, he was lured back into public service 2 years later, when he spent 6 months commuting to Washington as director of the Campaign for Military Service.

Since 1980, Tom has served on the adjunct faculty of NYU, where he has been a mentor to a generation of law students searching for a way to use their skills in the service of humanity. He is a vice president of the American

Civil Liberties Union and vice chairman of the American Foundation of AIDS Research.

Tom has also shown immense courage in his personal struggle with AIDS. He expresses gratitude—not for the disease, but for the way in which it has deepened his sense of connectedness to those he has represented so ably for so long. As he said to *The New York Times,* he has become the client as well as the lawyer: the "they" has become "we." His experience has broadened his perspective into what he has described as "an all-encompassing vista, one that connects the past to the future, one that ties me to all other people who have suffered."

In a similar way, Mr. Chairman, the Stoddard Foundation connects the aspirations of lesbian and gay Americans with the larger struggle for social justice and human dignity. I join with Tom's spouse, Walter Rieman, and their family, friends and colleagues, as they inaugurate this fellowship and celebrate the extraordinary man for whom it is named. May this endowment enable a new generation of leaders to further his vision of a society that is "fairer, more humane and more inclusive" of every human being.

November 16-19, 1995

The City, the Country, the World: Not What They Used to Be

Douglas Sanders

This is the keynote address given by Douglas Sanders of the law faculty of the University of British Columbia to the Eleventh Annual Conference of the International Network of Lesbian and Gay Officials (INLGO) meeting in Toronto, Ontario, in November 1995.

It is wonderful to come to lesbian and gay conferences these days and get official receptions, like the reception at city hall last night with the Mayor. Even if the hall clearly needed redecorating, it was very nice. I recall two years ago attending a reception for ILGA, the International Lesbian and Gay Association, hosted by the city of Barcelona. The reception was held in a small palace that General Franco used as his Barcelona residence during the years of the Franco dictatorship. There we were, drinking Spanish champagne in the garden, while a city councillor passionately declared that lesbian and gay equality was the great moral issue of the 1990s. Franco must have been spinning in his grave. And last year at Stonewall 25 in New York City the Seagrams Corporation gave a reception for ILGA in the Seagrams Tower on 5th Avenue, perhaps the finest modernist building of the great Mies van der Rohe. Very high class. I studiously sampled each and every flavour of Absolut Vodka (which advertises in every gay magazine on earth). There were gracious speeches. When the speeches ended, the microphone was left on. There I was, absolutely pissed [drunk] and just steps away from the microphone. So I gave a speech. I explained that I was the senior member of the Canadian delegation and that Seagrams was a Canadian company. I noted how Seagrams had prospered during prohibition by what some might call bootlegging. It was wonderful I said, that Seagrams and gays and lesbians had achieved respectability, symbolized so well by the fact that Seagrams could now host ILGA in class on 5th Avenue. I have not yet been invited back.

These high class official receptions for lesbians and gays show that there have been amazing changes. If I ever have doubts about the progress we have made, I remind myself that there is an out gay city councilor in Edmonton, Alberta, Canada, the city I grew up in. Amazing. Amazing. Who would have believed it?

The World

A friend said that when he told his mother he was gay she said "nice people won't invite you to their homes." Well there are still places where we are not welcome, still places where no open lesbian or gay has gone before. In 1992 I spoke in the United Nations Subcommittee on Prevention of Discrimination and Protection of Minorities in Geneva as the first openly gay man to speak at a UN meeting. The United Nations—what a closet! Joseph McCarthy said in the United Nations that the State Department was a hotbed of homos. Well I can tell you that there are lots of gay men around in the various diplomatic missions at the United Nations. One diplomat said to me, with some agony, it seemed, over my having gone over to talk to him: "I am a gay man. My country is opposed to what you are doing. We are a Catholic country." He could have added: "I do not want to be seen talking to you."

In the early 1980s the Netherlands criticized the United States in the United Nations Human Rights Commission for the immigration laws which barred homosexuals from even visiting the United States. Syria was delighted that a western country was criticizing the United States, but said to the Netherlands delegation that they hoped for criticism on something more substantial, something that they could support.

When I spoke at the UN in 1992, it was something new. An account of the 1992 session of the Subcommittee said that there was some "open hostility" in the room to my remarks. It was a small start in a not very friendly milieu.

ILGA was refused accreditation at the United Nations as a non-governmental organization in 1991. The liberal *New York Times* ran an editorial condemning the fact that Human Rights Watch had been denied accreditation. The editorial did not mention the fact that ILGA had been rejected at the same meeting.

But you never know what is going to happen. In 1993 we tried again. Three countries pushed our case in the committee. They were the most unlikely activists. The first country was super-Catholic Ireland, which still had a criminal prohibition of sodomy in defiance of the ruling of the European Court of Human Rights in the case brought by Senator Norris. Ireland repealed its sodomy law later the same year. The second country was Russia, which also had an anti-sodomy law. It turned out that Boris Yeltsin had repealed the law by a secret decree, made public a couple of months later. The third country was Cuba, notorious for repressive policies on homosexuality. A representative of Cuba said to me "we have learned from our mistakes."

Because of Ireland, Russia and Cuba the committee voted on our application. With absences and abstentions, a minority of the full committee carried the day. The recommendation then went to the parent body, the Economic and Social Council. In the ECOSOC there was a roll-call vote. I was at the meeting lobbying individual delegations. The delegation from Australia said their instructions from Canberra gave first priority to ensuring the accreditation of ILGA. Australia has been the leading supporter of our issues at the United Nations in recent years. When the roll-call vote came to Morocco, the Moroccan delegation was in obvious disarray. They had a choice of "yes," "no," "abstain" or "not participating." They couldn't figure out which alternative to choose. So they shouted out "absent." Everyone in the room laughed. But official records show Morocco absent. A minority of the full membership of ECOSOC approved our application. We were in.

But the roller coaster ride was not over. We were targeted by the religious right in the United States, using the fact that NAMBLA, the North American Man Boy Love Association was one of more than 300 member organizations of ILGA. NAMBLA had been the first U.S. group to join ILGA, back when ILGA was a much looser organization. ILGA does not support pedophilia, something that had been made clear in a resolution on the protection of children passed in Stockholm in 1990. But we were not being judged on our positions. It was guilt by association, thanks in large part to Senator Jesse Helms in the United States. We were tarred and feathered for having four member organizations who supported or condoned consensual intergenerational sex. Just as Pink Triangle Press was persecuted in Ontario in the 1980s for a serious article on intergenerational sex, we were hounded at the UN. The four organizations have been expelled or have left ILGA and we are about to apply to have the suspensions of accreditation lifted. Hopefully we will soon be back to our routine of fruits in suits and dykes in dresses at the United Nations. But we have paid a price for our respectability among the more liberationist elements of the lesbian and gay movement.

The United Nations has been changing. The Toonen decision of the Human Rights Committee in 1994 held that the sodomy laws in the state of Tasmania were a violation of the International Covenant on Political and Civil Rights. The Committee ruled on the basis of privacy rights. But it also said that discrimination on the basis of sexual orientation would be prohibited as a form of discrimination on the basis of sex. The Toonen ruling led the Committee to criticize the United States in 1995 for the anti-sodomy laws that continue in force in about half of the states. The Committee called those laws "a serious infringement of private life" with consequences for the enjoyment by lesbians and gay men "of other human rights without distinctions." They recognized how the sodomy laws have blocked progress on other civil rights issues. The Toonen decision means that we are now a legitimate part of United Nations Human Rights work—to the discomfort of many in Geneva and New York.

On the political level our biggest achievement occurred in September, 1995 at the women's conference in Beijing. Eleven lesbian and gay organizations were accredited to the conference. Four references to sexual orientation had been proposed for the final statement, The Platform for Action. The issue of including sexual orientation was debated in working group number two early on the morning of the last day. At 4 A.M., after an hour long debate, the chair intervened. She noted that this was the first debate on lesbian and gay equality rights in a United Nations forum. She ruled that if there was no consensus the references to "sexual orientation" would be dropped. In the process of the debate thirty-three governments expressed support for our issues. We had never had so many governments supporting our issues. We lost, but it was the best loss we have ever had.

The Country

Movement at the United Nations would not have been possible without developments in the more influential countries. Our strategy at the United Nations is to tell everyone who will listen about the most recent state actions repealing sodomy laws, extending antidiscrimination laws, recognizing same-sex relationships. The changes at the state level are real and sometimes quite dramatic. It is not smooth sailing at the state level, of course. We see both the Clinton administration in the United States and the Chretien government in Canada delivering less than they promised.

The Canadian story is interesting. In 1982 we were not able to get mentioned in the Charter of Rights and Freedoms. The disabled made it into the equality section, but we did not. But the section was "open-ended." It had a general prohibition of discrimination, followed by examples of prohibited grounds of discrimination. We were not named, but we were lurking in the closet. By 1986, for a combination of legal and political reasons, the Minister of Justice announced in the House of Commons that the government's lawyers had advised the government that the equality provision in the Charter would apply to homosexuals. The Minister of Justice pledged that the government would bring Canadian law into line with this understanding of the Charter. John Crosbie was Minister of Justice at the time. He was a truly conservative man who had introduced strong legislation against prostitution and pornography. He made it clear, in case there might be some misunderstanding, that by no means was he condoning homosexuality. He was simply opposing discrimination. There was a small but open back bench revolt over the policy statement (highly unusual in Canada where we have party discipline, totally unremarkable in the United States.)

John Crosbie did not deliver legislative change. Kim Campbell, a subsequent Minister of Justice, did not deliver. And now Alan Rock, as Minister of Justice, is not delivering. The tenth anniversary of the federal government's promise is just four months away, with no prospect of the Canadian Human Rights Act being amended by that time. But the Courts have compensated for the failure of successive Ministers of Justice. The Ontario Court of Appeal ruled in 1992 that the Canadian Human Rights Act had to be interpreted and applied as if discrimination on the basis of sexual orientation was expressly included in the statute.

In spite of broken promises, and repeated delays, the changes in the legal landscape in Canada and the United States are very impressive. The extension of adoption rights to same-sex couples in New York, Ontario and British Columbia in 1995 is the best example to cite at the moment. Let me talk briefly about two other States.

The Netherlands has been our best friend over the years. In October I was in the Netherlands and met the chief civil servant responsible for lesbian and gay "emancipation." Yes, "emancipation!" What other government would talk in such terms? Basically her role was limited to handling funding for seven lesbian and gay organizations in the Netherlands, the largest being COC, which was founded in 1946. What was remarkable was how unremarkable it all seemed. One gay spokesman said it was about time that gays stopped getting government funding. They should recognize that they were already "emancipated." The civil servant was turning her attention to more specific problem areas, such as the dilemmas facing the lesbian and gay children of Moroccan immigrants.

Another great development is the post-apartheid constitution of South Africa, which expressly forbids discrimination on the basis of sexual orientation, the first constitution in the world to do so. And South African representatives are wonderful at international meetings. They explain to whoever will listen that because of their history of racial discrimination they were determined to end all forms of discrimination in the new South Africa. They understand clearly the parallels between racism, sexism and homophobia. They are our first champion from the "South."

And who opposes us? China abstained in the vote on ILGA's accreditation in the Economic and Social Council, as did India. The opposition to us internationally is but now clearly very narrow. It is largely limited to Islamic states.

The City

I come, finally, to the cities and the wonderful fact of open lesbian and gay people on city councils, parks boards, boards of education and as appointed members of human rights bodies. This is the only level where people in North America who are already out can get elected. In Congress and in the Canadian House of Commons, the five out members all came out after they got elected. The local city level is proving to be much more tolerant, much more open in this historic period. Cities have often played this role of fostering diversity and freedom.

There was a spurt of energy on lesbian and gay issues at the local government level in the United Kingdom from about 1981 to 1988. This happened in a number of the larger cities. It found initial legitimation in Equal Opportunities Policies, there in the context of work against racism and sexism. The scope of the work grew beyond that initial context. The range of issues is interesting, and reflects a somewhat different role of local government in the United Kingdom. The activity involved:

- school curricula, including the promotion of "positive images" of lesbian women and gay men in regular school curricula;
- succession rights in public housing for surviving members of same-sex couples;
- adoption and fostering of children;
- funding of counseling services, help lines, lesbian and gay centres and cultural festivals;
- "pink plaques" commemorating important figures or buildings; and
- HIV/AIDS programs.

But by 1993 this work was essentially over, though elements like succession rights to public housing have been accepted nationally. But why was there such a rising and falling off in this work?

The urban political activity was caught up in rather specific party politics. It may have been, in part, a reaction to the increasingly conservative policies of Margaret Thatcher's government at the national level. It had a dangerously narrow political base. It represented the left wing of the Labour party, acting at the local government level, and dubbed in the national tabloids as the "looney left." There was an ability and a willingness of the national government in the 1980s to slap down the local governments. This occurred with the abolition of the Greater London Council, with funding cuts to local governments and with article 28 of the Local Government Act of 1988 which prohibited local governments from promoting homosexuality or teaching that homosexuality was acceptable as a "pretended family relationship." With this increasingly conservative political atmosphere, the national Labour party backed away from support of lesbian and gay issues. While there are out lesbians and gays on local government bodies in the UK, the loss of momentum on a lesbian and gay agenda in the 1980s is a sobering story.

And the local government activities of people at this conference are threatened in the United States by the state-wide ballot measures—the constitutional amendment in Colorado, presently before the United States Supreme Court—the constitutional amendment just defeated by voters in the State of Maine. The news stories always note that these measures will invalidate anti-discrimination laws already in place in some of the cities. Their aim is clear. The state-wide measures are aimed at ending innovations at the local level.

Local governments have so often taken a lead, so often challenged higher levels of government. The City of Toronto barred discrimination in city employment on the basis of sexual orientation in 1973. This was a pioneering move, followed quickly by the cities of Windsor and Ottawa. Around one hundred cities in the United States now ban such discrimination. Broader antidiscrimination laws are sometimes possible at the local level. Four cities in Brazil bar discrimination on the basis of sexual orientation including the largest cities of São Paulo and Rio de Janeiro. And on the extension of benefits to same-sex partners, cities often lead. Toronto, again, led in Canada, followed by Vancouver, Calgary, Edmonton, Ottawa, Carleton and now four provinces and one territory. Registration systems have been pioneered at the local government level. Over 70 local government jurisdictions in the Netherlands have registration provisions. Over twenty in the United States. Six Paris districts and two Belgium cities established registration systems in September of this year.

You who are out at the local government level have been responsible for this activism and I commend you for it. But you also deliver a special kind of visibility. Svend Robinson is, of course, our living national treasure, but you at the local government level are more real, more visible, virtually normal, with virtual equality. You are the homo next door, the local fruit in a suit, dyke in a dress.

We have the debate on assimilation and equality (on the one hand) and the transformation of society and liberation (on the other hand). And paralleling that debate is the debate on immutability and the search for the queer gene (on the one hand) and social construction and choice and sexual autonomy (on the other hand). And you can publish books on this stuff, as Andrew Sullivan and Urvashi Vaid have shown.

I think the dominant reality is that we are minorities. We will continue to live in a minority ethos as long as the larger society has its hang-ups about us. Your presence as out lesbians and gays in politics is important for it follows the history of other minorities coming to respectability, influence and power, usually first at the local government level. To earlier minorities this meant both some assimilation and some transformation of the larger society—not just one or the other. It is the same for us.

You dress well when you're on the job. You don't run around shouting "We're here, we're queer, get used to it!" But that is your message. Perhaps we have a special Canadian version of the line. Rene Levesque, the beloved hero of Quebec nationalism, was quoted widely after the seperatist [*sic*] Parti Quebecois came to power for the first time in Quebec. He said to the rest of Canada, the English majority—"relax, take a Valium."

I think I am with Levesque on this. All of us queers can say to the larger society. "darlings, take a Valium." I suppose you in the audience would add, "and vote for us."

1996

Introduction to the Film *Stonewall*

Barbara Gittings

This speech was given at the 1996 International Gay and Lesbian Film Festival, held that year in Philadelphia. Gittings was asked to speak about the film *Stonewall* as a veteran of the early gay rights movement.

Welcome to our International Gay and Lesbian Film Festival.

I've been a gay rights activist for 38 years. Tonight I've been plucked from the dustbin of history to introduce this film. But tonight's movie isn't meant to be a history lesson. It's a story, one person's story, with some engaging characters and imaginative play. After all, you did come here to be drawn into someone else's imagination.

Of course there are points of history in the movie story. For example, the police harassment and police brutality were real and were experienced by every one of us who ever entered any kind of gay bar or lesbian bar in the decades before Stonewall.

One of the plot lines is a gay picket march at Independence Hall. I was in the real Independence Hall picket line, not once but 5 times, every July Fourth from 1965 to 1969. These demonstrations were to tell the public that a large group of American citizens is not getting the benefit of "life, liberty, and the pursuit of happiness" as promised in the Declaration of Independence we celebrate on July Fourth.

Yes, those pickets were sedate. And yes, we had a dress code. We had to reckon with the popular image of us at the time as perverted and sick and weird. We wanted the public to gawk not at us but at the messages on our signs and in our leaflets.

Remember, this was 30 years ago. Picketing was not a popular tactic then as it is now. Certainly our cause wasn't popular. Even many gay people thought our efforts were foolish and outlandish.

What we did was scary because we were cracking the cocoon of invisibility. Only a tiny handful of us could take the risk of being so publicly on view.

You might lose your job if your boss saw you on the 6 o'clock news. Your picture might appear in your parents' hometown newspaper and cause shock waves. Certainly your picture would go into government files. We were always surrounded by government agents filming and photographing and tape-recording us. Also there was the risk that some bystander would toss a brick instead of a brickbat.

The early gay pickets were protests. Stonewall was an uprising. It was a welcome flash point, and it sparked a great surge of activism.

Some people say that nothing really happened for us until the Stonewall riot. But as a pre-Stonewall activist friend of mine says, "We built the airplane, and the drag queens flew it away." Not only that—they managed to razz the police and to inject humor into even the most awful situations. Watch for this in tonight's story.

Humor as social protest has a long tradition. But I'm convinced we do it better than any other minority group. I love belonging to a special people. And I believe that even when all the bigotries and barriers are overcome, we will always have twice as much fun in each other's company. We'll continue to have gay and lesbian film festivals so we can show ourselves and see ourselves, our many selves. Enjoy!

February 27, 1996

Philadelphia Gay News Celebrates Twenty Years of Service

Thomas M. Foglietta

This address was given on the floor of the House of Representatives by Representative Foglietta of Pennsylvania and entered into the *Congressional Record* of February 27, 1996.

Mr. Speaker, I rise today to recognize the 20 year anniversary of publishing for the *Philadelphia Gay News,* one of the oldest newspapers serving the gay and lesbian community in America.

I met a young activist named Mark Segal when I was a Republican member of the Philadelphia City Council many years ago. When Mark started the newspaper in 1975, he was a pioneer. In 1975, very few communities had any means for gays and lesbians to know about what was going on in terms of politics, government, health or social events. They had to depend on leaflets and word of mouth. Through the energy of people like Mark Segal throughout the country, that has changed. Lesbian and gay journalism helped that community become more cohesive, politically aware and active. Indeed, trailblazers like Mark Segal helped put the community in the gay and lesbian community. Now, Mark is respected as an elder statesman in gay and lesbian independent journalism in America, though he is anything but an elder. Nationally, Mark was deeply involved in the establishment of gay and lesbian journalists' and publishers' organizations, as well as putting some of their newspapers onto the Internet.

Through credible and independent journalism, the *Philadelphia Gay News* promoted pride in gay and lesbian self identity and educated the community about violence and HIV, AIDS, and other health concerns. The paper helped promote empowerment by giving an advertising avenue for burgeoning gay and lesbian business interests. It gave force to gays and lesbians in Philadelphia government and politics.

I congratulate Mark Segal, his partner Tony Lombardo, who acts as the paper's business manager, and the paper's editor Al Patrick for their commitment to adding to the vitality and diversity of the Greater Philadelphia community.

April 16, 1996

Gay and Lesbian Activist Alliance 25th Anniversary

Eleanor Holmes Norton

These remarks were given on the floor of the House of Representatives by Representative Norton of the District of Columbia and entered in the *Congressional Record* for April 16, 1996.

Mr. Speaker, Tuesday, April 16, 1996, marks the 25th anniversary of the Gay and Lesbian Activist Alliance [GLAA]. GLAA is the oldest consistently active lesbian and gay political and civil rights organization in the United States. I am proud to represent GLAA in Congress and to count its members among my friends.

Since its founding in 1971, GLAA has remained a nonpartisan organization and a consistent force advocating the civil and political rights of the lesbian and gay people in Washington, D.C., and across the Nation. GLAA has played a pivotal role in establishing a ban on discrimination against lesbian and gay public schoolteachers in Washington, D.C., the first in the Nation. Its efforts helped lead to the passage of DC's Human Rights Act, the founding of the Civilian Complaint Review Board, the reform of the District's sodomy statute, and the enactment of DC's domestic partnership law.

GLAA's work with elected officials in Washington, DC, has resulted in more effective AIDS prevention programs targeted to the public schools, to the prisons, to the homeless, and to underserved populations in the Nation's Capital. The alliance's tireless advocacy on behalf of persons living with AIDS increased local funding for AIDS services and programs.

I hope my fellow Members will join me in congratulating the Gay and Lesbian Activist Alliance on its 25th anniversary. I wish them every success in their future endeavors.

May 20, 1996

On Striking Down Colorado's Amendment 2

Suzanne B. Goldberg

At the time she issued this statement, Goldberg was a staff attorney for the Lambda Legal Defense and Education Fund. She later co-edited the 1998 book *Strangers to the Law: Gay People on Trial* with Lisa Keen and served as executive director of the Lesbian and Gay Immigration Rights Task Force (LGIRTF) in Washington, DC.

The Supreme Court ruling today in *Romer v. Evans* is a breakthrough for lesbians and gay men throughout the United States. This landmark, 6-3 ruling should shape the course of civil rights in the United States for decades to come and is the single most positive Supreme Court ruling in the history of the gay rights movement.

The Supreme Court decision makes clear that gay bashing by ballot initiative is unconstitutional. All Americans, gay and non-gay alike, share the same right to seek government protection against discrimination. The Court, relying on a hallmark of American justice, makes clear that a majority cannot trample the rights of an unpopular minority by amending the rules of political participation.

Amendment 2 would have barred all branches of Colorado's state and local government, including public agencies and public schools, from ever prohibiting discrimination against lesbians, gay men and bisexuals. For example, if a lesbian employee showed that she faced job discrimination, or a student experienced anti-gay harassment in public school, government officials would have been powerless to protect those individuals had Amendment 2 not been invalidated today.

This ruling shatters the "special rights" rhetoric of those who oppose equal treatment for lesbians and gay men.

The Court's majority says: "We find nothing special in the protections Amendment 2 withholds. These are protections taken for granted by most people, either because they already have them, or do not need them; these are protections against exclusion from an almost limitless number of transactions and endeavors that constitute ordinary civic life in a free society."

The Court's ruling marks an important shift in Supreme Court responses to anti-gay discrimination. Just ten years ago, the Court relied on the "moral disapproval of homosexuality" to justify upholding Georgia's "sodomy" law in *Bowers v. Hardwick.* Today the Court has said that anti-gay sentiment does not justify governmental discrimination.

We believe the ruling should have ramifications for other attempts to treat gay people as second-class citizens—including the military's ban on openly gay service members and proposals to prohibit legal recognition of same-sex couples' marriages.

While we are elated with the ruling, Americans should understand that in Colorado and 40 other states, lesbians and gay men remain without statewide anti-discrimination protections. This ruling simply leaves us free to continue the fight for anti-discrimination laws in our states, cities and towns.

October 11, 1996

Remarks at Walk Without Fear '96

Richard Rosendall

The following remarks were made in October 1996 during the Walk Without Fear demonstration in Washington, DC, which began with a rally on Du Pont Circle at 7 p.m. and concluded with a candlelight vigil on 17th Street. Rosendall was at this time the president of the Gay and Lesbian Activists Alliance of Washington, DC. Loron Lavoie and Ken Ludden, who are referred to in the text, were other speakers that evening, themselves recent victims of gay bashing. Tyra Hunter was a transgendered person of Washington, DC, who died in August 1995 due to injuries suffered in an auto acccident which an emergency medical worker refused to treat upon discovering Tyra's transgendered identity. A lawsuit brought against the city by Tyra's mother was decided in her favor on December 11, 1998, with an award of two million dollars.

Good evening. How many times have we heard public officials say that "public safety comes first?" Yet here in DC—despite the fact that our police and fire departments don't have the equipment and training they need to do their jobs—our government *does* have the money to go after victimless crimes, and to send ABC Board investigators into gay bars with flashlights and notepads watching out for people fondling each other. So in the 1990s we still have a Morals Division operating under a different name, while basic public safety concerns go wanting. Let me give you an example.

Until a couple of years ago, DC had something called the Civilian Complaint Review Board. It was designed to provide for independent civilian review of complaints of police misconduct. Unfortunately, all the CCRB could do was make recommendations. Repeatedly, CCRB findings were overturned by police trial boards. Adverse personnel actions were almost never taken against the problem officers.

How did the DC Council respond to this problem? Instead of giving the CCRB the teeth it needed to fulfill its mission, Councilmember Bill Lightfoot—with the acquiescence of his Council colleagues—simply abolished it. Over 800 unresolved cases were simply thrown back to the MPD's Internal Affairs Division, thereby completely undermining the whole purpose of independent civilian review.

There is now a bill pending before Lightfoot's Judiciary Committee which will rectify this situation. It is called the Police Conduct Review Board Act of 1995.

Please call or write Councilmember Lightfoot's office and urge him to report the PCRB Act out of his committee this year. And tell him and his colleagues on the Council to get their priorities right and find the money to pay for it. They created this mess, and we hold them accountable for rectifying it. You can use GLAA's letter to Lightfoot as an example—it's on our World Wide Web site at <www.glaa.org>.

Relations between the Police Department and the gay community have actually improved in recent years—through sensitivity training and implementation of the Hate Crimes Law. Much of the credit for this goes to Gay Men and Lesbians Opposing Violence, or GLOV, which I'm proud to say was spun off from GLAA's anti-violence project. I'm sorry that GLOV is not with us this evening. We hope they can join us again next year.

We are pleased with the progress that has been made. But we believe that a system of accountability is key to building public trust for the police who are sworn to serve us.

Another part of public safety is firefighting and emergency medical services. Since the death of Tyra Hunter over a year ago, many of us have been working with GLOV to reform the Fire Department. We have received some promises from the Mayor and Fire Chief Latin, but as Ken and Loron will tell you, we are still waiting for the situation on the streets to change.

What we expect as taxpayers is that misconduct by our public safety officers should be punished. There's an election coming up. Let's make it clear to those who seek to govern us that we hold them accountable.

Our numbers and our commitment give us power if we are willing to use it. Our cause is simple. The words are carved above the entrance to the Supreme Court: Equal Justice Under Law. We owe it to Tyra and to all the victims of hate violence and ignorance to accept no less. Those who advocate hatred must be held responsible for its violent consequences. We do this not as victims, but as proud citizens who will not tolerate anything less than the simple respect we deserve.

The reason why the Radical Religious Right is attacking us so viciously and desperately is because they can see that we are gradually winning the cultural war. The tide of history is with us. But we must choose to ride the tide of history; we must choose to live it. A recent example of people riding that tide is the gay and lesbian employees of a company called IBM. Like many other Fortune 500 companies, IBM has decided to grant domestic partner benefits—but in this case only to same-sex couples, because heterosexual couples already have the right to get the same benefits by getting married.

IBM granted those benefits not out of pure altruism, but out of a recognition that it was in their interest to do so. And their recognition didn't happen by magic—it happened because their gay and lesbian employees decided they deserved equal treatment. They organized. And they asked, they lobbied, and they pressed for what they wanted.

What those IBM employees learned—and what their counterparts at Disney and AT&T and so many others have learned—we must learn also. Power is not something outside us, that can simply be handed to us. We gain power by recognizing it within ourselves and asserting it. We gain freedom by exercising it. Frank Kameny didn't wait for permission four decades ago to exercise his constitutional rights—he went out and did it, and he never gave up.

Hate crimes and gay bashing do not occur in a social vacuum. Whenever lies and hatred and contempt go unchallenged, whenever we stifle our instinct to speak up, whenever we remain silent and fail to give witness to our lives, we become less safe.

So let us recommit ourselves as brothers and sisters here tonight to supporting one another in all our rich diversity, and to exercising our unalienable rights as human beings—which includes holding our public servants accountable. Unwavering self respect is a powerful political act. Perhaps it was best said by Rabbi Hillel two thousand years ago:

> If I am not for myself, who will be for me?
> If I am not for myself, what am I?
> And if not now, when?

March 7, 1997

Log Cabin Republican Address

Jim Kolbe

This speech was delivered by Representative Jim Kolbe (R-AZ) to the Log Cabin Republicans in Los Angeles on March 7, 1997. It reviews the events leading to his coming out as an openly gay member of Congress and subsequent career impacts. Bruce Bawer was a poet and neoconservative journalist, author of *A Place at the Table: The Gay Individual in American Society* (Poseidon Press, 1993) and *Beyond Queer: Challenging Gay Left Orthodoxy* (Free Press, 1996).

I remember the moment very well. It was a little more than a year ago, but it seems like a lifetime now. I was headed out the door of my Washington office, brief case in hand, bound for a pleasant, relaxing weekend in New York with friends. My secretary stopped me and said a reporter from *The Advocate* was on the phone.

I had spoken to this reporter before. So, when I picked up the phone and heard him say he needed to talk to me in person, I wasn't surprised. We agreed to meet the following Monday when I returned from New York. I hung up the phone and left the office, determined to enjoy my rare weekend "off duty." But at that moment I sensed my life was about to change—irrevocably and fundamentally. Or was it?

The conversation on Monday confirmed what I suspected. *The Advocate*—in an article about DOMA, the Defense of Marriage Act, intended to "out" me as a gay—but not openly so—member of the House of Representatives. Armed with that knowledge, I decided to beat them to the punch by making the announcement myself.

What followed was a kaleidoscope of decisions, activities and conversations that most gays and lesbians handle over the course of months—or years. In my case—my very public case—I only had five short days. Between Monday and Friday I had to lay out a game plan; inform my staff and colleagues in the House about my sexual orientation and why I was acknowledging it; write a press statement and letter to key supporters; and call to a seemingly endless list of friends, supporters and yes, family. You see, I come from a family—and I know many of you can relate to this—where we never discussed such personal things as "feelings."

No "operation" as complex as this, of course, ever comes off exactly as you plan it. Too many people had to be notified. The press got wind and Thursday evening—twelve hours ahead of schedule—the story broke on the late evening television news. That broke the dam and by the next morning every media outlet in the country had the story.

The phones rang, and they rang, and they rang—in Tucson and in Washington. Incidentally, by the time the calls and faxes tapered off and tallied the numbers, over 97 percent of everyone we heard from expressed support in one way or another.

All of this—this astonishing, compressed chain of events—occurred during the final week leading up to Congress' August recess. While I was trying to manage this life-changing event—politically and personally—Congress was considering, and voting on, Welfare Reform and the final version of illegal immigration legislation. All this, simultaneous with phone calls to my 86-year-old mother and to news outlets in Arizona. What a week!

Friday ended; Welfare Reform was on its way to the White House for Presidential signature, and Jim Kolbe had taken his place as the second openly gay Republican in the United States Congress. Saturday morning I flew home to Arizona, went to the office and did one-on-one interviews with each of the television news outlets in my community. The questions by now were boringly repetitious and predictable—but they had to be answered—patiently, honestly, candidly. I remember saying at the end of the last interview, half to myself and half to the assembled press, "That's it, folks. You've got your story. Now I am going back to being the Congressman I was before."

And I did. An hour later, I stood in front of an audience at the University of Arizona praising the Udall Foundation for its establishment of a Native American Intern Program. The next week, I conducted my usual August series of town halls, listening to voters praise or vilify Congress and me for what we had done—or not done.

Was I slipping back into denial, a habit I formed early in adult life and gradually shed as I came to terms with my own sexuality? I believe the answer is emphatically "no." I was simply reasserting myself as the Congressman from Arizona's Fifth District, the acknowledged Republican leader for free trade and open market, the new advocate of Social Security Reform, the proponent of less government, lower taxes and more individual responsibility. There were the issues I had been advocating for twelve years in Congress and six years before that in the Arizona Senate. Oh, yes, I happened to be a gay person, too. But, being gay was not—and is not today—my defining persona.

Which leads me to the substance of my remarks tonight. Are we—Log Cabin members and friends—Republicans first, or are we gay persons who happen to think our political views incidentally make us Republicans, also?

If I focus on the need to liberalize trade, cut taxes, and balance the budget, does that mean I cannot also be recognized as a quiet voice of reason on issues of civil liberties and individual rights for homosexuals in our society? Conversely, if I become a "poster boy" and talk mostly about gay/lesbian issues, do I reduce myself to irrelevance with my Republican brethren in the House and cause Republicans?

To answer these questions, I ask you to think back to the celebration we had this Spring, marking the 50th anniversary of Jackie Robinson's debut in major league baseball, the breaking down of the color barrier in America's national pastime. Can anyone here tonight doubt how Jackie Robinson paved the way for a generation of sports greats from the African-American community—from Jackie Robinson and Muhammad Ali to Michael Jordan and Tiger Woods? It wasn't because Jackie Robinson held frequent press conferences, or made speeches, or participated in boycotts. It was because he played baseball, and he played it well.

To his potential detractors, he left no room for doubt that he had been hired by Branch Rickey to do anything except play the best baseball the National League has to offer. Jackie Robinson succeeded in breaking the color barrier in baseball because he proved he was a great baseball player. He paved the way for countless other minorities in professional sports, not because he trumpeted his color but because he played baseball so well. That's what Muhammad Ali did with his right jab and that is what Michael does with his incredible slam-dunks and that is what Tiger Woods is doing for golf with an awesome, cool performance at the Masters. They hit baseballs, throw knock-out punches, shoot baskets flawlessly, and hit golf balls with deadly precision. And they just happen to be African Americans or people of color.

Do they deny their color with their acts of professionalism? Do we deny that we are gay or lesbian by being gathered here tonight as Log Cabin Republicans? Certainly not. And yet there are many in the gay community for whom "gay Republican" is a contradiction in terms.

I, for one, reject such narrow-minded thinking. Just as there are Republicans and Democrats with different points of view, African-Americans who disagree over affirmative action, veterans who differ about a flag burning amendment to the Constitution and Jews who passionately differ as to whether Israel should be supported at any price—so, too, will there be gays who differ about DOMA and ENDA—and, yes, about immigration policies and taxation of capital gains.

We are not monolithic. We are diverse . . . varied . . . individualistic. It is this latter characteristic—our belief in individual liberty—that brings us together as Log Cabin Republicans—Republicans who happen to be gay. This is a core value I dare say we share with the vast majority of fair-minded Americans. There is nothing intrinsically "gay" about it.

As I often remind my constituents in southern Arizona, our nation was founded on the proposition, stated so eloquently in the Declaration of Independence, ". . . that all men are created equal, that they are endowed by their Creator with certain unalienable rights, that among these are Life, Liberty, and the pursuit of Happiness." For more than two hundred years now we, the people of the United States of America, have struggled to realize the full meaning of our creed: to create an opportunity society that empowers **all** citizens to achieve the American Dream. And make no mistake: it **has** been a struggle.

I ask my constituents to consider the words of Abraham Lincoln, whom I revere as our greatest President. A century and a half ago—in 1855, when he was still a country lawyer—he dared to suggest that the nation was failing to live up to its promise that "all men are created equal." As Lincoln said,

> We now practically read it "all men are created equal, except Negroes." When the Know-Nothings get control, it will read "all men are created equal, except Negroes and foreigners and Catholics." When it comes to this, I shall prefer emigrating to some country where they make no pretense of loving liberty—to Russia, for instance, where despotism can be taken pure, and without the base alloy of hypocrisy.

Doesn't it seem strange, I ask my constituents, to think that Lincoln's words were considered radical at the time, and that such thinking would help provoke a civil war?

I remind my friends and neighbors in southern Arizona that personal liberty—the freedom to choose—is the cornerstone of our American democracy. If **each** of us is to fully enjoy the opportunities and blessings of liberty, then **all** of us must accept responsibility for our own actions, and for how our actions will affect the lives of others.

As Friedrich August von Hayek, the great Austrian economist, explained:

> Liberty not only means that the individual has both the opportunity and burden of choice; it also means that he must bear the consequences of his actions.

I believe proprietary self-interest and concern for one's fellow man are not mutually exclusive. Indeed, they go hand in hand, and I believe that together they comprise the "content of our character" by which Dr. Martin Luther King said each of use should be judged.

The American ideal of limited government of the people, by the people, and for the people is also a radical concept. Our founding fathers dared to believe that government should derive its authority from the consent of the governed, and not the other way around. Thomas Jefferson elaborated on his conception of "good government" when he took the oath of office as our nation's third President in 1801. He said:

> The sum of good government is to restrain men from injuring one another and leave them otherwise free to regulate their own pursuits of industry and improvement and shall not take from the mouth of labor the bread it has earned.

James Madison, who succeeded Jefferson as President, clearly saw the dangers inherent in unlimited government. He warned that:

> . . . there are more instances of the abridgment of the freedom of the people by the gradual and silent encroachments of those in power than by violent and sudden usurpations.

It is not that I and my fellow Republicans in Congress who seek to change the status quo believe the Federal government is some sort of malevolent agent, intentionally seeking to deprive us of our liberty. Rather, we believe the power of the federal government has grown far beyond anything our founding fathers could have imagined. More important, it has grown so large it gets in the way of citizens' ability to maximize their individual freedom and opportunities. Jefferson and Madison understood intuitively that government, in and of itself, cannot provide happiness. That is something you must pursue for yourself. What our government can ensure—and what your fellow American citizens ought to honor—is your liberty, in law, to live out your American Dream.

Ronald Reagan said it very well more than a decade ago in a speech he entitled "A Time For Choosing." He said these words:

> . . . for almost two centuries we have proved man's capacity for self-government, but today we are told we must choose between a left and a right or, as others suggest, a third alternative, a safe middle ground. I suggest to you there is no left or right, only an up or down. Up—to the

maximum of individual freedom consistent with law and order, or down to the ant heap of totalitarianism.

With those words, Ronald Reagan expressed what should be the credo of all Log Cabin Republicans—"individual freedom consistent with law and order." Isn't that what we as Republicans believe in? Surely, that expresses what **we** as Log Cabin Republicans—concerned with government intrusion into our private lives, devoted to maximizing individual liberties and responsibilities—must believe.

I am both fascinated and amused with the convergence in views of some Republicans on the right side of our Party with the views of gay, liberal Democrats. Neither would even admit their common philosophy, but it is there, nevertheless. The so-called conservative Republican deplores big government, welfare programs, erosion of personal liberties—and then votes for constitutional amendments to ban flag burning, or to proscribe specific medical procedures for a doctor performing an abortion, or to deny gays their rights to fully participate in our society.

Liberal, gay Democrats, on the other hand, deplore the intrusion of government into the bedroom or the doctors' examining room—and then proceed to wax eloquent for programs that would nationalize the entire health care delivery system, or compel poor people to live in sub-standard housing operated by the liberal bureaucracy, or decry programs to give education vouchers to lower income parents so that they might send their children to schools of their own choosing.

We might be excused for excessive hubris for thinking Log Cabin Republicans are the only gays who really understand that individual liberties are for everyone. Why is it, then, that as gay Republicans we have allowed gay Democrats, largely committed to the collectivist state, to speak for gay and lesbian rights? Why are the ones committed to expanding government control over our lives in housing and in education, the ones who would nibble at our freedom through use and abuse of the tax code and regulatory system—why—how are they presumed to speak for gay rights? What distortion of the definition of freedom and liberty has given them unfiltered access to the megaphone, claiming to express the views of all gays?

But, just as we must not abandon the battlefield of policy to the illiberal left, so we must not allow the religious fundamentalists to use "morality" as a cudgel against us. For many gays, the process of coming out involves shedding the guilt and shame associated with our sexuality. In that process, most of us conclude—rightly, I believe—that we are not "immoral" just because we are homosexual.

Unfortunately, many gays go a step further and reject any association of behavior and morality. A rejection of the hypocrisy of the rigid morality of the 1950s has led conservatives and liberals alike to flee from public discourse about what is right or wrong. And so, we have a society where divorce rates and illegitimate births are soaring, where teenage violence and drug use is rampant. We may invoke a moral position for ourselves, but we adopt moral neutrality for everyone else. The result is a backlash in society, for the simple fact is—people yearn for moral guidance.

As columnist Dan Perreten recently pointed out, we must not lose sight of the distinction between the words "moral"—principles of right and wrong in behavior—and "moralizing." We are, Perreten notes, so offended by the practitioners of the latter that we fail to acknowledge the importance of the former. Just as we must challenge liberal Democrats on policy issues where we know them to be wrong, so must we engage in an honest, candid debate with ourselves on moral issues that affect the gay and lesbian community.

The fact is, we belong to the party that really talks about concerns of the gay community. Ours is the party of Abraham Lincoln, of Theodore Roosevelt, of Ronald Reagan. It is the party of freedom, liberty and individual responsibility. We are a minority within the Republican party when we think of ourselves as gays. But when we add all those Republicans, and other Americans who won't be identified with a party—all those who do not want government telling them what to do—then we are a majority. When we understand this simple fact and act like majority Republicans, we will win.

Call it "safe middle ground" if you like, but it represents the historical mainstream of Republican thinking for 150 years. Republicans will support, and elected officials will vote, "our way" if the question is framed as one of "individual rights," not of "lifestyle." Opposing discrimination on the basis of one's sexual orientation is not a matter of defending a lifestyle; it is protecting our rights as individual American citizens, just as surely as all of us would oppose discrimination against Jews or women or African-Americans because such discrimination is contrary to the fundamental principles underlying our Constitution. Discrimination should be an abomination to all Republicans—Log Cabin Republicans and moral majority Republicans. But it is equally right for Republicans to oppose special privileges for any group—quotas or special legal protection.

Sometimes we must show special courage as gay Republicans, standing up to the conventional wisdom in both the Republican party and the gay community. But with a foot in both groups, true to the principles we know to be right, we can gain the respect and acceptance of gays and Republicans alike. When you argue the case to your Congressman or state Assemblyman for school choice—when you tell them this is an exercise of individual choice in education—you show them a face of gay Republicans they may not have seen before. When you talk to them about how lower taxes can expand job opportunities for Americans of all stripes, you speak a language they understand but have not heard from the gay community.

We gain acceptance and build our bridges, not by stressing that we are gay people who are Republicans, but that we are Republicans who happen to be gay or lesbian—that we are Republicans who care about families and schools, who believe in a strong national defense and laws that are tough on criminals, who worry about the environment and want to balance the budget so the next generation is not saddled with the fruits of our profligacy.

My constituents and my Republican colleagues in Congress respect me and support me because they know I am fighting for open markets, free trade and consumer choice, for a balanced budget, and for an honest overhaul of our Social Security system. To them, these issues are no less important, and I am no less qualified to make the case for them, now than before my announcement. Free trade is the engine of our economic prosperity and the ticket to future competitiveness. Balancing the budget—a feat Republicans achieved this year for the first time in 30 years—matters because it says we care about our nation's stability. And thinking honestly about transforming Social Security from a dead-end tax into a real retirement savings plan says that we care about the future for the next generation.

Log Cabin Republicans have already shown they can speak to the broad concerns of all Republicans. Four years ago, in the New York mayoral race, Log Cabin Republicans introduced an ad, the tag line for which was: "Who says crime is not a gay issue?" That simple message speaks volumes, both about ourselves as gay Republicans, and to the large majority of Republicans who have the same worries about crime and safety. "Who says crime is not a gay issue?" Of course it is. It's everybody's issue. The sooner we speak to it—and to similar issues—the sooner we speak to middle America, the sooner we enter the mainstream of American politics.

In the 1996 Republican presidential sweepstakes, Log Cabin Republicans demonstrated their moral courage and constancy, by taking on the prospective Republican nominee when a Log Cabin contribution was first accepted and then rejected. When Log Cabin stood its ground, Senator Dole's campaign changed its attitude, accepted the contribution, issued an apology, and conferred new respect to this organization. When Log Cabin Republicans endorsed Dole's Presidential bid, they demonstrated that they were an important part of the team.

The cause for all gay persons, Republicans and Democrats alike, will be advanced when we focus not on what sets us apart from our fellow Americans but on what we share in common; when we demonstrate our concern and our commitment, our expertise and our execution, on issues that matter to mainstream America.

Bruce Bawer, in a recent column, talks about a revolution that is taking place in America today—a revolution he says that is the worst nightmare of a far-left gay activist. It is a revolution brought about by people who work in corporations, worship in our churches, speak through our news media and teach in our schools. It is a revolution brought about by ordinary gay people who live their lives in ordinary ways on every ordinary day.

By doing so, Bawer says, other ordinary Americans "have grown from ignorance into knowledge, from lies into truth, from prejudice into love." There are still two Americas, he notes, one in which homosexuality is accepted as part of everyday life and another in which gays continue to be demonized and discriminated against. But, if we are ever to eliminate the division, it will be because of those ordinary people living their ordinary lives. It will also be because a few brave, extraordinary people, some of whom are gathered here tonight, choose to reject the politics of exclusion and group identity. You are here tonight because you have chosen to pursue the politics of inclusion and mainstream values.

Last December, just a few months after my announcement made big news, I was privileged to speak at the dedication of a statue commemorating the 150th anniversary of the peaceful arrival of the Mormon Battalion in the Presidio of Tucson during the Mexican War. I shared the dais that day with my friend and colleague from the Arizona Congressional delegation, Matt Salon, and Gordon Hinkley, President of the Church of Jesus Christ of Latter Day Saints. More than 7,000 people came from throughout Southern Arizona. Most were Mormons, and maybe a third were directly descended from members of the Mormon Battalion.

In my remarks, I noted that the men of the Mormon Battalion had volunteered to serve their country in spite of the fact that the federal government had done little to protect them from religious persecution. These were men who, along with their families, had been driven from their homes in the East by angry, intolerant neighbors. In many cases their property had been stolen or confiscated. Some of their brethren—including Joseph Smith, founder of the faith—had even been murdered for their beliefs. Despite all this, 500 Mormon men faithfully answered the call to enlist and march 2,000 miles from Iowa to California. This arduous, six-month trek remains the longest infantry march in U.S. Army history. And they accomplished this remarkable feat without a shot being fired in anger.

I noted that the statue honoring the Mormon Battalion was really a monument to peace . . . and tolerance. This was a message this audience could understand. At least three times they interrupted my remarks with their applause. And in the months that have followed my office has received more requests for that speech than for any other I have ever given.

Last spring, in the wake of Susan Molinari's resignation announcement, I joined a small group of my Republican House colleagues to discuss the leadership races. Names were being tossed around—moderates who might run for Conference Vice-Chairman or Secretary. Finally, someone turned to me and said "Well, Jim, why don't you run? You've got the seniority, you're a moderate, and you've shown your leadership on trade and other issues. You'd be a good candidate!"

"Oh, sure," I replied. "I'm sure our Republican caucus is ready to elect a pro-choice, gay person to the leadership."

"Oh, goodness," the first individual responded, "I had forgotten about that!"

Well, good. Perhaps, from time to time, this individual—and others—need to be gently reminded that I am gay, if only so that they remember how secondary it is in my political and everyday life.

Arizona Republic cartoonist Steve Benson got it right after my coming out when he did a cartoon—two identical drawings of Jim Kolbe, side by side. One was labeled; "Jim Kolbe, hard-working, fiscally conservative, socially moderate Republican Congressman from Arizona—before he announced he was gay." The second, same caricature, had the same label, except "After he announced he was gay." Looks like the same guy to me.

April 1997

Why Can't We All Get Together, and What Do We Have in Common?

Jim Kepner

This speech was given by Jim Kepner, veteran gay journalist and founder of the collection of gay and lesbian books, periodicals, and artifacts that would become ONE Institute's International Gay and Lesbian Archives.

Gays and lesbians often agonize because our movement doesn't move directly toward that ultimate goal they're sure all of us want. But—is our goal clearly agreed on? It is not, and nothing has so hampered our movement as our failure to understand our legitimate differences regarding goals. We'll continue to rip our movement apart unless we clearly understand this diversity and its consequences. Our movement's history suggests that our diversity is more than just something to be tolerated.

That history shows how religious Gays and atheists, conservatives and radicals, feminists, radical faeries, transsexuals, boy lovers, minorities and PWAs have built up the debate about our movement goals. Not until the late '60s did many activists admit that such differences are legitimate, and begin to see that our diversity has some advantages. Note that I generally use the terms Gay, homophile and homosexual as Gay men and women did then, to include both (or all) genders.

I don't like lazy speeches that take an hour to say what can be said in a few sentences, so I'm going to cover a lot of ground—and jump around a bit. I hope you'll jump when I jump.

I knew I was different by age four, but had a long search to define that difference and to relate my perceptions to the group I would seek out to share with. I define myself differently today from when, from age 12 to 17, I planned to be a Presbyterian missionary to the Congo. I came out in San Francisco in 1943, but took side trips through pacifism, militant atheism, science fiction fandom and the Communist Party before I found my way to our fledgling Gay movement in 1953. These "side trip" identities with other groups and causes helped shape my perceptions of who we are and what we might become. Memories of my former beliefs, and the emotional residue each has left in my gut, help me appreciate the diverse ways in which other Gays and Lesbians define ourselves and our goals.

Ulrichs and Hirschfeld

Most founders of the first stable U.S. Gay organization didn't know in 1950-51 that our movement was born in Germany in 1896, after 30 years of pioneering by Karl Ulrichs—and a few earlier persons who'd argued in our behalf. Many of our goals were first defined in the pre-Nazi German movement for homosexual rights.

Karl Heinrich Ulrichs responded to an immediate threat: the several independent German states were being swallowed by Prussia, which had a severe anti-homosexual law. Ulrichs, a civil servant in Hanover, opposed the unification which would criminalize all German homosexuals. He informed his relatives of his nature, and of his plan for a public campaign for education and justice, then appealed for justice for what he called "Urnings," at a Jurists conference, where he was shouted down. He said that having gone public, he and his cause could never turn back.

He took the term Urning from Plato's *Symposium,* mentioning Uranus as God of same-sex lovers. Ulrichs' first goal was to work out a theory as to Who are we? How do we get this way? And does nature have a reason for so regularly producing us?—an idea revived by Sociobiologists today. He was a prophet, but no organizer. The German movement got its real start the year after he died.

The first group was Der Eigene (community of the special), founded by Adolf Brand, Benedict Friedlander and publisher Max Spohr. Their goal was to build a separate and idealized male Gay culture, on the old Greek model. A radical German women's movement also started that year, and a hippie-like back-to-nature youth movement, rejecting bourgeois values and emphasizing erotic friendship. Socialism, spiritualism and health fads also blossomed until the Nazi takeover.

In 1897, the Der Eigene leadership joined Dr. Magnus Hirschfeld to form the Scientific Humanitarian Committee, which Hirschfeld led. SHC goals were scientific research to show that the "intermediate sex" (which Hirschfeld compared to being crippled) was inborn, and a campaign to solicit influential people to reform the law, arguing that homosexuals can't help being the way they are, and that the law encouraged blackmail. Friedlander and some women's leaders scorned the comparison to cripples, whom society might tolerate, but never accept as equals. They also spurned Hirschfeld's and Ulrichs' view that male homosexuals were by nature womanish.

Five thousand illustrious persons ultimately signed the law reform petition: Einstein, Hermann Hesse, Socialist leaders August Bebel and Karl Kautsky, Freud, Krafft-Ebing, Martin Buber, Karl Jaspers, George Grosz, Heinrich and Thomas Mann, Carl Maria von Weber, Stefan Zweig, Gerhardt Hauptmann, Rainer Maria Rilke, Arthur Schnitzler, even Berlin's police chief and the Prussian and Federal Ministers of Justice—but no publicly identified homosexuals.

In 1898 the issue came before Germany's Reichstag—supported only by minority Social Democrats. In 1907 a right-wing newspaper attack on Prince Eulenburg and other Gay intimates of the Emperor killed the reform, and hurt the movement, as Hirschfeld testified against the defendants as a police witness. Hirschfeld, frustrated by the failure of influential Gays to help the cause, had discussed the controversial strategy revived by some AIDS activists recently—of forcing such persons out of the closet.

The reform bill was diverted in 1914 by World War I, and in 1923 by runaway inflation. It passed the Reichstag's Criminal Justice Committee but not the whole Reichstag—just before Hitler's takeover signaled the quick, total destruction of the German gay community.

Gay groups had diversified greatly. The law hadn't changed but police pressure had relaxed, so before the Nazi takeover, there were Gay and Lesbian cultural, pen pals, health, political, religious and social groups. Novelist Sinclair Lewis, in *Dodsworth,* described Gay neighborhoods in major German cities patrolled by friendly policemen. Hirschfeld, emphasizing education, published his thick *Yearbook for Intermediate Sexual Types* and built a massive library and school in Berlin, which the Nazis burned. With actor Conrad Veidt, he starred in the first Gay rights film, *Different from the Others,* and collected massive research to prove that homosexuality was inborn and that homosexuals, though effeminate, were fine citizens, even fine soldiers in World War I. He thought this information would end discrimination. Just when Hirschfeld and others thought they stood on the brink of victory, the holocaust swept them away. Untold thousands were worked to death in concentration camps. The Nazis saw Hirschfeld—Jew, homosexual, socialist and feminist—as their ultimate enemy.

Homophile leader Kurt Hiller has said that homosexuals must free themselves, not wait for others to do it. He was sent to a concentration camp, ransomed out, taught in England during the war, and came back to lead the German law reform campaign to success in 1968-69.

Other Countries

Similar groups were started in other countries. Dutch and Czech SHC groups started in 1911, the Dutch interrupted only by World War II's Nazi occupation. The COC, now called the Dutch Society for Integration of Homosexuals, provided a safe meeting place and worked to lower age-of-consent laws. Most European groups assumed that homosexuals were middle or upper class, who sought boys or lower class men as partners.

Edward Carpenter, George Ives, Havelock and Edith Ellis, A.E. (and) Lawrence Housman, Radclyffe Hall and others tried starting an English movement during the fearful years after Oscar Wilde's trial—aiming mainly at sex education. England's real movement came only in 1970 after massive witchhunts and 16 years debate on the Wolfenden law reform proposals. The Homosexual Law Reform Society during the 1950s and 60s had argued that homosexuals couldn't help being that way, and ought not be imprisoned—imagining that homosexuals would gratefully become invisible once the law changed! Anglican, Catholic and British Medical Association reports supported this. Only the Quaker Report said that homosexuals were potentially as moral as heterosexuals.

A Zurich woman, Mammina, started the Swiss Friendship Bund in 1932 to provide social outlets and work modestly for law reform. The name became Der Kreis or The Circle in 1943, after she handed the group over to prominent actor Karl Meier a.k.a. Rolf. The only magazine and club to survive through World War II, Der Kreis added French and English sections during the fifties. With its Oktoberfests and other social activities, it was an international center for a select circle of gay men, many of them American.

There was a small movement among intellectuals in pre-Communist Russia. Leo Tolstoy, a guiltily repressed homosexual, castigated Gay rights advocates in his 1899 novel *Resurrection,* but he signed Hirschfeld's petition. By 1905, Gays like poet Mikhail Kuzmin had produced a small body of Gay advocacy literature. The Bolsheviks removed Czarist anti-homosexual laws, and Gays became briefly more open. Lenin and Trotsky stayed homophobic, but initially viewed the traditional family as a bulwark of reaction. Most open Lesbian and Gay poets hailed the Revolution, but most of them soon came under house arrest. Kuzmin issued his Gayest work after 1918—but in Amsterdam, not Russia. Some like the great poet Ann Akhmatova stood by their friends, until each was sent to Siberia. To survive, she had to publish fawning lines about Stalin.

At World League Congresses for Sexual Reform led by Hirschfeld from 1921 until 1930, Russian Health Minister Grigorii Batkis called the USSR a model of homosexual freedom, until he was silenced. The Soviets briefly promised a Gay homeland, in the far reaches of Siberia near Birobijan, the forgotten Jewish "homeland." The communists soon reverted to hetero conformity and ended talk of sex liberation. Gays were branded a sign of bourgeois decadence. Communists blamed fascism on homosexual excess, while the Nazi blamed us for the decadence of democracy.

Around 1913, anarchist Emma Goldman and Edith Ellis each lectured on homosexual rights to large responsive American crowds, according to contemporary press reports, and birth control advocate Margaret Sanger reportedly tried to set up some sort of organization. Hirschfeld toured the U.S. later, his talks enthusiastically reported for the Hearst press by pro-German gay writer George Sylvester Viereck.

Lesbians, prominent in several artistic and literary circles, such as that around Margaret Fuller in early 19th century Boston, Charlotte Cushman later in Rome and Margaret Anderson in Chicago about 1913, seemed less likely than men to organize politically—except in the 19th century abolitionist, prohibition and women's rights movements, where women-loving-women played leading roles but never publicly raised Lesbian issues. Few even defined themselves that way. They focused on freeing women from the worst tyrannies of marriage, endless childbearing and alcoholism, while opening to women social roles previously reserved for men.

Women fought to be able to attend and teach school, serve as nurses or foreign missionaries, dress more comfortably, build settlement houses to educate and assist immigrants, crusade for child labor laws, sanitation, etc., but most affectional relations were hidden behind "convenient" hetero marriages, or "Boston marriages" which were presumed to be romantic but sexless. The woman artists and writers who wanted to openly flout heterosexual expectations either moved to Europe or disguised themselves as men.

Gerber and Friends

Bavarian-born Henry Gerber, forerunner of America's movement, served in the U.S. World War I army in the Rhineland, discovering the thriving Gay movement there. Back in Chicago in 1924 he recruited eight ordinary guys for his Society for Human Rights, though he tried to win support from such leading sex reformers as Margaret Sanger. His group was all arrested and undistributed copies of their paper Friendship and Freedom were seized (two copies were recorded in European Gay periodicals). After two trials, Gerber returned to the army, ran Contacts, a pen-pals club, for ten years from New York, and in '34 wrote for *Chanticleer,* a mimoegraphed atheist publication in which at least half the space went to Gay concerns—the earliest U.S. periodical of which copies exist.

When Gerber folded Contacts in 1939, member Manwell Boyfrank pestered him to start some group through which like-minded men could meet. For some, that remains the primary goal of our movement. Gerber, Frank McCourt and Boyfrank corresponded for years, arguing how to organize and to what purpose. Their sharply differing views on the nature of homosexuality and of society left little room for them to agree on goals or tactics.

They hoped to educate opinion-makers about human sexuality, assuming that problems will vanish when people are informed of the truth. Gerber felt there always had been homosexuals and heteros, with undecided fools making things dangerous; yet he always cruised straight-looking servicemen. Convinced that religious superstition shackled sexuality, he advocated atheist propaganda as a prerequisite to homosexual freedom.

Boyfrank assumed that most men were drawn toward other men or boys, unless snared into providing for women's domestic needs. He sought sex with masculine-type men, but also argued to fathers (successfully, even in small towns) that their sons need a kindly older gent to provide the considerate love and guidance which fathers rarely have time for. He was proud when his boys grew up hetero. His atheism was milder than Gerber's. He saw marriage as the enemy. Later, recognizing the family's financial advantages, he urged men to form Federated Families, to save their property from relatives' clutches. (His own property went to his sister).

McCourt held prayer meetings in a large Riverside Drive house during World War II for Gay soldiers about to be shipped over the submarine-infested Atlantic. Gerber raged at this arrant pandering to superstition. But it had to be comforting to Gay servicemen who weren't getting family support as they headed to the war many would not return from. McCourt studied Gay history and literature and worked to build circles of Gay friends with shared interests. All three viewed women as the source of sexual repression.

In 1944, after homophobic press coverage of a murder case, they started answering press slurs as the Society Skirting Sexual Superstition, a name they used only among themselves. Their overlong letters were often printed. Gerber's "In Defense of Homosexuality" was one of the first articles I found in 1942—in a freethinking magazine.

In Los Angeles, Edith Eyde, whom I'd known earlier, typed out her carbon-copy magazine *Vice Versa—America's Gayest Magazine* in 1947-48 to inform Gay women about the subject. She hand-delivered them, mostly in a Lesbian bar, for fear of postal snoops who often seized or opened mail then. Two women readers later became editors of *ONE Magazine.* Edith later sang campy Gay folksongs at bars—as she did in the film *Before Stonewall.*

The Early Mattachine

In Los Angeles's Pershing Square in 1930, a friend of Gerber's told young Harry Hay about the Society for Human Rights, inspiring Hay to imitation—even though the friend thought Gerber was a damned fool for trying to organize. But to start a group, you need at least one other person, and it took Hay 20 years to find that other—the later famed fashion designer Rudi Gernreich. Hay had gained valuable organizing experience in the Communist Party, plus unique views on the nature of homosexuality from his study of the musical expression of peasant religions, in which he searched for Gay influences.

Having discovered the American Indian berdache, what followed Edward Carpenter's view that in tribal and medieval societies, we had been outsiders with special roles, and if we today seek assimilation, we sell our birthright for a mess of hetero pottage. He hoped to form underground mystic guilds, to reawaken ourselves to who we are and what we are for. In late 1950, he met three more men who shared his dream of gays working openly in a socialist-led united front.

He showed a prospectus he'd drawn up earlier to Bob Hull, a student in his Social History of Music class. Bob brought his friends Chuck Rowland and Dale Jennings to Hay's Silverlake house. Chuck, a former American Veterans Committee midwest organizer, supposedly ran up the hill waving the prospectus, saying, "I could have written this myself! When do we start?" (Chuck later denied that story.)

The fear-ridden society they faced was **very** different from that we live in today. People were being hounded, even arrested, for being different in any significant way. "Perverts" and subversives were considered largely the same—both threats to everything America stood for. Committed to making a socialist revolution, Hay and his new friends had to figure out how to make Gays part of this.

They began seeking consensus on how to create a movement **where none had seemed possible,** arguing over every idea to agreement, lest they risk setbacks. They were groping in the dark, exchanging what little they knew about homosexuality before they could even think of social action. Two young motorcyclists joined five months later, brought in friends, such as photographer Ruth Bernhard, and chose the name Mattachine—from 11th century guilds of wandering actors Hay had described in his class.

They were painfully aware that America was in a dangerous, witch-hunting mood, and that Gays were a prime target. Hay's music class had unwittingly involved a search for Gay roots and roles. Communists had devoted attention to the minority question, so Hay proposed the radical notion that homosexuals were an oppressed minority, needing to build a sense of community. Most new members wildly resisted this idea, wanting only to be like everyone else.

Then Dale Jennings was charged with propositioning a vice cop. Since Gays and other minorities were angry about entrapment, they launched a Committee to Outlaw Entrapment, to raise defense funds and to hold public discussion groups, from which they could hunt for promising recruits. They soon drew crowds of 20 to 150 gay men and a few Lesbians to weekly groups all over town, with topics very few Gays had ever before felt free to discuss in public:

> **Should I tell my parents, or my boss?**
> **Can a Gay person still be religious?**
> **Do we need a Gay ethics for special conditions in our lives?**
> **Do we have a group purpose, a special way of serving society?**
> **How can I meet nice responsible friends?**
> **Why aren't there more women here?**
> **Are swishes and bulldykes the cause of prejudice against us?**

Few of the new recruits shared the founders' vision. Most of them saw homosexuality as just a sexual habit. They wanted nothing to do with other minorities, or with communists. In early '53, just as Mattachine reached San Diego, northern California and Chicago, with inquiries coming in from all over, Chuck Rowland and others, realizing the creakiness of the old lodge-like structure, called a constitutional convention to devise new structures.

One hundred of us, hot with optimism, certain that we were going to win our battle against bias soon, met at a Universalist church in Los Angeles. Few of us in those two weekends understood the bitter issues which ripped us apart. While we voted on dozens of confused proposals for a new organizational structure, the conservative-conformist newcomers generally routed the founders.

Anything remotely radical-sounding was knocked out, such as a Statement of Purpose clause ". . . we hold it necessary that a highly ethical homosexual culture be integrated into society." The new leaders saw this as viciously communistic—I never understood how. One insurgent threatened to report us all to the FBI (saying that he'd already turned in hundreds of traitors). The resulting constitutions proved extremely contradictory, unstable and incomplete.

Optimism vanished and membership declined, though new chapters began in time in New York, Detroit and Denver. The Los Angeles council soon folded and headquarters moved to San Francisco. But there were also gains. The secretiveness was gone. *Mattachine Review,* several local newsletters and *Dorian Book Quarterly* along with *ONE Magazine,* brought an increasingly positive message to many isolated Gays. The most creative Mattachine chapter and newsletter was Denver's. Their 1959 national convention was our first professional-type event, the first to get fair, daily newspaper coverage.

ONE, Incorporated

The idea for a magazine, called *ONE,* came up at a Mattachine discussion group, but the magazine committee quickly chose to be independent. Too feisty for most timid Mattachinos, *ONE* soon began to balance male and female contents. The women of *ONE* felt that women had a different sensitivity, but didn't yet envision "women's issues" as such. Most staffers felt ONE, Incorporated existed **only** to produce a magazine "dealing with homosexuality from the scientific, historical and critical point of view," but business manager Dorr Legg had written in broader purposes: "to sponsor educational programs, lectures and concerts for the benefit of social variants and promote among the general public an interest, knowledge and understanding of the problems of variation . . . to sponsor research and promote integration . . . ," etc. He saw it as ONE's goal to create all the social service, cultural and educational institutions necessary for well-rounded community.

Legg as a youth had seemed alone in looking for a community, not just a lay or a lover. He chose Los Angeles as the place to share life with a black lover—not easy then. Before joining Mattachine, he'd helped launch the short-lived interracial club, the Knights of the Clocks. He exercised iron control over ONE, Incorporated until his death in late 1994.

By early 1956, though we meant to concentrate on the magazine, counselees were coming to ONE desperate to escape the hell they felt St. Paul had condemned them to. Ann Carol Reid and I proposed kicking off a series of Sunday morning events, where ex-ministers or metaphysicians who were part of our circle could do whatever seemed appropriate to them: pray, preach, hold seances, hear confessions, meditate or lead singalongs. Chuck Rowland, head of our promotions committee, broke away and organized the Church of One Brotherhood. It grew steadily for a year, despite our angry scorn, and collapsed suddenly. They **did** help Gays suffering religious guilt, and ambitiously proposed to start a retirement home, a university, a hospital, etc., "as soon as they'd raised $100." What they tried was brought off successfully a dozen years later by Troy Perry. Several Gay Orthodox clergy branching out from the late Bishop Michael Itkin, claim descent from a reported 1945 Gay church in Atlanta.

In '56 we at ONE organized America's first Gay studies, surveying the academic fields of biology, anthropology, sociology, history, literature, religion, law and philosophy, asking what each could contribute to understanding how Gays fit into the nature of things. In 1958, I produced *ONE Institute Quarterly of Homophile Studies,* the first U.S. Gay scholarly journal. Issue 38, based on court cases defending the Right of Association in Gay bars, was widely used as a text in British laws schools.

Don Slater, *ONE*'s chief editor and librarian after 1957, was a cantankerous individualist, denying that the state has a right to exist, much less to curb our behavior in any way. His sharp, campy style fit well with that of art editor Eve Elloree.

My Coming Out

From age four I was looking for a special friend, the brother I never had—in place of the marriage everybody said lay in wait. Not effeminate, I was uncomfortable with what a boy was supposed to be, and felt a common bond with tomboys. At 19, I first heard the word homosexual, loathesomely defined. With unusual luck, I found relevant books, which were rare and mostly awful then. I started the collection which ultimately grew into the International Gay and Lesbian Archives. It took me a year to find the Gay crowd, but because of a burst of police pressure, and because Gays expected one another to act effeminate, I later returned back to the closet.

In science fiction fandom, my closeted Gayness caused a minor scandal. From the radical movement, I was expelled in 1948 for being Gay. After several attempts to convince friends to join me in starting a Gay magazine or organization, I joined Mattachine in 1953 and ONE a bit later, helping edit *ONE Magazine* and other ONE publications through 1960. I helped start ONE's classes, teaching gay studies off and on since then in several cities.

At inter-group panels at annual meetings of ONE, Mattachine and the Lesbian Daughters of Bilitis during the late fifties, I likened the latter two to the cautious National Urban League, which sought quiet ways to up-grade Black social status. I compared ONE to the militant National Association for the Advancement of Colored People. Mattachine aimed to convince opinion makers that we were just like everyone else, so **they** would stop persecuting us. One Mattachine officer said their goal was to help cure us all. DOB aimed to provide nicer Lesbian meeting places than bars, urged members to avoid dress or behavior which might inflame bias, later argued that we must recognize that we are sick before society can respect us. ONE urged Gays to respect and understand themselves, to build the communal strength needed to win our rights. We looked for the social roots of prejudice, seeking tools to counter it.

In January '61, ONE planned a Constitutional Convention to write a **Homosexual Bill of Rights.** We mailed a questionnaire to subscribers. Dorr Legg and I agreed that some rights are general and some conditional. I'd hoped to analyze what Gays wanted. But Dorr, who despised the term Gay, composed a questionnaire whose answers couldn't be interpreted clearly or tabulated, and that asked irrelevantly (I felt) "what kind of sex acts do you prefer?" By conference time, I had left ONE for a complex set of reasons, and the DOB came down angrily opposed to even thinking about claiming any "special rights." The "Constitutional Convention" was a disaster.

After leaving ONE, I spent six years at cab driving and two at junior college, finding time to consider some general questions.

People often asked, "Why did Gays take so long to organize?" I recalled responses I'd had earlier when asking others to join me in organizing. Most Gays felt homosexuality was a sickness, a sin or both. Either way, organizing seemed inappropriate. Some longed for the conditions of ancient Greece, but without time machines, had no idea how to get back to that blessed state. Very few saw our problems as political, i.e., amenable to organizing, and most felt that while other social problems might be helped, society will always hate us. A few saw a need for organizing, but were fearful and unlikely to agree on a specific clear course. It was virtually a miracle that people came together for the original Mattachine as well as for the original DOB who could agree on the need to do something, and on what to do. That agreement was rather short-lived in both cases.

Mid-1960s Groups

In the early sixties, old groups stagnated and new ones brought new goals and strategies. After TV game shows were rocked in 1960 by payola scandals, the long-time habit of cops taking pay-offs in Gay bars backfired. San Francisco cops and state Alcoholic Beverage Control agents busted each other for taking protection money. After nearly every Gay bar in town was closed and reopened, bar owners formed the Tavern Guild, a mutual defense league which launched a revolution beyond their hopes.

They began doing community-building, with appeals to patrons, social outings and voter registration. Then several S.F. Mattachine members, tired of their volunteer time being used for one officer's private business, walked out. In '64 a second walkout produced SIR, the Society for Individual Rights. SIR was creative and aggressive, with jargonless practical programs to cultivate genuine Gay community consciousness. They built special interest groups, registered voters, helped elect candidates to public office, staged dances, plays and picnics, worked with the Tavern Guild and helped launch the Council on Religion and the Homosexual. They studied community organizing tactics (how to reach the corridors of power and influence those people who can move things) and helped create a [North American] Conference of Homophile Organizations, or NACHO, aiming to coordinate U.S. and Canadian groups.

A *Hollywood Citizen-News* campaign to "drive Sex Deviates out of town" created a flurry of new Los Angeles activity. The campaign, conceived ironically as a newspaper sales gimmick by a Gay staffer, eventually put the daily paper out of business—our first successful boycott.

PRIDE was a 1966 Los Angeles attempt to imitate SIR—but aside from one fine street protest against police brutality, and launching the newsletter which became *The Advocate,* PRIDE was torn apart by contrary goals and tactics—S.D.S.-like militancy competing with respectabilism and toadying to cure-peddlers.

Vanguard was started on San Francisco streets in 1966 by hustlers, some as young as 11, using Anglo-Saxon language, radical slogans and psychedelic art like later Gay Liberation Fronts. Until then, all NACHO groups, on strong legal advice, had refused to deal with minors, but these angry minors demanded we deal with them. We did.

An east coast coalition led by Dr. Frank Kameny, Barbara Gittings and Jack Nichols, began picketing the White House and Independence Hall annually to demand equal justice. Nichols had called for rejecting the negative, Uncle Tom, attitudes many movement leaders had, and had approached Churchmen to deal with the subject. Dick Leitsch and Craig Rodwell held sip-ins at bars, protesting state regulations that bars can't serve known homosexuals. The DOB turned to general women's issues after 1970, objecting to the homophile movement's focus on men's arrests for public sex (though that was not exclusively a male problem). A few Gays began criticizing some homophile groups' ties to cure-peddling shrinks.

Dr. Franklin Kameny of Washington planted Mattachine clone groups from New England to the Niagara Frontier. He insisted that we had no time for social activities, education and social service: "Until we get the law off our backs, we can't take time to pick up the flotsam and jetsam of a rotten society." Yet he was often charitable. He, Nichols and Gittings implacably fought military and civil service discrimination cases. Gittings later worked to get better images of Gays and Lesbians in libraries.

Not all Gays approached military counseling the same way; some used it to protect the right of privacy, some to oppose the war in Vietnam. Some began telling draft boards that they were Gay, whether they were or not. In some cities, Gays started VD clinics to halt the disease's spread. Others felt that VD couldn't be a special problem for us since Gays-are-just-like-everyone-else, and besides, they argued, VD tests served only to give police our names. These arguments resurfaced at higher pitch early in the AIDS crisis 20 years later.

Craig Rodwell, founder of the pioneering Oscar Wilde Memorial Bookstore, Randy Wicker and Bob Martin of Columbia University's Student Homophile League (a first) became militant young Turks on the east coast, upsetting the prissy conservative leaders. In San Francisco, young radicals attacked SIR and took the Black Panthers as models—Constantine Verlandt, who'd come out while editing UC Berkeley's *Daily Californian,* ABC reporter Leo Lawrence, radicalized when cops gassed him at Chicago's 1968 Democratic Convention, Vanguard veterans and the unstable Rev. Ray Broshears.

NACHO's founders in Kansas City and in San Francisco in 1966 tried to adjudicate between two factions claiming to represent ONE. Insurgent Don Slater (who'd moved everything of value from ONE's office in May 1965) insisted that all homosex acts are perverted, but we have a right of privacy. (Even today, many see defending our Privacy as our only legitimate goal.) The lesbian DOB, outnumbered in a mostly male movement, wanted their several city chapters separately represented. ONE loyalists then claimed to have previously unmentioned chapters in four cities.

In NACHO, most Easterners aimed to bar groups which they felt might tarnish our image, and to enforce a common strategy, emphasizing court appeals, for all homophile groups. They refused to admit prominent hetero friends to our conferences, and barred metaphysically-or-sex-oriented groups lest they hurt our image. It was proposed that groups receive representation proportionate to their membership, but the Credentials committee couldn't validate membership claims, so each certified group got five votes, whether it had one member or 1,000. Kameny insisted that small, dedicated groups were more effective anyhow. NACHO sunk in the endless struggle on credentials.

Every hot-shot leader in NACHO tried to steam-roller the six successive conferences to legislate the entire movement into doing things his or her way. Easterners wanted every participant group to be bound by any resolution the conclave passed. Eastern leaders demanded focus on litigation to end discrimination. "I don't give a damn if people don't like me," Dr. Kameny shouted, "so long as they can't discriminate against me." Most westerners were pluralists and emphasized education, community-building, and building Gay political clout. One narrowly-passed resolution canceled another, until in 1970, Gay Liberation crazies recruited by Morris Kight and others from the streets trashed and destroyed NACHO. The debates between NACHO's East and West blocs paled in comparison with the post-Stonewall, hippie-counter culture-New Left radicalism. Here was **real** diversity!

Patrons led by bartender Lee Glaze, had responded to an August '68 raid at Wilmington, CA's Patch II bar by pelting police at the station with flowers. Three new-type groups, Metropolitan Community Church, SPREE and HELP resulted. MCC, founded by recently excommunicated Pentecostal minister Troy Perry, was presented as a church open to Gays (they didn't dare say Gay church). Perry catered to his parishioners' mixed denominations and took a lead in new militancy. Few leaders then were as skilled as he at building Gay pride and community feeling. MCC's growth from the first 12 who showed up in Troy Perry's Huntington Park apartment was phenomenal. Even Gay skeptics and heteros found it inspiring. But the prime goals of MCC, to get Gays to heaven or to improve our conditions on earth, came in for years of debate. Cleaning out the sexism and racism from traditional religious liturgy were later and more difficult goals.

HELP was for ten years a sort of legal insurance club mostly for the leather crowd, with added social and legislative goals. It tried to establish a Los Angles Tavern Guild and to improve legal service delivery to Gays.

We started SPREE to honor film-maker Pat Rocco, who'd given us our first glimpse of Gay romantic films. For ten years as a film, theater and social club, SPREE was well represented in most Los Angeles Gay demonstrations. Though often operating at the giggly-gay level, we worked to encourage others to make Gay films and plays, providing a warm social climate for (most older) sentimental Gay men and a few women.

San Diego priest Pat Nidorf organized Dignity for Catholic Gays in early '69. It got rolling in Los Angeles and spread, with hierarchy support in some cities. It worked to heal Gays damaged by clerical homophobia, and to alter the church's anti-Gay stance, making much progress among theologians and priests' and nuns' associations before the shocking 1986 letter from Nazi-trained Cardinal Ratzinger, exiling open Gays from church support. Dignity however had made a generation of Gay Catholics strong enough to stand up against that.

The Gay Liberation Phase

Soon after the June '69 police raid on New York's Stonewall Inn, where customers angrily fought back, precipitating a weekend of revolt, the Gay Liberation Front started our movement's wildest transformation, previewed by San Francisco's Vanguard and its Committee for Homosexual Freedom and by Minneapolis' FREE. Where we had mostly focused on middle class values, new liberationists had vastly different mindsets—different goals and tactics.

The respectability drive gave way to wild self-indulgence. From suit-and-tie, we went to every costume extreme. From asking authorities to define us more nicely, we said we'd define ourselves—and the rest of society as well. Our movement burst out of the three coastal cities that had largely dominated it. In the months after Stonewall, groups started in Billings, MT, Gainesville, FL and Lawrence, KS. The "zap" was invented, a strategy of invading straight offices and meetings to angrily confront homophobes.

Meetings were often exercises in anarchy. Where *Robert's Rules of Order* had intimidated those unskilled at using them, now any call for orderly procedures was labeled elitist. A few Blacks began making demands, often getting pained silence even from Gay Civil Rights Movement veterans—though virtually all GLF's took radical positions in support of minority rights. Some new activists hoped to use gay Lib to advance other causes, such as sectarian left parties—and some socio-political conservatives joined GLF but would have been more at home in the older groups.

There was a flurry of experimentation with new social forms, rejecting the theory of monogamy, rejecting private property, building rural and urban communes, hoping their new life styles would alter all of society. Many Gay liberationists intended the total restructuring of society, thinking that if we all dropped out, the Establishment would topple and we could live in freedom. Our conferences often passed resolutions banning the military-industrial complex, the educational system, profit-making businesses, the churches and monogamy. Those institutions failed to lie down obediently and die.

New issues came forward which seemed essential to some, quite bothersome to others: sexism, racism, ageism, looksism, but sexism the most. Part of this wasn't new (racism surely wasn't) but its ramifications and its jargonizing were. Radicallesbians and male Effeminists announced that oppression of women is the basis of all oppression; homophobia is merely an aspect of that; liberation for men requires surrendering male privilege, and supporting whatever radical women say they want. Being male becomes a cardinal sin. Many men resisted the idea that sexism is rooted in language, battling over words that had long been in usage. Can we retain the organic integrity of our language and still remove the biases built into it?

Recognizing Our Diversity

The post-Stonewall era made it more essential to recognize that our differences were **more than mere personality clashes,** or temporary **impediments to be brushed aside.** The often clashing goals of Lesbians and Gay men became intense, separating us for a while. Still, many Gays, male or female, just wanted society to let us alone; just wanted to have a good time or find that perfect lover; wanted to be just-like-our-neighbors; to feel that our hope lies in putting on a good front, a polished image; to feel that if people only knew how many of us there are in important places, our troubles would go away—this last gambit did **not** work for German Jews.

A few talked about taking arms against the establishment—ignoring the fact that the other side has the heavy artillery; and some wanted to destroy all old Gay groups and businesses.

There are vast strategic differences (and many fail to distinguish between goals and the strategies we use to achieve them): there are those who are convinced we must get non-Gays to front for us, while a few Gays play power brokers. This strategy is regularly subverted by the fact that so many influential Gays stay deep in the closet. Others are convinced that a Marxist revolution would end all our oppression—but China, Cuba—and Russia and Eastern Europe until 1989—threw doubt on that. Some see Gay liberation as solely a sexual freedom issue, as in John Rechy's angry novel, *Sexual Outlaw.* A few feminists in the era of the "Political Lesbian" began to regard almost all sexuality as a form of male rape.

Many felt sure that if we all dropped out, smoked pot, chanted OM and joined the new Left or Counter Culture (which were never quite the same thing), the so-called Establishment would collapse quickly and our troubles would end. Many hope to build a rainbow coalition of minorities—always half negated by rampant respectabilism and prejudice in our own and other minorities. Most of these conflicting goals have at least partial validity, but none of their partisans will give up their views easily, if at all. Certainly, short term goals are easier to agree on—and the larger the city, the more pronounced the conflicts on goals and tactics are. We unite to picket an outstanding homophobe, or to push a specific piece of legislation, but the unity seldom outlasts a week.

Finally, there are those special interests, minorities within our minority: boy lovers, Lesbian separatists, drags, leather and kinky sex groups, transsexuals, ethnic groups, tearoom cruisers, punks, dopers—some of whom scandalize or scare many mainline Gays and Lesbians. Some of these often get excluded from our parades or centers, but if we exclude them today, we discard large parts of history and of our integrity. We become guilty of the same discrimination we have so long suffered. At any rate, the goals of these special groups introduces even more angry diversity into the mix. Not all of us defend the right to have whip-and-chain parties, or to have sex with minors or in the bushes, especially unsafe sex. Not all of us agree on abortion, though I think most Gay men support women's right to self-determination.

The joyous parades and other events held in many cities each June drew us together and sharpened our differences at the same time. Some wanted celebrations of freedom or diversity, others angry protests, public relations shows or Mardi-Gras-like parties. Many wanted drag queens kept out of the parades, ignoring the drags who kicked things off at Stonewall and the charity fund-raising that drag-ball groups have done for years. Some objected to right or left wing political slogans, or to religious or anti-religious groups—or to AIDS protests "spoiling the fun."

By 1971, Gay service centers were operating in several cities, and a year later, we organized the first heavily staffed multi-service agency in Los Angeles, which, despite most of its founders' apocalyptic anti-establishment ideas, was soon funded by several levels of government. Much radical energy in the movement was felt by some to be drained from confronting the powers-that-be, to providing consciousness-raising, jobs, housing, substance-abuse guidance, counseling for prisoners, the handicapped, transsexuals, seniors and youth. Radical staffers in 1975 nearly destroyed L.A's Center, feeling that the "Band-Aid approach" was draining off revolutionary energy.

Gays were starting softball and bowling leagues, ski clubs and professional caucuses and women's music was beginning to bloom. Gay and feminist bookstores (separate from "adult" stores) began in many cities, also Gay and women's publishing companies, Gay theaters, special interest caucuses, hiking and running clubs, choruses and bands. Gay publications diversified, some becoming very fancy by earlier standards. Many complained that the movement had sold out to consumerism.

The Chimera of Unity

In our desperation to escape the bind of ignorance and bias, we often scream out, "Why can't gays get together?" We blame our disunity on some defect in gay character. This is naïve. Wishing doesn't make it so—it more often leads to sideswipes at those who disagree with what others of us take for granted.

Anita Bryant's 1977 Miami attack on us (calling a Dade County Human Rights ordinance a threat to the nation's children) was a thunderbolt. Self important Gay power brokers converged on Dade County to run the campaign, driving out everyone whose strategy differed. They had their way, and the defeat was tidal. They blamed everyone but themselves. When Anita promised to take her campaign on the road, allied with anti-feminist Phyllis Schlafly, the shock half emptied the nation's middle class closets. Towns too small to have had a gay group before staged outsize anti-Anita rallies. It was as big a turning point as Stonewall. Human Rights Coalitions cropped up in many cities and became arenas for every sort of Gay extremist and power-grabber. We ripped each other apart.

In crises, we can often come up with a patchwork unity for fighting homophobic attacks or dealing with AIDS. Yet we rarely see eye-to-eye, and California's 1978 Briggs campaign showed surprising virtue in that. Because attempts failed to organize one big committee in each part of the state to carry out the "best" strategy, we won an election we'd probably otherwise have lost.

While the biggies raised the most money, paid one another lavish salaries and bought a few expensive TV spots, Gay radicals reached labor unions and ethnic minorities. Gay Catholics and other religious groups reached local hierarchy, which promised benevolent neutrality, a gain over other cities. By our usual practice, all would have been organized from Los Angeles and San Francisco, with most of the state overlooked. Instead, anti-Briggs groups started in many virgin areas. Each group reached its own constituency, swinging many voters which a unified committee would have ignored. The prime virtue of our diversity is that it gives us a chance to build bridges to **every** sector of the vastly diversified non-Gay community we come from. The Briggs fight taught us that, but the lesson was forgotten in later campaigns, which we lost.

Ex-stockbroker turned hippie, Harvey Milk, had come to San Francisco and run for office three times, building a half wacky grass roots organization, and bucking the Gay establishment led by Jim Foster and *Advocate* publisher David Goodstein. In 1978 Milk was elected Supervisor and became a national symbol. After he'd worked against the Briggs initiative, and called for a national Gay March on Washington, Milk and pro-Gay Mayor George Moscone were assassinated by ex-Supervisor and ex-cop Dan White.

The White verdict set off a large Gay riot outside San Francisco city hall. The massive 1979 March on Washington was partly a memorial for Harvey, but many older leaders had opposed that march, and efforts to follow it with a grass roots National Organization of Lesbians and Gays bogged down over the same credentials questions that had buried NACHO.

New national organizations emphasizing professionalism sidestepped the question of being representative, avoiding extreme disagreements by setting up self-perpetuating boards which undertook to speak for the entire Gay community in lobbying and public relations. They aim to do for us what they feel needs to be done, and the rest of us just have to send in the bucks.

In 1979, Harry Hay, Don Kilhefner, Mitch Walker and others launched the Radical Faerie movement (actually, it was already a few years old), exploring the spiritual dimensions of being Gay.

Faerie gatherings, in rustic settings, became excited exercises in new consciousness, a mix of guerrilla theater, Hindu mysticism, mud baths and splendiferous costumed dancing in the moonlight, making magic to restore childhood fantasies and the mystic brotherhood of tribal shamen, in an anti-masculine context. Could we recapture our primitive birthright and make it meaningful, or vital, for today's world? The diverse women's spirituality movement was far ahead of them, though both male and female seekers after spirituality were at times quite weird.

To Gay activists shaped by the sixties, it seems that our community has abandoned the fight and sold out for establishment norms, for buttering up elected officials, for rampant consumerism and respectability, for using the movement as a pool in which those on the make can fish for big salaries. Perhaps. But being on the winning team is often a temporary thing. Recent setbacks in the Democratic Party, where we had seemed to have it made, are a hint of that.

The rise of AIDS after 1981, agonizingly killing thousands of our brothers and some sisters, radically altered the styles and goals of our movement. Some felt that it made all the other issues irrelevant, at least for the duration.

Wishful thinking aside, there is almost no single course that will get all Gays and Lesbians marching in unison **for long**—though the '87 and '93 Marches on Washington were incredible highs—for almost a week each. Even on AIDS, some refuse to believe that sex contact has any part in spreading the disease, or that we should limit our sexual behavior in order to slow the plague. A few still think the whole AIDS crisis is "a media hype." And AIDS organizations differ on whether to focus on lambasting inadequate government response and pharmaceutical prices, on research, or on helping people with AIDS. They do focus on raising astronomical funds and paying extravagant salaries to executives. I think we need closer examination of alternate cause and treatment theories—even if only to lay them to rest. With our lives at stake, we **must** ask the unaskable questions. Many Lesbians feel, understandably, that too little attention is paid to health problems that kill women.

And there's intense disagreement as to whether the tactics of ACT-UP groups help or hurt our overall cause—though ACT-UP's "bad manners" have undeniably gotten results. Here especially, we need to discuss our disagreements, to try to iron them out.

I don't think politics is our natural game, and I'd gladly let the heteros have it all back—**except** as a Minority, we always **stand on the brink of holocaust.** Many Gays think that, except for AIDS, we've already won the brass ring, and never have to fight anymore. Not true. While Gay rights ordinances have passed in many unexpected places, while an increasing number of Gays and Lesbians have won public office in many areas, while we've helped elect many friendly officials, many victories still elude us, and none of our victories are written in stone. Any or all of our gains could be erased overnight. So we always will have to do the political thing, if only to protect our tails. I'd **rather** see us devoting full time to exploring our spirits and building our community—but we must play the straight world's game also.

Finding Our Common Core

We needn't leave this discussion with the assertion of our total diversity. We MUST give diversity proper attention, but after doing so, we can hope to understand better the things that draw us together, the threads of commonality in our experience and to bridge some of our differences. Commonality is not the same thing as homogeneity or unity. It won't press all of us into one mold, or into the same political campaign, or get us to agree on which are the right tactical moves for today. It won't erase all of our disagreements, or the anger that goes with them. But it should draw us into one river, even if it has diverse streams and eddies.

Many think we have only our sexuality in common. Others say we are tied together only by the persecution we suffer. I suspect we are hung up on these ideas because of how our own society defines the difference. Our commonalities lie deeper, but I can't define them. I can only give suggestions.

Growing up often with a feeling of being outsiders is an important element. Gays aren't the only outsiders in this society, but our estrangement goes deep and starts very early, often in our own family. From infancy on we struggle with social expectations about gender. This sets up in each of us **various** lines of accommodation, resistance, resentment or rebellion, shaping our characters by how much we resist, go along with, or deny. Our first goal was self-understanding, trying to figure out why and exactly how we differed from what our parents, peers and teachers expected, seeking others of our kind, and trying to understand what we shared with them.

This gives us some potential advantages, though many Gays fail to develop that potential: an ability for empathy with others; an ability for nonlinear thinking; a tendency to relate to others on an "I-Thou basis," rather than treating others as objects; and an ability to see around corners erected by the straight world to bridge all the differences in the world.

The first time I was Gay-baited in print, I was called "the man with the grasshopper mind," because I didn't stick to "A-leads-to-B-leads-to-C" thinking. I finally gave up apologizing for not having a straight mind, locked into the belief that everything has a beginning, turning point, and an end, that every effect has a single cause. I like to think we have a potential for holistic thinking, though our hetero education tries to beat it out of us.

Like Near Eastern Gnostics just before and after Christ, who believed that some people were born with a unique Spark which was a tiny fragment from the God of Light, who'd been shattered in a war with the god of this material world, and who worked to reunite each of its scattered Sparks into a Great Light, I feel that Gay love tends toward expansiveness, inclusiveness, and that our Gay love can eventually bind us together, and bridge all of the diversities in our own community and in the whole world.

Recap

Those who feel in their gut that we all want the same thing won't be satisfied. They'll still say we all want only to be able to live without prejudice, oppression or undue restriction.

Let me recapitulate:

Some feel that society will accept us if we behave like straights, if we convince them that we are just like them. Some want only to organize to fight discrimination or to win gay political clout.

Others feel we must educate the public about the varieties of affectional expression or sexual practice, so that prejudice will vanish and we'll be free to behave as our natures dictate. This group seeks more freedom than the first would care for. Some seek the right to have any kind of sex at any time or place with as many partners as we wish.

Others like Harry Hay feel we must earn social acceptance and respect by convincing society that we provide needed services which heteros can't provide. I don't feel we can permit ourselves to be dependent solely on the goodwill of non-Gays. Radical Faeries aim to cast off hetero conformity, and reawaken the shamanistic spirits that they feel are central to our nature; to revive the talents of witches and such, so we can heal the wounds of hetero society.

Other Gays and feminists believe our society is founded on oppression, and cannot help but oppress us until society itself is turned upside down. Restructuring goals differ endlessly, some seeking only a more peaceful and equitable society, others seeking to end capitalism, religion, racism, inequality, monogamy, gender roles and much else that distinguishes our society now.

Others feel we can't be free unless we get right with God. For some, that involves giving up our sexuality—or at least giving up non-monogamous sex.

Some of you may dismiss most of these differences of opinion as nonsense, but the differences won't go away easily, if at all. If we hope to work on **some** things together, we must try to understand these radically differing goals, and be aware that each goal dictates a unique line of strategies and tactics. So don't be surprised the next time another Gay or Lesbian starts saying or doing something which you are convinced will defeat "our goal." Take our diversity as a rich treasure and try to find ways to work with it. It ain't easy. **Lord, it sure ain't easy!**

June 29, 1997

Press Conference Remarks at New York Gay Pride March

Barbara Gittings

These remarks were made by Gittings at a press conference called on June 29 in New York City as part of the 1997 Gay Pride celebration.

Just five days from now, on July Fourth, we celebrate the Declaration of Independence, which proclaims the right to "life, liberty and the pursuit of happiness." And it doesn't say that it's for heterosexuals only. For too long our lives have been hidden, our liberty has been restricted, our pursuit of happiness has been tangled up in bigotries and barriers.

We want relief from the pain of wearing the mask. We want to be judged as individuals, on our merits. We want to be able to live and love and work and play, openly and safely, as ourselves.

Becoming visible is the key to our struggle for fair treatment and equal rights. We are everywhere, we are already part of every community—but we have to keep reminding others by our presence.

Today's march is one kind of presence. I'm thrilled to be part of this huge demonstration of gay pride and gay love, especially because this was unthinkable when I began working for gay rights almost forty years ago. Being here today, I'm convinced it won't take another forty years for us to have full equality. And we have a message for those who cannot afford to be visible on this march: Hang in there, folks, because those of us who are out are oiling those closet door hinges just as fast as we can!

July 8, 1997

Gay and Lesbian Pride Celebration 1997

Barney Frank

This address was given on the floor of the House of Representatives by Representative Frank of Massachusetts, an openly gay member of Congress, and entered into the *Congressional Record* for July 8, 1997.

Mr. Speaker, during the month of June, gay and lesbian people throughout this country celebrated our presence in this country. That is a tradition that has now gone on for more than 20 years, but this year there was one difference. As Herb and I prepared to go to New York to participate in the New York celebration, I carried with me a statement from the President of the United States in which he welcomed the gay lesbian pride celebrations and reaffirmed his commitment, the President's commitment, to fighting anti-gay and lesbian prejudice.

Bill Clinton is the first President in our history to confront this prejudice. Unfortunately, by the norms of American political discourse, you generally today get criticized by people when they are unhappy and ignored when you have done something that they should be applauding.

President Clinton is entitled to a good deal of praise for his willingness to confront one of the enduring prejudices that has blighted our ability as a nation to fully realize our constitutional ideals. I believe, Mr. Speaker, given the historic nature of this proclamation which I was pleased to get a copy of from Richard Socarides, a very able aid at the White House who worked on these issues, I think it is appropriate that the President's statement on Gay and Lesbian Pride Celebration be shared here in this Chamber. So I will now, with unanimous consent, proceed to read the President's celebration:

> Warm greetings to all those participating in the 1997 Gay and Lesbian Pride Celebration.
>
> Throughout America's history, we have overcome tremendous challenges by drawing strength from our great diversity. We must never believe that our diversity is a weakness. The talents, contribu-

tions and good will of people from so many different backgrounds have enriched our national life and have enabled us to fulfill our common hopes and dreams. As we stand at the dawn of a new century, we must all rededicate ourselves to reaching the vital goals of acceptance and inclusion. America's continued success will depend on our ability to understand, appreciate, and care for one another.

We're not there yet, and that is why our efforts to end discrimination against lesbians and gays are so important. Like each of you, I remain dedicated to ending discrimination and preserving the civil rights of every citizen in our society. We have begun to wage an all-out campaign against hate crimes in America, crimes that are often viciously directed at gay men and lesbians. I have also endorsed and fought for civil rights legislation that would protect gay and lesbian Americans from discrimination. The Employment Nondiscrimination Act now being considered in Congress would put an end to discrimination against gay men and lesbians in the workplace, discrimination that is currently legal in 39 states. These efforts reflect our belief in the right of every American to be judged on his or her merits and ability, and to be allowed to contribute to society without facing discrimination on the basis of sexual orientation. And they reflect our ongoing fight against bigotry and intolerance in our country and in our hearts.

My Administration's record of inclusiveness is a strong one, but it is a record to build on. I am proud of the many openly gay men and lesbians who serve with distinction in my Administration, and their impact will continue to be significant in the years ahead. I pledge to you that I will continue striving to foster compassion and understanding, working not simply to tolerate our differences, but to celebrate them.

Best wishes for a memorable celebration. Bill Clinton.

Mr. Speaker, I congratulate the President on his willingness to speak out. It is consonant with the many actions he has taken in a number of areas to ban discrimination and to fight for the right of all Americans, as he said, to be judged on their individual merits, without being held back by some irrational prejudice.

November 16, 1997

The Emerging Sex Panic Targeting Gay Men

Eric Rofes

These remarks were given by veteran activist and writer Eric Rofes at the National Gay and Lesbian Task Force's Creating Change Conference in San Diego, California, in November 1997.

Historian Allan Berube has defined a sex panic as a "moral crusade that leads to crackdowns on sexual outsiders." It is distinct from ongoing harassment and vilification of the sexual fringe. It requires the following components: ideology, the machinery and the power to transform ideology into action, and scapegoated populations, sites, and sexual practices.

During a sex panic, a wide array of free-floating cultural fears are mapped onto specific populations who are then ostracized, victimized, and punished. As Gayle Rubin has observed, historically we have seen that when moral panics are over, countless individuals and groups have suffered greatly and the original triggering social problems have not been remedied.

Gay men have no corner on the market on sex panics. In recent years, we have seen sexual terrors marshaled to create a stampede mentality to trample upon many groups including prostitutes and other sex workers, African-American men, welfare mothers, sex offenders as a class, and men who engage in consensual sex with male teenagers.

Are We Confronting a Sex Panic Today?

Currently debate rages among sectors of gay male communities about whether contemporary spates of police entrapments, closures of commercial sex establishments, encroachments on public sex areas, and vilification of specific gay male subcultures constitute a sex panic. It is important to distinguish between ongoing waves of harassment and victimization and a full-scale sex panic because, while both are destructive of lives and communities, a sex panic alone is characterized by a sustained period of intensified persecution of sexual minorities involving punitive state action, public disgrace, and a powerful cultural dynamic of scapegoating, shaming, and silencing of alternative viewpoints. While communists were harassed and persecuted in this nation during the 1940s, it took the coalescing of a variety of cultural factors in the late 1940s and early 1950s to create the moral panic we have come to know as "The McCarthy Period."

I believe we may be witnessing the early stages of an emerging sex panic focused on sexually-active gay men who do not organize their sex and relationships following heteronormative models. It is at different stages in different locations. For example, I believe this sex panic has emerged in New York City with a sustained, intensified period of policing, harassment, and closure of many gay sex spaces and an accompanying discourse in the media about the need to halt continuing gay male HIV infections. In places like Los Angeles, Miami, Washington, D.C., Austin, and Providence, it is clearly at an earlier stage. Sex panic looks different in urban, small city, and rural areas and will have different characteristics, contexts and trajectories.

What we are witnessing in 1997 are several powerful social shifts which could easily and swiftly fall into place, causing a full-scale sex panic to break out nationwide at any time. This is the way terror and scapegoating operate in a postmodern culture. At least four factors are contributing to a mounting sex panic:

The ascendancy and entrenchment of the Far Right and their development, testing, and successful utilization of sex as a wedge issue which speedily divides liberals and Leftists, their primary opponents.

The redistribution and intense concentration of wealth creating vast economic disparities and making the urban centers of our nation sites of contentious class-based battles over massive corporate land-grabs.

A shift in public awareness from the belief that gay men had stopped transmitting HIV to the realization that gay men continue to become infected with HIV at significant levels. This is accompanied by many gay men and lesbians' feelings of embarassment, shame, and outrage.

The relative success of gay rights efforts where certain victories are offered predicated on the sacrifice of certain sectors of our communities or the squelching of certain social, cultural, or sexual processes which seem different from heterosexual social norms.

Why Are the Current Debates Flaring into Sexual Civil Wars?

The emerging sex panic appears to be shaping up as characterized by an ideology which believes gay men's sex is not only sinful and predatory, but is responsible for an escalating AIDS epidemic. We are seeing the machinery and the power to transform ideology into action emerging in media frenzies over gay men's sex, the conceptualization of current health problems as public health emergencies, the use of exceptional measures to restrict sex spaces by public officials, and extreme actions by police officers and other representatives of state power to curtail the sexual activity and drug use of gay men. Media accounts are increasingly scapegoating specific populations—at the moment, circuit boys are the scapegoat-of-choice-sites such as bathhouses, sex clubs, and circuit parties, and activities such as "barebacking." It is also characterized by the active involvement and, in some cases, instigation and leadership of gay and lesbian journalists, political leaders, public officials, HIV prevention workers, and other public officials.

This is precisely what makes the current debates problematic and why many have such powerful feelings of rage and betrayal.

20 years ago we heard Anita Bryant and Paul Cameron insisting gay male sex is diseased and suicidal and these days we hear gay men saying the exact same thing.

20 years ago we fought heterosexuals in the mainstream media who invaded our sex spaces and wrote lurid, uninformed accounts of our sex cultures. These days it's gay men working in the mainstream media who invade the spaces and write the same lurid stories.

20 years ago it was heterosexual public officials who ordered crackdowns on gay bars, mass entrapment at rest stops, and the intense regulation, policing, and closure of sex clubs. These days it could be queer public officials ordering such actions.

Those of us defending gay male sex cultures are not indifferent to HIV prevention efforts. Many of us are leaders in both areas. We know that effective prevention is built on sexual empowerment and believe that decades of public health research show that tactics of guilt, fear and repression exacerbate public health crises rather than deter them. It is precisely because many people have become frustrated with HIV prevention and feel at a loss to chart new directions for our work, that the time is ripe for an escalation for coercive measures to stop gay men's sex.

Those of us standing up for sexual freedom are neither lost in a romanticized version of the golden age of the 1970s nor dick-hungry men who are selfishly seeking more power and more privilege. We have been condescendingly characterized as immature children who haven't grown up and need to get with the times, put our pricks back in our pants, and apply our energies to the real challenges facing our communities, like gays-in-the-military or gay marriage. Yet we believe that even a cursory look at the histories of our movement will show that sexual liberation has been inextricably bound together with gay liberation, the women's movement, and the emancipation of youth. Among the most effective ways of oppressing a people is through the colonization of their bodies, the stigmatizing of their desires, and the repression of their erotic energies. We believe continuing work on sexual liberation is crucial to social justice efforts.

Those of us taking action to monitor, de-track, and resist the emerging sex panic find ourselves increasingly at odds with mainstream gay efforts to present a sanitized vision of our people which has replaced butch/femme dykes with Heather and her two mommies and kinky gay men with domestic partner wedding cakes. Can we not advocate for a pluralistic queer culture where we affirm everyone's right to self-determination in the ways they organize their sexual relations and construct their kinship patterns?

How Can We Prevent a Full Scale Moral Panic over Gay Men's Sex?

People who want to stave off the emerging moral panic should go home and organize local activist groups like queers of all genders have done in New York and San Francisco. I hope you write letters and hold the media and public officials accountable for their actions and refuse to renounce our movement's historic linkage with sexual liberation. And I encourage you to continue our efforts at HIV prevention but refuse to support a panic-based response to continuing gay male seroconversions or feel that current infections diminish our communities' contributions to the fight against AIDS of the past 15 years.

For those of you who are ambivalent about such organizing, and for mainstream gay groups who are scared to touch these issues with a ten foot pole, let me say one thing: When full moral panics flare history has shown, in Lillian Hellman's words, it's "scoundrel time" and there are limited roles from which social actors can choose. There are the scoundrels who blow the whistle, point the finger, name the names. There are the resistors who take the risk, go out on the limb, take the fall, and get trampled in the mindless outraged stampede. And there are the vast masses who find themselves locked in silence by confusion, misgivings, self-protection, ambivalence, and fear. When the panic is over and attention has shifted to other issues, when we all shake our heads and say "How did we ever let it get to that stage?" these people are complicit in the destruction. There is no neutral here.

Please consider three final points.

Regardless of your confusion or misgivings stand up firmly against any efforts which mobilize arms of the state to restrict the right of sexual and reproductive self-determination. You don't like sex clubs, don't go to sex clubs. But do not ask your local authorities to shut them down. You don't like sex areas in parks, don't go to sex areas in parks, but don't invite police to bust the men who enjoy such activities.

Refuse to cast off any section of our community in order to gain privileges and social acceptance. Demand a continuing commitment to a pluralistic vision of community.

Try to understand the historic role sex cultures have played in the formation of queer identities and communities and resist seeing them simply as an unfortunate by-product of antigay oppression. Are our sex cultures evidence of our stigmatization, abuse, and reprobation? Or, to borrow James Baldwin's language about a parallel matter, can they be understood as "cultural patterns coming into existence by means of brutal necessity" and can they be seen as strategies for survival?

Perhaps the real trouble with gay men's sex cultures, in a time when many in our communities are replicating heterosexual patterns of social organization, is that they alone give testimony to the fact that gay men as a class have not completely assimilated.

January 28, 1998

Congregation Beth Simchat Torah

Eliot L. Engel

This address was given on the floor of the House of Representatives by Representative Engel of New York and entered into the *Congressional Record* for January 28, 1998.

Mr. Speaker, Congregation Beth Simchat Torah is New York City's only, and the world's largest, gay and lesbian synagogue, and on February 7 is celebrating its 25th anniversary.

This remarkable congregation started with barely enough for a minyan (ten people) in a borrowed room at a neighborhood Episcopal Church. The Kiddush cup, some candles and a challah used in the ceremony were carried to the services in a shopping bag.

The congregation grew by word of mouth and small ads in the local weekly newspaper. Slowly, at first, the number of congregants grew so that it was large enough to have to move to another church in the neighborhood on the High Holy Days. By 1975 it was clear that they needed still more space so a large loft was rented and the congregation moved into it that year. The following year it got its first Torah on "permanent loan" from a Bronx congregation. In 1977 Congregation Beth Simchat Torah hosted the Second International Conference on Lesbian and Gay Jews and that year a second Torah was acquired.

Talmud and Hebrew classes were expanded and over the next few years the High Holy Day crowds approached 1,000. By 1992 Rabbi Sharon Kleinbaum was hired and more than 2,200 people attended Yom Kippur services.

This dynamic congregation has served its community with distinction. With Rabbi Kleinbaum, it looks forward to greater community involvement, future growth and a continuance of its traditional/creative liturgy.

March 5, 1998

Why a Millennium March on Washington?

Troy Perry

This is the text of the statement issued by Reverend Perry, founder and moderator of the Universal Fellowship of Metropolitan Community Churches. UFMCC and the Human Rights Campaign were the two organizations which first proposed the idea of the Millennium March on Washington, subsequently held in April 2000. This statement was issued to clarify the reasons UFMCC believed in the worth of such an event.

I am excited by the strong grassroots support the proposed Millennium March on Washington is receiving, and pleased with the growing number of local, regional and national organizations which are endorsing the "first human rights march of the new millennium."

I warmly welcome the growing number of organizational endorsers, and I also welcome the healthy debate as some of our national gay, lesbian, bisexual and transgendered organizations continue to explore their options for participation in this national human rights event.

As a human rights activist with 30 years of experience in the gay, lesbian, bisexual and transgendered communities, I believe the Millennium March on Washington for Equality in April of 2000 is a vital step in consolidating our gains, mobilizing our community, and taking the next step toward justice in the new millennium.

Why do I believe this? Why a Millennium March?

It's already been too long. Seven years will have passed since the last March on Washington. I believe in the value of demonstrating to our nation the strength of our numbers and the passion of our commitment to justice. If we have learned any lesson, it is how quickly and easily our elected officials forget. It's time to remind our government and our nation that millions of her citizens are still denied equality.

The new millennium presents a strategic opportunity. The dawn of a new millennium, by its very nature, heightens society's sensitivity. Commentators, pundits, the press and society at large will be looking for messages and trends for the new millennium. We have an opportunity at this strategic time to move our message to the forefront.

The year 2000 is a presidential election year. In our society, much of our progress is contingent upon getting the ear, and then the support, of our elected officials. The presence of one million gay, lesbian, bisexual and transgendered persons is designed to make our voice heard—by Democrat, Republican, reform and other political party candidates. In addition to the Millennium March itself, one million gay, lesbian, bisexual and transgendered Americans will have an opportunity to walk the halls of Congress, to meet with their Congresspersons and Senators and to make a compelling and personal case for equality for all citizens.

It will birth a new generation of activists. Each of our previous marches has served to birth new activists. In fact, as with many g/l/b/t organizations, there are several members of my own staff whose first taste of activism came through the previous Marches on Washington. With two years of lead time, we have an opportunity to become intentional about using this Millennium March to inspire and birth new activists who will continue to work toward the dream of equality for all our citizens.

It will energize our movement. I am convinced that this March, along with the 1999 50 State Initiative, will energize the g/l/b/t/ rights movement, strengthen all of our organizations, and present untold opportunities for gay human rights, justice and spiritual organizations to grow in terms of members, influence, accomplishments and media access.

The march's theme is focused, simple and understandable. Our society still hasn't got the message. We need look no further than the recent repeal of the equal rights law in Maine to know that the message of simple equality has been neither heard nor embraced. The theme of this Millennium March is simple—and designed to build allies. To accomplish this goal of equal human and civil rights, it is imperative that we strategically build allies and support throughout society. One million gay, lesbian, bisexual and transgendered persons have an opportunity to call upon our nation and its citizens to live out our nation' s creed of "liberty and justice for all." Every element of this march will be focused on the call for equality, and every sub-theme will directly relate to the march's purpose.

For 30 years, I have lent my voice and strength to the work of building a just and equitable society for all of our citizens. Three decades of this work have taught me two lessons:

We must use every means at our disposal to get our message out and
We must not rest until our nation's highest ideals have transcended promise and become reality for all our citizens.

Through the Millennium March, I will stand with one million of my brothers and sisters, and each of us will proclaim:

This is our country, too.
This is our flag!
This is our Constitution!
This is our military!
This is our nation's promise!
This is our contribution to America!
This is our spirituality!
This is our love!
This is our freedom!
This is our life!
This is our dream!

Until that day, I will continue to join hands with my gay, lesbian, bisexual and transgendered brothers and sisters—and with our enlightened allies—to raise my voice . . . to call for justice . . . to tirelessly work for equality and yes, to march on our nation's capital—to use every means at our disposal until we, too, are "free at last." That's why I passionately believe in the Millennium March on Washington for Equality.

May 22, 1998

A Celebration of Jim Kepner's Life

Franklin E. Kameny

Given at an event titled "A Celebration of Jim Kepner's Life and the Past 50 Years of the Gay and Lesbian Rights Movement," held at the Samuel Goldwyn Theater of the Academy of Motion Picture Arts and Sciences in Beverly Hills, California, by Dr. Kameny, the founder of the Mattachine Society of Washington, DC, on May 22, 1998. Kepner died on November 14, 1997.

While it is hardly my wont to resort to anything religious under any circumstances, it is not inappropriate to do so just this once. In the New Testament, one of the reasons given for setting out the history narrated there was the passing from the scene of the first-hand witnesses to the events which had occurred.

That is singularly relevant to this truly remarkable gathering of the slowly dwindling numbers of those of us who remain from the creation of one of the most uniquely successful efforts at profound social change which has ever occurred—at least in recent generations.

And successful it has been! Beyond the wildest dreams of those of us who were there three, four and five decades ago—and more. Not only beyond our wildest dreams, but beyond even the ability to dream those dreams back then. We started with nothing, and look what we have wrought!

Who would have imagined upwards of a million gay people marching in Washington and filling the Mall? Who would have imagined not merely the fading of anti-gay discrimination, but laws affirmatively prohibiting such discrimination? Who would have imagined personal appearances by the President and Vice-President of the United States at major gay events, and congratulatory statements by the President supportive of gay pride festivals? In fact, who then would have imagined gay pride, much less public celebrations of it? In an era when the government was our enemy and was out to get us, who would have imagined organizations of gay federal employees supported by government agencies, departments and departmental Secretaries—even the FBI? And who would have imagined that THE front-burner social issue of the day, taken seriously by friend and foe alike, would be same-sex marriage?

That listing was just a haphazardly-assembled illustrative sampling of the kind of progress which we have made over the past half-century—progress for which much of the credit must go to the people who are here this evening, and those who have left us.

Of course we haven't won all the battles yet. We still have the military. One third of the states still have anti-sodomy laws—but then they all did until 1962. We haven't actually achieved same-sex marriage yet, but who would even have imagined domestic partnership laws and policies back then? There are still very deep reservoirs not merely of prejudice, but of overt virulent hatred. There are organized powerful structures of what I call "the nutty fundamentalists," who have declared war on us, and are waging it vigorously. They didn't have their act together even twenty years ago.

But as even the nutty fundamentalists realize, they are losing their war. The tide is with us. We are winning because without a doubt, we are right and they are wrong. We are moral and they are immoral. We are American and they are un-American and anti-American. All of us have always known that, of course. It has been our driving motivation. Our success has been in significantly persuading the American public that that is so. And there we have pulled off a coup of the most incredible proportions, for which all of us can rightly congratulate ourselves.

Sadly, as we all know, one of the old stalwarts, one of the indispensable foot soldiers, is no longer with us. Jim Kepner had a longer history in this effort than almost anyone here, if not everyone here. While I did not get to know him as well as I might have—we were perpetually 3,000 miles apart and operated in parallel but somewhat different universes—we were always on friendly terms. I last saw him unexpectedly in 1993 in Washington, when by sheer chance, we marched near each other. Fortunately, he lived long enough to have seen and have helped to chronicle and preserve the record of the successes which he helped so much to achieve.

While all the battles are far from won, there is one major difference between the current situation, and that which faced us in past decades. We were then almost alone—a small handful of people, without troops and without allies. Nowadays, the troops are there in vast numbers, and allies are emerging from every quarter up to and including the very highest levels of government.

In 1968, I coined the slogan "Gay is Good." We have always known that; acceptance of it represents the indispensable bottom-line rationale for everything that we have done over the past half-century. We here have made it much better. And we pass the torch to those who will make it perfect. I am confident they will. And soon.

May 22, 1998

Remembering Jim Kepner

Barbara Gittings

This is the speech made by Barbara Gittings on May 22, 1998, in the Samuel Goldwyn Theater of the Academy of Motion Picture Arts and Sciences at the memorial celebration of the life of veteran gay activist, historian, and archivist Jim Kepner.

My life partner Kay Lahusen and I were simply astonished when we first met Jim Kepner in 1963 at his home in Los Angeles. We saw books, *books,* BOOKS, and files, *files,* FILES, from floor to ceiling!

Jim and I clicked immediately. I too was a gay book buff, because in 1950 when I needed to learn about myself and what it meant to be gay, there was no one I could ask, so I instinctively turned to books.

Jim's library impressed us, but so did his dedication to activism, which we shared, and his passion for chronicling our movement.

The author George Eliot in her novel *Middlemarch* said, "The growing good of the world is partly dependent on unhistoric acts." I think of Jim's great legacy as those unhistoric acts, in the sense that his work wasn't headlined in the mainstream press, seldom even in gay/lesbian chronicles.

Jim was a sweet and low-key person who kept on plugging at his dream, never abandoning it, always tending it. The notion of burn-out wasn't in his cosmos. And even when his health faltered, Jim didn't.

Jim put his time and energy and what little money he had into creating a better life for all of us, and he took the change he created as its own reward.

To Kay and me, Jim seemed self-effacing in many ways. In 1983, the gay group in the American Library Association put on a program at the annual librarians' conference called "Why Keep All Those Posters, Buttons and Papers?" Jim Kepner was one of our speakers.

I needed publicity photos of the flier to promote the event. Jim didn't have a publicity photo. The picture he sent was a tiny snapshot and in the picture Jim is, appropriately, submerged in papers.

The last time I saw Jim wasn't a gay movement event. I was visiting in Los Angeles, and Jim took me to the Huntington Library and Botanical Gardens. Naturally we ooohed and aaahed over the exotic rare books and manuscripts, but Jim also proved an enthusiastic guide to the specialty gardens around the library. A man of many interests and wide knowledge.

What a legacy Jim has given us—worth having a hell of a celebration for! So here we are tonight, ancient activists and some newer ones, for a grand hurrah.

Jim, we love you, we honor you.

October 23, 1998

Introduction to the Documentary *Out of the Past*

Barbara Gittings

This address was given by veteran activist Gittings in Chicago, Illinois, at a screening of the documentary film *Out of the Past* sponsored by GLSEN, the Gay Lesbian Straight Education Network.

This film is what I should have had in Social Studies in high school.

As a teenager in the late 1940s, I had to struggle all alone to learn about myself and what it means to be gay. Homosexuals then were completely invisible: even the word "homosexual" was still in the closet. Back then, most homosexuals were isolated for years until we managed to find others and eventually build up a circle of friends. And it was hard to feel right about yourself when you had no others like yourself to look to, not even at the distance of history books.

So, opening up our history has been a favorite part of my 40 years of work in the gay rights movement.

For example, in the early 1960s my partner Kay and I had the privilege of editing *The Ladder,* the first lesbian magazine with a national circulation. We published many articles about lesbians and maybe-lesbians throughout history.

In the 1970s when we worked with the gay group in the American Library Association, we searched for gay history materials to include in our gay reading lists. We also drew attention to gay and lesbian poets and artists. For example, at the ALA's conference in 1972 in Chicago, our gay group had a program of readings from Sappho, Walt Whitman, Gertrude Stein, and Constantin Cavafy, to remind our listeners that these writers whose works we value on our library shelves had this homosexual dimension to their lives and their art.

Also in the 1970s, I was on a committee trying to find a major library willing to collect and preserve the unique materials being produced by our civil rights movement. This idea was ahead of its time. Of the 13 university and research libraries we contacted with our proposal, all of them with track records for having collections on minority and social change issues, only one even bothered to respond—and that response was a rejection.

The world has moved ahead since then. Still, two decades later, Kelli Peterson, the high school student whose battle against prejudice in Utah is the framework for this documentary, tells us she started the Gay-Straight Alliance at her school "to end the misery and isolation of being gay in high school." Unlike me in the 1940s, Kelli in the 1990s was in fact hearing some messages about homosexuality, but they were very negative.

Fortunately, help was on the way in the form of GLSEN, the Gay Lesbian Straight Education Network. Kevin Jennings, founder and executive director of GLSEN, had reviewed high school curricula to see what, if anything, was being taught about us. He came up with a Big Blank. So he wrote a book called *Becoming Visible: A Reader in Gay and Lesbian History for High School and College,* and he prepared a gay history slide show and took it around to schools. The huge demand for this exciting fresh material sparked the making of the film we're about to see.

The section of the film on me is called Becoming Visible. Now you might think that because I've been visible all my 40 years in the gay rights movement, that's not an issue for me. Yes, I'm out—but I'm still dealing with the consequences. For instance, I have an elderly aunt who lives in a retirement community near me in Wilmington, Delaware. She is 102. She grew up in a time when "One knew there were people like that, but one never talked about it." She does not like it that I'm so public. She understands that living a hidden life has a cost and is dishonest, but she still wants us to stay hidden because to her, being open amounts to being public about your private sex life. Every time I'm due to appear in public such that I'm likely to be seen on TV, I have to tell her so she won't be surprised if a friend calls to comment. But she always gets upset about it. And at age 102, an upset could be serious. Still, she loves me and I love her, and we muddle through the distress every time.

How I deal with my aunt's cultural bias is my responsibility. But we all have a responsibility toward students in school, both gay and non-gay, to change the cultural bias that affects them.

I hope you enjoy the film. And I hope you'll find ways to use it to Teach Our Schools a Lesson.

November 13, 1998

Building a Movement for Sexual Freedom During a Moment of Sexual Panic

Eric Rofes

This address was delivered in November 1998 to the Second Annual Summit to Resist Attacks on Gay Men's Sexual Civil Liberties, meeting in Pittsburgh, Pennsylvania. Megan's Law (named for seven-year-old Megan Kanka, a victim of sexual assault and murder) was enacted on October 31, 1994, by the state legislature of New Jersey and required certain convicted sex offenders to register with law enforcement and provided for community notification of the risk they might pose.

One year ago in San Diego, over 100 activists came together to organize a visible resistance to what we'd experienced as an emerging Puritanical gay male consensus about sex and morality. Three key forces were the engines behind the meeting: (1) the repeated failure of most national and local gay groups to consider sex and sexual freedom as a central part of their agenda; (2) a rising anti-sex fervor in newspaper articles and books written by self-identified gay men; (3) a growing response to continuing HIV infections among gay men by many AIDS organizations and gay leaders which was marked by an acceleration of strategies heavily dependent on moralizing, hysteria, and shame.

We called our meeting the National Sex Panic Summit and that weekend we made valuable connections, grappled with key theoretical questions, and educated ourselves about the history of moral panics during this century. Isolated organizers working in different parts of the nation met new comrades. We debated the distinction between ongoing patterns of harassment and an escalating moral panic. We spent endless hours drafting and debating a document called "A Declaration of Sexual Rights" linking the history of our movements with the current attacks on sexual self-determination. In short we did organizing work: the good, hard, grunt work required to define an issue, ignite activism, and begin to chart out an agenda.

We did this work under stressful conditions. The National Gay and Lesbian Task Force appeared embarrassed by our presence and its leaders trivialized our concerns. A number of mainstream gay and lesbian activists accused us as undercutting efforts to achieve gay marriage, protect the rights of gays in the military, and promote a portrait of gay men as repentant and chaste. A few leading progressive organizers saw our work as simply a patriarchal attempt to win more sexual privileges for men and understood our efforts as about dick-dick-and-only-dick rather than about social change and human freedom.

The Backlash of 1997

None of us were prepared for the backlash we would face in the weeks and months following the summit. Our modest organizing efforts became the focus of a million news stories, editorials and opinion pieces which misrepresented who we were, mischaracterized our work of the weekend, and willfully mislead [*sic*] the public about our politics and our vision. The lead organizer of the summit—Tony Valenzuela—was pilloried in the local and national press and positioned as our summit's sacrificial lamb. In an action reminiscent of the McCarthy period, the president of the Log Cabin Republicans issued a very public call demanding every national gay organization publicly distance themselves from our summit and denounce our efforts. Our small gathering became the focus of the lead news story in that week's *New York Times* section "The Week in Review," where we were mocked and derided as sexual renegades, diseased pariahs, and a throw-back to the 1960s.

I understood the backlash in two ways. First, we'd committed heresy. By daring at the public level to value sex, pleasure, and the benefits which emerge from our sexual cultures—and to argue that the Monogamites have no corner on the market on ethics, values, or morality—we broke ranks with the gay rights movement's primary strategy of assimilationist politics and showed it for what it really is: a bankrupt, Faustian bargain which opts for a narrow package of concessions rather than authentic human rights, privileges cultural conformity over cultural pluralism, and affirms the status quo over the status queer.

The second way I understood the backlash was that we had hit a nerve, punched a button, unleashed a fury which Freud might call the "return of the repressed." By discussing sex openly and explicitly, and by publicly discussing anal sex as a valuable, meaningful act for many gay men, we shattered a powerful taboo which had taken root during the crisis years of the AIDS epidemic. We'd become accustomed to expecting fags to maintain a public silence about the wide discrepancy between the ways many AIDS groups publicly represented gay men's sex lives, and what we knew was really occurring in gay communities throughout the nation.

To hear a young man talk about getting fucked and taking semen up his butt, without the usual expressions of horror, regret, or "I've learned my lesson!" was more than many people could stand. We shattered the silence and punctured a lie that was the foundation upon which so many people constructed their public identities as "respectable" gay men during this gay rights era. By standing as examples of gay men who appear before the public unapologetically as neither members of monogamous gay couples nor de-sexed celibates sacrificing personal lives to the demands of community work, we achieved a bad-boy status among those who continue to grovel before a community self-image as the best little boys in the world.

Hence last year's sex summit achieved what we set out to achieve. We met one another and began to share strategies, tactics, and organizing tips. We supported each other personally and professionally to continue our principled work in gay communities even as the social supports for our politics and our visions continued to erode. And, perhaps most importantly, we created an alternative voice within gay male communities, a critical voice of resistance to the demonization of gay men's sex. During an era when many forces discourage from speaking out those who believe in the power of the erotic as a central component of social change, we found a way to assert our vision and our values into the community dialogue.

The Challenges We Face in 1998

We come together this weekend, just one year later, to continue our efforts to transform the position of sex and desire in gay men's communities. I know how difficult this work is today. It was one thing to speak out on behalf of promiscuity or open relationships in 1969 during a cultural moment which valued freedom, personal transformation, and communitarianism; it is quite another thing to do this work just 30 years later, during an era which considers the 1960s a failed experiment and places productivity over pleasure, caution over adventure, the nuclear family over the tribe. Have no illusions: those of us in this room do not share a singular vision, nor do we agree on a range of controversial issues related to our work. But we are here because we have chosen to continue the work of sexual liberation during a time of increasing repression, escalating moral panic, and the return of sexual shame.

My aim for us today and this weekend is three-fold. I want to show those who thought a media-trashing would destroy our efforts and force us underground, that we are here for the long haul and will continue to do the methodical, plodding work of building a resistance to their narrow, misguided agenda. We are not going away. I also want to show that—contrary to what our critics say—many of us do this work out of a commitment to gay men's health. Over half of the collective organizing the summit this year works each day to improve the health and safety of gay men—at AIDS and public health organizations, gay community centers, and gay men's health projects. We believe the use of shame, terror, and punishment as central tools of disease prevention is a key cause of men's alienation from their bodies and desires. We have no doubt that our work at this summit focused on empowerment will contribute to improving the sexual health—and the mental and spiritual health—of gay men.

My final aim for this summit is for us to find a way to break through the barriers that prevent us from successfully organizing our resistance in every part of this country. We must consider seriously the profound roadblocks we face doing this kind of work at the current cultural moment. I want us to share tactics, lessons learned, resources, and bright ideas which will help us create savvy organizing responses and mobilize a mass movement in support of sexual civil liberties and the rights of all people to organize their sex and relationships outside traditional family values.

To achieve these ends, it's important for us to think back over the last 12 months since we last convened and assess the state of sex panic facing gay men throughout the nation. I want to highlight critical incidents and what I consider to be the central core issues emerging in 1998 and I want to suggest some lessons we might take away from specific case studies of our organizing efforts. So settle back in your seats and let me take you on a highly-subjective tour of the past year.

Four Core Issues

I want to start by flagging four core issues which have seized center stage during the past year. When we last convened, New York City was in the throes of a major effort led by Mayor Giuliani to rid the city of commercial sex businesses. We debated whether New York was experiencing the usual ongoing harassment and crackdowns or whether a sex panic had emerged. Over the past 12 months I believe it is clear that a multi-pronged, and amazingly pernicious attack on sexual freedom has occurred to benefit commercial real estate interests and a smug, moralistic mayor. While New York's Sex Panic group continued to meet and organized several effective actions and public education campaigns, pro-sex forces have faced tremendous barriers, splintered and lost membership at precisely the moment of most urgent need for resistance. Many have understandably feel [*sic*] dispirited and pessimistic about the potential to hold the line against the police, zoning boards, media hacks, and politicians. As the situation in New York City continues to intensify, I believe it is appropriately understood as the key urban site of moral panic in the nation today.

The second core issue of the past year involves the moral panic churned up by the media in response to cruisers in bathrooms, parks and truck stops. To borrow Keith Griffin's analysis, this year over 40 television stations and hundreds of newspapers thought a great way to gain viewers during sweeps week was to report "normal" behavior which has occurred for decades, as if it were noteworthy, shocking, and a danger to respectable citizens. Many chose the "sexual predator" angle and insisted they were coming to the defense of innocent children. The leading trade publication for television producers which annually creates a list of hot story ideas, fanned the flames by suggesting TV news shows run pieces on public sex in their local areas. These journalistic forays into the "underworld" of men's sex cultures, have been an explosive challenge for local organizers.

The third hot issue—and one with which all of us must grapple, however difficult it may be—involves the escalation of attacks on adult men involved in consensual relationships with young men in their teens. I am talking here about 22 year old men imprisoned for having sex with 16 year olds, the profound ramifications which homophobic enforcement of age of consent laws have on gay male youth isolation and identity-formation, and the escalating campaigns which criminalize and demonize a very wide range of people, relationships and behaviors under the guise of protecting "childhood innocence."

In an era in which Megan's Law is used not only to persecute gay men who got busted for bathroom sex 30 years ago, but also non-violent adult men who formed consensual relationships with sixteen year old gay identified youth, we have to recognize that the moral panic facing gay men is not limited to bathroom cruisers, circuit boys, or sex workers. The hysteria surrounding this issue has led to life-time parole or extended sentences for some sex offenders who have already served their time in prison, sweeping new censorship laws, mandatory reporting laws that turn health providers and counselors into arms of the state police, and efforts to perpetually hound sex offenders who had served their prison time out of jobs and housing anywhere in the nation. Because the "save our children" rhetoric is a powerful tactic in a range of sex panics, I believe it is time—perhaps past time—to open dialogue with gay men and others who have been organizing in this important area.

Finally, we must look at the ways in which current panic surrounding HIV is leading to repressive measures against sexually-active people with

HIV, measures we fought long and hard to defeat just a decade ago. What does it mean, during a moment in which many gay men no longer experience AIDS as a crisis, that communities of color and indigent populations are hit with the passages of laws which gay men successfully resisted a decade ago? A legislative backlash has instituted laws which report the names of people with HIV, notify partners, and imprison people with HIV who engage in unprotected sex. Why are some white gay leaders who lead [*sic*] the opposition to such laws a decade ago, now the leading advocates for such laws? What are the implications of these new laws for the sexual freedom and civil liberties of people with HIV—including gay men with HIV, including gay men of color with HIV?

Key Successes of 1998

I want to highlight a number of successes we've achieved this year because I believe, as Saul Alinsky frequently insisted, "We need wins." I choose to highlight three efforts here where gay men—through a process of grassroots, collaborative organizing—brought about some key victories which offer lessons for all of us.

First I want to highlight the work of a small group of gay male health workers in Portland, Maine. In March, shortly after the citizens of Maine became the first state to repeal a statewide law protecting people from discrimination on the basis of sexual orientation, the police chief, perhaps sensing an opportunity to strengthen morality codes, put forward a proposal to the city council for an ordinance that would criminalize and crackdown on consensual, out-of-view sexual activity, the kind of activities that may occur in a car or a dark corner of a dance club. Savvy activists immediately moved to establish a small, grassroots committee to generate resistance, spread the word through the community, engaged in intense lobbying and media work, and succeeded in getting this so-called lewd activity ordinance defeated by a vote of 7-2.

What worked here was that local AIDS leaders used the connections garnered through their AIDS work to get public testimony from the former director of the state's health department, key civil rights leaders, and even the grande dame socialite of Portland, a 94 year old blueblood woman who's been a leading volunteer and AIDS philanthropist. What also worked here was that a critical mass of gay men who felt no shame about their sex and the sex cultures of their community, pulled together quickly, did the grunt work of organizing, and then celebrated a victory.

The second achievement I want to highlight is the important work done by a small group of health activists at this year's National Lesbian and Gay

Health Conference in San Francisco. I was a member of this group and we wanted to create a presence at this key national event which was different from the organizing-in-exile we are forced to do around Creating Change. By working collaboratively, paying attention to the details of organizing and marketing, and building bridges to people with whom we agree 80% of the time, rather than making them into "the enemy," we were able to shift the conference discussions about gay men's sex and drug use away from the punitive, just-say-no approach so popular these days among anxious, exhausted health providers, and towards more complicated understandings of issues such as barebacking, muscles, circuit parties, and public sex. We raised the level of public discussion up several huge notches.

Third is the truly impressive work done in Detroit by the Triangle Foundation and its attorneys. By forming an active and aggressive strategizing group comprised of lawyers—including former prosecutors—activists, and former victims of entrapment, the group has staged informational outreach programs at rest areas and parks, met with police officials, waged a savvy media campaign to counter the police rhetoric on public sex, and begun to put together ground-breaking legal challenges to entrapment. This energetic and principled group have been able to prevent legislation aimed at censoring the Internet, halt the use of Megan's Law for men entrapped at public sex venues, and put on trial the entrapment practices of the police and the moral panic practices of the media.

What's especially wonderful about the work of the Triangle Foundation is that thanks to the leadership of Jeff Montgomery, we are able to witness a single mainstream gay organization which, in 1998, has taken on entrapment and sexual civil liberties as a key part of its agenda. What's also impressive here is that people occupying a range of positions which carry some stature and hence some risk—attorneys, executive directors, community organizers, were willing to put themselves on the line and stand up for what they believe. By forging a working group with a commitment to ending entrapment, I believe the Triangle Foundation offers us a model which should be adapted to local gay male communities throughout the nation to address not only entrapment, but also sex club closures, media moral panics, and the overarching moralizing suffusing our communities.

I also want to flag for you some of my personal heroes and heroic events of the past year because they show how individual gay men—and key community organizations—can make a valuable contribution to our efforts to resist shaming and sexual repression. Here I think of Edmund White who published a piece in an otherwise awful issue of *The Advocate* which offered no apologies for a lifetime of promiscuity and nailed sex-negative critics for their contradictions, self-delusions, and mendacity. I think of Michael Bronski, whose new book *The Pleasure Principle,* cuts to the heart of our culture's sexual repression and should be required reading for all activists for sexual freedom.

I want to applaud the new leadership of *OUT Magazine* for bringing on board Dan Savage and Pat Califia, two social critics who write about sex shamelessly and in all its complexity. I also want to affirm the work of HIV prevention workers at Gay Men's Health Crisis who have withstood repeated attacks by a local gay paper aiming to replace their harm reduction approach to gay men's sex and drug use with simple-minded shaming and downright dumb social marketing campaigns. I also want to highlight the work of a group of Boston-area educators, health activists, criminal justice workers, and organizers who have crafted a thoughtful and powerful statement called "A Call to Safeguard Our Children and Our Liberties," which begins to tackle the "Save Our Children" construct and confront the real challenges facing children and youth in our nation.

Finally I want to highlight my celebrity hero of the year, George Michael, who responded to his very public entrapment by not only coming out of the closet (finally!) as a gay man, but by appearing in television talk shows unashamed and unrepentant, and for producing a new single and a video titled "Outside," which is a powerful statement affirming sexual freedom and denouncing police repression.

Dangerous Trends

Perhaps it would be useful to point out two other dangerous trends which we've faced this year. First I want to highlight the continuing challenge we face working on sex issues not only with the mainstream media, but with the queer press as well. *The Advocate* continues to lead the way, sensationalizing gay men's sex to sell papers, and encouraging readers to link public sex, fetishism, and multipartnerism with danger, disgrace, and disaster. They are not alone.

Yet the winner in this year's contest for most horrifying commentary in the gay press must go to columnist Jennifer Vanasco who used the suicide of a gay man in Arkansas after he'd been outed in the local paper for public sex, to express her "happiness" that such men get busted, applaud the use of shame and disgrace as methods of policing, and blame the victim for his own demise. Showing no knowledge of the long history of such suicides or the unequal enforcement of public sex codes, and no empathy for the dead man, Vanasco reaches her lowest point when she insists, "Lesbians should get a big chuckle out of the idea that these men have sex in public because they're oppressed," and attempts to create a wedge between lesbians and gay men. It takes every bit of my will to resist saying, "Vanasco: Shame on *You!*"

The second dangerous trend is the rise of Sexual McCarthyism we've witnessed this year. This is a complicated matter and one which is linked to Kenneth Starr's public release of Grand Jury documents about the President to the media. I use the term "Sexual McCarthyism" as sort of a dangerously misguided extension of "outing." In this case, you don't out someone's sexual orientation, you out their sexual interests, activities, or desires. Just a month ago, a New Hampshire paper linked a state Democratic leader in a legislative race to defeat an incumbent Republican to a gay organization which sponsors "leather nights" and "rubber orgies." The paper atttempted to defeat Rick Trombly by portraying what they suggested were his "quaint homosexual fetishes." In this case, it didn't work: with 94% of the vote in, Trombly was ahead of his opponent with 52 to 48% of the vote, and I believe he won the race. No suicide, no disgrace, no defeat.

In Lawrence, Massachusetts, a local paper outed a member of the city's school board for engaging in Internet searches for a three-way with his girlfriend. He was forced to resign his post. This is Sexual McCarthysim. On hearing that a gay male watersports club was planning a Palm Springs weekend of parties, local officials in Cathedral City unsuccessfully attempted to ban the Waterboys from their area. This is another form of Sexual McCarthyism.

Activists for sexual freedom might argue that if sexual diversity is good, what's wrong with outing an individual's fantasies, sexual practices and kinks? Perhaps we should all walk around with our desires printed in black marker on our forehead? Perhaps its okay to "out" the contradictory practices of our opponents? One sex activist in San Francisco sent a public letter to newspapers and zapped it out over the Internet after he saw a city official who'd opposed the opening of a bathhouse in San Francisco at a local porn theater. When I visited Provincetown this summer, tongues were abuzz because a popular writer who embraces marriage and neo-conservative morality supposedly had spent his vacation in leather bars and on the Dick Dock. When a Board member at GMHC [Gay Men's Health Crisis] died recently, a local gay paper found it useful public health strategy to expose that he had died of drug overdose, not AIDS, and use his particular circumstances to undermine the organization's credibility and deride their work.

These are complicated matters. I don't pretend there are easy answers here. But I do fear that our organizing efforts will be hurt rather than helped if we feed into the frenzy to expose, embarrass, and publicly disgrace people on the basis of their sex. People on "our side" of these issues love to gossip about the supposed sex lives and imagined or real contradictions of those with whom we disagree. When I'm exhausted by these sex debates within our communities, I sometimes want to enumerate which lesbian activists cheat on their lovers, which executive directors love to be tied up, and which gay male public officials fetishizes specific body parts, races, or articles of clothing. But I resist this urge to use the tactics of the Right to further our progressive agenda because at night, when I go to sleep, I have to face myself and be accountable for the tactics I've used. And ultimately, I want to celebrate all of our sex—from vanilla to kink—and not demonize specific interests and acts as part of a narrow, short-sighted agenda.

Rather than respect our opponents' rights to their opinion and tackle their thinking head on, some of us mock their ambiguities and have no empathy for any conflicts they might have. I cite this here because I believe that Sexual McCarthyism is escalating and that those who stand to lose the most are those with transgressive desires. I encourage us to resist the urge to use such tactics and trust that those who disagree with us, do so primarily out of their intellectual position.

Why Is Organizing So Difficult?

There is much we can learn from less-than-successful efforts of the past year which force many of us to confront precisely how difficult it is to organize a resistance to attacks on sex and sexual cultures. It is important to realize how tough it is to do any kind of grassroots organizing these days on any issue outside the mainstream. Many of us like the identity of being community organizers but when the grunt work gets tiresome, when the conflicts between individuals get ugly, when racism, classism, and sexism divide us and leave us enraged and dispirited, many of us would rather stay home and watch *Ally McBeal* or *South Park.* So we retreat into roles as journalists, health workers, nonprofit managers, public officials, business people, and tell ourselves we're still doing activist work.

There are many ways to contribute to social change, but there is a difference between grassroots organizing and writing a book. I want to be a voice affirming the value and heroism of long-term commitment to democratic processes of community organizing. We may hate the endless meetings, be sick of licking envelopes, feel frustrated working across different identities and political visions, and be drained by community cannibalism, but we've got to keep going. No one will give you rewards for your work, but social change cannot happen without old-time grassroots community organizing.

There is a particular challenge these days organizing around sex. Because of the rise of Sexual McCarthyism—inside and outside the gay communities—the stigma of speaking out, defending principles, or participating at meetings like our summit, is more than many people can bear. For some it's a matter of risk and cutting their losses. We all have to consider ways in which defending buttfucking or sex in parks sits alongside our current employment and our future job prospects. While I want to be a voice urging us to be bold, I also want justice-minded people to approach this work with open eyes and I trust each of us to decide what kinds of risks we can take. While we need to gently push each other to be courageous, we also need to withhold our judgements and accept that a range of legitimate factors besides being chickenshit, keeps many people from participating in this work. We must take this into account in our organizing.

For others, the primary barrier to speaking out and organizing around sex issues is a five letter word: shame. Many people believe their desires are wrong, their turn-ons are sick, and the way in which they organize their sex is shameful. You might love sucking dick through a glory hole or spending hours in the AOL dungeon chat room, but not only do you not want anyone to know about it, but you won't ever take steps to fight for your right to continue to enjoy these activities. Just as the shame about being gay limited our movement in the 1970s to a handful of people willing to openly own their gay and lesbian identities, shame about getting fucked, licking boots or good old vanilla promiscuity limits participation in efforts to support sexual freedom.

A final major challenge to this work that I want to cite is the difficulty conveying messages about sexual liberation to a hostile media and a public—which increasingly includes a queer public—which hears of our work and thinks, "What planet are they on?" During an era where the Right has so successfully undermined and redefined concepts of liberty, freedom and democracy, and the Left has run from issues of the body, desire, and sex, how do we frame our arguments in language which is neither esoteric nor trite. When sex has been so devalued and so demonized that placing the word "sex" alongside "freedom," makes many people smirk, how do we articulate our beliefs that promiscuity may be as moral as monogamy, that the right to choose an open relationship may be as ethical as choosing celibacy?

A Strategy for 1999

The current cultural moment is ripe for our organizing efforts. Our work will be neither easy nor simple, but the public debates about the President's sex life has taught me a great deal about the American public's view of sex. I argue the fact that the public has continued to support the President despite powerful attempts by Kenneth Starr, Newt Gingrich, and the mainstream media to discredit and shame him, has everything to do with our work of gay liberation of the past 25 years. We have been in the vanguard of insisting that people's right to hold jobs is independent of the way they organize their sex and relationships. We have argued that this separation is key to democracy and pluralism. While it is clear that the media has never embraced this position, I believe we've impacted the public in a major way. This gives me hope.

Our work will not be easy. I find it ironic that Het Amerika may be becoming more open-minded on certain sex issues—and that the public clearly understands that marriage and sex are often complicated, untidy matters—just as gay communities are becoming increasingly narrow-minded. Alan Wolfe's recent sociological report on middle-class morality shows that an influential sector of the public is liberal and tolerant about all populations except lesbians and gay men. They believe sex is inherently dangerous, volatile and best kept private. This leads Wolfe to advocate for the de-sexing of homosexuality and spurs forward a Human Rights Campaign vision of gay people who prioritize faith and family over the alternative forms of organizing sex and kinship which are where most gay men live their lives. Our biggest challenge is finding a way to make sure groups which were often founded and built by transgressive queers—groups like GLAAD, and the National Gay and Lesbian Task Force, and Lambda Legal Defense, and local gay and AIDS organizations—continue to do some small amount of work which is risky, outside-the-box, and beyond-the safe-and-status quo.

I want to close this talk by suggesting four key directions for our organizing over the next year. First, creating a coalition of all the different groups facing the threat of a moral panic over sex seems important to me. We must continue our internal efforts focused on gay men's communities, but we need to link up with allies organizing sex workers, pornographers, sadomasochists, and others, as well as those working for sexual and reproductive freedom for women. I believe next year's summit might best be conceived of as a broad-based coalition effort where we play one small part. With this in mind, I offer two suggestions for our own continuing efforts. First, we must find a way to overcome or resolve powerful divisions within our group concerning coalition work with gay men organizing around intergenerational relationships. Second, we must examine why our efforts and our participation are so white, and how racism and whiteness together shape what we prioritize and with whom we work.

Next, I recommend that we become involved in local efforts building towards the 50 state marches next spring and that we use these efforts as a way to create networks of activists who are working toward sexual freedom. At the very least, these marches must make the repeal of sodomy laws a top demand. We might use these marches to meet colleagues sharing a similar vision, or inject into the march some pro-sex visibility.

Third, I believe that the work they've done in Detroit organizing an ongoing strategy and response group focused on entrapment and preserving gay men's sexual civil liberties should be replicated in every part of this country. During our work this weekend, I urge you to seek out folks from the Triangle Foundation, learn how they organized their resistance efforts, and consider folks in your hometown who might want to contribute to a similar ongoing effort in your area. I'd like to meet again a year from now and hear that there are at least dozen of "entrapment action groups" or similar efforts in different parts of the country.

Finally, I want to encourage our work over the next year to continue to highlight prominently the linkage we see between sexual liberation, public health, and social change. Over the past 20 years I've worked on a range of gay men's health issues. I've written a book on gay people and suicide, directed a multi-purpose gay health center, led AIDS organizing efforts, and founded programs for gay youth. In every case, the repression of sexuality through guilt, shame moralizing, and terror has been a major barrier to health promotion. There is no need to create a false opposition between health and freedom, sex and the spirit. Nor is there any need to pretend that sexual cultures do not face their own specific health challenges. Yet to allow those who advocate for the displacement of sex from a central position in gay cultures to represent themselves as health-minded and us as disease-promoting, is not only wrong, it is dangerous. Let our work this weekend continue to integrate a commitment to democratic freedoms, social change, and sexual health.

February 5, 1999

Why We Are Going to the Millennium March on Washington for Equality

Troy Perry

This public statement was issued by Reverend Perry of the Universal Fellowship of Metropolitan Community Churches as a position paper addressing the rationales for the holding of the April 30, 2000, March on Washington.

We're marching to state capitals in March of 1999!

We're marching to our nation's capital in April of 2000!

We're marching to the ballot box in November of 2000!

On April 30, 2000, more than one million gays, lesbians, bisexuals and transgendered persons will gather along with our friends and families on the Mall in Washington, DC to call for equality under the law for all citizens.

This will be the fourth national March on Washington in the history of the GLBT Movement—and follows in the tradition of earlier marches in 1979, 1987 and 1993.

For some, the March has been controversial. For others, it has been embraced as a powerful way to present our GLBT message to the nation.

Here's why the Universal Fellowship of Metropolitan Community Churches is supporting and will be attending the Millennium March on Washington for Equality:

The March advances the GLBT movement.

The Millennium March represents a key element of a three-pronged strategy for advancing our movement. We must advance in three areas: the state government, our national government, and the ballot box. That's why we're supporting the marches on state capitals through the Equality Begins At Home events and the Millennium March. Each event will support and sustain the other. And that's why UFMCC has embraced this powerful theme: "We're marching to the our state capitals in March of 1999. We're marching to our nation's capital in April of 2000. And in November of 2000, we're marching to the ballot box."

The March follows in the tradition of Dr. Martin Luther King Jr.'s Civil Rights advances.

Dr. King knew the value of marching on the nation's capital, and galvanized support for civil rights by an overwhelming presence in Washington, DC. We believe in the value of demonstrating to our nation the strength of our numbers and the passion of our commitment to justice.

The March will demonstrate the broad diversity of the GLBT communities.

This is a March for all of us. Every segment of the GLBT movement will be represented. AIDS activists, civil rights workers, families, leather folk, community organizers, children, military service members, transgendered people, people of faith, same-sex marriage proponents, youth—everyone is invited! Together we'll demonstrate the diversity of our movement.

It's already been too long.

Seven years have passed since the last March on Washington. If we have learned any lesson, it is how quickly and easily our elected officials forget. It's time to remind our government and our nation that millions of her citizens are still denied equality.

The new millennium presents a strategic opportunity.

The dawn of a new millennium, by its very nature, heightens society's sensitivity. Commentators, the press and society at large will be looking for messages and trends for the new millennium. We have an opportunity at this strategic time to move our GLBT message to the forefront.

The year 2000 is a presidential election year.

In our society, much of our progress is contingent upon getting the ear, and then the support, of our elected officials. The presence of one million gay, lesbian, bisexual and transgendered persons is designed to make our voice heard—by all of our national elected officials, In addition to the Millennium March itself, one million gay, lesbian, bisexual and transgendered Americans will have an opportunity to walk the halls of our national government and make a compelling and personal case for equality for all citizens.

The March will birth a new generation of activists.

Each of our previous national marches has served to birth new activists. In fact, as with many GLBT organizations, there are many UFMCC members whose first taste of activism came through the previous Marches on Washington. We have a strategic opportunity to become intentional about using this Millennium March to inspire and birth new activists who will continue work toward the dream of equality for all our citizens.

The Millennium March will energize our movement.

The Millennium March on Washington will energize the GLBT rights movement, strengthen all of our organizations, and present untold opportunities for gay human rights, justice and spiritual organizations to grow in terms of members, influence, accomplishments and media access.

The Millennium March's theme is focused, simple and understandable.

Our society still hasn't heard the message. We need look no further than the recent repeal of the equal rights law in Maine to know that the simple message of equality has not yet been heard and embraced. The theme of this Millennium March is simple—and designed to build allies. To accomplish the goal of equal human and civil rights, it is imperative that we strategically build allies and support throughout society. One million gay, lesbian, bisexual and transgendered persons have an opportunity to call upon our nation and its citizens to live out our nation's creed of "liberty and justice for all." Every element of this March will be focused on the call for equality, and every sub-theme will directly relate to the march's purpose.

These are some of the reasons the Universal Fellowship of Metropolitan Community Churches supports the Millennium March on Washington. We must use every means at our disposal to get our message out. And we must not rest until our nation's highest ideals have transcended promise and become reality for all our citizens.

May 6, 1999

First Annual GBLT Memorial Day

Jerrold Nadler

These remarks were made on the floor of the House of Representatives and printed in the *Congressional Record* for May 6, 1999. Nadler represented New York.

Mr. Speaker, I rise today in recognition of the first annual Memorial Day for the Gay, Lesbian, Bisexual and Transgender community. This special day has been established to remember the many who have lost their lives due to killings, beatings, and suicides that have resulted from the homophobic attitude prevalent in our society and throughout history.

Every year, on the anniversary of the Warsaw ghetto uprising, the world commemorates Yom HaShoah or the Day of Remembrance for the Holocaust. Although several museums throughout the United States and Europe include exhibits recalling the homosexual experience during the Nazi era, most Yom HaShoah services fail to mention that part of Hitler's reign of terror was the systematic attempt to eliminate homosexuals from Germany. It is estimated that, under his plan, tens of thousands of homosexuals were arrested and thousands were confined to death camps along with others he deemed "undesirable." Today's solemn remembrance is part of an effort to remove the veil of silence about this tragic history of persecution and killing, underscore the seemingly endless chain of hate crimes, and provide education aimed at eradicating intolerance and violence against gay, lesbian, bisexual and transgender persons.

I salute Congregation Beth Simchat Torah, the Church of the Holy Apostles, the International Association of Lesbian and Gay Children of Holocaust Survivors and the many other religious and community organizations that have joined in coalition to cosponsor today's solemn commemoration of the many lives lost as a result of a national reaction to homophobia. May their lives serve as reminders of the horrors of prejudicial acts of this kind. Let us honor their memory by committing ourselves to ending bigotry toward all people regardless of who they are or who they love.

June 7, 1999

The Spirit of Stonewall

Carolyn B. Maloney

These remarks, made on the floor of the House of Representatives, were printed on page E1144 of the *Congressional Record* for June 7, 1999. Carol Maloney was a representative from New York State.

Mr. Speaker, I rise to commemorate the thirtieth anniversary of the modern gay rights movement. On Friday, June 27, 1969, the New York City Police Department raided and attempted to close the Stonewall Inn for the perceived crime of operating a dance bar that catered to homosexuals. Recall, that in 1969 it was illegal for men to dance with men, although, oddly, it was legal for women to dance with women.

In New York City and almost everywhere, police raids on gay bars were routine. Usually, the patrons scurried, fearful of the repercussions of being caught in a gay bar. On this night, brave young men and women stood up to the police. They were no longer willing to accept daily harassment and the abridgment of their civil rights.

The Police operated in their customary fashion, hurling a string of homophobic comments, as they evicted the bar patrons one by one. As patrons and onlookers gathered outside, the crowd grew. A parking meter was uprooted and use to barricade the door. Thirteen gay people were arrested that first night.

This was the beginning of a number of nights of demonstrations that drew national attention. Moreover, it demonstrated to the gay community that there was an alternative to continued oppression. It also showed the community at large that gays were no longer willing to be silent in the face of injustice. After that night the movement to protect the rights of gays, lesbians, bisexuals and the transgendered gained strength and respectability.

In the last thirty years much has changed. Gay bars can be found in almost every town—from Anchorage, Alaska to Wheeling, West Virginia. More important, bookstores, hotlines and support groups have appeared in smaller communities to ease the isolation previously felt by many gays. The legacy of Stonewall can be seen in the lives of hundreds of thousands of men and women who are able to live their lives honestly and out of the closet. The Stonewall Revolution inspired men and women to "come out" and showed young gays and lesbians that they are not alone. Today, an openly gay person is no longer automatically disqualified from holding public office or other positions of trust. Now, numerous communities have embraced the post-Stonewall reality by passing laws specifically protecting against discrimination based on real or perceived sexual preference.

I am proud to represent thousands of gays and lesbians, in Manhattan and Queens, and I am proud of my close relationship with and support of the Stonewall Veterans Association, a group of those actually present on that fateful night.

As we celebrate the anniversary of the modern gay rights movement, we recognize the expansion of freedom has not been uniform and much remains to be done. So we celebrate the important, but incomplete, steps toward equality for those previously banished to the closet. Much more remains to be done to eliminate irrational prejudice against those who are different. And we must recommit ourselves to the fight against all types of bigotry, whether based on race, religion, national origin, sex or perceived sexual preference.

June 17, 1999

Gay and Lesbian Democratic Club 25th Anniversary

Carolyn B. Maloney

These remarks were delivered on the floor of the House of Representatives by Representative Maloney of New York and printed in the *Congressional Record* for June 17, 1999, on page E1308.

Mr. Speaker, I rise to salute the Gay and Lesbian Democratic Club, on its twenty-fifth anniversary.

The Gay and Lesbian Independent Democrats (GLID) began as the Gay Independent Democrats five years after the Stonewall demonstrations.

GLID has played a central role in the fight for gay rights and in the election of openly gay candidates. An early leader of GLID, Christopher Lynn served as the head of New York's Taxi and Limousine Commission and later as NYC Transportation Commissioner. More recently, GLID leaders such as Tom Duane and Deborah Glick, two of the first openly gay persons elected to office in New York, used GLID as a springboard to elected office. In recent years, GLID played pivotal roles in the elections of three gay City Council Members: Christine Quinn, Margarita Lopez and Phil Reed.

As fighters for gay rights, GLID has been in the forefront of the effort to enact an appropriate domestic partnership bill in New York City. At the Federal level, GLID has worked to promote civil rights for gays, including efforts to pass the Anti-Hate Crimes Bill. GLID is one of the leading organizations fighting anti-gay measures like the Defense of Marriage Act and the Religious Liberties Freedom Act.

As part of their celebration GLID will honor three outstanding gay leaders in the city and state of New York. Two of these honorees, Tim Gay and Harry Wieder, are long time members of GLID. Through their work with GLID, they have helped to reach out and mobilize gays and lesbians to elect progressive candidates. They have manned the barricades to protest injustices like the murder of Matthew Shepard and discrimination in the military.

Tim Gay is a long time district leader in the Chelsea area of New York City. Tim Gay's diligence in fighting to improve the quality of life for his constituents has greatly contributed to the revitalization of Chelsea.

Harry Wieder in addition to his activities as a gay activist has served as a leading advocate for the physically and mentally disabled. As founder and board member of the 504 Democratic Club (named for a key provision in the Rehabilitation Act of 1973), Harry Wieder has fought tirelessly for the disabled and the reform of our health care system.

Barbara Kavanaugh was one of the first openly lesbian officeholders in New York State. A true trailblazer, Barbara was elected to the Buffalo City Council as an openly gay candidate. She currently serves as the Assistant Attorney General for Buffalo and has been active in the National Stonewall Democratic Federation.

I salute GLID for leading the fight to ensure full rights for gay and lesbians. This battle may take another twenty-five years, but with strong efforts of GLID and others we can succeed.

June 19, 1999

Jacksonville, Florida, Gay Pride Rally Speech

Barbara Gittings

> This speech was given by Barbara Gittings upon the occasion of her serving as co-grand marshal of the Jacksonville, Florida, Gay Pride Rally on June 19, 1999.

I've been fighting the good gay fight for 41 years!

When I joined the gay rights movement in 1958, it was already ten years old. What was it like then?

There were only half a dozen gay & lesbian organizations in the whole United States. There were maybe 200 of us activists. It was like a little club—we all knew each other, even 3,000 miles apart. Most people in the movement then used false names to protect their jobs and their families.

The three gay magazines in existence in 1958 couldn't be sold anywhere. And there were few subscribers because people were afraid to have their names on any kind of gay list.

We were completely invisible on television and we had just begun appearing on radio talks shows—the ones late at night, after children were in bed. The rare mentions of us in newspapers were under headlines like "Perverts Dismissed From State Department" or "Dozens Caught in Raid on Homosexual Bar."

We invited lawyers and clergy and psychotherapists who weren't gay to address our public meetings and conferences. Our own lawyers and clergy and psychotherapists were still deep in the closet. We were in the wake of the McCarthy witch-hunts, when an accusation of being "Commie-Pinko-Queer" could and did ruin the lives and careers of many decent people. In that climate of fear on top of the stigma of being gay, most of our people couldn't afford to be linked with anything concerning homosexuality.

We did have an occasional mad moment of triumph. For example, our longtime Washington gay activist Frank Kameny used to give a talk called "Tweaking the Lion's Tail, or, Constructive Fun and Games With Your Government." One of his stories was about how in 1963 the lone gay organization in the nation's capital stood up to FBI director J. Edgar Hoover. Since the gay group often had to deal with the government's anti-gay policies, it wanted to keep top officials informed of its activities, so it routinely sent its newsletter, unasked, to everyone at the White House and in the Cabinet and in Congress.

J. Edgar Hoover didn't appreciate this. J. Edgar Hoover desperately wanted his name *off* that gay group's mailing list! He tried to bully, he tried to scare. But the group stood firm and made Hoover back down. The organization's newsletter continued to be sent to Hoover along with all the other federal bigwigs. It must be the only time in the career of that powerful man he didn't get his way—and WE did it!

In 1965—yes, four years before Stonewall—we tore off the shroud of invisibility when a handful of us walked in the first gay picket lines at the White House and the Pentagon and the Civil Service Commission in Washington, and at Independence Hall in Philadelphia.

It was scary. Picketing was not a popular tactic 34 years ago. Certainly our cause wasn't popular. Even many gay people thought our efforts were outlandish and unseemly. Only a few of us could take the risk of being so public. What if my boss sees me on the 6 o'clock news and fires me? What if my picture appears in the front page of my parents' hometown newspapers and causes them grief/What if passersby throw insults at us—or worse, bricks and stones? And what is the government going to *do* with all those photos and recordings they're making of us?

What a great change this crowd today signals!

We're here to celebrate gay pride, gay love, and gay rights.

Do you think we'll have our rights once ENDA, the Employment Non-Discrimination Act, is passed by Congress and when gay marriage is finally legal? These WILL happen—after all, you are writing and calling your state and federal lawmakers, aren't you? Such laws give us a legal leg to stand on and to challenge the most blatant kinds of discrimination against us. But laws alone can't end the personal prejudice behind the discrimination.

Gay rights means much more than getting good laws and policies and practices, though that's a key step. We also have to change the hurtful messages that still come from many religious leaders and many public officials including school board members. Progress on paper is fine but we can't stop there. The struggle for equal treatment has to be won in people's hearts and minds where it really counts.

We want relief from the pain of wearing the mask. We want freedom from those big and little compromises that pinch the spirit. We want to be judged as individuals, on our own merits. We want the right to live and love and work and play, without being denounced and penalized for being true to ourselves.

One way to secure that right is to live and love and work and play as ourselves when we can, to exercise our right openly, to let this city and the whole country know that we are here, we are everywhere.

We are everywhere—but lest they forget, keep reminding them. We're fortunate to have the visibility of Barney Frank in politics and Martina Navratilova in sports and Ellen DeGeneres in show business and the visibility of Ellen Hayes and Tony Suscynski here at home. But we need also the everyday visibility of people like you, a constant presence, always reminding others that we're at the next desk at work and at school, we're in the next pew at church or temple, we're in the next chair at the family dinner table. We're already part of every community. We won't go away and we won't be converted, and more and more of us are refusing to hide and pretend.

Being visible takes courage and persistence. You're here today because you want to make difference, to leave a legacy. And we have a special message for those who can't yet appear at a Gay Pride march: Hang in there folks, because those of us who are out are oiling the closet door hinges just as fast as we can!

I was invited to be part of your Gay Pride celebration partly because I've acquired a high profile as an activist. But George Eliot wrote in her novel *Middlemarch* that "the growing good of the world is partly dependent on unhistoric acts." So I want to acknowledge the contributions of dozens of Jacksonville people who have done special jobs for our growing good—but whose names usually don't turn up in the written stories about our work. I salute all of you who, for a day, for a month, or for years, have given your time and talent just for the fun of it and as its own reward.

Our goal is equality in society, but there's no one best way to achieve it. We advance thanks to a thousand different talents and interests. We are everywhere and everybody. You know, this is very frustrating for those who oppose us. It's like punching pillows: they squelch us here—and we just pop up somewhere else!

Sometimes I'm asked for advice on how to avoid burn-out. I have a two-part prescription.

Don't be daunted. Over the long haul, for every setback and every stubborn problem, we've made three or four giant strides forward. Be patient, be persistent, be persuasive. Remember that success comes in little moments as well as in grand events. Take care of minor issues along with the main job, and you'll have the satisfaction of seeing results every week, not just once in two or three years.

Keep and use your sense of humor. Gay rights is serious business, but it doesn't always have to be grim. And a light touch often helps to push our message. So let loose your sense of fun.

In a world in which we are often despised and rejected, in which we are put down, harassed, hounded and even killed for being who we are, we refuse to buckle. We believe in the rightness of our lives, our loves, and our cause. Despite the bigotries and barriers we have to cope with, most of us lead wonderful lives useful to ourselves and to society.

In the face of the AIDS epidemic, we have been constructive, innovative, caring, and heroic. We have not been defeated.

And we are loving. How well *we* know the power of love! The world needs more love, and we're contributing our share of love—without waiting for approval.

Just fifteen days after this march, on July Fourth, we celebrate the Declaration of Independence which proclaims the right to "life, liberty and the pursuit of happiness." And its doesn't say that's for heterosexuals only. Its *your* life. It's *your* liberty. It's *your* pursuit of happiness. It's up to you—go get them!

July 29, 1999

A Gay Men's Health Movement Is Born

Eric Rofes

This is the text of the opening plenary address to the founding conference of the gay men's health movement, known as the Boulder Summit: Building a Multi-Issue, Multicultural Gay Men's Health Movement, given to the over 300 attendees of the meeting in that Colorado city on July 29, 1999. Veteran AIDS activist Rofes was one of the collective members who planned the conference.

On behalf of the four-person collective which organized this event, welcome to the Boulder Summit: Building A Multi-Issue, Multicultural Gay Men's Health Movement! Over 300 people are registered for the Summit, coming from throughout the United States as well as from Canada, Denmark, and Australia.

We welcome all of our gay, lesbian, bisexual, transgender and heterosexual participants committed to strengthening gay men's health and wellness. Amid this sea of men, I extend a special welcome to the two dozen women who have joined in as presenters, volunteers, and participants.

Thanks to all of you, we offer over 100 sessions over the next three days on issues ranging from anti-gay violence to alcoholism to anal cancers, STDs to smoking cessation to steroid use, mental health to microbicides to masculinities.

We think our Summit program is comprehensive, timely, and bold. We have sessions targeting the health needs of men of color, rural men, gay male youth, aging gay men, homeless men, men in prison, and gay men with HIV; programs focus on specific subcultures including bears, circuit boys, leathermen, and sex workers.

We address provocative issues such as barebacking, public sex, and promiscuity and emerging health challenges such as hepatitis C, tobacco use and the needs of gay men with chronic illnesses distinct from HIV. Our program raises uncomfortable though critical questions such as:

Can we create healthy gay cultures without challenging promiscuity?
What role should U.S. gay men play in the health of our brothers worldwide?
What should our relationship be to the women's health movement?

We believe that collectively the women and men in this room have come forward to create a program which could easily overwhelm any of us and leave us pulled in a zillion directions.

Tonight we suggest you take the time to look over the Summit book and sketch out your own agenda. We recommend creating a schedule which meets your interests but also draws you into new arenas and challenges your current perspective.

I will be upfront with you about one of our overarching goals for this Summit: we want you to leave Boulder with a deeper understanding of gay men's health, a broader commitment to activism, and a burning desire to strengthen and create gay men's health projects in your local community.

We want the people at this Summit to inspire our communities to prioritize gay men's health and wellness and spark specific organizing efforts which will make gay men's health as central to our lives over the next two years as HIV/AIDS has been for the past two decades. And we are delighted to include a track of "model programs" which highlights successful efforts already underway throughout our nation.

Because our collective unabashedly has called for increased attention to issues such as substance abuse, prostate cancer, and hepatitis, some have depicted us as believing that AIDS is over.

Let me make one thing clear from the outset: the Summit organizers believe HIV/AIDS remains a central part of our agenda and our program this weekend certainly reflects this commitment. While we believe major shifts are occurring in the ways gay men experience and make sense of HIV, we do not believe the medical condition called AIDS has been cured or that continued activism in this area is not needed.

We also believe gay men of different races and classes are forging increasingly distinct relationships to HIV based on distinct experiences with access to treatments, prevention efforts, and institutionalized racism.

We do believe that future AIDS prevention work with all gay men will only be effective if it is embedded in a broader, holistic gay men's health movement, and if it takes seriously the range of mental, physical, emotional and spiritual health needs of gay men.

While we have received supportive comments on the breadth and quality of our sessions this weekend, we want to acknowledge that there are gaps and silences.

For example, there is limited programming on the health challenges facing old gay men in our culture and there are no sessions at all on eating disorders, gaps we tried unsuccessfully to fill.

We'd hoped to convene a session on the health implications of rimming—we planned to call this the Rimming Roundtable—but our best intentions came to naught. Given our proximity to Littleton, Colorado, we attempted to create more sessions on school-based violence against gay youth, but the presenter who'd championed this part of the program found himself faced with a job-related conflict which forced his cancellation. While these gaps may disappoint us, overall we are very grateful to the broad range of innovative sessions which you have created for all of us.

I want to be candid with you about the genesis of this Summit and lay out our objectives in organizing this event.

This event did not emerge out of a vacuum: it grew out of the National Gay and Lesbian Health Conference, an annual convergence of health activists which celebrated its 20th anniversary last July in San Francisco. Many of us have valued our time together at that conference and the many activist projects which it has generated.

When we learned last November that the sponsoring group had undergone organizational crisis and that this summer's conference was not likely to occur, we began discussing possible ways to continue some of our work together.

For the last few years, a group of people had organized a track of sessions at that conference which had attempted to grapple with emerging gay men's sexual cultures and new directions for HIV prevention.

We began to discuss hosting our own mini-conference this summer to move our work forward. As we passed the word around, we found others shared our interest in seizing the opening left by the demise of the health conference to tackle what we saw as a central organizing challenge; breaking the stranglehold HIV/AIDS held on gay men's health organizing.

We believed this was a moment with the potential to catalyze organizing and broaden our focus in a powerful and much-needed way.

Several of us committed to organizing this Summit last November, but we spent three months trying to find an organizational sponsor; a host organization which would be the funnel for our finances and which wouldn't meddle in the program content.

We approached several gay and AIDS organizations which we believed might be amenable to our project and while they all supported our efforts, none felt they had the time or organizational capacity to host such an event.

In fact, we had given up all hope for holding the event this summer, when, in March, the Boulder County AIDS Project heard of our plight and approached us about working together.

Because we were aware of the Boulder Project's innovative work with gay men's sex and had been impressed with their commitment to cutting-edge work, we readily formed a solid partnership.

We made an early strategic decision about this Summit which has caused a bit of controversy and for which our collective takes responsibility. We considered attempting to organize an event not only focused on gay men, but on lesbians, bisexuals and transgender people (LGBT).

Indeed, many of us here tonight consider ourselves part of a broad LGBT health movement and have learned much from the cross-fertilization such a movement has encouraged. We made a tough call back in February to focus this year's event narrowly on gay men and we stand by our decision despite the criticism directed our way.

For while we believe in solidarity among lesbian, gay, bisexual and transgendered people—and while we will be delighted to join efforts to initiate a new annual LGBT health conference—we also believe there are times when circumstances and limited resources compel us to organize separately. We believe this is one of those times.

While many of us have been excited by the surge of organizing among transgendered and bisexual organizers over the past few years, and the incredible strides made by lesbian health activists as their movement has blossomed this decade, we have not experienced parallel excitement when we've considered gay male health organizing. Instead, we have felt frustrated as we've watched AIDS become a totalizing metaphor for gay men's health, to quote Chris Barnett.

We knew gay men faced other pressing issues and we knew that our AIDS work itself was hampered by our inability to focus resources and attention broadly.

We'd attend the annual health conference seeking cutting-edge sessions on gay men's mental health, youth issues, or substance abuse and find little that was not narrowly focused on HIV.

As we stood in awe of lesbian, bisexual and transgender organizing in the 90s, we wondered what had happened to the gay men's health movement of the 1970s? Where had our creativity, insights and talent gone?

For those of you who might be unaware, there was a gay men's health movement before AIDS, albeit a small, under-resourced and nascent movement. Its most prominent manifestation were community-based sexually-transmitted disease clinics which emerged out of the free clinic movement of the 1960s.

Many of our most prominent mainstream AIDS service organizations—Whitman-Walker in Washington, D.C., Howard Brown in Chicago, Fenway Community Health in Boston—existed as gay male STD clinics in the 1970s.

The 1970s were also a time when gay men developed models of peer-based counseling, addiction recovery programs, and suicide prevention services to meet our communities' needs.

The development of a gay men's health movement was interrupted by the onslaught of AIDS. Many of our leaders and institutions applied their energies and resources to the burgeoning epidemic—and we are grateful that they did.

The first major AIDS conferences were convened as part of the National Gay and Lesbian Health Conference, and most of our major AIDS organizations were created out of existing networks of gay, lesbian, bisexual and transgender health activists.

Our communities' extraordinary response to AIDS in the 1980s was made possible by our organizing work of the 1970s, our early networks of queer social workers, doctors, psychologists, and activists, and the existence of gay community centers, gay newspapers, early men of color networks and gay bars, bathhouses and discos.

Two new books begin to capture this important community history: John-Manuel Andriote's *Victory Deferred,* which captures for the first time the leadership gay men have provided in leading our nation's effort against AIDS, and Cathy Cohen's groundbreaking book *The Boundaries of Blackness,* which documents the critical early leadership provided by African-American gays and lesbians in igniting a response from Black communities throughout the nation.

By stating that the resources and talents of the 1970s were redirected to fighting AIDS, I do not mean to suggest that the gay men's health movement died in the 1980s.

Instead, I'd argue that the work continued in quieter, less-prominent ways, and often with very limited funding. Often the gay health movement was intertwined with HIV organizing in surprising and sometimes confusing ways.

For example, the number and size of community centers have expanded impressively over the past 15 years, and many have become full-scale social service agencies meeting a broad range of health needs of our communities.

The expansion of services focused on gay youth and gay men of color also occurred during this time, as savvy proposal writers convinced funding sources that strengthening the overall health of our communities was effective prevention work.

And this brings us to the point we are at now, in 1999, and questions we hope to confront here in Boulder:

Do gay men's health issues merit attention, resources, and activism in and of themselves, or only when they are implicated in the spread of HIV?

Should we demand that the health bureaus of our local, state, and federal governments include gay men's health—as well as lesbian, bisexual and transgender health—prominently in their health initiatives, and never again create entire mainstream health campaigns which ignore the specific needs of our communities?

We have created a range of national organizations overseeing our nation's AIDS response, advocating for community needs, and troubleshooting emerging threats related to the epidemic. What national organization oversees gay men's health needs beyond AIDS? What organization serves as our sentinel, troubleshooting new and emerging health threat areas?

To tackle these daunting questions, four of us took the lead and formed a collective which organized this Summit. We began with no financial resources and knew of no deep pockets who would fund this Summit, so we chose a low-key grassroots organizing strategy. It might surprise you but, until this morning, our collective had never held a face-to-face meeting, or even held one of those expensive and, to my mind, confusing conference calls.

We communicated almost entirely by e-mail. By crafting our Call to the Boulder Summit, and promoting it through the Internet and gay newspapers, we generated participation in the Summit, an impressive array of sessions and, earlier this month, a grant from DuPont Pharmaceuticals.

As someone who came of age as an organizer during the 1970s and endured endless meetings where we even processed our processing, I am delighted with this move into postmodern, high tech organizing.

In a few minutes, I want to shift and ask you to tell us what brought you to Boulder this week? What inspired you to spend your time here, and not on the beach, in the woods, or hanging out with your friends? What local issues were the impetus to get you to this Summit and what projects would you like to invite others to participate in with you? How did you feel when you first heard about the goals of this Summit?

Because we hope that each of you will bring home at the end of the weekend something valuable to contribute to your local community, we want to begin our Summit asking you for something valuable which your experience in your local community can offer all of us here today.

But allow me to focus finally on our own vast ambitions. While we are thrilled you've come to Boulder and excited by the program, we maintain five specific work objectives for our time together:

First, we very much hope to see the energy of this Summit trigger the expansion of gay men's health projects throughout the nation. We want to see conferences, organizations and networks formed which champion broadly-defined gay men's health issues.

Learning from our AIDS efforts, we want to see projects emerge from various gay male ethnic and racial groups which define and prioritize specific communities' health agendas. We want local and national groups to form which take responsibility for oversight and planning for the health needs of our diverse populations.

We hope some of you will leave here eager to organize a local summit on gay men's health, establish a gay men's health project, or research gay men's health beyond HIV.

Second, we want to see gay activism come alive and focus as much on issues such as anti-gay violence or access to health care or STD treatment as HIV/AIDS. If a decade ago, we united under banners proclaiming Silence = Death, today the silence surrounding non-HIV related gay men's health issues is deafening.

We want gay men out in the streets demanding universal health care for all, full funding for mental health services and the development of new technologies to promote gay men's sexual health. And we want the gay media to take all gay male health issues seriously, and not limit their focus to HIV.

Third, we have planned action sessions throughout the Summit which are our attempt at a "product-oriented" agenda. We urge you to consider participating in sessions which will attempt to create a publication focused on gay men's health, an algorithm for doctors to use when gathering a sexual history from gay men, a public statement from gay men 35 or under, or mechanisms to continue our work after this Summit has ended.

Ultimately, underlying this Summit is an anarchistic spirit of optimism: we believe that the simple mix of 300 extraordinary people will produce countless organizing projects over the next few years. We urge you to be part of making that happen.

From the start of organizing this Summit, we have been upfront about our fourth objective: we want to support men 35 years old or younger to take on leadership roles in our health movement, reframe existing questions to fit their own interests and needs, and assert their voices loud and clear.

It strikes me as ironic that during the gay liberation period, our movement's leaders were primarily in their teens, twenties, and early thirties. When I was a young gay man, few thought it odd that a 22-year-old would be the editor of a gay paper, leader of an activist group, or author of a political manifesto.

The vanguard of the women's movement, the civil rights movement, Chicano organizing, and anti-war efforts was teeming with young people.

Today, gay people 30 and under are often classified as youth and offered mentorship programs to learn from activists of my generation. It has been exciting for me that with one exception (me!) the four-person collective organizing this Summit are age 30 and younger.

While we want this Summit to confront generational tensions head-on, but kindly, our ultimate goal is to network and energize young health activists from all over the nation.

And finally, fifth, we want to transform the ways in which we think about and evaluate gay men, shifting away from a perspective which exoticizes, demonizes, and pathologizes our bodies and our lives into a model which recognizes the tenacity, survival skills, and overall resilience of our cultures and communities.

What would it mean to understand openly gay men as the resilient portion of our community, that portion which has suffered physical assault, religious abuse, and political violence yet emerged emotionally intact and spiritually strong? What would it mean to understand our gender play, kinship networks, and sexual cultures not as pathetic products borne of a homophobic society but as adaptive survival strategies which have served us well?

Hence we hope to examine several sides of the issues and cultures which commonly are scrutinized in one limited way.

We might decry the substance abuse occurring at circuit parties, but also understand that rank and file gay men by the thousands find something valuable—something life affirming—about the mixture of music, drugs, and men dancing together.

We might read drag queens or leathermen as sexual caricatures born out of patriarchal culture, or we might understand them as radical subversions of gender norms and attempts to perform more nurturing forms of masculinity.

Some among us might be concerned at the failure of most gay men to organize their relationships as long-term monogamous couples, but as Peter Nardi's book on gay male friendships suggests, by prioritizing friendship networks over nuclear families as the primary unit of gay male social organization, we may, in fact, have strengthened the bonds of community in ways quite uncharacteristic of most cohorts of American men.

These five objectives guide our work this weekend. By the end of our time together, we hope the phrase "gay men's health movement" will roll off our tongues as easily as phrases such as "HIV/AIDS," or "protease inhibitors," and that we will bring back to our hometowns a renewed commitment to nurturing an activist health movement for gay men.

Let me be clear about one final point. At several times during the organizing of this Summit we were tempted to articulate our motivation for organizing this event by utilizing what has become the traditional American way of generating support around health issues: the crisis construct.

We felt pulled to deploy the murder of Matthew Shepard, or the rise in reports of rectal gonorrhea, or alarming reports about Hepatitis C to fan the flames of crisis in order to draw people to our event.

We did our very best to resist this temptation because we are clear about one thing: we want to create a gay men's health movement that will build momentum outside the toxic cycle of crisis and resolution which frames most contemporary health organizing.

Join with us in igniting a movement that will sustain itself against the capricious whims of media attention and the inexplicable shifts in interest by funders.

Join with us to create a multi-issue, multicultural gay men's heath movement which will sustain us for many, many decades.

September 1, 1999

Australia's First Openly Gay Senator Speaks

Brian Greig

This speech was given by Senator Greig, the first openly gay member of Australia's legislature, on September 1, 1999. The lines by Armistead Maupin come from his novel *More Tales of the City,* specifically Michael Tolliver's coming-out letter to his parents.

I spent my youth on the coast at Lancelin, where my parents were involved in the crayfish industry. I recall with affection the many times I worked as a deckhand on my father's cray boat, miles out to sea, in the wee hours of the morning, surrounded by rotting cow hocks and fish heads, and crashing face first into strong headwinds.

Some might say this was good preparation for a career in politics. It was there, growing up on the windswept coast north of Perth during the late 1970s and early 1980s, that I developed my love of the sea and of the coastal sands and bushlands which hug the Western Australian coastline, a region rich in the history of the early exploration by the Dutch.

Growing up in Lancelin introduced me to the wonders of natural history and instilled in me a deep respect for native flora and fauna. My early years were in some ways mirrored by the life of one of my favorite authors, Gerald Durrell, who as a child grew up on the sun-drenched shores of Corfu in Greece. He later wrote with great clarity and humor about his love of wildlife and the need to protect and preserve it.

In later years, as a student activist I campaigned in defence of free education and in opposition to tertiary fees. I also fought strongly for compulsory student unionism, and am proud of the role that the Democrats have played in defending this principle, once again, from attack.

At one point during my student days, I could be found waist deep in muddy swamp water trying to stop a road bypass being constructed through the Farrington wetlands at the southern edge of Murdoch campus. However, the road went through, as roads so often do, and it was a road that eventually brought me all the way to Canberra.

However, I would be painting an incomplete picture if I did not detail the most profound aspect of that journey. That is the fact that, since the age of 12, I have known that I am gay.

This has profoundly influenced my life and given me personal insight into intolerance, prejudice and the hatred that I might not otherwise have experienced. Equally, it has made me determined to stand against this and to fight all unjust laws by confronting law and opinion makers with the reality of their intolerance.

As a young person coming to terms with my sexuality, I found it to be an alienating and lonely experience. Schools ignore their gay and lesbian students for fear of being seen to promote homosexuality. But, of course, a person's sexuality is innate.

It cannot be taught and it is not contagious. As a consequence of this conspiracy of silence, gay and lesbian youth live in an environment of denial and rejection, with no support, counseling, validation, or role models. And then we wonder why it is that up to one third of all young people who attempt suicide do so because of the anguish or uncertainty over their sexuality.

Lesbian and gay youth are a normal and healthy part of the diverse human family. They need to know that and to know that they are not alone. As the author of *Tales of the City,* Armistead Maupin, said more succinctly:

> I wish someone older than me, and wiser than me, had taken me aside and said: You're all right kid. You can grow up to be a doctor or teacher just like anyone else. You are not sick or crazy or evil. Most of all though, you can love and be loved without hating yourself for it.

It came as a shock to me to learn in 1989 that I was a criminal. And in the views of the Western Australian parliament I remain a criminal, because there is no statute of limitation on this type of prosecution. Prior to 1989, all gay men in Western Australia were considered criminals and faced 14 years in prison for consenting sex in private.

Little has changed and, although this law has partly been repealed, gay males in my home state under the age of 21—the highest consent age in the world—are still regarded as criminals. These laws are worse than any that exist in Western or Eastern Europe—with the exception of Romania.

In WA, gay men are still being arrested, still being charged, still being fined and still being imprisoned under laws that do not apply to heterosexual people—laws similar to those which saw Oscar Wilde imprisoned in Reading Jail more than 100 years ago.

While anti-gay laws also exist in New South Wales and the Northern Territory, they are most draconian in WA. Additionally, WA holds the dubious distinction of being the only state where discrimination against gay and lesbian people remains legal. We can be refused employment, accommodation and the provision of goods and services. This happens frequently and with impunity. There is no state or Commonwealth redress, Federal human rights laws exclude us.

As a nation, Australia maintains appalling laws against gay and lesbian people. We live under a regime of apartheid. It is an apartheid not based on the colour of our skin, but on the colour of our sexuality. Homophobia is nothing less than sexual racism. But homosexuality is not a behaviour to be regulated. It is an identity to be respected. We are people, first and foremost. We work, we have lives, we love and have relationships. We are family.

Yet, despite being citizens, voters and taxpayers, lesbian and gay Australians do not have the same rights—or in many cases have no rights—to those things in life that heterosexual people take for granted. As a gay man, I can be denied access to a hospital to visit my partner if he is sick or injured—because I am not considered next of kin.

If I should die, my partner has no legal claim to my superannuation death benefit, despite the fact that I have nominated him as my beneficiary. I cannot claim my partner as a dependant or split our incomes for taxation purposes and, if we should separate, there is no legal mechanism to ensure fair and reasonable property settlement—we are denied access to the Family Court. And so it is for all same sex couples.

These complications are even more pronounced for the many gay and lesbian families raising children. It may come as a surprise to the Senate that many gay men do in fact have children and that about 30 per cent of lesbian couples either have or plan to have children.

Despite this, some people still promote arguments and laws in opposition to what is the reality of many people's lives. But the fact remains that, no matter how many obstacles you place in front of women trying to have children, those women who really want children will have children, as is their right. Heterosexual people do not have a monopoly on good child rearing practices. It is those people who really want children who make the best parents.

The systemic denial of our relationships is evident even here in the Senate. I am required to fill out the senators' register of interest, including notation of any assets and shares belonging to "spouse or defacto partner."

And yet as recently as May of last year, the Senate determined that these definitions must apply only to heterosexual relationships. Lesbian and gay MPs are precluded from registering their partner's interests. When I inquired as to what I should do in relation to Keith, my partner of 13 years, it was suggested to me that I may simply want to comply with the spirit of the register and to provide Keith's details anyway. As a matter of principle, I cannot.

Gay and lesbian people fighting for compensation and superannuation death benefits find that the spirit of those acts cannot be applied to same sex relationships. And so it is with unfair stamp duty payments and other taxation imposts, property settlement, family payments and spousal recognition within the defence forces and Public Service.

Gay and lesbian people seeking to be regarded as next of kin for hospital visits or funeral arrangements can find that the spirit of those acts cannot be applied to them, and the immigration process for same sex couples applies differently and to our disadvantage. The spirit does not apply here either. No, the spirit of Commonwealth legislation towards same sex relationships is decidedly mean spirited. We are excluded.

I give notice that I will move to amend the orders of the Senate relating to spousal definitions in the register to ensure that gay and lesbian MPs will also have the same responsibilities as other members of parliament. The legal recognition of same sex relationships is a human rights priority that must be addressed by the Commonweath.

The New South Wales government has already done this. The Queensland government has indicated it is set to follow, and the Tasmanian government is looking at doing so following the sweeping changes to gay and lesbian reform that have occurred in the island state.

In his victory speech in 1998, Prime Minister Howard spoke of the need for a more caring and tolerant Australia. At their national conference in Hobart two years ago, the Australian Labor Party unanimously passed a motion recognising the need for equality and justice for gay men and lesbians. If these parties are serious about this, as the Democrats are, then now is the time for them to act.

The Democrat Sexuality Discrimination Bill currently before the Senate will remove all discrimination from Commonwealth legislation as it currently applies to the sexuality of all Australians. Further, it will impose national antidiscrimination laws on the basis of sexuality or gender status, and make it unlawful to incite hatred on the same grounds. It deserves cross party support.

Discrimination against gay and lesbian people is as morally repugnant as racism or anti-Semitism. As a nation we have fallen behind comparable jurisdictions, such as New Zealand, Canada and South Africa, in terms of protecting the human rights of homosexual people.

For as long as governments condone this apartheid, they are creating the social and political environment that leads to harassment and violence towards gay and lesbian people. While parliaments continue to deny our relationships, deem us to be criminals, and render us to be second-class citizens without legal protections, then some people will take this as their cue to continue to treat us badly.

Australian research shows that almost half of all gay and lesbian people report some form of discrimination or harassment at work, including sackings. Roughly 30 per cent of lesbian and gay people experience harassment at school. And, worst of all, 70 per cent of gay and lesbian people report being verbally abused, threatened or bashed in a public place.

I wish to take a moment now to briefly tell the story of a young man named Matthew Shepard. Matthew was a slightly built 21-year-old student in Wyoming in the United States. About a year ago he was lured from a campus bar by two men. They drove him to a remote area outside the town of Laramie, where they viciously beat him.

As he lay there bleeding, begging for his life, he was bound to a fence and left in near freezing temperatures to die. He had been beaten so badly that his limp body, when found, was at first thought to be a scarecrow, His attackers had stolen his shoes and robbed his apartment. After being struck in the head 18 times with the butt of a hand gun, he remained in a coma for five days without regaining consciousness, before dying. Matthew Shepard was murdered because he was gay.

Before anyone here is tempted to think that this could only happen in America, I remind the Senate that no fewer than 30 men have been bashed to death in Sydney since 1990, simply because they were gay or presumed to be so.

This violence does not occur in a vacuum, it is not spontaneous. Hatred of this kind takes years to mature within societies. It is nurtured through a culture of invisibility and fear towards gay and lesbian people and the neglect and indifference of parliaments.

Each time a piece of legislation comes before the parliament and touches on human rights and human relationships but excludes gay and lesbian people and denies our relationships, it perpetuates this culture of invisibility.

Each time a public figure or religious speaker denounces our existence or seeks to justify our differential treatment, it perpetuates this culture of fear. As Justice Michael Kirby said on this topic recently, "The game of shame is over."

I stand here today, on this first day of spring, and on the dawn of a new century, as a representative of the last generation of gay and lesbian people who will tolerate the injustices of the past being carried into the future.

To the thousands of gay, bisexual and transgendered citizens who know the pain of abuse and discrimination and to those who have been unjustly arrested and jailed, I pledge my support and the support of my party.

Throughout my 10 years as a human rights activist, I was inspired by the dedication and tenacity of small groups of people fighting for change against overwhelming odds. These groups have very few resources, other than a passion for justice and a strong desire for change.

At times these groups face opposition so fierce it can lead to violence, as we have seen recently in the forests of Western Australia, and it is deeply personal. Yet it is these tiny community groups which change community attitudes, which in turn change laws.

I salute the Tasmanian Gay and Lesbian Rights Group which, through a 10-year campaign, brought about the repeal of offensive anti-gay laws in that state, a state which now leads the world in sexuality education programs, and leads the nation with antidiscrimination laws.

And I offer my respects to Rodney Croome and Nick Toonan, the public faces of that movement. Their legacy is a United Nations resolution affirming the human rights of all gay and lesbian citizens, a resolution which has shone a light into some of the darkest corners of the world and which can now be built on.

I also salute the Gay and Lesbian Equality group in my home state which, after 11 years of fighting, is on the brink of achieving change. Its legacy is the shift in community attitudes it has brought about through reasoned arguments, truth and persistence.

Senator Tchen, in his first speech, spoke of the generational change taking place in parliament. Specifically, he referred to the election of himself, a Chinese born Australian, and of my colleague Senator Ridgeway, an indigenous Australian, as indicative of this generational change.

I agree, but I would go further and add that the election to the Australian parliament of a gay and lesbian rights advocate is also indicative of this generational change. It is also indicative of the maturity of the Australian Democrats as a party of representation and reform. Let us hope that as a nation we enter the new millennium a society not simply of greater tolerance but of greater acceptance.

Finally, I offer my sincere thanks to the many thousands of Western Australian citizens who voted for me, and in doing so have asked me to represent them and their interest in the Senate through the prism of Democrats' policy and philosophy. I accept that challenge.

In closing, I want to express grateful thanks to my parents, both of whom worked hard to provide better opportunities for their children, and to my partner, Keith, who taught me that the personal is political. Keith, never short of an opinion, knows exactly what is wrong with the world and what it is that politicians need to do to fix it—but then he is a cab driver, so you have got to expect that.

I also express thanks to Lucy, for her unconditional love, but then she is a kelpie, so you have got to expect that too; to John, a fellow traveller who shares this journey with me; to Sophia, for teaching me that everything changes; to Joan, for pushing; to Melinda, for being there; to the Democrats, for their trust; to the Western Australian gay and lesbian community for its support; and to the late Chris Carter, a gay man and founding member of the Australian Democrats, who showed the way.

October 14, 1999

20th Anniversary of the First National March on Washington for Gay and Lesbian Rights

Malcolm Lazin

This statement was issued on October 14, 1999, by Lazin, at that time the executive director of the Millennium March on Washington planning group.

Today, October 14, 1999, marks the 20th anniversary of the our nation's first gay and lesbian March on Washington, an historic and seminal event in the ongoing struggle for social justice—and an event which energized our movement and birthed a new generation of activists.

This is an appropriate day to honor the early visionaries who first dreamed of a national March for gays and lesbians and to recognize the more than 100,000 women and men who gathered in Washington, DC for that historic event. It is also fitting to remember the strength and energy they brought to the struggle for civil rights for all gay and lesbian people.

But today is also a time for sober reflection.

The truth is that our community has not yet achieved one of the goals we sought in 1979—goals which simply sought equality under the law for sexual minorities. The demands of that first March were both simple and profound:

Repeal all anti-lesbian and gay laws.

Pass a comprehensive lesbian and gay rights bill in Congress.

Issue a Presidential executive order banning all discrimination based on sexual orientation in the Federal government, the military and federally-contracted private employment.

End discrimination in lesbian mother and gay father custody cases.

Protect our lesbian and gay youth from any laws used to discriminate against, oppress, and/or harass them in their homes, schools, jobs or social environments.

While we've made great strides these past 20 years, there is much unfinished work yet to be done. That's why on behalf of the MMOW Board of Directors, the more than 150 GLBT organizations endorsing the Millennium March on Washington, and the 4000 grassroots MMOW volunteers across the country, I encourage all people who passionately believe in equality under the law to join more than one million gays, lesbians, bisexuals, and transgendered persons, along with our families, friends and allies on Sunday, April 30, 2000, in Washington, DC for the largest GLBT civil rights march and rally in history.

Together we'll lobby the members and staffs of Congress. We'll have unprecedented opportunities to participate in conferences, workshops and informal networking events. We'll honor our past and mobilize for the future, and yes, we'll celebrate. We'll organize our community to prepare for the upcoming presidential and congressional elections. And we'll march through the streets of our nation's capital and rally on the Mall to demonstrate to our nation the power of our numbers and the justness of our cause.

For those who have wondered whether you should attend the Millennium march on Washington, I invite you to make the decision—the commitment—to join one million of your brothers and sisters for the largest GLBT gathering in history. This is a unique historical opportunity for our community to come together around the one issue that unites us all: Full equality under the law for gays, lesbians, bisexuals and transgendered persons.

Together, we'll boldly demonstrate the strength of our diverse communities, we'll further the goal of equality under the law for all people, and we'll call on our nation to live out the promise of her creed: liberty and justice for all.

And together we will honor the dream of those visionary men and women who called for and organized the first national GLBT March on Washington on October 14, 1979.

October 14, 1999

Celebrating the Memory of Matthew Shepard

Mark Udall

This address was given on the floor of the House of Representatives by Representative Udall of Colorado and entered into the *Congressional Record* for October 14, 1999.

Mr. Speaker, I rise today to celebrate the memory of Matthew Shepard. One year ago, this 21-year-old college student died in a hospital bed in Fort Collins, Colorado, the victim of a brutal and senseless act of hate. I don't think anyone will ever forget the imagery of him being pistol-whipped, beaten, robbed, tied to a rough-hewn fence and left for dead on a cold October morning outside of Laramie, WY. And all this because he was gay.

It is ironic that his life would be taken in such a violent way, considering the fact that Matthew wanted to dedicate his life to creating a world of peace and promoting human rights. He did not die in vain. His death shook us by our shoulders and forced us to deal with the issue of hate crimes and come to grips with the hate that brews in so many people's hearts. A crime motivated by hate is more than just another crime committed against an individual—it is intended to put fear into a whole community, whether it is the African-American, Asian, Latino, disabled, gay and lesbian or senior communities.

Mr. Speaker, enough is enough. Every person is entitled to respect and human dignity, and no person should live in fear for being who they are. Our nation is strong because of our diversity, not in spite of it. We must speak with one voice to erase violence and hate from our communities and from our hearts. And we must pass the Hate Crimes Prevention Act. This piece of legislation may not end all hate violence, but it will send a strong message that this Congress will not tolerate hate crimes, and that people who commit such acts will be met with swift and equal justice. And it will renew our commitment to creating an America where there is "liberty and justice for all."

October 18, 1999

The Tragic Death of Matthew Shepard

Nancy Pelosi

This address was given on the floor of the House of Representatives by Representative Pelosi and printed in the *Congressional Record* for October 18, 1999.

Mr. Speaker, with great sadness I rise to recall that 1 year ago, Matthew Shepard, a gay college student, was murdered. We should all deplore his tragic death. He was a lovely young man and was courageously willing to be open about who he was. He suffered because of who he was. This is simply wrong. It is a tragedy when a young man has the courage to be open about who he is, and his life is taken for it.

Unfortunately, Matthew is not alone. His tragic death and violence toward others point out the need for hate crimes legislation. According to the National Coalition of Anti-Violence programs, in 1998, 33 Americans were murdered because they were gay or lesbian. In the United States last year, there were at least 2, 552 reports of anti-gay or lesbian incidents. The number of serious assaults in which victims sustained major injuries grew by 12 percent. How many more deaths, how many assaults on the personal integrity of people, need to happen before this Congress will see the need for hate crimes legislation?

The statistics and Matthew's individual personal story demonstrate that these incidents are not isolated. Harassment of gays, lesbians and bisexuals is not isolated to one geographic area nor to any one factor. As our country knows all too well, hate crimes take many forms and affect many different kinds of victims. We all remember the 1996 horrible murder of James Byrd, Jr., an African-American man in Texas. We all remember earlier this year, when a gunman opened fire at a Jewish Community Center and then singled out an Asian-American and shot him. These harsh stories are troubling and unfortunately, recent shootings are a constant reminder of the hate that still exists in our society.

The Hate Crimes Prevention Act would provide law enforcement officials with needed tools, and would serve as a lasting tribute to the lives of

Matthew Shepard, James Byrd, Jr., and the others who have been victimized by hate crimes. The Hate Crimes Prevention Act would not end all violence against people because they are gay, or African-American, or Jewish, or come from another country. Nonetheless, this legislation would allow the Federal Government to investigate and punish crimes motivated by hate.

The murder of Matthew Shepard is the manifestation of the enduring bigotry that still prevails in our society. Our Nation should take action and pass this responsible legislation which would enable Federal law enforcement officials to fight these crimes and punish the perpetrators.

November 16, 1999

Recognizing Amnesty International-USA for Its Leadership in Promoting LGBT Human Rights

Tom Lantos

These remarks were made on the floor of the House of Representatives by Representative Lantos on November 16, 1999, and printed in the *Congressional Record* for this date on page E2391.

Mr. Speaker, I rise today to commend Amnesty International-USA for its foresight in establishing the Amnesty OUTFRONT Program this past year. OUTFRONT is Amnesty's program and membership network which is focused on promoting the human rights of lesbian, gay, bisexual and transgender people around the world.

The human rights of lesbians, gay men, bisexuals and transgender people are violated daily, Mr. Speaker. Not only are people beaten, imprisoned, and killed by their own governments for engaging in homosexual acts, but those suspected of being lesbian, gay, bisexual or transgender are routinely the victims of harassment, discrimination, intimidation and violence. Many of those who speak up for lesbian and gay rights—regardless of their sexual orientation—are themselves persecuted with impunity and thus pressured to remain silent.

Mr. Speaker, the OUTFRONT Program will work with similar programs being developed in Amnesty divisions throughout the world and with Amnesty's research department to insure that human rights violations committed against lesbian, gay, bisexual and transgender people are documented and actions are taken to combat these violations. The effort will promote human rights standards at the international and national level that recognize the basic human rights of all people. In the United States, Amnesty OUTFRONT will launch a public campaign to raise awareness of the human rights violations faced by lesbian, gay, bisexual and transgender people around the world and will work to build an activist membership committed to combating these violations wherever they occur.

As Co-Chair of the Congressional Human Rights Caucus, Mr. Speaker, I have long admired the human rights activity of Amnesty International and am proud to work with the organization in combating human rights violations. I welcome Amnesty's special concern for the human rights concerns of lesbian, gay, bisexual and transgender people. This important aspect of human rights has not been given adequate attention, given the dimensions of the problem. I welcome the fact that a renowned human rights organization like Amnesty is taking a lead in this area.

Mr. Speaker, I urge my colleagues to work with me and with Amnesty International in promoting awareness of human rights violations on the basis of sexual orientation and mounting a forceful campaign against such injustices. I look forward to working closely with Amnesty and its OUTFRONT Program in the coming years, and I wish them great success in developing this important program.

SECTION VII: 2000

February 20, 2000

Speech at the Dedication of the Leather Archives and Museum

Joseph Bean

This address was given by veteran activist Joseph Bean in the theater later known as the Etienne Center at the dedication of the building of the Leather Archives and Museum on Greenview Avenue in Chicago, near Loyola University. Bean was at this time serving as executive director of the institution, a position he held until early 2002.

How does this feel to you? All of this? Viola Johnson cried. I did too, a few times. Several people have just stepped back, speechless. I have done that too and more than once. What you have done by believing in the Leather Archives and Museum, and supporting it, and putting the records of your lives into the collections of the Leather Archives is an unprecedented thing. You have done in next to no time what other communities in this country and the world have take a century or more to do. We have made a footprint in the mire of our bigoted times that can be forever measured and scrutinized, tested and examined by anyone and everyone who cares to. If the curious come asking what is this leather thing, is it what I am looking for? they will discover that we are everywhere in time and space, that we are of every sort, that we are a generous and loving family ready to welcome and teach and support them. If other leatherfolk like ourselves come here, they will discover how very NOT alone they are, and they will discover a community of people like themselves, and they will go away more able to live their lives in the world free of shame and guilt. If our enemies come—and they will come—they will find little to support their view of our debauchery or our moral bankruptcy, but they will find that most powerful of all antidotes for hatred: The Truth. This will not make them love us, but neither will it give unalloyed fuel to their disgust.

Until now, we and those seriously curious about us and even our enemies, have had no one place to go to find out the truth about leather and leathersex, about leather lives and the leather community or, certainly, about leather love.

From today, people all over this country and the world people will know that we are unashamed of our lives. Indeed, we will put them on display in a museum. We will put the truth about ourselves in an archives and, for that matter, in the *Chicago Tribune* and *The New York Times* if we get half a chance. The Leather Archives and Museum has many tasks to do: Supplying the news media with the truth about leather, providing leather newcomers with a home for the desires of their untried hearts, making a lasting home for the records of leather lives, supporting those students and scholars who want to examine and explore our way of living and loving, but above all, I believe, our job is to stockpile pride and love and self-assurance so that those who experience shame or loneliness or self-doubt because of their leather realities will, for generations to come, find here what they are lacking.

If Jewish Americans need to be reminded of what is special about themselves and their forebears, they can find shows in many museums, and especially the Holocaust Museum in our nation's capital. If Native Americans need to be reassured that what happened to their forefathers will never be forgotten or repeated, they will soon be able to go to the last new museum making up the national capital mall for that reminder. If African Americans lack certainty that their troubled times and their achievements will be remembered, they have museums across the country, and more being built all the time, where they can bolster their sense of self and reassert the long-since abandoned but true anthem "Black Is Beautiful." You and I know better than to wait. There is no Museum of Sexual Differences planned for Washington, D.C. There are no government bodies set up to explore our need or to fund our protection. We knew all along that if we would have the things without which a community has no real center, we would have to build them ourselves. And we have done that.

Of course, we are probably about five years and a million dollars away from insuring that our realized dream remains secure for all time, but I feel sure that our commitment will last as long as it is needed. So resting on my personal faith in you, I am inviting you now to attend the Leather Archives and Museum's Fall 2004 mortgage burning party. Come on back!

If we can come this far, we can go all the way. That million dollar figure I just mentioned was no wild guess. The budget that will pay for this building and keep it running, and give us the footing we need to attract funding from foundations and governments, requires nine hundred and eighty thousand dollars between now and August 2002, and we can do that. Let me put this in perspective. There are 164 seats in this theater. If the person assigned to each seat would donate or raise for the LA&M just $1,493.90 for these four years, we'd have done [it] exactly. The building would be paid off, the museum would be furnished, and we would have the time and community support required to become attractive to other funding sources, to begin to reap the benefits of our work, to cease being a begging charity and become—in every way—a community resource. I won't harangue you further about the money we need. There are jugs all over this building into which you can put gifts. Any one of the people helping out this weekend will gladly accept your check or credit card information or your IOU, for that matter. What I want you to see is not the NEED but how close we are now to filling the need completely and for all time. This can be done. In fact, you have in a sense already done it with your promises and the faith you have shown in what we are doing here.

So secure in the faith I have in you, I invite you here and now to stand with me and warm this building, this new home for leather history, with an ovation that will ring down through the years of its service to leathermen and leatherwomen for all time. Just once first, after you are standing, let this building hear the mantra that reminds me every day what I am doing in Chicago. This is our new and permanent Leather Archives and Museum. . . .

LOCATED IN CHICAGO AND SERVING THE WORLD!

March 8, 2000

Human Rights Violations Based on Sexual Orientation

Tom Lantos

These remarks were given on the floor of the House of Representatives by Representative Lantos of California and entered into the *Congressional Record* for March 8, 2000.

Mr. Speaker, with the support of 30 of our colleagues—including both Republicans and Democrats—I introduced House Concurrent Resolution 259, a bill decrying human rights violations based on sexual orientation and gender identity. I did this, Mr. Speaker, because I believe very strongly that we in the Congress must send a strong message that—no matter what any of our colleague's views may be on the question of the lifestyle of gays and lesbians—that gay, lesbian, bisexual and transgender people must be treated with dignity and respect, not with hatred and violence.

All around the world, Mr. Speaker, unacceptable violations of human rights have taken place against individuals solely on the basis of their real or perceived sexual orientation. These ongoing persecutions against gay people include arbitrary arrests, rape, torture, imprisonment, extortion, and even execution.

The scope of these human rights violations is staggering, and for the victims there are few avenues for relief. Mr. Speaker, some states create an atmosphere of impunity for rapists and murderers by failing to prosecute or investigate violence targeted at individuals because of their sexual orientation. These abuses are not only sanctioned by some states, often, they are perpetrated by agents of the state.

Mr. Speaker, in Afghanistan, men convicted of sodomy by Taliban Shari'a courts are placed next to standing walls by Taliban officials and subsequently executed as the walls are toppled upon them, and they are buried under the rubble. Police in countries such as Turkey, Albania, and Russia, among others, routinely commit human rights abuses such as extortion, entrapment, and even physical assaults.

In Brazil, a lesbian couple was tortured and sexually assaulted by civil police. Despite the existence of a medical report and eye-witness testimony, their case remains unprosecuted. Many of us in the Congress protested when, in Zimbabwe, members of "Gays and Lesbians of Zimbabwe" were threatened and brutally assaulted for forming an organization to advocate for social and political rights. In Uganda, the president ordered police to arrest all homosexuals, and the punishment for conviction of homosexual activity is life in prison.

Mr. Speaker, around the world, individuals are targeted and their basic human rights are denied because of their sexual orientation. The number and frequency of such grievous crimes against individuals cannot be ignored. Violence against individuals for their real, or perceived, sexual orientation violates the most basic rights this Congress has worked to protect and defend.

H. Con. Res. 259 puts the United States on record against such horrible human rights violations. As a civilized country, we must speak out against and condemn these crimes. Our resolution notes the violence against gay people in countries as wide ranging as Saudi Arabia, Mexico, China, El Salvador, and other countries. By calling attention to this unprovoked and indefensible violence, this resolution will broaden awareness of human rights violations based on sexual orientation.

H. Con. Res. 259 reaffirms that human rights defined in international conventions include protection from violence and abuse on the basis of sexual identity, but it does not seek to establish a special category of human rights related to sexual orientation or gender identity. Furthermore it commends relevant governmental and non-governmental organizations (such as Amnesty, Human Rights Watch, and the International Gay and Lesbian Human Rights Commission) for documenting the ongoing abuse of human rights on the basis of sexual orientation. Our resolution condemns all human rights violations based on sexual orientation and recognizes that such violations should be equally punished, without discrimination.

This legislation is endorsed by a broad coalition of international human rights groups, gay rights groups, and faith-based organizations, among others. They include: Amnesty International, International Gay and Lesbian Human Rights Commission, Human Rights Watch, National Gay and Lesbian Taskforce, Human Rights Campaign, Log Cabin Republicans, Liberty Education Fund, National Council of the Churches of Christ in the USA, Equal Partners in Faith, the United Church of Christ, the National Organization of Women (NOW), NOW Legal Defense and Education Fund, and the Anti-Defamation League.

Mr. Speaker, the protection of gender identity is not a special right or privilege, but it should be fully acknowledged in international human rights norms. I ask that my colleagues join with me in wholeheartedly embracing and supporting basic human rights for all people, no matter what their sexual orientation might be. It is the only decent thing to do.

Mr. Speaker, I ask that the text of H. Con. Res. 259 be included in the RECORD.

HOUSE CONCURRENT RESOLUTION 259

> Expressing the concern of Congress regarding human rights violations against lesbians, gay men, bisexuals, and transgendered individuals around the world.
>
> Whereas treaties, conventions, and declarations to which the United States are a party address government obligations to combat human rights violations, and the overall goals and standards of these treaties, conventions, and declarations in promoting human rights of all individuals have been found to be consistent with, and in support of, the aspirations of the United States at home and globally, as well as consistent with the Constitution of the United States;
>
> Whereas articles 3 and 5 of the 1948 Universal Declaration of Human Rights, articles 6 and 7 of the 1966 International Covenant on Civil and Political Rights, and the 1984 Convention against Torture and Other Cruel, Inhuman or Degrading Treatment or Punishment, guarantee all individuals the right to life, liberty, and security of person, and guarantee that no one shall be Subjected to torture or to cruel, inhuman, or degrading treatment or punishment;
>
> Whereas the fundamental human right not to be arbitrarily deprived of life is violated when those convicted of homosexual acts in Afghanistan are sentenced to be executed and are crushed by having walls toppled over them, and there remain a number of other countries around the world that call for the possible execution of those convicted of homosexual acts, including Saudi Arabia, Yemen, Kuwait, Mauritania, and Iran;
>
> Whereas the fundamental right not to be subjected to torture or other cruel, inhuman or degrading treatment is violated when gay men, lesbians, bisexuals and transgendered individuals are subjected to severe beatings while in police custody in Turkey and Albania, and individuals in these groups are also routinely the victims of human rights abuses, such as extortion, entrapment, physical assaults, and rape,

committed by the police in Mexico, Argentina, and Russia, among other countries;

Whereas a number of lesbians, gay men, bisexuals, and transgendered individuals are targeted and tortured or killed by paramilitary groups in Colombia and El Salvador, which operate in collusion with the military, police, and government officials;

Whereas articles 2 and 7 of the Universal Declaration of Human Rights and articles, 2, 14 and 26 of the International Covenant on Civil and Political Rights guarantee all individuals freedom from arbitrary discrimination and equal protection before the law;

Whereas in many countries arbitrary detention or cruel, inhuman, or degrading treatment or conditions in detention directly result from the application of penal laws criminalizing same sex behavior between consenting adults, such as a 5-year sentence for private same sex behavior between consenting adults in Romania, and some of those individuals who have been convicted in Romania report torture, including rape, in prison, and all are unable to seek redress for abuses in detention;

Whereas in Pakistan and Saudi Arabia the sentence for same sex behavior between consenting adults includes "flogging" and in Singapore and Uganda the sentence for same sex behavior between consenting adults can extend to life in prison;

Whereas many governments, on the basis of vague laws, may target and persecute lesbians, gay men, bisexuals, and transgendered individuals: in the People's Republic of China individuals in these groups are imprisoned under laws against "hooliganism," in Argentina, individuals in these groups are imprisoned under the laws against "vagrants and crooks," and the vagueness of these laws makes it difficult to monitor governmental persecution;

Whereas articles 19 and 20 of the Universal Declaration of Human Rights and articles 19 and 22 of the International Covenant on Civil and Political Rights guarantee all individuals freedom of expression and freedom of association;

Whereas the fundamental rights of freedom of expression and association are violated when governments deny the right of lesbians, gay men, bisexuals, and transgendered individuals to form organizations or advocate for rights, such as in Zimbabwe where members of Gays and Lesbians of Zimbabwe (GALZ) have been threatened and brutally assaulted;

Whereas in some countries agents of the government are directing or are complicitous in abuses committed on the basis of sexual orientation and gender identity and investigations and prosecution of those agents for violations often do not occur;

Whereas due to failure by governments to investigate and prosecute human rights violations based on sexual orientation and gender identity, private individuals feel encouraged to violently attack lesbians, gay men, bisexuals, and transgendered individuals with impunity, contributing to the atmosphere of fear and intimidation;

Whereas lesbians and bisexual women who suffer human rights violations are often abused because of their sexual orientation while their gender often incites, compounds and aggravates this abuse, and, moreover, since their gender is not recognized as a factor, their abuse often goes unrecorded;

Whereas violations of internationally recognized human rights norms are to be considered crimes regardless of the status of the victims and are to be punished without discrimination;

Whereas fundamental access to legal protection from violations of internationally recognized human rights norms is often unavailable to the victims;

Whereas lesbians and bisexual women face additional obstacles in these countries when seeking assistance from police, judges, and other officials due to pervasive gender bias;

Whereas the preceding clauses constitute only a few examples of the violations suffered by lesbians, gay men, bisexuals and transgendered individuals, the full range and extent of such violations are not known because governments create an atmosphere of immunity for those perpetrating such human rights violations and prevent victims from seeking effective protection and just redress and thus their suffering remains undocumented and unremedied; and

Whereas many governmental human rights organizations, including Amnesty International, Human Rights Watch, and the International Gay and Lesbian Human Rights Commission, as well as the United States Department of State and the United Nations, have documented, and are continuing to document, the ongoing violations of the human rights of lesbians, gay men, bisexuals and transgendered individuals: Now, therefore, be it

Resolved, by the House of Representatives (the Senate Concurring)

condemns all violations of internationally recognized human rights norms based on the real or perceived sexual orientation or gender identity of an individual, and commends nongovernmental human rights organizations, including Amnesty International, Human Rights Watch, and the International Gay and Lesbian Human Rights Commission, as well as the United States Department of State and the United Nations, for documenting the ongoing abuse of human rights on the basis of sexual orientation and gender identity; and

(A) recognizes that human rights violations abroad based in sexual orientation and gender identity should be equally punished without discrimination and equally classified as crimes, regardless of the status of the victims and that such violations should be given the same consideration and concern as human rights violations based on other grounds in the formulation of policies to promote and protect human rights globally; and

(B) further recognizes that the protection of sexual orientation and gender identity is not a special category of human rights, but it is fully embedded in the overall human rights norms as defined in international conventions.

March 9, 2000

An Open Letter to the Lesbian, Gay, Bisexual, and Transgender Community

This letter was originally printed in one of Chicago's weekly gay and lesbian community newspapers, *Windy City Times,* on March 9, 2000, and is signed by eleven Illinois activist organizations. They are the Chicago Democratic Socialists of America's Queer Commission, the Chicago Metro Area Gay Youth Coalition, the Coalition for Positive Sexuality, Equality Illinois, Homocore Chicago, Hysterical Women, It's Time Illinois, Khuli Zaban, Queer to the Left, Transsexual Menace Chicago, and Women in the Director's Chair. *OUTlines* refers to the other newspaper serving the Chicago gay and lesbian community at this time.

We are writing to register our outrage with the process by which a so-called Millennium March on Washington (MMOW) is being organized, and to explain why we think participation in this march is actually detrimental to our community. Many of us have participated in past Washington marches. We are dismayed to see how a small group of people with corporate financial backing have appropriated this historically important means for mobilizing people at key political moments for their own purposes.

From the beginning, the process used to call, organize and conduct this march has been corrupt and exclusionary. Despite sentiments against a national march at a 1997 Creating Change Conference (a gathering of activists who work at the state and local levels of the political process around the country) top leaders of the Human Rights Campaign (HRC) and the Universal Fellowship of Metropolitan Community Churches (MCC) unilaterally decided to hold and name the march without consulting other national, state, or local LGBT organizations.

Faced with mounting criticism regarding a lack of accountability and community input, march organizers announced that they would hold "town hall" meetings across the country to solicit grassroots input. But these meetings were not publicized and few were actually held. Only 25 people showed up at the first meeting in Minneapolis, home to one of the march co-chairs.

The second meeting was scheduled for Chicago. There were no announcements in the local LGBT press about the event, but approximately 75 people showed up (most learning about the event through email posts), almost all voicing opposition to holding a march.

Simultaneously, MMOW organizers said that folks could use the Internet to cast ballots for issues the march should take up. As *OUTlines* reported recently, MMOW organizers have subsequently disregarded these votes. Large numbers of people suggested that AIDS and reproductive rights be a part of the march platform, but these issues are, incredibly, not part of what is now being called the "working vision" for the march. A final political agenda has yet to be set, and the march is less than two months away. Why even begin planning a march before having an agenda? Why expect folks to make plans to attend the march now when they don't even know what they are to be marching for?

There has also been no financial accountability. Despite suspicions that some people would be inappropriately profiting from this march, the MMOW board refuses to release financial information. Moreover, the MMOW board has held no open bids for any contracts.

Given the lack of accountability and democratic input regarding any element of this event, it is not surprising that no Chicago or statewide Illinois LGBT groups have signed on as sponsors of this march. On a national level, the National Black Lesbian and Gay Leadership Forum, Pride At Work, BINET USA, It's Time America, the National Stonewall Democratic Federation, and the National Association of Black and White Men Together have refused to support the march. Welcomed to the MMOW board in the face of criticism that the march was being organized by a narrow elite, the executive directors of National Gay and Lesbian Task Force and the National Youth Advocacy Coalition ultimately ended up resigning because of the board's inability to address meaningfully its credibility problems regarding democratic input and fiscal accountability to LGBT communities.

Since the substantive issues to be taken up by this march have never been made clear, and the process so exclusionary, it is hard to imagine what the purpose of this event is other than to advance the power of march organizers, with a substantial turnout being used to parlay themselves into the role of the principal, if not exclusive, voice for the LBGT community. But we are a diverse community, and no one or two organizations can ever pretend to speak for all of us. It is particularly unconscionable to us that a national march allegedly representing the aspirations of all LGBT people can proceed without the leadership and support of a single national organization of African-American, bisexual or transgendered folks—people who have traditionally faced exclusions in heterosexual and LGBT communities.

Participation in this march uncritically replicates and propagates the racism, elitism and consumerism that need to be confronted if we are to achieve the justice our movement seeks. We urge our fellow LGBT brothers and sisters to sit this march out, and to instead hook up with one of the many local and state LGBT organizations that are already doing important work in our communities.

April 25, 2000

The GLBT Movement at a Crossroads

Elizabeth Toledo

This address was given at the National Press Club in Washington, DC, in April 2000 by Toledo, who was at that time the incoming executive director of the National Gay and Lesbian Task Force.

Good morning. I am here this morning to discuss the state of the gay, lesbian, bisexual and transgender movement for equality in the United States.

As many state legislators across the land wrap up their work and adjourn, we are seeing a frenzied pace of legislative activity surrounding GLBT issues. For only the second year in our movement's history, we have seen bills favorable to our community outnumber unfavorable bills—and the ratio is rapidly increasing. So far this year, the National Gay and Lesbian Task Force has tracked 466 bills, of which 288 are favorable and 178 are unfavorable. By comparison, last year, we tracked 269 favorable bills and 205 unfavorable ones.

A trend has emerged which shows that although the gay, lesbian, bisexual and transgender population remains under fierce attack, the movement toward civil rights for all is steadily gaining strength.

Today the Vermont House of Representatives is poised to give that final approval to a bill that would allow same-sex couples the right to enter into official civil unions sanctioned by the states. If approved and signed into law, the Vermont bill will do what no state has ever done before—it will provide same-sex couples with all of the rights, benefits and responsibilities of marriage that a state can offer.

Vermont has garnered a lot of attention, and rightfully so. But did you know about Georgia? Indiana? Maine? Alabama? Georgia this year for the first time ever has passed and enacted a hate crimes law. Indiana has passed and enacted a hate crimes data collection law. While not a full-blown hate crimes law, it represents the first time Indiana legislators have ever reacted favorably to a GLBT issue. Maine has passed and forwarded to the voters a full-scale civil rights law that includes sexual orientation. In Alabama, the House has passed an historic bill adding sexual orientation to the existing hate crimes law. The bill is scheduled to come up for a hearing in the Senate tomorrow.

Five states—Mississippi, Nebraska, New Hampshire, New Mexico, Wisconsin—have defeated attempts to either pass or strengthen anti-same-sex marriage laws.

The pace of activity this year continues a trend we first noticed in 1999, a breakthrough year for the GLBT movement. Last year's legislative victories included historic advances in such disparate states as California, Kentucky, New Hampshire and Nevada. In California, legislators passed and the governor signed a trio of bills that established a statewide registry for same-sex couples, added sexual orientation to the nondiscrimination clauses under the state Fair Employment and Housing Act and offered public school students some protection against discrimination on the basis of sexual orientation.

In Kentucky, two cities and two counties adopted pro-GLBT civil rights measures. In New Hampshire, a law preventing same-sex couples from adopting children was repealed. And Nevada became the 11th state to ban job discrimination on the basis of sexual orientation.

While we have largely picked up in the year 2000 where we left off, the news is not all good. Two states—Utah and Mississippi—have passed bills preventing same-sex couples from adopting children. Two state legislatures—Colorado and West Virginia—passed laws preventing same-sex couples from marrying, and California voters approved a measure banning the state from recognizing same-sex marriages in other states. The number of states that have explicitly passed laws banning same-sex marriage will reach 33 if the Colorado governor signs that state's legislation.

Such activity reflects that unfortunate reality of our movement. There is a checkerboard quality to the legal and cultural victories for the LGBT movement, and too often the difference between legitimacy and illegitimacy in the eyes of society may rest on something as arbitrary as a state boundary. Many residents of this country assume that the great strides of the civil rights movement have afforded broad protection against discrimination for all. In fact the legal reality is that those of us in same-sex relationships have not been fully protected from discrimination in housing, jobs, family law, education—virtually every aspect of our lives is subject to discrimination and sadly, hate violence or harassment remains a reality in every state in the nation.

Too often the cultural strides that are made in the media, in places of worship, in schools and universities and in the workplace are misinterpreted as a sign that equality has been won.

I'll give you an example. The National Gay and Lesbian Task Force frequently receives phone calls from same-sex couples asking for a list of states in which they can legally marry. These individuals see shows like *Will and Grace* or *Dawson's Creek.* They worship in churches or synagogues that welcome them. They are out in the workplace or at school. They just assume, like many heterosexual Americans, that the barriers of discrimination have been eradicated.

The reality, of course, is quite different. Not a single state allows same-sex marriage. 39 states allow gay, lesbian, bisexual and transgender employees to be fired from our jobs. 28 states lack hate crimes laws that include sexual orientation. 18 states criminalize loving, same-sex relationships.

Today the GLBT movement is at a crossroads. We are under open assault by those who would deny us basic human rights, and at the same time the nation is witnessing a surge in support for our cause. Our lives, our liberty, our pursuit of happiness depend upon our ability to build strong political infrastructure and organize on the state and local level.

Local organizing has always been the trademark of the National Gay and Lesbian Task Force. Fortunately, we are not alone. Today, the state and local political infrastructure of the GLBT movement in the United States is stronger than it has ever been before.

In 1996, NGLTF helped found the Federation of Statewide LGBT Political Organizations. This federation consists of political groups that fight for equality. In just four years' time, the Federation has grown to represent members in every state in the union, an incredible rate of growth in such a short period of time.

With the Federation's help, last year NGLTF was able to produce the largest grassroots mobilization in our movement's history. We helped organize some 350 rallies and other events in all 50 state capitols [*sic*], plus D.C. and Puerto Rico, during a one-week period. Our campaign—called "Equality Begins At Home"—and the work of the Federation paved the way for the wonderful successes we have seen in the past year.

Now many state legislatures are wrapping up their business and adjourning. Attention will soon shift to the November election—and what could be the most important election of our generation. The GLBT voting bloc has proven to be one of the most powerful constituencies in the country in recent election cycles. If our voters are motivated to the polls and elect supportive leaders, we could have the opportunity to shape groundbreaking legal protection. If the nation elects leaders who are hostile to all that NGLTF stands for, we could witness a serious backlash to our hard-won gains.

Dr. Martin Luther King once said that the moral arc of the universe is long but bends toward justice. Dr. King was right—but with our continued organizing and mobilization, we can make that moral arc bend much more quickly.

April 30, 2000

Keep the Flame Alive for Rights

Tammy Baldwin

This is the speech given by U.S. Representative Tammy Baldwin (D-WI), representative from Wisconsin's 2nd congressional district, to the Millennium March for Gay and Lesbian Rights in Washington, DC, on April 30, 2000.

If I close my eyes, I can remember being here in 1987. I came to this city, this historic place, these steps. Why did I march?

I was 25 years old and just one year into my first term in elective office. I was out. I was at the point in my life where I had just realized that I did not have to choose between being honest about who I am and pursuing the career of my dreams. I could do both.

And that moment of decision was at once one of the most terrifying and one of the most freeing of my life. So I marched to replace my fear with courage, my isolation with belonging, my anger with hope.

If I close my eyes, I can remember being here in 1993. I came to this city, this historic place, these steps. Why did I march? I was 31 years old and had just been elected to the Wisconsin legislature.

I had just gotten a touching glimpse of the power of our visibility.

After a statewide new story announced that I was the first openly gay or lesbian person to be elected to state-level office in Wisconsin, I received a telephone call from a young man.

His voice was wavering. He was from northern Wisconsin and he said, "I read the story and I feel differently about myself today." So I marched, so that he and others might be able to replace fear with courage, isolation with belonging, anger with hope.

If I close my eyes, I can remember coming to this city, this historic place, these steps in January 1999. Only this time, I climbed these steps to take the oath of office. And as I climbed these steps, I remembered all those who had marched and mobilized—those who helped pave the way for my election and the election of those who will come after me. You are with me every time I pass through those doors.

And the lessons learned from you, from my participation in this civil rights movement, and from organizing against AIDS are now being applied, empowering me as I fight every day the battle for health care for all, increasing educational opportunities, and fighting for many others who lack a voice in our democracy.

Now, with open eyes, I am experiencing this march. I come to this city, this historic place, these steps. I'm 38 years old and I'm a member of Congress.

Why do I march? I march to challenge the naysayers, the cynics, and the keepers of the status quo. And I march for a promising, inspiring, and incredible new generation—so they might replace their fear with courage, their isolation with belonging, their fear with hope.

And I can say with conviction: Never doubt that there is reason to be hopeful.

Never doubt that Congress will pass legislation that expands the definition of hate crimes.

Never doubt that the states will grant us equal rights, including all the rights afforded couples through marriage.

Never doubt that we will enact legislation ensuring nondiscrimination in the workplace.

Never doubt that America will one day realize that her gay, bisexual, and transgendered sons and daughters want nothing more—and deserve nothing less—than the rights accorded every other citizen.

But we must make it so—by daring to dream of a world in which we are free.

So, if you dream of a world in which you can put your partner's picture on your desk, then put his picture on your desk—and you will live in such a world.

And if you dream of a world in which you can walk down the street holding your partner's hand, then hold her hand . . . and you will live in such a world.

If you dream of a world in which there are more openly gay elected officials then run for office . . . and you will live in such a world.

And if you dream of a world in which you can take your partner to the office party, even if your office is the U.S. House of Representatives, then take her to the party. I do, and now I live in such a world. Remember, there are two things that keep us oppressed: them and us. We are half of the equation.

There will not be a magic day when we wake up and it's now OK to express ourselves publicly.

We must make that day ourselves, by speaking out publicly—first in small numbers, then in greater numbers, until it's simply the way things are and no one thinks twice.

Never doubt that we will create this world, because, my friends, we are fortunate to live in a democracy, and in a democracy, we decide what's possible.

April 30, 2000

Remarks at the Millennium March for Equality

Troy Perry

This is the text of the address made to those attending the Millennium March on Washington by Reverend Troy Perry, founder and moderator of the Universal Fellowship of Metropolitan Community Churches, on the Mall in Washington, DC, on April 30, 2000.

We've gathered today on the National Mall with incredible diversity!
We've gathered here today:
Those ready to fight for justice,
And those who are weary from the battle.
I come here today as a person of faith.
Many of us gathered here today are people of faith.

Let me also quickly acknowledge that too many of us in the gay, lesbian, bisexual and transgendered communities have been hurt by organized religion.

In spite of that:
Many of us have found strength and hope in our spiritual faith.

So we gather here today:
Jew and Christian, Islamic and Hindu, Pagan and Wiccan, as well as those who have rejected any faith system.
And today I proclaim this message that I have preached during my 30 years of activism:
Believe that God—the God of the Universe—loves you just the way you are!

There are some things I believe with all my heart. These are the things I believe with unshakeable faith:

I believe that we don't owe an apology to anyone for who we are!
I believe that God loves me, And if God loves me, I KNOW that God loves YOU!
I believe every one of us can come to terms with our own spirituality without the control of any other person, church, temple, group or organization.

Let me make it clear:
In Metropolitan Community Churches we believe in *freedom of religion* for all people. And we believe just as passionately in *freedom from religion* for those who choose another path.

But this is my witness: In my own life, my faith has kept me going.
What a battle this struggle for justice has been!

For many of us in these diverse communities, our spiritual faith has kept our hope alive in the midst of the struggle.

This is my witness: in the ongoing battle for social justice: *We've come this far by faith!*
But I tell you the truth: Some days its been hard to keep the faith.
When our gay, lesbian, bisexual and transgendered communities continue to suffer the oppression of hate crimes; it's hard to keep the faith.

In my own church—the Metropolitan Community Churches: more than 21 of our congregations have been firebombed or arsoned. In New Orleans, 12 of our members died in a terrible fire. In California, Rev. Virgil Scott was murdered solely because he was gay. And just six moths ago, our associate pastor in Sacramento, Rev. Ed Sheriff, died after being stabbed 24 times. The police say it was "just" a robbery, but I'm not so sure.

I am so conscious that as we gather here today, we are surrounded by a great cloud of witnesses:
We are surrounded by our own gay, lesbian, bisexual and transgendered martyrs: Those who have paid for this struggle with their own lives and who inspire us to keep on keeping on.

So some days it's hard to keep the faith, when our people are still oppressed and harassed and murdered. Some nights I awake up in the middle of the night, and I can see them—I can see them just as clearly as if they were standing in front of me. I see the people I have met during 30 years of activism for our community:

Too many high school students taunted and branded as "faggots" and "dykes."
Too many people who've attempted to end their lives too soon because society heaped shame and humiliation upon them.
I think of the man who walked away from his spirituality because his faith community rejected him.
I see the mother in tears because the court took her baby.
I think of the partner of 35 years denied access to his lover's hospital room because no laws protected their relationship.

Listen, America:
It's time to end the division!
It's time to end the oppression!
And it's time to stop the hate crimes against our people!

Listen, America:
Holy Scripture tells us it is a sin to murder!
It is a sin to oppress!
It is a sin to deny or destroy God's creation!

God didn't create us so God could sit around and have someone to hate!

Listen, America:
It's time for this nation to repent of her sins against gays, lesbians, bisexuals and transgendered persons.

Listen, America:
It's time to welcome all of the human family to our rightful place at the table of understanding.

Listen to me:
Until those who seek to oppress us have ceased from their ways:
WE MUST NOT REST!
Until the government leaves our families alone and protects our children:
WE MUST NOT REST!
Until we can marry those we love:
WE MUST NOT REST!
Until hatred and prejudice are banished from our vocabularies:
WE MUST NOT REST!
Until the doors of all churches and temples and houses of faith open wide in welcome to all people:
WE MUST NOT REST!

Until the Matt Shepards and the James Byrds and the Billy Jack Gaithers are no longer taken from us:
WE MUST NOT REST!

Oh yes, there are days it's hard to keep the faith. But just when I think I can no longer go on, faith stirs inside me. Hope is reborn. And new strength arises.

Today, each of us must renew our commitment to "fight the good fight."
Until all our people are free from oppression;
Until this nation grants equality to all our people;
Until all our people experience the promise of our nation's ancient creeds;
Until that day, I'll continue to cling to the words of the old hymn, words we all know;

"Through many dangers, toils and snares,
I have already come."

"Tis grace that brought me safe this far,
And grace will lead me home."

Until that day for which we work and strive:
Keep the faith!
Keep the faith!
Keep the faith!

May 2, 2000

Honoring Dr. Franklin Kameny and the GLAA

Eleanor Holmes Norton

This speech was given on the floor of the House of Representatives by Representative Norton, the delegate from the District of Columbia, and entered into the *Congressional Record* for May 2, 2000.

Mr. Speaker, today I recognize two Washington, D.C. institutions that have been in the forefront of the lesbian, gay, bisexual and transgendered civil rights movement, and that I have the distinct honor and pleasure of representing in this body: the Gay and Lesbian Activists Alliance of Washington, D.C. (GLAA), the oldest continually active gay and lesbian rights organization in the United States and its charter member, Dr. Franklin E. Kameny.

Since its founding in April, 1971, GLAA has been a respected and persistent advocate in District politics tirelessly asserting equal rights and social equality for lesbians and gay men living in the city. In the last two years, its advocacy with the city government helped reestablish an independent Office of Human Rights and the Citizen Complaint Review Board; implementation of a unique identifier system for reporting cases of HIV/AIDS to help protect the privacy of people who test positive for HIV; and the establishment of an antiharassment policy by the District of Columbia Public Schools.

On April 27, GLAA held its 29th Anniversary Reception honoring the year 2000 recipients of its Distinguished Service Awards: Steve Block of the American Civil Liberties Union/National Capital Area; Jeffrey Berman of the Public Defender Service; local and international gay activist Barrett L. Brick; Food and Friends; Dr. Patricia Hawkins, Associate Director of the Whitman Walker Clinic; and Jessica Xavier, a local and national transgendered activist. GLAA also celebrated Frank Kameny's 75th birthday.

Dr. Kameny's resume reflects the history of the gay and lesbian movement in the District of Columbia. He remains an indefatigable and outspoken gay activist. Dr. Kameny holds a BS in Physics from Queens College and an M.A. and a Ph.D. in Astronomy from Harvard University.

In 1957, Dr. Kameny began an 18-year struggle to end the civil service ban on the federal employment of gay men and lesbians that achieved success in 1975 and was recently formalized by President Clinton with Executive Order 13087. In 1961, Dr. Kameny founded the Mattachine Society of Washington, the first local gay and lesbian organization in the District. The following year, he initiated an the ongoing effort to lift the band on gay men and lesbians in the military.

By 1962, Dr. Kameny had become the nationally recognized authority on security clearances for lesbians and gay men. His efforts resulted in lifting of the absolute ban on gay and lesbian security clearances in 1980, which President Clinton made formal with Executive Order 12968. In 1965, Dr. Kameny organized the first lesbian and gay demonstration at the White House; and a year before the "Stonewall Rebellion" in New York City, in 1968, he coined the slogan "Gay Is Good."

In 1971, Dr. Kameny ran for Congress in the District of Columbia, the first openly gay person to seek such an office in the country. His campaign committee became the nucleus of the Gay and Lesbian Activists Alliance of Washington, D.C. He subsequently helped draft the D.C. Human Rights Law, one of the strongest civil rights laws in the country, which codified gay and lesbian civil rights in the District.

Dr. Kameny's 10 year fight to have homosexuality removed from the American Psychiatric Association's classification as a mental illness succeeded in 1973. He was a founding member of the National Gay and Lesbian Task Force (1973), the Gay Rights National Lobby (1975), which ultimately became the Human Rights Campaign, and the Gertrude Stein Democratic Club (1976).

Dr. Kameny became D.C.'s first openly gay municipal appointee when Mayor Washington appointed him to the Human Rights Commission (1975). He drafted the legislation which repealed the D.C. Sodomy Law in 1993.

Dr. Kameny continues to be a revered and effective activist. He lectures, writes, and testifies on behalf of gay and lesbian issues. He has become the institutional memory of D.C.' s gay and lesbian rights movement.

I ask the House to join me in congratulating the Gay and Lesbian Activists and Dr. Franklin E. Kameny.

July 5, 2000

Boy Scouts of America Rally

Ken South

This speech was delivered before a crowd of more than 100 demonstrators outside the local Boy Scouts of America headquarters in Baltimore, Maryland, on July 5, 2000. The Supreme Court decision Reverend South refers to was handed down on June 28, 2000.

I stand before you today a 54 year old white American citizen, a middle class, male. I'm also a child of God, created in God's image, a United Church of Christ minister, a brother, a spouse, a friend, a nephew, a home owner and tax payer, and a registered Democrat. I live among the "haves" and I move easily through this society because I resemble those who have the power, those who are straight, white men. In the reality of a society still struggling with racism and sexism, I am perceived as a person of privilege.

Last week the United States Supreme Court, reinforcing and supporting the fear and prejudice called homophobia, of the Boy Scouts of America, reminded me of one more thing about myself—one aspect of my life that, in their minds, changes everything—one fact that, in their minds, is the total substance of my being, the fact is, I am also a gay man.

I am seen by them and the others of their kind as a queer, a faggot, a fag, a homo, a fairy, and several dozen other names I don't even know. And now in the holy writ of a Supreme Court decision I am reduced to being defined by my "homosexual conduct."

Well Mr. Chief Justice and Mr. Chief Scout Executive I'd like you to know that it was this "homosexual's conduct" that earned him the rank of Eagle Scout, and Vigil Chief of the Order of the Arrow, and a BA from the American Humanics Foundation when my life's dream was to be a District Scout Executive.

For ten summers I directed programs at the Onteora Scout Reservation, run by Nassau County Council where this "homosexual's conduct" meant that 4,000 boys and men had a scouting experience that fulfilled the goals of the Boy Scouts of America, those of physical fitness, character building and citizenship training.

Scouting meant a great deal to my family as well. My Dad and I found a very special bond through our Scouting activities. And contrary to ex-gay movement propaganda, I did not have a distant or hostile relationship with him to "cause" my homosexuality. He loved me as a total person, unconditionally, sexuality included. He was active in Scouting his whole life, a Scoutmaster, district commissioner, Wood Badge Scout Master, and Silver Beaver recipient. Hundreds of his fellow scouters came to his funeral. Because Scouting meant so much to him we buried him in his uniform.

I stand here today to say how deeply ashamed I am of the corporation called the Boy Scouts of America. This multi-million dollar institution is supposedly dedicated to instilling character building in young men and boys but is now boasting its promotion of deceit, dishonesty, fear and prejudice. Where in the definition of "morally straight" as pledged in the Boy Scout Oath, is the part that says to gay youth that you need to "lie to get by"? Where does it say it is "morally straight" for young boys and men to embrace ignorance and the worst of stereotyping by insinuating that gay scout leaders are by definition pedophiles? In what part of the definition of "character building" does it remind young men to demonize anyone who is not like themselves? And since when I am I no longer trustworthy, loyal, helpful, friendly, courteous, kind, obedient, cheerful, thrifty, brave, clean or reverent because of who I love?

The question before us is what to do now. In my experience with large organizations like the church, for instance, I know there is a big difference between the policies of the official institutions and the lives and hearts of those within it.

The recovery movement has a wonderful, liberating saying: "take what you like and leave the rest!" I have to believe that the misguided and prejudicial views of the leadership of this corporation called the Boy Scouts of America does not have to effect [*sic*] the good will of many of its rank and file members who understand what justice is and what "morally straight" should mean. I encourage all the gay Scouts, gay adult leadership, including gay professionals who can find the courage within themselves, to continue the struggle from within. Those of us who are gay or bisexual, lesbian or transgender know who we really are, we know that we have nothing to be ashamed of, and we know that we have an incredible capacity to love and be loved. We also know that our commitment to justice will not be stopped by this corporation and certainly not by the five justices of the Supreme Court.

Surely there are many men and women of goodwill and courage within the Scouts who will continue to support and nurture young men. Who will be there when these young boys seek counsel and advice about some of the most personal and critical moments in their identity development. Who will be there when they seek out the support of the adult leaders in their troops because it may be much too dangerous for them to confide in their own parents.

To those Scouters past and present who want to remind the BSA that this current policy is totally unacceptable, that discrimination and prejudice have no place in a free society, I urge them to demand sponsoring organizations withdraw the charters of individual troops until the outrageous policy is rescinded.

And now I will engage in another form of "homosexual conduct" as I send my Eagle award back to Boy Scout Headquarters in Texas. I invite others to do the same. This symbol of achievement has represented an important part of my life, but I can no longer keep it. Since they will not acknowledge my total personhood, I can't keep it under these false pretenses, it wouldn't be morally straight.

Our gathering here today is not about the end of this issue. It's about the beginning of a new level of commitment. An imperative to challenge the conscience of the people of this country to embrace all their young people, black, white, red, brown and yellow, rich and poor, boys and girls, gay, lesbian, bisexual, transgender and questioning. Each and every one is deserving of our respect, support, trust and love, to do anything less is to shame us all.

July 19, 2000

What Is a Healthy Gay Man?

Eric Rofes

This is the text of the opening plenary address delivered by convener and veteran activist Eric Rofes at the Gay Men's Health Summit II, which met in Boulder, Colorado, July 19-23, 2000.

The three hundred or so people who attended the first Gay Men's Health Summit last July in Boulder shared in a spirit of exchange and mutual support across differences in identity, politics, and experiences. I was fascinated as I watched small groups of men and women gather during our morning breakfast breaks to talk through the morning plenary sessions. I was delighted to hear different viewpoints put forward in a spirit of mutual exchange rather than in a competition to see who was right or who would win.

We were very clear last year—as we are this year—that if we want to continue to create a multi-issue, multicultural gay men's health movement that tackled heart disease as well as HIV, anti-gay violence as well as addiction, syphilis as well as suicide, we cannot find ourselves only talking to those with whom we fully agree. A spirit of loving can envelop our gathering—a huge kiss, if you will—even as we tackle with sincerity our differing viewpoints on gay men's health.

Over the Past 12 Months: Facing an Outbreak of Epidemics

Last year's opening plenary address was entitled "Why Gay Men's Health? Why Now?" We put forward the need to blanket the nation with gay men's health and wellness projects, much as we did with HIV prevention programs in the mid-1980s. We want to see a gay men's health project in every state and a gay men's health summit to occur in every part of this country.

I feel more determined now than I did one year ago, to be part of creating a broad, holistic approach to gay men's health and wellness. While aggressive work on HIV and AIDS must remain critical, we need to expand dramatically beyond a narrow focus on HIV and address the many, many health issues faced by gay men of all colors and all generations. We need to replace bankrupt tactics of fear-mongering and terrorizing as our primary ways of reaching out to gay men and adopt a long-term strategy that is not vulnerable to the toxic cycle of crisis/cure we regularly foist on the gay male population.

Since we came together in Boulder a year ago, we've all heard reports that gay men are facing a broad array of threats to our health and wellness. First, we read about alarming outbreaks of syphilis among gay men in over a dozen U.S. cities, often linked to Internet chatrooms. Next, the Gay and Lesbian Medical Association sounded the alarm on a "club drug epidemic," highlighting a "severe increase in the abuse of methamphetamine, ecstasy, ketamine, gamma-hydroxyburyate (GHB) and nitrates (poppers)" by gay men. More recently, the web site GayHealth.com announced "New Epidemic Threatens Gay Community," and highlighted a study showing a "startling increase in anal cancer" in gay men. And over the last three weeks, San Francisco's AIDS leadership and mainstream media declare that San Francisco's "long-feared and often predicted new wave of HIV infection is here" for gay men and highlighted an alleged "surge" in new infections among the city' s gay men.

These reports raise critical issues worth talking about this weekend. First, do they reflect an accurate interpretation of the epidemiological data, or does the need to grab media attention, funding opportunities, or the ears of policy-makers lead to overstated claims, sensationalistic headlines, and problematic interpretations. The same health officials who initiated media reports about the "surge" of infections and triggered international headlines about a *tripling* of HIV among San Francisco gay men, already have backpedaled from their initial statements and apologized for their exaggerated claims. Yet the "second wave" of HIV among San Francisco gay men has already been accepted uncritically and endlessly repeated by journalists internationally. Even though we have no convincing corroborating empirical data, the world now believes gay men in San Francisco have tripled their infection rate and brought onto themselves a new cycle of cataclysm and destruction.

The second issue raised by these reports of new epidemics involves the painting of simplistic portraits of a diverse community or complicated subculture. Many gay men in San Francisco felt health department officials last week mis-used data to put forward to the world a vision that maligned gay men in our city. Whether we are talking about the gay community at large, or specific subcultures including gay men of color, circuit party participants, young gay men, or barebackers, journalists, researchers, policy-makers and activists too easily offer uninformed perspectives without any deep knowledge of the population they are talking about. Is it any wonder gay men feel defamed by the ways their cultures are discussed in health circles?

How do we know what we know about the lives, sexual practices, attitudes towards health, and identities of young gay men? Very little funded research has been allowed to occur with this population, and most people read news clippings rather than actual research studies. Yet it's so easy to extrapolate from one's own twisted adolescent memories or jump to conclusions based on tired cliches about youth that bear no resemblance at all to the day-to-day experiences of queer youth in the year 2000.

If you doubt homophobia and moralizing play a continuing role in the way gay male subcultures and sexual practices are discussed just compare the horrified tone of the coverage devoted this year to gay men who fuck without condoms to the empathic coverage devoted to uninfected women who are impregnated by their HIV-positive husbands. Journalists seem wholly able to sympathize with women who take health risks because having a baby is meaningful to them (and many of us here strongly support the rights of women to choose even when HIV is involved), yet these same journalists appear fully unable to fathom that some gay men take risks because specific sex acts are valuable to them and receiving semen might carry profound meanings. Sex acts that produce babies are easily seen as valuable. Sex acts that simply produce pleasure and identity—especially the act of anal sex for many gay men—are seen as disgusting and diseased.

The third issue kicked up by these reports involves what happens when gay men are told on an almost-monthly basis that they are the targets of distinct, new epidemics—first syphilis, then circuit drugs, then anal cancer, then a new wave of HIV. Does the overuse of the crisis construct dull sensitivity to authentic emergencies? Who is served by the constant chain of crises branded onto the foreheads of gay men and at whose expense does this occur? Does a repeated use of epidemic threats save lives or take lives?

All these reports lead me to believe that gay men are either the targets of an outbreak of epidemic panics on the part of medical authorities or the codependent victims of a public health system deeply addicted to crisis approaches to public health. And they lead me to feel even more determined to be part of a large and powerful gay men's health movement that is neither crisis-driven nor reliant on tactics of terror and shame. They lead me to be here in Boulder this week where we can make a long-term commitment to community health and wellness.

I say this because gay men do not need a new state-of-emergency declared—about drug abuse, anal cancer, or HIV/AIDS. At the same time, we do not need to pretend that significant health challenges do not threaten some of our subcultures. We need a broad, multi-issue gay men's health movement that reaches beyond HIV and values our cultures and our lives while working with us over the long haul. We need a movement that will support aggressive research to explore the factors that contribute to some gay men's risk-taking behavior and examines the value we place on sex, health, and our lifespans, while refusing to stigmatize us because our priorities may diverge from white, middle-class, heterosexual norms. We need a movement that recognizes not only our risk-taking but also our determination and resilience in the face of adversity.

Our Not-So-Hidden Agenda: Galvanizing the Organization of Local and Regional Gay Men's Health Summits

This week, we invite you to become active supporters of our not-so-hidden agenda. Our vision is to take the energy, creativity, and spirit of the folks converging on Boulder and use it to galvanize a gay men's health movement throughout the United States. We seek your help—your *active* help—in making this happen. We ask you to consider using the next few days to generate ideas and make connections that will allow you to organize gay men's health summits in your local area. Pay particular attention to the sessions described in the program guide that focus on "organizing local summits." Our aim is to come out of this weekend with a list of several dozen summits that will occur over the next 18 months and that collectively will reposition health and wellness in the agenda of gay men's communities from Key West to Kentucky, from Macon, Georgia to Missoula, Montana, from West Hollywood to Western Massachusetts.

Our organizing collective does not hold a single perspective on what these summits should look like. You can see how we conceptualized and structured this national summit, but we don't pretend to know what best meets the needs of the gay men in your area. Perhaps in your rural county, it would be most beneficial to host a health summit focused not only on gay men but also on lesbians, bisexuals, and transgender people. You have our support to head in that direction! Maybe the racial politics of your urban community are such that you believe your energy would be best spent organizing a summit on the health needs of gay men of color. Go for it! Or perhaps what really gets your energy flowing is organizing a summit that is more like a health fair, and that offers ordinary gay men the opportunity to learn about an entire range of health concerns and wellness programs that they might find helpful; a fair where they can get tested for STDs, experience a chiropractic adjustment, participate in a support group focused on a single middle-age gay man, get their blood pressure checked, and dialogue with health professionals and other gay men about their experiences with Viagra. Again, we say to you, go forward and organize it! Our greatest hope is that folks will leave Boulder on Sunday and become a vast network igniting gay men's health organizing all over the country!

While we support you in conceptualizing a summit that meets the needs of gay men in your local area, we ask you to consider—just consider—a few issues that we have struggled with as we've organized the program for the next few days:

Before the organizing gets started, bring together a broad group of people working with various populations and subcultures of gay men you hope to target. If you are aiming for a broad summit spanning diverse populations of gay men, pay particular attention to those who are not usually in the room and make a special effort to create a local gay men's health movement that is racially diverse, spans generations, welcomes men with a range of disabilities, and that includes poor and working-class men. And please recognize that a long-term approach to gay men's health means not only tackling the politics of homophobia and sexism, but also grappling with racism, classism, ableism and—increasingly—ageism. This isn't about being politically correct, it's about ensuring that our health movement includes those gay men who have historically had the least access to health care and medical services.

If there's anything we've learned from two decades of AIDS organizing it's that improving the health of marginalized populations necessitates political advocacy. So when the head of HIV prevention at the Centers for Disease Control becomes alarmed and points her finger at young gay men becoming infected with HIV, let's hear her, but let's also help her see how the failure of the CDC and the entire federal health system to take greater pro-active measures to improve the wellness of young gay men, creates conditions that place them at risk for many health challenges. Next time CDC leaders express shock that a group of young gay men test HIV-positive, let's remind them that in almost every state in this nation, precisely zero federal dollars are directed to supporting gay youth programs, that our nation's annual federally funded health survey of America's youth continues to occur without a question asking respondents to identify their sexual orientation, and that during eight years of the current Democratic administration, the FDA has not approved a single condom for anal sex. Our gay men's health movement must always play a fearless role redirecting policymakers from pointing their fingers at individuals and subcultures, to confronting the social and political forces that collude in creating "at-risk"populations.

Our local and regional summits must reach beyond the "true believers" and capture the interest and participation of those gay men who have the power to influence the behavior, risk-taking, and quality of

life of significant subcultures of gay men. We must engage the popular men, the opinion leaders, trendsetters, and local hunks. We need to remember that our early HIV prevention efforts were successful precisely because we had very little public health infrastructure to rely upon: we had to move boldly into gay male communities and subcultures to create a huge cadre of leaders and activists who could tackle the challenges we faced. As you begin to envision those who will make up the rank-and-file of a gay men's health movement in your area, don't primarily think of nurses and social workers and policy-makers and psychologists: instead think of bartenders and chorus members and popular drag queens, and tough leather daddies. Consider enlisting producers of circuit parties, Internet web masters, organizers of a local gay bowling league, and local MCC ministers. My point here is that we limit ourselves by separating our movement for gay men's health and wellness from the ordinary men who make up the day-to-day life of our communities. We need to involve them centrally in all our efforts, not as followers but as our leaders, our creative brain trust, and as colleagues who often have a clear sense of how to inspire their friends to become involved in a significant way.

What Is a Healthy Gay Man?
What Is a Healthy Gay Community?

Ultimately, we wanted to begin this Summit by asking you to think about "What is a healthy gay man?" Is it someone who is physically fit, but not too skinny and not too muscle-bound? Can a gay man be considered healthy if he's overweight? Smokes? Is HIV-positive? Is he someone who never drinks alcohol or uses drugs? Would you consider someone to be healthy if he regularly took allergy medication? Anti-depressants? Ecstasy?

We want you to think tonight—and think deeply—about the beliefs and the biases you bring to this question. How do you determine if YOU are healthy? What relationship do your own values and everyday social practices have to your perspective on this question? We want you to ponder this deeply because we believe that behind all of the contentious gay male debates about health, sex, and identity are radically different assumptions about what we consider to be "healthy." By becoming more mindful of our own beliefs here, we can better come together in a broad, inclusive gay men's health movement.

Can you be a healthy gay man at the age of 85? At the age of 16? Do healthy gay men have sex at rest stops? Do they go to sex clubs? Are all healthy gay men sexually versatile or can you be a total bottom and still be considered healthy? Can you be into SM? Can you be attracted to guys who are much older than you and still be healthy? Can you be attracted to much younger men? Do you know any gay men living on public assistance that you consider healthy? Are members of the new tribe of Abercrombie men appearing in gay communities everywhere wearing Abercrombie t-shirts or sweatshirts, healthy? What about any 300-pound bears? Can they be considered healthy? Do you know any immigrants who do not yet speak English whom you'd consider to be a healthy gay man? Can you be a healthy gay man and be transgendered?

Behind these queries lie some powerful existential questions. Is there a relationship between healthiness and length of lifespan? Will I have lived a healthier life if I live until 97, rather than dying at the age of 45? What relationship does quality of life have to healthiness? Could a short life filled with meaning and pleasure be considered healthier than a long life absent of joy?

What makes an HIV-positive man healthy or unhealthy? Can a gay man with HIV be healthy if he has only 20 T-cells and has a high viral load? Where would you consider positive men on protease inhibitors on the healthy scale? What about an HIV-positive man who has been infected for a dozen years and never been on a single medication? Are positive men healthier if they treat their HIV with Chinese herbs, acupuncture, and yoga? Would you consider a gay man with HIV healthy if he did not believe that HIV causes AIDS?

Is a healthy gay man someone who has sex once a day? Once a week? Once a month? Could you consider a celibate gay man to be healthy? Do you know any gay men involved in a monogamous relationship that you'd consider to be healthy gay men? Any men in open relationships? Any single gay men? Do healthy gay men use a condom every time they have anal sex? Are there any barebackers whom you'd consider healthy? Are all healthy gay men spiritual? Do they all attend religious services regularly? Are there gay men who attend Catholic church services whom you'd consider healthy? Do you think a gay man who's married to a woman could be healthy?

I've spent a great deal of time this month wondering if I am a healthy gay man. I've tried to take an inventory of my health condition over the past few weeks. When I consider myself healthy, I think of certain everyday activities in my life. I go to bed at 9 PM most nights and get up around 5 to go to the gym. I work out with weights and spend 30 minutes on the Stairmaster. I try to eat healthy foods, avoid red meat, and try to avoid sweets. I don't smoke and don't drink and haven't used recreational drugs for over twenty years. I attend regular meetings of several support programs. I am HIV-negative, have never been hospitalized and my cholesterol and blood pressure are normal.

At the same time, I have allergies and take Allegra to control them on almost a daily basis. I am prone to skin rashes, which I treat with acupuncture and herbal treatments. I have lower back problems and see a chiropractor each week for an adjustment. I tend to over-eat and wish I could lose a few pounds. While I generally think of myself as a happy person and have worked to minimize stress in my life, occasionally something throws me for a loop and I'm overwhelmed by depression, panic attacks, and worse. I've never tested positive for syphilis or gonorrhea, but I've had crabs and scabies many times.

Am I a healthy gay man if I am often attracted to men who look much like me: other white Jewish or Italian men? Other bears? Am I healthy if I like guys my own age? Yet if I've lately been messing around with a guy in his early 70s, and another one who is 23, does this make me unhealthy or more healthy? Would a new interest in men of other racial and ethnic backgrounds suggest that I am becoming healthier?

If I eat too much junk food, is this an indication that I have low self-esteem? I drink at least three Diet Cokes a day: does consuming the artificial sweeteners and caffeine suggest I am not very healthy? My lover thinks that I work all the time and don't take enough "down time" away from my teaching, writing and organizing. Am I actually a workaholic?

Do I gain points on the "healthy scale" if I do not fuck without condoms? Do I gain more points if I only fuck or get fucked these days? Or would a lack of fucking cause me to lose points and a not-so-healthy gay man? Do I lose points if I rimmed a stranger last weekend? If I tied someone up and called him nasty names? Do I lose even more if someone tied me up and talked real dirty to me? Am I a healthy gay man if I seem to have relatively little sexual energy and only climax a few times a week? Or does this suggest I am not healthy? If I fantasize about getting penetrated without condoms, does this indicate I am generally unhealthy and self-destructive? Would I be even more unhealthy and self-destructive if the person I fantasize about penetrating me was a straight man? A police officer? An HIV-positive man?

These queries and others run through my mind as I consider the question, "What is a healthy gay man?" I do not believe there are easy answers to these questions, but I think they are worth all of us considering as we begin to work together at this Summit. As I close this talk and we move into an activity that probes these questions, I want to leave you with a few final thoughts to mull over. When we say that we are aiming to promote the health and wellness of gay men, what are we actually talking about? When we participate in community with people with a broad range of values, desires, identities and social practices, is it essential that we talk together candidly about our bottom line assumptions about health? And finally, should we initiate a process whereby our communities and subcultures struggle openly with these identical questions?

September 16, 2000

Accepting the SPARC Lifetime Achievement Award

Barbara Gittings

This is the address of thanks and challenge given by longtime activist Barbara Gittings upon the occasion of being honored with an award recognizing her lifelong activism from the Statewide Pennsylvania Rights Coalition (SPARC), meeting in State College, Pennsylvania, on September 16, 2000.

I'm thrilled to be receiving this award. For those of us who put our energy and time and money into creating a better life for gay people, a big pat on the back is always welcome, even if you believe that the change you bring about is its own reward.

I have been chosen for this award partly because I've acquired a high profile as a gay activist. But George Eliot wrote in her novel *Middlemarch* that "the growing good of the world is partly dependent on unhistoric acts." So I want to acknowledge the contributions of thousands of people who've done special jobs for our growing good—but whose names usually don't turn up in the stories about our work.

I salute all of you who, for a week, for a month, or for years, have pushed for our visibility and our equality, who have given your time and talent for the fun of it and the satisfaction of making a difference.

A few years ago I was being introduced by someone who wanted to emphasize that I had the longest track record of all the gay activists in Philadelphia. But he got flustered and it came out as "Barbara is the oldest living lesbian."

Not quite! But I'm working on it. And I've been fighting the good gay fight for 42 years!

Our gay rights movement got started in this country over 50 years ago, with a handful of people who met in someone's apartment in Los Angeles to discuss homosexuals' problems in society. They had the blinds drawn and the door locked and a lookout posted for the police, because they feared they might be arrested just for gathering to talk about the taboo topic of homosexuality.

But they persisted and gained courage, and soon there were 3 organizations: ONE, Inc. in Los Angeles, Mattachine Society which started in L.A. then moved to San Francisco, and the lesbian organization Daughters of Bilitis in San Francisco. For a while these 3 groups were the only ones, even though each group did have a few chapters elsewhere in the country. Each organization started publishing a magazine or newsletter.

When I joined the Daughters of Bilitis in 1958, ten years after our movement started, there were only about eight organizations in the whole U.S. There were maybe 200 of us activists. It was like a little club—we all knew each other, even 3,000 miles apart. Most people in the movement at that time used false names to protect their jobs and their families. The word "gay" wasn't used even by us, let alone outside our groups.

The 3 gay publications in existence in 1958 couldn't be sold anywhere. There were few subscribers because people were afraid to have their names on any kind of gay list.

The subject of homosexuality was still shrouded in silence. We were invisible on television news and talk shows and we had just begun appearing on radio talk shows—the ones late at night, after children were in bed. The rare mentions of us in newspapers were under headlines like "Perverts Fired From State Department" or "Dozens Caught in Raid on Homosexual Bar."

When our groups began having public meetings and conferences in the 1950s, we invited lawyers and clergy and psychotherapists who weren't gay to address us. Our own lawyers and clergy and psychotherapists were still deep in the closet. We were in the wake of the McCarthy witch-hunts, when Communists and liberals and homosexuals were lumped together as subversives who threatened national security. An accusation of being "Commie-Pinko-Queer" could and did ruin the careers and lives of many decent people. In that climate of fear on top of the stigma attached to being gay, most of our people couldn't afford to be linked with anything concerning homosexuality. They denied they were gay, they tried to pass, they tried to hide their true nature from the world and even from their families and close associates.

Our movement started with 3 objective problems to tackle:

We were considered *sick,* so we had to labor under the albatross of the sickness label, which infected everything we said and did. They said you're sick, we said no we aren't, they said that's your sickness talking.

We were considered *sinful,* so we had to start dialogue with the churches and make a presence in the churches.

> We were considered *criminal,* so we had to cope with the sodomy laws, which were still on the books in all the states. And by extension with any problems connected with the law or the courts.

One of our earliest legal victories was the case of *ONE Magazine* which began publishing in 1951. In 1953 and 1954 the Los Angeles postmaster stopped issues from going out in the mails because he objected to the content. The organization ONE, with the help of an established law firm, challenged this censorship in the federal courts, all the way to the U.S. Supreme Court, which issued in 1958 a ruling that guarantees forever the right of gay periodicals to travel in the mail.

Remember the country was still hurting from the ugly time of Senator McCarthy's purges. It took a lot of courage for that gay organization to stand up against official censorship with no popular support. It must have been difficult too for those heterosexual lawyers who stuck their necks out for us.

We did have a few other shining moments of triumph. For example, our longtime Washington gay activist Frank Kameny used to give a talk called "Tweaking the Lion's Tail—Or, Constructive Fun and Games With Your Government." One of his stories was about how in the 1963 the lone gay organization in the nation's capital stood up to FBI Director J. Edgar Hoover. Since the gay group often had to deal with the government's anti-gay policies, it wanted to keep top officials informed of its activities, so it routinely sent its newsletter, unasked and free, to everyone at the White House and in the Cabinet and in Congress.

J. Edgar Hoover didn't appreciate this courtesy notification. J. Edgar Hoover desperately wanted his name OFF that gay group's mailing list! He tried to bully, he tried to scare. But the group stood firm and made Hoover back down. The organization's newsletter continued to be sent to Hoover along with all the other federal bigwigs. It may be the only time in the career of that powerful man that he didn't get his way—and WE did it!

We love and need those shining moments. But we realize that our mission is to make real and permanent changes in the conditions of our everyday lives. I'll come back to this.

I've mentioned the early movement's 3 big objective problems: sin, sickness, criminality. (I call them objective because you could get a handle on them, there was something concrete you could go after.) But the overriding problem in our early days was invisibility. How can you organize people to do something about their problems if they're invisible?

Breaking out of invisibility was tough and it was scary.

For instance, in 1965, several years before Stonewall, a handful of us picketed at the White House and the Pentagon and the Civil Service Commission in Washington, to protest the government's anti-gay policies in employment, security clearances, and the military. Also there were pickets at Independence Hall in Philadelphia every July 4th from 1965 to 1969. These demonstrations were to tell the public that a significant group of citizens is not getting the benefits of "life, liberty and the pursuit of happiness" as promised in the Declaration of Independence we celebrate on July 4th.

As you see from the picture on my shirt, those pickets were sedate and we had a dress code. We had to reckon with the popular image of us at the time as perverted and sick and weird. We wanted the public to gawk not at us but at the messages on our signs and leaflets.

Remember, this was 35 years ago. Picketing wasn't a popular tactic then as it is today. Certainly our cause wasn't popular. Even many gay people thought our efforts were foolish and outlandish.

Only a tiny handful of us could take the risk of being so public. What if my boss sees me on the 6 o'clock news and fires me? What if my picture appears in my parents hometown newspaper and causes them grief? What is the government going to DO with all those photos and recordings they're making of us? And what if bystanders throw insults at us—or worse, bricks and stones?

Becoming visible could sometimes be fun. For instance, I was involved in the first-ever gay kissing booth, held at a librarians' convention in Dallas in 1971. Our gay librarians group called it "Hug a Homosexual" and we offered free same-sex kisses and hugs. Let me tell you, the aisles were jammed. But no one came in. They all wanted to ogle the action, not be a part of it. They were a bit shy because two Dallas TV crews were filming and a *LIFE* magazine photographer was snapping pictures. So the four of us on duty kissed and hugged each other, and we handed out copies of our gay reading list and encouraged the onlookers, and then kissed and hugged some more to show them How It's Done!

The shock value of our kissing booth brought us the attention we needed in the American Library Association to promote our solid professional work about gay books and discrimination in libraries. Just as important, we got out the message that gay men and lesbians shouldn't be held to a double standard of sexual privacy, that we're entitled to be just as open as heterosexuals—no more, no less—in showing our affection.

Our greater visibility nowadays has really advanced our cause and helped many lesbians and gay men to come out of the closet. It also has brought a lot of heterosexual hostility out of the closet.

There are still plenty of people who heartily wish we would just disappear off the face of the earth. Or if not that, they want us to hide and pretend to protect their sensitivities. Even some of our non-gay friends and family who claim they support our rights find our visibility a stumbling block. They say, why make such an issue of your lifestyle? Why can't you just live your lives without announcing it to the world? Why do you flaunt yourselves?

We have an old joke that if we had a nickel for very time we've been accused of flaunting, we'd be a rich movement, not a shoestring effort. For these people, a little homosexuality goes a l-o-o-o-n-g way!

Heterosexuals flaunt themselves all the time, only it isn't called flaunting, it's just the standard social scenery, it's taken for granted. They wear wedding rings. They proudly show pictures of their spouses or opposite-sex partners. They kiss and embrace in public. Why they even announce their relationships in the newspapers for thousands of strangers to see. How much more public can you get about your sexual interests?

If we do hide and pretend, we're usually assumed to be heterosexual and treated as such. And we don't get our rights as gays. So we have to explain and show what's important to us—thus making an issue of our private lives. We are not yet part of the official picture of life, and we have to keep drawing attention to our situation until we're thoroughly woven into the fabric of life. We can't continue to live our lives under a rock.

While I believe that our visibility is the engine that drives us to secure our rights, I also believe high visibility isn't for everyone. Some of us have problem situations or other priorities. But there's no shortage of behind-the-scenes jobs for those who are willing. You should do what you can, and enlist others to do what they can, to support the cause. And no one should feel that her or his contributions counts for less because its less public.

A side note on visibility: Many of you may not know that SPARC has a sort of old-auntie ghost behind it. That was the Pennsylvania Council for Sexual Minorities, the first official government body in the country set up to deal with gay issues. It was launched in 1976 by Governor Milton Shapp who also issued an executive order banning discrimination on the basis of sexual orientation. Gay men and lesbians and transgender persons were appointed to the Council. It was not a high-profile group. Its members focused on working quietly with state agencies to make real changes in Pennsylvania's regulations and policies on everything from education to health to prisons to welfare to youth services to state police to employment. The Council lasted only about 3 years—but it was a start and a good model.

However, gay rights means much more than getting good laws and policies and practices, though that's a key step. We also have to change the hurtful prejudice that still comes from many religious leaders and many public officials including school board members and many of our neighbors and fellow citizens. Progress on paper is fine, but we can't stop there. The struggle for equal treatment has to be won in individuals' hearts and minds, where it really counts. That is transformation at the roots!

We want relief from the pain of wearing the mask. We want to be judged as individuals, on our own merits. We want to live and love and work and play, openly and safely, as ourselves.

Does this seem an impossible dream? Just think how far we've come since the old days I've told you about. If you still feel daunted, here's a four-part prescription to give you fresh energy: Practicality, Perseverance, Presence, and Playfulness.

Practicality—This means, look ahead but keep your feet moving on the ground. And remember that success comes in small moments as well as grand events. Take care of minor issues along with the main job and you'll get the satisfaction of seeing results every month, not just once in 2 or 3 years.

Perseverance—If you expect our work to change the world overnight, you might get discouraged. One reason I haven't burned out is that I'm always happily surprised by each advance, each victory, each creation—and I want to be around for the next great turn. When I joined the movement I never dreamed we would soon have parents-of-gays groups, or gay caucuses in the professions, or full-scale gay community centers, or gay choruses and marching bands, or openly gay elected officials, or gay documentary films. Marvelous changes, unthinkable to me 42 years ago! Over the long haul, for every setback, we've made 4 or 5 giant strides forward. So whatever you set yourself to do, keep at it, be persistent, be persuasive.

Presence—This is closely tied to perseverance. We are everywhere—but lest they forget, keep reminding them. While we're fortunate to have high-profile Barney Frank in politics and Martina Navratilova in sports and some show-business celebrities, what we most need is the everyday visibility of people like you, a constant presence, always reminding others that we're at the next desk at work and at school, we're in the next pew at church or temple, we're in the next chair at the family dinner table. We're already part of every community. We won't go away and we won't be converted.

Our goal is equality in society, but there's no one best way to achieve it. We advance thanks to a thousand different talents, a thousand different interests. It's really a blessing that our movement is not centralized or like a disciplined army, that gay individuals can erupt into whatever they do best to make a presence. You know, this is very frustrating for our opponents. It's like punching pillows. They squelch us here—and we just pop up somewhere else!

Playfulness—Gay rights is serious business, but it doesn't always have to be grim. Humor can cut through homophobia. A light touch often helps to get our message across. And we can have fun doing good!

When we've achieved equality, when all the bigotries and barriers have been erased, we'll continue to enjoy being a special people. I'm glad to be with you. Thank you for your dedication and work, for SPARC and for our cause and our lives.

September 30, 2000

The Future of Leather

Joseph Bean

This address was delivered as the keynote speech at the Great Lakes Leather Conference in Louisville, Kentucky, on September 30, 2000. Bean, a longtime activist, artist, and writer for and in the leather community, was at this time the director of the Leather Archives and Museum in Chicago. *The Rose Exterminator* was written by William Carney and published in 1982. It belongs to a group of novels and short stories set in the leather community that began to appear in the late 1960s.

If you think of leather/SM/fetish as a way of being, as a way your life can be ordered and made sensible, you may find my message valuable. If, on the other hand, you see SM as *just* a way to get off, leather as *mostly* a way to be fashionable, and fetishes as the inexplicable kinks found among "crazies" . . . you may save yourself the bother of listening to my ranting. Go, be safe, do something else, you won't miss anything by missing this speech.

I'm glad to see you didn't all dash from the room.

I want to start by talking about my favorite subject: Me. Relax. It's personal history, but I'll try to keep it interesting, or at least painless for you. People ask about my personal history all the time. Maybe—while serving another purpose—this speech will be a first installment towards telling my story . . . so you will know who is speaking to you.

I was born in Humansville, Missouri, a very small crossroads in the Ozarks. So small, in fact, it didn't even have a significant crossroads. Besides, we lived on a farm, miles from Humansville. Anyway, even though I was born in 1947, because of *where* I was born, I got to experience the amazing world-transformation generally called The Turn of the Century or Fin de Siecle. In most of the world, that moment in history, the beginning of the 20th Century, generally took place at least 40 years before I was born, but the changes hadn't trickled down much to the hill folk of the Ozarks yet in 1947.

The miracle of gas lighting inside homes, for example, was surprising in my childhood. We had kerosene lamps and candles . . . electricity, indoor plumbing and gas cooking came to my family when we moved into town, meaning Bolivar, still in Polk County Missouri. But telephones took a little longer, and I didn't see a television until we moved to Kansas City in preparation for our Grapes-of-Wrath style westward trek in 1956: with 25 people and 6 cars, none of them less than 15 years old.

Then, bang! There were radios with dials instead of crystals and needles. There were televisions. There were streams of cars, not to mention trucks so big they could haul houses down the highway . . . and you can imagine my reaction to highways. There were also people who looked and acted and sounded different. They didn't say "full of piss and vinegar" when they meant peppy, they never said "that boy ain't right" even when they knew it was true . . . and they threw away the greens from their turnips and couldn't tell a tasty poke weed from bitter ditch grass.

The point of this early-childhood confessional—and I do have one—is that I adjusted. Dragged from a Victorian infancy in which all babies and toddlers were in dresses and curls, through the terror of discovering I was a boy and I had to figure all that out, I was then thrust into a world that was half-a-century ahead of my family . . . and I adjusted.

OK. More about me, but we're getting closer to the Future of Leather and to what I suspect is your favorite subject: You.

Before I was 20—17 years and 3 months to be exact—the world crumbled and phoenix-like raised itself in a whole new form before my eyes. You've guessed it. It was sex, and for me, sex shot off like big guns with all three barrels fully loaded. This was genuine sex, not the child's play with penises I knew so well. It was also gay sex, male to male, my frightening and irresistible dreams come true. And, it was SM, the take me while I'm hot, do with me as you will, no-holds-barred, I'll do my best to explain the bruises later . . . full-on SM. And, not that this is on the same scale, but it was also dangerously public and extremely illegal. Wham! I was there: New world, new Joseph, thank you, SIR!

Soon, everything in my new world of gay SM sex seemed in order. Each of us knew our place; out of the way until called, silent until ordered to speak, available to be used or ignored by the men towering over our cowering forms.

Was this safe? I survived it. Was it sane? I'm still permitted to walk the streets. Was it consensual? Well, yes. The only thing we feared more than being singled out by one of the men was NOT being noticed by them. Week after week, whenever I was invited, I was at the apartment where the whips and chains and the MEN would be. If you sit by the telephone for hours waiting for the invitation phone call, whatever you're waiting for, if you get it, is consensual.

Besides, when there were no get-togethers to go to in Los Angeles, I could always go to the docks at San Pedro or in San Francisco, as I often did, to have strangers (goaded as much as necessary) do the same things to me on the piers or in the backs of trucks. At least among the men in Los Angeles there was one safety valve. Nothing could destroy a man's reputation so completely or guarantee his exile from the group more certainly than having it said of him that "he won't take no for an answer." Never mind that no one ever gave me permission to say no. Never mind that I wouldn't have considered saying it. The fact remains that, in those years, the mid-60s to mid-70s, I felt safe because I heard of men disappearing simply because they wouldn't "take no for an answer."

Things change.

By 1975, bars and back-rooms and sex clubs and bathhouses were more common than the gatherings I had so eagerly waited to be invited to at the homes of older men with names like "The Captain" and "Ranger Leader."

I adjusted again.

In fact, I took to these new commercial venues like a duck to water, especially the ones with "bad" reputations, the ones about which it was whispered that "the wrong kind" go there. Before, we used no names, although most of us KNEW the names of the others around us. In the commercial setting, using no names was raised to the level of genuine anonymity. Safety and some version of sane behavior were pretty much guaranteed, in a sense, by the fact that there was a business owner worried about keeping his business license. And consensuality was easy. You open the cubicle door or close it. If you reject someone, he can go do the thing you didn't want with someone else around the next turn in the maze. No problem.

This is the beginning of the end, you know. Maybe you didn't notice then if you were there, but this was the first completely false step for SM in America.

This equation that included business owners and business licenses, bottoms saying no and Tops moving like bees from spot to spot till they got what they wanted instead of just beating some sense into the nay-saying boy at hand . . . well, it was the turn that led into the unfortunate by-way we're exploring now.

Over the next ten years, we got leather title contests which were both good and bad, but all very much a part of the path to today. Soon the first rule of the SM world I'd come out in was being broken everywhere. "Don't frighten the villagers," we were told, god knows how many times. Suddenly, the SM men I knew were being confronted by the leather-wearing SM men from the bars and bike clubs, and these guys were wearing their leathers on the streets, in the grocery stores . . . everywhere! I didn't know how to take this. It was shocking enough to discover there was supposed to be a connection between leather and SM, but now this connection was somehow sweeping away the Big Rule.

Things change. Again, I adjusted.

I got myself some leathers which the men I respected most said I had every right to wear. "If those fucking bike freaks do, boy, you can too, but remember . . ." and I promised, I wouldn't frighten the villagers.

Just as the marvels of the Twentieth Century had been evolving outside the Ozarks when I was born, the LEATHER-SM world had been evolving as a universe next door to my own yes-sir/anything-you-say-sir world since the mid-50s, but I knew nothing of it. Where the men in my world worked only with those they knew well, the new-to-me leathermen PLAYED with anyone who'd agree to it. We had been devoted to the brotherhood, "making in the scene," and had done sessions: they were loners, doing scenes and giving names to everything in sight. Bottom and Top, boy and slave, Master and player were all new words to me, naming things I barely recognized. "Toys" was the hard one . . . or maybe "play" was. Whatever, it was a new world that opened to me when I slipped into chaps and tiptoed into a leather bar.

For as long as I could, I was with my Old Buddies whenever I could be, but I found a place for myself in the leather-SM world too. Here, I became a contributor to the changes which, later and now, I would consider Big Mistakes.

In the 1980s there were at least two, maybe three genuinely tectonic shifts. This first was a great expansion of something I've already mentioned. People began to have "parties" instead of sessions, musters or gatherings. More and more people picked up the idea of calling whips and restraints and paddles TOYS. And the names that had cropped up here and there—especially boy as the name for male bottoms—became pretty widely used.

I began to sense a discomfort here. To feel it might be wrong to adjust. I really distrusted this evolving world where the bottoms admitted out loud they wanted to hurt and everyone thought of SM as FUN.

The next world transmuting shift was the infamous advent of gay cancer, GRID, AIDS, which was very much the property and even the "fault" of SM men in the beginning . . . so said the gay press and so the official safer-sex guidelines seemed to imply as well. I absolutely didn't want to adjust to this, but friends began dying, and I learned to live with that *in a way* while fighting the whole thing in whatever ways I could.

Then came the third revolutionary change in SM. It took a while for us to give it a name. It even took a while to notice what we were doing, and we WERE doing it. In time, we called it pansexuality and inclusiveness, and watched as it became the greatest of the 1980s earthquakes. Language is only language. AIDS somehow became a human problem instead of an SM problem, but the expanded population was not just language and it really had its epicenter at the heart of SM.

Things change. I adjusted. Hell, I didn't adjust. I dived in. Maybe I was finally grieving for the lost SM world I had loved, or maybe I was crazy, or maybe I was doing the right thing. I honestly don't know any more.

Since I had already broken ranks, in a sense, by actually teaching SM technique classes as early as 1978, I was already able to see myself as something of an outsider, although I had another SM connection I would not lose until the end of the 80s in which I found a very comforting touchstone.

Pansexuality and the coincident population explosion didn't just mean doing SM with women and heterosexuals in the room. It also meant classes and conferences on a major scale and it involved ideas I had tried not to think about. Things like legal rights had meant nothing when we all accepted that being arrested from time to time was "just the price of being different."

With pansexuality and AIDS and the language shifts came also the questions about our SM predecessors and the history of such institutions as chaps, the bike clubs and the leather bar. They brought us the idea of the Old Guard, maybe because the community's founders were dying (AIDS), maybe because their language was disappearing (working, sessions, making the scene), maybe because the new people of all genders and sexualities who were coming in ever-increasing numbers needed a way to trivialize their forebears who would otherwise seem too great and be too important and would have too much authority. But, the naming of the Old Guard was a giant step toward where we are today.

This, my patient listeners, is where most of you come in. You may have experiences like mine in the 60s, 70s, 80s, or not. Most of you will recognize the next decade—the 90s—from experience. And however alike or different your experience and mine were before, we became entwined in the 90s, you and I. I invented and edited magazines and wrote articles that some of you read, always pushing you and pulling myself toward today . . . one way and another. I did art and illustration and classes and demonstrations; editorials and speeches . . . all of them committed to making the new, more free, more open world of SM as accessible as possible. I apologize if you see that as a mistake, but I remind you that you as readers, event package buyers, art buyers and the rest made choices and gave feedback that encouraged and directed me and the others on my side of things. We were involved, you and I, throughout the 90s, feeding and guiding each other. And now I have come to believe we were very much in the wrong.

I'm sorry. That's the most I can say. I'm sorry for the part I played in confirming and creating an SM world where newcomers are abused and undersocialized; where the spirit of camaraderie is subordinated to the glee of party-time; where the life of the human spirit is often no less crushed in the dungeon than it is in the cubicle-farm office.

We're on a dead-end here. The problem is NOT the language, although I'm old-fashioned enough to think it matters. The problem is certainly not AIDS, although there is nothing I want more than my dear friends and slaveboys back. The problem is not pansexuality or the population explosion, because there certainly and genuinely is strength in unity so long as it is a unity with a broad embrace and heart enough to countenance real diversity.

The problem is simpler. Maybe it is too simple really to be noticed, but it is vitally important. What we have lost, what we have to regain if we are to be anything more than a flash in the Senate or a lightening bolt in the occasional TV-sit-coms is easily named, but not easily understood. Before I go that last step, however, let me read to you very briefly from William Carney:

In *The Rose Exterminator,* Carney has the character Symonds walking down a street in San Francisco where he runs into an old SM acquaintance. These are guys from the *leather*-SM world. Symonds asks Faulkner if he still "makes the scene," meaning does he still do SM.

> (Symonds narrates) ". . . he almost smiled, shaking his head in reply."
>
> "It's not the same you know." There was neither sadness nor scorn in his voice . . . "Leather is IN, and everybody's into it. It's not what it used to be."
>
> I replied. "It probably never was."
>
> "No," he said, "you know better than that."
>
> His eyes, which through glasses lent the severity of his face a scholarly cast, still held that old, secret flame of age burning like points of light deep dancing, beckoning with equivocal glints past the pale portals of the iris.
>
> "There's no concentration or quietness in it anymore," he said. "It's all parody."
>
> And, looking around, I saw that it was so. The passion was gone, and the darkness with it. The guilt, the fear, and the uncertainty are done away with and there is nothing to shiver at any more. But people continue to get their skin peeled . . . everything is common now to all . . . boredom has succeeded passion, and there remains now only order.

The story goes on,

> Symonds sees he was never one to suffer gladly the common man . . . when the choice was forced upon him to become a parody or remain

> forever an enigma in the minds of those who knew him whom he cared about, he chose what his special wisdom told him he must choose, knowing that he could not have both, and that he was not made for a common end, and that anyway parodied enigma is enigma no more . . ."

The Rose Exterminator is set largely in the 1960s. These guys were already saying it was not like the old days, not worth the whip-cleaning, not what it once was . . . and they did not adjust.

Carney's other SM book, *The Real Thing,* ends even more loudly on the very same note. And that is where, with a little bit of a twist, I want to end tonight.

The Future of Leather, now your future very much more than it is mine, is in grave danger if we pursue the paths that are becoming well-worn today.

I say that leather is a gypsy thing. If it has grown roots, they should be harvested. If it has settled on a foundation, that should be broken and abandoned. What we should be longing for is, in Carney's words, the passion, the darkness, the guilt, the fear, and the uncertainty which are done away with as leather and SM become a respectable, monitored subculture. If we are no longer rebels, so be it, but don't let us stop tasting what is forbidden and daring what is impossible and repeating what is unsavory. If we are no longer criminals, so be it, but let us place before all other values the pursuit of self-transformation which can include sex and sexuality only if they are bliss-inclined which means they have to be aimed at the darkness.

If there is a Future of Leather that has a place for the likes of me as I was 30 years ago, it will not be discovered or made by the likes of me as I am today.

More true and more important than anything else I can say about the future of leather, there is this one thing that I can say which is directed only to the new and the young: Don't adjust. Bend not the slightest bit. Find what answers the yearning of your own passion and accept nothing else . . . nothing less.

The Future of Leather is either something new, invented, and ruled by the young, or it is nothing of leather/SM at all. To go on along the path of least passion as we are going today is to become what we imagine our grandparents to have been—dull to say the least. But, to stand aside and allow the newcomers and the young to create around you a new SM world may well rekindle in you the very instincts and urges that drew you into leather to begin with.

I say "you" not us, because I believe that I have another leather destiny. I won't be one of the people populating the parties or playing for fun. I won't continue to adjust. But I will do the things I believe will give the greatest liberty to the creators of the next and forward looking world of leather/SM, so long as no one asks me for the kind of instructions or advice that usually misleads the young hotheads into the path of the old farts.

I come from a time and world in which leathersex was a life apart—not a thing apart from life. It's all very well to have a museum and lobbyists and committees and conferences, but the time has come to ask what are we lobbying for the right to do, and is it worth *that?* To ask seriously what is the future of the historic reality recorded in the Leather Archives and Museum and is there something important that is different now—not better, not even intentionally changed—just lost?

I can not tell you what will be the future of leather, but I would ask you to ask yourselves as you make and live in it: Don't you want lives in leather to be something *more*?

Bring back the darkness. Bring back the passion, and give leathermen and leatherwomen hereafter something to *live for,* something to anticipate and fearfully shiver about. Only then will the museums, art shows, legal battles and conferences be justified.

October 10, 2000

The Twenty-Fifth Anniversary of the Lesbian/Gay Community Service Center of Cleveland

Dennis J. Kucinich

These remarks were made on the floor of the House of Representatives by Kucinich, a former mayor of the city of Cleveland, and entered in the *Congressional Record* of October 10, 2000.

Mr. Speaker, I rise today to celebrate the twenty-fifth anniversary of Cleveland's Lesbian/Gay Community Service Center. For the past twenty-five years, the Center has served the community's gay, lesbian, bisexual and transgender people and their supporters in the Greater Cleveland area.

Driven by the belief that all people have a right to pursue life, liberty and happiness in America, and because gay, lesbian, bisexual and transgender (GLBT) people have been denied these basic rights, the Center has distinguished itself as a respected educator, advocate, social services provider and community builder.

In 1975, the Center's founders, Ethan Ericsen, Michael Madigan, and Arthur MacDonald, opened the Gay Education and Awareness Resource Foundation, or GEAR. In 1988, GEAR's name was changed to the Lesbian/Gay Community Service Center and the "Living Room," a drop-in center for men with AIDS, was opened. The Living Room was the only center of its kind in the Midwest United States—establishing the Center's position as not only a preeminent advocate for the gay and lesbian community but as a pioneer in GLBT services. The Center has served Cleveland in many capacities, including the encouragement of GLBT people to vote with "Promote the Vote" programs, the creation of a Speaker's Bureau to inform and educate the general public about the Center and its gay/lesbian issues, and the training of law enforcement agencies regarding GLBT issues. Recently, the Center was awarded the Human Rights Campaign's Equality award for outstanding service to the GLBT community in Greater Cleveland. Now, arriving at its twenty-fifth year celebration, the Center is still thriving with various activities and plans to serve [the] Greater Cleveland Community.

Mr. Speaker, I ask that my fellow members join me in honoring the outstanding community service of the Lesbian and Gay Community Service Center of Greater Cleveland.

Copyright Acknowledgments

Anonymous (January/February 1955). "An Open Letter to Senator Dirksen." Originally printed in the *Mattachine Review,* published January/February 1955. Permission to reprint courtesy of Ben Heath.

Bean, Joseph (February 20, 2000). "Speech at the Dedication of the Leather Archives and Museum." Speech given in Chicago, Illinois. Permission to reprint courtesy of Joseph Bean.

Bean, Joseph (September 30, 2000). "The Future of Leather." Speech given at the Great Lakes Leather Conference, Louisville, Kentucky. Permission to reprint courtesy of Joseph Bean.

Burns, Ken (August 1956). "The Homosexual Faces a Challenge." Originally printed in the *Mattachine Review,* published August 1956. Permission to reprint courtesy of Ben Heath.

Call, Hal (August 25, 1962). "A Decade of Progress in the Homophile Movement." Originally printed in the *Mattachine Review,* published October 1962. Permission to reprint courtesy of Ben Heath.

Call, Hal (November/December 1964). "Open Letter to the Florida Legislature's 'Johns Committee.'" Originally printed in the *Mattachine Review,* published November/December 1964. Permission to reprint courtesy of Ben Heath.

Cerullo, Margaret (April 11, 1994). "A Moment of Great Crisis, Great Potential, and Great Danger." Speech given for the Gay/Lesbian and Straight Teachers Network of Massachusetts. Permission to reprint courtesy of Margaret Cerullo.

Credle, James (November 28, 1983). "Police Brutality: The Continual Erosion of Our Most Basic Rights." Speech given at congressional hearings on police brutality, Brooklyn, New York. Permission to reprint courtesy of James Credle.

Deacon, Jay (June 26, 1981). "Speech at Daley Plaza." Speech given at ILGTF Rally, Daley Center, Chicago, Illinois. Permission to reprint courtesy of Jay Deacon.

D'Emilio, John (June 1988). You Can't Build a Movement on Anger." Editorial. Originally printed in *Gay Community News.* Permission to reprint courtesy of John D'Emilio.

Drake, Timothy (May 23, 1980). "Presentation to the Temporary Committee on Resolutions." Permission to reprint courtesy of Timothy Drake.

Ellis, Albert (January 26, 1957). "How Homsexuals Can Combat Anti-Homosexualism." Speech given at ONE Midwinter Institute, Los Angeles, California. Permission to reprint courtesy of Albert Ellis.

Gay Day Committee (August 28, 1971). "We Demand." Document of the August 28 Gay Day Committee, published in *Flaunting It!: A Decade of Gay Journalism* from the Body Politic, Pink Triangle Press, 1982, pp. 217-220. Permission to reprint courtesy of Pink Triangle Press.

Gearhart, Sally Miller (February 1972). "The Lesbian and God-the-Father." Speech given at pastors' conference, Pacific School of Religion, Berkeley, California. Copyright Sally Miller Gearhart. Permission to reprint courtesy of Sally Miller Gearhart.

Gittings, Barbara (June 8, 1977). "Prayer Breakfast." Speech given at Coalition for Human Rights Prayer Breakfast. Permission to reprint courtesy of Barbara Gittings.

Gittings, Barbara (October 13, 1982). "Speech at the Human Rights Campaign Fund Banquet." Speech given in Philadelphia, Pennsylvania. Permission to reprint courtesy of Barbara Gittings.

Gittings, Barbara (October 22, 1983). "Speech at the Philadelphia Gay Walk-A-Thon." Permission to reprint courtesy of Barbara Gittings.

Gittings, Barbara (June 2, 1990). "Philadelphia Gay and Lesbian Pride Parade Speech." Permission to reprint courtesy of Barbara Gittings.

Gittings, Barbara (June 15, 1990). "Toasting Troy Perry." Speech given at the Philadelphia MCC Dinner, Philadelphia, Pennsylvania. Permission to reprint courtesy of Barbara Gittings.

Gittings, Barbara (August 19, 1991). "Memorial to A. Damien Martin." Permission to reprint courtesy of Barbara Gittings.

Gittings, Barbara (February 11, 1994). "Abraham Lincoln Award Acceptance Speech." Speech given for Log Cabin Club of Philadelphia, The Union League, Philadelphia, Pennsylvania. Permission to reprint courtesy of Barbara Gittings.

Gittings, Barbara (1996). "Introduction to the Film *Stonewall*." Speech given at the 1996 International Gay and Lesbian Festival, Philadelphia, Pennsylvania. Permission to reprint courtesy of Barbara Gittings.

Gittings, Barbara (June 29, 1997). "Press Conference Remarks at New York Gay Pride March." Permission to reprint courtesy of Barbara Gittings.

Gittings, Barbara (May 22, 1998). "Remembering Jim Kepner." Speech given at memorial celebration for James Kepner, Los Angeles, California. Permission to reprint courtesy of Barbara Gittings.

Gittings, Barbara (October 23, 1998). "Introduction to the Documentary *Out of the Past*." Permission to reprint courtesy of Barbara Gittings.

Gittings, Barbara (June 19, 1999). "Jacksonville, Florida, Gay Pride Rally Speech." Permission to reprint courtesy of Barbara Gittings.

Gittings, Barbara (September 16, 2000). "Accepting the SPARC Lifetime Achievement Award." Speech given at the Statewide Pennsylvania Rights Coalition Conference, State College, Pennsylvania. Permission to reprint courtesy of Barbara Gittings.

Goldberg, Suzanne B. (May 20, 1996). "On the Striking Down of Colorado's Amendment 2." Permission to reprint courtesy of Lambda Legal Defense and Education Fund.

Greig, Brian (September 1, 1999). "Australia's First Openly Gay Senator." Permission to reprint courtesy of Brian Greig, senator.

Grier, Barbara (September 19, 1975). "The Possibilities Are Staggering." Speech given at the Second Annual Lesbian Writers Conference in Chicago. Permission to reprint courtesy of Barbara Grier.

Grier, Barbara (March 1977). "Neither Profit Nor Salvation." Speech given as keynote to the San Jose State University Women Together Day. Permission to reprint courtesy of Barbara Grier.

Hiller, Kurt (1928). "Appeal . . . on Behalf of an Oppressed Human Variety." Translation of speech in *The Early Homosexual Rights Movement (1864-1935)* by John Lauritsen and David Thorstad (New York: Times Change Press, 1995). Permission to reprint courtesy of John Lauritsen, translator.

Hyde, Sue (April 30, 1988). "We Gather in Dubuque." Speech given at Dubuque, Iowa's, Second Annual Gay and Lesbian Pride March. Permission to reprint courtesy of Sue Hyde.

Kameny, Franklin E. (July 22, 1964). "Civil Liberties: A Progress Report." Speech given at Freedom House, New York City. Permission to reprint courtesy of Franklin E. Kameny.

Kameny, Franklin E. (May 22, 1998). "A Celebration of Jim Kepner's Life." Speech given at A Celebration of Jim Kepner's Life. Permission to reprint courtesy of Jack Nichols, Senior Editor, *GayToday*.

Kepner, Jim (April 1997). "Why Can't We All Get Together, and What Do We Have in Common?" Permission to reprint courtesy of Jack Nichols, Senior Editor, *GayToday*.

Kolbe, Jim (March 7, 1997). "Log Cabin Republican Address." Speech given at Log Cabin Republican meeting, Los Angeles, California. Permssion to reprint courtesy of Jim Kolbe, congressman.

Larsen, John Eric (1990). "Song to My Master." Permission to reprint courtesy of Alexis Keppeler.

Lazin, Malcolm (October 14, 1999). "First National March on Washington for Gay and Lesbian Rights 20th Anniversary." Permission to reprint courtesy of Malcolm Lazin.

Lehtikuusi, Hannele (December 24, 1994). "Welcoming Speech at the ILGA Opening Plenary." Permission to reprint courtesy Hannele Lehtikuusi.

Martin, Del (October 1956). "President's Message." Printed in *The Ladder,* 1(1), 6-7, October 1956. Permission to reprint courtesy of Del Martin.

Mattachine Society (May 15, 1955). "Resolution." Printed in the *Mattachine Review,* published July/August 1955. Permission to reprint courtesy of Ben Heath.

McFeeley, Tim (July 13, 1990). "Chicago Speech." Permission to reprint courtesy of Tim McFeeley.

McFeeley, Tim (September 18, 1993). "Dallas/Fort Worth Speech." Speech given at Dallas/Fort Worth black-tie dinner. Permission to reprint courtesy of Tim McFeeley.

Moldenhauer, Jearld (February 13, 1972). "Waffle." Speech given at the New Democratic Party Waffle Convention, Hamilton, Ontario. Permission to reprint courtesy of Jearld Moldenhauer.

Morgan, Robin (April 14, 1973). "Lesbianism and Feminism: Synonyms or Contradictions?" A speech given by Robin Morgan, April 14, 1973, West Coast Lesbian

Feminist Conference, Los Angeles, California. Copyright © Robin Morgan, 1973. Permission to reprint courtesy of Edite Kroll Literary Agency, Inc.

Nestle, Joan (April 24, 1982). "The Fem Question, or We Will Not Go Away." Speech given at "The Scholar and the Feminist" Conference at Barnard College, New York, New York. Permission to reprint courtesy of Joan Nestle.

Nestle, Joan (June 24, 1984). "Passion Is Our Politics." Speech given at the New York City Lesbian and Gay Pride celebration. Permission to reprint courtesy of Joan Nestle.

Nichols, Jack (May 1967). "Why I Joined the Homophile Movement." Speech given at Bucknell University. Permission to reprint courtesy of Jack Nichols.

Nichols, Jack (March 16, 1973). "Walt Whitman: Poet of Comrades and Love." Speech given at the University of Colorado. Permission to reprint courtesy of Jack Nichols.

Nichols, Jack (September 5, 1981). "The Gay Tradition: Strategies for the Decades Ahead." Permission to reprint courtesy of Jack Nichols.

Parkerson, Michelle (October 9, 1983). "Jericho: A Call for Activism in the Black Gay Community." Speech given at Black Gay Men's and Women's Conference, Washington, DC. Permission to reprint courtesy of Michelle Parkerson.

Perry, Troy (February 5, 1999). "Why We Are Going to the Millennium March on Washington for Equality." Permission to reprint courtesy of Troy Perry.

Perry, Troy (April 30, 2000). "Remarks at the Millennium March for Equality." Speech given in Washington, DC. Permission to reprint courtesy of Troy Perry.

Rofes, Eric (April 25, 1993). "Unashamed, We Embrace the Traditions of the Broad Civil Rights Movement in America." Permission to reprint courtesy of Eric Rofes.

Rofes, Eric (November 16, 1997). "The Emerging Sex Panic Targeting Gay Men." Permission to reprint courtesy of Eric Rofes.

Rofes, Eric (November 13, 1998). "Building a Movement for Sexual Freedom During a Moment of Sexual Panic." Permission to reprint courtesy of Eric Rofes.

Rofes, Eric (July 29, 1999). "A Gay Men's Health Movement Is Born." Permission to reprint courtesy of Eric Rofes.

Rofes, Eric (July 19, 2000). "What Is a Healthy Gay Man?" Permission to reprint courtesy of Eric Rofes.

Rosen, Susan (June 20, 1979). "Community and Power: Building Gay Services for the Next Ten Years." Speech given at gay town meeting, Faneuil Hall, Boston, Massachusetts. Permission to reprint courtesy of Susan Rosen.

Rosendall, Richard (October 11, 1996). "Remarks at Walk Without Fear '96." Permission to reprint courtesy of Richard Rosendall.

Rueling, Anna (October 8, 1904). "What Interest Does the Women's Movement Have in Solving the Homosexual Problem?" Speech given for Scientific Humanitarian Committee, Berlin. Permission to reprint courtesy of Michael Lombardi-Nash, translator.

Sanders, Douglas (November 16-19, 1995). "The City, the Country, the World: Not What They Used to Be." Speech given at the Eleventh Annual Conference of the International Network of Lesbian and Gay Officials, Toronto, Ontario. Permission to reprint courtesy of Douglas Sanders.

South, Ken (July 5, 2000). "Boy Scouts of America Rally." Permission to reprint courtesy of the National Gay and Lesbian Task Force.

Stoltenberg, John (December 9, 1983). Speech given at NOW gathering in 1974 reprinted from "Refusing to Be a Man" by John Stoltenberg in *For Men Against Sexism,* edited by Jon Snodgrass (Albion, CA: Times Change Press, 1977), by permission of John Stoltenberg.

Taylor, Valerie (September 13, 1974). "For My Granddaughters . . ." Speech given at First Annual Lesbian Writers Conference, Chicago, Illinois. Copyright © Womanpress. Permission to reprint courtesy of Womanpress.

Toledo, Elizabeth (April 25, 2000). "The GLBT Movement at a Crossroads." Speech given for National Press Club. Permission to reprint courtesy of the National Gay and Lesbian Task Force.

Tyler, Robin (June 8, 1989). "A Love Letter to the Movement." Originally published in *Southern Voice,* June 8, 1989. Permission to reprint courtesy of Robin Tyler.

Vaid, Urvashi (April 27, 1991). "The National Lesbian Agenda." Speech given at the National Lesbian Conference, Atlanta, Georgia. Permission to reprint courtesy of Urvashi Vaid.

Vaid, Urvashi (April 25, 1993). "Speech at the March on Washington." Permission to reprint courtesy of Urvashi Vaid.

Vida, Ginny (August 17, 1976). "Statement on Sex and Violence on Television." Speech given to the Subcommittee on Communications of the House Committee on Interstate and Foreign Commerce, Los Angeles, California. Permission to reprint courtesy of Ginny Vida.

Wertheim, Aubrey (November 14, 1984). "Why Aren't More Gay Men Feminists?" Speech given at New York University Women's Center Conference on Men and Feminism. Permission to reprint courtesy of Aubrey Wertheim.

Whitlock, Kay (June 25, 1978). "Speech at Gay and Lesbian Pride Rally, New York City." Permission to reprint courtesy of Kay Whitlock.

Williams, A. Cecil (November 16, 1964). "On Getting and Using Power." Permission to reprint courtesy of A. Cecil Williams.

Woolard, Cathy (January 1989). "Time Is Not Right to March on Washington." Permission to reprint courtesy of Cathy Woolard.

Index